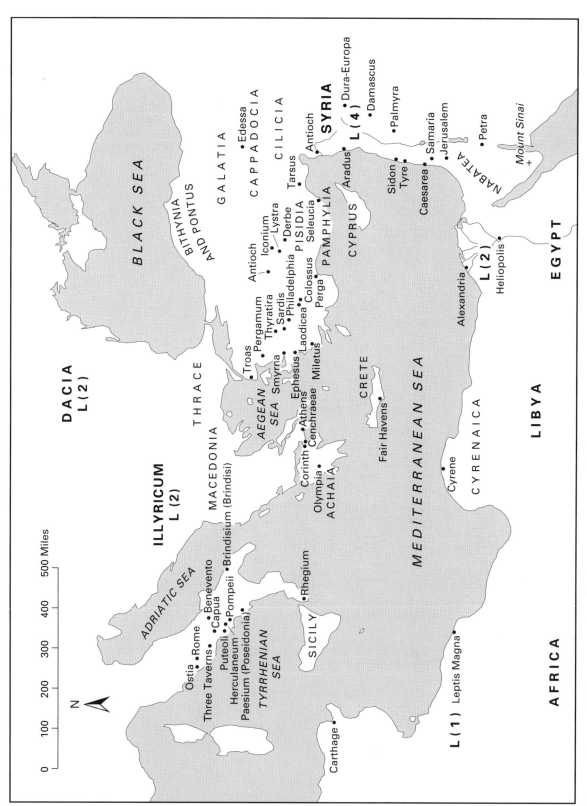

Roman Eastern Mediterranean World, First Century C.E. The location of legions is indicated by **L** followed by their number (23 C.E.) The four legions of Syria were: In the north, X *Fretensis*; in the center, III *Galica* and IV *Ferrata*; in the south, XII *Fulminata*.

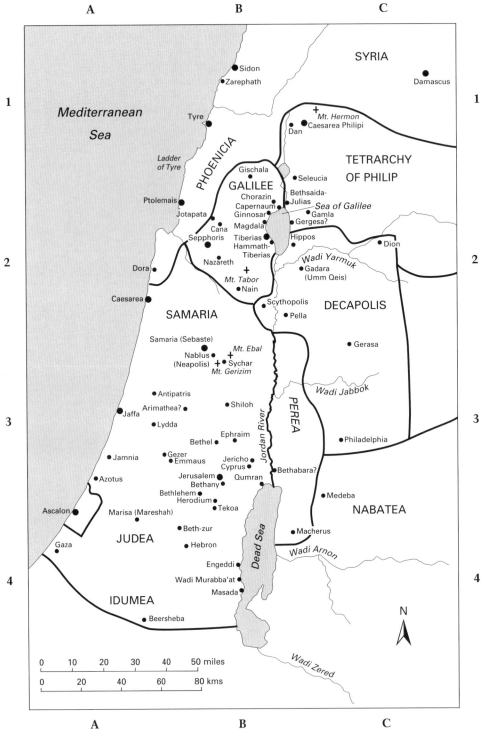

Palestine from 6 to 44 C.E.

Map of Palestine Key

Arimathea	B3	Hippos	B2
Ascalon	A4	Jaffa	A3
Azotus	A3	Jamnia	A3
Beersheba	A4	Jericho	B3
Behtabara	B3	Jerusalem	B3
Bethany	B3	Jotapata	B2
Bethel	B3	Macherus	B4
Bethlehem	B4	Magdala	B2
Bethphage (dot between		Marisa	A4
Jerusalem and Bethany)	B3	Masada	B4
Bethsaida-Julias	B2	Medaba	C4
Beth-Zur	B4	Mt. Ebal	B3
Caesarea-Maritima	A2	Mt. Gerizim	B3
Caesarea-Pilippi	B1	Mt Hermon	C1
Cana	B2	Mt Tabor	B2
Capernaum	B2	Nablus	B3
Chorazin	B2	Nain	B2
Cyprus	B3	Nazareth	B2
Damascus	C1	Pella	B2
Dan	B1	Phildelphia	C3
Dora	A2	Ptolemais	B2
Emmaus	B3	Qumran	B3
Engeddi	B4	Samaria	B3
Ephraim	B3	Scythopolis	B2
Gadara	B2	Seleucia	B2
Gamla	C2	Sepphoris	B2
Gaza	A4	Shiloh	B3
Gerasa	C3	Sidon	B1
Gergesa	B2	Sychar	B3
Gezer	B3	Tekoa	B4
Ginnosar	B2	Tiberias	B2
Gischala	B2	Tyre	B1
Hammath-Tiberias	B2	Wadi Murabba'at	B4
Hebron	B4	Zarephath	B1
Herodium	B4		

Jesus and His World

Jesus and His World

AN ARCHAEOLOGICAL AND CULTURAL DICTIONARY

John J. Rousseau
Rami Arav

SCM PRESS LTD

Scripture quotations, some of which coincide with the Revised Standard Version or the New Revised Standard Version of the Bible, are the authors' translations.

Cover design: Peggy Lauritsen Design Group. The cover photograph in upper left is of Alec Garrard's Temple Model and is used by his permission. The bottom left cover photograph is of a pair of sandals, Bar-Kochba Caves. Used by permission of the Israel Museum, Jerusalem, The Shrine of the Book, D. Samuel and Jeane H. Gottesman Center for Biblical Manuscripts. Interior design: *By Design*/Wendy LaChance. Illustrations on pp. 23, 32, 45, 48, 79, 111, 148, 160, 168, 174, 197, and 272 by Parrot Graphics/Patricia Isaacs; all other illustrations by Thomas Goeke. Photographs by John Rousseau.

Copyright © 1995 Augsburg Fortress

0 334 02626 1

First published in Britain 1996
by SCM Press Ltd
9-17 St Albans Place, London N1 0NX

Printed and bound in the USA

Contents

✦ Foreword ✦

A Down-to-Earth Jesus

by James M. Robinson

The present volume is neither a life of Christ nor a guide book to Israel but rather an effort to combine the two: Locations, artifacts, and customs relevant to Jesus are treated alphabetically in the light of archaeology, to which John Rousseau and Rami Arav append at the end of each entry a section highlighting their relevance for the study of Jesus. This not only draws the attention of tourists visiting an archaeological site to relevant references in the Gospels, but also provides for students of the Bible access to the archaeological dimension often neglected in the study of Jesus.

Palestinian archaeology for the century leading up to the Jewish War of 66–70 C.E. is coming into focus with considerably more precision both in terms of time and space and with regard to archaeological sophistication than was possible in the past. Hence one can hope that information will emerge that will, as Ernest Renan romantically put it, make of the Holy Land a "fifth Gospel" for critical scholarship as well as for the all-too-gullible pilgrim.

The pious have been sold a bill of goods ever since Constantine's mother Helena first began the locating of such sites, three centuries after the fact, beginning with Golgotha, on which Constantine erected the Church of the Holy Sepulchre (unless one prefers the Garden Tomb identified a century ago by the British general Gordon), down to today's hawking of "the house of St. Peter" in Capharnaum and the tourist bus stop "Mount of Beatitudes" at the traditional location of the Sermon on the Mount (this mount is the outcome of Matthew's editing of Mark and Q, not a place in Jesus' biography). Such pious Franciscan archaeology as these two Galilean locations typify is being replaced today by the kind of serious scientific archaeology capable of being coordinated in a very productive way with New Testament scholarship.

I have been asked to provide this brief foreword from the perspective of New Testament scholarship, especially that part of it which of late has built a new access to Jesus by means of the Sayings Gospel Q, a collection of sayings ascribed to Jesus that was used by the Evangelists Matthew and Luke, but then no longer copied (because the church preferred the two revised and enlarged editions that are in the New Testament). This most important primitive Christian text, unknown for more than a millennium and a half, was itself not unlike an archaeological discovery, dug up a century and a half ago imbedded in the two canonical Gospels. And it fits well into the current archaeological findings in Galilee.

The Sayings Gospel Q does not contain so much theology from on high as it does down-to-earth pithy sayings. Its two main "theological" categories, "kingdom of God" and "son of man," turn out not to be technical scholarly terms of the day, but rather favorite idioms that Jesus developed in trying to score his point. The text is in significant places oriented even to such down-to-earth realities as stones the size of the small rolls of bread that were the staple of the Galilean menu: John said God could change one into the other, Jesus said God was the kind of parent who would not give one when asked for the other, the devil said Jesus should change one into the other. Such stones are not only the weapon of David against Goliath and more recently of the Intifada, but also the daily bread of field archaeology. Hence it is at this low level that one must begin if one wishes to build a foundation that will not collapse with the next storm.

How then does Jesus look from this rather humble vantage point of the Sayings Gospel Q?

Jesus was raised in Nazara,[1] a hamlet in the hill country of Lower Galilee. He heard about a holy man named John,[2] and went to him to undergo his rite of initiation, baptism (by immersion),[3] into a completely new lifestyle, where the givens are basically changed: When the ideal becomes real[4] and God rules,[5] there are no poor[6] or hungry,[7] no handicapped or sick,[8] no exploiter[9] or enemy,[10] no mentally disturbed[11] or force of evil.[12] Jesus believed that all this ideal was the basic reality, and acted accordingly.[13]

In the rite of passage administered by John, Jesus may have taken off all his identifying garb,[14] an intentional loss of identity, and then resumed, perhaps only out of modesty, the basic shirt and cloak of his day.[15] But he may not have resumed wearing sandals,[16] perhaps as a symbol of penance.[17] He carried no coin purse,[18] for he had no coins and earned no money. He wore no backpack,[19] for he had no change of clothes or provisions of food. He carried no club,[20] the weapon of the poor, for he turned the other cheek[21] and gave muggers the shirt off his back,[22] defenseless. He counted on life's necessities being provided with-

out his working[23] or otherwise concerning himself for his own physical well-being.[24] All this, at least if we may assume he practiced what he preached. (Central to his preaching was the insistence that one practice what one preaches.)[25]

This involved Jesus moving away from home and family ties.[26] He set up a base camp at the northern edge of the Sea of Galilee.[27] There, well below sea level, the climate may have been more tolerant of such an exposed existence as that which Jesus advocated and practiced. Here, along the shore and in the alluvial plain, where the Jordan flows into the Sea of Galilee, and in the rugged hill country behind, he worked both sides of the river.[28] He developed a circuit of three villages, Capharnaum,[29] Bethsaida, and Chorazin, all in close boating or walking distance of each other, where he cured sick people,[30] laid out his thoughts,[31] and motivated a few to abandon their customary lifestyle and join up with him.[32] At some juncture this base camp was repudiated, presumably because it had turned on his movement and had to be abandoned.[33]

His procedure seems to have been as follows: He would walk along the shore, catch an occasional ride in a fishing boat, hike through the hilly terrain from house to house,[34] hamlet to hamlet,[35] knocking on doors.[36] When someone opened the door, he would say "Shalom,"[37] and, if received hospitably, would show the reality of the ideal he kept talking about[38] by the way he cared for the sick.[39] The "Peace!" of the normally hollow greeting (equal to no more than our "Good morning!") would thus become concrete reality,[40] which the host, who had at least already responded positively to the initial advance at the door,[41] might well come to take literally.

Jesus ate as moderately or sumptuously as was provided.[42] But on leaving the next day or so, he would accept no provisions for the road.[43] This not because he was ascetic—he had, after all, eaten what was put before him—but perhaps because carrying one's own provisions through the day would involve selfishly depriving those in need whom he passed on the way. For he was constantly on the go,[44] starting over each time to implement the ideal, leaving it to God to care for the practical side of things.[45] When a door was slammed in his face, he went to the next house, and when he was run out of town, his parting gesture was to the effect that they, not he, had lost out.[46]

If what he had to say ever got a wider hearing,[47] it and the corroborating conduct would amount to a direct threat to the system that kept the ruling class on top. Although his activity was not explicitly political, he did realize that the problem was systemic.[48] For he advocated an alternative life style that presupposed a different, utopian kind of world. By calling it the kingdom/reign of God, he by implication defrocked the temple cult and the state religion. He was thus in effect a revolutionary, and shared the fate of John and others before them who had spoken up for that ideal as real. Cut short almost before he had begun, Jesus may hardly have had time or occasion to cope with the impracticalities that were inherent in implementing such a utopian ideal, or to revise in the light of experience. The problem of reaching a *modus vivendi* with the given establishment was left to his successors.

The Jordan River was not only a geographical marker, at places often not navigable (especially north of the Sea of Galilee); it was also a political frontier. Because a centurion stationed at the border town Capharnaum had a high regard for Jesus as a faith healer,[49] such a powerful Gentile may well have functioned on the local level as a patron, producing in effect for Jesus a haven from political oppression. Jesus also got along well with the customs officials.[50] It may have been the termination of this privileged position, perhaps as a repercussion of the elimination of John,[51] that led to the abandoning of this base camp and its resultant condemnation,[52] but this is mere speculation.

No other location attained a status comparable to that of Capharnaum and its immediate environs, from which one may infer that no alternative base camp could be set up. Scenes are usually not identified by place name, and those that are (all outside of Q) are isolated occurrences: Nain in Luke; Cana in the Semeia Source and hence in John; Sychar and Ephraim in John; Nazareth and Jericho in Mark. Jerusalem and its surroundings (Bethany) form a case for themselves; in any case they are absent from Q, with the exception of Jerusalem's rejection of Wisdom's envoys from the dawn of time to the end of the canon, and hence its resultant abandonment by God to its fate at the time of the Jewish War 66–70 c.e.[53]

Jesus lived in a religious culture and hence, although he may not have been learned in his religious tradition (in contrast to the Qumran scribes and the Evangelists), naturally experienced and expressed his idealistic humane orientation in religious terms. The ideal that again and again became real he called God ruling, and his abandon regarding practical matters of self-interest came to expression as prayer, turning those matters over to God to handle. But his movement actually became organized as a functional religion only after his death, when it seemed to imitate the more highly organized religious movement of John; this is not yet evident in Q.[54] During his lifetime Jesus functioned within (even when against) a given religious culture with which he was familiar, Galilean Judaism.

The horror, consternation, confusion, and dislocation attendant upon the brutal elimination of Jesus probably surpassed that which may have taken place among Jesus and his followers upon the death of John (about whose own followers we know even less than the scanty information about Jesus' followers). Perhaps John's death was less of a crisis due to the fact that Jesus had already distanced himself geographically from John and had his own practice and message. Jesus was in any case able to carry on after John's death, whereas Peter apparently was not prepared in a comparable way. For he floundered and retreated with the others back to Galilee, only then to return to Jerusalem, no doubt a bit sheepishly, to set up headquarters there. Of all this Q says nothing.

Q apparently does not reflect the Jesus movement's headquarters in Jerusalem, but rather its remnants in Galilee. This is suggested not only by the distinctive gospel of Q and the absence of Holy Week and its gospel, both of which set Q apart from the standard forms of primitive Christianity, but also by the absence from Q of any of the names of Jesus' family or followers, and even of any titles for them. The possible exception is the term "worker," which however is used by Paul *in malam partem*, perhaps with reference to much the same kind of itinerants.[55] Yet Q does not speak of the Twelve.[56] Nor does it speak of the Apostles.[57] Thus the Jerusalem leaders from Galilee and their titles are eloquently absent. Similarly the non-Christology of Q seems archaic.[58]

This may be in part due simply to the temporal primitiveness of Q, but may well be more due to geographical isolation from the mainstream of emerging Christianity.[59] One may assume that the central core of followers, who had actually broken with their former lifestyles and accompanied Jesus on his way, tended not to be those who continued to live in Galilee, but rather those who made Jerusalem and beyond their orientation. Those left in Galilee lacked leadership and ultimately failed. Most of the remnants who did not get absorbed into emerging normative Judaism were ultimately absorbed along with their text into the thriving Gentile Christian church (perhaps as the Matthean church).

A few may have stuck it out with their outdated lifestyle, in Gentile Christian eyes almost like the Amish in American Christendom today. Such hold-outs of the Q movement may have continued a shadowy existence under what became heretical designations, such as Ebionites and Nazarenes,[60] not to speak of "heretical" precursors such as the Judaizers: "those of circumcision"[61] who would "Judaize" the Gentiles if they could.[62] But for all practical purposes the Q movement survived only as a text used by the Gentile-Christian Gospels of Matthew and Luke.

James M. Robinson

Notes

1. Q [4:16]. (Q is cited by Lucan chapter and verse numbers. Double square brackets [ ] indicate doubt as to whether the reference is in Q.) This spelling is only found here in Matthew and Luke, which is the reason for ascribing it to Q.
2. Q 3:2; [3:21/Matt. 3:13]. Whether this verse belongs to Q has been often contested, because Luke almost completely deletes it in his program to periodize history, but it seems to be presupposed in the Temptation.
3. Q [3:21/Matt. 3:13].
4. Such imprecise, not to say fuzzy, use of technical terms is not inappropriate. The term that Q elevates to its central abstraction, kingdom or reign of God, similarly says, generally, everything but, precisely, nothing.
5. The kingdom or reign of God, actually a quite rare, non-technical term, dominates the abstract conceptualizing of Q: 6:20; 7:28; 10:9, 11; 11:2, 20; 12:31; 13:18, 20, 29; [14:16/Matt 22:2]; 16:16. The common assumption that, in terms of the history of religions, it is derived from Jewish apocalypticism, is inaccurate, because it does not occur there. The historical problem the term poses is rather that of its sudden appearance here, without an immediate background. The situation is similar with regard to the other most prominent idiom, son of man, which also presents the history-of-religions problem of lacking an immediate background. See my essay, "The Son of Man in the Sayings Gospel Q," in *Tradition und Translation: Festschrift Carsten Colpe* (Berlin and New York: Walter de Gruyter, 1994).
6. Q 6:20; 12:28; 12:29/Matt 6:31.
7. Q 6:21; 10:7; 11:3, 11-12; 12:24, 29; 13:28-29.
8. Q 10:9.
9. Q 6:29-30.
10. Q 6:27, 35.
11. Q 11:14.
12. Q 4:13; 11:14, 20, 21-22.
13. Q 6:43-49.
14. The metaphor of the believer spiritually disrobing and rerobing familiar in the Pauline and Gnostic traditions is absent from Q, which hence provides no metaphors from which to draw inferences about John's baptismal rite.
15. Q 6:29.
16. Q 10:4.
17. The injunction not to wear sandals fits poorly with Q 3:16 and Mark 1:7, when understood as John being unworthy to perform a servant's task of taking on and off a master's sandals, which, when applied to Jesus, would indicate he continued to wear sandals. But it could have referred to removing his sandals permanently prior to immersion, with John's unworthiness to do this being a stage in the subordination of John to Jesus picked up and amplified by Matt 3:14-15. Norbert Krieger, "Barfuß Busse Tun," *New Testament* 1 (1956) 227–228, followed by Walter Bauer, *A Greek-English Lexicon of the New Testament and Other Early Christian Literature*, trans. William F. Arndt and F. Wilbur Gingrich, second edition revised and augmented by F.

Wilburg Gingrich and Frederick W. Danker from Walter Bauer's fifth edition, 1958 (Chicago and London: The University of Chicago Press, 1979), s.v. *bast'axo*, i.e. "remove," citing also K. Preisendanz et al., eds., *Papyri Graecae Magicae: Die griechischen Zauberpapyri*, Sammlung wissenschaftlicher Commentare, vol. 4 (Stuttgart: Tübner, 1928], 1058: *bast'axo tò stefánion âpó tês Kefalês"*.

18. Q [10:4].

19. Q [10:4].

20. Q [10:4/Matt 10:10]. Luke 22:36 confirms indirectly that a weapon had been forbidden, although what is here restored is a more middle-class weapon than is a club. The requirement of a sword is here necessitated by the following Marcan story of the cutting off of an ear in Gethsemane. The RSV translation "stave" at Q ·10:4, obscures somewhat the defensive meaning that a student from Kenya first brought to my attention as thoroughly obvious. At el-Kasr near Nag Hammadi I have seen this formidable weapon in the hand of a peasant in a situation in which he felt called upon to be able to defend himself. The *Los Angeles Times* of 17 Dec. 92, reporting on the new sense of security provided by the arrival of U.S. military forces in the famine-ridden town of Baidoa in Somalia, provides the anecdote: "Wednesday, the feeding center was filled with optimism and a new sense of security, commodities as rare as grain in this parched land. 'Where's your gun?' Rice teased Abduhakim, 19, one of the center's security guards. Only a day before, he had been carrying an automatic weapon. Wednesday, he was carrying a walking stick." The stick was obviously not due to sudden lameness, but rather was a weapon permissible in the presence of U.S. forces in a way that a gun would not be. The *Los Angeles Times* of 11 March 93 published a picture with the caption: "Two Somali men walk through the ruins of what was once the Hotel Aruba in the capital, Mogadishu. They carry sticks for protection."

21. Q 6:29a.

22. Q 6:29b.

23. Q 12:24,27. The ethos is more that of a mendicant order than that of the Calvinistic work ethic.

24. Q 12:29-31.

25. Q 6:46.

26. Q 11:27-28. The move of the family with him to Capharnaum (John 2:12) may not be early tradition, but rather a redactional transition from the Wedding in Cana (John 2:1-11), where his mother had been present, to the Healing of the Official's Son (John 4:46b-54), which in the Semeia Source followed the Wedding immediately.

27. Q 7:1; 10:13-15.

28. Capharnaum (Q 7:1; 10:15) and Chorazin (Q 10:13) are just west of the river, Bethsaida (Q 10:13) just east. See Rami Arav and John J. Rousseau, "Elusive Bethsaida Recovered," *The Fourth R*, (January 1991): 1–4; Heinz-Wolfgang Kuhn and Rami Arav, "The Bethsaida Excavations: Historical and Archaeological Approaches," *Early Christianity: Essays in Honor of Helmut Koester*, ed. Birger A. Pearson (Minneapolis: Fortress Press, 1991), 77–106.

29. Jonathan L. Reed, "The Population of Capernaum," *Occasional Papers of The Institute for Antiquity and Christianity* 24 (1992): 15, 19, concludes, after sifting through the various kinds of meagre evidence, that population estimates beyond 1700 inhabitants are unfounded.

30. Q 7:1-10; 10:9.

31. Q 10:9. Q 6:20-49 is a secondary collection.

32. Q 9:59-60; 22:28.

33. Q 10:13, 15. Q 9:58 would, to the extent it is accurate, reflect better the subsequent homelessness.

34. Q 10:7.

35. Q 10:8, 10-11.

36. Q 10:5; 11:9-10. Being locked out became a painful metaphor, Q 13:24-29.

37. Q [10:5].

38 Q 10:9b.

39. Q 10:9a.

40. Q 10:6.

41. Q 10:6.

42. Q 7:34; 10:8; 13:26. This stands in contrast to the asceticism of John (Q 7:33; Mark 1:6). The caricature by "this generation" that Jesus is "a glutton and a drunkard" is presented as an invidious distortion of him coming "eating and drinking" (comparable to John having a demon as the caricature corresponding to him coming neither eating nor drinking). Leif E. Vaage, "Q¹ and the Historical Jesus: Some Peculiar Sayings (7:33-34; 9:57-58, 59-60; 14:26-27)," *Forum* 5/2 (June 1989): 159–76, infers Jesus is a "real party animal" (p. 165), "a bit of a hellion and wanderer on the wild (or, at least, illicit) side of things" (p. 166), "a bit of an imp, in Socrates' terms a social gad-fly" (p. 175), a characterization designed (p. 175) to increase the "notoriety" of the Jesus Seminar (which, to judge by newspaper reports, turned out to be a success). As such, one can join in his "enjoyment" (p. 175). But his more serious effort (p. 165) is inadequate: "Far from worrying about where his next meal would come from (as 12:22 admonishes not to do), Jesus, according to 7:34, apparently ate and drank well and often enough to be suspected of overindulgence. Perhaps for that reason, he saw no reason for concern about these things. In any case, his behavior in this regard seems not to have conformed to the conventional image of religious seriousness and uprightness." Somewhere between being conventional and being a hellion is where Jesus is, in terms of the Q texts, to be placed. The serious task is to seek to interpret the texts in a way that does justice to them in their context of early Q material, and thus to "place" Jesus' posture toward the necessities of life, a task which Vaage in this essay does not actually undertake.

43. Q [10:4].

44. Q 9:58.

45. Q 11:3, 9-13; 12:29-31. The concept of being provided by one's superiors with a day's ration of (perishable) bread was common in the ancient world. The relevant texts are collected by Erwin M. Yamauchi, "The 'Daily Bread' Motif in Antiquity," *The Westminster Theological Journal* 28 (1966): 145–56

46. Q 10:10-11.

47. Q 11:33; 12:3/Matt 10:27.

48. The systemic nature of the problem is reflected in the term kingdom of God. This is not just because a contrast is being drawn to a diabolical kingdom (Q 4:5-7; 11:15, 17-18, 21-22). It is rather that the surfacing of the good, be it of varying sorts, such as food, clothing, healing, exorcism, deliverance from trial, is brought together in the ascription of it all to God. One such instance is thus symptomatic of the others. The activation of the good exposes the basic impotence of evil. The apparent prevalence of evil thus is unmasked as an unreal sham, and thus as a system is broken. For this will surely come to light all over. Thus it is the systemic nature of the kingdom of God that leads to eschatology, which is functionally more an inference from than a presupposition of what is taking place.

49. Q 7:1-10.

50. Q 7:[29], 34. The frontier position suggests that what one usually translated "tax collectors" may have been "customs agents." See Gerd Theissen, *The Shadow of the Galilean* (London: SCM, 1987), Chap. 12, "Men on the Frontier," 109–17, featuring a Capharnaum "toll collector" and his converted predecessor. *See* TAX AND TAX COLLECTORS.

51. This may be implied in the prominence of Herod especially in Luke 9:7-9; 13:31-32; 23:6-16 (all missing from Q).

52. Q 10:13-15.

53. Q 11:49-51; 13:34-35.

54. Though the baptism of Jesus was probably in Q, there is no reference to him or his disciples baptizing. John 4:1 makes a passing reference to Jesus baptizing, which is promptly corrected in John 4:2, to the effect that not Jesus, but only his disciples, baptized. *The Testimony of Truth* (NHC IX,3: 69,15-17) reports: "For [the Son] of [man] did not baptize any of his disciples." Luke 11:1 uses John teaching his disciples to pray as a context for the Lord's Prayer (Q 11:2-4). Mark 2:18 uses John's (and the Pharisees'!) disciples fasting as the occasion for calling on Jesus' disciples to fast. Secondary though such settings for sayings no doubt are, they together do convey the impression that John's religion was in such formal matters ahead of the Jesus movement.

55. Q 10:2; Q 10:7 (par. 1 Tim 5:18; *Did* 13:2); Q 13:27; 2 Cor. 11:13; Phil. 3:2; 2 Tim. 2:15. See Dieter Georgi, *Die Gegner des Paulus im 2. Korintherbrief: Studien zur religiösen Propaganda in der Spätantike* (Neukirchen-Vluyn: Neukirchener Verlag, 1964), English, *The Opponents of Paul in Second Corinthians* (Philadelphia: Fortress, 1986), 40, 68, 165–67, 224–26.

56. Q 22:30 is moving toward this title, in referring to Jesus' followers sitting on thrones judging the twelve tribes of Israel. It is the parallel Matt 19:28 that adds that there were "twelve" thrones, moving a step closer to "the Twelve."

57. Q 10:2; 11:49 use the verb "to send," Q 10:16 the active participle "sending," and Q 13:34 the passive participle "those sent." "Apostles" in Q 11:49 is apparently a reference to pre-Christian "emissaries," like the "prophets" of the Old Testament ("from the blood of Abel to the blood of Zechariah," Q 11:51). If Luke had inserted the term to refer to Christian apostles (Matt. 23:34 refers to "wise men and scribes"), he would probably have followed his custom of including the definite article. Thus Q usage is moving toward, but not quite attaining, the Christian concept "apostle." The rough synonym "to cast out" in Q 10:2, meaning to send out, is moving in the same direction.

58. See my essay, "The Son of Man in the Sayings Gospel Q."

59. Paul Hoffmann, "QR und der Menschensohn: Eine vorläufige Skizze," *The Four Gospels 1992: Festschrift Frans Neirynck* (Leuven: University and Peeters, 1992), 421–56, esp. "V. Der Menschensohn und der Fall Jerusalems," 450–56, has renewed persuasively the argument that Q 11:49-51; 13:34-35 reflect the crisis mood of the siege of Jerusalem, as do comparable passages in a roughly contemporary Mark. This would tend to date the redactional layer of Q, but not the preceding layer(s).

60. See my essay, "The Sayings Gospel Q," *The Four Gospels 1992: Festschrift Frans Neirynck* (BETL; Leuven: Leuven University and Peeters, 1992), 1, 361–88, esp. 366–68, 373–82.

61. Gal. 2:12.

62. Gal. 2:14.

✦ Acknowledgments ✦

We are grateful to the many theologians, scholars, historians, archaeologists, epigraphists, numismatists, and other specialists who preceded us in the area of Jesus research or contributed to it. We especially tried to give credit to the archaeologists, to whom we owe so much, by providing their names whenever possible. Among those to whom we are more directly indebted are the Fellows of the Jesus Seminar, the participants of the Historical Jesus Section of the Society of Biblical Literature, and the excavators of Bethsaida, Capernaum, Chorazin, Gamla, Jerusalem, and Sepphoris. Conversations with many of them facilitated our work.

We greatly appreciate the enlightened contribution of Professor James M. Robinson, Director of the Institute for Antiquity and Christianity at Claremont, who wrote the Foreword. We are indebted to Fred Strickert, who contributed most of the entry "Coins as Historical Documents," to Professor H.-W. Kuhn and Monika Bernett for providing most of the information on the entry "Pantera's Tombstone," and to those who read drafts of the entries and gave constructive criticism: Carol Meyers, Marjorie Meret, Amy L. Wordelman, Kevin Kaiser, and Deborah von Bolschwing.

Tom Goeke, artist and draftsman who worked for the Bethsaida Excavations, provided most of the maps, diagrams and drawings. Unless otherwise indicated, the photographs are from John Rousseau. Barbara Orme, a word processing specialist of great ability, diligently produced the final manuscript and diskette. Above all, we are most grateful to Dr. Marshall D. Johnson, Publishing Director, Pamela J. McClanahan, Managing Editor, and Julie Odland, Production Editor, of Fortress Press for their professional guidance and encouragement.

Without them, this book would have been impossible.

Rami Arav   *John J. Rousseau*

List of Abbreviations

For the sake of the reader, abbreviations are avoided except when the title of the publication is very long or recurs frequently. The few abbreviations used are the following:

ABD	*Anchor Bible Dictionary.* Garden City, N.Y.: Doubleday, 1992.
AEHL	*Archaeological Encyclopedia of the Holy Land.* New York: Putnam, 1972.
ANET	*Ancient Near-Eastern Texts.* (Pritchard)
Antiq.	*Jewish Antiquities* (Josephus)
ASOR	American Schools of Oriental Research
b.	Babylonian Talmud
BA	*Biblical Archaeologist*
B.A.R. International	*British Archaeological International Studies Reports*
BAR	*Biblical Archaeology Review*
B.C.E.	Before Common Era. Equivalent of B.C. (before Christ)
C.E.	Common Era. Equivalent of A.D. (*Anno Domini*)
G. Thom.	Gospel of Thomas
IEJ	*Israel Exploration Journal*
JSOT	*Journal for the Study of the Old Testament*
m.	Mishnah
Nat. Hist.	Natural History (Pliny)
NEAEHL	*New Encyclopedia of Archaeological Excavations in the Holy Land.* New York: Simon and Schuster, 1993.
SBL	Society of Biblical Literature
t.	Tosepta
War	*Jewish War* (Josephus)
y.	Jerusalem Talmud

List of Figures

✦ List of Tables ✦

✦ Introduction ✦

The Quest of the Historical Jesus

The fewer data, the more theories!

The early biblical texts pertaining to Jesus, his life, teaching, and death represent only some 150 pages. But in the two millennia that followed his crucifixion, millions of pages have been written about him, in ancient and modern languages, by thousands of theologians, scholars, and other writers. In the last two centuries, under the influence of eighteenth-century critical rationalism that began with the publication of Hermann Samuel Reimarus's work, Jesus research increasingly came to be detached from faith. It gained momentum and spread throughout the Western world. After much activity that led to meager results, scholars became discouraged:

> There is nothing more negative than the results of the critical study of the life of Jesus.[1]

> No one is any longer in a position to write a life of Jesus. . . . In truth, this state of affairs has deeper causes and compels us to affirm the futility of any renewed attempt at Lives of Jesus now and in the future.[2]

Yet a renewed quest followed the publication of Bornkamm's challenge. Perhaps it will not produce a biography of Jesus, but it can retrieve the core of his most probable sayings and deeds. In 1957, James M. Robinson delivered an address at Oxford on "The Four Gospels in 1957." It was entitled "The Kerygma and the Quest of the Historical Jesus," and developed into a book, *A New Quest of the Historical Jesus*, in which Robinson, carrying further the position of Rudolf Bultmann in *Jesus and the World* (1926), expanded on the possibility, legitimacy, and procedure of the new quest. Subsequently, since the mid-1960s a resurgence of interest in Jesus studies began among scholars and clergy. In the United States, this interest led to the creation, in the mid-1980s, of the Historical Jesus Section of the Society of Biblical Literature and the Jesus Seminar of the Westar Institute. The goals and procedures of the latter deserve special explanation.

The Fellows of the Jesus Seminar centered their work on the Greek texts of the canonical Gospels and of the Gospel of Thomas. Their project has been aimed at identifying the "authentic" sayings of Jesus through collective consideration of a set of criteria relating to authenticity. The result of their research is published in *Forum* and in *The Five Gospels*.[3] After presentation, discussion and vote, the sayings attributed to Jesus were rated as follows:

I

- red = most probably authentic
- pink = probably authentic
- gray = probably not authentic
- black = not authentic

The method, which uses weighted averages, gave results statistically comparable with those obtained in the past by New Testament critics. Out of 1,544 sayings examined, including parallels,

- 31 are rated *red* (2 percent)
- 211 *pink* (14 percent)
- 416 *gray* (27 percent)
- 886 *black* (57 percent)

Thus, only 16 percent of the sayings ascribed to Jesus, mainly aphorisms and parables, would be most probably or probably authentic. By comparison, John Dominic Crossan, a member of the Jesus Seminar who published his results independently, recognizes 105 sayings out of 522 in his data base as "actually going back to the historical Jesus."[4] His method, relying heavily on multiple attestation, yields a percentage of authenticity of 20 percent. Currently, the work of the Jesus seminar continues for the deeds of Jesus.

The research done by these groups and individuals is not without limitations. Its major handicap is that it is based almost exclusively on the analysis of the four canonical Gospels and the Gospel of Thomas with little attention to other sources, such as the Hebrew Bible and other ancient Jewish and Christian writings, or other means of recovering the past, such as biblical archaeology, social-science paradigms, and others. Such a narrow field of inquiry can lead, not unexpectedly, to flagrant errors. For instance, in a recent book on the Galilean Jesus, the respective locations of Tyre and Sidon are inverted. Its author indicates that the harbor of Ptolemais (Acco) was situated at the modern site of Haifa, whereas it was at the other end of the bay, ten miles to the north. Distances between landmarks of Palestine are grossly wrong. Another specialist states in an article that the total area of the Jerusalem Temple platform was 145 acres instead of 35. A leading New Testament authority writes that the Samaritan temple was towering over the heads of Jesus and the Samaritan woman (John 4:1-26) when, in reality, it had been razed by John Hyrcanus some 140 years before and had never been rebuilt. The same specialist proposes a scenario in which two Roman procurators, one for Samaria, Cumanus, another for Judea, Pontius Pilate, together repress a rebellion in Samaria. In fact, there were never two prefects ruling concurrently in that region, but only one prefect for Judea, Samaria, and Idumea, with Pilate in power from 26 to 36 C.E. and Cumanus from 48 to 52 C.E. Other Jesus specialists place Taricheae-Magdala south of Tiberias, although it is to the north, and specify that the Temple tax, actually owed only by men twenty or older, was to be paid by all persons of the house of Judea. As for Jesus, he has been presented as a rabbi, a revolutionary, a Pharisee, a peasant, a magician, a marginal Jew, a Cynic, a charismatic religious leader, an apocalyptic prophet, a noneschatological sage, an Essene, a social reformer, a liberator.

The presence of such misinformation and of an abundance of theories points to a need for the enlargement of the sources of information about the life of Jesus. This work is intended to make available the wide variety of extrabiblical sources related to the quest of the historical Jesus. Our opinions and suggestions are meant solely to direct the reader's attention toward new possibilities and areas of research. In order to remain as much as possible in the world and circumstances of Jesus, we avoid drawing on conceptions born two millennia after the events, thousands of miles away, in a totally different culture, shaped by religious dogmas and philosophies foreign to first century Palestine. For example, the people of Jesus' time knew nothing of a distinction between "illness" and "disease." Wounds were inflicted in battle, in accidents, or by robbers. Ailments were thought to be caused by demons, among which were what we call psychological dysfunctions. Other ailments were attributed to some obvious natural causes or divine punishment, all in agreement with the beliefs of the time among that people.

The Authors and the Procedure

Rami Arav, an Israeli scholar and archaeologist, holds a Ph.D. from New York University. He is the son of a Galilean farmer. He lives in Haifa, participated in the Archaeological Survey of Israel, directed several excavations, and initiated the excavations of Bethsaida in 1987. John Rousseau, of Huguenot origin, is a Fellow of the Jesus Seminar who has long been concerned with the study of the historical Jesus. For this purpose, while living in Semitic countries, he observed firsthand the life and activities of Arab fishers, villagers, farmers, Bedouins, and Jewish artisans, and merchants. He studied their ancestral customs as they existed after World War II. He holds a doctorate from the Sorbonne and another from Claremont, California. He lives in Israel for two or three months every year and is a staff member of the Bethsaida excavations. These backgrounds allow for an intimate understanding of the material culture of Palestine.

We have often been asked how we managed to write a book together, one working in Berkeley and the other in Haifa. The task was not easy. Rousseau started the book alone and about midway realized that much information published in Hebrew was not accessible in the United States. After Arav accepted the invitation to participate in the project, Rousseau sent him the entries already drafted, and Arav returned them with his input.

Rousseau then blended their respective contributions into one text that, at first, was rather uneven and needed careful editing. The same process continued for the remaining entries. The authors also met twice a year in order to review the work accomplished and to work out differences that emerged.

Several persons whose input is much appreciated are named in the Acknowledgments. These extra efforts were worthwhile in order to present a view of Jesus' life and world that would be influenced as little as possible by christological, theological, and Western concepts.

In the culture of the time of Jesus, with normative principles such as the collective consciousness of being a chosen people bound to God by a covenant, obedience to Torah as the divine law of the land, the centrality of the Temple, and a widespread patriarchal system, techniques and ideas evolved slowly. We thus felt that our focus on a specific period, namely 4 B.C.E. to 36 C.E. would be enhanced by using methods of extrapolation, interpolation, and "retropolation": extrapolation from the times of the Maccabees and Herod the Great, with the use of sources preceding 4 B.C.E. (death of Herod), interpolation from noncanonical sources between 4 B.C.E. and 36 C.E. (such as Philo), and also retropolation from the period following 36 C.E. (banishment of Pilate and dismissal of Caiaphas). In addition, we believe that first and second century sources such as Josephus may shed light on the first part of the first century C.E. and thus deserve our attention. By these methods and within these boundaries, the deeds and sayings of Jesus can be better understood.

We found that the resulting picture is much more complex than previously imagined, especially with respect to what can be safely dated to the time of Jesus. In fact, for areas such as Galilee, there are very few data from the first century B.C.E. and the first century C.E. Most archaeological discoveries date from the Late Roman and Byzantine periods (see Chronological Tables at end). Sites such as Nazareth and Capernaum have yielded meager relevant remains for the study of Jesus' time. Because of the strong influence of Roman culture visible in the material remains from the second century C.E. through the Byzantine period, some scholars have retrojected this phenomenon into the first half of the first century C.E. However, a more likely situation may be represented by the case of Bethsaida, where there is no significant stage of occupation after the destructive First Jewish War of 66–70 C.E. As a result, a clear Late Hellenistic–Early Roman layer could be identified. The same situation exists at Gamla, destroyed early in 67 C.E. and never rebuilt. In Jerusalem, extensive and prolonged archaeological research indicates that Hellenization, until the mid-first century C.E., was superficial and limited to the wealthy elite. Qumran, destroyed in 68 C.E. by the Romans, is a good example of a Jewish community that rejected all aspects of Hellenism, in contrast to the situation a few miles away in the royal palaces of Jericho.

Herod the Great, in building Greco-Roman temples, placed them in Samaria (Sebaste), Caesarea, and Paneas (Caesarea Philippi), outside Jewish areas. If stadiums and hippodromes dating from Jesus' time were discovered in Jericho, Caesarea, Samaria, and possibly Scythopolis, no remains of theaters existing in this period have been identified. Unlike stadiums and hippodromes, theaters required involvement of the audience in the Greek rituals and a good understanding of the Greek language by a large number of the population. As for visible traces of Greek education, despite the statements of 1 Maccabees, no remains of gymnasia have been found in Palestine, not even in Jerusalem, for the Late Hellenistic–Early Roman period. Nevertheless, this does not prove that they did not exist.

On the other hand, rural settlements 20 to 150 acres in size from the first century were not as tiny and humble as is often supposed. Nor did fishers around the Sea of Galilee live in poverty. The fisherman's house of Bethsaida extends over 400 square meters (4,300 square feet) and, although it contains no Hellenistic architectural elements, it does contain fine pottery, some imported from Asia Minor. In Gamla, only seven miles from Bethsaida, lower class houses stood next to patrician residences and did not differ substantially from them. Tombs of the upper class of the first century C.E. were surprisingly simple, as indicated by the tomb of Caiaphas the High Priest. Without his name engraved on his ossuary, it would have been impossible to imagine that he was buried there. By providing such information, field archaeology, despite its limitations, contributes significantly to our information about life in Jesus' time.

Archaeology, while thus contributing enormously to our understanding of life in the first century C.E., also has its limitations. It is most useful in its direct relevance to sites, objects, and other aspects of material culture. Archaeology can also re-

veal aspects of the social milieu of a given period. However, the process by which social relations and dynamics are reconstructed is a complicated and evolving one. The "new archaeology" of the 1960s and later, and the more recent processual and post-processual methodologies and interpretive strategies, have raised hopes that a better knowledge of past societies will become available but also have led to an acute awareness of the painstaking interdisciplinary work needed in order to establish viable paradigms and construct reliable models.

Sources, Format, and Use of the Book

This book presents entries arranged in alphabetical order. Sources of information include the Hebrew Bible (Old Testament); the canonical Gospels; other early Christian writings, especially the Acts of the Apostles and the Gospel of Thomas; the Apocrypha, particularly 1 Maccabees; the Mishnah and other rabbinic writings; the works of ancient writers such as Josephus, Philostratus, Suetonius, Tacitus, Strabo, Philo, and Origen; the contributions of scholars in New Testament studies and in early Judaism; the findings of archaeology, epigraphy, and numismatics. In our integrative approach, archaeology is to be understood both in its original sense of the study of what is ancient and in its modern sense of the recovery of the material culture of the past through excavation. By considering Jesus' Jewish background and environment as a most important source of information, we hope to give the reader a more accurate knowledge of Jesus' life, attitudes, and teaching.

Each entry ends with a section called "Implications for Jesus Research" in which we explore the relationship of archaeological data to the investigation of the life of Jesus. Sometimes firm correlations can be made. At other times we draw inferences and suggest hypotheses to be tested or questions to be raised. In the Implications, some aspects of Jesus' personality are portrayed; but they represent only possible renderings of the reality, for, in the current state of our information, it is impossible to obtain certainty. Nevertheless, the background and environment of Jesus, insofar as they can be reconstructed, provide information without which his image would be vague at best and inaccurate at worst. They give points of reference allowing for a more probable and plausible characterization, and they safeguard against gross distortion and misrepresentation.

Entries vary in length and depth of study, in relation to their importance for the understanding of Jesus' life. Regarding sites, longer developments are given to JERUSALEM, THE TEMPLE; CAPERNAUM; BETHSAIDA; and GOLGOTHA, TRADITIONAL SITE. For artifacts, features, and documents, CAVE OF LETTERS; COINS AND MONEY; COINS AS HISTORICAL DOCUMENTS; DEAD SEA SCROLLS; GOSPEL OF THOMAS; received more attention. In the area of human activities, AGRICULTURE; CRUCIFIXION; EXORCISM; BOATS; FISHING, NETS; MAGIC AND MIRACLES; OINTMENTS, PERFUME; MEDICINE, PHYSICIANS; and TRADITIONAL HEALING are among the more substantial.

In order to increase understanding and perhaps facilitate further research, a variety of other materials is included in this volume: maps, distances, a conversion table, chronological and genealogical tables, lists of rulers, a general bibliography, and more. The term *Scripture references* is used in a broad sense and includes some noncanonical texts. Cross-references appear in most entries next to the words or phrases for which more information may be needed. Unfamiliar words not usually found in college and office dictionaries are marked with an asterisk and briefly defined in a glossary. A general bibliography complements the more specialized ones following each entry. Sometimes we were unable to attain complete bibliographic information due to differing standards between America and other countries in reporting data.

For the sake of the general reader, notes have been avoided, and references deemed necessary are incorporated into the text. The same concern led to the elimination of most abbreviations of scholarly publications. The repetition of such expressions as "according to," "is said to," "apparently," which

otherwise would appear more than five hundred times, is avoided. But the use of the indicative tense does not ipso facto imply authenticity. For example, "Jesus went to the Decapolis" must be understood as, "According to the Gospels, Jesus went to the Decapolis." If a word such as *Pharisee* is not found in the entries, the reader should consult the Index to find out where information pertaining to it is situated. Many quotations are translated from the original biblical texts and may not exactly agree with existing English versions. For instance, the Greek *ptusas eis ta ommata autou* (Mark 8:23) is translated according to its true meaning, "spitting in his eyes," while the NRSV renders it in a edulcorated form, "put saliva on his eyes."

In our effort to be as accurate as possible, we have kept the original wording of the Hebrew and Greek texts in our translations. The language we use is therefore not always inclusive when we report events and life-styles of the past.

As a rule, we do not engage in direct criticism. Opinions and theories with which we disagree are normally given without the names of their authors. The informed scholar will recognize what is alluded to, but the general reader will not be annoyed by what could be understood as a polemic. Our ambition is to provide a useful tool at a time when interest in the historical Jesus is growing and to disseminate little-known or unpublished information. We hope that, in the future, biblical scholars and archaeologists can cooperate more closely for a more fruitful use of all available data.

Rami Arav   *John J. Rousseau*

[1] Albert Schweizer, *The Quest of the Historical Jesus*. German 1906. New York: MacMillan, 1968.
[2] Günther Bornkamm, *Jesus of Nazareth*, trans. by Irene and Fraser McLuskey. Minneapolis: Fortress Press, 1994. (First edition New York: Harper, 1956.)
[3] Jesus Seminar, *Forum* 6.1 (1990) to 7.2 (1991); *The Five Gospels*. New York: Macmillan, 1993.
[4] John D. Crossan, *The Historical Jesus*. San Francisco: Harper Collins, 1991.

Aenon and Salim

Importance

According to the Fourth Gospel, John baptized at Aenon near Salim while Jesus was in the Judean countryside.

Scripture Reference

John 3:23.

General Information

The exact location of Aenon is unknown. According to the Fourth Gospel, John continued baptizing there after Jesus' baptism while Jesus was ministering in Judea and making converts in great numbers (John 3:26; 4:1). Eusebius mentions the place (*Onomasticon* 40:1–4), which he locates on the western side of the Jordan, as does Jerome (*Epistle* 73). The Madaba map indicates another location on the eastern side, opposite Bethabara (*see* BETHABARA). According to a Christian tradition dating from the sixth century and coming from the pilgrim guide Antonius and Cyrillus Scythopolitanus, there was a cave on the eastern location (named Saphsaphas or "Willow" on the Madaba map) where Jesus dwelt at the time of his baptism.

Aetheria (385–388 C.E.) reports that the cave was situated in a garden.

Archaeological Data

Several sites have been proposed for the locations of Aenon and Salim:

- Tell Abu Sus, for Salim, 6 miles south of Beth-Shean, the Scythopolis of Jesus' time.
- Tell er-Ridgah for Salim, south of Beth-Shean; the name would be preserved in the name of the Arab village Sheikh Salim.
- Ainum, for Aenon, 8 miles northeast of Nablus, near the source of Wadi Far'ah.
- On the east side of the Jordan, at the ford of Jericho, near the place where the cave is located in the Wadi Kharrar; a church was built there by Elias, bishop of Jerusalem (494–518).

It is impossible, at this time, to determine the correct location of either Salim or Aenon.

Implications for Jesus Research

Jesus probably took shelter in caves (*see* GALILEAN and JUDEAN CAVES), although none can be specified except perhaps for the caves at the Mount of

Olives. The tradition designating the cave of Wadi Kherrar as the place of Jesus' shelter at the time of his baptism is not reliable because its first century origin cannot be ascertained. Such traditions are to be questioned (*see* BETHSAIDA and GOLGATHA, TRADITIONAL SITE) and it seems doubtful that Jesus and John would have stayed in Herod Antipas' territory for a long period of time.

BIBLIOGRAPHY

Albright, W. F. "Recent Discovery in Palestine and the Gospel of St. John." *The Background of the New Testament and its Eschatology*, edited by W. D. Davies and D. Daube. Cambridge: Cambridge University Press, 1954:153-55.

Boismard, M. E. "Aenon près de Salim (Jean III, 23)." *Revue Biblique* 80 (1973): 218–29.

Conder, R. C. "On the Identification of Aenon." *Palestinian Exploration Fund, Quarterly Statement* (1874): 191–92.

Mackay, C. "Salem." *Palestine Exploration Quarterly* 80 (1948): 121–30.

Agriculture, Cereals

Importance

Palestine was primarily an agricultural country and the Gospels refer to many aspects of agricultural life. Cereals were the most important staple food.

Scripture References

Matt. 3:10, 12; 6:26, 28, 30; 9:37-38; 11:29-30; 13:3-9, 18-23, 24-30, 31-32, 37-40, 44; 15:13; 22:5; 24:18, 32, 40-41; Mark 4:3-9, 14-20, 26-29, 31-32; 11:12-13; 13:16; Luke 3:9, 17; 6:43-44; 8:5-8, 11-15; 9:62; 10:2, 12:24, 28; 13:6-9; 14:18-19; 15:25; 16:7; 17:6, 7, 28; 19:21-22; 22:31; John 4:35-38; 6:9, 13; 12:24.

General Information

Except for a few fertile plains or valleys (Esdraelon, Netofa, Sharon, Sorek and Elah in the Shephalah, and the Jordan Valley), the land of Israel is comprised mostly of rocky hills. It took enormous efforts over centuries, as population expanded, to remove the rocks and build terraces where crops could grow. It is estimated that, by the Roman period, nearly half of the hilly ground had been cleared of rocks and was under cultivation. Even desert farming flourished in Southern Judea: stone walls were built across wadis, a few hundred feet apart, in order to form artificial fields, which were flooded during the rainy season and planted. In the Negev, the Nabateans developed elaborate ways to make the most of the four to five inches of rain that fell for only a few hours each year. In the hills of Galilee and Samaria, the soil of the terraces was fertile and two crops of wheat could grow every year. The yield was low by today's standards: no more than five bushels for one bushel of grain planted.

The farmers' main concern was the lack of sufficient and stable water supply. The dry season lasts five months, from April or May to mid-October; and water had to be stored in cisterns, artificial ponds, lakes, or reservoirs. A few perennial streams allowed for some artificial irrigation. Toward the end of the dry season, the nocturnal dew of August and September brings relief. Farmers feared the hot wind or sirocco from the desert that, in Judea, could blow for several days in a row between mid-September and late October. Other dangers such as damage from insects, especially locusts, fungi, and mildew also threatened crops.

Wheat was the most important staple food. The main sowing season was in late October or early November for a harvest time in May or June, to which corresponded the Feast of Weeks (*see* fig. 1 and TEMPLE, SERVICE AND RITUAL). Barley was second in importance. It grew best in the dry areas of southern Samaria and Judea; it was planted at the same time as wheat but was harvested a month earlier. Spelt, a wheat of lower quality but more rugged, was sown in the poorer soil surrounding the fields of wheat and barley. Flax (harvested in March or April, *see* TEXTILE), olives, grapes (*see* VITICULTURE and OLIVE OIL INDUSTRY), dates (mostly in the plain of Jericho), lentils, beans, peas,

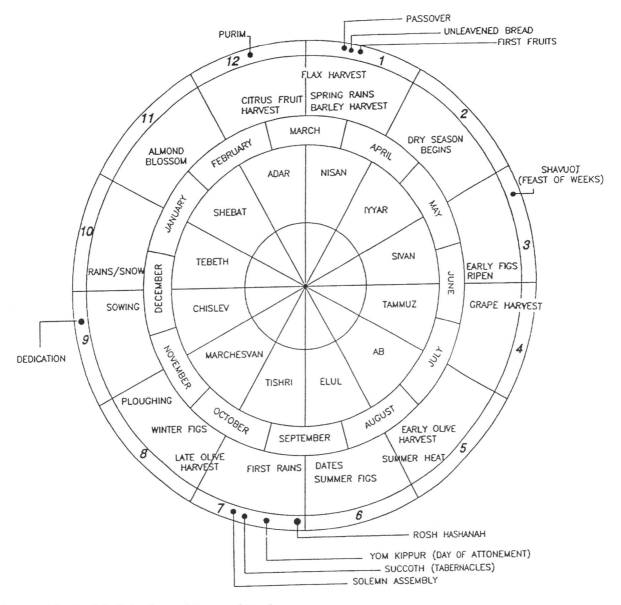

Figure 1 The Jewish Calendar and Seasonal Cycle

cucumbers, onions, leeks, garlic, figs, pomegranates, and sycamore figs also were grown and contributed to the welfare of the people.

Prosperity was seen as dependent upon land ownership and farming: "under their own vines and under their own fig trees" (Mic. 4:4; Zech. 3:10), "those who till their land will have plenty of food: (Prov. 12:11), but the destitute had certain rights to share the fruit of the land with the landowners. The hungry were allowed to eat directly from the crop in the field provided nothing was taken away, as Jesus and his disciples did (Matt. 12:1 and parallels).

> When you go into your neighbor's vineyard, you may eat your fill of grapes, as many as you wish, but you shall not put any in your basket. When you go into your neighbor's standing grain, you may pluck the ears with your hand, but you shall not put the sickle to your neighbor's standing grain (Deut. 23:24-25).

The edges of the field and its corners were not usually harvested. The grain was left standing there for the benefit of the poor; all that was left in the field itself, even a forgotten whole sheaf, belonged to the "sojourner, the orphan, and the widow." Similar policies applied to the harvest of olives and grapes (Deut. 24:19-21). The story of Ruth illustrates this humanitarian regulation in the case of a barley harvest (Ruth 2:3, 7, 8, 15-19).

Life and religious cycles closely followed the seasons and the agricultural calendar. The three most important religious feasts corresponded to specific agricultural events: The Feast of Unleavened Bread, the seven days following the night of *pesah*, "Passover," had its origin in a Canaanite seasonal feast and an offering of barley was made. The "Feast of Weeks," *shavuot* or Pentecost, marked the end of the grain harvest and the beginning of the bringing of the first fruit. The "Feast of Booths," *succoth* or Ingathering, corresponded to the end of the vintage season and agricultural year (*see* fig. 1). Offerings were expressed in terms of agricultural production: tithing of harvests, first born males of the flock, first fruit.

According to Joshua, the land had been divided among the tribes and then allotted to clans and families. Every parcel was supposed to stay in the same family forever. If it was sold, it was to return to the original owner at the time of the Jubilee year (Lev. 25:8-12), but it is difficult to ascertain whether this legal prescription was followed in the Israelite period or in later times, especially during the Hasmonean and Roman periods. Rich priestly families and the aristocracy had managed to gather

large estates either by legal proceedings, for instance in the case of debt, or by forceful purchase as in the case of Naboth's vineyard (1 Kings 21:1-16). The dispossessed owners, if they wanted to continue farming, had to work as hired hands or slaves. The most common process of elimination from ownership was descendant multiplication. The oldest son received a double share of the land and the rest was divided evenly among his brothers (daughters inherited only if there was no male child). After a few generations, the parcels became so small that they could not sustain a family or even a single individual. The legal owner of such a small parcel had to sell it, usually to his older brother. A number of young people were thus eliminated from land ownership. They could work for the older brother, hire themselves as farm workers, indenture themselves as slaves (*see* SLAVES AND SERVANTS), learn a craft, start a trade, live on hunting and fishing, work on construction sites like Tiberias or the Temple, sell or beg in the streets of Jerusalem, join a band of brigands or the armies of Herod's sons, Antipas and Philip, or the Roman auxiliary forces, or leave the country and perhaps become a merchant or a magician in the Diaspora (*see* EXORCISM and MAGIC, MIRACLES).

Galilee was a special case. The country had been conquered from the Seleucids by the Maccabees, its people converted to Judaism and the land reallotted. Thus, in the first century C.E., there were a majority of small freeholders and small flock owners using the open grazing land of the hills. It was a prosperous region (Josephus, *War* 3, 3. 2/41–43). The climate and the soil allowed for diverse farming; families could be self-sufficient—owning a field, a few sheep and goats, olive and fruit trees, a vegetable garden, chickens, a donkey, and perhaps a cow. Doubtless taxes, tribute, and offerings represented an important portion of the family's income (*see* TAX AND TAX COLLECTORS). In addition to the Temple tax paid by every male aged twenty-one and older (*see* TEMPLE, TREASURY) and the mandatory offerings of crops and animals there were civil taxes. But it seems unlikely that there was widespread starvation among the lower class as suggested in some recent books about Jesus and his time. In fact, the reign of Herod Antipas was apparently a peaceful one, only disturbed in 6 C.E. by the call of Judas the Galilean and the Pharisee Zadok against the census and the payment of the tribute. Similar observations could be made for Samaria, Judea and Jerusalem, which came under direct Roman rule in 6 C.E. In these regions, it was only under the prefectorate of Pontius Pilate and under an increasingly corrupt High Priesthood that the situation began to deteriorate.

Archaeological and Technical Information

A number of metal parts of agricultural implements such as sickle blades and plowshares, and stone objects such as grinding mills dating from the first centuries B.C.E. and C.E., have been discovered in excavations and by chance find. Through ethnoarchaeology—comparison with modern cultures using similar techniques—wooden instruments such as forks, yokes, plow frames, threshing sleds, and the like, have been reconstructed. They can be seen, for example, in the display of farming instruments in the restored village of ancient Qatzrin in Lower Golan. Although Qatzrin is a fifth-century C.E. village, the tools were substantially the same for centuries and provide a good idea of their first-century C.E. appearance.

The plow with an iron share was pulled by two oxen or asses and could dig furrows up to five inches deep, which is too close to the surface by modern standards. It seems that no harrows were used. Instead of harrowing after seeding, the farmer plowed his field a second time, going across the original furrows in order to cover the seeds with the soil. He would finish the work by raking the soil with a large broom made of small branches. The farmer's collection of tools also included picks, shovels, spades, and hoes. Threshing was done on flat hardened earth or preferably on the horizontal surface of a large natural slab, such as several that can still be seen today. The operation consisted in separating the grain from the stalks by beating the plants with long sticks, or by driving

Grain Grinder (Qatzrin)

cattle over the stalks, or by dragging over them a threshing sled made of a heavy board studded with pieces of iron or stones on its lower side. After the bulk of the straw was removed, winnowing separated the grain from the chaff. It was done with a wooden fork or a shovel in the afternoon, when the wind was strong enough and steady. Workers tossed the husks in the air, the wind blew the light chaff away, and the heavier grain fell back on the threshing floor. The last operation, sifting, was done in two steps with two different round sieves: one with a large mesh to eliminate small rocks and pebbles; another with a fine mesh to eliminate dust. The grain was then poured into large storage jars. What was owed to the Temple and the tax collector was set aside and the rest taken away for storage in a corner of the family house or, for large crops, in granaries, dry cisterns, or silos.

Implications for Jesus Research

Because the population of Palestine was mostly agrarian, Jesus used images borrowed from the lives of the farmers or shepherds in several of his parables. Thus it is intriguing that, while fishers were a small minority in the country, Jesus used a large number of expressions referring to fishing. There is a noticeable disproportion in this connection, which tends to indicate that he had stronger ties with sailors than with peasants (*see* FISHING, NETS and BOATS). According to the Gospels' accounts, Jesus had the charismatic ability to relate to people from all walks of life and from all levels of society. Besides farmers and fishers, other parables or Gospel narratives show him referring to or addressing women, rich owners, political extremists or assassins (G. Thom. 98), scribes, Pharisees and Sadducees, tax collectors, prostitutes, people with leprosy, people who could not walk, synagogue leaders, Samaritans, a centurion, and Gentiles. Jesus' use of agrarian images is illustrated in the Parable of the Sower, which received a *pink* rating by the Jesus Seminar in 1986: "Other seeds fell on good soil and brought forth grain, some a hundredfold, some sixty, some thirty" (Matt. 13:8, Mark 4:8). Compared with the then current yield of the crop, a maximum of five times the quantity sown, a yield of thirty times seemed miraculous; yields of sixty and one hundred times were inconceivable. The power of faith in the Kingdom was certainly carried through.

As noted above (*see* General Information), the period between 6 and 30 C.E. was relatively stable in Palestine. Disturbances, if any, may have been caused by nationalistic and religious feelings rather than by widespread poverty. In these circumstances, we should not retroject into Jesus' time situations described by Josephus for the years 50 to 70 C.E., when Palestine was under Roman and priestly oppression. Only toward the end of Jesus' life is a reference found in the Gospels to rebels and to an insurrection most certainly caused by Pilate's highhanded ways (Mark 15:7).

BIBLIOGRAPHY

Applebaum, S. "Types of Agricultural Settlements in Eretz Israel in the Hellenistic, Roman and Byzantine Periods." *Fifth Archaeological Conference in Israel* (1978): 23 ff.

Avery-Peck, A. J. "Scripture and Mishna: The Case of the Mishnaic Division of Agriculture." *Journal of Jewish Studies* 38 (1987): 56–71.

Bergheim, S. "Land Tenure in Palestine." *Palestinian Exploration Fund, Quarterly Statement* (1894): 191–99.

Borowski, O. *Agriculture in Ancient Israel*. Winona Lake, Ind., Eisenbrauns, 1987.

Colomb, B. and Y. Kedar. "Ancient Agriculture in the Galilean Mountains." *IEJ* 21 (1971): 136–40.

Edelstein, G. and S. Gibson. "Ancient Jerusalem Food Basket." *BAR* 8 (1982): 46–54.

Rohrbaugh, R. L. "The Social Location of the Markan Audience." *Interpretation* 47.4, 380–95.

Turkonski, L. "Peasant Agriculture in the Judean Hills." *Palestine Exploration Quarterly* 101 (1969): 21–33, 101–12.

Antonia, Pavement *(Gabbatha, Lithostrotos)*

Importance

The fortress Antonia may have been the location of the *praetorium* where Jesus was sentenced by Pilate.

Scripture References

Matt. 27:2, 27; Mark 15:2, 16; Luke 23:1; John 18:28, 33; 19:9, 13.

General Information

King Herod must have built the fortress Antonia at the northwest corner of the Temple Mount some time before 31 B.C.E. because only then would he have named the fortress after his patron, the triumvir Marcus Antonius, who was defeated that year at the battle of Actium* by Octavian. The Antonia was a rebuilding and enlargement of the *birah*, "citadel," which had a long history. It was destroyed by the Seleucids but rebuilt shortly after by Antochius IV Epiphanes, who kept a garrison of Syrian soldiers there. The fortress was taken and then lost again by the Hasmoneans until John Hyrcanus conquered it and rebuilt it in 134 B.C.E. It probably remained intact until the reign of Herod.

Josephus describes the Antonia as a high fortress with a tower at each of its four corners

(*War* 5, 5.8/238–47). A large, spacious, and splendid complex, it could easily accommodate a cohort. It was in fact a palace with porticoes and baths, and Herod resided there for at least eight years until he built his new palace around 23 B.C.E. on the western hill. Josephus reports that the corner towers of the fortress were 50 cubits high (75 feet) with the exception of the southwestern one, which was 70 cubits (105 feet) high. This highest tower was manned by a century.* During the pilgrim festivals, the soldiers were positioned on top of the fortress and roofs of the porticoes surrounding the Temple court of the Gentiles. This at times caused humiliation for the worshipers. Sometimes the soldiers on duty insulted people. A serious offense of this sort occurred during the time of prefect Cumanus (48–52 C.E.): on the Feast of Unleavened Bread (Passover), a soldier on top of one portico "turned his back to the Jews, bent forward, raised his skirt in an indecent manner and broke wind noisily while keeping his posture." The people were enraged and hurled stones at the soldiers. They called on Cumanus who, fearing for himself, sent reinforcements who poured into the porticoes. The crowd panicked and more than 30,000 were trampled to death according to Josephus's account (*War* 5, 7.1/223–27), which may be an exaggeration.

An underground passage led from the southeastern tower to the sanctuary. This was used by Herod when he lived in the fortress and then by the High Priest when his sacred vestments were kept in the tower (*see* TEMPLE, STAIRS AND GATES, and *Antiq.* 15, 11.7/424). On the western side of the fortress was a large open-air pool oriented northwest to southwest called *Strouthion* ("swallow" in Greek), probably because swallows flew over it to catch mosquitoes and other insects attracted by the water. In 70 C.E., the soldiers of the Fifth Legion erected a ramp from the bottom of the pool to ram the wall above it. The Strouthion pool can be seen today under the Convent of Notre Dame de Sion.

Archaeological Data

The rocky height, leveled as a plateau on which the Antonia was built, has been identified. It rests about 75 feet above its surroundings. Today, the el Omariyyeh School, at the northwest of Haram esh-Sharif* stands upon it. It also extends to the areas of the Convent of the Flagellation, the Convent of Notre Dame de Sion and of the Hadrian Arch (*Ecce Homo* Arch). Its overall measurements were about 270 x 115 meters (885 x 377 feet).

From 1931 to 1937 L. H. Vincent and M. Godelene of the Ecole Biblique excavated the area under the Convent of Notre Dame de Sion. In 1955, the Franciscans began their own excavation under the Convent of the Flagellation. Under Notre Dame de Sion, the excavators found an extensive water system with large pools and cisterns. It covers an area about 170 feet long and 45 feet wide, with depths reaching 33 feet in some places. There is little doubt that this was the *Strouthion*. During the Hadrianic destruction of Jerusalem (135 C.E.) and its reconstruction as the Roman city *Aelia Capitolina*, vaults were built over the pool to support a large courtyard (156 x 117 feet) paved with stone slabs. Some of the stones were scratched to make a large game board.

Several reconstructions of the floor plan of the Antonia have been proposed; none is entirely satisfactory. Contrary to what is often explained to Christian pilgrims, the pavement seen under Notre Dame de Sion cannot be the *Gabbatha* (in Hebrew), or *lithostrotos* (in Greek), where Jesus was taken to be sentenced by Pilate. The board game on the slabs was probably not a human-sized board where the game of *baselikios*, "king," was played by Roman soldiers. It cannot indicate the location where Jesus was ridiculed as the King of the Jews, cloaked in purple with a crown of thorns. These elements simply were not at the location where they are today. However, it may be that the slabs were taken from the original pavement of the Antonia's courts.

Implications for Jesus Research

The location of the fortress Antonia is well established, although its exact floor plan and measurements are uncertain. An important controversy developed regarding the location of the *praetorium* where Jesus was taken to appear before Pilate. The traditional Christian opinion is that Pilate resided in the Antonia; but several scholars argue that he stayed in Herod's new palace. Because the *praetorium* was wherever the prefect resided, the traditional course of the *Via Dolorosa*, from the Antonia to the Church of the Holy Sepulchre, is questioned.

When Pilate left his usual residence of Caesarea Maritima to go to Jerusalem, he probably would have preferred to stay in the Antonia during the festivals for two reasons:

1. The Temple was the center of attraction for the pilgrims who flocked there in large numbers; the most likely location for any emerging rebellion was thus the Temple. It seems natural that the prefect would stay where the concentration of soldiers and the potential for popular unrest were greatest. There, he could be informed immediately and react without delay should any sign of violence be detected.
2. The Antonia was a royal palace properly fit to be the residence of a prefect.

The only convincing reason for Pilate to have resided in Herod's new palace is that it was adjacent to the city wall in the west and connected to the gate leading to Jaffa and Caesarea. In case of an insurrection, Pilate could have left Jerusalem safely with his personal guard, leaving the tribune in charge of the situation. But in the eyes of the emperor such an attitude would have been an act of desertion and, according to the accounts of his character in Josephus and Philo, it is unlikely that he would have abandoned his post. It seems, then, that Jesus was sentenced in the Antonia and that the general orientation of the *Via Dolorosa* is correct, assuming that Golgotha was indeed located in the area of the Church of the Holy Sepulchre, which is not established (*see* GOLGOTHA, TRADITIONAL SITE).

BIBLIOGRAPHY

Benoit, P. "The Archaeological Reconstruction of the Antonia Fortress." *Qadmoniot* 5 (1972): 127–29.

———. "The Archaeological Reconstruction of the Antonia Fortress." *Jerusalem Revealed*, edited by Y. Yadin, New Haven: Yale University Press, 1976.

———. "L'Antonia d'Hérode le Grand et le forum oriental d'Aelia Capitolina." *Exégèse et Théologie*, vol. 4, Paris: Le Cerf, 1982.

Peters, P. E. *Jerusalem*. Princeton, N.J.: Princeton University Press, 1985.

Bethabara/Beth Araba/Bethany

Importance

Bethabara could be the place where Jesus was baptized.

Scripture Reference

John 1:28.

General Information

The canonical Gospels all indicate that Jesus was baptized by John at the river Jordan. Josephus describes the activity of the Baptizer in a passage that is considered authentic by most scholars (*Antiq.* 18, 5.2/116–17). Only the Fourth Gospel gives a name for the place where John baptized, "Bethany beyond the Jordan." No known record or tradition indicates a place or village by that name on the east side of the Jordan.

In contradiction to the Gospel's information, the Madaba map shows a spot for the baptism of Jesus on the west bank of the Jordan, at about the latitude of Jericho, with the name Bethabara. Madaba is a small town in Jordan, 15 miles east of the river, where a mosaic map of the Holy Land was found on the floor of an ancient church. This evidence leads most New Testament scholars to conclude that the name Bethabara was changed to Bethany in the course of successive transcriptions. Origen (185–253 C.E.) had already indicated that the place of the baptism was Bethabara on the west side of the river, and on his authority older manuscripts bear this name. Emperor Anasthasius (491–518) followed Origen when he built the church of Saint

John the Baptist near the west bank on a site identified with Qasr el Yahud, the "Fort of the Jews."

Archaeological Data

Madaba (Medeba or Medaba) is an old Moabite town that was occupied by the Israelites and is mentioned several times in the Hebrew Bible, in 1 Maccabees, and in Josephus (*Antiq.* 13, 2.4/11,19; 13, 9.1/255). In the Byzantine period it was an important city whose bishop participated in the council of Chalcedon (451). In 1896, during the excavation of a sixth-century church, a well-preserved mosaic floor was found. It depicts a map of the Holy Land from Beth Shean to the Nile, with corresponding quotations from Scripture. It dates from the sixth century, but gives information from an older tradition. Ruins of a sanctuary at Qasr el Yahud probably belong to the church built by Anasthasius.

Implications for Jesus Research

Scholarly discussions of John 1:28 go back to the time of Origen. Rudolf Bultmann summarizes them in a long footnote to his commentary on this verse. Based on geographical and socio-historical considerations, it seems probable that John baptized in a place that was easily accessible, because his call was for everyone, and in a place where it was convenient to enter the water. A ford is the most likely possibility. John may have preferred to stay on the west side for reasons of security. There he could perform his task without being in immediate danger of being arrested by the soldiers of Herod Antipas who, eventually sent him to prison and had him beheaded. Most scholars recognize that Jesus started his ministry as a disciple of John the Baptist. In his own independent mission, which he may have initiated after John's imprisonment, he followed some of the Baptizer's principles, the most important being repentance as a condition of salvation (*see* DEAD SEA SCROLLS).

BIBLIOGRAPHY

Avi-Yonah, M. *The Madaba Mosaic Map.* Jerusalem: Israel Exploration Society, 1954.

Bultmann, R. *The Gospel of John: A Commentary.* German, 1964. Translated by G. R. Beasley-Murray, 93 n. 3. Philadelphia: The Westminster Press, 1971.

Conder, C. R. "The Site of Bethabara." *Palestine Exploration Fund, Quarterly Statement* (1875): 72–74.

Dockx, S. "Béthanie au-delà du Jourdain." *Chronologies Néotestamentaires et vie de l' Eglise Primitive.* Paris: Duculot, 1976.

Piccirillo, M. *The Mosaics of Jordan* (American Center of Oriental Research Publications 1.) Amman: American Center of Oriental Research, 1993.

Webb, R. L. "John as Baptizer: His Activity of Immersing in the Context of First Century Judaism." In *Jesus Seminar Papers.* Sonoma, Calif.: Polebridge Press, 1991.

Wiefel, W. "Bethabara jenseits des Jordan." *Zeitschrift des deutschen Palästina-Vereins* 83 (1967): 72–81.

Bethany

Importance

Jesus had friends in Bethany and, according to the Fourth Gospel, he raised Lazarus from the dead there.

Scripture References

Matt. 21:17; 26:6; Mark 11:1; 14:3; Luke 24:50; John 11:1, 18.

General Information

Bethany is a village on the eastern side of the Mount of Olives. Some scholars have identified it with ancient Ananiah (Neh. 11:32). It was the last stop before reaching Jerusalem, less than 2 miles away, for travelers coming from Jericho. Bethany holds a special place in Christian tradition: There stood the house of Simon the Leper, Martha, Mary, and Lazarus. Lazarus was raised, Mary anointed Jesus, and Jesus washed the feet of his disciples there. According to Luke, it was the place of the Ascension (Luke 24:50-51).

A sanctuary of Lazarus, the "Lazarium," was already visited by the Bordeaux Pilgrim in 333 C.E. Its name is preserved in the name of the Arab village of el-Azarieh. By the end of the fourth century a church was built over the crypt (Eusebius, *Onomasticon*). This church stood until the times of the Crusaders, who built another basilica to mark the place where Mary would have anointed Jesus' feet. After the expulsion of the Crusaders from the Holy Land, the Arabs built a mosque over the site, and the original passage leading to the tomb was walled. At present one enters through a staircase cut in the rock by the Franciscans in the seventeenth century.

Archaeological Data

S. J. Saller excavated the site of Bethany from 1949 to 1953. He found the remains of four superimposed churches built to the east of "Lazarus's tomb," all decorated with mosaics. The most ancient was from the fourth to fifth centuries, the second oldest was from the Byzantine period, and the most recent were medieval. Numerous rock-hewn tombs were found in the same area, some of them within the very precincts of the churches. The excavations also revealed remains of the ancient city: houses, cisterns, silos, and winepresses. The associated pottery belongs to the Persian, Hellenistic, Roman, Byzantine, and later periods.

The cave that is shown as Lazarus's tomb is comprised of an antechamber and a burial place, which is accessible only through a hole in the floor of the antechamber and a few steps on which one must crawl. The cave does not accord with the design of other tombs of the period: walls of masonry line the bare rock and there are no platforms, benches, or niches typical of Jewish tombs. Nevertheless, the possibility remains that it was originally a tomb and that, in later times, it was enlarged and reconstructed to form a small undergound chapel.

Implications for Jesus Research

Archaeological research in Bethany to date reveals the existence of a village or small city in the first century C.E. near the present "tomb" of Lazarus. The cave itself cannot be dated as a tomb of that period. Even if it could be dated to the first century

C.E., no evidence indicates that it was indeed the tomb of Lazarus. The location of the house of Simon the Leper and Lazarus in Bethany was perhaps in observance of purity rules regarding the Temple: there should be no source of defilement windward of the sanctuary, that is, in the west (*see* JERUSALEM TOMBS and GOLGOTHA, TRADITIONAL SITE).

BIBLIOGRAPHY

Brunot, A. "Béthanie et ses environs." *Bible et Terre Sainte* 163 (July–Aug. 1974): 357–70.

Perkins, L. J. "Bethany." *ABD* 1: 702–3.

Saller, S. J. "Bethany." *Annual of the Department of Antiquities of Jordan* (1951): 44; (1952): 82–83.

———. "Excavations at Bethany (1949–1953)." *Publications of the Studium Biblicum Franciscanum* 12 (1957): 9–33.

Storme, A. "Les lieux saints évangéliques: Qu'en est-il aujourd'hui de leur authenticity?" *La Terre Sainte* 9 (1991): 165–76.

Taylor, J. E. "The Bethany Cave: A Jewish-Christian Cult Site?" *Revue Biblique* 97 (1990): 453–65.

Bethlehem

Importance

Birthplace of David; traditional location of Jesus' birth.

Scripture References

Matt. 2:1, 5, 6, 16; Luke 2:4, 15: John 7: 42.

General Information

Bethlehem was a city of Judea located about 5 miles south of Jerusalem. Its name is ambiguous; it can mean house (or place) of bread, food, fighting, or of the god Lahamu. J. Murphy-O'Connor indicates that the town is first mentioned in the fourteenth century B.C.E. when the king of Jerusalem wrote to Pharoah asking for archers to help him recover *Bit-Lhami*, which had rebelled. Bethlehem plays an important role in the history of the ancient Israelites and of the Jewish people: the clan of Perez, son of Tamar and Judah, settled there; from the line of Boaz came David, the great hero and king of Israel, who became the prototype of the Messiah. It was the scene of the story of Ruth, an ancestor of David and Jesus, according to Matthew (Matt. 1:5). Above all, it was David's birthplace and the place where Samuel anointed him. Because Bethlehem was the city of origin of David, it became the focus of messianic hope according to Matthew 2:6, which quotes Micah 5:2-4.

From a military perspective, Bethlehem had considerable strategic importance in ancient times. It lay on the caravan route linking Jerusalem to Egypt via Hebron, and at the end of Saul's reign it was occupied by a Philistine garrison (2 Sam. 23:14). The story of David's men bringing him water from the "well of Bethlehem that is by the gate" suggests that it was a fortified city. Less than a century later, Rehoboam built a new fortress there as part of a line of fortifications to protect Jerusalem against invaders coming from the south and southeast (2 Chron. 11:5-12). By the second half of the eighth century B.C.E., Bethlehem seems to have lost its importance. In 135 C.E., the Romans stationed a garrison there in order to eliminate the last fighters of Bar Kokhba's army.

Early in Christian tradition, Bethlehem became highly venerated because, according to Matthew and Luke, Jesus was born there. But Paul, author of the earliest written Christian documents known to this day, does not mention this. Neither Matthew nor Luke indicates that Jesus was born in a cave, as a tradition first recorded by Justin Martyr (*circa* 110–165 C.E.) indicates. The cave tradition became official when, about 330 C.E., after the pilgrimage of his mother (Queen Helena) Emperor Constantine ordered the first church of the Nativity to be built over a cave. The Bordeaux Pilgrim reports that he had seen the basilica when he visited the Holy Land in 333 C.E. The Christian monk and scholar Jerome, who translated the Hebrew Bible into Latin, lived in a cave at Bethlehem from 386 to his death in 420. He indicates that emperor Hadrian had erected a temple to Adonis in a nearby sacred wood planted over a grotto (Jerome, *Epistle 58, to Paulinius*). According to him, both Jupiter and Adonis were worshiped at Bethlehem until the time of Constantine.

Under the reign of Justinian (527–565), the church of Constantine was destroyed during the Samaritan revolt of 529 and rebuilt in its present form. The first two Crusader kings of Jerusalem, Baldwin I and II, were crowned in the Church of the Nativity, which remained in Christian hands during the rule of the Mamluks and Turks despite fierce Muslim oppression. For security reasons, the Christians kept reducing the size of the main entrance so that, even today, only one person at a time can enter, by bending. Unending conflicts between the denominations in charge of the building caused its deterioration. The rivalry has even motivated international frictions: the silver star, which marked the presumed place of Jesus' birth, was stolen in 1847; this theft was one of the causes of the Crimean War (1854–1856). The situation became so bad that, in the mid-nineteenth century, the Turks officially divided the building among the Christian denominations in charge, and determined the order of their respective ceremonies. The Turkish ruling is still observed today, yet it does not prevent occasional fights between priests of the rival denominations. In 1990, the Israeli government had to repair the roof of the church because the two main rival denominations could not agree on who was to be in charge of the work and how to share the cost.

Archaeological Data

The grotto located under the apse of the church is not open to archaeological research and the natural rock cannot be observed, covered as it is with marble slabs and religious ornaments. In 1934 W. Harvey, followed by the Franciscans from 1948 to 1951, excavated parts of the church. The main structure as seen today dates from the time of Justinian (527–565). Except for the columns and carved wooden architraves above the capitals of the columns, however, almost nothing remains of the original decoration. It is said that when the Persians destroyed part of the church in 614, they kept the paintings of the columns representing the magi in a nativity scene because their costumes were Persian.

Implications for Jesus Research

Archaeology provides no evidence that could shed light on the role of the Bethlehem grotto in the traditions about Jesus' birth. Indeed, those traditions can be criticized on the following points:

- Besides the specific mentions of Matthew and Luke, the other references, direct or indirect, to the birthplace of Jesus point to Nazareth (see NAZARETH).

- Paul, the earliest New Testament writer, does not mention a birth at Bethlehem. If Jesus had been born in Bethlehem, this factor would have been a strong argument to support Paul's statement that Jesus was of Davidic descent (Rom. 1:3).

- Luke indicates that Joseph and Mary went to Bethlehem because of the census, which in fact happened in 6 C.E., at least ten years after Jesus' birth.

Two more observations can be made:

- Because the Persians had built a network of caravansaries along the well-kept roads linking together the different parts of their immense empire, there could have been an "inn" at Bethlehem in the first century C.E. Nevertheless, there is no evidence of such a caravansary near this town. Even if there had been an inn, the underground grotto would have been too small to give shelter to the animals of travelers. Caravansaries had vast enclosures to keep camels, horses, and donkeys.

- If Joseph's family (the whole Perez clan) was from Bethlehem, it is more likely that he would have stayed with relatives than in an inn. In fact, Matthew indicates that Mary and Jesus were in a house in Bethlehem at the time of the magi's visit (Matt. 2:11). The legend of Jesus' birth at Bethlehem appeared after the time of Paul, perhaps to convince potential Jewish converts that Jesus was the Messiah they expected.

BIBLIOGRAPHY

Dalman, G. *Les Itinéraires de Jésus*. German, 1922. Paris: Payot, 1930.

Cazelles, H. "Sur l'histoire de Bethléhem." Edited by R. Laurentin. *Kecharitoméné* (1990): 145–52.

Dinur, U. "Bethlehem." *Excavations and Surveys of Israel* 5 (1986): 15–16.

Harrison, R. K. *Major Cities of the Biblical World*. Nashville: Thomas Nelson Publishers, 1985.

Leconte, R. "Bethle'em aux jours du roi Hérode." *Bible et Terre Sainte* 15 (1958): 4–9.

Livio, J. B. "Bethléhem Cité de David." *Bible et Terre Sainte* 186 (1976): 8–15.

Murphy-O'Connor, J. *The Holy Land*, pp. 146–52. New York: Oxford University Press, 1980.

Stekelis, M. and Avi-Yonah, M., and V. Tsajeris. "Bethlehem." *NEAEHL* 1:203-210.

Storme, A. "La Gruta de la Natividad de Belèn." *Tierra Sancta* 65 (1990): 284–89.

Bethphage

Importance

Jesus found a donkey in Bethphage to ride for his entry into Jerusalem.

Scripture References

Matt. 21:1; Mark 11:1; Luke 19:29; John 12:12-15.

General Information

Bethphage (place of the green figs) was a village on the Mount of Olives between Bethany and Jerusalem, about one mile east of the Temple. It has been identified with the village of et-Tur. A church was built there in modern times to commemorate the story of the colt and the triumphant entry. According to the Gospels, Jesus, on his way to Jerusalem for his official entry, sent two disciples ahead of his group to find a colt that was waiting for him, tied at the entrance of the village. The writer of Matthew, who did not understand the use of doublets in Hebrew literature, indicates that there were two animals, a donkey and her colt and that Jesus "sat on them" (Matt. 21:7; cf. Zech. 9:9).

Archaeological Data

Various excavations were carried out in the vicinity of et-Tur over the last century. Caves, tombs of different types, cisterns, pools, a winepress and coins were found; all of them point to an occupation of the site from the second century B.C.E. to about the eighth century C.E. Crosses on the walls of a tomb indicate that Christians lived in Bethphage in the Byzantine period or that pilgrims visited the place.

Implications for Jesus Research

Archaeology indicates the existence of a village in the first century C.E. at the site recognized as that of ancient Bethphage. If the story of the borrowed colt happened as recorded in the Synoptics, it implies a prearranged agreement between Jesus and friends or supporters unknown to the Twelve and other disciples. The story, however, could have been inserted to connect Jesus' visit to Jerusalem with the messianic understanding of Zechariah 9:9.

The Matthew account raises a question regarding the relative dating of the Gospel of Matthew and Gospel of Thomas (see GOSPEL OF THOMAS). Some scholars date Thomas, or at least some of its components (G. Thom. 1) earlier than Matthew while others maintain that Thomas was composed by adding some gnostic sayings to material contained in the Synoptics. A possible argument in favor of the posteriority of Thomas might be found in The Gospel of Thomas 47.1: "Jesus said 'It is impossible for a man to ride two horses' [. . . and it is impossible for a servant to serve two masters]."

Could it be that the writer of Thomas, in introducing saying 47.1, wanted to react against the absurdity of Matthew 21:7? If this were the case, Matthew would be anterior to Thomas. Even if the horse saying were part of the common wisdom tradition, the possibility of this hypothesis remains.

BIBLIOGRAPHY

Barrois, G. A. "Tombes récemment découvertes à Jérusalem, 2. Tombe Chrétienne à Bethphage." *Revue Biblique* 37 (1928): 262.

Kloppenborg, J. S., M. G. Steinhauser, M. W. Meyer, and S. J. Patterson. *Q. Thomas Reader*, 88–90. Sonoma, Calif.: Polebridge Press, 1990.

McArthur, H. K. "The Dependence of the Gospel of Thomas on the Synoptics." *Expository Times* 71 (1959–60): 286–87.

Saller, S. J. "The Archaeological Setting of the Shrine of Bethphage." *Liber Annuus* 11 (1960/1961): 172–250.

Sukenik, E. L. "Notes on the Jewish Graffiti of Bethphage." *Journal of the Palestinian Oriental Society* 4 (1924): 171–74.

Bethsaida

Importance

Bethsaida is the place in the Gospels most frequently mentioned after Jerusalem and Capernaum in connection with Jesus' activity. According to John, it was the birthplace of Peter, Andrew, and Philip.

Scripture References

Matt. 11:21; Mark 6:45; 8:22; Luke 9:10; 10:13; John 1:44; 12:21.

General Information

Bethsaida, located north of the Sea of Galilee, was originally a settlement of fishers, as its name (House of Fishing) indicates. This is substantiated by references in the Gospels to the occupation of Peter and Andrew and by archaeological finds. According to R. Arav, the *zer* of Joshua 19:35 may be an ancient form of the name Bethsaida. The *r* (*resh*) closely resembles the *d* (*dalet*) in Hebrew. For this reason the two letters often are confused; *zer* originally could have been *zed*. Following the death of Herod the Great in 4 B.C.E., the region of Bethsaida, east of the Jordan, became part of the tetrarchy of his son Philip (Josephus, *Antiq.* 17, 189). Jesus came to Bethsaida and performed mighty works there (Matt. 11:20-24; Luke 10:13-15), possibly the feeding of the multitude (Luke 9:10), and the healing of a man who was blind (Mark 8:23). But when he realized that the people of Bethsaida would not repent, he condemned them together with those of Chorazin and Capernaum. In 30 C.E., Bethsaida was elevated to the status of a Greek *polis* by Herod Philip and was named Julias in honor of Livia-Julia, Tiberius's mother. Josephus's statement that the city was renamed after Augustus's daughter (*Antiq.* 18, 2.1/28) does not agree with the historical and numismatic evidence (Khun and Arav; *see* COINS AS HISTORICAL DOCUMENTS).

At the beginning of the First Jewish War of 66–73 C.E., the army of Agrippa II clashed with the rebels led by Josephus near Bethsaida with neither side emerging as a clear victor (Josephus, *Life*, 71–73). Archaeological evidence shows that the city was destroyed at that time, probably just before or after the fall of Gamla, and was never rebuilt. A few pilgrims mentioned visiting Bethsaida from the fifth century onward, but the exact site was lost and most of their descriptions pertain to different locations. A scholarly dispute began in 1590 when the Dutch priest Adrichomius published a work called *Theatrum Terrae Sanctae* with a map showing Julias to the east of the Jordan and Bethsaida to the west. The Papal legate to Syria and Mesopotamia, Francisco Quaresmio, supported that view in his 1639 publication, *Elucidatio Terrae Sanctae* . More than half a century later, J. Lightfoot, a British Presbyterian theologian, contended in *Chorographia in Marcum* (1699) that Josephus and the Gospels were referring to the same city. The German theologian and philosopher Cellarius, who examined both positions, concluded in *Notida Orbis Antiqui* (1706) that "this

question is one of the most difficult in all of sacred geography."

The quest for the site of Bethsaida reemerged with the rise of modern biblical research. The American scholar E. Robinson (1794–1863) visited the area and reassessed the literary sources. He identified Bethsaida with a large mound named et-Tell situated about 2 kilometers (1.25 miles) from the north shores of the Sea of Galilee and 500 meters (545 yards) east of the Jordan. A few decades later, the German scholar G. Schumacher maintained that a fishing village could not be located at such a distance from the water, and he indicated two possible locations near the shore. One was el Araj, a few hundred yards away from the mouth of the Jordan, on the east side; the other was a small ruin, el-Mesadiyeh, a little further to the southeast (*see* fig. 2). He did not consider that alluvial deposits and tectonic movements (the Jordan runs along the Syro-African rift) could have altered the course of the river and the shape of the shoreline. Some even more elaborate opinions, like that of the French historian V. Guérin, claimed that the Gospels were referring to two different cities: on the one hand, Bethsaida-Julias or Golanian Bethsaida in Luke 9:10 and Mark 8:23, and on the other hand Bethsaida in Galilee in Mark 6:45 and all other Gospel references. An article published in 1985 by B. Pixner stated that there were two Bethsaidas, Bethsaida-Julias at et-Tell and Bethsaida of the Gospels at el Araj; the same information was published in Germany in 1991.

Archaeological Data

R. Arav made a series of probe excavations at el Araj and et-Tell in 1987; the site of el-Mesadiyeh is too small to be a valid candidate. He determined that et-Tell is Bethsaida on the evidence that no construction existed at el Araj prior to the fourth century C.E. Excavations continued at et-Tell from 1988 onward.

Et-Tell, now Tell Bethsaida, is the largest mound on the northern shore of the Sea of Galilee. Its ruins lie on a basalt hill extending from the

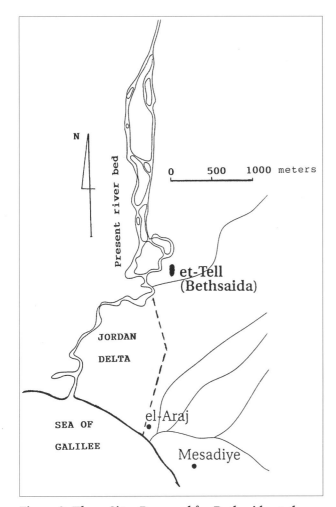

Figure 2 Three Sites Proposed for Bethsaida at the Beginning of the Twentieth Century

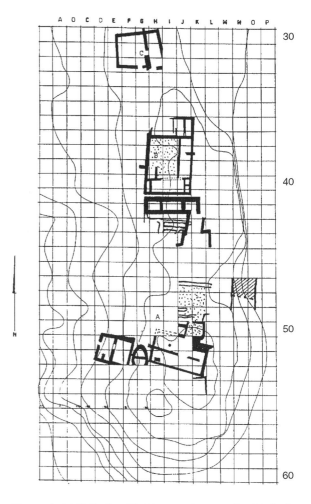

Figure 3 Tell Bethsaida Excavations at the End of the 1993 Season. The squares are 5 x 5 meters.

basalt plains that form the Lower Golan. The mound measures 450 x 200 meters (1,360 x 660 feet) and rises 25 meters (80 feet) above its surroundings. The longer dimension is oriented north-south, parallel to the Jordan. A spring, now hidden by bushes, flows from its western slope toward the river. Excavations were begun in two areas, Area A in the south of the central depression and Area B in the center; they revealed four different periods of occupation (see fig. 3). The first settlement dates to

the Early Bronze Age I (3300–3000 B.C.E.) and continues without interruption through the Early Bronze Age II (3000–2700 B.C.E.). At this time the settlement was surrounded by a thick wall built of huge boulders. Parts of this wall have survived to a height of 1.3 meters (4.25 feet) and still existed in the first century C.E.

The next period of occupation is the Iron Age II (1000–586 B.C.E.). During this period the area of Bethsaida was part of the Land of Geshur, a small kingdom that had a relationship with Israel during the reign of King David. As a result of a treaty between the two kingdoms, David married a Geshurite princess, Maacah daughter of King Talmai. David and Maacah had a son, Absalom, who later found refuge in Geshur for a period of three years after he killed his half brother Amnon (2 Sam. 3:3; 13:38). A large complex seems to include a temple, a plaza, and a palace.

The mound was resettled in the beginning of the Hellenistic period, circa 300 B.C.E. The new settlement covered the entire area and became one of the largest towns on the shores of the Sea of Galilee until it was destroyed by the Romans during the first Jewish War (66–70 C.E.). The Iron Age building was reused and, during the early first century C.E., was altered and adorned with architectural decorations. North of this building in Area B stood a residential complex built around a courtyard in a manner typical of Hellenistic houses. Fishing implements found by this house indicate that its owners were fishers. The house also contained a large number of imported Eastern Terra Sigilatta ware.

Excavations in Area C, opened on the north of the tell in 1992, revealed an 11 x 5.5 meter (36 x 18 foot) room with a number of kitchen implements perhaps used for fish processing. In 1993, in a trench excavated near the spring at the foot of the tell in the southwest, alluvial deposits indicated that the Sea of Galilee or a branch of the Jordan was close to the city. Carbon 14 analysis confirmed their dating to the first century C.E. A wall, which could indicate the existence of an ancient harbor was discovered there (see fig. 4).

Implications for Jesus Research

Of particular interest to the student of the historical Jesus are the finds in the house of Area B: net lead weights, a 15 cm (5 inch) long curved bronze sail needle, two basalt line sinkers, two stone anchors, and a fisher's seal. The seal apparently depicts two men casting a throw-net from a flat bottom boat with a horse-shaped prow. The boat is near a leafy reed identical to those found in the marshy area at the Jordan's mouth today. Under the reed is a fish (see fig. 5). Among the coins found at Bethsaida are two bronze coins minted by Herod Philip in 29–30 C.E., shortly before Jesus' crucifixion. On one side they bear the head of Tiberius turned to the right and on the other the façade of a temple (see COINS AND MONEY and COINS AS HISTORICAL DOCUMENTS).

The pilgrim Theodosius (circa 530 C.E.) indicates that Zebedee and his two sons were from Bethsaida; unfortunately he does not give his source. If Theodosius is right and if we can rely on the information given by John, five disciples out of twelve could have been from Bethsaida: Peter, Andrew, Philip, and James and John, sons of Zebedee. The evidence of archaeology, topography, and hydrology indicates that Bethsaida no doubt was an important center of fishing and fish processing (drying and salting) in the time of Jesus. The fact that the Synoptics indicate that Peter had a house in Capernaum (Mark 1:29 and parallels) does not necessarily contradict the information given by John that Peter and Andrew were from Bethsaida.

According to the Gospels, Jesus was active at Bethsaida and perhaps resided there for a while in the friendly territory of Herod Philip, which also included the region of Caesarea Philipi. From Bethsaida it was easy to reach the Decapolis only 6 miles away. The Gospels report that Herod Antipas married his brother's ex-wife, that he executed John the Baptist, and that Jesus did not hold him in high esteem (Luke 13:32). By contrast, Herod Philip was a "person of moderation and quietness" and was always ready to render justice with the help of his tribunal (Josephus, *Antiq.* 18, 4.6/106–7). Jesus did not seem to fear him or have a bad opinion of him. It may be the reason that he resided at or near Bethsaida.

The December 1985 issue of *Biblical Archaeologist* shows a quarter-page photograph of "the Stone of Bethsaida," the location of which figures on a map (pages 208–15). A short text accompanies the photograph:

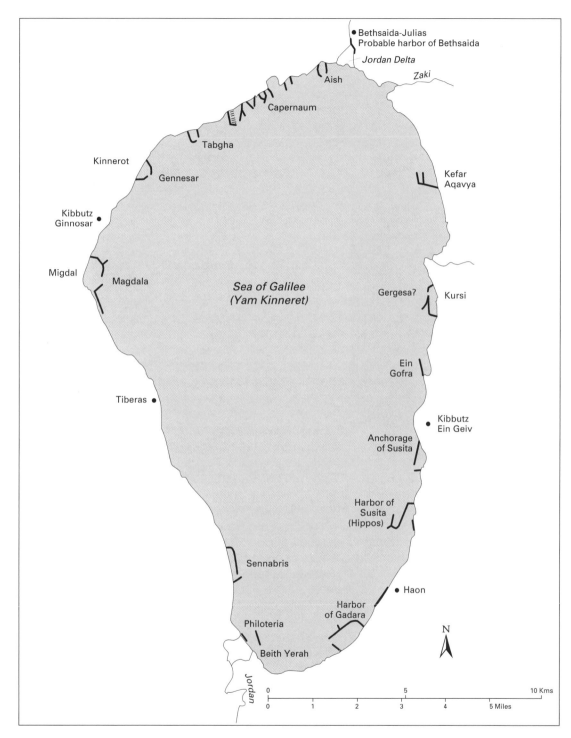

Figure 4 Ancient Harbors of the Sea of Galilee (Yam Kinneret). *Harbors not set to scale.*

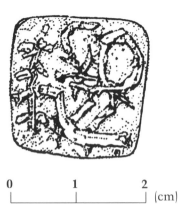

0   1   2 (cm)

Figure 5 The Bethsaida Fisherman's Seal. The seal dates from the Late Hellenistic-Early Roman period. Its actual size is about 3/4 by 3/4 of an inch. It represents a flat bottom boat near a leafy reed. The figure above has been interpreted as symbolizing two men casting a throw net.

The Leafy Reeds of the Jordan Delta as Represented on the Fisherman's Seal

Basalt stone with petroglyphs, located at the northern entrance of et-Tell. The symbols carved into the stone include two eyes—one open and one closed—symbolizing the miracle of the blind man who regained his sight at Bethsaida (Mark 8:22-25); a tree branch, which is a Judeo-Christian symbol for the tree of Jesse, indicating Jesus' descendency from David; and the cross with a rainbow over it, representing for Christians God's successive covenants with man.

There is no mention of the origin of this stone, which, in fact, is not an ancient landmark showing the place where Jesus healed the blind man, as many visitors are now led to believe. Instead, this stone was planted there and decorated in 1981. It is mentioned here only to illustrate how traditions may originate and how unreliable they can be.

BIBLIOGRAPHY

Arav, R. "Et-Tell and el-Araj." *IEJ* 39 (1989): 99–100.

Arav, R. and J. J. Rousseau. "Elusive Bethsaida Recovered." *The Fourth R*. (1991): 1–3.

————. "Bethsaide, ville perdue et retrouvée." *Revue Biblique* 100 (1993): 415 ff.

Dalman, G. *Les Itinéraires de Jesus*. German 1922. Paris: Payot, 1930.

Heidet, L. *Dictionnaire de le Bible*, s.v. "Bethsaide." Paris: Letouzey et Ané, 1895.

Kopp, C. *The Holy Places of the Gospels*. New York: Herder and Herder, 1963.

Kuhn, H. W., and R. Arav. "The Bethsaida Excavations: Historical and Archaeological Approaches." In *The Future of Christianity, Essays in Honor of Helmut Koester*. Minneapolis: Fortress Press, 1991.

Pixner, B. "Searching for the New Testament Site of Bethsaida." *BA* 48 (1985): 207–16.

Theodosius. "De Terrae Sanctae." In *Itinera Hiorosolymitana et Descriptiones Terrae Sanctae*. Geneva: Titus Tobler and M. A. Molinier, 1879.

Boats

Importance

Jesus was familiar with boats and sailed across the Sea of Galilee several times with his disciples.

Scripture References

Matt. 4:18, 21; 8:18, 23-24; 9:1; 13:2; 14:13, 22, 29, 32; 15:39; Mark 1:19-20; 3:9; 4:1, 35, 37-38; 5:2, 18, 21; 6:32, 34, 45, 47, 51, 53-54; 8:10, 13-14; Luke 5:3, 7; 8:22, 27, 37; John 6:16, 19, 21-23.

General Information

There are no less than forty-five references to boats and fishing in the Gospels in connection with Jesus' activities. He spoke to fishers and was familiar with boats; he addressed the crowds from boats and crossed the Sea of Galilee at night with his disciples. This was not surprising, as life was intense on and around the sea. The number of remains of breakwaters and small harbors show that the use of boats, for fishing or commerce, was common (*see* fig. 4, HIPPOS and SEA OF GALILEE). Josephus mentions boats several times in reference to his activities as commander of the rebels' army in Galilee in 66–67 C.E. He provides evidence that boats were also used for military purposes. At the beginning of the First Jewish War, when the insurgents had established a stronghold at Gamla, King Agrippa II sent Sylla, the captain of his guard, with an army to Bethsaida-Julias in order to cut off the supply line of the fortress. Josephus engaged him but had to abandon the battle when an accident caused Josephus's medical evacuation. Sylla did not pursue his good fortune further when he learned that rebel reinforcements had sailed from Magdala to Bethsaida (*Life* 73/406). In another instance, when the Romans had sent a cavalry detachment to Tiberias, its citizens revolted openly against Josephus whose headquarters were in Magdala-Taricheae, a few miles north of Tiberias. Josephus used a clever maneuver: He ordered all available boats, 230 according to his account, to be gathered at Magdala with their crews of five, at which point he sailed with his fleet at dusk and anchored near Tiberias. Taking with him the crew of his boat, the only seven soldiers he had and some friends, he entered the city and convinced the Tiberians that his boats were loaded with soldiers. The Tiberians submitted and Josephus took with him 2,600 notables as hostages (*War* 2, 11.10/645). Although his numbers are not to be accepted uncritically, they nevertheless give an idea of the capacity and size of the boats. Taking into account the standard crew of 5, and assuming that the prisoners were evenly distributed among the boats, an average of 16 or 17 persons would have been in each boat. In Josephus's boat there were, besides himself, 5 sailors, 7 soldiers, and at least 2 friends for a total of 15. These figures correspond well to the size of the boats used for commercial fishing in the Sea of Galilee (*see* FISHING, NETS) and with the size of the first-century boat or Kinneret boat found in Ginosar in 1986.

When the Romans had finally occupied Tiberias, while Josephus was still entrenched in Magdala, Yeshua ben Shafat who had been the head of the rebels at Tiberias led a nocturnal attack against the Roman camp, tore down a segment of their wall and retreated in his boats (*War* 3, 10.1/466–69). In the end, the superior Roman forces took Magdala, and Josephus evacuated his army in his large fleet. Vespasian immediately ordered rafts to be built quickly, a task achieved thanks "to the abundance of wood and carpenters." The outnumbered Jews were defeated and "the beaches were strewn with wrecks, the dead . . . numbered six thousand seven hundred" (*War* 3, 10.9/530–31). The number of craft involved and the local availability of wood and carpenters suggest that boating flourished on the Sea of Galilee during the first century C.E.

What kind of boats were used? The Greek words most often used in the Gospels are *ploion* and its diminutive *ploiarion*, used interchangeably to mean "small boat." Under the entry FISHING, NETS, it is explained that a boat able to carry the heavy dragnet and a crew of eight to sixteen should have been at least twenty feet long. In fact, the Kinneret boat found in 1986 is 8.2 meters (27 feet) long. These were considered small boats compared to the Mediterranean ship *naus*, which could be more than one hundred feet long and displace more than eighty tons. The Sea of Galilee boats were propelled by oars or sails. The boat on a first-century mosaic found at Migdal has one mast and a square sail with three oars on each side, two for rowing and one for steering at the stern. There is a watercutter at the stem that seems somewhat exaggerated in size in the reproduction (*see* fig. 6).

Although no specific text describes boat building activity on the shores of the Sea of Galilee in the first century C.E., there is little doubt that such activity existed. The discovery of the Kinneret boat raises the possibility that the area of Magdala-Taricheae was a boat building center for the following reasons:

- Reusable parts of the Kinneret boat were removed from the hull before it was abandoned. Parts of the hulls of other boats and a cluster of nails were located in the same place (Steffey, *'Atiqot*, English Series, vol. 6 [1966]: 43–47).

- As noted above, Josephus indicates that Vespasian found an abundance of wood and "no lack of carpenters."

- Some of the wood used in the Kinneret boat came from local trees: Aleppo pine (one strake), jujube (aft part of keel), oak (frames), hawthorn (one frame), willow (one frame), redbud (one frame). (*see* WOOD, FURNITURE.)

Archaeological Information

Two mosaics and a graffito found in Israel depict boats probably similar to those of the Sea of Galilee in the first century C.E. Perhaps the best evidence is the boat of the Migdal mosaic. The Franciscans under the direction of Father Corbo excavated the site of Magdala-Taricheae where they found the first century C.E. mosaic. Seen in profile, the boat is oriented to the left and its entire hull is depicted (*see* fig. 6). The back-curved stern is probably oversized as is the cutwater stem. The number of oars indicates that a crew of at least five was required: four rowers and one skipper-helmsman. The superstructure consists of one mast with a horizontal yard and a square sail shown reefed up, one forestay, and one yard brace. The information provided by the mosaic accords with other data, including the remains of the Kinneret boat. Because technology did not change much over the centuries in the ancient world, it is also possible to consider as relevant the fifth-century mosaic of Beth-Shean, which represents the same type of boat. The same is true of a graffito in the Beth She'arim catacombs; it represents a one-masted boat with a curved stern and raising stem, which could help to supply on a drawing the missing parts of the Kinneret boat.

The major archaeological discovery of recent years pertaining to sailing and fishing in Palestine is the Kinneret boat, which has been alluded to above. In January 1986, when the waters of the Sea of Galilee were at their lowest after a severe drought, two members of Kibbutz Ginnosar, while walking on the newly uncovered part of the lake bottom, noticed a spot shaped like a boat. It was in fact an ancient boat buried in mud. The Department of Antiquities of Israel undertook a survey followed by a probe excavation that revealed a boat 8.2 meters (27 feet) long and 2.3 meters (7 feet 7 inches) wide (*see* fig. 7). A cooking pot outside the prow was dated to a period between the mid-first century B.C.E. and the mid-second century C.E. An oil lamp inside the boat was dated to some time between the first century to the mid-second century C.E. A few coins including one of Herod Philip dating from 29–30 C.E. and similar to the one found at Bethsaida (*see* BETHSAIDA), were also recovered. Full excavation began on February 16, 1986, and was conducted as quickly as possible in order to reimmerse the fragile soft wood in a large water tank prepared especially to receive it. It was the beginning of a conservation process that was to last at least nine years. During this time the water of the

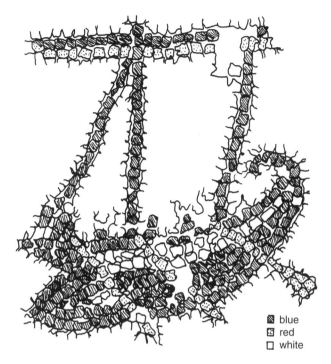

blue
red
white

Figure 6 The Magdala Boat. This illustrates basic features of the time: ram type bow, rounded stern, two pairs of oars, quarter rudder(s), and a square sail. It was a five man workboat like the Kinneret boat.

wood cells was gradually replaced with synthetic wax.

Several different species of wood are represented in the construction of the boat, which is unusual. It may mean that the owner made the most of the local and less expensive resources. Most of the strakes (side planks), about 3 centimeters thick (1¼ inch), are made of cedar imported from Lebanon. The planks are carefully edge-joined and locked by tenons and mortises kept in place with hardwood pegs (*see* fig. 8). The frames, made mostly of oak, are irregular in size, and the planks are fixed to them with iron nails. Some important pieces, stern post, stem, internal timber, and topside parts, seem to have been removed on purpose probably to be reused. The boat was old when it

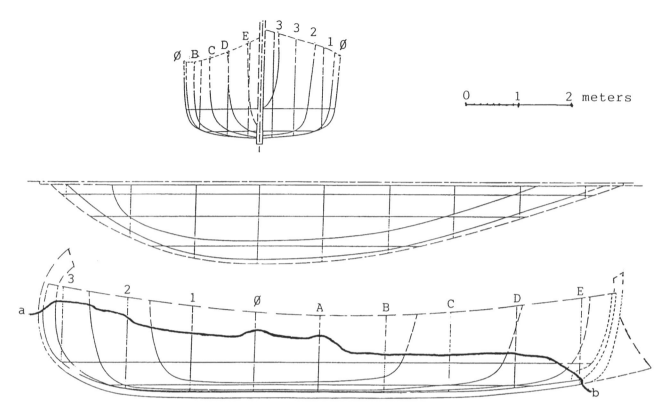

Figure 7 The Kinneret Boat. Total length: 8m (26 feet), maximum breadth: 2.5m (8 feet), depth: 1.25m (4 feet). The party recovered is under line a-b.

sank and had been repaired many times. The various methods used to date the boat (study of construction techniques, Carbon 14, and pottery types found in the boat) point to a period between 100 B.C.E. and 70 C.E. This boat was surely typical of those used by first-century fishers and by Josephus and his troops.

The fisher's seal found at Bethsaida (see this entry) represents a boat of a different type. It seems to be a flat-bottomed boat fit to sail in the shallow waters of the marshy Jordan delta, which was particularly rich in fish easily caught with a throw net. By the prow of the boat stands a leafy reed similar to those still found today in the northern part of the Sea of Galilee. The uprising stem is shaped like a horse head characteristic of the Greek Hippos-type boat (*see* fig. 5).

Implications of Jesus Research

This brief study of first-century C.E. boats contributes to the interpretation of certain Gospel passages relating to Jesus' lifestyle.

Matt. 8:23-24; Mark 4:37-38. While Jesus and his disciples cross the Sea of Galilee at night, a windstorm arises and waves swamp the boat. But Jesus continues to sleep undisturbed. The frightened disciples wake him up and Jesus calms the storm. Mark is more specific than Matthew and probably more authentic in saying that Jesus "was in the

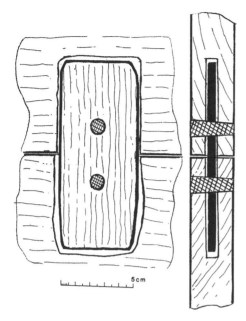

Figure 8 The Minute Tenon and Mortise Joint of the Kinneret Boat's Strakes

stern, asleep on the cushion." These few words convey the reality of the situation. The boat was undoubtedly designed for seine fishing and had a deck on its aft part where the net was placed and prepared, ready to be spread (*see* FISHING, NETS). Because the boat was about four feet deep, there was ample space under the aft deck for one or even several people to sleep. The cushion mentioned by Mark was not exactly a cushion or a pillow as sometimes translated. Rather it probably was a sandbag used for ballast as was still the case in seine boats in the Mediterranean in the first half of this century. Its purpose was to trim the boat when under sail. Two types were known: a ballast sack of 100 to 120 pounds (Arabic *kis sabura*) and a pair of ballast pillows of about 50 pounds each, easier to handle (Arabic *mehadet sabura*; *see* Wachsmann, 111). Probably it is one of the latter type to which Mark refers.

John 6:1-24. The author of the Fourth Gospel locates the scene of the feeding of the Five Thousand on the northwestern side of the lake in the area of Magdala-Ginnosar. The geographical information in the Synoptics is uncertain, but that of John is quite coherent, placing Tiberias on one side and Capernaum on the other. According to Josephus, as noted above, there were many boats in the area; "boats from Tiberias" could well have come on the day following the feeding to try to find Jesus (John 6:23). Because Magdala-Taricheae was an important fishing and fish processing center (*see* MAGDALA and FISHING, NETS), the location given by John for the feeding of the Five Thousand makes sense.

What can this information indicate about Jesus' social milieu in Galilee? If the Gospels are accurate, he was familiar with fishing (*see* FISHING, NETS) boats, and sailing, and he could sleep through a storm when professional fishers were frightened. This behavior is certainly not typical of a "peasant" attached to his land and usually afraid of large bodies of water. The psychological traits of peasants and sailors are quite different. Perhaps Jesus was connected with the fishing industry before his baptism by John. There is no reason to doubt that he had been trained as a *tekton* (carpenter or construction worker, Matt. 13:55, Mark 6:3), so he may have worked in boat construction or repairs in a harbor of the Sea of Galilee. Some of his acquaintances there became his disciples when he began his own ministry.

BIBLIOGRAPHY

Bash, L. "De la survivance de traditions navales phéniciennes dans la Méditerrannée de nos jours." *Mariner's Mirror* 66 (1975).

———. "Bow and Stern Appendages in the Ancient Mediterranean." *Mariner's Mirror* 69 (1983).

Corbo, V. "Scavi archeologici a Magdala (1971–1973)." *Liber Annuus* 24 (1975).

———. "La Città Romana di Magdala." *Studia Hierosolymitana* 1 (1976).

Rabban, A. "The Boat from Migdal Nunia and the Anchorages of the Sea of Galilee from the Time of Jesus." *The International Journal of Nautical Archaeology and Underwater Exploration* 17 (1988): 311–29.

Reich, E. "A Note on the Roman Mosaic from Magdala on the Shore of the Sea of Galilee." *Qadmoniot* (1989): 85–86 (Hebrew).

Tilley, A. F. "The Survival of Ancient Boat Designs." *Mariner's Mirror* 59 (1973).

Wachsmann, S., et al. "The Excavations of an Ancient Boat in the Sea of Galilee." *'Atiqot,* English Series, vol. 19. Jerusalem: Israel Antiquities Authority, 1990.

Caesarea Maritima

Importance

Caesarea Maritima was the seat of the Roman prefect of Judea and Samaria; Philip, Peter, and Paul visited it.

Scripture References

Acts 8:40; 9:30; 10:1, 24; 11:11; 12:19-23; 18:22; 21:8; 23:23; 25:1-13.

General Information

Caesarea Maritima, named in honor of Augustus, was the realization of "Herod's Dream," one of the greatest construction feats of Near Eastern antiquity. Ptolemy II Philadelphus first built a small settlement on the site in the middle of the third century B.C.E. for military and economic purposes. It was a *stratopedon* ("army camp," Arav 1989). The anchorage of the city has been wrongly attributed to one of the two Sidonian kings of the fourth century C.E. named Straton because of the similarity with *stratopedon*. During the Maccabean rebellion, Alexander Jannaeus took it (circa 96 B.C.E.), and a few decades later Augustus gave it to Herod. Between 22 and 10 B.C.E. Herod built a city and a harbor, which became a successful competitor to Alexandria. When Judea was ruled by the Romans, the prefects or governors resided in Caesarea; and the legions proclaimed Vespasian emperor there. The First Jewish War began in Caesarea in 66 C.E. when violence erupted between Jews and Gentiles (Josephus, *War* 2, 13.7/266–70; *Antiq.* 20, 8.7–9/173–81).

Christianity came to Caesarea just a few years after the Crucifixion: Philip preached there (Acts 8:40), Peter converted the centurion Cornelius (Acts 10:1, 24; 11:11), and Paul stayed at Caesarea on his way to Tarsus (Acts 9:30) and again when coming back from his first two missionary journeys (Acts 18:22; 21:8). He appeared before Felix and Festus (Acts 23:23; 25:12) when he was in prison and finally sailed from Caesarea for Rome after being heard by Agrippa II (Acts 25:13—27:2). After the destruction of Jerusalem, Caesarea became the capital of Judea and, later, the capital of the whole country, when it was renamed Palestine by Hadrian. Toward the end of the second century the city had a bishop. A Christian school and its library developed and gained international fame. Origen (185–254), Pamphilius (240–309), and Eusebius (260–340) wrote and taught there. The Jewish community had several synagogues, and it is at Caesarea that the tractate *Zeraim* of the Jerusalem Talmud was written. Like most cities in Palestine, Caesarea had a tumultuous history: It was captured by the Persians in 614, was destroyed by the Arabs in 639, fell to the Crusaders in 1101, and was finally razed in 1265 by the Sultan Baybars in order to prevent a new Christian settlement.

Archaeological Data

C. R. Conder and H. H. Kitchener in 1873 carried out the first comprehensive exploration of Caesarea Maritima during their survey of western Palestine. The first excavations of the site took place in 1945 under the auspices of the Department of Antiquities of Palestine. In 1951 excavations revealed a church and a street from the Byzantine period. From that time on, a period of intense archaeological activity developed involving the Hebrew University with M. Avi-Yonah, an Italian expedition that worked on the Roman theater, an underwater team with E. Link, the Israeli National Parks Authority in the Crusaders' town with A. Negev, Drew University with R. Bull, the University of Haifa with A. Raban and E. Linder, the University of Victoria with J. Oleson, and the University of Maryland with L. Vann. Ultimately two consortiums were formed to coordinate the research of the site: one for land exploration, the Joint Expedition to Caesarea Maritima (J.E.C.M.) in 1972; one for maritime research, the Caesarea Ancient Harbor Excavation Project (C.H.E.P.), which began in 1980. Although the total excavation work may seem minimal—the overall area of the ancient city was 8,000 acres and only 5 have been dug—architectural and artifactual discoveries have been voluminous. It will take many years of work to publish all the information gathered at Caesarea. We will mention only the most important finds pertaining to the Early Roman period in Palestine, which encompasses the time of Jesus.

1. *Harbor*. The harbor, named Sebastos (Greek for Augustus), was protected by two breakwaters 200 feet wide, one 250 yards long in the north, another 600 yards long in the south, sheltering an area of 40 acres (*see* fig. 9). According to Josephus, it was larger than Piraeus, the harbor of Athens (*War* 1, 21.5/410). The excavators also found that an inner harbor had been dug out, closer to the temple platform. Herod made an international emporium known as "Caesarea" that lies in front of Sebastos. The name "Maritima" is a modern creation to distinguish it from Caesarea Philippi.

2. *Warehouses*. Forming a large wall against the water and the wind, a series of large vaulted chambers, each 90 feet long, on the southern breakwater, opened on a quay. In the third century, one of these warehouses was transformed by the Roman soldiers into a sanctuary to Mithra.* A hole had been opened in the ceiling in such a way that on the summer solstice (June 21) the ray of the sun would fall on the altar.

3. *Temple of Augustus*. Facing the harbor, the temple was built on an artificial mound supported in part by vaulted chambers 65 feet long and 21 feet wide. It contained two colossal statues of Augustus and Roma. A three foot long, white marble foot belonging to one of these statues was found. The location of the temple was within the presently accessible Crusader city where palaces were also built. Because Caesarea was a totally new creation, its planners took advantage of the available space to design a perfect north-south, east-west grid of streets.

4. *Theater*. At the southern end of the city, facing the sea, a theater that could seat 4500 spectators was erected on a concrete pad. Its floor was of fine plaster painted with vivid colors, and more than a dozen layers of paint showed that it had been used over a long period of time. Indeed, the theater had been modified and partially rebuilt several times. In one of these reconstructions, a stone bearing the name of Pontius Pilate was reused (*see* PONTIUS PILATE'S STONE). According to Josephus and Acts, it was in Caesarea that Agrippa I found his sudden death (*Antiq.* 19, 8.2/343–50; Acts 12:21-23). The spectacles he gave in honor of Caesar could not have been offered in this theater, which is dated to the Late Roman period.

5. *Amphitheater*. This could be another example of Herod's megalomania; the arena of the amphitheater was larger than that of the Colosseum in Rome. However, the date of its construction cannot be ascertained without further excavation.

6. *Water system*. There are no natural water sources in the area, and rainfall alone would not have provided enough to satisfy the needs of a large population. To solve the problem an aqueduct was built to bring water from the springs of Mount Carmel. As the city grew a second one was built, parallel and adjacent to the first, in the time of Hadrian. It bears inscriptions acknowledging the work of the second, sixth, tenth, and fifteenth legions. In the fifth century, the water supply had to be increased again, and a tunnel was built to connect the city with an artificial reservoir created by a dam on the Crocodile River. The reservoir was known as Lake Caesarea; thirteen water mills were built on its dam.

7. *Sewer system*. Herod's architects built an elaborate sewer system under the city (see Josephus, *Antiq.* 15, 9.6/340). The effect of the tides and the

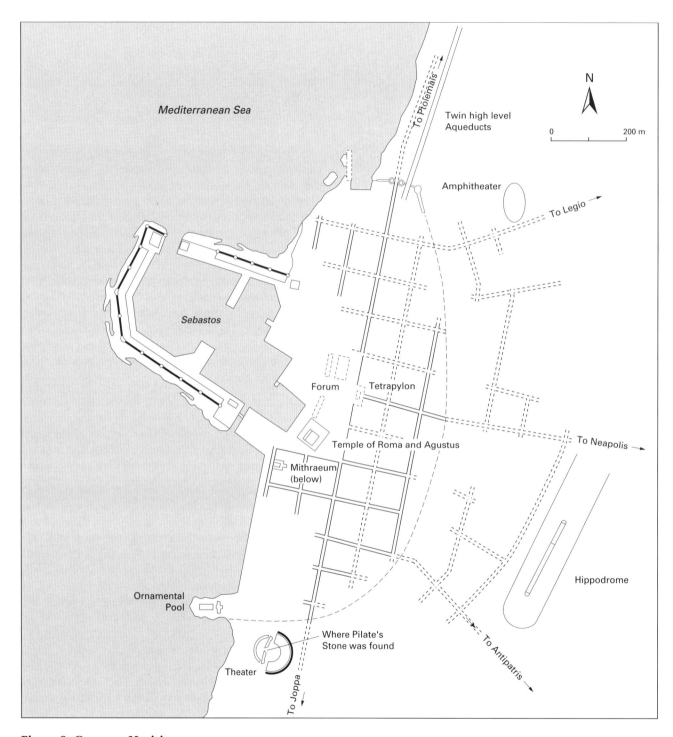

Figure 9 Caesarea Maritima

prevailing current coming from the south drained away "the filth of the citizens." A section of an underground canal 10.5 feet high was found.

8. *Hippodrome*. A large hippodrome stood east of the harbor; its access ramps and central *spina*˙ are still visible.

It is almost impossible to imagine the splendor of the city and harbor, where the less noble building material was white limestone. Mosaic sidewalks, with long rows of columns, led from the city to the theater. Thousands of columns standing in parallel rows along the main streets formed majestic promenades throughout the city. More than 1,300 column fragments were found on the bottom of the harbor alone. They were made of marble imported from Italy and Egypt; columns of pink granite came from Aswan. Large slabs covered streets and sidewalks. Maritime trade was extensive: large warehouses facing the harbor contained amphorae of garum (a sauce made of decaying herrings seasoned with spices, which was much liked by the Romans), wine, olive oil, fruit syrups, and nails. The presence of Chinese porcelain attests to the geographical reach of Herod's commercial activities.

Implications for Jesus Research

As far as we know, Caesarea Maritima was not directly related to the life and ministry of Jesus, although early Christians were active there. The Pilate Inscription can be linked to parts of the Gospel narrative. In addition, shortly after the Crucifixion, Caesarea Maritima played a major role in the life of the nascent Church with the evangelistic activities of Philip, Peter, and Paul. The splendor of the city and the prosperity of its harbor reflect the wealth and the life-style of the Herodians and upper class of Jesus' time. There was clearly a significant gap between the extreme affluence of the rich and the economic level of the rest of the population. The same contrast probably characterized urban centers such as Ptolemais, Sepphoris, Tiberias, Sebaste, Jericho, and Jerusalem's Upper City. Such disparity may be reflected in the tradition of Jesus condemning the rich and ministering to the poor, a "flock without shepherds."

BIBLIOGRAPHY

Arav, R. "Some Notes on the Foundation of Straton's Tower," *Palestine Exploration Quarterly* 121 (1989): 144–48.

Beebe, H. K. "Caesarea Maritima. Its Strategic and Political Significance to Rome." *Journal of Near-Eastern Studies* 42 (1983): 195–207.

Bull, R. J. "Caesarea Maritima. The Search for Herod's City." *BAR* 8 (1982): 24–40.

Fransen, I. "Césarée Maritime au temps de St. Paul." *Monde de la Bible* 12 (1980): 5–13.

Hohlfelder, R. L. "Caesarea Beneath the Sea." *BAR* 8 (1982): 42–47.

———. "Sebastos Herod's Harbour at Caesarea Maritima." *BAR* 9 (1983): 133–43.

Holum, K. G. et al. "Caesarea." *NEAEHL* 1: 170–86.

Holum, K. G., et al. *King Herod's Dream*. New York, London: W. W. Norton and Co., 1988.

Raban, A. "Maritime Caesarea." *NEAEHL* 1:286-.91.

Vann, R. L. "News from the Field: Herod's Harbor Construction Recovered Underwater." *BAR* 9 (1983): 10–14.

Caesarea Philippi (Banias)

Importance

Caesarea Philippi was an important Greco-Roman center of worship at the foot of the Hermon range. Jesus visited the area and Peter acknowledged him as the Messiah there.

Scripture References

Matt. 16:13; Mark 8:27.

General Information

Caesarea Philippi was a strongly Hellenized city at the foot of Mount Hermon on the southern side, near the main source of the Jordan, 25 miles north of the Sea of Galilee. The location, one of the most pleasant in Israel, is on a large terrace 1,150 feet high overlooking a fertile valley. In the Hellenistic period, a sanctuary to the god Pan was built in the large grotto where the water of one of the Jordan sources comes to light. Accordingly, the names Paneion, Panias, Paneas (today: Banias) were given to the city. The sanctuary may have been dedicated to other gods before Pan, because cultic places already existed on Mount Hermon for the worship of Baal-gad or Baal-hermon (Josh. 11:17; Judg. 3:3; 1 Chron. 5:23). The cult of Pan, god of fields, forests and mountains, flocks and shepherds, originated in Arcadia, a pastoral region of Greece. Greek travelers or settlers, finding that the landscape was like that of their homeland, established a sanctuary to Pan. It is possible that the holiness of the Jordan derived from the fact that the sources of the river were consecrated to several deities (*see* JORDAN RIVER, FORDS).

At Paneas Antiochius III defeated the Ptolemies of Egypt in 200 B.C.E., thus establishing Seleucid rule in Palestine and Syria (Polybus XVI, 18:2; XVIII, 1:3). In 20 B.C.E., Augustus gave Paneas to King Herod who erected there a temple of white marble dedicated to his patron (Josephus, *Antiq.* 15, 10.3/360); but the city was built only later by his son Herod Philip. During the First Jewish War (66–70 C.E.), Vespasian together with Titus and his army encamped there, and were entertained by King Agrippa II (Josephus, *War* 3, 9.7/443–44). After the death of Agrippa II, Caesarea Philippi was attributed to the province of Syria, and later to Phoenicia. It was conquered by the Arabs in the seventh century. In the Talmud it is referred to as Qisariyon, "Little Caesar" (*b. Sukka* 1:9).

Only two Gospels, Matthew and Mark, mention Caesarea Philippi as the place where Peter or all the disciples acknowledged Jesus as the Christ. Luke (9:18-22) and John (6:69) omit this geographical information.

Archaeological Data

Two expeditions sponsored by the Israel Antiquities Authority have been excavating at Caesarea Philippi since 1987. One, directed by V. Tzaferis, is digging in the section of the city that was in existence from the Roman to the Medieval periods; the other, conducted by U. Z. Maoz, is investigating the Roman sanctuary next to the grotto dedicated to Pan. The Tzaferis excavations have uncovered remains from the time of Herod Philip (early first century C.E.). They include a public building that was decorated inside and outside with stucco and frescoes. Heart-shaped columns were discovered as well. These columns were developed in Asia Minor in the Hellenistic period and were introduced to Judea by Herod the Great or perhaps even earlier by the Hasmonean kings, as is evidenced by the presence of such columns in the fortress Alexandrium at the north of the Judean Desert. During the Late Roman period, the town of Caesarea Philippi–Paneas flourished, possibly as a result of the cultic activity at the sanctuary of Pan. Among the finds of this period are a large basilica and a large vaulted structure that may have been part of a massive commercial complex adjacent to the city forum. During the Byzantine period, when the pagan cult centers all over the Empire were closed down by an imperial decree, the town suffered a sharp decline. It was only during the Crusades that the city returned to its former grandeur when, because of its location on the highway between Damascus and Tyre, the town was rebuilt and protected by majestic fortresses.

Excavations at the grotto of Pan have uncovered an enclosure containing two or perhaps three shrines, an altar, and possibly a sacred pool. The reconstruction of the sanctuary is based on three main sources of information: the description of Josephus, archaeological excavations, and coins. Below the grotto, at the sources of the Jordan River, there was a large pool from which the water gushed forth. The pool was surrounded by columns. In its center stood a statue of Pan leaning on a column and playing the syrinx (the seven-pipe flute). Above the pool was a platform used for the service of the shrines. Inside the cave stood the main shrine dedicated to Pan and his consort, the nymph Echo. Other archaeological remains indicate the existence of an elaborate propylaeum* opening to a corridor. Presumably, this was the temple built by Herod the Great in honor of Augustus, as mentioned by Josephus. The temple is described as decorated with marble, and marble was indeed found in the dig.

Implications for Jesus Research

In Jesus' time, Caesarea Philippi was an important Greco-Roman city, and its population was mostly pagan (Josephus, *Life*, 13). Were the inhabitants of the villages around the city Jews? Probably not, because in the same text Josephus informs us that no kosher olive oil was available for the Jewish minority in the city. Thus, a question arises: If Matthew 16:13-16 and its parallels are authentic, what was Jesus' purpose in asking his disciples a question about his true identity or mission in a mostly pagan environment? Because the texts may not be authentic, according to the Jesus Seminar in its 1990 deliberations, the question becomes: Why did the evangelists choose such a locale, which was probably unfamiliar to them, for such a story? An obvious answer would be that the evangelists wanted to demonstrate that Jesus was superior to a much-celebrated pagan deity. If this is the answer, then the story is probably a creation of the Gospel writers because, according to the Gospels, Jesus apparently did not attack foreign religions. Except perhaps for his action in the Temple, it seems that he was not a religious activist. The Gospels do not give any indication that Jesus preached against false gods or attempted to destroy idols. His neutral attitude is in sharp contrast with that of the Israelite prophets, who condemned the worship of foreign gods and idols, and also with some contemporary groups like the Qumranites.

BIBLIOGRAPHY

Beyer, D. *Miscellanea Babylonica—Mélange Offert à Maurice Birot*. Paris, 1985, 39–44.

Lackenbacher, S. *Miscellanea Babylonica—Mélange Offert à Maurice Birot*. Paris, 1985, 153–60.

Maoz, U. Z. "Banias the Temple of Pan, 1989." *Excavations and Surveys in Israel 1989/90.* (1990): 85.

———. "Banias the Temple of Pan." *Hadashot Arkheologiot* 9 (1991): 2–4. (Hebrew)

———. "Banias." *NEAEHL* 1: 136-43.

Tzaferis, V. and T. Mutlat. "Banias, 1987." *Excavations and Surveys in Israel 1987–88* 6 (1987–88): 2–3.

Tzaferis, V. and R. Avner. "Banias, 1988." *Excavations and Surveys in Israel 1988–89* 7–8 (1988–89): 10–11.

Tzaferis, V. and R. Avner. "Banias, 1989" *Excavations and Surveys in Israel 1989–90* 9 (1989–90): 3–4.

———. "Banias 1990." *Hadashot Arkheologiot* 96 (1991): 1. (Hebrew)

Camps, Siege Banks

Importance

According to the Synoptics, Jesus predicted the destruction of the Temple and of Jerusalem, which would be surrounded with a siege bank. It is debated whether this was a true prophecy or a *post eventum** prediction.

Scripture References

Matt. 24:2; Mark 13:2; Luke 19:43; 21:6, 20, 24.

General Information

When a city was too strong for direct attack, and if it was not possible to use either ruse or surprise, the only recourse was to besiege it, a technique as old as the construction of city walls. By surrounding the city and isolating it from the rest of the world, starvation would eventually force the defenders to surrender or weaken them to the point that they would not offer much resistance in battle. The process could take several years as was the case when the Assyrians besieged Samaria. That siege lasted three years, from 725 to 722 B.C.E. (2 Kings 17:1-6). The attackers built siege banks or even walls around it, except where the terrain offered natural obstacles. Another biblical example involves Joab, David's commander, who besieged Abel Beth-maacah (2 Sam. 20:15); Isaiah prophesied that Nebuchadnezzar would not have the time to build such a bank around Jerusalem (2 Kings 19:32-

33; Isa. 32:33-34). Other prophets clearly knew about this method used by all armies (Jer. 6:6; 32:24; Ezek. 4:2; 17:17; 21:22; Dan. 11:15, and again Isa. 29:3).

The Romans used siege banks very effectively. Unlike the Greek army, which relied on slave labor, the legionaries were also construction workers, and the Roman armies included engineers. When arriving at the site to be besieged, the legions would first organize a fortified camp according to a uniform square or rectangular plan. The soldiers would then dig and fill as needed to make a level platform on which to pitch their tents. Several camps were set around the besieged city and were connected by the siege bank. The extent of the work could reach enormous proportions. For example, in order to isolate Spartacus's army of slaves and gladiators, Marcus Licinus Crassus, in 72–71 B.C.E. had his legions dig a 30-mile-long ditch backed by a wall across the Italian Boot. (This work was in vain, however, because the insurgents crossed the ditch and wall during a snow storm).

In 66 C.E., at the outset of the First Jewish War, Vespasian arrived at Ptolemais and first conquered Galilee by the end of 67. Vespasian then moved to the south, occupied Jericho in 68, and started to install garrisons in the existing citadels (Josephus, *War* 4, 9.1/486). After the death of Nero in the same year, Vespasian was made emperor by his legions, and his son Titus took over the direction of the operations. Titus set his camp on Mount Scopus to the north of Jerusalem and started to build a siege bank around the capital. The siege was relatively short; it began in the spring of 70 and the Temple, main citadel of the resistance, fell in September of the same year (Josephus, *War* 4, 3–5.6/121–290).

Archaeological Data

From October 1963 to May 1964 and from November 1964 to April 1965, Y. Yadin led the archaeological excavations of Masada under the auspices of the Hebrew University, the Israeli Department of Antiquities and the Government of Israel (*see* MASADA). The site provides a striking example of Roman siege techniques. The remains of the eight camps and siege bank are exceptionally well preserved. The 6-foot-thick wall is a little over two miles long and is fortified by towers every 60 to 80 yards. Of the eight camps, two large ones are outside the circumvallation itself, one (140 x 180 yards) on the east, and one (130 x 160 yards) on the west. The latter served as headquarters for Silva, the commander of the Tenth Legion. Four of the other small camps, which would quarter up to five centuries,* were integrated in the circumvallation. The last two camps were set in locations to guard possible places of escape from the fortress. The siege system of Masada was thus absolutely tight. The siege bank and towers built three years before around Jerusalem (Masada fell in 73 C.E.) were certainly as well organized. Among others, the Tenth Legion, which besieged Masada, was also at Jerusalem (*see* fig. 10).

Implications for Jesus Research

Because of the long history of siege walls as a military technique and also because of their mention in the Hebrew Bible, there can be no doubt that the Jews of Jesus' time and Jesus himself knew about them. Consequently, Mark 13 and its parallels—a prediction made by Jesus—may very well have been composed around an authentic core. He announced the destruction of Jerusalem: "Do you see these great buildings? Not one stone will be left here upon another; all will be thrown down . . . [as it is done when a city is conquered]": (Mark 13:2 and parallels). The Jesus of Luke wept over the city, saying: "If you, even you, had only recognized on this day the things that make for peace! . . . for the days will come upon you when your enemies will set up ramparts around you, and surround you, and hem you in on every side. They will crush you to the ground" (Luke 19:42-44).

Most scholars see these two sayings as probably not authentic; the Jesus Seminar rated both of them *gray*. For this reason, Mark is usually dated to "about 70 C.E." It is believed that such statements could have been written only after the fall of Jerusalem in September 70 C.E. But the histor-

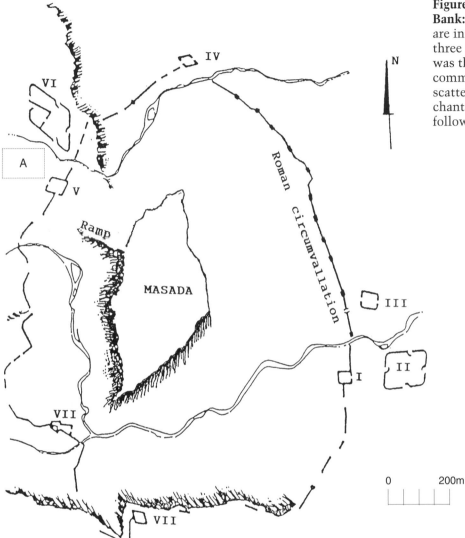

IV

VI

A

V

Ramp

MASADA

Roman circumvallation

N

III

II

I

VII

VII

0   200m

Figure 10 Example of Roman Siege Bank: Masada 70 C.E. Five camps are integrated in the wall, and three are set behind. Camp VI was the headquarters of the commander, Silva. Area A contains scattered remains of the merchants' houses and brothels which followed the legion (*Rami Arav*).

ical context and the biblical texts mentioning siegework indicate that, if the nation followed the militant nationalists, a catastrophe would certainly occur (*see* MASADA and CONSTRUCTION). In fact, Mark could have been written much earlier (*see* COINS AS HISTORICAL DOCUMENTS)— a "Proto-Mark" without the apocalyptical elements—probably no later than 60 C.E. Such a date would still allow for the inclusion in Mark of Paul's conception of the Last Supper as expressed in 1 Corinthians, which is generally dated to about 54 C.E. (*see* WOOD, FURNITURE and UPPER ROOM).

Jesus' eschatology was probably not apocalyptic/cataclysmic as were those of many of his contemporaries; rather, he was expecting people of his time to turn their hearts to God and to accept divine rule in a new theocratic covenant (see SON OF MAN). His prediction of a natural disaster was made in consideration of then-current historical circumstances, as his predecessors had done. In consideration of the information provided by history and archaeology, this view deserves some attention.

BIBLIOGRAPHY

Allison, D. C. "Matthew. 23:39 = Luke 19:35b as a Conditional Prophecy." *Journal for the Study of the New Testament* 18 (1983): 75–84.

Borg, M. "Luke 19:24-44 and Jesus as Prophet?" *Jesus Seminar Papers*. Sonoma, Calif.: Polebridge Press, 1990.

de Camp, L. S. *The Ancient Engineers*. New York: Ballantine Books, 1960–63.

Mark, B. *A Myth of Innocence: Mark and Christian Origins*. Philadelphia: Fortress Press, 1988.

Yadin, Y. *Masada*. 1966. Reprint. New York: Random House, 1985.

Cana

Importance

According to John, Jesus performed two miracles in Cana, the city of Nathanael.

Scripture References

John 2:1, 11; 4:46; 21:2.

General Information

The Fourth Gospel is the only one to mention the name of "Cana in Galilee," so called by John because there were other places with the same name. Two locations have been proposed for the Cana of Jesus' time: Kefr Kenna, the present day Cana, about 5 miles northeast of Nazareth, on the road to Tiberias; and Khirbet Qana, some 9 miles north of Nazareth on the northern side of the Netofa Valley, 12 miles west of Magdala. The second site is more likely for several traditional or historical reasons: the Arabic spelling, Qana, is closer to that of the Gospel and the full name, Qana el-Jelil, means "Cana in Galilee." Pilgrims of the twelfth century and later reported that they had visited this site presented to them as the Cana of the Gospel. In fact, the ruins of an ancient village are to be found there. Finally, Josephus resided in Cana while he was living in the plain of Asochis (*Life* 16, 41). This information points to Khirbet Qana, which is less than two miles from Jotapata where he was defeated by the Romans and surrendered to them.

According to John, the only Gospel to mention Cana, Jesus performed two miracles in that city: changing water into wine (John 2:1-11) and healing at a distance the son of an official (John 4:46-54). In the last chapter, generally recognized as a late addition, Cana is said to be the city of origin of the disciple Nathanael.

Archaeological Information

Archaeological data suggest that Khirbet Qana is New Testament Cana. Most of the finds at Kefr Kenna, the "touristic" Cana near Nazareth, do not predate the Byzantine Period. Surveys of Khirbet Qana indicate that the site was occupied in the first century. Khirbet Qana is thus a better candidate than Kapher Kenna.

Implications for Jesus Research

Josephus and the Fourth Gospel attest to the existence of a village named Cana in Galilee in the first century C.E. Because of its proximity to Nazareth, Jesus' family may have had friends or relatives there, making it possible that he and his mother were invited to a wedding in that village. For the same reason, Jesus may have lodged there on some occasions (John 4:46). This proximity would also explain why one of the Twelve, Nathanael, was from Cana. Stone jars of a size comparable to those described in John 2:6 have been found in several locations in Herodian Jerusalem (see JERUSALEM, UPPER CITY and STONE, STONING). Such vessels indicate that the primary author of the Fourth Gospel was accurate in giving the material details of his stories. Incidentally, he may have pointed to an ancient Jewish tradition, which is to perform weddings on Tuesday, the third day of the week, Sunday being the first (John 2:1). This tradition is based on Genesis 1:9-13, where the word "good" (*tov*) is used twice for the third day of creation instead of once only for the other days. Accordingly, important matters like weddings were decided, settled, or celebrated on the third day of the week to call for a double blessing from God.

BIBLIOGRAPHY

Avi-Yonah, M. "Gazetteer of Roman Palestine." *Qedem* 5 (1976).

———. *The Holy Land from the Persian to the Arab Conquest*. Grand Rapids, Mich.: Eerdmans, 1977.

Bagatti, B. and S. Loffreda. "Le Antichita de Khirbet Qana e di Kefar Kanna in Galilee." *Liber Annuus* 15 (1969): 251–92.

Mackowsky, R. M. "Scholars' Qanah." A re-examination of the Evidence in favor of Kirbet-Qanah." *Biblische Zeitschrift* NF 23.2 (1979): 278–84.

Masterman, E. W. G. "Cana of Galilee." *Palestine Exploration Fund, Quarterly Statement* (1914): 179-83.

Pilter, W. T. "Where is Cana of Galilee?" *Palestine Exploration Fund, Quarterly Statement* (1883): 143–48.

Storme, A. "Caná do Galilea: Lugar del primer milgro de Jesus." *Tierra Sancta* 66 (1991): 176–79.

Strange, J. F. "Cana of Galilee," *ABD.* 1: 827.

Capernaum (Capharnaum) [Hebrew, *Kfar Nahum*]

Importance

Jesus established his headquarters in Capernaum, at least for some time.

Scripture References

Matt. 4:13; 8:5-10; 11:23; 17:24; Mark 1:21; 2:1; Luke 4:23; 7:1; 10:15; John 2:12; 4:46; 6:17, 24, 59.

General Information

Capernaum (Village of Nahum) has been identified with Tell Hum. It was built on the northern shore

Capernaum. *Milestone of the Via Maris.*

of the Sea of Galilee, about two miles west of the Jordan River on the "Via Maris," the highway from Damascus to Ptolemais and Caesarea Maritima, two miles east of Tabgha (the place of seven springs, from the Greek *Heptapegon*). According to Josephus, the village was engaged in the First Jewish War against the Romans. When he was commander-in-chief of the rebels' army in Galilee, he was evacuated to Capernaum after an accident that occurred during the battle of Bethsaida (Josephus, *Life* 72; *see* BETHSAIDA).

Among the activities of Jesus in Capernaum or its area were the recruiting of Peter, Andrew, John, and James (Matt. 4:18-22, apparently contradicted by John 1:40 for Peter and Andrew), his teaching in the synagogue (John 6:59), the miraculous payment of the half-shekel tax (Matt. 17:24-27), and a number of healings and exorcisms including the healing of Peter's mother-in-law (Mark 1:29-31, 34; 2:1-12). Despite these mighty works, Capernaum did not repent and Jesus condemned it along with Bethsaida and Chorazin (Matt. 11:23; Luke 10:15).

According to Josephus and rabbinic literature, *minim* (sectarians, heretics) lived in Capernaum, Tiberias, and Sepphoris. This could be a reference to Jesus' followers or to early Jewish Christians. Jerome indicates that the Pharisees used to call them Nazarenes and that they were still strong in his day (fourth to fifth centuries) "in the synagogues of the east." In his opinion, they were neither faithful Jews nor true Christians. About 335 C.E., the Christian convert Joseph obtained from Constantine permission to build "churches for Christ" in Tiberias, Sepphoris, Nazareth, and Capernaum. Then gentile Christians joined the first Jewish Christians already settled there and built a sanctuary on what had been recognized as Peter's house. Archaeological data provided evidence that Capernaum was occupied continuously from the first to the seventh centuries.

Archaeological Data

In 1838 the American scholar E. Robinson recognized remarkable ruins, which he later (1855) identified as a synagogue. In 1866, C. Wilson rightly claimed that it was the site of ancient Capernaum. The Franciscans purchased the land in 1846: they own about two thirds of the site, while the Greek Orthodox Patriarchate owns the other third on the east side. H. Kohl and C. Watzinger explored the site in 1905, and the Franciscan G. Orfali excavated and partly restored the synagogue from 1921 to 1925. He also continued the excavation of the octagonal church begun by W. von Menden, who worked on the site from 1906 to 1915. Fr. V. C. Corbo and Fr. S. Loffreda resumed work in 1968 and continued until 1985. They opened a number of trenches in the synagogue and extended the excavation around it. Pavements, streets, and houses dating from the first century B.C.E. were uncovered (*see* fig. 11). Directly beneath the remains of the Byzantine octagonal church, south of the synagogue, they found a large room apparently used as a place of meeting or worship as early as the end of the first century C.E. The excavators concluded that the room was part of Peter's house for the following reasons:

1. Synagogues in the first century often were simple meeting places in private homes. It might be that Jesus had started his own synagogue in Peter's house.

2. Several early pilgrims identified the place as Peter's house. Among them was Egeria or Aetheria (381–384 C.E.), who wrote, "the house of the chief of the apostles has been turned into a church." The pilgrim of Piacenza (*circa* 570) gave the same information (*see* fig. 12).

3. Scores of graffiti in Aramaic, Greek, Hebrew, Latin, and Syriac, as well as crosses and one boat, scratched or drawn on the plastered walls indicate that the place had a special significance for the first generations of Christians.

4. Ancient peoples tended to build new sanctuaries over preexisting ones, even if they were dedicated to a different god. In this case, the Byzantine octagonal church was built exactly over the ancient large room.

5. Artifacts discovered there (Herodian coins and lamps, fish hooks) show that the house was occupied as early as the first century B.C.E. and that people involved in fishing lived in or around the house.

6. The floor and the walls of the room had been plastered at least three times, the first coating being dated to the middle of the first century C.E.

7. No traces of domestic activity, such as ashes, kitchenware, loom weights, and the like, were found in this room.

The excavators' conclusions are widely accepted today. Most scholars agree that the most significant witness of Jesus' activity is in Capernaum. Unfortunately, in 1987–88, a huge sanctuary shaped like a flying saucer was built to mark the site. It hovers a few feet over the octagonal

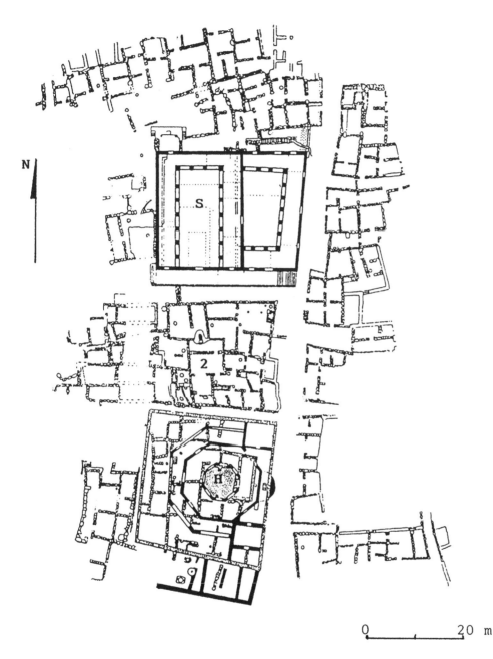

Figure 11 Capernaum. Excavations in the Franciscan property. S = Synagogue; 2 = Insula No. 2; H = Octagonal church over house.

N

0 ⎯⎯⎯ 20 m

church and makes new aerial photographs or observations impossible. The isometric view of a reconstructed insula is shown in figure 13.

Because of Luke 7:5, the synagogue deserves special attention: Was it really built by the centu-

rion? In consideration of its type, ornaments, dedicatory inscriptions in Greek and Aramaic, and other stylistic features, some Jewish scholars—among whom N. Avigad and G. Foerster—have dated it to the second or third century C.E. In oppo-

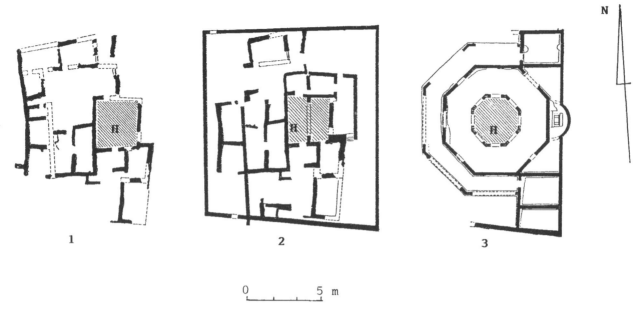

N

1   2   3

0 ___ 5 m

Figure 12 The Three Stages of Development of the "House of Peter" at Capernaum.
H = "House of Peter." 1) First to fourth centuries C.E., house with drystone walls.
2) First half of the fourth century, the complex around the house is enclosed, with
one entrance in the north and one in the south. 3) Middle of the fifth century, the
buildings are leveled and an octagonal church centered on the house is built. Its
floor is covered with a mosaic. *(After V. C. Corbo)*

sition to this view, the Franciscan excavators, V. Corbo and S. Loffreda, estimate that it cannot be older than the late fourth or fifth century. They base their opinion on the discovery of thousands of coins and potsherds unearthed during the 1968–1985 excavations. The controversy is not yet resolved, but one thing is certain: the present white synagogue, beautiful as it is, cannot be that of Jesus' time. The "centurion's synagogue" of the first century was probably a more modest edifice made of local black basalt like the buildings around it, or like the synagogue of Gamla (*see* GAMLA). The basalt foundation of the present limestone synagogue may include some of the elements of the synagogue Jesus knew.

A most distinctive feature of the present synagogue is the absence of a Torah niche in the middle of the wall facing Jerusalem as was the usual practice in Roman-Byzantine synagogues. Interestingly, a fragment of a cornice presents the well-preserved sculpture of a Torah shrine on wheels. It may represent the biblical story of the Ark being carried on a cart (1 Sam. 6:11, 2 Sam. 6:3) or, more likely, it may represent a movable receptacle for Torah scrolls. According to some scholars, among whom are J. Milgrom and the late E.L. Sukenik, it could have been a practice that, in this type of synagogue, the Torah was wheeled in at the beginning of the worship service, symbolizing God's presence. The destruction of the Temple by Titus in 70 C.E. may have led to the custom of keeping the Torah scrolls in a fixed place within the synagogue itself. It seems that the synagogue of Gamla, only ten miles away, did not have a Torah

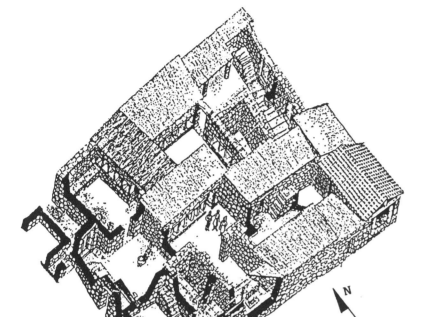

Figure 13 Capernaum. Isometric view of insula No 2 (Franciscan Custody of the Holy Land).

niche on its back wall either. If it is in fact a first-century synagogue, it may serve as a model for the ancient synagogue of Capernaum, because it is the only one in the area that is dated with certainty to the first century.

On the Greek Orthodox property, the excavations of 1978 to 1987 were directed by V. Tzaferis of the Department of Antiquities, with the participation of several universities from Canada and the United States. A Roman bathhouse from the second to third centuries C.E., 64 by 20 feet in size, was found. Beneath lay the remains of older walls dating from the first century C.E., but they were not investigated. Other first-century remains were a few small wall and floor sections of a building adjacent to the bathhouse. All other structures, a storehouse, a private house, and two large buildings, belong to the late second to eighth centuries C.E. (*see* fig. 14).

The results of both excavations indicate, somewhat surprisingly, that archaeological witnesses dating back to the first century are scarce. Just a few remains in the Greek Orthodox section and some more in the Franciscan area are the only clues to what Capernaum looked like in Jesus' time. It seems that it was only a small settlement in that period. There were probably a few rows of houses along the seashore, with the core of the village in the area where the octagonal church and synagogue stand. No large structure dating from the time of Jesus has been recovered. The excavators report that they found the remains of a basalt structure dating from the first century C.E. under the white Byzantine synagogue. Their main argument for identifying this structure as a synagogue is that houses of worship were often built one above the other in consecutive periods. This is generally true, especially for synagogues of the Middle

Capernaum. The Torah Ark represented on a freize. The Ark is not on a cart but has its own wheels.

or Late Roman and Byzantine periods, but at present not a single example exists of a first-century synagogue replaced by a Late Roman or Byzantine one, except perhaps for the successive synagogues at Nebratein in Upper Galilee. The remains under the Byzantine synagogue are too fragmentary to be conclusive and do not resemble the contemporary synagogue of nearby Gamla. The segments of walls under the white synagogue thus may have been part of a private house rather than a synagogue.

The white Byzantine synagogue and the adjacent octagonal church present several peculiarities that raise questions about the circumstances of the former's purpose and function. These peculiarities are as follows:

1. This is one of the largest, most decorated synagogues in all of Israel. It is commonly accepted that the economic strength of a community often correlates to the size of the public buildings it erects. In Capernaum it would mean that this town was larger and richer than any other community in Is-

rael either in rural or urban areas during the Late Roman-Byzantine period. This could not have been the case at the beginning of the first century C.E. Factors other than the size of the local population however, may have contributed to the size and grandeur of the synagogue.

2. This may be the only synagogue where development over the long course of its use is not evident. Normally there are always a few phases of reconstruction and modifications; here, not a single change seems to have been made.

3. In front of the synagogue and at a short distance from it is the octagonal church surrounded by a wall. This type of structure was used primarily for memorial churches not to serve local communities but, instead, to suit pilgrims. The fact that the large church appears modest in comparison with the large synagogue is intriguing. The circumstances of their construction seem very strange, especially if we consider that they were both built during the Byzantine period when there was hostil-

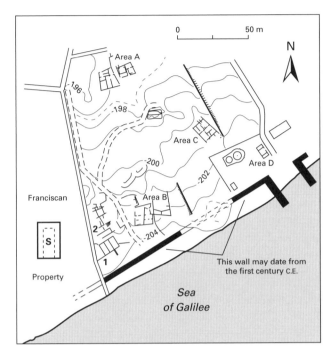

Figure 14 Capernaum. Excavations on the Greek Orthodox property. S = Synagogue *(Israel Antiquities Authority and Consortium)*

ity toward Jews in some places. How can this seemingly pacific coexistence in Capernaum be explained? Even if such coexistence is not unique in the Byzantine period, as the evidence from Sepphoris indicates, it might still be suggested that the splendid synagogue may have been a Christian monument erected to commemorate the ministry of Jesus in Galilee and to satisfy the religious fervor of pilgrims. This possibility would also explain why thousands of coins of the period were found under its floor, although similar hoards have been found elsewhere in synagogues.

4. The excavators date the synagogue to the late fourth or fifth century C.E. However, the style of the building is typical of the second or third century as mentioned above. This apparent anachronism may be significant in assessing the nature of the building. Taking into account that the syna-

gogue was of primordial importance to Christians and especially to new converts, and that it was built when pilgrimages were at their peak, this peculiar feature would further support the hypothesis that it was a Christian shrine rather than an active Jewish house of prayer. Another view, however, is that Capernaum was indeed a totally Jewish community and that the memorial church was imposed by the Byzantine emperors.

5. The *insula*-type houses were discovered only in the Franciscan area. Excavations in the Greek Orthodox section revealed a different pattern of settlement: The more ancient houses are situated along the shoreline and the community expanded inland. Instead, the *insula* pattern, according to the Franciscan archaeologists, suggests a preplanned community, which started at some distance from the waterfront. The reasons for this difference are not yet clear (*see* fig. 13).

Thus, the archaeological finds at Capernaum, significant as they are, are associated with major problems that cannot easily be solved. Perhaps further excavation and study will bring greater understanding.

Implications for Jesus Research

There is little doubt that Capernaum was, at least for a while, Jesus' center of activity. The discovery of the plastered room under the octagonal church startled the Christian community. It increased the authenticity of many statements referring to Capernaum in the Gospels and it made others more comprehensible. For example, the size of the plastered room is such that a roofing technique using arches or inner walls to support basalt beams of about six feet long, as was common in the region, could not be used. Instead, the span between the walls required wooden beams covered with palms or reeds. Thus Mark 2:4 becomes plausible, whereas the use of *keramon* "tiles," in Luke 5:19 seems improbable. Similarly, the uneven floors paved with rough stone slabs in private houses allow us to understand how a coin could easily fall in the interstices and become invisible in the darkness of a room having only a door and sometimes a small window to let in the light (Luke 15:8-10).

A difficult, isolated statement like Gospel of Thomas 42, "be(come) passers-by," may perhaps be understood as a reference to a wheeled-in Torah, which symbolically brought God's presence to his people wherever they happened to be. This possibility is supported by the view of C. S. Feller that "The Babylonian experience of exile implied a Talmudic tradition that knows without a doubt that we can be a holy people anywhere . . . The Torah . . . was, in Neusner's words, a mobile land" (*Land of Israel* 159, 180). Separation from the Temple contributed to the development of local congregations: "The Most High does not dwell in houses made with hands" (Acts 7:48-50). Jesus' claim that he would rebuild a temple not made with hands, may show that he probably had a spiritual understanding of the reign of God that he was announcing. He is even said to have proclaimed the destruction of the Temple (Mark 13:1-2). His eschatological concepts were presumably very different from those of the Qumranites, John the Baptist, and other first century groups.

Can the location of Capernaum and the biblical and archaeological records give some indication about why Jesus chose this place to establish his headquarters? Perhaps. First, it is obvious that Galilee, familiar to Jesus and distant from the religious center, was preferable to Judea or Samaria for basing his activities and recruiting disciples. Nazareth was too small and landlocked; in case of repressive action by Antipas' police there was no way to escape. There was also a shadow of doubt about the legitimacy of his birth (*see* PANTERA'S TOMBSTONE), and the Nazarenes did not welcome him back. Capernaum had the advantage of being close to the political border of Galilee with the tetrarchy of Herod Philip, which could easily be reached by boat should trouble come. Chorazin and Bethsaida, by themselves, probably could not provide many long-term followers. In contrast, Capernaum was a place of transit with a tax or toll office

and probably a small garrison. The proximity of the Via Maris would have afforded Jesus the opportunity to reach far more people in Capernaum than just the local population.

BIBLIOGRAPHY

Baarda, T. "Jesus Said: Be Passers-By, On the Meaning and Origin of Logion 42 of the Gospel of Thomas." In *Early Transmission of Words of Jesus: Thomas, Tatian and the Text of the New Testament*, edited by J. Helderman and S. J. Noorda, Uitgeverij: VU Boekhandel, 1983.

Bagatti, B. "Capharnaum, la ville de Pierre." *Monde de la Bible* 27 (1983): 8–16.

Corbo, V. C. *Cafarnao.* 3 vols. Jerusalem: Franciscan Printing Press, 1975.

Dewey, A. J. "A Passing Remark: Thomas 42." *Jesus Seminar Papers.* Sonoma, Calif.: Polebridge Press, 1990.

Feller, C. S. "Land of Israel: Sanctified Matter or Mythic Place." *Three Faiths, One God*, edited by Hick and Meltzer. New York: SUNY Press, 1989.

Fisher, M. "The Corinthian Capitals of the Capernaum Synagogue: A Late Roman Feature in Eretz Israel." *Eretz Israel* 17 (1984): 305–11 [Hebrew, with English summary].

Foerster, G. "Notes on Recent Excavations at Capernaum." *Ancient Synagogues Revealed.* Jerusalem: Israel Exploration Society, 1981.

Grant, R. M. and D. N. Freedman. *The Secret Sayings of Jesus.* New York: Doubleday, 1960.

Jeremias, J. *Unbekannte Des Thomas-Evangeliums.* Berlin: Alfred Topelmann, 1961.

Kasser, R. *L'Evangile selon Thomas.* Neuchâtel, 1961.

Laughlin, J. C. H. "Capernaum. From Jesus' Time and After." *BAR* 19 (1993): 54–61.

Loffreda, S. "The Late Chronology of the Synagogue of Capernaum." *Ancient Synagogues Revealed.* Jerusalem: The Israel Exploration Society (1981).

———. *Recovering Capharnaum.* Jerusalem: Edizioni Custodia Terra Sancta, 1985.

Loffreda, S. and V. Tzaferis. "Capernaum." *NEAEHL* 1: 290-96.

Meyers, C. "Temple, Jerusalem." *ABD* 6:350–69.

Milgrom, J. Oral comments at the consecration of the Torah Scroll and Ark of Synagogue Netivot Shalom in 1990 at Berkeley.

Patterson, S. J. "*The Gospel of Thomas within the Development of Early Christianity*" Ph.D. diss. Claremont Graduate School, 1988.

Rousseau, J. J. *A Plea for Reconsidering Thomas 42.* Jesus Seminar. Sonoma, Calif.: Polebridge Press, 1991.

Seidler-Feller, C. "Land of Israel: Sanctified Matter or Mythic Place." *Three Faiths, One God*, edited by Hick and Meltzer, 159, 180. New York: SUNY Press, 1989.

Strange, J. F. and H. Shanks. "Has the House Where Jesus Stayed in Capernaum Been Found?" *BAR* 8 (1982): 26–39.

———. "Synagogue Where Jesus Preached Found at Capernaum." *BAR* 9 (1983): 24–31.

Tzaferis, V. "New Archaeological Evidence on Ancient Capernaum." *BA* 46 (1983): 198–204.

Tzaferis, V. and M. Peleg. "Excavation at Capernaum." *Qadmoniot* 16 62–63 (1983): 72–75.

Weis, H. "Gold Hoard Found at Capernaum" *BAR* 9 (1983): 50–53.

Wison, R. M. *Studies in the Gospel of Thomas.* London: A. R. Mowbray and Co., 1960.

Cave of Letters

Importance
Artifacts and documents from the Cave of Letters shed light on the life and languages of first-century Palestine.

Scripture References
Matt. 10:3-4; 11:20-24; Mark 3:18; Luke 6:14-15; 10:13-15; 13:1; 23:25: John 19:20, 23.

General Information
The material in the Cave of Letters is relevant to the Second War, the War of Bar Kokhba (132–135), which erupted in Palestine in 132. At the beginning of this conflict, the Jews conquered Jerusalem, established an independent state and coined their own money. The situation became so critical that Emperor Hadrian (117–138) sent his best legions to Palestine under the command of Julius Severus, governor of Britain.

Little is known about this devastating confrontation, which led to the complete destruction of Jerusalem, the deportation en masse of the Jerusalemites, who were scattered all over the Roman Empire, and the interdiction for them to ever come back to Jerusalem except for a one-day visit once a year. A Roman city, Aelia Capitolina, was built over the ruins of the Holy City. This limited information about the Bar Kokhba War comes from a few references by Roman historians who wrote about the reign of Hadrian, from some comments by early Church Fathers and from some legendary, obscure mentions in the Talmud. Even the name of the revolt leader was uncertain: Bar Kokhba, "Son of a Star," in Christian sources; Bar Koziba, "Son of a Liar," in Jewish writings.

After the accidental discovery of the first Dead Sea Scrolls, local Bedouins realized that it might be profitable to find other materials in the caves of the Judean desert (*see* DEAD SEA SCROLLS and QUMRAN); they explored more of the caves in that area. By the end of 1959, a group of them offered to sell a few pieces of leather bearing Hebrew and Greek inscriptions to the Rockefeller Museum in Jerusalem. The source, they said, was an inaccessible cave in Wadi Murabba'at. The following year, more leather and papyrus fragments were offered to different institutions and antiquities dealers. One such document began with the words, "From Shimeon ben Kosiba to Yeshua ben Galgoula and the people of the fort, shalom . . . " The news generated excitement in Israel and eventually caused the creation of a systematic research program.

In 1960, Y. Yadin, professor of archaeology at the Hebrew University of Jerusalem, met with David ben Gurion, Prime Minister and Secretary of Defense, to discuss the matter. They decided to make a comprehensive and systematic inventory of all caves of the Judean Desert, examine all of them, and thoroughly search all those that could have been used for inhabitation or storage. They hoped to recover more information about the circumstances of the Bar Kokhba War and the character of its leader. The directors and sponsors of the expedition represented the highest level of government and academia: David ben Gurion himself, army Chief of Staff Rav-Aluf Haim Laskow, and Professor Benjamin Mazar, then president of the Hebrew University.

Archaeological Information

The area surveyed, located south of en-Gedi, was about 14 kilometers (9 miles) long, from north to south, and 7 kilometers (4.5 miles) wide, extending westward from the eastern edge of the chain of cliffs overlooking the Dead Sea (*see* fig. 15). Three canyons were to be explored. Y. Aharoni, N. Avigad, P. Bar-Ardon, and Y. Yadin each led a team of investigators. The most important discoveries were made in Nahal Hever in the northern area assigned to Yadin. The work began on March 23, 1960 and lasted two weeks.

In the northern wall of the Nahal Hever canyon, some 100 meters (328 feet) below the top of the cliff right under a Roman century* camp, which itself was 700 meters (2,300 feet) above the canyon floor, was the largest cave of all those in the area surveyed, with two entrances close to each other. Refugees in the cave had apparently been trapped and had died of starvation. A wealth of artifacts and ecofacts* were recovered together with the skeletal remains of three men, eight women, and six children (*see* fig. 16).

The artifacts include an assortment of early-second-century textiles and thus represent the technology of the early centuries C.E.: clothes, rugs, skeins and balls of yarn, and spinning whorls of thirty-four different colors. Among the clothes were women's mantles, a child's linen shirt, and bundles of unspun purple wool used to make the *tsitsith* (tassels) for the fringes of prayer shawls. Written documents included a number of parchment fragments with verses from Psalms and a bundles of letters on papyrus stuffed in a waterskin along with other precious objects. The articles in the waterskin and others found near it included jewelry, a powder box, an engraved bone handle, a glass vial, precious stones, a glass jug, and a brass mirror in a wooden frame. Scattered elsewhere in different caches of the cave were fine metal vessels, coins, incense shovels, glassware, a bird-catching net, keys, and more written documents.

Laboratory analysis of the dyes revealed sophisticated techniques, especially in the way they were

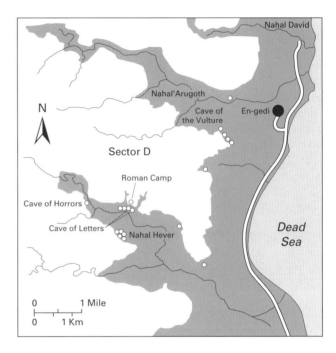

Figure 15 Sector D *(attributed to Yigael Yadin)*

stabilized and fastened with mordants of various metal salts. Only three basic dyes were used to produce the thirty-four identifiable colors: saffron yellow from *Crocus Sativus* (Pliny mentions that it was in great demand and often imitated), indigo blue, and alazarin red from the roots of *Rubia Tinctorium*, the only one able to dye wool and leather (*see* TEXTILE). The woven materials indicate that weavers and wearers did not use fabric blends (see Lev. 19:19, which forbids mixing fibers of different kinds). The weaving, especially that of several tunics, was of high quality (*see* TUNIC WITHOUT SEAM, DICE).

The written documents are especially important for the story of Bar Kokhba. One of the wooden slats between which the papyrus letters were folded bears the words "Shimeon bar Kosiba, President (or Prince) of Israel." Professor G. Bierberkraut, a Hebrew University expert on manuscript preservation, unfolded the bundle and found fifteen

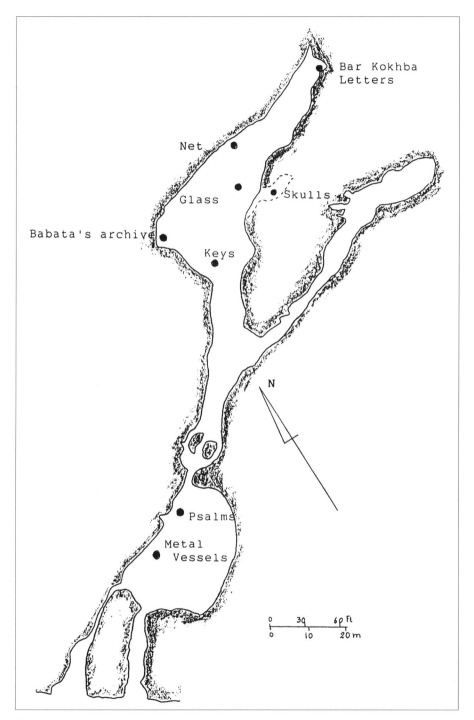

Figure 16 Cave of Letters. Map showing the locations of the finds.

Cave of Letters. The goatskin containing precious objects.

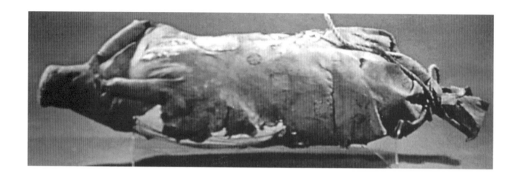

letters, most of them well preserved. They contain information about Bar Kokhba's life and struggle and are also a source of linguistic data in that they were written in several languages: Aramaic, Hebrew, and Greek. One Greek letter announced that "The letter is written in Greek as we have no one who knows Hebrew." Perhaps this indicates that non-Jews fought with Bar Kokhba and his supporters ("Many outside nations were joining for eagerness of gain" [Yadin, *Bar Kokhba*, 132]). It also shows that the addressee, although a Jew, could read Greek or had a translator at hand. That the letters were dictated, not all in the same handwriting, means that they reflect the spoken language. All bore an indication of the sender, "From Shimeon bar Kosiba," but without his signature. The explanation of the uncertainty about his name emerged: his true name was Kosiba; people made puns on the wording, his supporters changing it to Bar Kokhba and his detractors to Bar Koziba (Son of a Star versus Son of a Liar). Among the latter, his contemporary, Rabbi Akiba, believed that the messianic deliverer would not be defeated and that failure was the equivalent of imposture.

One letter contains evidence of the religious practices of the rebels. This letter, written in Aramaic, the Palestinian vernacular of the time, requests the "four species" specified for the Feast of *Sukkoth* (Booths or Tabernacles): the *lulav* (palm branch), *ethrog* (a kind of large lemon), *hadas* (myrtle), and *arava* (willow):

Shimeon to Yehuda ben Menashe, at Qiriyath 'Arabya: I have sent you two donkeys that you shall send two men to Yehonathan ben Be'ayan and Masabala so that they shall pack and send to the camp *lulavim* and *ethrogim*. And you, from your place, send others who will bring *hadasim* and *aravim*. See that they are tithed and sent to the camp. This request is made because the army is big. Be well.

A second expedition, launched in 1961, recovered more artifacts, including a goatskin in a cache. It contained some of the possessions of a widow, Babata, who had taken refuge in the cave with other persons during the Bar Kokhba Revolt. Among the objects in the goatskin were thirty-five legal documents written on papyrus. They had been neatly wrapped, tied together in a piece of cloth, and placed in a leather pouch. When the package was opened, it appeared that the papyri were methodically grouped in different bundles, each dealing with a specific subject. Thus, the name "archive" was given to the find. The dates of the documents ranged from 93 to 132 CE.

Twenty-three of these documents were of the "double deed" or "tied deed" type used to prevent falsification. The text was written on one side of the sheet, which was rolled and tied with five or seven rings of string. The upper part of the sheet, several inches long, was let free. It bore a brief description of the deed and the signatures of witnesses, one for each ring (*see* fig. 17). When needed,

Figure 17 A "Tied Deed" as Found in Babata's Archive. Note the witnesses' signatures under each ring.

the document was opened before a court or an official in the presence of witnesses whose function was to observe that the text, in the inner side of the rolled sheet, had not been tampered with. Other documents, not tied, were summons to appear in court, before the Roman governor who had jurisdiction over En-Gedi, where Babata had most of her properties.

Another systematic investigation of all the Judean Caves made in 1993 did not yield materials shedding any more light on Bar Kokhba or Babata.

Implications for Jesus Research

If Greek was a common language in Palestine in 135 C.E. and earlier, *a fortiori*, was it so at the beginning of the first century. Many Jews were in close contact with Greek speakers. No village in Galilee was more than 12 miles—a four hour walk—from a center of Greek-speaking Roman culture: Caesarea Philippi, Tiberias, Ptolemais (Acco), Sepphoris (less than 4 miles from Nazareth), Scythopolis (Bet Shan), the Decapolis,

and Phoenicia. In order to sell various agricultural products to Greek-speaking city dwellers, the Jews from nearby villages had to have a rudimentary knowledge of the language of their patrons. The same was undoubtedly true for the rest of the country in places such as Caesarea Maritima, Sebaste (Samaria), Ashkelon, Joppa, and Jerusalem at the time of the pilgrimages. Koine* Greek was the lingua franca of the Mediterranean Basin. The warning signs on the *soreg** of the Temple itself were written in Greek and Latin (*see* TEMPLE, WARNING SIGN). The *titulus* on Jesus' cross was written in Hebrew, Latin, and Greek (John 19:20). Documents written in Greek were even found in the caves around Qumran, the stronghold of those who considered themselves the eschatological remnant of Israel (*see* QUMRAN and DEAD SEA SCROLLS).

Probably at least one of Jesus' disciples was a native Greek speaker: Philip from Bethsaida (he had a Greek name). When Jesus was in Bethsaida, the Decapolis and Phoenicia he was in contact with Greek speakers and perhaps could express himself in their language (Matt. 10:3; 11:20-24; Mark 8:22; Luke 10:13-15; John 1:44; 12:20-21). Pilate may have communicated with Jesus in Greek during his examination before judgment.

The discoveries of the Cave of Letters also may be relevant to Jesus' life because revolutionaries or Zealots were present among his followers. The period of Jesus' life was one of relatively peaceful coexistence among the local population, the gentile settlers and the Roman auxiliary forces. Yet, there is evidence of an underlying Zealot spirit in Palestine. Those opposed to the Romans and their allies were present and ready to take action, as indicated by the involvement of the sons of Judas the Galilean in the First Jewish War (*see* MASADA). The parable of the assassin (G. Thom. 98), the incident of the Galileans whose blood Pilate mingled with their sacrifices (Luke 13:1), and the allusion to "rebels" and "the insurrection" in which Barabbas was arrested (Mark 15:6; Luke 23: 19, 25) point to a latent hostility toward the Romans. Thus Simon the Zealot (or Cananaean) could indeed have been a political-religious militant; a Zealot current apparently existed well before 66 B.C.E.

Among the various Jewish groups of first-century Palestine were nationalist activists who may have considered Jesus a potential leader. Yet they would have abandoned him if they thought that he was not the Messiah they expected. His disciples disbanded at the time of his crucifixion. As was the case for Bar Kokhba a century later, most Jews of Jesus' time did not recognize Jesus as the Redeemer of Israel, because, in their view, God's Anointed could not fail; crucifixion was a form of death believed to be a curse from God (*see* CRUCI-FIXION). In their eyes, Jesus was not a true messianic figure.

BIBLIOGRAPHY

Abramsky, S. *Bar Kokhba, President of Israel*. Tel Aviv, 1981 (Hebrew).

Benoit, P., J. T. Milik, and R. de Vaux. *Les Grottes de Muraba'at*. Discoveries in the Judean Desert 2. Oxford: Clarendon, 1961.

Fitzmayer, J. A. "The Bar Kokhba Period." *Saint Mary's Theology Studies* 1 (1962): 133–68.

Horsley, R. A. *Jesus and the Spiral of Violence*. San Francisco: Harper and Row, 1987.

Horsley, R. and J. S. Hamon. *Bandits, Prophets and Messiahs*. New York: Winston Press, 1985.

Howard, G. and J. C. Shelton. "The Bar Kokhba Letters and Palestinian Greek." *IEJ* 23 (1973): 101–2.

Lewis, N., ed. *The Documents From the Bar Kokhba Period in the Cave of Letters*. Jerusalem: Israel Exploration Society and Hebrew University, 1984.

———. (English ed.), Y. Yadin, and J. C. Greenfield (Hebrew eds.). *The Documents from the Bar Kokhba Period in the Cave of Letters*. Jerusalem: Israel Exploration Society, 1989.

Mantel, H. "The Caves of the Bar Kokhba Revolt." *The Jewish Quarterly Review* 58 (1968): 224–42, 274–96.

Polotski, Y. "The Judean Desert Expedition, 1961. The Greek Documents from the 'Cave of Letters.'" *Yedot* 26 (1962): 237–41 (Hebrew).

Vermes, G. *Jesus the Jew*. Philadelphia: Fortress Press, 1973.

Yadin, Y. "The Judean Desert Expeditions, 1962. Expedition D. Cave of letters." *Yedot* 26 (1962): 204–36 (Hebrew).

———. "The Finds from the Bar Kokhba Period in the Cave of Letters." *Judean Desert Studies* 1 (1963).

———. *Bar Kokhba*. 1971. Reprint. London: Weindenfeld and Nicolson, 1978.

———. "Cave of Letters." under "Judean Desert Caves." *NEAEHL* 3: 829-32.

Chorazin

Importance

One of the places Jesus visited where he performed "mighty works." The city did not repent, however, and Jesus condemned it.

Scripture References

Matt. 11:20-22; Luke 10:13-14.

General Information

Chorazin, identified with Khirbet Karaze, is located two-and-a-half miles north of Capernaum. Besides being mentioned in the Gospels, it appears in rabbinic literature from the third to fourth centuries as one of the "medium-size towns" of Palestine (*t. Makkot* 3:8). The town is also mentioned in connection with the first harvest offering ('*omer*), which should have been brought to the Temple had the city been closer to Jerusalem (*b. Menahot* 85a). Eusebius indicates that the city was destroyed in the fourth century. It was probably destroyed by an earthquake and rebuilt in the fifth century.

Archaeological Data

In 1869, C. Wilson identified the remains of a synagogue, which was first excavated in 1905–7 by H. Kohl and C. Watzinger, and later, in 1926, by J. Ory and N. Makhouly. Z. Yeivin excavated in 1962–64 and, when Chorazin was included in the Israel National Park Service, returned to continue excavation and do restoration in 1980–84. Today the synagogue and the reconstructed city form an impressive complex, open to the public.

Synagogue of Chorazin
Northwest corner.

This restored city, however, is not the Chorazin of Jesus' time because no remains from the first century C.E. were found. A few potsherds dated from that earlier period were gathered on the other side of the modern road. The original Chorazin should probably be sought there. The current city dates from the third to fourth centuries. The excavations revealed domestic complexes with cisterns and *miqva'ot* (ritual baths), streets and channels, a large public building, and a majestic synagogue. All the buildings are made of the same local, hard, volcanic basalt as is found in Capernaum, Bethsaida, Qatzrin, and Gamla. The building complexes are larger than the *insulae* of Capernaum; one of them is comprised of fourteen rooms around a courtyard. In the center of the building is a large *miqveh*, in a partly covered courtyard, with a cistern probably used to store rain water.

In the center of the city stands a large (70 x 50 feet) synagogue, "a masterpiece of stone work," to quote Z. Yeivin. Its basilical floor plan, with two parallel rows of columns, is comparable to that of the synagogues of Capernaum and other Galilean villages. Also, as at Capernaum and elsewhere in Galilee, the southern façade has three portals, the central one being the largest. Inside, as at Nabratein, there is a *bema*, "platform" on each side of the main entrance. The right *bema* (when entering) was probably for the reader and the left one for the Torah scroll. This could be in accordance with a practice that succeeded the putative "wheeling-in" of the Torah shrine (*see* CAPERNAUM). Another interesting discovery is the "Moses' seat" found in 1926. In Yeivin's reconstruction, it is placed on the *bema* located between the main and western entrances. Hellenistic and Roman influence, as in other synagogues of the same period, can be seen in the decoration, which includes human figures, a lion attacking a centaur, another one devouring an animal, an animal suckling a cub, and a Medusa. More than two thousand coins were found under the fifth-century floor, with dates ranging from the fourth to the seventh centuries. They include two gold coins of Heraclius, from 612. It cannot be a foundation deposit or an ordinary coin hoard, as found in some other synagogues, because the synagogue did survive into the seventh century. One explanation, proposed by Yeivin, is that the coins were thrown into a hole in the floor over the centuries by pilgrims, just as it is done today in some places.

Figure 18 Site of Chorazin.
M: Miqvaoth area. *(After Z. Yeivin)*

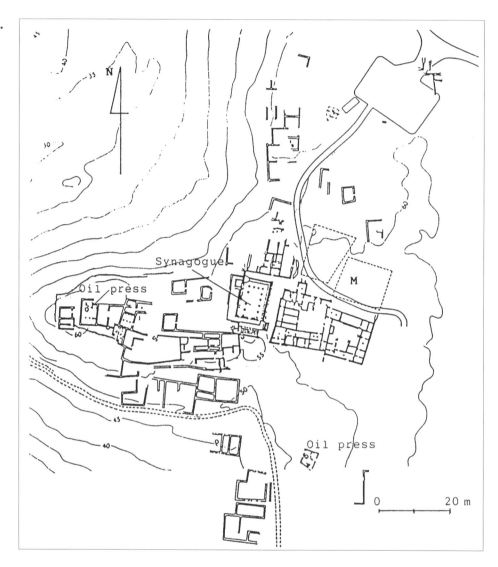

Implications for Jesus Research

The existence of a town called Chorazin in the Capernaum area in the first century C.E. is indicated by Matthew 11:20-22 and Luke 10:13-14. Implications for Jesus research are limited to the discovery of the so-called "Moses seat" (*see* MOSES SEAT). Nevertheless, because construction techniques and building materials were the same, the present restored Chorazin provides a general idea of what the towns of Bethsaida and Capernaum were like in the first century. The same may be said of Qatzrin, about ten miles in the northwest of Chorazin (*see* fig. 18).

BIBLIOGRAPHY

Kohl, H. and C. Watzinger. "Chorazin." *Synagogen*, 41–58.

———. "Two Lintels with Menorah Reliefs from Chorazin." *Ancient Synagogues Revealed*. Edited by L. I. Levine. Jerusalem: The Israel Exploration Society, 1981.

Yeivin, Z. "Has Another Ark Been Found?" [Chorazin Synagogue]. *BAR* 9 (1983): 75–76.

———. "A Ritual Bath (Miqveh) at Chorazin." *Qadmoniot* 17 (1984): 66–67, 79–81 (Hebrew).

———. "Ancient Chorazin Comes Back to Life." *BAR* 13 (1987): 22–36.

———. "Chorazin." *NEAEHL* 1: 301-4.

Coins and Money

Importance

Coins and money are mentioned several times in the Gospels. Jesus expressed opinions about the use of money and employed it as an image in some parables.

Scripture References

Matt. 2:11; 5:26; 6:24; 10:9, 29; 17:24, 27; 18:23-25; 20:2, 13; 21:12; 22:19; 23:16-17; 25:14-30; 26:14; 27:6; 28:12, 15; Mark 6:8; 11:15; 12:15, 41-42; 14:11; Luke 9:3; 10:35; 12:6, 59; 15:8; 16:9-13; 19:11-27, 45; 20:24; 22:5; John 2:14-15.

General Information

Originally, economic activity was conducted by way of the barter system: services and goods were exchanged directly in two-way transactions. For the sake of convenience and in an effort to better compare and standardize values, certain commodities were attributed a buying power and became a third term of exchange in the barter. It was the beginning of a crude form of money where shells, hides, cattle, certain quantities of grain became units of exchange. This system greatly facilitated multilateral transactions. Further progress involved the use of precious metals measured by weight as the intermediary term of exchange. Until the end of the Iron Age, in the sixth century B.C.E., barter with or without intermediary commodities and the use of precious metals by weight remained the only means of economic exchange. Accordingly, the Hebrew word *kesef* which means "silver," is often translated as "money" in most versions of the Bible. It is worth noticing that only one reference to shekels of gold appears in the Hebrew Bible (1 Chron. 21:25). The shekel as a unit of weight was the equivalent of about four tenths of an ounce. Where there is no other indication, the word shekel always refers to a weight of silver.

The first coins of the Near East appear to have been minted at the end of the seventh century B.C.E. at Lydia in Asia Minor. Made of electrum, a natural alloy of gold and silver (Herodotus, I.94), they were small pieces of irregular shape stamped with a royal imprint as a guarantee of their weight and content of precious metal. Currency issuers soon realized that coins, especially the good ones, travel far. Coin minters took advantage of this fact to convey messages, ideas, and propaganda to the most remote areas. Coins announced new appointments of governors, the supremacy of deities, the construction of new monuments, and special events. Alexander the Great established a mint at Acco and the Ptolemies added three more at Joppa, Ashkelon, and Gaza. The Hasmoneans received from the Seleucids the right to mint Jewish coins. During this Hellenistic period, payments with coins became the rule, and the old barter system was relegated to minor local transactions.

By the end of the first century B.C.E., the new monetary system was well established and organized. The best and most favored pieces were the gold and silver coins of the Roman emperors, the older coins of the Roman Republic, and the coins of the Hellenistic rulers. The Roman emperors minted in gold and silver, the Phoenician cities continued to mint in silver, and local kings and autonomous cities like those of the Decapolis were limited to bronze coins. Two main monetary systems, the Roman and the Hellenistic, existed concurrently, with a special place for the Phoenician coins, especially those of Tyre. The Hellenistic system was based on the silver drachma as the main unit. Its weight varied from one area to another. According to the Attic standard, a coin of four drachmas (*tetradrachmon*) weighted 17.4 grams, but its weight was only 14.5 grams in the Phoenician standard. Four drachmas were the equivalent of one Phoenician stater or one Jewish shekel. The half-shekel per capita Temple tax levied on Jewish males was thus the equivalent of two Phoenician drachmas (Matt. 17:24). This was the equivalent of 7.25 grams per person (*see* table 1). For an estimated population of two million Jews subject to this tax, the Temple revenue in silver alone was the equivalent of 14.5 tons every year (*see* TEMPLE, TREASURY).

Archaeological and Typological Information

In the time of Jesus, the emperors Augustus and Tiberius had a monopoly on issuing gold coins, which were minted in Rome and in some provinces. A few Hellenistic gold coins, which had been kept in people's possession for generations, were probably also still in circulation. Silver coins were much more abundant and have been found in the excavations of most of the important sites of the period. All three types are represented: Hellenistic, Roman, and Phoenician, with the Tyrian type being most abundant. The didrachma or half-shekel from Tyre, exclusively recognized for payments to the Temple treasury, was minted from 126 B.C.E. to 66 C.E., the year of the first Jewish Revolt, when it was replaced by the Jewish shekel. The Tyrian shekel tetradachma displays on the obverse the head of Melkart, the main god of Tyre, and on the reverse an eagle standing on the prow of a galley with the legend, "Belonging to Tyre the Holy and Asylum City" in Greek. These coins bear the date of minting and the mark of the mint and were greatly favored for their high content of pure silver, 98 percent. Numismatist Y. Meshorer argues that Herod the Great and his successor, Archelaus, minted Tyrian tetradrachmas in Jerusalem for the payment of the Temple tax. A hoard of 4,560 Tyrian coins was discovered on Mount Carmel in 1960: 3,400 tetradrachmas and the rest didrachmas. It has been suggested that it was a shipment that did not make its way to the Temple.

The bronze coins used in Palestine during the first century came from different sources. In general use were old coins minted by the Seleucid kings at Antioch, Damascus, and other cities of the kingdom, and newer coins issued by the Roman prefects and the autonomous cities. Jews used coins minted by the Hasmonean and Herodian dynasties. The most common of these were the coins of King Alexander Jannaeus. John Hyrcanus, Judah Aristobulus, and Matthias Antigonus also minted Jewish coins, mostly in the lepta and half-lepta denominations. Usually, the Hasmonean coins show a double cornucopia on the reverse and on the obverse a paleo-Hebrew inscription in which the only variant is the name of the High Priest: "Yehonatan (or Yehudah, Yehohanan, Yonatan, Matitiah) the High Priest and the Jewish Assembly." This last expression probably refers to the Sanhedrin, in which case the legend would be the only evidence available today of a collaboration between the Sanhedrin and the High Priests. One reason that the coins of Alexander Jannaeus were so popular may be that they had different symbols. A Jannaeus coin bore a star with the inscription "To the King Jannaeus" between the rays. It may have symbolized the messianic hopes and expectations of political autonomy aroused by the new Jewish kingship. Other Jannaeus coins feature an anchor, which has been interpreted as a way to commemorate his capture of the port city of Jaffa, a lily representing the people of Israel, and a palm symbolizing the country. The last of the Hasmoneans, Matthias Antigonus (40–37 B.C.E.) issued a new series of coins with what became a typical Jewish symbol: the seven-branched menorah of the Temple. These coins probably were meant to affirm his priestly status at the time of the rise of his most threatening adversary, Herod.

The Herodian dynasty did not use Hebrew letters on coins and favored neutral, nonprovocative symbols: cornucopias, pomegranates, palms, the prow of a ship, and a helmet. On the third year of his appointment to kingship by the Roman Senate (the first year of his effective reign), Herod the Great minted coins representing utensils from the Temple, probably to indicate that he was as respectful of the people's religious feelings as was

Table I Equivalence Table

Drachme or Dinarius Equivalent	Phoenician (Tyrian)	Greek	Roman	Jewish
6,000		TALENT=34kg or 75 pounds of silver	(240) aurei	
100		MANEH=0.45kg or one pound of silver		
25			(G) AUREUS	
4	(S) STATER or TETRADRACHMON	(S) TETRADRACHMON		"shekel"
2	(S) DIDRACHMON	(S) DIDRACHMON		"half-shekel"
1		(S) DRACHME	(S) DENARIUS	
¼			(B) SESTERTIUS= ¼-denarius	
⅛			(B) DUPENDIUS= ½-sestertius	
¹⁄₁₆		"assarion"	(B) AS= ¼-sestertius	
¹⁄₃₂			(B) SEMIS= ½-As	
¹⁄₆₄			(B) QUADRANS= ¼-As	
¹⁄₁₂₈				(B) LEPTON or PRUTA= ½-quadrans

Notes:
- *Minted coins are framed.*
- *Accounting units have their values between parentheses.*
- *Names of units that were not always minted are between quotation marks.*
- *G = gold; S = silver; B = bronze and other copper alloy.*

Matthias Antigonus whom he had defeated. In 4 B.C.E., Herod's kingdom was divided between his sons. Archelaus ruled for ten years over Judea and Samaria before being deposed and replaced by Roman prefects. His coins show a helmet, the grapevine of the Temple (*see* TEMPLE, HISTORY, DESCRIPTION), and the prow of a ship. Antipas received Galilee and Perea, he built a new capital at Tiberias (*see* TIBERIAS), where he established a mint. His coins represent the emperor Tiberius on the obverse and on the reverse a palm or a reed, symbol of Tiberias. Philip inherited the territory east of the Jordan, north of the Decapolis. He founded two cities, Caesarea Philippi at Paneas and Julias at Bethsaida. One of his coins represented the façade of a temple, probably the Augusteum built by his father at Paneas. In 30 C.E. he issued another series of coins to commemorate the foundation of Julias. They show the heads of Tiberius, Livia-Julia (Tiberius' mother) and his own. He was the only Jewish ruler whose picture ever appeared on a coin (*see* COINS AS HISTORICAL DOCUMENTS).

The Roman prefects followed Herod's example by avoiding the use of symbols that could have offended the Jewish population. Those who minted coins, Coponius (the first one, 6–9 C.E.), Valerius Gratus (15–26), and Pontius Pilate (26–36) did not represent the head of the emperor as was customary in the rest of the empire, but instead used symbols of authority or images representing the country.

Implications for Jesus Research

The extreme variety of coins in circulation in the time of Jesus, the differences of standard, the plurality of origins, and the large spread of minting periods from the fourth century B.C.E. to the first century C.E. explain why money changers flourished. The obligation to pay the Temple tax in Tyrian coins was thus not the only reason for the proliferation of these dealers. It is remarkable that coins from a foreign country with the representa-

tion of a pagan god were preferred by the High Priests; practicality and dependability took precedence over God's commandments (Exod. 20:4). In secular life, private contracts stipulated payments in "Tyrians," even two generations after the destruction of the Temple, as illustrated by the marriage contract of Babata (*see* CAVE OF LETTERS). The Gospels refer to two types of persons dealing with money: the *trapezitai*, "bankers" (Matt. 25:27) and the *kollybiston* (Matt. 21:12; Mark 11:15; John 2:15, with *kermatitas* "coin dealers," in John 2:14), who were the changers authorized to operate in the Temple precincts. The Mishna, in *Seqalim*, indicates that the changers took a commission. Jesus' action against them was possibly justified by their abuses, especially at the times of the pilgrimages, and by their bribing of the High Priest and Temple officials (*see* TEMPLE, ROYAL STOA).

Most translations of the Gospels do not render the variety of designations in Greek. The following table indicates the different types of coins and values found in the original text.

Coins and Money in the Gospels

talent of silver	Matt. 18:23-25; 25:14-30
maneh (pound)	Luke 19:11-27
aureas	Matt. 10:9 ("gold"?); Matt. 23:16-17
Tyrian stater (tetradrachma)	Matt. 17:27; 26:15 (?)
Tyrian didrachma	Matt. 17:24
dinarius	Matt. 10:9 ("silver"?); 20:2, 13; 22:19-21 = Mark 12:15 = Luke 20:24. Luke 10:35; 15:8-9
as (Assarion)	Matt. 10:9 ("copper"?); Mark 6:8 ("copper" in girdle); 12:41; Luke 12:6
quadrans	Matt. 5:26; Mark 12:42
lepton	Mark 12:42; Luke 12:59; 21:2
silver (*argyrion*)	Mark 14:11; Luke 9:3; 22:5

Table 2 Ratings of the Parable of the Entrusted Silver

1986	The entire story	Luke 19:12b-17	*gray*
		Matt. 25:14-30	*gray*
1987	Reduced story; the criticism of the master	Luke 19:12b, hr#14, 25	*black*
		Luke 19:13, hr#15-24	*pink*
		Matt, 25:14-28	
		(less 21c and 23)	*pink*
1989	"Have and Receive"	Luke 19:26 and	
		Matt. 25:29	*gray*
1990	Same (reevaluation)	Same	same

The parable of the "entrusted silver" (either talents or pounds), which is thought to have derived from Q*, is rendered differently by Matthew and Luke. Luke refers to a king and pounds, Matthew to an unspecified man and talents. Matthew has the man giving five, two, and one talent respectively to three slaves, whereas Luke has the king giving only one pound to each of ten of his slaves. Trying to determine which story is the most authentic is a difficult task, and the Jesus Seminar took five years to analyze these texts (*see* table 2).

From the social-historical and archaeological data pertaining to coins and money, it appears that Luke turned the original story into a satire against Archelaus, who was accused of oppression by a Jewish delegation in Rome and banished soon after. Thus Luke 19:14 would correspond to the historical reality. Although it is an event Jesus probably knew about, it may be part of Luke's rewriting. More disturbing is the lack of logic in both stories. It is hardly conceivable that even a rich individual of the time could have a liquid disposability of 8 talents = 600 pounds of silver = 3.6 million dinarii (keeping in mind that a dinarius was the wage for a day's work in the fields) to entrust with his slaves. On the other hand, a ruler over Judea, Samaria, and Idumea who could collect a tribute of 400 talents a year (Josephus, *War* 2, 6.3/97) would certainly have the ability to distribute more than ten pounds of silver or 1,000 dinarii among his

slaves. Besides, the point of the story is not as clear as it would have been in an authentic parable from Jesus. Is it "Be diligent and increase what you have received" (spread the good news? . . .)? Is it "The rich will get richer and the poor poorer" (this would contradict the great reversal teaching, "the first will be last")? If there was an authentic core in both versions, it is impossible to reconstruct it with the information currently available. An insight may be given by Eusebius, who reports that a somewhat similar story existed in the Gospel of the Nazareans: One servant spent his master's money with harlots and was cast in prison, another made his talent multiply and was rebuked by his master, the last one who had simply hidden the money was rewarded. Unfortunately, Eusebius does not indicate what the lessons were in the cases of the second and third slaves (*Theophania* 22, on the corresponding story of Matthew).

By contract, the story that shows Jesus tested about the payment of the tribute is much more plausible. Because the three Synoptic versions are almost identical, a common origin can be assigned to Mark (Mark 12:13-17 = Matt. 22:18:22 = Luke 20:20-26). The Greek texts specifically refer to a dinarius, the smallest silver coin, which was widely circulated because it was a day's wage for an agricultural worker. It was certainly readily available in the girdles or pouches of those who tested Jesus.

**Figure 19 Sampling
of Coins from
Hasmonean to
Roman Times**

Hasmonean Coin. Bronze

Obv: Ivy wreath. "King Antigonus"
Rev: Double cornucopia. "Mattathias the high
        priest and the community of Israel"

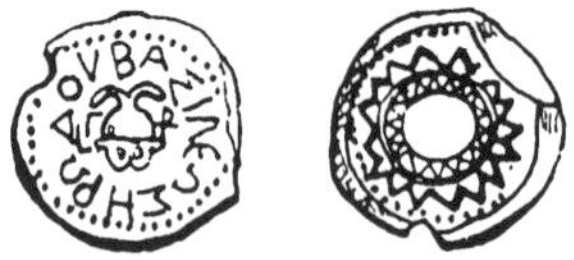

Herodian Coins. Bronze

Obv: Helmet with cheek flaps. "King Herod"
Rev: Circular shield.

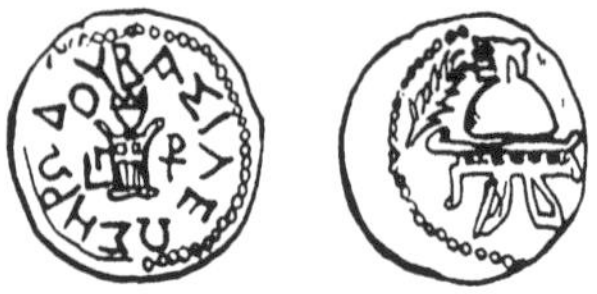

Obv: Bowl on tripod. "Year 3" "King Herod"
Rev: Incense burner between two palm branches.

Roman Coins.

Silver denarius
Obv: Head of Tiberius. "Tiberius Caesar, son of the
        divine Augustus, Augustus."
Rev: Pax seated. "High priest."

Bronze coin
Obv: Lituus. "Tiberius Caesar"
Rev: Wreath. "Year 17" (30/31 C.E.)

Herod Antipas. Bronze

Obv: Palm branch. "Year 33" (29/30 C.E.)
Rev: Wreath. "Tiberias"

Herod Philip. Bronze

Obv: Head of Tiberius "Caesar Augustus"
Rev: Temple façade with four columns. "Philip,
        Tetrarch" "Year 12" (8/9 C.E.)

Tyrian. Silver

Obv: Head of the God Melqart
Rev: Eagle with palm branch. "Year 152" (26/27
        C.E.) "Tyre, sanctuary and asylum"

On its obverse a profile of Tiberius is finely impressed. The scene and the dialogue prior to Jesus' final saying are perfectly coherent with the social-historical circumstances. Jesus' teaching, "Render to Ceasar . . . , render to God . . . ," is in agreement with his neutral attitude toward the dominant foreign power and his lack of nationalistic militantism.

Logion 100 of the Gospel of Thomas presents a shorter version of the story of Jesus being tested on the payment of the tribute:

> They showed him a gold (coin) and said, "Caesar's men ask taxes from us." He said to them, "Give the things of Caesar to Caesar, give the things of God to God and to me what is mine" (parallels: Mark 12:13–17; Matt. 22:15–22; Luke 20:20–26).

This abbreviated saying without context can hardly reflect the true situation. Someone in the crowd ("they") is unlikely to have pulled a gold *aureus* worth 25 dinarri out of his girdle. It is more likely to have been the common silver dinarius on which the emperor's head was minted with great precision. Mark's version, which is reproduced almost word for word a generation later by Matthew and Luke, is probably authentic. Mark's context and dialogue fit perfectly in the social-historical context of Jesus and could well represent the report of an eyewitness. In this specific instance, Gospel of Thomas 100 seems to be a compacted form of a story that lost significant details in the transmission process. The addition of the last phrase, "give me what is mine" is, perhaps, a Gnostic addition. The Jesus Seminar rated this later addition *black* in 1989 but preferred the Gospel of Thomas's version, rated *red*, eliminating the dialogue of Mark 12:15–16 (*see* fig. 19).

BIBLIOGRAPHY

Hanson, R. S. *Tyrian Influence in Upper Galilee.* Cambridge, Mass.: ASOR, 1980.

Hill, G. F. *Catalogue of Greek Coins of Palestine.* London: British Museum, 1914.

———. *Catalogue of Greek Coins of Phoenicia.* London: British Museum, 1910.

Maltiel-Gerstenfeld, J. *260 Years of Ancient Jewish Coins. A Catalogue.* Tel Aviv: Minerva, 1982.

Mandel, S. "Who Paid the Temple Tax when the Jews Were under Roman Rule?" *Harvard Theological Review* 77 (1984): 277–99.

Meshorer, Y. *Ancient Jewish Coinage.* New York: Amphora Books, 1982.

——— "One Hundred Ninety Years of Tyrian Shekels." *Studies in Honor of Leo Mildenberg,* 171–79. Wettern, 1984.

Negev, A., ed. "Money." *AEHL.* Rev. Ed. New York: Thomas Nelson, 1986, 265-68.

Strocker, W. D. *Extracanonical Sayings of Jesus.* SBL Resources for Biblical Studies 18: 45. Atlanta, Ga.: Scholars Press, 1989.

Coins as Historical Documents

Importance

The study of coins often provides information about certain aspects of history not present in other written sources. This is the case for the political relationships between Pontius Pilate and Herod's sons in the time of Jesus.

What the Coins of Bethsaida Can Tell

[The following text is for the most part the work of Dr. Fred Strickert of Wartburg College, a staff member of the Bethsaida Excavations Project.]

Among all the rulers who figure in Jesus' life and time and in his immediate historical background, Herod Philip is the only one to have used human images on his coins, a liberty that even Herod the Great and the Roman prefects did not dare to take. That he took this liberty may have been because the concentration of Jewish population was lower in his tetrarchy and the concern about using human forms had lessened. In his early coinage Philip was influenced by Lysanias and Zenodorus, who ruled over the same area from 30 to 20 B.C.E. In 27 B.C.E. Zenodorus had issued a coin with his own portrait on the obverse and that of Octavian on the reverse. Philip's first coins included images of both himself and Augustus. This practice was then abandoned in favor of using only the emperor's image on the obverse and a temple on the reverse. Although Philip was the first Jewish ruler to issue such coins, there is no evidence that he met disapproval. In fact, he may have been the most popular of the Herodian rulers.

The Temple of Augustus. Even more striking than the use of human images is the depiction of a pagan temple. While none of the coins specifically identifies this temple, it surely represents the temple to Augustus in Paneas–Caesarea Philippi. Josephus reports that this temple was constructed by Philip's father, Herod the Great, after Augustus visited this territory and annexed it to the kingdom of Herod. After Herod had accompanied Augustus to the coast, he proceeded to have it built in Augustus's honor (*Antiq.* 15, 10.3/363; *War* 1, 21.3/404). Because of the temple's significance, Philip renamed the city Caesarea Philippi to parallel the coastal city of Caesarea where Herod had built a second temple to Augustus.

The human images and the temple depiction are unique in themselves, and the absence of Jewish symbols is also noteworthy. The one exception is a lily, which appears on the temple pediment in the first issue of this type of coin. On Jewish coins, the lily often symbolized the Jerusalem Temple.

The significance of the imagery of Philip's coins is important in any discussion of Christian origins. A case is often made from silence that Jesus avoided towns like Tiberias, where Antipas minted coins of a conservative Jewish design (*see* TIBERIAS). Nevertheless, Jesus went to Bethsaida and also to the region of Caesarea Philippi, the two main centers of Philip's rule (*see* CAESAREA PHILIPPI). The imagery on Philip's coins shows not only his openness to non-Jewish cultural forms, but also the dominance of Roman religion in his territory.

Dating Philip's Coins, Political Factors. With one exception, dates are included on all of Philip's coins. A Roman "L" standing for "year" is followed by one or two Greek letters having a numerical value. This, of course, represents the year of Philip's rule, which began after Herod's death in 4 B.C.E., but possibly not until 3 B.C.E. On the majority of coins the date is located between the columns of the temple, on several it occurs within a wreath, and on others it occurs in the field next to the image.

The following chart shows the relation of the issue dates of Philip's issues of coins to some events:

Year	Coins of Philip	Event
4 B.C.E.		beginning of Philip's reign
1 C.E.	first issue	Caesarea celebrated
6 C.E.		Coponius as Prefect (reaction to census?)
8 C.E.	second issue	
9 C.E.		Ambibulus as Prefect
12 C.E.	third issue	Annius Rufus as Prefect
15 C.E.	fourth issue	Valerius Gratus as Prefect
26 C.E.	fifth issue	Pontius Pilate as Prefect
29 C.E.	sixth issue	first Pilate coinage
30 C.E.	seventh issue	second Pilate coinage
31 C.E.		third Pilate coinage
33 C.E.	eighth issue	
34 C.E.		death of Philip

It seems that issuing coins served to publicize the legitimacy of Philip's own authority in the face of foreign domination.

An intriguing question arises from the sequence of issues: Why did Philip issue coins in only four of his first twenty-nine years and then four times in the next eight years (26, 29, 30, and 33 C.E.)? For New Testament scholars, this is of special interest because this latter period is the time of Jesus' activity in and around Bethsaida.

The timing of the first four mintings is quite logical. Philip did not mint coins during the first years of his rule, perhaps not until the city of Caesarea Philippi had become well established. Antipas similarly did not mint his first coins until 20 C.E., after Tiberias was established. Subsequent mintings were not brought about merely by monetary needs; rather, they were primarily political. The second minting may have been a reaction to the introduction of the Roman prefects in Judea. Upon arrival in Judea, the first prefect, Coponius, issued his own coinage in 6 C.E. This was a time of great unrest, with revolts taking place in the north at the instigation of Judas the Galilean and Pharisee Zadok (*see* MASADA). Philip's decision to mint a new series of coins in 8 C.E. may well have been an attempt to reassert the independence of his rule from that of the Roman prefects in Judea. The next three mintings of Philip all occur in a year when a new prefect arrived: in 12 C.E., Annius Rufus; in 15 C.E., Valerius Gratus; and 26 C.E., Pontius Pilate.

An eleven-year gap, coinciding with the longest tenure of the prefects by Valerius Gratus (15–26 C.E.), occurred between the fourth issue and the coins minted in 26 C.E. During the ten-year tenure of Pilate (26–36 C.E.) Philip minted coins in four different years: 26, 29, 30, and 33 C.E. In this situation, one might expect the number of denominations of currency, which was two per minting up to this point, to decrease. Instead, Philip continued to mint two denominations in 26 and 29 C.E., and even increased the number of denominations to three or four in both 30 and 33 C.E. The time of Pontius Pilate was the most productive in coinage for Philip.

The Philip and Julia Coins. Recent discoveries have brought to light two new coin types minted by Philip dating to the last period of his reign. Up to 29 C.E., Philip's coins were relatively standard, depicting the images of Caesar and the Paneas temple. However, in both 30 and 33 C.E., Philip issued a coin with his own image and another with the image of Livia-Julia. Careful analysis shows that these particular coins were produced with Pilate's coinage in mind.

Figure 20 The Symbols of Pontius Pilate's First Coin

In the year 29 C.E., Pontius Pilate issued his first coin. As was the custom of the prefects, he made use of symbols and avoided human images. The obverse shows a *simpulum*, which was a ladle used by Roman priests to pour wine over sacrificial animals. The reverse show what appears to be a common, neutral symbol: three ears of wheat bound by stalks (*see* fig. 20).

The key to understanding this coin is the inscription on the reverse: "IOULIA KAICAROS." The year 29 C.E. marked the death of Julia, and this coin type was produced to commemorate the event. A different coin type was substituted in both 30 and 31 C.E. Although ears of grain had been used on Jewish coinage before, this coin shows a major difference: in this case, the two outer ears are drooping. Julia was dead. Livia-Julia was frequently associated with Abundantia (Euthenia), the goddess of agricultural plenty; coins of Augustus from 2 B.C.E. to 14 C.E. depict Livia seated and holding ears of corn and a scepter. In addition, Livia was sometimes depicted as priestess of Augustus. Thus the obverse depiction of a Roman cultic theme was quite appropriate for this memorial to Livia.

On another coin issued by Pilate an augural staff represents the authority of the Roman state. This staff is surrounded by the inscription "TIBERIOU KAISAROS." On the reverse is the date within a wreath, another symbol frequently associated with the Caesars.

For the first time since the initial mint, Philip issued in 30 and again in 33 C.E. a coin with his own image on the obverse and the date within a wreath on the reverse.

Philip's Coin:

Figure 21

Pilate's Coin:

Figure 22

The connection between the two coins is clear. Philip simply substituted his own image for the *lituus*[*]—both symbols of authority. The reverse is virtually identical with Pilate's coin. One can conclude that Philip was influenced during these years by the minting patterns of Pontius Pilate, with regard to both the frequency and the symbols used on his coins.

Denominations. The Pilate coins also affected another aspect of Philip's coinage—their size. Prior to the year 30 C.E., Philip produced two denomina-

tions per year of mintage; the smallest coin weighed 3.80 g with a diameter of 16 mm. In the years 30 and 33 C.E., Philip produced three or four denominations of coins with the addition of smaller coins. The four coins weigh 1.61, 1.75, 2.51, and 3.50 g. respectively, and have diameters of 10.5, 11.7, 14.0, and 15.2 mm. This radical change in minting pattern appears to be a response to Pilate flooding the market with small coins with weights from 1.2 to 2.3 g. and diameters from 14 to 16 mm.

Looking at the denominational standards for ancient mints will be useful here. The Roman system of this time was made up of five denominations:

1. *sestertius*   27g
2. *dupendius*   14g
3. *as*   7g
4. *semis*   3.5g
5. *quadrans*   1.8g

The precision of these measurements was due to the use of a yellow alloy of copper and zinc called orichalcum. Because this alloy was unavailable in Palestine, such precision was impossible there. Nevertheless, Palestinian mints made the effort to follow the Roman standard to some degree.

In six mintings through 29 C.E., Philip issued coins in two denominations: the *as* and the *semis*. The evidence from the first two issues (1 B.C.E. and 8 C.E.) is clearest because Philip issued two different coin types in each year (*see* table 3).

Table 3   Philip's Issues of 1 B.C.E. and 8 C.E.

Year	Denomination	Obverse	Reverse	Weight	Diameter
1 B.C.E.	*as*	Philip	Augustus	9.39 g	23.4 mm
	semis	Philip	temple	3.82 g	18.0 mm
8 C.E.	*as*	Augus. head facing right	temple	9.61 g	22.0 mm
	as	Augus. head facing right	temple	8.90 g	21.0 mm
	semis	Augus. head facing left	temple	5.96 g	18.0 mm
	semis	Augus. head facing left	temple	4.62 g	16.0 mm

(from Maltiel-Gerstenfeld catalogue)

Philip changed his minting pattern in 30 C.E. In 30 and 33 C.E., he issued two additional denominations, the *quadrans* and *half-quadrans*, while continuing to issue a *semis* (*see* table 4).

The Tiberius coin is a continuation of the most common coin type with the temple on the reverse. The example from 30 C.E. weighing 5.16 grams fits the standard for the *semis*, although the 33 C.E. coin weighing 7.05 reaches the upper limit. Note, however, that both of these coins also include the laurel branch, which designated the *semis* in 26 and 29 C.E.

In both 30 and 33 C.E., therefore, Philip issued three denominations. Only an *as* appears to be missing; otherwise there are four full denominations, as was the minting pattern of both Herod and Antipas.

Coins With No Date. There is one final type of coin of Philip that does not include a date. This coin has the tetrastyle* temple on the reverse, with a double image of Augustus and Livia on the obverse. Even without a date, it can be assigned with some certainty to 30 C.E.

The year 30 C.E., unlike the previous six years in which coins were minted, included four different denominations (*see* table 5):

Why was the date omitted on the Augustus-Julia *as*? Not only does it differ from other coins in other years, but it also differs from the three other coins minted in 30 C.E., which did include dates. It is unlikely that the omission was accidental. Like most coins of Philip, this coin also portrays the Paneas temple on the reverse. Yet, instead of including the dates between the four columns, the

Table 4   Philip's Issues of 30 and 33 C.E., Tiberius Coins

Year	Denomination	Obverse	Weight	Diameter
30 C.E.	*as*	?		
	semis	Tiberius	5.16 g	18.5–19 mm
	quadrans	Julia	3.5 g	15–15.2 mm
	half-quadrans	Philip	1.61 g	11.7 mm
Year	Denomination	Obverse	Weight	Diameter
33 C.E.	*as*	?		
	semis	Tiberius	7.05 g	19 mm
	quadrans	Julia	2.51 g	13–15 mm
	half-quadrans	Philip	1.75 g	10.5 mm

Table 5   Philip's Augustus-Livia Coin with No Date

Year	Denomination	Obverse	Weight	Diameter
30 C.E. (?)	*as*	Augustus/Julia	7.0 g	19–24 mm
	semis	Tiberius	5.16 g	18.5–19 mm
	quadrans	Julia	3.5 g	15–15.2 mm
	half-quadrans	Philip	1.61 g	11.7 mm

inner columns have been moved adjacent to the outer columns, leaving no space in between for dates. This alteration was made to depict a round object in the center of the temple—an object that does not appear on any of the dated coins. Maltiel-Gerstenfeld refers to it as a "shield" (*260 Years of Ancient Jewish Coins*, p. 143).

The round object would have been identifiable by the populace in Philip's day and was probably related to a particular event near the time of minting, because it was never repeated on any of the other issues of this coin. One event that is well known from this period is the famous "shields episode," when Pilate attempted to set up commemorative shields in Jerusalem. Philo relates these events as follows:

> One of his lieutenants was Pilate, who was appointed to govern Judea. He, not so much to honor Tiberius as to annoy the multitude, dedicated in Herod's palace in the holy city some shields coated with gold. They had no image work traced on them nor anything else forbidden by the law apart from the barest inscription stating two facts, the name of the person who made the dedication and one of him in whose honor it was made. (F. H. Colson, The Embassy to Gaius, 38.244)

Philo concludes his account by stating that the shields were returned to Caesarea where they were hung in the Temple of Augustus. Although there should be no attempt to confuse two distinct temples, the fact is that Philip's father Herod built two temples, both in honor of Augustus and both in cities named Caesarea. Would not a symbolic depiction of a shield in a temple of Augustus on Philip's coin serve to remind people of Pilate's fiasco? Because this event probably took place around 29 or 30 C.E., a date of 30 C.E. for this coin is reasonable.

KTISTES. Another coin in the 30 C.E. series is of special interest. The *semis*, which bears the image of Tiberius and the tetrastyle* temple, has a unique inscription. Basically three types of inscriptions mention the name of Philip on this common coin type:

Inscription	Year
PHILIPPOU TETRARXOU	1, 8, 12, 15 C.E.
EPI PHILIPPOU TETRARXOU	26, 29, 30, 33 C.E.
EPI PHILIPPOU TETRARXOU KTIS	30 C.E.

This last inscription is of special interest, because the additional *KTIS* is an abbreviation for *KTISTES*, "founder." This coin calls attention to the role of Philip as the founder of cities. In fact, this is the very word used by Josephus in his description of the founding of Caesarea and Julias:

> Philip founded [KTIZEI] the city of Caesarea at the sources of the Jordan in Paneas and Julias in lower Gaulantis. (War 2, 9.1/168).

Numismatic scholarship has generally noted the *KTISTES* in inscription as a reference to the founding of Caesarea Philippi. Yet the fact that *KTISTES* occurs only once on a single issue of coin in 30 C.E. is ignored. Caesarea had been founded in the early years of Philip's rule. Why had *KTISTES* not been used on earlier coins? There is no reason to maintain the interpretation as a reference to Caesarea.

It is more likely that the occurrence of *KTISTES* on a single coin type refers to the founding of a city in the very year, 30 C.E., that the coin was issued. This is supported by the presence of the *KTISTES* coin in a series of four coins issued in the same year—the only year that Philip issued four denominations. The series not only includes coins with the image of the emperor and Philip himself—something that had not been previously done—but also has two new coin types: one with Julia alone and the other with Julia alongside Augustus. The attention given to Julia in this series may suggest that this issue was minted to commemorate the founding of Bethsaida-Julias.

Classical historians have long noticed that Herod Philip could not have named Bethsaida Julias in honor of Julia, daughter of Augustus, who had been banished to an island in 2 B.C.E. Although married, she "had been indulging in every sort of vice . . . Whenever her name came up in conversation, he [Augustus] would sigh deeply, and sometimes quote a line from the *Iliad*: 'Ah, never to have married, and childless to have died!' " (Suetonius, *The Twelve Caesars*, Augustus, 65). Livia-Julia, wife of Augustus, who was revered throughout the Roman world, was a more likely candidate; Josephus (or a scribe after him) made an error in referring to the younger Julia as the person Philip wanted to honor. A. Negev, for instance, reports that Bethsaida-Julias was renamed "Livias in honor of Livia, wife of Augustus" (*AEHL* 51. Josephus *Antiq.* 18/27). R. Arav and H. Kuhn presented the case anew after Arav's discovery of Philip's coins (*The Future of Early Christianity*, 77–106).

Julia, ex-Livia, had been an extremely popular figure who was honored with Augustus her husband in the imperial cult. Upon his death in 14 C.E., she was adopted into the Julian clan according to the directive of the will of Augustus. She thus received the title Augusta-Sebaste and the name Julia, which guaranteed succession to her son Tiberius and also raised her to a level equal with the next emperor himself. The timing of this event is significant. One might expect the naming of the town Julias to have happened in 29 C.E., the actual year of Livia-Julia's death. Why might it not have taken place until a year later? One must understand that controversy surrounded her death. While Livia-Julia sought deification as had been the case with Augustus, this was not granted by her son Tiberius. In fact, being away from Rome at the time of her death, he delayed his return long enough so that only a simple funeral could be carried out without him. In contrast to Tiberius's command that mourning be forbidden following the death of Augustus, which entailed subsequent deification, he ordered that the country mourn Livia-Julia's death as a recognition of her mere humanity. The coin issued by Pilate in 29 C.E. (mentioned earlier) is thus a sign that mourning was taken seriously; even the ears of grain are drooping on that coin. Pilate was responding favorably to his political appointment by Tiberius.

The actions of Philip following the death of Livia-Julia, however, suggest that he did not mourn her death as that of a mere human. Rather, like many others, he favored her deification—a process that culminated during the rule of Claudius in 41 C.E. Thus the absence of a Julia coin in 29 C.E. is not surprising. Philip would not produce a coin that focused on themes of mourning. At the same time, he would not offend Tiberius by publicly disregarding the period of mourning.

A year later, however, such honors for Livia-Julia could be considered appropriate. Thus the coin of Livia-Julia emphasizes divinity, with the representation of the hand holding ears of grain—the goddess Abundentia continuing to provide blessings. Likewise a second coin juxtaposes Livia-Julia and Augustus, and the inscription *SEBASTWN* connotes equality in status. This coin is also an important reminder that Philip had initially received his rule not from Tiberius—as was the case with Pilate—but from Augustus, who had favored honors for Livia-Julia. It is thus ironic that the *KTISTES* inscription occurs on the coin in that series that displays the image of Tiberius. The ultimate honor bestowed by Philip upon Livia-Julia was not the issuing of coins, but the founding of a city named for her.

Implications for Jesus Research

Coins contribute greatly to an understanding of political conditions in first-century Palestine. In particular, they provide information about the power struggle between Pontius Pilate and Herod's sons, especially Philip. Because Jesus is said to have been active in Bethsaida (named seven times in the Gospels; *see* BETHSAIDA), and visited the region of Caesarea Philippi (*see* CAESAREA PHILIPPI), we may infer that he had no problems with Herod Philip. In contrast, the Gospels do not mention any visit by Jesus to Tiberias (*see* TIBERIAS); he had little respect for Antipas, "that fox," who wanted to arrest him (Luke 13:31-32). While he was ministering in Galilee, he had his fixed residence either in Bethsaida or in Capernaum from which he could easily flee to the other side of the Jordan (*see* CAPERNAUM). Incidentally, the expression "that fox," with a negative connotation, is not found in the

Hebrew Bible. The word *fox* is used only once in the Hebrew Bible (in a different context) in Nehemiah 4:3. This does not mean, however, that the expression was not popular in Palestine during Jesus' time.

The dating to 30 C.E. of the elevation of Bethsaida from village (*kome*) to city (*polis*) confirms what some scholars have already hypothesized: Mark uses the term *village* (8:23, 26) because Jesus was active there before the locality became a city. Mark's account is thus accurate and the date of its source, oral or written (proto Mark?), must be close to 30 C.E. (*see* CAMPS, SIEGE BANKS). On the other hand, Matthew and Luke, probably dated to ca. 80–90 C.E., use the term *city* because this was the status of Bethsaida-Julias at the time these Gospels were composed (Matt. 11:20, 21; Luke 9:10; also John 1:44).

BIBLIOGRAPHY

Arav, R. and H. W. Kuhn. "The Bethsaida Excavations: Historical and Archaeological Approaches." *The Future of Early Christianity*, edited by B. A. Pearson, 77–106. Minneapolis: Fortress Press, 1991.

Hendin, D. *Guide to Biblical Coins*. New York: Amphora Books, 1987.

Maltiel-Gerstenfeld, J. *260 Years of Ancient Jewish Coins*. Tel Aviv: Kol Printing Service, 1982.

Meshorer, Y. *Ancient Jewish Coinage*. Vol. 2. New York: Amphora Books, 1982.

Negev, A. "Bethsaida." *AEHL*. Rev. ed New York: Thomas Nelson, 1986, 58-59.

Negev, A. "Money." *AEHL*. Rev. Ed. New York: Thomas Nelson,1986, 265-68.

Vermes, G. *Jesus the Jew*. 1973. Reprint. Philadelphia: Fortress Press, 1988.

Construction, Cities

Importance

The Gospels contain a number of references by Jesus or others to various construction projects: the Temple, a synagogue, tombs, private buildings, and cities.

Scripture References

Matt. 7:24-27; 16:18; 21:33, 42; 23:29; 24:1-2; 26:61; 27:40; Mark 12:1, 10; 13:1-2; 14:58; 15:29; Luke 4:29; 6:48–49; 7:5; 11:47–48; 12:18; 13:4; 14:28, 30; 19:44; 20:17; 21:5-6; John 2:19-21; G. Thom. 63, 71. In addition, the words *city* and *cities* appear fifty-two times in the Gospels.

General Information

Construction figures prominently in the Bible, both literally and figuratively. Because stone is available in abundance almost everywhere in Palestine, it was the preferred building material (*see* STONE, STONING). With the appearance of iron tools, stone dressing and fitting improved considerably. Techniques of stone construction reached their apogee in the time of Herod the Great as can be seen in surviving examples of Herodian construction in Jerusalem, Caesarea Maritima, and Hebron, among others. Where stone was less readily available, especially in the area of Jericho and southern Judea, mud brick was most commonly used. Mud for brick was first produced by filling a hole dug in the ground with water; when the mud was thick enough, straw was added and incorporated in it by treading. When the substance was ready, it was removed and placed in wooden molds where it took its final shape. The fresh bricks were then spread on the ground to dry in the sun. In the Roman period the technique became more elaborate; bricks were fired and gained more strength. Roof tiles, which were first used in Palestine during the Persian period, were also improved by the Romans. Mortar and plaster had been in use since the Iron Age and possibly earlier; they too were much improved during the Roman Period, as will be seen below.

Most monumental buildings of first-century Palestine were erected by Herod the Great and his sons under Augustus (24 B.C.E.–14 C.E.) and Tiberius (14–37 C.E.). Many highly qualified Roman architects and civil engineers were undoubtedly hired by Herod and his sons and by the wealthy people of Palestine. The Romans contributed little to the advancement of science and philosophy; but they were certainly leaders of their time in the fields of applied sciences and technology, law, public administration, and even social politics. Many of their construction projects were meant to provide work for the people. For instance, Vespasian, who had been offered the plans for a machine that would have saved much labor, answered that his constant concern was first to ensure that "the working classes earn enough money to buy food" (Suetonius in *Vespasian* 18, De Camp, 179, 413). The same concern was expressed by Agrippa II when, at the end of the construction of the Jerusalem Temple, he ordered the streets of the city to be paved with slabs of white stone in order to provide new jobs for the 18,000 workers who had been laid off (Josephus, *Antiq.* 20, 9.7/219–22). Employment was an effective way to maintain political stability.

The Romans were well organized in carrying out construction projects. For the erection of public buildings, a government official—the emperor himself, a consul, or governor; in Palestine the king, tetrarch, or prefect—ordered the work. He hired an *architectus*, "civil engineer," who had authority over a team of specialists: *agrimensores*, "surveyors," *libratores*, "levelers," contractors, and others. Civil engineers were held in high esteem and members of the imperial family, like Tiberius's son Drusus, claimed the honor of being an *architectus*. One of the greatest architects was Marcus Vipsanius Agrippa, who had studied in Greece with the future emperor, Augustus (Octavian). During his relatively short life (63–12 B.C.E.), he served as a military commander in Gaul and Germany, commanding Octavian's fleet against Pompeius in 37 B.C.E. and also against Marcus Antonius at Actium in 31 B.C.E. When Octavian was finally established as emperor, Agrippa devoted all his life and private fortune to the enlargement and beautification of Rome, the most famous of his accomplishments being the Pantheon.

The technical improvements made by the Romans in matters of civil engineering include the mortarless wall, concrete, arches and vaults, water and drainage or sewer systems, all of which are represented in Herodian construction. They succeeded in trimming ashlars so accurately that no mortar or cement was needed, as can be seen with the large stone blocks of the Temple Mount in Jerusalem. If the stone blocks were not heavy enough to be considered immovable by virtue of their own weight, they used metal cramps to hold them together. They discovered that a sandy volcanic ash, which is abundant in Italy, when mixed with lime mortar, sand, and gravel, formed a concrete harder than rock. It could even harden under water, as was the case with the concrete used in the harbor of Caesarea Maritima. Used as cement (without the addition of sand and gravel) it produced a watertight lining for aqueducts and cisterns. The Roman technique of building arches and vaults can be seen in the gigantic vaults that support the southern part of the Temple platform. Sections of the aqueducts built by the Romans still stand near Caesarea Maritima and between Bethlehem and Jerusalem. The Roman techniques for building sewer and drainage systems were used in Caesarea, where automatic flushing was done by use of the tides, and in the Tyropoeon Valley where rain water was collected under the street and drained off to the pool of Siloam (*see* JERUSALEM, POOL OF SILOAM) and other places.

Roman construction techniques are visible in Palestine not only in individual projects but also in the establishment or rebuilding of entire cities. Cities of Phoenician and Greek origin existed in Palestine when Pompey arrived in 63 B.C.E. He conquered them; they then counted their date of foundation from 63 B.C.E. They were the coastal cities built by the Phoenicians and also the Hellenistic cities founded by the Ptolemaic dynasty in the late fourth and third centuries B.C.E. Among these were Scythopolis (Beth Shean), Ptolemais (Acco), Stratonos Pyrgos (Caesarea), Philoteria (Beth Yerah), and a few others. The Seleucids continued their policy and sold the right to establish such cities. In this manner, cities of the Decapolis were formed as was the "Antiochians in Jerusalem" on the western hill. Herod the Great and his successors also founded or enlarged several cities: Caesarea and its harbor, Antipatris (Arethusa-Pegei), Phasaelis in the Jordan Valley, Sebaste (Samaria), Sepphoris renamed Autokratis, Tiberias, Livias-Julias (Betharamtha), Caesarea Philippi, and Bethsaida-Julias.

In addition to these cities numerous towns, villages, and hamlets, where native inhabitants conducted their life according to ancient patterns, were ultimately altered by the introduction of Roman techniques and styles. These communities had developed organically, without a master plan. They were normally located next to a spring and their streets and lanes were developed from sheep paths and property limits. Until the second century C.E. they lacked most of the features of the Greco-Roman urban style. These elements were introduced gradually through public buildings such as synagogues, fountains, and bathhouses.

Archaeological Information

The best-known construction remains of the first century are the Temple platform walls in Jerusalem; but many others exist, still standing or recently excavated: the houses and ritual baths of the Ophel (see JERUSALEM, CITY OF DAVID, OPHEL), the walls of the Tombs of the Patriarchs at Hebron, the fortification wall, synagogue, ritual baths, olive mills, presses, and private houses of Gamla, some of the houses of Capernaum and Bethsaida, the houses of Jerusalem's Upper City, some of the buildings at Caesarea Maritima and Caesarea Philippi, the buildings and ritual baths of Qumran and Masada, the Judean desert fortresses, and more. The most extraordinary feature of Roman construction is the colossal size of some of the stones and the precision of their cutting, dressing, and adjusting, which allows them to fit perfectly together without mortar. One block at the base of the Western Wall of the Temple measures 46 x 10 x 10 feet and weighs about 415 tons. Another at Hebron is 22 x 5 x 5 feet and weighs about 50 tons. By comparison, the largest monolith at Stonehenge

A Hoist for the Construction of a Wall (Qatzrim)

weights 40 tons, and the stones of the Great Pyramid of Cleops weigh no more than 15 tons. Scholars have several hypotheses about how these gigantic blocks could have been cut from the quarries, transported to the construction site, and placed exactly where they would fit. One theory is that they were first cut as huge circular columns, rolled as cylinders, and squared on site. A strong objection to this method comes from 1 Kings 6:7: "The house was built with stone finished at the quarry, so that neither hammer nor ax nor any tool of iron was heard in the temple while it was being built." Herod could not have been less careful than Solomon about not disturbing the service of the Temple by the noise of heavy metal tools. Another theory, more plausible, is that the stones were cut

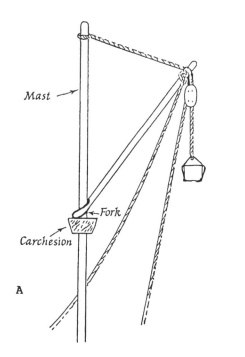

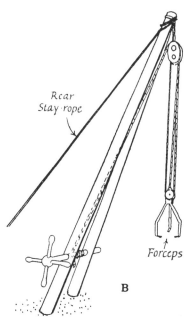

Figure 23 Two Types of Ancient Cranes: A= Rotating; B = Fixed. **Two Types of Roman Walls:** C = *Opus incertum;* D = *Opus reticulatum. (After J. C.Landells, and Sprague de Camp)*

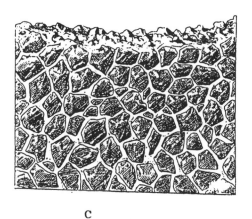

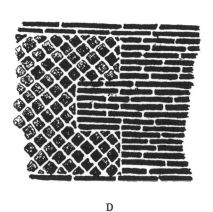

and dressed at the quarry, and then pulled, rolling on cylindrical logs, to their final location. In both cases, ramps would have been used to take them up to the desired height.

An abundant labor force, either military (the legionaries were also builders) or hired and servile, did not preclude the use of machinery. Hoists and cranes spiked the landscape of every construction site. As with all ancient machines made of wood, no actual remains are left; but detailed descriptions are found in technical writings and on relief sculptures, such as the one on the tomb of the Haterii family (*Atti della Accademia Nazionale dei Lincei*, series 8, vol. 13, 1968, figs. 15, 17). Among the literary sources, the work of Marcus Vitruvius (toward the end of the first century B.C.E.) is the most complete and informative. He gives descriptions of machines that could lift blocks of 9 tons to a height of more than 30 feet. Figure 23 represents two types of cranes that he describes: the two-leg and the one-leg jib cranes. The second type allowed sideways tilting by means of a *carchesian*, which could take the form of a circular block of wood supporting a forked gaff. A few simple instruments based on the principle of the plumb line were used to determine vertical and horizontal lines and right angles, but water levels made of oblong containers carved in wood also existed. In order to determine right angles in a horizontal plane, the Romans used the *groma*, a horizontal cross, with branches at ninety degrees, placed on top of a vertical post. Plumb lines hanging at the four ends of the cross allowed the surveyor to ascertain the perfect horizontality of the sight lines when the post was perfectly parallel with all four plumb lines. (*See* entries under HOUSE; JERUSALEM; TEMPLE; CAPERNAUM; SYNAGOGUES, RITUAL BATHS (*miqvaoth*); QUMRAN; MASADA; HERODIUM; HEBRON; MACHAERUS; CAESAREA MARITIMA; CHORAZIN; STONE, STONING; WOOD, FURNITURE).

Implications for Jesus Research

Jesus lived in a period of building activity that followed the monumental architectural feats of Herod the Great. The construction of the court and porticoes of the Temple continued during all of Jesus' lifetime and beyond. Herod Antipas enlarged Sepphoris and Tiberias (*see* SEPPHORIS and TIBERIAS), Herod Philip built Caesarea Philippi and toward the end of Jesus' ministry Bethsaida-Julias. Pontius Pilate built the lower aqueduct of Jerusalem, which he financed with money from the Temple Treasury (*Antiq.* 17, 3.2/60; *War* 2, 9.4/175). Because Jesus' original trade was probably that of a *tekton* (*See* WOOD, FURNITURE), he was no doubt familiar with building techniques, tools, and

machines. It would have been natural for Jesus to use images from construction activities to convey his message: the building of towers (Matt. 21:33; Mark 12:1), granaries (Luke 12:18; G. Thom. 63), houses (Matt. 7:24-27; Luke 6:48-49); estimating the cost of a tower (Luke 14:28); and accidental collapse of a tower (Luke 13:4). The rating of the Jesus Seminar has fluctuated from *pink* in 1986 to *black* in 1987 for Luke 14:28-30; it is *black* for Luke 6:47-49 (1989), *gray* for Matt. 21:33-39 and Mark 12:1-8 (1987), *pink* for Luke 12:16-20 and G. Thom. 63 (1986) and *black* for Luke 13:1-5 (Tower of Siloam, 1990). These sayings should be considered authentic because they cohere with the material culture of the times and because Jesus apparently used such images for didactic purposes.

One of the greatest scholarly controversies concerns Jesus' sayings or the accusations against him regarding the destruction of the Temple and his rebuilding it in three days. The different Gospel passages pertaining to this issue can be presented as follows with their respective ratings by the Jesus Seminar:

Prediction of Destruction:

Matt. 24:1-2	*gray* 1989
Mark 13:1-2	*gray* 1989
Luke 19:42-44	*gray* 1990 (all of Jerusalem)
Luke 21:5-6	*gray* 1989
G. Thom. 71	*black* 1987, 1990

"I will raise it again in three days:"

John 2:19-21	*black* 1987

Accusations by others:

Matt. 26:61	*black* 1987
Mark 14:58	*gray* 1987
Acts 6:14	*black* 1987

Accusations and Jeering:

Matt. 27:40	*black* 1987
Matt. 15:29	*black* 1987

A majority of the members of the Jesus Seminar thus doubt that Jesus predicted the destruction of the Temple and that he threatened to destroy it and rebuild it in three days. While it is tempting to see the prediction as a *vaticinium ex et post eventu*,* two remarks have to be made: First, it was easy for informed and sagacious persons of the time to foresee the danger of a destruction of the Temple and Jerusalem; second, Jesus was seen by many and perhaps saw himself as a prophet.

One argument in favor of considering the prediction as *ex et post eventu* is that the method of the siege bank actually used by the Romans in 70 C.E. is described in Luke 19:42-44. It was, however, an ancient and well-known military technique (*see* CAMPS, SIEGE BANKS). People had heard stories of siege and destruction of cities; they knew about the predictions of Isaiah 29:3 and Ezekiel 4:2, about the Babylonian siege of 586 B.C.E., the battles over Jerusalem between the Seleucids and the Hasmoneans, and the siege and conquest of Jerusalem by Pompey in 63 B.C.E. A rebellion against the Romans would certainly bring war, siege, and destruction. This may be why Romans had supporters among the Jews. In any event, predicting such an event would not have been difficult, and Jesus was not the only one to do so; the Qumranites expected the destruction of the Temple and its rebuilding under an idealized form, as set forth in the Temple Scroll of Qumran.

There is little doubt that Jesus was considered a prophet by many of his contemporaries and perhaps saw himself as such—like Isaiah and Ezekiel, capable of warning people of imminent danger. Several Gospel verses, a few of which have been rated *pink* by the Jesus Seminar, point to this conception: Matthew 13:57; 21:22; 26:68; Mark 6:4 (changed from *gray* to *pink*), 15; 14:65; Luke 4:24; 7:6, 39; 22:64; 24:19; John 4:19, 44; 7:40; 9:17. Despite the current view of New Testament scholarship that Jesus was a nonprophetic, noneschatological but sapiential figure, a majority of the Jesus Seminar gave positive answers to the following questions: "Did Jesus say some anti-Temple words?" (69 percent, yes) and, "Did Jesus predict

the destruction of the Temple of Jerusalem?" (53 percent yes, Spring 1987).

Regarding the question of the rebuilding of the Temple, it appears that Jesus had an eschatological conception of his role (*see* EXORCISM), except that it was probably not in the framework of a general cataclysmic, apocalyptic end of the world. Otherwise, it would be difficult to explain why he joined the Baptist's movement and then left to start his own. It seems, that, in his view, the end of the evil order was to come under the form of a spiritual change with the advent of the Reign of God. His new Temple was probably an ideal one made of faithful worship detached from any geographical location. That was the old concept of Exodus: where the people are, God is (John 4:21-23; G. Thom. 42; Acts 7:48-50). Jesus' concept would have been more immaterial than the eschatological temple of the Qumranites, the temple that God would build (*see* DEAD SEA SCROLLS, HOUSES, and TEMPLE, HISTORY, DESCRIPTION).

BIBLIOGRAPHY

Arav, R. "Settlement Patterns and City Planning in Hellenistic Palestine, 337–31 B.C.E." Oxford: *BAR International*, 1989, 4–85.

Borg, M. "Luke 19:42-44, Jesus as Prophet?" *Jesus Seminar Papers*. Sonoma, Calif. Polebridge Press, 1990.

de Camp, L. S. *The Ancient Engineers*. New York: Ballantine Books, 1988. (First edition 1960.)

Finch, J. K. *The Story of Engineering*. Garden City, N.Y.: Doubleday, 1960.

Forbes, R. J. *Man the Maker (A History of Technology and Engineering)*. New York: Abelard-Schumann Ltd., 1958.

Jones, A. H. M. *The Cities of the Eastern Roman Provinces*. Oxford: Oxford University Press, 1971.

Landels, J. G. *Engineering in the Ancient World*. Berkeley: University of California Press, 1978.

Seeman, C. "The Herodian Urbanization of Galilee." Master's thesis, Graduate Theological Union, Berkeley, 1993.

Stambaugh, J. E. and D. L. Balch. *The New Testament in Its Social Environment*. Library of Early Christianity, 2. Philadelphia: Westminster, 1986.

Vitruvius, Marcus. *De Architectura*. Loeb Classical Library.

Crucifixion

Importance

Jesus died by crucifixion, a method of execution that had long been practiced in the Near East and was adopted by the Romans.

Scripture References

Matt. 10:38; 16:21; 20:19; 23:34; 26:2; 27:22-44; 28:5; Mark 8:34; 10:34; 15:13, 20-32; 16:6; Luke 9:23; 14:27; 23: 21, 23-32; 24:7; John 19:6, 15-41.

General Information

Crucifixion, as a method of execution, probably originated in Mesopotamia. Practiced by the Persians, the Phoenicians, the Greeks, the Jews, and the Romans, it may have been a development of Assyrian impaling; the Hebrew and Aramaic word *sbl* means both "to hang" and "to impale" and, by extension, "to crucify." The Gospels use only the verb form *stayroo*, "to crucify." The Romans employed crucifixion for the capital punishment of noncitizens (Cicero, *Defense of Rabinius*, 5.16). But some officials, such as Gessius Florus in Jerusalem in 66 C.E., occasionally applied it to citizens of the lower class and provincials. Some of the Jews he had scourged and nailed on crosses before his tribunal were Roman citizens of equestrian rank (Josephus, *War* 2, 14.9/308).

Contrary to common thought, crucifixion was not an exclusively Roman procedure in Israel. Joshua 8:29 and Deuteronomy 21:22 refer to "hanging on a tree," an expression that came to designate crucifixion in later times. Josephus reports that the Hasmonean king Alexander Janneus (103–76 B.C.E.) ordered a mass crucifixion of hundreds of his people. In 88 B.C.E., his enemies (probably Pharisees) invited the Seleucid king Demetrius III Encenus to intervene in the affairs of Judea. He set camp at Shechem, won a battle against Alexander Janneus, but lost the support of those who had called him, and left. Josephus describes Janneus's revenge: "He had eight hundred of his captives crucified in the midst of the city and their wives and children butchered before their eyes while he looked on, drinking, with his concubines reclining beside him" (*Antiq.* 13, 14.2/380; *War* 1, 4.6/97). After his death, Simon ben Shetah, brother of Queen Salome Alexandra, hanged or crucified eighty "witches" near Ashkelon. M. Hengel, however, suggests that these were actually Sadducees executed by the Pharisees taking their revenge during the reign of Simon's sister (*m. Sanhedrin* 6:4; M. Hengel, *Crucifixion*, 77–78).

Under Roman law, robbers, deserters, traitors, and rebels were subject to punishment by crucifixion. A slave owner had the right to scourge and crucify his slaves. If the owner of an estate was murdered and the murderer could not be found, all of his slaves were crucified. The largest mass crucifixion happened at the end of the Spartacus revolt (73–71 B.C.E.): six thousand gladiators and slaves were crucified along the road of Capua to Rome. When the Jews rebelled at the death of Herod the Great in 4 B.C.E., Quintilius Varus, legate of Syria, had two thousand of them crucified (Josephus, *War* 2, 5.2/75). Between this event and the beginning of the First Jewish War, only two crucifixions in Palestine are reported by Josephus: that of Jesus (*Antiq.* 18, 3.3/64) and that of the sons of Judas the Galilean during the great famine in the prefectorate of Tiberius Alexander (ca. 42–48 C.E.). At the beginning of the war, Vespasian crucified at least one prisoner who resisted torture at Jotapata (*War* 3, 7.33/321). Titus crucified another prisoner before the walls of Jerusalem as a warning (*War* 5, 6.5/289); thereafter executions became more frequent (*Life* 75). Mass crucifixions increased during the siege of Jerusalem in 70 C.E.: "Out of rage and hatred the soldiers amused themselves by nailing their prisoners in different postures, and their number was so great that spaces could not be found for the crosses nor crosses for the bodies." Five hundred or more were crucified daily (*War* 5, 11.1/450–51). These executions—carried out in view of the rebels standing on the ramparts—probably were meant to provide a deterrent: "Whenever we crucify criminals, very crowded highways are chosen so that many see it and may be moved by fear of it, because all punishment does not pertain so much to revenge as to example" (Quintilian, *Declamations*).

Roman crucifixion normally consisted of three elements: scourging, carrying of the cross by the condemned, and nailing and lifting. A *titulus* indicated the nature of the crime as was the case for Jesus ("Jesus of Nazareth, the king of the Jews;" John 19:19 and parallels). It was a board covered with gypsum, inscribed with black letters, and carried before the condemned at the head of the procession to the execution ground.

There were two main types of crosses: T-shaped and dagger-shaped. In either case, the upright beam was normally planted in a fixed position, and the *patibulum* "crossbar," was movable and carried by the condemned. J. J. Collins distinguishes between the *crux humilis*, "low cross," on which the feet of the victim were from ten to eighteen inches above the ground, and the *crux sublimis*, "high cross," on which the feet were about three feet above the ground ("The Archaeology of the Crucifixion" 154–55). The low cross would have been used for common criminals so that they easily could be devoured by beasts. At the whim of the executioner, a peg or *sedecula*, or a short crossbar forming a narrow seat, could be added to allow the victim to sit for a while. A footrest, which appears in some paintings, is not attested in the first century C.E.

The hands or wrists were nailed or the arms tied to the *patibulum,* which was lifted, with the victim hanging, by means of ladders and *forcillae* (poles ending with a Y-shaped fork). The *patibulum* was secured in a mortise of the upright in the case of a dagger-shaped cross or on top of it for a T-shaped cross. The feet were usually nailed to the upright beam but could be kept loose. Death was not always quick, and the victim might agonize for several days before dying. Josephus reports that during the siege of Jerusalem, when coming back from Tekoa, he recognized three of his friends on crosses. He obtained permission from Titus to have them taken down, and one of them survived (*Life*

75). Medical studies suggest that crucifixion death was caused by asphyxiation (LeBec, Barbet, W. D. Edwards, et al; *see* Bibliography). F. Zugibe questions this view ("Two Questions about Crucifixion," 1989), but his short experiments on volunteer students are inconclusive.

The probability that death was the result of asphyxiation appears likely because of what is known of certain German practices. A 1937 book by Dr. Hynek of Prague describes a military punishment, the "aufbinden," which he witnessed when serving in the German army in 1914–18. The punished soldier was hanged by the hands on a post, the tips of his toes barely reaching the ground. After a while, the muscles of the arms, thorax, and legs began to contract violently. Because the thorax muscles commanding inhaling are stronger than those commanding exhaling the lungs filled to the maximum, but they could not expel the air turned into carbon dioxide. To avoid death by asphyxiation, the tortured soldier was let down for a short time and then lifted up again. The Nazis used this method for torture and execution in their deportation camps according to former Dachau prisoners (Barbet, 110–13).

Constantine abolished crucifixion in the fourth century C.E.

Archaeological Information

Two major discoveries in Israel provide evidence of the existence of crucifixion in first-century Palestine and of how it was perceived by some of Jesus' contemporaries. One consists of the remains of a crucified man, and the other involves passages in Qumran texts.

In June 1968, three burial caves were found northeast of Jerusalem, near the Nablus road, on the site of Giva'at ha-Mitvar, a large necropolis dating from the Second Temple period. Excavated by V. Tzaferis, they appeared to be typical rock-hewn Jewish family tombs. They contained five ossuaries,* which were published by J. Naveh, who dated two of them to the first century C.E. One of the first-century ossuaries* contained the bones of two men and of a three- to four-year-old child. The skeletal remains were first discussed by N. Haas in 1970 and then by J. Zias and E. Sekeles in 1985. One of the men was twenty-four years old and was about five feet five inches tall. The tibiae and fibulae of his legs were apparently broken, and his right heel bone (calcaneum) was pierced by a 4 1/2-inches-long nail. The nail first had been driven through a small piece of olive wood, probably to prevent the foot from moving off the narrow head of the nail. A scratch on one of the wrist bones may have resulted from the contact with a nail driven through the forearm, near the wrist. The nail in the heel, when driven into the hard olive wood of the upright beam, bent at its sharp end, forming a hook. According to Haas, when the body was taken down, the foot was cut off and stayed attached to the upright for some time until it could be removed; Zias and Sekeles contest this interpretation. The ossuary bore two inscriptions, probably names, on one of its long sides: *yhohnn yehohanan* and *yhohnn be hggval*. There is no consensus on the interpretation of the last word, *hggval*.

The second discovery is that of two references to crucifixion in Qumran texts. One, the *pesher* (commentary) of Nahum (4QpNah), was published by J. M. Allegro in 1968. Fragments 3–4, column 1, lines 7–8, which comment on Nahum 2:11-13, read: "The Lion of wrath . . . hangs live men [on the tree as it was done] in Israel from of old." The last phrase may refer to Joshua 8:29 and Deuteronomy 21:22. The "Lion of wrath" probably designates Alexander Janneus, who had crucified eight hundred Pharisees (*see* "General Information" above). In addition, the Temple Scroll, 11QTemple, gives an interpretation of Deuteronomy 21:22-23 in column 64, lines 6–13. It considers capital punishment by "hanging upon the tree" for those who are guilty of treason and have fled to the Gentiles. It adds the curse of men to the curse of God, "For a hanged man is accursed by God [Deut. 21:23] *and by men.*" These two texts indicate that crucifixion was called "hanging on a tree" by some Jews of first-century Palestine. Originally, in a country with many oaks and olive trees, crucifixion may

have been carried out by nailing or tying the arms of the victims to branches forming a cross, while the feet were tied or nailed to the trunk.

Implications for Jesus Research

Jesus' crucifixion is the one prominent feature of the Gospels accounts that is not challenged. At least four independent sources—Paul, Mark, Acts, and John—agree on this point. Josephus also refers to Jesus' crucifixion. Two sources, Mark and John, attest that Pontius Pilate ordered Jesus' crucifixion for a crime (rebellion) punishable under Roman law. But Mark and its Synoptic parallels, also suggest that Jesus was condemned for blasphemy (Mark 14:64) by a Jewish court and that the religious leaders demanded his execution (*see* CAIAPHAS'S HOUSE).

Archaeology provides evidence for crucifixion in first-century Palestine and indicates that the bodies of the condemned were not necessarily thrown into a common grave, as has been proposed as the fate of Jesus' body. Families and friends could claim the bodies and give them the customary burial, as was done for Yhohnn Yehohanan, a contemporary of Jesus. Thus Mark 15:43 and its parallels correspond to archaeological discoveries. But from the nature of the fractures of the lower leg bones, as established by forensic medical analysis, it cannot be concluded that John 19:31-35 describes a practice followed at the time. The study of 4QpNah and 11QTemple establishes that, in the first century C.E., the expression "hanging on the tree" referred to crucifixion. Texts such as Acts 5:30; 10:39; Gal. 3:13, and 1 Pet. 2:24 thus indicate the execution of Jesus on a Roman cross.

It is impossible to describe exactly how Jesus was crucified and in what position (*see* fig. 24). Because his crucifixion was not likely part of a mass execution (despite the reference to an insurrection in Mark 15:7) Jesus was probably subjected to the regular Roman procedure of scourging, *patibulum* carrying, and nailing on an upright beam bearing a *sedecula*. In a period when Roman authorities seem to have been more lenient, it is possible that he was not naked on the way to Golgotha but

Figure 24 Different Methods of Crucifixion. An artist's view.

rather wore a loin cloth. The Gospel account of the *titulus* conforms to historical information: It could indicate that Jesus was crucified on a dagger-shaped cross, although it is possible for a *titulus* to be nailed on the cross beam of a T-shaped cross, directly above the head of the condemned.

The Gospels give no evidence that Jesus was crucified on an elevated and isolated place like the narrow top of the rock of Golgotha (*see* GOLGOTHA, TRADITIONAL SITE) and on a *crux sublimis*. He apparently could talk to persons present at his execution (John 19:26-27), and passersby could hear his words (Mark 15:34-35). It is impossible to determine whether the sponge dipped in a mixture of water and vinegar was presented to him on a reed or a spear. *Hysso* means spear, *hyssop* means reed and hyssop (Mark 15:36 and parallel in Matt.; John 19:29). Both are possible, because reeds in Israel can have stems as rigid as bamboo. Another source of uncertainty is that spears and javelins could be made of reed stems, thus the name *hysso* could derive from *hyssop*. Because the author of John is usually well informed, the term *hyssop* or reed might be preferred.

The pericope Mark 15:42-45 evokes two remarks. First, the possibility that Joseph of Arimathea asked for the body of Jesus in view of his burial is strengthened by information from Philo. Bodies normally remained on the crosses until they were completely eaten by rats or beasts and vultures. But in Egypt, as in Palestine (*see* "Archaeological Information" above), Jews were allowed to remove and bury the corpses of crucified friends and relatives. Philo complained that Flacus, prefect of Egypt, in 38 C.E., refused this favor to the Jews (J. J. Collins, 158). Second, the surprise expressed by Pilate at the quick death of Jesus was authentic in that death on a cross could take several days, as indicated by Josephus's story about his surviving crucified friend (*Life* 75).

BIBLIOGRAPHY

Bammel, E. "Crucifixion as a Punishment in Palestine." *Studies in Biblical Theology.* Second Series 13. London: S.C.M. Press Ltd., 1970.

Barbet, P. *La Passion de Jésus Christ selon le chirurgien.* 1950. Reprint. Paris: Editions Paulines, 1965.

Baumgarten, J. M. "Hanging and Treason in Qumran and Roman Law." *Eretz Israel* 16 (1982): 7–16.

———. "Does TLH in the Temple Scroll Refer to Crucifixion?" *Journal of Biblical Literature* 91 (1972): 472–81.

Briend, J. "La sépulture d'un crucifié." *Bible et Terre Sainte* 133 (July–Aug. 1971): 6–10.

Charlesworth, J. H. "Jesus and Jehohanan: An Archaeological Note on Crucifixion." *Expository Times* 84 (1972–73): 147–50.

Collins, J. J. "Exegetical Notes: The Archaeology of the Crucifixion." *Catholic Biblical Quarterly* 1 (1939): 154–59.

Edwards, W. D. et al. "On the Physical Death of Jesus Christ." *The Journal of the American Medical Association* (March 21, 1986).

Fitzmayer, J. H. "Crucifixion in Ancient Palestine, Qumran Literature and the New Testament." *Catholic Biblical Quarterly* 40 (1978): 493–513.

Ford, J. M. " 'Crucify Him, Crucify Him' and the Temple Scroll," *Expository Times* 87 (1975–76): 275–78.

Haas, N. "Anthropological Observations on the Skeletal Remains from Giv'at ha-Mivtar." *IEJ* 20 (1970): 38–59.

Hengel, M. *Crucifixion in the Ancient World and the Folly of the Message of the Cross.* German, 1976. Translated by J. Bowden. Philadelphia: Fortress Press, 1977.

Moller-Christensen, W. "Skeletal Remains from Giv'at ha-Mitvar." *IEJ* 26 (2976): 35–38.

Naveh, J. "Report on Five Ossuaries Found at Giv'at ha-Mivtar." *IEJ* 20 (1970): 33–37.

O'Collins, G. G. "Crucifixion." *ABD.* 1:1207-10.

Sava, A. F. "The Wound in the Side of Christ." *Catholic Biblical Quarterly* 19 (1957): 343–46.

Thorton, T. C. G. "The Crucifixion of Maman and the Scandal of the Cross." *Journal of Theological Studies* 37 (1986): 419–26.

Tzaferis, V. "Crucifixion. The Archaeological Evidence." *BAR* 11 (1985): 44–53.

———. "Jewish Tombs at and near Giv'at ha-Mivtar." *IEJ* 20 (1970): 18–32.

Zias, J. and J. H. Charlesworth. "Crucifixion: Archaeology, Jesus and the Dead Sea Scrolls." *Jesus and the Dead Sea Scrolls*, edited by J. H. Charlesworth. New York: Doubleday, 1992.

Zias, J. and E. Sekeles. "The Crucified Man from Giv'at ha-Mivtar: A Reappraisal." *IEJ* 35 (1985): 22–27.

Zugibe, F. T. "Two questions about Crucifixion: Does the Victim Die of Asphyxiation? Would Nails in the Hand Hold the Weight of the Body?" *Bible Review* 5 (1989): 35–43.

Dead Sea Scrolls

Importance

The Jewish sectarians of Qumran left manuscripts providing significant information for New Testament scholarship.

Scripture Reference

Matt. 3:6-12; 12:18; 19:6, 12, 21; Mark 1:3-6; 2:28; 10:2-9; Luke 3:2-4; 6:1-5; 7:33; 12:33; 16:8; John

1:23; 12:36; Acts 2:42-47; 4:34-37; 5:1-11; 2 Cor. 6:14-15; Col. 1:12-13.

General Information, Chronology of the Field Research

In 1947, a young Ta'amireh Bedouin, Mohammed ed-Dib (the Wolf), while looking for one of his sheep, found ancient manuscripts in a cave located some 1,300 meters (about 1,400 yards) north of the ruins of Khirbet Qumran. A Bethlehem dealer bought seven manuscripts. He sold three of them to E. L. Sukenik for the Hebrew University: an Isaiah Scroll in bad condition, the Hymn Scroll, and the War Rule. Four others were sold to the Metropolitan of the Syriac Convent of Saint Mark and were subsequently purchased in the United States by the government of Israel in 1954. They were an Isaiah Scroll in good condition, the Habakkuk *pesher* (commentary), the Rule of the Congregation, and the Genesis Apocryphon. Excavations began in 1949, after the War of Independence, with Qumran then located in Jordan. A Belgian UN officer, Philip Lippens, initiated the archaeological work, which was conducted by G. Lancaster Harding, director of the Jordanian Department of Antiquities, and R. de Vaux, director of the French Ecole Biblique et Archéologique of Jerusalem. The field work, from 1948 to 1958, can be summarized as follows:

15 February–5 March 1949: Excavation of the first cave. Despite previous visits by the Bedouins, it still contained remnants of about fifty jars and their lids, bowls, cooking pots, juglets, four oil lamps, some six hundred pieces of parchment from at least seventy manuscripts, some forty fragments of papyri, a few pieces of linen cloth used to wrap the scrolls, one phylactery* and six leather cases for phylacteries.

24 November–12 December 1951: First excavations at Khirbet Qumran. At that time, the Bedouins brought to Jerusalem new manuscripts found in the caves of Wadi Murabba'at, south of Qumran.

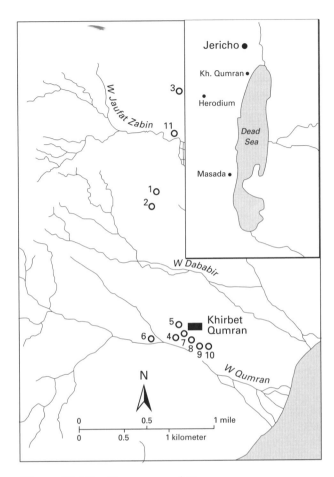

Figure 25 The Caves around Qumran

21 January–3 March 1952: Excavation of the caves of Wadi Murabba'at. They contained documents from the time of the Bar Kokhba Revolt (132–135 C.E.) not related to the Qumran scrolls.

March 10–29: Exploration of the Qumran cliffs and excavations of caves 2 and 3. The exploration extended from a point 1.5 miles north of Qumran to the south of Ras Feshkah (*see* fig. 25). A total of 270 caves and cracks were located, 40 of which contained artifacts. More than half of them contained pottery of the same type as in the Qumran caves. The Copper Scroll was found in cave 3.

September 22–29: Exploration of the terrace on which the settlement was built and excavation of caves 4 to 6.

9 February–24 April 1953: Second excavation campaign at Khirbet Qumran.

13 February–14 April 1954: Third excavation campaign at Khirbet Qumran.

2 February–6 April 1955: Fourth excavation campaign at Khirbet Qumran and excavation of caves 7 to 10. Fragments of Greek papyri were found in cave 7.

18 February–26 March 1956: Fifth excavation campaign at Khirbet Qumran. The excavation of cave 11 yielded, among other finds, the Leviticus Scroll, the Psalms Scroll containing 37 "canonical" psalms and 7 unknown ones, the Targum* of Job, and an iron tool shaped like a pick-hatchet, perhaps a tool used in connection with Deut. 23:12–14.

25 January–21 March 1958: Excavation of Khirbet Feskha, after the Suez Canal conflict.

The containers used to hold the scrolls were of two types: the high jar, about 25 inches high and 10 inches in diameter, and the low jar, 18 by 9.5 inches. The scrolls themselves were 6.5 to 13.5 inches high and 2 to 5 inches in diameter. Most manuscripts were written in biblical Hebrew adapted to the vernacular of the time as, for example, by the use of the letter *vav* as a vowel for "o." It seems that, besides Palestinian Aramaic, the sectarians knew a language similar to Mishnaic Hebrew and Samaritan Hebrew. A few manuscripts were written in Greek. Among those in Aramaic are Daniel, the two targums* of Leviticus and Job, Tobit, Enoch, the Genesis Apocryphon, the prayer of Nabonidus (*see* EXORCISM), and Jubilees. An often recurring word, *kittim*, designates the enemies of God and the sect. It is interpreted as applying to the Romans in consideration of the historical situation and on the basis of information found in the War Scroll: the shields of the eschatological warriors are similar to those of the Roman army, with large rectangular ones for the infantry and smaller circular ones for the cavalry (*see* WEAPONS).

Inventory of the Scrolls. The scrolls were numbered according to the cave where they were found. The most important and best preserved are summarized in table 6.

Similarities and Differences between Qumran and the Christian Tradition. Affinities and differences between Qumran and Christian tradition have been widely explored, and an abundant literature exists on these issues. One of the most recent works on this subject is that of J. H. Charlesworth (1992, *see* Bibliography).

For the sake of clarity, but with the risk of oversimplification, we distinguish between John the Baptist and Jesus in examining some of the implications of the Dead Sea Scrolls texts for Jesus research.

Similarities and Differences between John the Baptist and the Qumranites. Because the Essenes adopted children to instruct them (Josephus, *War* 2, 8.2/120; 1QSa 1:4–6), John may have been raised by the sect and then left the community when the time came for him to officially join the congregation at age twenty. This scenario would explain his ascetic habits (the Damascus Document indicates how to cook and eat locusts; CD 12:14; Mark 1:6). But the same habits could derive from a Nazirite vow involving fasting and abstinance from wine (Luke 1:15; 7:33). Note that the Essenes drank wine and ate meat and that they wore white linen clothes whereas John wore a tunic of camel hair.

One obvious similarity between the Baptist and the Qumranites is their common understanding of the eschatological* symbol of the desert. It was only a few hours walk between Qumran and the traditional remote site of John's activity on the Jordan (*see* BETHABARA); he shared their preference for isolation. The symbolism of Isaiah 40:3 seems to have inspired both Qumran and John (1QS 8:13; 9:19b–21a; John 1:23; Mark 1:3, and parallels). For both, the end was near; both announced the wrath of God. But John did not consider a final cosmic

Table 6 Dead Sea Scroll Inventory

Scroll Number	Name
Rules	
1Qs	*Serek hayyahad,* Rule of the Community
CD	Damascus Document
4Q266	— — Fragment a
4QCDb	— — Fragment b
4Q268	— — Fragment c
4Q272	— — Fragment g
1QSa = 1Q28a	Messianic Rule or Rule of the Congregation
1QM = 4QM	*Milhamah,* War Rule
11Q Temple	Temple Scroll
4Q181	Wicked and Holy
4Q280–2, 286–7	Curses of Satan and His Lot
5Q13 = 4Q Régle	A Rule of the Sect
Hymns, Poetry, Liturgy	
1QH	*Hodayot,* Thanksgiving Hymns
1QSb	Blessings
1Q27	The Triumph of Righteousness
1Q34, 34bis	Liturgical Prayer
4Q174 = 4QFlor	*Florilegium* (Poetry)
4Q179 = 4Q501	Lamentations
4Q184	The Seductress
4Q185	Seek Wisdom
4Q380–1	Pseudepigraphic Psalms
4Q400–407 = 11Q5–6	Songs for the Holocaust of the Shabbath
4Q503	Daily Prayers
4Q504	The Words of the Heavenly Light
4Q507–9	Prayers for Festivals
4Q510–11	Songs of the Sages
11QPs^a	Apocryphal Psalms

Scroll Number	Name
Texts and Interpretation, Other	
1Q14	Commentary on Micah
1Q22	The Words of Moses
1QpHab	*Pesher* (Commentary) on Habakkuk
1QapGen	Genesis Apocryphon
3Q15	Copper Scroll
4QAmram	Testament of Amram
4QprNab	Prayer of Nabonidus
4QpsDan = 4Q246	Pseudo-Daniel
4QPBless	Blessings of Jacob
4QTob	Tobit Fragment
4Q159, 513–14	Commentaries on Torah
4Q160	Samuel Apocryphon
4Q161–4	Commentaries on Isaiah
4Q166–7	Commentaries on Hosea
4Q169	Commentaries on Nahum
4Q171, 173	Commentaries on Psalms
4Q174	Midrash on the Last Day
4Q175 = 4QTestim	Testimonies on the Messiah
4Q176	Consolations
4Q180	Ages of Creation
4Q186	Horoscopes
4Q375	Moses Apocryphon
4Q394–9 = 4QMMT	*Miqsat Ma'aseh Torah,* Some Rules of the Torah
4Q502	Marriage Ritual (?)
11QtgJob	Targum of Job

battle; he was more in line with the prophets. His image of the axe may have been inspired by Isaiah 6:13 and 10:34, that of the wheat and chaff by Isaiah 17:13; 29:5, and Jeremiah 13:24. In his diatribes against the religious establishment, however, the Baptizer shared the sentiments of the sectarians (1QH 2:27; 3:12, 17, 18; 4:27; CD 4:14; 8:9 *et passim*; Matt. 3:7-12). Both announced the final judgment in terms apparently derived from Malachi 3:1-5.

Purification by water was understood differently by John and the Qumranites. At Qumran, if the initiate took a first formal purification bath on the day of Pentecost, at the occasion of the Covenant celebration, the practice was renewed daily. According to the Gospels and Josephus (*Antiq.* 18, 5.1/117) the followers of the Baptist immersed only once. Subsequent ablutions may also have occurred in accordance with the purity rules of the Torah. The Qumran documents use the word *thr*, the biblical (Hebrew Bible) word for purity: the Babylonian Talmud (in *Yoma*) uses *tbl* for the priest's bathing and *tbyh* for the baptism of the proselytes. The Gospels employ *baptizein* as in 2 Kings 5:14, when Naaman dipped himself in the Jordan without any help. Josephus uses *bapt* and derivatives for the baptism of John; but for the Essenes, he uses *loytron*, "washing," *agnein* "purifying," and *apoloyesthai*, which means "to wash oneself." Thus, it would seem that those John baptized immersed themselves in the water without his direct involvement, as was the practice for purification bathing (*see* RITUAL BATHS). In both cases, repentance, confession, and change of heart were the substance of conversion (1QS 1:24; 2:1, 25; 3:12; Matt. 3:6; Mark 1:5; Luke 3:10-14). The main difference for John is that no probationary period was required as it was in Qumran.

Although there are some clear similarities between John and practices found in the Qumran documents, the differences are important. Few scholars still adhere to the notion that John was directly involved in the Qumran community.

Similarities and Differences between Jesus and Qumran. No clear indication appears in the Gospels that Jesus either expected a Messiah or saw himself as the Anointed One and Final Judge (*see* SON OF MAN). By contrast, the Rule of the Community indicates that the Qumranites expected "the Prophet" and the "Messiahs of Aaron and Israel" (1QS 2:25; 3:12). The Baptist may have expected a Messiah identical to the "one like a son of man" (Dan. 7:13) and to the final judge (1 Enoch 45:3). But his question, most embarrassing for the Church, about the role of Jesus indicates that he was not convinced that the Nazarene was indeed "the one who is to come" (Matt. 11:13; Luke 7:19). The Gospels themselves, even in the postresurrection narratives (Matt. 13:57; 12:11, *et passim*; Luke 24:19), frequently refer to Jesus as a prophet. What can be reasonably inferred is that, in a time of widespread messianic expectation, Jesus probably saw himself as having a certain role to play (*see* EXORCISM).

The Last Supper and Jesus' eschatological banquet with Abraham, Isaac, and Jacob have been compared to Qumran's communal meal. There are differences, however, in the meals of the Qumran texts. Although the Rule of the Community and the Rule of the Congregation (1QS and 1QSa), dated to 100–75 B.C.E., were written by the same hand, their focuses diverge. The Rule of the Community (1QS) 4:4–5 refers to the regular daily meals for which a ritual must be observed if at least ten attend, including one priest. The priest first blesses the bread and wine together in one single act; the meal has no sacramental character; thanksgiving and brotherhood are the dominant features. The other text, the Rule of the Congregation (1QSa/2:17-22), deals more specifically with the eschatological meal at the end of time, when the Messiah is born. It specifies the order of sitting and describes a more detailed ritual: the High Priest first places his hands on the bread and wine, the Messiah (who comes in second place) then gives the blessing and, after him, everyone else in turn according to rank does the same thing. Jesus' Last

Supper, then, seems to be more similar to the daily communal meal of Qumran than to the eschatological one; but the statement, "I shall not again drink of the fruit of the vine until that day when I drink it new in the Kingdom of God" (Mark 14:25) gives it an eschatological overtone (*see* UPPER ROOM).

A dualistic conceptualization of the world is to be found both in the Qumran texts and in the Gospels. The War Scroll distinguishes between the Prince of Light and sons of light on one side and the Angel of Darkness and sons of darkness on the other. Jesus announces the reign of God and the defeat of Satan, ruler of this world. But Jesus does not envision an eschatological battle, nor does he adhere to the concept of predestination found in the Rule of the Community and in the Horoscopes. At Qumran, the sign of the Zodiac under which people are born is seen as determining their physical characteristics and their fate according to a light-darkness ratio, which is received at birth. The spirit of a son of light is at least "six parts in the house of light against three in the house of darkness" (1QH 3:7–8). "God divides them lot by lot until the last day" (1QH 4:15–17). One does not become a son of light by training but rather by birth. Jesus probably did not use, as a tenet of his teaching, the light versus darkness opposition, which appears first in Paul's letters (2 Cor. 6:14–15, with the use of the Qumranite word "Belial" for Satan; Col. 1:12–13; Eph. 5:8–14). The expression "sons of light" appears only in the later Gospels (Luke 16:8; John 12:36), where it is not contrasted with "sons of darkness." Also, Jesus' kingdom of God is opened to all those who repent—women, men, even prostitutes and tax collectors—rather than to those predestined for a certain fate as in the Qumranite concept.

The idea of a new covenant appears in both Qumran and the Gospels. Nevertheless, it must be noted that the covenant is a central theme of the Hebrew Bible and that the idea of a new covenant, as found in Jeremiah 31:31–34, was part of the common background of both Jesus and Qumran

and does not indicate a link between them. The same idea of a common heritage is true for other similarities in their spiritual life. Prayer or call to God, rather than recourse to strange practices, paraphernalia, and rituals, was the method of exorcising demons for both Jesus and the Qumranites (*see* EXORCISM). Both prayed regularly, and Jesus recommended prayer as a normal form of communication with God (1QS 10:9–17); 1QH; 4Q503; Matt. 11:25–27; Luke 10:21–22, *et passim**).

Both Jesus and the Qumranites condemned divorce (11QTemple 57; Mark 10:2–9; Matt. 19:6 *et passim**). Despite the claims of pseudoscholarly sensationalists, there is no evidence that Jesus was married. On the contrary, he indicated that some men could become eunuchs, figuratively or literally, for the sake of the kingdom of heaven (Matt. 19: 12). While voluntary castration was practiced by devotees of Cybele and others, the only Jews for which there is evidence of a commitment to celibacy, besides the Therapeutae of Egypt, were the Qumranites (Josephus, *War* 2, 8.2/121; CD; 1QSa; 4Q502; 11QTemple). Whether Jesus included himself in his reference to sexual abstinence is uncertain. What Jesus and the celibate Essenes of Qumran had in common was their absolute dedication to God.

The Qumranites apparently had a strong dislike for the corrupt priesthood of the Temple (CD; 1QS). Nevertheless, it appears that, although they did not offer sacrifices there, they continued paying the half-shekel Temple tax (Josephus, *Antiq.* 18, 1.5/19). In a similar fashion, although Jesus visited the Temple, he does not seem to have offered a sacrifice, and he performed a symbolic act of cleansing (*see* TEMPLE, ROYAL STOA); but he may have paid the Temple tax (Matt. 17:24). Another similarity between Jesus and the Qumranites is reference to the Holy Spirit, which is otherwise seldom mentioned in the Hebrew Bible or rabbinic writings. The Spirit is the thread that unites the Gospels and Acts; similarly, it appears frequently in the Dead Sea Scrolls with, however, a major difference: In the latter, it is a hypostasis, a distinct angelic person *from* God while, in the New Testament, it is the Holy Spirit *of* God. The hypostasis concept was introduced later in the Church with the appearance of the dogma of the Trinity. The Holy Spirit may have been a concept known only to some Palestinian Jews, because at Ephesus Paul found some disciples who had not received it when they believed and had never heard of such a thing (Acts 19:2). This may imply that Jesus and the Evangelists acquired this belief in the Holy Spirit through contact with those Jews, probably the Qumranites.

Major differences between Jesus and Qumran beliefs indicate either that he broke from the Qumranite community, if he ever was part of it, or that, more likely, he had a different, albeit related, formative background. One such difference concerns the attitude toward enemies: love, for Jesus (Matt. 5:44; Luke 6:27, 35); hatred, for the Qumranites (*War* 2, 8.7/139; 1QS 1.4, 10; 2.5–8), who may have been inspired by some of the Psalms (Pss. 79:11; 137:8–9; 139:19–22). Also, while the Qumranites rigorously respected the *shabbat*, Jesus taught that the *shabbat* was made for people and not people for the *shabbat* (Mark 2:27), and that he had authority to establish a new *halakah** regarding the *shabbat* (Matt. 12:8 and parallels). A major difference also existed in the methods of teaching or interpreting: the favorite method of the Qumranites was the *pesher*, "commentary," while Jesus used parables extensively. Perhaps more striking is the precise description of the Qumranites' eschatological temple (*see* fig. 67) as opposed to the universal vision of Jesus expressed in John 4:21–24 and Acts 7:48–49.

In conclusion, both John the Baptist and Jesus possibly had been in contact with Qumran and personally knew Essenes established in cities and villages (*see* HOUSE and TEXTILE). Jesus had affinities with them but also obvious differences. Since the second half of the nineteenth century (e.g., A. Schweitzer, *The Quest of the Historical Jesus*), many scholars have proposed that John the Baptist and Jesus were Essenes. Although unlikely, such a possibility can be entertained only if it is understood that at a certain point in their respective careers they separated from the covenanters in order to follow their own practices and beliefs. Any Essene affinity or influence evident in the Gospels, Acts, and Paul may simply indicate that Essenes joined the primitive Church. Another indicator of this possibility is that no references to Essenes occur in the New Testament, while they were known to Josephus, Philo, and Pliny as a distinct Jewish sect with members in every town and village. A logical inference would be that most books of the New Testament were written or edited by Essene scribes. Perhaps some of the priests who joined the Church (Acts 6:7) were Essenes from Qumran after their buildings were razed by the Romans in 68 C.E. They may have introduced the Qumranite term "Way" in Acts and in the Didache* (1QS 8:13–16; 9:16–21; Acts 19:23; 22:4; 24:14, 22; Did. 1:1–2).

Controversies about Qumran and the Dead Sea Scrolls have recently stirred the academic world and brought Qumran into prominent public view. The popular media have examined the issues of an alleged conspiracy not to publish some fragments, the "unauthorized" publication of the photographs of the complete texts, the claim that the Qumranites were not Essenes, and others. As indicated in the introduction, our purpose is not to engage in polemics, but to help make available data from ancient writings and archaeological discoveries. However, works dealing with some of these issues are included in the bibliography. As regards the Qumranites, a valid hypothesis, in consideration of the Dead Sea Scrolls texts, is to consider them as the "sons of light," the eschatological warriors recognized among the Essenes according to their astrological references.

BIBLIOGRAPHY

Allegro, J. M. "Jesus and Qumran: The Dead Sea Scrolls." *Jesus in History and Myth*, edited by R. J. Hoffman and G. A. Larue, Buffalo, N.Y.: Prometheus Books, 1986.

Baumgartner, J. M. "Does TLH in the Temple Scroll Refer to Crucifixion?" *Journal of Biblical Literature* 91 (1972): 472–81.

Benoit, P. "Note sur les fragments de la grotte 7 de Qumran." *Revue Biblique* 79 (1972) 321–24.

———. "Nouvelle note sur les fragments de la grotte 7 de Qumran." *Review Biblique* 80 (1973): 5–12.

Brownlee, W. H. "Jesus and Qumran." *Jesus and the Historian*, edited by F. T. Trotter, Philadelphia: Westminster Press, 1968.

Charlesworth, J. H., ed. "Jesus and the Dead Sea Scrolls." *Jesus Within Judaism*. Anchor Bible Reference Library 1. Garden City, N. Y.: Doubleday, 1988.

———. *Jesus' Jewishness: Exploring the Place of Jesus within Judaism*. New York: Crossroad, 1991.

———. *Jesus and the Dead Sea Scrolls*. New York: Doubleday, 1992.

Collins, J. J. "Dead Sea Scrolls." *ABD* 2: 85–107.

———. "Essenes." *ABD* (1992), 2:614-26.

Emerton, J. A. "The Problem of Vernacular Hebrew in the First Century A.D. and the Languages of Jesus." *Journal of Theological Studies* 24 (1973): 1–23.

Fitzmayer, J. A. *The Dead Sea Scrolls: Major Publications and Tools for Study, Rev. ed.* Atlanta, Ga.: Scholars Press, 1990.

———. "The Qumran Scrolls and the New Testament after Forty Years." *Revue de Qumran* 13 (1988): 609–20.

Flusser, D. "The Sons of Light in Jesus' Teaching and in the New Testament." *Biblical Archaeology Today*. Proceedings of the International Congress on Biblical Archaeology. Jerusalem, April 1984. Jerusalem: Israel Exploration Society, 1985.

———. "Jesus' Opinion about the Essenes." *Judaism and the Origins of Christianity*, 1988.

Fujita, N. L. *A Crack in the Jar. What Ancient Jewish Documents Tell Us about the New Testament*. Mahwah, N.Y.: Paulist Press, 1986.

Golb, N. "Who Hid the Dead Sea Scrolls?" *BA* 48 (1985): 68–82.

Groh, J. E. "The Qumran Meal and the Last Supper." *Concordia Theological Monthly* 41 (1970): 279–95.

Kee, H. C. "The Bearing of the Dead Sea Scrolls on Understanding Jesus." *Jesus in History and Myth*, edited by R. J. Hoffman and G. A. Larue, 54–75. Buffalo, N.Y.: Prometheus Books, 1986.

Laperousaz, A. M. "Qumran. Archéologie du Khirbet Qumran et de la Région." *Dictionnaire de la Bible*, Paris: Letouzey et Ané, 1979.

Lapide, P. "Insights from Qumran into the Languages of Jesus." *Revue de Qumran* 8 (1975): 483–501.

Murphy-O'Connor, J. and J. H. Charlesworth. *Paul and the Dead Sea Scrolls*. New York: Crossroad, 1990.

Newsom, C. A. "Apocalyptic and the Discourse of the Qumran Community." *Journal of Near Eastern Studies* 49 (1990): 135–44.

Schiffman, L., ed. *Archeology and History on the Dead Sea Scrolls*. The New York University Conference in Memory of Yidael Yadin. Sheffield: JSOT Press, 1990.

Schiffman, L. H. *The Eschatological Community of the Dead Sea Scrolls: A Study of the Rule of the Congregation*. Atlanta, Ga.: Scholars Press, 1989.

———. *Sectarian Law in the Dead Sea Scrolls: Courts, Testimony and the Penal Code*. Chico, Calif.: Scholars Press, 1983.

———. *The Halakah at Qumran*. Leiden: Brill, 1975.

Schweitzer, A. *The Quest of the Historical Jesus*. German, 1906. New York: Macmillan, 1968.

Shanks, H. *Understanding the Dead Sea Scrolls*. Washington, D.C. Biblical Archaeological Society, 1993.

Stegeman, H. "Some Aspects of Eschatology in Texts from the Qumran Community and in the Teachings of Jesus." *Biblical Archaeology Today*. Proceedings of the International Congress on Biblical Archaeology. Jerusalem, April 1984. Jerusalem: Israel Exploration Society, 1985.

Vermes, G. "The Impact of the Dead Sea Scrolls on the Study of the New Testament." *Journal of Semitic Studies* 27 (1976): 107–16.

———. *The Dead Sea Scrolls*. 1977. Rev. ed. Philadelphia: Fortress Press, 1985.

———. *The Dead Sea Scrolls in English*. 1962. Rev. ed. London: Penguin Books, 1987.

———. "Bible Interpretation at Qumran." *Eretz Israel* 20, Yigael Yadin Volume (1989): 184–91.

Yadin, Y. *The Temple Scroll*. New York: Random House, 1985.

Decapolis

Importance

People from the Decapolis came to listen to Jesus and he visited the country.

Scripture References

Matt. 4:25; Mark 5:20; 7:31.

General Information

The Decapolis (from the Greek *deca*, "ten") originally may have been a league of ten cities with independent status, all on the east side of the Jordan except for Scythopolis, the Beth She'an of the Hebrew Bible. At least from the first century C.E. onward, however, it was more of an administrative region than a confederation of cities. Ancient authors do not agree on the actual number of cities involved. Josephus mentions ten but does not give their names. Pliny (*Nat. Hist.* 5, 16.74) names ten cities but recognizes that other writers give different lists. According to him, they are Damascus, Philadelphia (ex Rabbah, today's Amman), Raphana, Scythopolis, Gadara, Hippos, Pella, Dium, Gerasa, and Canatha. Josephus indicates (*War* 3, 9.7/446) that Scythopolis was the most important, which seems improbable if Damascus was part of the group. Ptolemy (*Geography* V, 14–18) gives a list of twelve cities, and Stephan of Byzantium names fourteen. What probably happened is that, in the course of time, more cities joined the original ten in their regional affiliation.

Most of the cities of the Decapolis were ancient settlements, some dating to the Iron Age, that had been rebuilt and resettled by the Ptolemies and Seleucids. The Hasmoneans annexed several of them, but Pompey, when he conquered Palestine, restored their autonomy, gave them the right to mint coinage, and placed them under the control of the governor of Syria (Josephus *War* 1, 7.7/155–56; *Antiq.* 14, 4.4/74–75). Augustus gave Hippos and Gadara to Herod; other transfers to other kings or provinces led to the disappearance of the Decapolis by the end of the second century C.E. In the time of Jesus, the ten (or more) cities were sumptuous places with colonnaded paved streets, forums, theaters, amphitheaters, temples, and water and sewer systems. They had their own festivals and athletic games. Crowds from the Decapolis followed Jesus (Matt. 4:25). At the break of the Jewish War of 66–70 C.E., according to tradition, the first Jewish Christian church withdrew from Jerusalem to Pella. The site of Jesus' entry into the Decapolis (Mark 5:1–2) cannot be ascertained, because different manuscripts give various readings: "the country of the Garasenes," "of the Gergesenes," and "of the Gadarenes."

Archaeological Information

Most of the cities of the ancient Decapolis have been excavated. Among them, the excavations of Beth She'an (ex Scythopolis), Gadara, and Geresa (today's Jerash) have yielded monumental treasures testifying to the splendor of the Late Roman and Byzantine periods of the cities that had accepted the *Pax Romana.* Hippos and Gadara are especially significant for the study of the historical Jesus (*see* HIPPOS and GADARA).

Implications for Jesus Research

The number of references in the Gospels to Jesus' journeys in foreign or pagan territories—Phoenicia, the region of Caesarea Philipi, the Decapolis, "beyond the Jordan"—tends to indicate that these visits were intentional. What might have been the reasons for such visits? One or more answers are possible:

1. His personal safety.
2. Bringing the good news to the Jews in these territories.
3. Bringing the good news to the Gentiles; if so, Jesus' instructions in Matthew 10:5–6 could be seen as an interpolation of the early Jewish Christian church.
4. Keeping ties with individuals or groups he had previously known.

The first option is more readily acceptable, but the other three must not be dismissed at first sight, new discoveries may elucidate the matter.

It is remarkable that the earliest references to the Decapolis are found in the Gospels, which antidate the works of historians and geographers like Josephus, Pliny, Ptolemy, and Stephan of Byzantium. The Gospels contain historical materials although they were not intended as histories.

BIBLIOGRAPHY

Bientenhard. "Die Dekapolis von Pompeius bis Traian." *Zeitschrift des deutschen Palästina-Vereins* 79 (1963): 24–58.

"Glorious Beth She'an." *BAR* 16 (1990): 17–31.

Rey-Coquais, J.-P. (translated by S. Rosoff). "Decapolis." *ABD* 2: 116-21.

Sussman, A. and M. Greenberg, eds. "Beth She'an." *Excavations and Surveys in Israel: 1988–1989*. Vol. 6. Jerusalem: Israel Antiquities Authority, 1990.

Ephraim

Importance

According to the Fourth Gospel, Jesus withdrew to a town named Ephraim before returning to Jerusalem for his last Passover.

Scripture Reference

John 11:54.

General Information

Ephraim was the name of Joseph's younger son and the name of the tribal territory west of the Jordan River, north of Jerusalem. The origin of the name is uncertain. The traditional explanation that it derives from the Hebrew *prh*, "to be fruitful, fertile," is based on Genesis 41:52 and Hosea 13:15 and may not be the only explanation. Another explanation is the derivation from *eper*, in the sense of "region."

Ephraim is also the name of an important town near Baal Hazor. At Baal Hazor, Absalom kept his sheepshearers and assassinated his half-brother Amnon (2 Sam. 13:23). It is commonly identified with Jebel el-Asur, the highest peak north of Jerusalem (1,016 m).

A few scholars identify Ephraim with the town where Jesus retreated after raising Lazarus from the dead at Bethany when he incurred the wrath of Caiaphas, the chief priests, and Pharisees in Jerusalem (John 11:45-54).

Despite the significant difference in the initial vowels, the village of Ephraim sometimes is equated with Ophra (Josh. 18:23). Eusebius identified it with the cities of Mount Ephron (Josh. 15.9) and placed it 20 miles north of Jerusalem and 5 miles east of Beth El. Most scholars today identify Ephraim with modern Tayibeh, 15 miles north of Jerusalem.

Indeed, perhaps all biblical towns named Ophra should be identified with modern villages named Tayibeh. The most common explanation for the unusual shift from Ophra to Tayibeh was because *Ifrit* means "demon" in Arabic, and the Arabs changed it to *Tayibeh*, meaning "favor, goodness." However, *Taba* means "gazelle" in Aramaic, which is the same meaning as *Ophra* in Hebrew. It is more plausible that the name Ophra was translated into Aramaic. Other toponyms similarly were translated into Aramaic and Greek (Migdal into Magdala, Hippos into Susita).

From 1 Maccabees 11:34 we learn that King Demetrius confirmed the boundaries of northern Judea and included the regions of Aphairema and two others taken from Samaria in its territory. On his way to Jerusalem, Vespasian took Bethel and Ephraim and left garrisons in them (Josephus, *War* 4, 9.9/551).

Archaeological Information

No archaeological excavations have been carried out at Tayibeh. Albright distinguished between Ephraim-Aphairema and Ophra-Ephron. He suggested identifying the latter pair with Tayibeh and the former pair with Ain Samieh, 3 miles northeast of Tayibeh and closer to the Jordan valley. He proposed that Jesus needed a warm place in February to winter with his disciples. Ain Samieh is warmer and had numerous caves that would have been ideal for him; it would have been preferable to Tayibeh, where the temperature is often colder than in Jerusalem.

Implications for Jesus Research

Although the site has not been exactly located nor excavated, the city by the name of Ephraim probably existed in the first century C.E. near the Samaritan border. The author of the Fourth Gospel either knew the geography of Palestine in Jesus' time or had good sources.

Jesus' decision to retreat near the Samaritan border would have been a logical one in a time of danger (John 8:59; 10:31; 11:8). The possibility of escaping in Samaria at a moment's notice offered more security than taking refuge in Perea, east of the Jordan, a territory under the jurisdiction of Herod Antipas (*see* SAMARIA, SAMARITANS).

BIBLIOGRAPHY

Albright, W. F. "Ophrah and Ephraim." *Annual of the American Schools of Oriental Research* 4 (1922–23): 125–33.

Mazar, B. "The Early Israelite Settlement in the Hill Country." *Bulletin of the American Schools of Oriental Research* 241 (1981): 75–85.

Thompson, H. O. "Ephraim." *ABD* 2:556.

Exorcism

Importance

Various New Testament passages, especially the Gospels, report that Jesus performed exorcisms.

Scripture References

Matt. 4:11, 23, 25: 7:28-29; 8:14-16, 28-34; 10:1-8;12:15-16, 22-50; 15:21-28; 17:14-20; Mark 1:12-13, 21-34; 3:7-15, 20-35; 5:1-20; 6:7, 13; 7:24-30; 9:14-19, 38; 16:9, 17; Luke 4:1-13, 31-41; 6:17-19; 8:2, 26-39; 9:1-6, 37-43, 49; 10:17-20; 11:14-21; 13:32; John 7:19-20; 8:39-52; 10:21; 12:31; 14:30; Acts 13:6, 8; 16:16-18; 19:13-16, 19.

General Information

Exorcism is one of the most ancient and universal practices in the history of humankind. In first-century Palestine it was widely practiced, and it is reported as one of Jesus' normal activities. The Gospels contain thirty-six references to demon possession and exorcism, no less than twenty-four

if parallels are discounted. The first Christians were also familiar with casting out demons, and a number of exorcisms and references to demons are found in the rest of the New Testament and in early Christian literature.

Exorcism presupposes the belief in the existence of invisible, hostile entities and in the phenomenon of possession. In the course of time, hostile entities took on different aspects: gods, demons, ghosts of the dead, a living enemy, and animals.

Hostile possession can be defined as the occupying of a person by an adverse invisible entity. In the Judeo-Christian tradition, demons usually represented hostile possession. Hostility is a necessary characteristic of the invisible entity in this tradition, because it was believed that individuals could also be possessed by the Holy Spirit. In *By the Finger of God*, S. V. McCasland suggests that possession is either a cohabitation in the same body of both the human and evil spirit or its replacement by the evil entity. Possession can be considered permanent (as in the case of the Gerasene demoniac, Matt. 8:28 and parallels), intermittent (as in the case of the epileptic boy, Matt. 17:18-20 and parallels), or temporary (when the demon departs of its own accord and never returns). One person could be possessed simultaneously by several hostile spirits as in the case of Mary Magdalene (Mark 16:9; Luke 8:2).

Possession results in a complete change of personality, even in the case of possession by the Holy Spirit. At Pentecost, the disciples spoke in other tongues and appeared to be drunk. Those possessed by demons are said to have erratic behavior, speak languages they did not learn, and mention places and people they did not know. They may use a different voice and scream as if under torment.

Given the nature of hostile possession, exorcism as performed by one or several exorcists can be defined as the act of compelling the hostile entity or entities to leave the possessed person and not to return.

The origin of Jewish exorcism can be traced back to the ancient practices of Sumer, Akkad, Assyria, and Babylon. Perhaps while in Babylon, the exiled Judeans of the sixth century B.C.E. became acquainted with such Babylonian-Iranian beliefs as:

- Supremacy of the Most High God, *Ahura-Mazda*, creator of both the good spirit, *Spenta Mainyu*, and the evil spirit, *Angra Mainyu*.
- Cosmic struggle between *Angra Mainyu* and his progeny, the *daevas*, opposing *Spenta Mainyu* who would eventually prevail.
- Existence of heaven, the place of eternal reward and hell, the place of eternal punishment.

Exorcism called on the power of *Spenta Mainyu* to subdue *Angra Mainyu* and his hoards of *daevas*. These beliefs influenced Judeo-Christian demonology, angelology, and exorcism.

The techniques and methods of ancient Mesopotamian exorcisms earlier transmitted to Israelite and then Jewish tradition were quite elaborate. They included oral rites, pharmaceutical recipes, ties and knots, running water, substitution, appeasement, obtaining the help of another hostile entity, liturgies, intervention of a god, and negotiation. Many others, used throughout the world, will never be known because they were considered esoteric knowledge and were never recorded. Like the secret rites of the Greek mysteries, they are lost forever. Take the story of the young and beautiful Sarah in Tobit. It does not present a case of exorcism *strito-sensu*.* She is not possessed by the demon Asmodeus (the *Aeshma Daeva* of the Persians) and does not behave like a typical possessed person, but Asmodeus killed several of her would-be husbands. The story is notable because it indicates the intervention of an angel, Raphael, and an unknown method of repelling demons evidently used in the early second century B.C.E.: the burning of a fish's viscera, namely the heart and liver. The stench was so unbearable that "the demon fled to the remotest parts of Egypt," where Raphael bound his "hand and foot" (Tob. 8:2-3).

Other methods and techniques of exorcism involved incantations, music, noise, and magical objects. Hundreds of ancient incantations have been found. The following Babylonian chant invokes the gods Marduk and Shamash:

In my body do not dwell,
On my body do not press.
By Shamash the Mighty, be exorcised.
By Marduk, chief exorciser of gods, be exorcised.
By the fire god who burns you, be exorcised.
From my body, be taken away
(S. M. Langdon, *Semitic Mythology*, p. 366–78)

The sun-god Shamash of Akkad had been appropriated by the Babylonians and associated with their own Most High God, *Marduk*, chief exorciser. Shamash is still preserved in the modern Hebrew word, *Shemesh*, meaning "sun."

The power of music in exorcism is illustrated by the references to David's harp, which had a soothing effect on the troubled Saul (1 Sam. 16:14-23). The evil spirit returned but this was seen as the will of God. Magical objects such as stones, rings, bracelets, amulets, and phylacteries are probably very ancient and are used in exorcisms to this day, as is the crucifix in Roman Catholic exorcism.

Many Jews of first-century Palestine probably believed in one god and also in angels, in demons or evil spirits led by Satan, master of this world, in a final judgment, in the resurrection of the dead, and in eternal reward or punishment. Certain groups like the Qumranites and the Baptist's followers believed in the imminence of God's judgment, with or without a cosmic battle between the armies of God and the forces of evil, with or without the destruction of the Temple and the disappearance of the corrupt priesthood. One or two Messiahs were expected to introduce the reign of God; and believers collected the bones of their dead in ossuaries in family tombs so they could be raised when the Messiah came. The old Iranian belief that demons could possess individuals and cause diseases had gained wide acceptance; therefore, techniques of exorcism were used for the treatment of illnesses. Nevertheless, a distinction was made between exorcism and healing, as will be seen below. For the Sadducees, most of these beliefs were heretical. The Qumranites and the Pharisees, the latter being perhaps the most influential group, practiced exorcism as did some priests.

Of interest with respect to Jewish exorcism are Josephus' remarks about Solomon. He wrote about Solomon's knowledge of exorcism, and the presence of his methods in first century C.E. Palestine.

> God also enabled him to learn that skill which expels demons. . . And he left behind him the manner of using exorcisms by which they drive away demons so that they will never return, and this method of cure is of great force into this day, for I have seen a certain man of my own country . . . Eleazar, releasing people that were demonical in the presence of Vespasian . . . He put a ring with a root of these sorts mentioned by Solomon to the nostrils of the demoniac, after which he drew the demon through his nostrils; and when the man fell down immediately, he abjured him to return to him no more, making still mention of Solomon and reciting the incantations which he composed . . . He set a little way off a cup full of water and commanded the demon, as he went out of the man, to overturn it; and when this was done, the skill and wisdom of Solomon was shown very manifestly (*Antiq.* 8, 2.5/46–48; trans. W. Whiston).

Certain aspects of Jewish exorcism preserved ancient Mesopotamian practices: use of a ring, the root of a plant, or an incantation; the collapse of the patient; command to the demon not to return and to show a sign of his departure. Exorcism tradition was probably at least two millennia old in Solomon's time and was revered as his 1,000 year later.

In addition to Jesus' exorcisms, the New Testament refers to demon possession and to Jewish practices of magic and exorcism:

Source	Description
Source	*Description*
Mark 9:38/Luke 9:49	man casting out demons
Luke 11:19	sons casting out demons
Acts 13:6, 8	Bar-Jesus/Elymas
16:16-18	the slave girl
19:13-16	itinerant Jewish exorcists, sons of the High Priest, Sceva
19:19	magical books burnt

The first text indicates that Jesus was not the only one to cast out demons in Galilee; according to both versions, the unknown exorcist was already using Jesus' name to threaten evil spirits, which may indicate that Jesus' special power was already recognized.

In the Q* recording of the Beelzebul controversy, the Pharisees (Matthew), or some in the crowd (Luke), or their sons engaged in exorcism. In Acts 13:6-8, Paul and Barnabas, while in Paphos in Cyprus, came upon "a certain magician, a Jewish false prophet named Bar-Jesus" (Elymas). In Philippi of Macedonia, where there was a Roman colony, a slave girl who had "a spirit of divination" followed them day after day until Paul ordered the spirit out of her "in the name of Jesus Christ." It seems that there were itinerant Jewish exorcists at Ephesus because "some" of them began to pronounce the name of the Lord Jesus over those who had evil spirits. Among them, the seven sons of Sceva were not recognized by the evil spirit and had to flee, beaten up and naked. As a result of their failure, many new converts confessed that they had practiced magic, gathered their magical books, and burned them publicly. There must have been a large number of these books, for their total value was estimated at fifty-thousand pieces of silver. It would appear then that in the Greco-Roman world exorcism and magic were commonly practiced. Even members of priestly families may have been exorcists (*see* Luke 11:19). Nonscriptural sources such as Philostratus, *Life of Apollonius of Tyana*, the works of Lucian of Somosata, and early Christian writers also testify to the widespread practice of exorcism in the first century C.E.

Much more significant, because they come directly from Jesus' time or immediately before, are four well-preserved texts on exorcism and incantations among the Dead Sea Scrolls. Two exorcisms have been studied by A. Dupont-Sommer, and E. Puech reconstructed two incantations. Josephus indicates that the Essenes were expert healers of souls and bodies:

> They also take great pains in studying the writings of the ancients, and choose out of them what is more advantageous for their souls and bodies, and they enquire of such roots and medicinal stones as may cure their illness (War 2, 8.6/136).

Archaeological Data

Archaeology reveals the extent of the practice of exorcism in the ancient Near East and in the Greco-Roman world. Large numbers of amulets, texts of incantations, recipes, and accounts of exorcisms have been recovered. Three documents from Qumran are particularly informative:

1. Aramaic Scroll, Genesis Apocryphon from Cave 1, published by N. Avigad and Y. Yadin in 1956 and interpreted by Dupont-Sommer in 1959. The scroll is a midrash* on Genesis 12:10-20 with a story of exorcism: For having taken Abram's wife, Pharaoh is struck by the plague; when Pharaoh returns Sarai to her husband, Abram prays and imposes his hand on Pharaoh "and the plague was removed from him and the evil [spirit] was expelled and he lived" (Genesis Apocrypha XX:11-32).

2. Fragments of an Aramaic Scroll from Cave 4 called The Prayer of Nabonidus, first published by J. T. Milik in 1956 and completed and interpreted by Dupont-Sommer in 1959. After he had abdicated in favor of his son Nabu-na'id, the King of Babylon retired a Teima in Arabia in 552 B.C.E. because he was struck by a malignant inflammation. After seven years he was healed by a "Jewish exorcist" who "forgave his sins."

3. Scroll 11 QPs Apa, a leather manuscript from Cave XI, published by the Royal Academy of Netherlands. It contains one psalm and three incantations translated and interpreted by E. Peuch in 1990. The incantations are typical of the Qumranite style and vocabulary, and are made in the name of YHWH against Belial.

What is remarkable in these texts is that no devices and no magical terms are used; rather only a prayer with or without imposition of hand is found in the first two texts and a simple declaration in the name of YHWH appears in the other. These documents most likely describe the methods used by the Qumranites. Like the Qumranites, Jesus did not use any accessories; he operated only by command.

Implications for Jesus Research

Jesus certainly performed exorcisms as they were practiced in the first century; it would have been natural for an itinerant charismatic healer and teacher to do so. That many others practiced exorcism is widely accepted by New Testament scholars. When the proposition, "Jesus exorcised what were thought to be demons," was submitted to the Fellows of the Jesus seminar, only 5 percent disagreed.

The distinction between exorcism and healing is not self-evident, because demons were seen as the cause of many ailments: dumbness, lameness, epilepsy, infirmity, blindness, madness, hysteria, fever, paralysis, and others. But some New Testament passages mention exorcisms and healings together, which indicates that the writers made a distinction between the two (see Mark 1:32-33; 3:10-11; 6:13; Luke 6:18-19; 7:21; 13:32). The second ending of Mark distinguishes between "cast out demons" and "lay their hands on the sick" (Mark 16:17-18).

Besides general statements about Jesus performing exorcisms, the Gospels record a few instances in which his actions surely can be labeled as exorcism:

1. *The Beelzebul Controversy.* Mark 3:20-35; Matt. 12:22-50; Luke 11:14-21. Jesus' opponents do not deny the reality of Jesus' exorcism; they only argue that they are performed by the power of Satan.

2. *Exorcism in the Capernaum Synagogue.* Mark 1:21-28; Luke 4:31–47; Matt. 7:28-29.

3. *Evening Exorcisms.* Mark 1:32-34; Matt. 8:16; Luke 4:40-41.

4. *Galilean Exorcisms.* Mark 1:39; Matt. 4:23-25.

5. *Crowds are Cured.* Mark 3:7-12; Matt. 12:15-16; Luke 6:17-19.

6. *The Gerasene Demoniac.* Mark 5:1-20; Matt. 8:28–34; Luke 8:26-39. This is the only instance where there is a dialogue between the evil spirit(s) and Jesus. A request by the demons is granted.

7. *The Daughter of the Syrophoenician Woman.* Mark 7:24-30; Matt. 15:21-28. This is the only case in which Jesus exorcises without seeing the patient. The mother's faith is a factor.

8. *The Epileptic Boy.* Mark 9:14-29; Matt. 17:14-20; Luke 9:37-43. Here too, the faith of a parent is a factor.

9. *Mary Magdalene.* Mark 16:9; Luke 8:2. This is an incidental remark that Jesus exorcised seven demons.

This inventory gives the impression that Jesus is not an ordinary exorcist. His authority is presented as complete; he is seen by the demons as being closely related to God, and thus they fear him and obey him at the first injunction. Unlike common practice, he does not use paraphernalia, formulas, incantations, or lists of powerful names. He does use long and complex liturgies. This was a unique development, and the people had never witnessed anything like it before. It was so unusual that the religious authorities decided to investigate.

In the Beelzebul controversy, the investigators from Jerusalem did not deny that Jesus had the power to perform exorcisms. Neither did the rabbinic writers of later generations; like their predecessors of the first century, they claimed that his power was sorcery:

It has been taught: On the eve of Passover they hanged Yeshu. And an announcer went out, in front of him, for fourteen days (saying): "He is going to be stoned because he practiced sorcery" (Baraitha, *b. Sanhedrin* 43a. Tannaitic period. Goldstein, 22).

From the above list of individual exorcisms or general statements about them, it is also obvious that Mark is the main source of information for the subsequent Gospel writers. Thus, the criterion of multiple attestations is missing for specific instances of exorcism, but the widespread beliefs and practices of the time and the testimony from Qumran may be taken as alternative attestations about Jesus and exorcisms.

How did Jesus perceive himself in connection with his activity as an exorcist? Luke 10:18, John 12:31, and John 14:30 refer to the ultimate exorcism: the fall of Satan, or the end of his reign, or the end of his power over Jesus. These concepts are in harmony with the Qumranite expectations of the eschatological victory over Belial (*see* DEAD SEA SCROLLS) and may have been inspired by them. The exorcisms performed by Jesus according to the Gospels include the following features:

- The demons fear being destroyed or tormented: 3 times
- They acknowledge that Jesus is the "Holy One" or "son of God": 4 times
- Jesus operates by simple injunction (by virtue of special power): 4 times

These features tend to indicate that Jesus' exorcisms are seen as part of a wider battle against Satan, whose total destruction or final banishment is in process. Jesus is shown acting as if he had a definite role to play in Satan's defeat. The Jesus Seminar attributed a *pink* rating to Luke (Q) 11:19-20, "If it is by the finger/power of God that I cast out demons, then the reign of God has come to you." The same rating was given to Luke 10:18, "I saw Satan fall like lightning from heaven." In their opinion, Jesus' purpose was probably to defeat Satan. In Qumranite literature, it was the role of the Messiah to destroy Belial, but the analogy cannot be pushed too far. Jesus never proclaimed that he was the Messiah, except perhaps at his trial, as others did afterwards.

BIBLIOGRAPHY

Arav, R. "Architectural Manifestations in the Texts of the Aramaic Magic Bowls." *Studies in the Archaeology and History of Ancient Israel*, edited by Heltzer and Ali. (Hebrew, English summary). Haifa: University of Haifa Press, 1993.

Bonner, C. "The Techniques of Exorcism." *Harvard Theological Review* (1943): 39–49.

Borg, M. *Jesus. A New Vision.* San Francisco: Harper and Row, 1987.

Bottero, J. "Les morts et l'audelà dans les rituels en Accadien contre l'action des revenants." *Zeitschrift fur Assyroilogie und Vorderasiatische Archäologie* 73 (1983): 153–203.

Dupont-Sommer, A. "Exorcism et guérisons dans les écrits de Qumran." Supplément, *Vestus Testamentum* (1959–60): 246–61.

Edelstein, L. *Ancient Medicine*, edited by O. Temkin and C. L. Temkin. 1967. Reprint. Baltimore: Johns Hopkins, 1987.

Eliade, M. *Shamanism.* Bollingen Series 76. New York: Pantheon Books, 1974.

Goldstein, M. *Jesus in the Jewish Tradition.* New York: Macmillan, 1950.

Howard, J. K. "New Testament Exorcism and Its Significance Today." *Expository Times* (1984–1985): 105-9.

Isabell, C. D. *Corpus of the Aramaic Incantation Bowls.* SBL Dissertation Series. Atlanta, Ga.: Scholars Press, 1975.

Kee, H. C. "Short Studies: The Terminology of Mark's Exorcism Stories." *New Testament Studies* 14 (1967–68): 232–46.

———. *Miracles in the Early Christian World.* New Haven: Yale University Press, 1983.

———. *Medicine, Miracle and Magic in New Testament Times.* Cambridge, Mass.: Cambridge University Press, 1983.

Kirchschlager, W. "Exorcisms in Qumran." *Kairos* 18 (1976): 135–53.

Langdon, S. H. *Semitic (Mythology).* The Mythology of all Races Series. New York: Cooper Square, 1964.

Leeper, E. A. "From Alexandria to Rome: The Valentinian Connection to the Incorporation of Exorcism as a Pre-baptismal Right." *Vigilae Christiane* 44 (1990): 6–24.

McCasland, S. V. *By the Finger of God: Demon Possession and Exorcism in Early Christianity in the Light of Modern Views of Mental Illness.* New York: Macmillan, 1951.

McCullough, W. S. *Jewish and Mandaean Incantation Bowls in the Royal Ontarion Museum.* University of Toronto Press, 1967.

Neusner, J. *The Rabbinic Tradition about the Pharisees before 70.* 3 volumes. Leiden: E. J. Brill, 1971.

Philostratus. *The Life of Apollonius of Tyana*, translated by F. C. Conybeare. 2 volumes. Loeb Classical Library, Cambridge, Mass.: Harvard University Press, 1912–60.

Peuch, E. "IIQ Ps Apa: Un rituel d'exorcismes, Essay de reconstruction." *Revue de Qumran* 14 (1990): 377–408.

Rousseau, J. "Jesus in the World of Exorcism." *Jesus Seminar papers.* Sonoma, Calif.: Polebridge Press, 1992.

———. "Jesus, an Exorcist of a Kind." *SBL Seminar Papers*, 1993. Atlanta: Scholars Press (1993): 129–59.

Sabourin, L. S. J., "The Miracles of Jesus, 2. Jesus and the Evil Powers." *Biblical Theology Bulletin* 4 (1974): 115–75.

Tamborino, J. "De antiquorum doemonismo." *Religiousges chichtliche Versuchen & Verarbeiter* 7/3. Giessen Topelmann, 1909.

Tresson, P. "Mélanges. I. Un curieux cas d'exorcisme dans l'Antiquité. La stèle égytienne de Bakhtan." *Revue Biblique* 42 (1933): 57–78.

Vermes, G. "The Etymology of 'Esseness.'" *Revue de Qumran* 2.7 (1960): 427–43.

———. "Essenes, Therapeutai, Qumran." *Durham University Journal* (1961): 97–115.

———. "Essenes and Therapeutai." *Revue de Qumran* 3 (1962): 495–504.

Fishing, Nets

Importance

Jesus recruited fishermen as his first followers, was knowledgeable in matters of fishing, and applied the metaphor "fishers of men" to his disciples.

Scripture References

Matt. 4:18-21; 13:47; 17:27; Mark 1:16-19; Luke 5:1-7, 9-10; John 6:9; G. Thom. 8; (*see* BOATS).

General Information

Fishing was a significant economic activity in northern Palestine around the Sea of Galilee and in parts of the Near East. Tyre acquired international fame for its fishing; in the time of Nehemiah, Tyrians had settled in Jerusalem and imported fish, which they sold even on Sabbath (Neh. 13:16). The fish trade was certainly active before the Exile, for a gate of Jerusalem was named "Fish Gate" (2 Chron. 33:14). Within Palestine, fresh-water fish abounded in the Sea of Galilee, Lake Huleh, and the upper Jordan. Most of the fish sold away from their point of origin were salted, dried, smoked, or pickled and kept in jars (*see* MAGDALA and BETH-SAIDA).

Both archaeology and the Gospels represent fishing as a prosperous activity. Families or groups owned several boats, and worked as partners, employing hired hands. Some boat owners had special seals to imprint their trademarks on the handles of fish jars (*see* BETHSAIDA). Josephus writes that during the First Jewish War a certain Yeshua ben Shafat, who led the rebel forces out of Tiberias in the fall of 66 C.E. when the Roman legions arrived, was the leader of the Tiberias fishers and chief magistrate of the city (*Life* 12.66; *War* 2, 11.3/559). If this information is correct, the fisherman's seal of Bethsaida may have belonged to a guild and not to an individual or family. Fishing implements included spears, lines and hooks, wicker traps, dragnets or seines, throw nets, and trammels. Fish ponds were also used to trap the fish in shallow waters, especially in the reefy Jordan delta. Fishing methods did not change much from biblical times until shortly after World War II. What was observed in the late 1940s could be traced back to the Egypt of the third millennium B.C.E.

The ancient population of edible fish is still partly represented today by three surviving groups: the musht, the barbel, and the fresh water sardine. The name *musht* in Arabic means "comb," referring to the long dorsal fin characteristic of this kind of fish. The best-known representative of this group is the *Tilapia Galilea*, improperly called "Saint Peter's fish." It can be as long as sixteen inches and weigh as much as three pounds; it feeds only on plankton. During the warm months, from spring to fall, the musht population is distributed around the lake, but in winter musht move closer to the shore in schools to seek warmer waters. The area near Tabgha attracts many of these fish because of the warm springs; they can be caught there in large quantities with dragnets.

The barbel or carp (*cyrinidae*) is also called *biny*, a word of Semitic origin, which means "hair," referring to the barbs that hang at the corners of its mouth. The main survivors of this group in the Sea of Galilee are the long-head barbel (*kersin* in Arabic), shaped like a trout, and the *Barbus Canis* (*kishri* in Arabic). The former can reach 24 inches in size and weigh up to fifteen pounds. It stays near the bottom of the lake where it feeds on mollusks and small fish. The *Barbus Canis* is smaller, with a maximum size of sixteen inches and maximum weight of eight pounds; it has large scales. Feeding exclusively on small fish, it clings to schools of sardines (*see* fig. 26).

The most abundant fish in the Sea of Galilee, the fresh-water Kinneret sardine (*Anacanthobrana Terrae Sanctae*), represented about 50 percent of the fishing production of the lake. As the staple fish of the region, it was exported in salted, smoked, or pickled form. The main center of fish processing was Magdala called Migdal Nunia, "tower of fish," in Hebrew and Tarichae, "place of smoked fish," in Greek. Another fish is worth noting because it may have been referred to by Jesus, as will be seen below. It is the catfish (*Claries Lazera*) or *sfamnun*, "the mustached fish," in Hebrew. It is the largest of the lake fish, up to 40 inches in length and 20 pounds in weight. Because it lacks scales, it falls under the prohibitions of Leviticus 11:10 and Deuteronomy 14:11.

Commercial fishing was done with nets of three types: the dragnet or seine, the trammel, and the throw net. The seine (Hebrew *herem*, Greek *sagene*) was a large net, up to 1,000 feet long and 12 feet high in its center part. It formed a vertical wall in the water; its lower side was kept to the bottom by lead weights, and the higher side was pulled up with cork floats. At each end was a long triangular section making a transition between the higher center part and a pulling rope. At the beginning of the operation, the seine was loaded on the aft half-deck of a boat, one pulling rope remaining ashore with half of the crew. The boat then moved perpendicularly from the shore to a distance of at least 300 feet, turned at a right angle, spread the net parallel to the coastline, and made another right angle toward the shore bringing back the other pulling rope. The remaining crew left the boat, pulled it ashore, and started pulling its rope in unison with the other half of the crew at the other rope. As needed, the boat was pulled back to the water and one person dove from it to lift the bottom edge of the net over obstacles that stopped the motion of the net toward the shore. When the seine was near the shoreline, the fishers picked up the fish caught in it and hauled up the net on the boat as it emptied. Then they started for another location where the operation was repeated. This method of fishing was very popular in the ancient Mediterranean world, as attested in Egyptian tomb paintings of the third millennium B.C.E. and in a number of other sources. A boat capable of carrying such a heavy load and crew would have been at least 20 feet long (*see* BOATS).

Used individually, the throw net (Hebrew *kela*) was circular, 18 to 25 feet in diameter, with a rope in its center and lead weights on its circumference. It was cast by one person standing in a boat or on a rock near the lakeshore. The net was laid on one arm and shoulder and was then thrown with a large swing of the other arm. The net fell, fully deployed, like an opened parachute in the water, its weights pulling it down to the bottom. The fisher then dove in and picked up the fish one by one; or he pulled all the weights together and brought them out of the water, the net forming a sack with the fish in it. The throw net could be used from a boat in conjunction with a larger net like the trammel to catch more of the fish in the shoal encircled or trapped between the shore and the wall-like net. This method of fishing

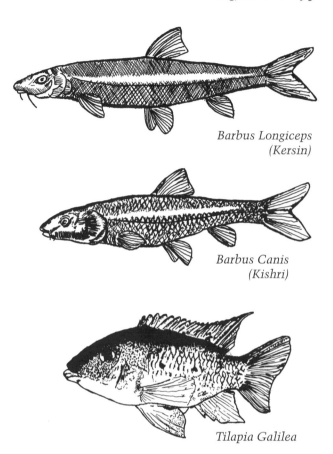

Barbus Longiceps (Kersin)

Barbus Canis (Kishri)

Tilapia Galilea

Figure 26 Common Fish on the Sea of Galilee. The two upper ones are bottom fish, feeding on molluscs. They are caught with lines and hooks (Matt. 17:27). The tilapia, a surface fish caught in nets, is erroneously sold under the name of "Saint Peter Fish."

was already ancient; complete throw nets were found in Egyptian tombs dating from the second millennium B.C.E.

Both the throw net and dragnet are mentioned in the Talmud. In one remarkable text the Babylonian Talmud tells of the existence of fishing rights, namely the rights to spread the *herem* and cast the *kela*, given by Joshua ben Nun to the tribe of Naphtali around the entire shoreline. For this purpose a strip of land at the south of the lake had been taken from the tribe of Gad and added to the territory of Naphtali, its width was "a full seine rope" (about 150 feet). According to M. Nun, the Hebrew Bible reference to seine fishing in Habakkuk 1:14-15 should read, in order to correspond to the reality of the operations: "And you make men as the fish of the sea, as the creeping things that have no rulers over them. They take up all of them with a fishing line, they drag them in their seine and gather them in their trapnet, therefore they rejoice and are glad" (*The Sea of Galilee and Its Fishermen*, 20–21). Other references to fishing nets found in the Hebrew Bible include Ezekiel 12:13; 17:20; 26:5, 14; 32:3; 47:10.

Another large net was the trammel, used for night fishing; it is still used today in the Mediterranean and in the Sea of Galilee. It is made of three nets attached to the same top and bottom ropes. There is a center net with a small mesh of 2-inch squares sandwiched between two nets with a large mesh of 5-inch squares. The center net is much higher than the two others to allow for its extension outside the large squares. The fish swim through a large square of the first net, push the center mesh until it goes through a large square of the third net forming a trap bag in which the fish are caught. The trammel comes in units about 115 feet long and 5 feet high. Several units were tied together and spread in the water to form a fence at the bottom of the lake. Lead weights and gourds maintained its vertical position. A series of trammels was set parallel to the shore; then, taking the boat halfway between the coastline and the net, the fishers splashed the water with their oars and made much noise to frighten the fish, which would dive to the bottom and swim away from the coast and be caught in the trammel. The operation was repeated several times during the night, and in the morning the crew washed the net. Because of its complex structure, the trammel was the only type of net that needed to be washed every day. The trammel could also be used in daytime in combination with a "veranda net." It was set in a circle, hanging by floats. On its edge, outside, all around the circle, another net was supported horizontally on the surface of the water by reeds. Seen from

above, the appearance of the two nets could have been that of a huge straw hat without a bottom. This system was used to catch musht. When a shoal of such upper-water fish was seen from the shore, boats went to encircle it with the combined nets. The fish jumping to escape from the vertical round net fell into the horizontal one.

Archaeological Information

We have already referred to several paintings of fishing scenes and entire throw nets found in Egyptian tombs. Many other scenes on reliefs, friezes, murals, vases, and lamps have been unearthed in Egypt, Mesopotamia, Greece, and the rest of the Mediterranean world, giving ample testimony to diverse ancient fishing methods, some of which are still in use today.

Directly relevant to first-century Palestine are the underwater remains of a number of breakwaters and small harbors around the Sea of Galilee (*see* fig. 4), and an immersed tank, made of plastered stones to store the fish caught in a seine, at Gergesa. Lead weights for nets have been discovered near Magdala and at Bethsaida, fish hooks at Capernaum and Bethsaida, a sail needle at Bethsaida and a net needle at Magdala, two line sinkers at Bethsaida, and several stone anchors and mooring stones in various places around the lake, the last one at Bethsaida in 1993. The most significant find has been the fisherman's seal of Bethsaida, found in 1989, and dated to no later than 67 C.E. (*see* BETHSAIDA).

A remark needs to be made regarding the well-known and widely duplicated mosaic of the Byzantine Church of the Multiplication at Tabgha. It depicts a basket of bread between two fish; but the fish has two dorsal fins while all the known fishes of the Sea of Galilee had only one. Two explanations are possible: either the fish of the mosaic belonged to an extinct species that still existed in the fifth century C.E., which is improbable; or the artist created a purely imaginative work without inquiring about the fishes of the lake. The latter explanation is more plausible, because other mosaics in the church represent plants and birds that were conventional decorations in an artistic genre inspired by Egyptian scenes.

Implications for Jesus Research

A study of ancient fishing techniques illumines several Gospel passages centered on fishing activities:

Mark 1:16–18. Jesus passing along the lake saw Simon and Andrew casting nets. The proximity of the two fishermen to the shore indicates that they were casting throw nets.

Matthew 13:47-48. The parable uses the image of a dragnet and the Greek word for net, *sagene*, a seine, is correct. The "bad fish" were likely of the catfish type, fish without scales that were forbidden in Pentateuchal law.

Matthew 17:24-27. The large fish caught with hook and line could not have been a musht, for this kind feeds only on plankton. Rather, it was a barbel, a voracious carp-like fish feeding on mollusks and fry. It is only for commercial purpose that the name "Saint Peter fish" has been attributed to the musht. The real fish caught by Peter would have been a barbel, and the bait on the hook a sardine.

Luke 5:1-7. Two boats, one belonging to Simon and Andrew, the other to James and John, were working in partnership. After a disappointing night, the fishermen came back, left their boats on shore and started washing their nets. All these details clearly point to musht fishing with a trammel. Jesus asked to borrow one of the empty boats to speak to the people from the water because sound carries better when its source is near the surface. While he was speaking, Jesus noticed a shoal of musht approaching the coast (thus it was winter) and informed Simon, who took advantage of the situation.

The same story appears in John's epilogue (John 21:4-8), but the absence of a telling detail, the washing of the trammel in the morning after a night's work, makes it less authentic. The situation is made worse by the addition of another element: "Simon Peter went aboard and hauled the net ashore, full of large fish, a hundred-fifty-three of them" (John 21:11). A heavy trammel full of fish could not have been brought ashore by one person. As seen above, the fish were taken out of the trammel by hand, one by one. Only with a throw net could Simon have brought his catch ashore, and the quantity of fish would have been much smaller. While the primary author of John is usually correct in his descriptions of sites or actions, here it seems obvious that this passage was written by a different author or editor. This observation supports the conclusions of a majority of Johanine textual critics that the twenty-first chapter of John is a later addition.

Jesus was apparently knowledgeable in fishing and had a close relationship with families involved in the fishing trade. In these circumstances it seems difficult to categorize him as a mere peasant (*see* SEA OF GALILEE and BOATS). In Matthew 13:47-48, Jesus describes a true-to-life fishing scene: he tells how the forbidden fish are discarded according to the proscriptions of Leviticus and Deuteronomy. In his teaching Jesus seems to have been respectful of the Torah as long as human welfare was not threatened.

BIBLIOGRAPHY

Goffen, M., ed. *The Lake Kinneret*. Tel Aviv, 1992.

Hornell, J. *Report on the Fisheries of Palestine*. London, 1935.

——. *Fishing in Many Waters*. Cambridge, 1950.

Nun, M. *Ancient Jewish Fisheries*. Tel Aviv, 1964 (Hebrew).

——. *The Sea of Galilee and Its Fishermen in the New Testament*. Kibbutz Ein Gev: Kinneret Sailing Co., 1989.

——. "Cast Your Net Upon the Waters." *BAR* 19 (1993): 46–56.

Gadara, Kursi

Importance

Jesus exorcised a demented man in the Decapolis, probably in the territory of Gadara.

Scripture References
Matt. 8:28; Mark 5:1; Luke 8:26, 37.

General Information
Gadara is mentioned indirectly in the Synoptics under the designation "country of the Gadarenes" or "Garasenes" or "Gergesenes." It was a city of the Decapolis, about 4 miles south of the Yarmuk and 7 miles east of the Jordan. It is identified with today's Umm Qeis. During the Hellenistic period, Gadara was one of the major cultural centers, the home town of the poet Meleager and of the Cynic philosopher Menippus (Strabo, *Geography* 16, 758). Under Ptolemaic rule, Gadara became the capital city of the district of Gilead, which became known as Galaaditis. When the Seleucids took control of Palestine and Syria, the city also was called Antiochia or Seleucia. During his first campaign the Hasmonean Alexander Jannaeus conquered it (Josephus, *Antiq.* 13, 15.4/396). Later, it was taken by Pompey, who rebuilt it and made it a government center (*Antiq.* 14, 5.4/91). Augustus granted it to Herod, and after the exile of his son Archelaus it was placed under the authority of the governor of Syria with the rest of his tetrarchy (*Antiq.* 17, 11.4/320).

Archaeological Data
In Roman times, Gadara was renowned for its hot springs. The remains of two theaters, a colonnaded street, and an aqueduct testify to its past splendor. The territory of the "Gadarenes" extended north of the Yarmuk, included the hot springs of Hammath Gader (Eusebius, *Onomasticon*), and perhaps stretched as far as the Sea of Galilee, south of Hippos. Thus, the location of the exorcism of Mark 5:1-17 and parallels would have been in the area east of the southern part of the Sea of Galilee.

Implications for Jesus Research
Although Kursi, with its Byzantine church and monastery on the northeastern shore of the Sea of Galilee, has been identified as Gadara or Gergesa and as the site of the exorcism and drowning of the swine, no remains dating from the first century C.E. were found there, which makes the site a most improbable location. However, the discovery of a tower and a chapel 200 meters (656 feet) south of the Byzantine church may support the identification of the site with the location of the miracle of the Gadarine swine.

Nevertheless, the pigs episode may be interpreted as an added satire mocking the Roman legions, which the storyteller envisioned as driven back to the Mediterranean, for the enjoyment of a Zealot audience. In this hypothesis, the original story would have been only the simple reporting of a dramatic exorcism performed by Jesus in the region of Gadara. Then, at the time of the First Jewish Revolt, a storyteller would have grafted on the basic fact his hilarious creation of a legion of pigs rushing to the sea and drowning because, as everyone would have understood, in the swiftness of the rebels' victory, there would not have been enough time for the Romans to bring a fleet to evacuate them. Pigs as Roman soldiers, and their debacle, that would have been a double hit! The date of such an addition might have been 66 C.E., when news of Vespasian arriving with his legions spread among the people—a date that fits with the date generally accepted for the final redaction of the Gospel of Mark.

In a different line of reflection, it has been suggested that Jesus could have been a Cynic in consideration of his life-style and attitude toward wealth and power. Although there is no scholarly consensus on the matter, Jesus may have been aware of Cynic philosophy, which had an influential center in Gadara, only eight miles from the Sea of Galilee.

BIBLIOGRAPHY

Applebaum, S. and A. Segal. "Geresa." *NEAEHL* 2: 470-79.

Blomme, Y. "Inscriptions Grecques à Kursi and Amwas." *Revue Biblique* 87 (1980): 404–7.

Burkett, F. C. "Gergesa. A Reply." *Journal of Biblical Literature* 27 (1908): 128–33.

Clapp, R. G. "A Study of the Place Names Gergesa and Bethabara." *Journal of Biblical Literature* 26 (1907): 62–63.

Livio, J. B. "L'Enigmatique pays des Géraséniens." *Bible et Terre Sainte* 152 (1973): 6–16.

Tzaferis, V. "Kursi." *NEAEHL 3: 893-96.*

Tzaferis, V. and D. Urman. "Excavations at Kursi." *Qadmoniot* 6 (1973): 62–64.

Galilean Caves

Importance

A number of natural caves in Galilee were used as hiding places in time of war or rebellion, as tombs, as cultic places, or even as dwellings in prehistoric and historical times.

General Information

Rocky hills with hundreds of natural caves exist throughout Israel: in Galilee, Mount Carmel, Samaria, the Shephelah , Judea, and the Negev. Many caves were used for different purposes such as shelter, rituals, storage, burials, hideouts. In Galilee, the most important caves are those of Arbela, Hayonim, Qafzeh, the Amud caves, and the cave discovered at Cana in 1990. (For the cave of Banias *see* CAESAREA PHILIPPI.)

Arbela or Arbel was a village a few miles west of Magdala in what is known today as Wadi el-Hamman. According to 1 Maccabees 9:2, a battle was fought in the plain of Arvel between the Maccabean insurgents and Bacchides, who defeated them. Later, when Herod conquered his kingdom, the Galilean rebels hid in the caves above the plain. In order to subdue them, he lowered his men down from the top of the vertical cliff in boxes and baskets to smoke the rebels out (Josephus, *Antiq.* 14, 15.5/422-24). The priestly family of Yeshua established its residence in Arbel after the destruction of the Second Temple.

The Hayonim Cave is located some ten miles west of the Sea of Galilee on the right bank of Nahal Izhar. Remains of several levels of occupation were found there.

Closer to Nazareth is the cave of Jebel Qafzeh, which was located in a narrow ravine descending to the plain of Jezreel. It contains evidence of prehistoric and historic occupation.

A complex system of caves exists in the gorges of Wadi Amud, a mountain stream that runs from the Safed area east to the Jordan Valley. The 60-to-90-foot-deep limestone gorges are situated about 5 miles west of the Jordan. An impressive natural limestone pillar (*amud* in Hebrew, thus the name of the Wadi) stands more than one mile from the lower entrance of the gorges.

Archaeological Data

At Arbela, the caves have been explored in 1987-89 by a team under Z. Ilan. Some 120 caves used from the Iron Age to the Roman Period were recorded. Four *miqvahot* were identified. The synagogue of Arbel was excavated by H. Kohl and C. Watzinger in the early twentieth century and by N. Avigad in 1968. Other Israeli teams have excavated the ancient village.

The Hayonim Cave was explored by O. Bar Yoseph and E. Tchernov beginning in 1965. They found several levels of occupation dating from prehistoric times to the Byzantine period; the remains included burials and numerous artifacts of stone, bone, and horn.

The Qafzeh Cave near Nazareth was first excavated in 1932 by R. Neuville and M. Stekelis, who discovered two historic and ten prehistoric levels of occupation. B. Vandermmeersch resumed the excavation in 1967 and added a wealth of information about prehistoric levels.

Historic and prehistoric layers were also found in the four caves of Wadi Amud thus far explored: the Emireh Cave by Turville-Petre in 1925, the Zattiyeh Cave by the same archaeologist in 1925-26, the Amud Cave A by Suzuki and Watanabe of the University of Tokyo in 1963–64, and Shaqbah Cave A by Binford in 1962.

Caves were used throughout the country for protection and to hide against enemies all through the ages. The most famous among these are: the Chalcolithic Cave of the Treasure in the Judean Desert, and the caves in the Shefelah and the

Judean Desert dating from the Second Jewish War (*see* JUDEAN CAVES).

Implications for Jesus Research

The Galilean caves may have had a role in the life of Jesus in several ways: as a boy, he perhaps heard the story of the rebels trapped in the Arbela Caves; in his youth he may have played in the caves around Nazareth, quite possibly in the Qafzeh Cave; as a man, during his ministry, he may have found shelter in caves, especially on his way to and from Phoenicia. He knew about the cave of Caesarea Philippi dedicated to the cult of Pan (*see* CAESAREA PHILIPPI), and he may have visited it. It is also possible that, when he withdrew to "isolated places" for his frequent moments of prayer, he used caves as retreats. Very early, a "cave theology" developed in the Christian tradition; caves of Mary and Joseph are shown in Nazareth, a cave of the Nativity in Bethlehem, and other caves on the Mount of Olives that Jesus is said to have visited (*see* JUDEAN CAVES; NAZARETH; BETHLEHEM; MOUNT OF OLIVES).

BIBLIOGRAPHY

Avi'am, M. "Secret Hideaways in Judea and Galilee." *Israel Land and Nature* 9, 3.4 (1983–84): 100–3.

Bar-Yosef, O. and E. Hovers. "Amud, Nahal." *NEAEHL* 1: 56-58.

Ilan, Z. and A. Izdarechet. "Arbel." *NEAEHL* 1.

The Society for the Research of Caves. *Migrot Zurim* (Hebrew).

Gamla, Gamala

Importance

The synagogue of Gamla is the only one known in or near Galilee that dates from the first century C.E.

General Information

Gamla is located in the Lower Golan, a region that was linked geographically to Galilee in ancient times, as indicated by Isaiah 9:1 and Matthew 4:15 ("across the Jordan, Galilee of the Gentiles,") and by Josephus, who reports that the revolutionary leader Judas the Galilean was from Gamla (*War* 18.1.1/4). The site is only 7 miles east of the Jordan and Bethsaida, at about the same latitude as the northern shore of the Sea of Galilee. A fortified settlement was built there on a nearly impregnable, isolated steep peak, shaped like a camel's back (*gamla* is Aramaic for "camel"), in the Daliyot Valley. The city is notable, among other things, for its role in the First Jewish War, and for its synagogue which, on the basis of coins of Alexander Jannaeus (103–76 B.C.E.) and John Hyrcanus II (63–40 B.C.E.) found there, is dated to the Hasmonean period. Gamla's perimeter wall followed the abrupt topography of the terrain in a way that made an attack on the site extremely difficult. Because of the steep slope, houses were built one against the other, half dug in the side of the hill, the retaining wall of one, mountain side, becoming the free standing wall, valley side, of the next house above it.

Access to the site is extremely difficult except on the northeast side where the top of the northern rim of the Daliyot Valley can be reached by a winding narrow path. Only three narrow flat areas were available to the city's builders. Two are on the eastern side of the city; the larger one near the only gate was chosen as the site of the synagogue, and the smaller one, well below it, contains the remains of an oil press. The third one is on a higher spot, at the western end of the ridge served as an acropolis.

In 66 C.E., when a general rebellion broke out against the puppet king Agrippa II, the Romans sent Vespasian to Palestine with two legions to support him. Flavius Josephus was appointed commander of the rebels' army in Galilee and began to reinforce the fortifications of all cities before the Romans arrived at Ptolemais (Acco). At Gamla, he ordered the obstruction of the gate and the widening of the wall. From Ptolemais, the Romans advanced through Galilee, conquering the rebel cities one after the other. The final battle occurred at Gamla. At first the Romans succeeded in breaching the wall; they rushed into the city, pursuing its defenders from roof to roof. But the roofs collapsed, and the attackers retreated precipitously, suffering severe losses. A second attempt, involving the sapping of the northwest tower, was successful. Rather than surrender, the defenders, taking their families with them to their death, plunged from the top of the wall into the deep ravine. Josephus (*War* 4, 1.10/83) describes at length the heroic resistance of Gamla and its tragic end in November 67 C.E. As in Masada, only two women are reported to have survived. Because the story of its tragic capture is similar to that of Masada, Gamla has been called the Masada of the north.

Archaeological Data

Gamla, first identified with eh Ahdab, a few miles to the southeast, was recognized in 1967 by Y. Gal, who spotted the camelback spur between two branches of the Daliyot. The same year, following Gal's suggestion, S. Gutmann began excavations on behalf of Israel's Department of Antiquities and Museums. The excavators soon realized that the site and its ruins corresponded to Josephus's description of Gamla. Furthermore, the site was fully visible from Magdala-Taricheae where Josephus had his headquarters and so could communicate with it by signals. The finds make sense in light of much of Josephus's account. The wall was indeed reinforced and the gate obstructed; in some places, the wall is 20 feet thick. The site was strewn with stone catapult balls and iron arrowheads. Remains of walls, stone stairways, doorposts, and lintels of the houses were unearthed. Basalt, locally abundant, served as the main building material as in the rest of the Golan and eastern Galilee. No limestone material was imported (*see* fig. 27).

Because the building generally identified as a synagogue certainly dates to Jesus' time, it will be examined in some detail. Just south of the only gate, inside the city and abutting the fortification wall, lie the ruins of a rectangular structure, 65 x 53 feet. On the short side, away from the fortification wall, is a narthex or exedra, 10 feet wide x 29 feet long, protecting the main entrance, which is oriented toward Jerusalem. On the southern long side, running along the wall, is a street about 10 feet lower than the floor of the building; a staircase at the back of the synagogue leads to this street. At the western end of the building, against the slope and north of the narthex, are several rooms and a *miqveh* receiving water by a channel. This last find may indicate that the building was a synagogue.

Four levels of the stone benches set in steps run along the four walls of the synagogue, except at the main entrance. The interior is divided by two rows of columns into a central nave and two aisles, one on each side; the corner columns, three of which, heart shaped, were found in situ. An additional bench runs along the back wall, which is on the eastern side. Only the space between the columns and the walls was paved with large slabs; the floor of the central area was of beaten earth as in other buildings of the same period. This is perhaps because only the peripheries areas were submitted to heavy foot traffic; the central area was probably covered with woven rugs. Some stones in the nave between the third columns from the back may have served as the base for two columns supporting the roof. Or, alternatively, they may have been part of a podium, from which Scriptures were read. A small recess in the north wall, near the northwest corner and slightly above the floor was perhaps the station of a warden watching the entrance or a niche for the Torah Scroll. The façade had two entrances: the main one in the center, about 5 feet wide and a narrower one, 3 feet wide, between the main entrance and the northern wall. The few fragments of decoration did not include representations of humans or animals, as were common in synagogues of later periods (*see* fig. 28).

In looking at the Gamla synagogue or public building along with those of Masada and Herodium, which were built by the Zealots (*see* MASADA and HERODIUM), three basic architectural features of these large first-century structures can be noted:

- There are three or four rows of columns parallel to the side and back walls.

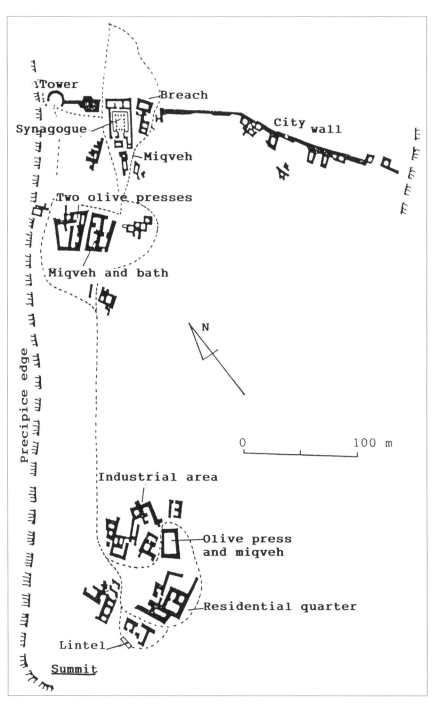

Figure 27 Gamla Excavations *(Israel Department of Antiquities and Museums)*

Gamala. *The synagogue as seen in 1993.*

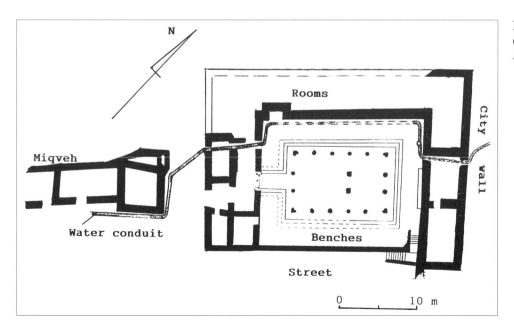

Figure 28 The Synagogue of Gamla *(After Zvi 'Uri Ma'oz, 1992)*

- The entire area between the columns and the walls is occupied by benches arranged in steps along the walls.

- The benches extend around the four walls, which allows the persons in attendance to face each other and to focus their attention on the center of activity.

As in the Hellenistic assembly halls (ec*celesiasterion* of Priene, *bouleteria* of Heraclea and Notium, and *telesterion* of Eleusis), the primary factor taken into consideration is the seated public. Individuals are able to interact freely and to hear the speeches or readings made at the center of the hall at the level of the lowest benches. It is noteworthy that these early Jewish public buildings apparently followed the model of a Greek public assembly house.

Implications for Jesus Research

There is no explicit record that Jesus visited Gamla, even though it was only a two-hour walk from Bethsaida and a Jewish city in the tetrarchy of the benevolent Herod Philip.

The features of the public building or synagogue of Gamla, also found in Masada and Herodium, may represent the physical conditions in the synagogues where Jesus is said to have spoken or performed healings and exorcisms. The congregation was not sitting in rows or pews as in most modern synagogues and churches, with everyone facing a focal point—Torah cabinet, cross, altar, pulpit, reading or communion table—at or near the end wall. Instead, the focal point was the center of the building, and all those in attendance could see clearly what was happening and hear what was read or said. They could also perceive the physical or verbal reactions of all around them and share or oppose the feelings so expressed. The basic concepts were that of mutual awareness and freedom of expression among participants, which would make the meetings lively and sometimes even rowdy (*cf.* Jesus' visit at Nazareth and the reactions in the synagogues visited by Paul).

BIBLIOGRAPHY

Unfortunately, detailed reports in English of the Gamla excavations have not been published at the date of this writing.

"Gamla, the Masada of the North, The Fall of Gamla by Flavius Josephus." *BAR* 28 (1992): 21–37; 5 (1979): 12–27.

Gutmann, S. "Gamla, First Three Seasons Excavations." 1981 (Hebrew).

———. "Gamla, First Eight Seasons Excavations." 1986 (Hebrew).

———. "The Synagogue at Gamla." *Ancient Synagogues Revealed*, edited by E. I. Levine, 30–34. Also in English: *Ariel* 52 (1982): 18–25.

———. "Gamla 1983." [Short Report]. *Excavations and Surveys in Israel* 3 (1984): 26–27.

———. "Gamala." *NEAEHL* 2: 459-63

Gutmann, S. et al. "Gamla 1987–88." *Excavation and Surveys in Israel* 9 (1989–90): 9–11.

Levine, L. I. "Synagogues," *NEAEHL* 4: 1421-24.

Maoz, A. "The Synagogue of Gamla and the Typology of Second Temple Synagogues." *Ancient Synagogues Revealed*, edited by L. I. Levine. Detroit: Wayne State University Press, 1982.

Garden Tomb

Importance

The Garden Tomb is considered the site of Jesus' burial by some Protestant denominations.

Scripture References

Matt. 27:32, 60; Mark 15:22, 46; Luke 23:32, 53; John 19:17, 20, 41-42; Heb. 13:11-12.

General Information

In Jerusalem, north of the Damascus Gate between Nablus Road (Derekh Shekkem) and Salah-ed-Din Street, is a Muslim cemetery on a low hill. On the south, next to the eastern side of the Dominican Convent and French Ecole Biblique, the hill was quarried for limestone, and an artificial vertical wall there has an opening to what is called the Garden Tomb. Near the top of the cliff at a short dis-

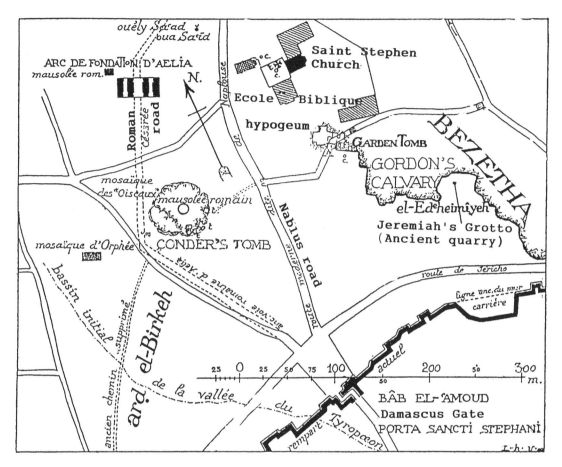

Figure 29 Garden Tomb. Ancient map showing the respective locations of the hypogeum in the Dominican property, the Garden Tomb and Gordon's Calvary. (*Ecole Biblique et Archéologique*)

tance to the east, two large caves, side by side, and fissures in the rock give the appearance of a gigantic skull when seen from the top of the city fortification wall (*see* fig. 29).

A tomb at the foot of this hill was discovered in 1867 by the landowner while he was removing refuse dumped on his property. The removal of a 5-foot deep heap of trash accumulated at the foot of the cliff revealed two openings into the rock. The owner reported the discovery to the German architect, B. C. Schick, who was then working in

Jerusalem. The two openings were the narrow, low entrance to a cave and a small window. The cave was filled with human bones and skulls up to 2 feet below its horizontal roof. On the eastern side, a red cross with Greek letters between its branches was painted on the wall. After the owner removed the skeletal remains, a second door leading to a second chamber was noticed. The owner died in 1870 and the property was sold. General Gordon of Britain visited the site in 1883 and became convinced that it was Jesus' tomb and that the cliff with the image

The Garden Tomb. *The groove at the foot of the wall. Notice the slope at the left end.*

of the skull was Golgotha. He initiated the creation of the Garden Tomb Association in England in 1894, and the association purchased the property. The ground was cleared, and excavations revealed a large cistern and a wine press. The property was eventually developed into a pleasant, peaceful garden.

The Dominicans excavated their own property adjacent to the Association's garden. They exposed the remains of a medieval chapel next to Nablus Road in 1881. In 1885, they discovered an underground hypogeum* hewn in the rock extending to about 10 feet from the Garden Tomb. This large necropolis* was last surveyed in 1975. The tombs do not have the typical *kokhim* and *arcosolia* (*see* JERUSALEM, TOMBS) of the end of the Second Temple period. Their features are characteristic of the Late Iron Age (800–600 B.C.E.). The burial chambers have benches on the back and side walls with headrests hewn in the rock. Some of them were reused

at a later period. During their excavations, the Dominicans found a slab bearing a Greek inscription, "Private tomb of the deacon Euthymios Pindiris." In the fifth century C.E., this tomb became part of the first monastery built around what is known as the *martyrium* of Stephen where, according to tradition, the first deacon of the Church had been stoned to death (Acts 7:58). In the fifth century, the Iron Age tombs had been transformed into a typical Byzantine necropolis,* characterized by hewn troughs covered with horizontal slabs and by crosses scratched on the walls. These tombs contained oil lamps of the period, which allowed for the dating of the Euthymos epitaph. During the Crusaders period, a number of Christian tombs, with scratched or red painted crosses, were added around the hypogeum. They are all in the area of what is known as Jeremiah's tomb, between Stephen's place of execution and the northern wall of the old city. There, the excavators uncovered many stone troughs, possibly those of the Crusader's *Asnerie* (donkey stables), and a large cistern.

Also found on the Dominicans' property were the remains of the first basilica built by Empress Eudocia, where the relics of the martyr Stephen were kept. In 1889, under an ancient pavement in the same area, another slab inscribed in Greek was found. Its many abbreviations made deciphering difficult, but Papadopoulos-Karameus read it as follows: "Private tomb of the deacon Nonnus Onesimus of the Holy Anastasis of Christ and of this monastery." Since Constantine's time, the name of the rotunda of the Church of the Holy Sepulchre had been *Agia Anastasia*, "Holy Resurrection," thus the name used by some denominations, "Church of the Holy Resurrection." This discovery evoked a series of far-fetched claims, such as:

> "There are strange rumors afloat about an inscription found at St. Stephen's . . . It is said that the Romanists are anxious to hush up the discovery, as it would damage the credit of the Church of the Holy Sepulchre. A person who has seen and read it informs me that its contents are somewhat to the following effect: 'I, Eusebius (sic), have desired to be buried in this spot, which I believe is close to the place where the body of my Lord lay' " (*Northern Christian Advocate*, Syracuse, N. Y., 7 November 1889).

The supporters of the Garden Tomb apparently had won their cause. A long polemic followed and continues to this day. A "task force" led by W. B. McBirnie from California investigated the matter in Jerusalem in 1974 but ignored the findings of the hypogeum.* He concluded that the Garden Tomb was most probably the true sepulcher of Jesus.

Archaeological Information

The burial cave of the Garden Tomb has no features of a first-century Jewish tomb. Instead of the typical *kokhim* or *arcosolia*, it contains only trough tombs identical to those of the nearby necropolis* with, on its walls, crosses accompanied by the Greek letters Alpha and Omega typical of the Byzantine period. During the Crusaders period, it was perhaps transformed into a pilgrims' shelter with a window hewn in its façade to give light to the second chamber. It is clear that the Crusaders transformed the tomb because the top of the façade was shaped like a Gothic arch according to the well-known formula of medieval French architects: R=3B/5, with R=radius and B=base (*see* fig. 30). The beginning of another arch is visible on the right. The top of the hill crumbled and the arch is not as clearly visible today as it was at the beginning of the century. The Crusaders also hewed grooves for shelves in the walls.

In its current state, the tomb contains two adjacent chambers hewn along the façade of the quarry wall. The first one may be entered from the south through an enlarged opening in the vertical wall of the hill. Two steps lead to the floor below the door sill. An inner entrance on the eastern side leads to the second chamber, but the partition wall now is not higher than the top of the trough graves. Its floor is about eighteen inches below the floor of the first room. The inner surfacing of the walls and ceilings is rougher than that of the hypogeum,* which could have been the result of Crusader reworking. In the first chamber, 10 x 8 feet and 6.5 feet high, are traces of an early trough grave opposite the entrance. The second chamber contains three large trough graves. The side of the one along the north wall was destroyed and a niche was hewn in the wall, at the eastern end, perhaps to bury the body of a person taller than the original length of the tomb. Remains of painted crosses and Greek monograms were still visible on its walls when it was found. Inside, three oil lamps and shards of a burnished deep bowl were unearthed. The bowl dates to the late Iron Age, and the Byzantine date of the oil lamps suggests a later use of the chamber.

At the base of the façade runs a rock-cut groove, 26 feet long. It has been suggested that this groove may have been hewn by the Byzantines as a trough for watering their animals and was used later for the same purpose by the Crusaders. However, it is too long, narrow, and low for such a use. Besides, on

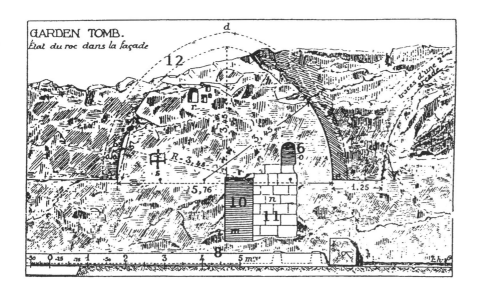

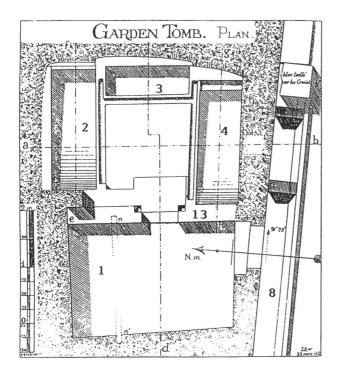

Figure 30 The Garden Tomb As It Was In 1925 (*Ecole Biblique et Archéologique, Jerusalem*)

1, 2, 3, 4: Trough tombs; 1 was destroyed.

5: Byzantine cross; under it, the wall is hewn in an arcosolium shape.

6: Opening probably made by the Crusaders.

7: Extension of tomb hewn in the rock.

8: Groove hewn in the rock. It slopes to the east at 1° 25′ below the horizontal level.

9: Western extremity of the groove showing a difference of level.

10: Entrance. It had been enlarged. The vertical distance between lien XY and the bottom of the groove may indicate the maximum diameter of a disc-shaped stone perhaps used to close the entrance.

11: The original facade collapsed and was walled up.

12: The arch made by the Crusaders.

13: Interior wall torn down to the level of the trough tombs.

the left end it slopes downward as do grooves used to hold the large stone discs used to close tombs in the first century C.E. around Jerusalem. Moreover, the façade of the wall was chiseled to make it a perfectly flat, vertical surface, an operation not needed for an animal water trough. The width of the groove is exactly the same (about two feet) as that of the groove for the rolling stone door of the so-called Tomb of the Kings, which is in fact the tomb of Queen Helena of Adiabene and her family, dated to the first century C.E. (*Palestine Exploration Fund, Quarterly Summary* [1889]: 130). The arguments in favor of the Garden Tomb thus may seem to balance those against it with respect to its possible first century C.E. date and its reuse as a burial place.

Implications for Jesus Research

The overall conclusion is that there is no evidence that the Garden Tomb was that of Joseph of Arimathea in which Jesus was temporarily buried. It originally dates from the late Iron Age, as do the nearby tombs of the hypogeum.* Because it was reused in the Byzantine and Crusaders periods, it could have also been reused in the first century C.E. But no coins or pottery have been found to support this hypothesis. The only positive indication of a first-century-C.E. date is the groove, with an inclined section at its western end, and the well-dressed, plain, vertical façade in analogy with the groove of the tomb of Queen Helena of Adiabene. Even if its use in the first century C.E. could be established, it would not mean that it was indeed the tomb of Joseph of Arimathea.

Nevertheless, the general location of the Garden Tomb is more plausible than that of the traditional site of the Holy Sepulchre and Calvary. The place was undoubtedly outside the city wall, a fact not archaeologically established for the Holy Sepulchre. It also meets the requirement of high visibility for executions (*see* CRUCIFIXION). The Romans and the Jews (stoning of Stephen) may have used the same execution ground. The location, north of the main gate from which two roads branched out toward Samaria, Galilee, Phoenicia, and Damascus, was the site of heavy traffic. The strongest argument in favor of this general location is the absence of first-century Jewish tombs, clearly identified as such, west of the Temple Mount within a 2,000 cubit (about 1,100 yards) radius from the sanctuary (*see* GOLGOTHA, TRADITIONAL SITE).

BIBLIOGRAPHY

Barkay, G. "The Garden Tomb. Was Jesus Buried Here?" *BAR* 12 (1982): 40–53.

Barkay, G. and A. Kloner. "Notes and News. Burial Caves North of Damascus Gate." *IEJ* 26 (1976): 55–57.

Heydet, J. "Où se trouve à Jerusalem le lieu de la Lapidation de St. Etienne? Etude Critique et Topographique." Jerusalem: Imprimerie des P. P. Franciscains, 1887.

McBirnie, W. S. *The Search for the Authentic Tomb of Jesus.* Montrose, Calif.: Acclaimed Books, 1978.

Murphy-O'Connor, J. "The Garden Tomb and the Misfortunes of an Inscription." *BAR* 11 (1985): 54–57.

Vincent, L. H. "Chronique. Garden Tomb. Histoire d'un Mythe." *Revue Biblique* 34 (1925): 401-31.

See also the Bibliographies under GOLGATHA, TRADITIONAL SITE and JERUSALEM, TOMBS.

Gennesareth (Hebrew, *Ginosar*)

Importance

Jesus visited the area of Gennesareth and performed healings there.

Scripture References

Matt. 14:34; Mark 6:53.

General Information

Gennesareth is probably to be identified with Chinnereth, one of the fortified towns of Naphtali (Josh. 19:35), for which the fertile plain where it stood was named. Its proposed location is that of Khirbet el-Oreimeh, six miles north of Tiberias. This site may have guarded part of the Via Maris between Hazor and Hattin. In the Roman period the area was known as the plain of Gennessar. According to Matthew and Mark, Jesus performed healings there and many were cured by touching "even the fringe of his garment." Josephus considered the plain of Gennesareth one of the most fertile areas in the Land of Israel. He describes at length its qualities, its favorable climate, and the abundance of its fruits (Josephus, *War* 3, 10.8/506–21).Talmudic sages made similar statements. In one passage it is asked why such a rich and fertile plain does not exist near Jerusalem. The answer is that the pilgrims coming to Jerusalem should not make delicious fruits the reason for their pilgrimage.

Archaeological Data

Exploratory excavations at Khirbet el-'Ureime identified as the site of Chinnereth, took place under P. K. Rephaim (1911). A. E. Mader and Schneider continued the work (1931–32). A. Bea excavated on behalf of the German Oriental Institute (1939). Large scale excavations were carried out by V. Fritz of the University of Mainz, Germany from 1982 to 1985. These projects show that the site was first settled in the Early Bronze Age (thirtieth to twenty-sixth centuries B.C.E., when it was surrounded by a thick wall. The next period of habitation, the Iron Age II (eleventh to eighth centuries B.C.E.), represented the major occupation of the site and may have obliterated evidence of the Middle and Late Bronze Age (eighteenth to twelfth centuries B.C.E.). The Bronze Age cities were mentioned in the Egyptian sources. The Iron Age city consisted of a lower town and a fortified acropolis surrounded by a strong wall. This town was destroyed, perhaps by the Assyrians, in the eighth century B.C.E. The Gennesereth of the time of Jesus was a small hamlet situated within the remains of the Iron Age acropolis walls. By the Roman period, the population around the Sea of Galilee had shifted to Magdala, Capernaum, Chorazin, and Bethsaida.

Implications for Jesus Research

Jesus visited both sides of the Sea of Galilee, often by boat (*see* BOATS), from the plain of Bethsaida to the plain of Gennesareth. The territory around the northern half of the Sea of Galilee was occupied by a largely Jewish population; it is perhaps one of the reasons why Jesus lived there for a while. It may be in that area, not too far from Tiberias (John 6:23) and on "the other side" from Capernaum (John 6:1, 24-25), that the feeding of the multitude occurred.

BIBLIOGRAPHY

Fritz, V. "Kinneret." *IEJ* 32 (1982): 255–56; and 34 (1984): 190–91.

Koeppel. "Der Tell 'Ore' me und die ebene Genesareth. Vorbereitende Untersuchungen zu einer Grabang." *Biblica* 13 (1932): 298–308.

Mazar, B. "Kinneret." *NEAEHL* 3: 872-73.

Negev, A. "Chinnereth." *AEHL*. Rev. ed. New York: Thomas Nelson, 1986, 86.

Gethsemane

Importance

Gethsemane is the place where Jesus was arrested.

Scripture References

Matt. 26:36; Mark 14:32; Luke 22:39-40; John 18:1.

General Information

The name Gethsemane derives from the Hebrew *gath sehnanim*, "oil presses." In the Gospels, it designates the place where Jesus agonized and was arrested. Two parallel traditions point to an area in the lower part of the Mount of Olives, across the Kidron Valley from the city and Temple, at a short distance from the city gates. It was probably an olive grove with an oil press. One tradition is centered on a cave near the "Tomb of the Virgin" or "Tomb of Mary," and a shrine was built there in the fourth century. Egeria (or Aetheria) indicates that the Jerusalem Christians, at the time of her pilgrimage (385–88), revered two locations: the cave where they said Jesus withdrew to pray, "where a fine church was built," and the Garden of Gethsemane where he was arrested. Arculf, the seventh century pilgrim, visited the cave and describes a rock bearing the imprint of "Jesus' knees." The Franciscans keep a "Grotto of the Agony" at this location, which began to be used for burials in the fourth century.

Another tradition locates the Garden of Gethsemane a few hundred feet to the south of the cave and slightly higher on the slope; the Armenian, Greek, Latin (Franciscan), and Russian Orthodox churches all own properties there. The two main landmarks are the Russian Church of Magdalene and the Church of All Nations (or the Franciscan Basilica of the Agony). Adjacent to the latter is an olive grove about 55 yards square, with some of its large trees perhaps more than a thousand years old. The grove was enclosed by the Franciscans in 1884 but is open to the public. This area corresponds to that given by Eusebius and Jerome (see fig. 31).

Archaeological Data

In 1937, trenches were cut in the area of the Grotto of the Agony and the site was excavated in 1972–73. Byzantine tombs were found near a fifth-century church known as the Church of Saint Mary in that location. Channels in the floor of the grotto and a hole in the ceiling, probably cut to give light, indicate that it was originally an oil press site. Farther south, under the Church of All Nations (built in 1924), are the remains of two ancient churches. The older one, built by Emperor Theodosius I (379–383), was excavated in 1902–1920 by the Franciscans under P. G. Orfali, who later worked at Capernaum. This Byzantine church was 65 x 54 feet; several capitals, column bases, and

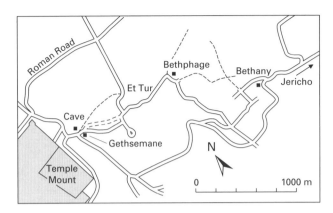

Figure 31 Respective Locations of Bethany, Bethphage, and Gethsemane on the Mount of Olives *(After Murphy-O'Connor)*

remains of mosaic floors were unearthed. The altar was built over a large flat rock, which has been designated as the "Rock of Agony." The church was destroyed by the Persians in 614 and a contiguous one was built by the Crusaders in the 12th century.

Implications for Jesus Research

The exact place where Jesus was arrested cannot be located with certainty. Nevertheless, the general area of the foot of the Mount of Olives fits the description given by the Gospels and also the topographic and economic data. Olive processing would have been done there, in a location easily accessible from the city. An olive press owner could well have offered hospitality to Jesus and his disciples (John 18:2).

BIBLIOGRAPHY

Murphy-O'Connor, J. *The Holy Land.* New York: Oxford University Press, 1980.

Thorsen, D. A. D. "Gethsemane." *ABD.* 2:997–99.

Wilkinson, J. *Jerusalem as Jesus Knew It.* 1978. Reprint. London: Thames and Hudson, 1982.

Golgotha, Traditional Site

Importance

According to a tradition dating to the beginning of the fourth century C.E., Golgotha and Jesus' tomb lie under the Church of the Holy Sepulchre.

Scripture References

Matt. 27:32, 60; Mark 15:22, 46; Luke 23:33, 53; John 19:17, 20, 41-42; Heb. 13:11-12.

General Information

Before the First Jewish War (66–70 C.E.), the members of the primitive Church in Jerusalem seem to have congregated in the area, wrongly called Mount Zion today, between the building where David's Tomb and the Upper Room are shown and the ancient Gate of the Essenes. According to Eusebius, the first Christians of Jerusalem, under the leadership of Shimeon ben Clopas, left for Pella in the Decapolis before the siege of Jerusalem by Titus (*History of the Church* 3.5, 11, 32). There is no evidence of their return in Jerusalem and of the continuity of the tradition regarding the location of Golgotha. After the Bar Kokhba War (132–135), Emperor Hadrian razed Jerusalem and built a new Roman city, Aelia Capitolina, from which Jews were banned under penalty of death, except for one day a year. Hadrian erected various temples and shrines, among which was a shrine to Venus on the location of today's Church of the Holy Sepulchre. For this purpose a quarry, which occupied most of the area, was filled with earth and debris and was paved.

There is no evidence, before the fourth century C.E., that Christians showed a special veneration for certain holy places. Origen visited Palestine about 230 and mentions only Bethlehem and some wells near Ashkelon (Jerome, *De Virus Illustribus* 3.54). Eusebius (ca. 260 to ca. 340), who became bishop of Caesarea, is the first to indicate the possible location of Golgotha in his account of the origins of the Church of the Holy Sepulchre:

[Constantine] realized that he ought to display the most blessed place of the Savior's Resurrection in Jerusalem in a worthy and conspicuous manner. So without delay, he gave orders that a house of prayer should be erected. As soon as he had issued his order, this false device [Venus' shrine] was cast to the ground with its images and gods. The Emperor also commanded that . . . a large area of the foundation soil, defiled as it was by devil worship, should be dug away to a considerable depth and removed . . . As layer after layer of the subsoil came into view, the venerable and holy memorial of the Savior's resurrection, beyond all our hopes, came into view. Thereupon the Emperor . . . gave orders that a house of prayer should be built in the precincts of the Saving Cave, rich, royal and magnificent. It was as though he had long foreseen all this and had by some superior acumen known what was going to happen (John Wilkinson, *Egeria's Travels to the Holy Land*, 164–68).

The wording of the second half of this passage seems to indicate that the discovery of a cave was fortuitous; the shrine of Venus was torn down along with other pagan shrines and temples in Jerusalem. There is no description of the cave that was found, and it is impossible to know if it was a typical Jewish tomb of the first century C.E. However, by 333, the tradition was well established according to an account of the Bordeaux Pilgrim:

As you leave there [Zion] and pass through the wall of Zion toward the Gate of Neapolis [Damascus gate], down in the valley on your right you have some walls where Pontius Pilate had his house . . . on your left is the hillock of Golgotha where the Lord was crucified and, about a stone's throw from it, the vault where they laid his body, and he rose again on the third day. By order of the Emperor Constantine there has now been built a basilica—I mean a place for the Lord—which has beside it cisterns of remarkable beauty, and beside them a bath where children are baptized.

Incidentally, the Bordeaux Pilgrim also indicates that, in his time, the residence of Pilate, thus the *praetorium*,* was probably believed to be in the Antonia (*see* ANTONIA, PAVEMENT), east of the main street going to the northern gate of Neapolis, and not in the former palace of Herod in the west.

In his sermon on the death of Theodosus in 395, Ambrose is the first to mention Helena, mother of Constantine, in connection with the alleged discovery of three crosses, the *titulus*, and two nails in a nearby cistern. Six years later, Rufinus added details on how the true cross was recognized from that of the two robbers (Matt. 27:38 and parallels): a funeral passed by; Helena ordered that the three crosses be presented one after the other over the body; at the last one, supposedly that of Jesus, the dead man rose up. Later, other versions of the pseudo-miracle circulated.

One of the key factors for determining the authenticity of the tomb tradition for Golgotha is whether it was inside or outside the fortification wall. According to the Jewish rules of the times it could not have been within the city. Most reconstructions of the period on maps or models accordingly show a sudden change of direction of the second wall eastward so that the Church of the Holy Sepulchre is left outside the city (see JERUSALEM, WALLS AND GATES). But no archaeological find substantiates this theory. As early as 1883, Colonel C. R. Conder of the British Corps of Engineer testified:

No military man could, for one moment, admit that the second wall ran down into the deep valley instead of occupying the saddle to the west . . . [also] there remains the fact that the traditional sites are certainly within Aprippa's wall which was built only eleven years after the crucifixion to defend the suburbs which could probably have taken in those days more than eleven years to attain the extent necessitating a new line of fortification ("The Holy Sepulchre," 73).

Even a strong supporter of the theory, R. M. Mackowsky, admits that, "His [Josephus's] summary description, moreover, is much too brief to delineate a wall with any degree of exactness, and it leaves many important questions unanswered, especially with regard to any gates and special towers that certainly must have been built into it. We must rely on the logic of strong Middle East traditions in this case" (*Jerusalem City of Jesus*, 49).

As seen above, there is no such strongly historically established tradition to determine with certainty the location of the site. Other significant factors must be considered:

• The only reference to an existing tomb in early Christian literature is to that of David (Acts 2:2). All other texts that can be dated to the period 30–313 C.E., except for the Gospels, are silent about the existence and location of the tomb of Joseph of Arimathea.

• No Jewish tomb that can be dated with certainty to the first half of the first century C.E. has been found in the area. A monument dedicated to Joseph Hyrcanus who died in 104 B.C.E. is the nearest, about 230 yards in the southwest of the hillock proposed as Calvary, in a location which, in his time, could have been outside the city wall (see fig. 32).

• Three tombs dated to the late first century B.C.E.-first century C.E. are located farther west or south: Herod's family tomb above the western rim of the Valley of Hinnon, Jason's tomb one and a half miles southwest of Jaffa Gate, and the tomb of Caiaphas more than two miles south of the Temple Mount.

• Tradition cannot be taken as evidence because there are too many examples of incorrect locations or name attributions in ancient traditions: for instance, the tombs of David, Absalom, Zechariah, the Kings, the Patriarchs and others, and more recently, the Stone of Bethsaida (see BETHSAIDA).

• The Church of the Holy Sepulchre is not near a gate historically known in the time of Jesus. The Ganneth Gate of Josephus (Garden Gate), as its name indicates, could have been a gate opening to a garden, not on well-traveled roadways as was customary for a Roman-style crucifixion. This gate was probably a mere postern, because its location is unknown and it is not otherwise mentioned in early literature.

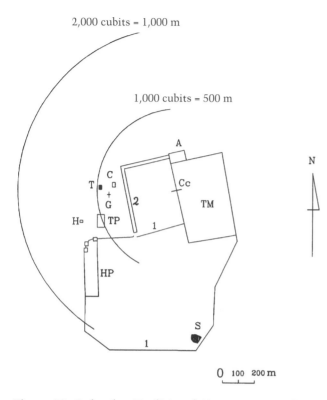

2,000 cubits = 1,000 m

1,000 cubits = 500 m

0   100   200 m

Figure 32 Golgotha, Traditional Site. Respective locations. G: Golgotha; T: Tomb; C: Helena's cistern; H: Hyrcanus monument; TP: Towers Pool; A: Antonia; TM: Temple Mount; S: pool of Siloam; HP: Herod's Palace: 1: First wall; 2: Hypothetical second wall; Cc: Center of circles.

• An execution ground at the site of the Church of the Holy Sepulchre would have been too close to Herod's palace, not a pleasant sight for his courtiers and guests enjoying the scenery from the top of the three high towers north of the palace.

• Even if they are wrong, established traditions tend to be respected, especially if they are supported by religious fervor. Until 1990, the model of Herodian Jerusalem next to the Holy Land Hotel in Jerusalem showed a green Hill of Calvary close to the fortification wall ("On a Hill, Faraway," as the popular hymn goes). From the military standpoint, it was absurd; it would have allowed attackers to find shelter and help them build a ramp for war ma-

chines. In 1990 common sense and the results of archaeological work led to the replacement of the green hill by a quarry. However, the rock hillock was reconstructed rising above the level of the ground measured at the top of the quarry which could not have been the case (*see* fig. 33). Besides, it would have been impossible to erect three crosses on the rounded top of the rock; there would not have been room for the executioners and the condemned. The Romans, in expectation of future Christian beliefs, would hardly have taken the extra pain to plant three upright posts on the top of a rocky dome eight feet in diameter in order to create an elevated Calvary.

• The 1980 survey by A. Kloner of the first-century tombs of Jerusalem revealed that no tombs were within 2,000 cubits (about 1,100 yards) west of the Temple. This was in accordance with the Jewish belief that no source of impurity could exist west of the Temple because the prevailing winds would carry the miasma to the holy site and defile it (*see* JERUSALEM, TOMBS and fig. 47). The Temple Scroll stipulates: "You shall make three areas, divided from one another, where the lepers, those suffering from a flux, and men who had a (nocturnal) emission (will be set apart). . . . You shall set apart in the midst of your land areas where you shall bury your dead" (col. 46, 48). Y. Yadin compared these stipulations with two later rabbinical statements: "Rabbi Yohanan said: One is not permitted to pass within four cubits of a leper. Rabbi Simon ben Lakhish said: Within a hundred cubits. There is no contradiction . . . [The first] meant when there is no wind blowing" and . . . [the second] meant when there is wind blowing" (m. Leviticus Rabbah 16). The other is: "Rabbi Mana would walk with people afflicted with boils. Rabbi Abaya said to him: Do not walk east of him, but rather to the west of him." Yadin concluded:

> There can be no doubt that the stress that the lepers were to be isolated in a separate place east of the city was prompted by the belief that this disease was contagious and carried by the wind (*The Temple Scroll*, 177).

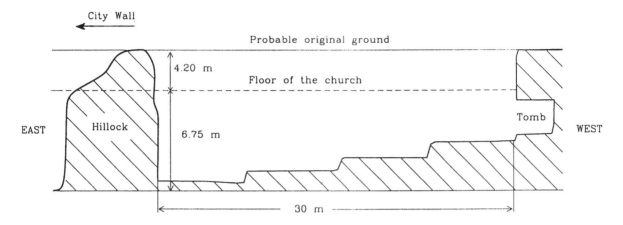

City Wall

Probable original ground

4.20 m

Floor of the church

EAST   Hillock   Tomb   WEST

6.75 m

30 m

Figure 33 Rock of Golgotha and Tomb. Traditional site. Section seen from the north. Dimensions and scale are approximate.

The distribution of burials in fig. 47 shows that the same interdiction was observed for tombs. This is a most important argument against the authenticity of the site.

• A Roman Catholic archaeologist, C. Coüasnon, who worked as codirector of the restoration of the Church of the Holy Sepulchre, commented in his 1972 Schweich Lectures that:

"One cannot actually prove that the present site which has been considered the authentic one since the year 326 is beyond any doubt the same as that venerated by the Christian community . . . In spite of everything [in the tradition] there remains some room for uncertainty" (*Schweich Lectures for 1972*).

Interestingly, in an article for Roman Catholic laity written the following year, Coüasnon mentions "The rock of Calvary . . . near the Gate of Ephraim . . . this mound of earth [sic] where stand the gallows of the city. Three upright posts." (*Bible et Terre Sainte*, 10-15). In these few lines he indirectly states: a) that it was improbable that the crosses could be planted on a rock, because he replaces "rock" by "earth," b) that the most likely site was beyond the northern wall, because the Gate of Ephraim was in the north, most likely on the site of today's Damascus Gate.

• Another Catholic archaeologist, F. Diez, concludes a 1984 article on the Holy Sepulchre with these words: "The work of Corbo, Coüasnon, Economopoulos gave information of the Byzantine and Crusaders periods, very little on Aelia, nothing on the prior period. The main Christian problem remains unchanged" ("Le Saint Sepulchre. La recherche archéologique," 28–37).

Archaeological Information

The excavations of the Muristan* and in the foundations of the Lutheran Church of the Redeemer by K. Kenyon and D. V. Lux revealed no traces of a Hasmonean or Herodian wall that would that provide evidence that the site of the Church of the Holy Sepulchre was indeed outside the city. In 1960, an agreement was reached between the three main denominations, Latin Catholic, Armenian, and Greek Orthodox, for the restoration of the Church of the Holy Sepulchre. The work was conducted from 1961 to 1981. In 1961, fourteen soundings were made to locate the foundations of the building. Most went down to bedrock and provided

Figure 34 Reconstructed Holy Sepulchre.
(according to Florentino Diez) A: Block
detached from cliff; B: Original cliff; 1: Stairs;
2: Entrance and hypothetical rolling stone;
3: Antechamber ("Chapel of the Angel");
4: Burial chamber; 5: Hypothetical arcasolium
and marble slab; c-d: Hypothetical line of separation; 1 and 2 would have been eliminated.

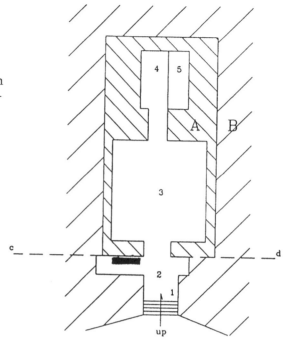

information for the construction of a model by T.
Ball. It appeared that the surface covered by the
present building was a quarry from the Iron Age II
until the time of the Exile (586 B.C.E.). It descended
in successive levels from the west to the hillock in
the east (*see* fig. 33). In order to isolate the sepulchre, the artificial wall of the quarry had been
hewn as was also done for the so-called Tombs of
Absalom and Zechariah. The volume below the
horizontal plane corresponding to the top of the
cliff had been filled with earth and debris. The
maximum depth of the quarry was about 36 feet
(11 meters).

Implications for Jesus Research

It cannot be archaeologically or historically established that the Church of the Resurrection stands
on the site of the Golgotha of the Gospels and that
it was outside the fortification wall of Jerusalem as
it existed in the time of Jesus.

The heavily decorated tomb shown today to pilgrims is only a tentative reproduction of that
which was carved out of the cliff in the fourth century. The tomb designated as that of Joseph of Arimathea was first destroyed in 614 by the Persians.
Rebuilt by Modestos, it was destroyed again by
the Fatimid Al Hakin in 1009. The Crusaders
built another one that was consumed by fire
in 1808. The edicule existing today is the fourth
version of the tomb (*see* fig. 34). Nevertheless, it is
still revered by many Christians, especially the
Greek Orthodox. The Roman Catholics center
their devotion on the rock hillock that can be seen
behind glass panes. Near the tomb, a slab of imported marble, the "Stone of Unction," is en-
shrined. It was brought there in 1810, but it is said

that it is on this slab that Joseph of Arimathea and Nicodemus embalmed Jesus. Significantly, no remains of marble have so far been found in or near first-century Jewish tombs. Even the houses of the wealthy did not contain large objects of marble (*see* UPPER CITY).

The proponents of the authenticity of the site rely heavily on a reconstructed Christian tradition:

• James, brother of Jesus, who became leader of the Jewish Christians in Jerusalem some time between 41 and 44 C.E., must have known the location of Golgotha.

• Luke visited Jerusalem *circa* 57 C.E. (Acts 21:15-18) and met with James. He certainly learned about the location and passed the information to the members of his church. Thus, when James, brother of Jesus, was executed by the High Priest in 62 C.E. (Josephus, *Antiq.* 22, 9.1/199–203), the tradition was not broken.

• James was succeeded by Shimeon ben Clopas who also certainly knew about the location. He led the Jewish Christians out of the country to Pella at the beginning of the First Jewish War in 66. The tradition was preserved by this group of Christians and their descendants.

• According to Eutychus, Patriarch of Alexandria in the tenth century, these Christians returned in the fourth year of Vespasian, which coincided with the fall of Masada, in 73. Consequently, the Palestinian tradition would have been all the more reliable.

• If, after the Second Jewish War of 132–135, the city was razed, the quarry filled, a new Roman city built over it, and the Jews excluded from it (except on the ninth of Ab every year), it may be assumed that the tradition was not broken: gentile Christians who had lived in Jerusalem before 132 remained there; they assured the continuity of the tradition and Eusebius mentions the existence of a gentile bishop of Aelia named Marcus soon after the construction of the new city (*Church History*, 4.6; 5.12).

• According to Epiphanus (*Panarion* 66.20), the last Jewish Christian bishop, Judah *Kyriakos* (from the family of Jesus?) lived until the eleventh year of Antonius Pius (148/149). He would have had a memory of the site and transmitted it to others.

• Julius Africanus (ca. 160–240) and Origen (ca. 185–254) both knew of a tradition according to which the "tomb of Adam" was located at Golgotha. This tradition perhaps inspired Constantine and his mother Helena (R. Riesner, "Golgotha").

• Gentile Christians were indeed interested in holy places before 313; Origen's friend Alexander, future bishop of Cappadocia, visited Palestine ca. 212 in order to pray and "investigate the places" (Eusebius, *Church History* 6.11, 12).

This is the array of arguments on which the supporters of the authenticity of the traditional site of Golgotha base their claim. Clearly more research must be done in order to find, if ever possible, archaeological or literary evidence that will clarify the location of Golgotha.

BIBLIOGRAPHY

Bahat, D. "Does the Holy Sepulchre Church Mark the Burial of Jesus?" *BAR* 12 (1986): 26–45.

Broshi, M. "Evidence of Early Christian Pilgrimage to the Holy Land Comes to Light in the Holy Sepulchre Church." *BAR* 3 (1977): 42–44.

———. "Recent Excavations in the Church of the Holy Sepulchre." *Qadmoniot* 10 (1977): 30–32 (Hebrew).

Broshi, M. and G. Barkay. "Excavations in the Chapel of St. Vartan in the Holy Sepulchre." *IEJ* 35 (1985): 108–28.

Conder, C. R. "The Holy Sepulchre." *Palestinian Exploration Fund Quarterly Summary* (1883): 73.

Coüasnon, C. "Le Saint Sepulchre. Les fouilles de 1971–1977," *Le Monde de la Bible* 2 (1978): 44–45.

———. "Le Golgotha, maquette du sol naturel." *Bible et Terre Sainte* 149 (1973): 10–15.

———. "The Holy Sepulchre. Excavations." *Schweich Lectures for 1972*. London: Oxford University Press, 1974.

Diez, F. "Le Saint Sepulcre—La recherche arachaeologique." *Le Monde de la Bible* 33 (1984): 28–37.

Kenyon, K. *Digging up Jerusalem*. London: Ernest Benn, 1974.

Kloner, A. *The Necropolis of Jerusalem in the Second Temple Period*. Ph.D. diss. Hebrew University, 1980 (Hebrew, English summary).

Mackowski, R. M. *Jerusalem City of Jesus*. Grand Rapids: Eerdmans, 1980.

Manns, F. "Saint Sepulchre III. La tradition littéraire pré-Constantinienne (Ier-IIIème Siècles)." *Dictionnaire de la Bible*, 1987.

Nicholson, O. "Holy Sepulchre, Church of the," *ABD* 3:258-60.

Riesner, R. "Golgotha." *Das grosse Bibellexikon*.

Wilkinson, J. *Egeria's Travels to the Holy Land*. rev. ed. Jerusalem: Ariel, 1981.

Yadin, Y. *The Temple Scroll*. New York: Random House, 1985.

———. *Jerusalem Revealed. Archaeology in the Holy City 1968–1974*. New Haven: Yale University Press, 1976.

Gospel Of Thomas

Importance

The Gospel of Thomas, discovered in 1945, reveals a new aspect of Jesus' teachings as recorded in a Christian Gnostic community of the first four or five centuries C.E.

Scripture References

Matt. 10:3; Mark 3:18; Luke 6:15; John 11:16; 20:24-28; 21:2; Acts 1:13.

General Information

As the Church struggled to define its orthodoxy, many early Christian texts were lost; some were systematically destroyed as heretical. For example, the Gospels of the Nazareans and of the Egyptians survive only in some quotations in the writings of the Church Fathers. The collection of sayings called the Gospel of Thomas (not to be confused with the Infancy Gospel of Thomas) was known to have existed because it is mentioned in the works of Jerome, Origen, and Hippolitus. In the fourth century it was considered heretical by Cyril of Jerusalem and subsequently disappeared. Thanks to a chance discovery by a peasant in 1945, near Nag Hammadi in Upper Egypt, a Gnostic library of thirteen codices, came to light (see "Archaeological Data" below). Among them was, in codex 2, the Gospel of Thomas, a collection of 114 sayings attributed to Jesus. Some seventy of them have parallels or near parallels in the canonical Gospels; but several have a simpler form, which leads a number of scholars to argue that they are more primitive and perhaps more authentic.

An international team of five scholars, A. Guillaumont, H.-Ch. Puech, G. Quispel, W. Till and Y. 'Abd Al Masih, produced the first translation simultaneously in English, French, and German in 1959. The language of Thomas was Sahidic Coptic, an Egyptian language of the first centuries C.E., transcribed by Christian missionaries with the Greek alphabet. Although the codex can be dated to the fourth to fifth centuries C.E., the original was much earlier. It probably was written first in Greek about 140 C.E. from even older sources; a majority of scholars today agree that most of those sources go back to the last two thirds of the first century C.E. Several of the *logia** could be traced back to Jesus.

After the publication of the Gospel of Thomas, Puech connected it with papyri fragments found in the late 1890s by British archaeologists in an ancient trash depository about 95 miles downstream from Nag Hammadi. The location was Oxyrhynchus and the fragments were named after the place. The most important is POxy 1, a complete sheet with a Greek text reproducing sayings attributed to Jesus dated to about 300 C.E. Substantial texts were also contained in POxy 654 and 655. Puech noticed that POxy 654 contained the prologue and first seven sayings of the Gospel of Thomas; POxy 1 contained sayings 28 to 33; and POxy 555 contained sayings 37 to 40. He concluded that the three fragments were part of the original Greek text of the gospel of Thomas. That at least some of the sayings originated in Jesus' time is indicated by the presence of logion 12, which refers to James, brother of Jesus and head of the Jerusalem Church, who was stoned in 62 C.E. by order of the High Priest Ananus (Josephus, *Antiq.* 20, 9.1/197–203): "The disciples said to Jesus, 'We know that you will leave us; who is going to rule over us?' Jesus said to them. 'Wherever you are you will go to James the Righteous for whose sake heaven and earth came into being . . .' "

Archaeological Data

Like the Dead Sea Scrolls discovered at about the same time, the Nag Hammadi Library and especially the Gospel of Thomas are among the most important finds of this century in providing new perspectives on the historical Jesus and on early Christianity. Muhammed Ali, the Egyptian farmer, who made the discovery in December 1945, had left with his brother to go to a certain place at the foot of the cliff of Jabal at Tariff, near the village of Hamra Dom, some 6 miles northwest of Nag Hammadi. Local farmers used to mine the nitrogen-rich soil there in order to fertilize their fields. They found a jar containing thirteen codices of papyrus bound in leather. Inscriptions deciphered later indicated that they came from the area of Chenoboskion, which was a center of ancient monastic life. The documents, sold in Cairo, did not attract much attention until three years later when Jean Doresse, a French scholar temporarily working for an antiquities dealer, made an inventory of all the sayings of the codices and recognized their historical and theological value. Due to political and international circumstances, photographs of the documents were not published until 1957, when the translators could at last begin their work (*see* fig. 35).

Implications for Jesus Research

The importance of the Gospel of Thomas discovery is still far from being fully evaluated with respect to its implication for the knowledge of the historical Jesus. Still, a few reasonable inferences can already be made. Here we will limit ourselves to a discussion of the identity of Didymos Judas Thomas, the primitive form of some *logia,** Jesus' concept of the Kingdom or Reign of God, Jesus' concept of salvation, and information about female disciples.

The text begins with this *incipit*: "These are the secret sayings that the living Jesus spoke and Didymos Judas Thomas recorded." Who is this Judas? First, it must be noticed that only Judas is a real name, Didymos (Greek) and Thomas (Aramaic) are the same nickname, Twin. This reflects the fact that the Near East was a multilingual world in the time of Jesus; both Aramaic and Greek were commonly used together with other languages according to location (*see* CAVE OF LETTERS). Thus, the author to whom the book is attributed is Judas the Twin, but which Judas and whose twin? Was it Judas Iscariot? Although this possibility seems unlikely in light of current information, it cannot be discarded a priori.* Also in the Gospels is a "Judas (not Iscariot)" (John 14:22), who is specifically called "Judas Thomas" in the Syriac version of John 14:22. Another Judas, brother of Jesus, appears in Mark 6:3 and Matthew 13:55; the Letter of Jude (Judas) begins with "Judas, a servant of Jesus Christ and brother of James." Because James was a brother of Jesus and became the first "bishop" of Jerusalem, it is possible that this Judas claimed brotherhood only with James and presented himself as a servant of his oldest brother Jesus out of modesty and reverence for the venerated founder of the new movement. The Fourth Gospel refers several times (John 11:16; 14:5; 20:24-26) to Thomas "the Twin," which is redundant. Consequently, this Judas may have been the twin brother of Jesus, as some have proposed. With the limited data available, it may be just logical to infer that Judas was the twin brother of James.

The apocryphal Acts of Thomas, which is sometimes cited in the debate, is of no help. It does not explicitly state that Judas-Thomas was Jesus' twin; it only says that "The king . . . saw the Lord Jesus bearing the likeness of Judas-Thomas . . . The Lord said to him, 'I am not Judas which is also called Thomas, but I am his brother' " (not "his twin," Acts of Thomas 11). Because Jesus and Judas were brothers, they did not have to be twins to look

Log. 1–4

80 10 These are the secret words which the Living Jesus spoke and Didymos Judas Thomas wrote.

12 (1) And He said :

Whoever finds the explanation (ἑρμηνεία) of these words will

14 not taste death. (2) Jesus said:

Let him who seeks, not cease seeking until he

16 finds, and when (ὅταν) he finds, he will be troubled, and when he has been troubled, he will

18 marvel and he will reign over the All. (3) Jesus said: If

20 those who lead you say to you: "See, the Kingdom is in heaven",

22 then the birds of the heaven will precede you. If they say to you: "It is in the sea (θάλασσα),"

24 then the fish will precede you. But (ἀλλά) the Kingdom is within you and

26 it is without you. If (ὅταν) you (will) know yourselves, then (τότε) you will be known

and you will know that you are

81

2 the sons of the Living Father. But (δέ) if you do not know yourselves, then you

4 are in poverty and you are poverty. (4) Jesus said: The man old in days will not

6 hesitate to ask a little child of seven

8 days about the place (τόπος) of Life, and he will live. For many who are first shall become last

Pl. 80^10–81^9

80 10 ⲛⲁⲉⲓ ⲛⲉ ⲛ̄ϣⲁϫⲉ ⲉⲑⲏⲡ̅ ⲉⲛⲧⲁⲓⲥ ⲉⲧⲟⲛϩ̅
ϫⲟⲟⲩ ⲁⲩⲱ ⲁϥⲥϩⲁⲓⲥⲟⲩ ⲛ̄ϭⲓ ⲇⲓⲇⲩⲙⲟⲥ

12 ̈ⲓⲟⲩⲇⲁⲥ ⲑⲱⲙⲁⲥ (1) ⲁⲩⲱ ⲡⲉϫⲁϥ ϫⲉ ⲡⲉ
ⲧⲁϩⲉ ⲉⲑⲉⲣⲙⲏⲛⲉⲓⲁ ⲛ̄ⲛⲉⲉⲓϣⲁϫⲉ ϥⲛⲁ

14 ϫⲓ ϯⲡⲉ ⲁⲛ ⲙ̄ⲡⲙⲟⲩ‘ (2) ⲡⲉϫⲉ ⲓⲥ̅ ⲙⲛ̄ⲧⲣⲉϥ‘
ⲗⲟ ⲛ̄ϭⲓ ⲡⲉⲧ‘ϣⲓⲛⲉ ⲉϥ‘ϣⲓⲛⲉ ϣⲁⲛⲧⲉϥ‘

16 ϭⲓⲛⲉ ⲁⲩⲱ ϩⲟⲧⲁⲛ‘ ⲉϥϣⲁⲛϭⲓⲛⲉ ϥⲛⲁ
ϣⲧⲣ̄ⲧⲣ̄ ⲁⲩⲱ ⲉϥϣⲁⲛϣⲧⲟⲣⲧⲣ̄ ϥⲛⲁⲣ̄

18 (blank) ϣⲡⲏⲣⲉ ⲁⲩⲱ ϥⲛⲁⲣ̄
ⲣⲣⲟ ⲉϫⲙ̄ ⲡⲧⲏⲣϥ̄ (3) ⲡⲉϫⲉ ⲓⲥ̅ ϫⲉ ⲉⲩϣⲁ

20 ϫⲟⲟⲥ ⲛⲏⲧⲛ̄ ⲛ̄ϭⲓ ⲛⲉⲧ‘ⲥⲱⲕ ϩⲏⲧ‘ ⲧⲏⲩⲧⲛ̄
ϫⲉ ⲉⲓⲥ ϩⲏⲏⲧⲉ ⲉⲧ‘ⲙⲛ̄ⲧⲉⲣⲟ ϩⲛ̄ ⲧⲡⲉ ⲉ

22 ⲧⲡⲉ ⲉⲓⲉ ⲛ̄ϩⲁⲗⲏⲧ‘ ⲛⲁⲣ̄ ϣⲟⲣⲡ‘ ⲉⲣⲱⲧⲛ̄ ⲛ̄ⲧⲉ
ⲧⲡⲉ ⲉⲩϣⲁⲛϫⲟⲟⲥ ⲛⲏⲧⲛ̄ ϫⲉ ⲥϩⲛ̄ ⲑⲁ

24 ⲗⲁⲥⲥⲁ ⲉⲓⲉ ⲛ̄ⲧⲃⲧ‘ ⲛⲁⲣ̄ ϣⲟⲣⲡ‘ ⲉⲣⲱⲧⲛ̄
ⲁⲗⲗⲁ ⲧⲙⲛ̄ⲧⲉⲣⲟ ⲥⲙ̄ⲡⲉⲧⲛ̄ϩⲟⲩⲛ‘ ⲁⲩⲱ

26 ⲥⲙ̄ⲡⲉⲧⲛ̄ⲃⲁⲗ‘ ϩⲟⲧⲁⲛ ⲉⲧⲉⲧⲛ̄ϣⲁⲛ
ⲥⲟⲩⲱⲛ ⲧⲏⲩⲧⲛ̄ ⲧⲟⲧⲉ ⲥⲉⲛⲁⲥⲟⲩⲱ

ⲧⲏⲛⲉ ⲁⲩⲱ ⲧⲉⲧⲛⲁⲉⲓⲙⲉ ϫⲉ ⲛ̄ⲧⲱⲧⲛ̄ ⲡⲉ

81

2 ⲛ̄ϣⲏⲣⲉ ⲙ̄ⲡⲉⲓⲱⲧ‘ ⲉⲧⲟⲛϩ̅ ⲉϣⲱⲡⲉ ⲇⲉ
ⲧⲉⲧⲛⲁⲥⲟⲩⲱⲛ ⲧⲏⲩⲧⲛ̄ ⲁⲛ ⲉⲓⲉ ⲧⲉⲧⲛ̄

4 ϣⲟⲟⲡ‘ ϩⲛ̄ ⲟⲩⲙⲛ̄ⲧϩⲏⲕⲉ ⲁⲩⲱ ⲛ̄ⲧⲱⲧⲛ̄
ⲡⲉ ⲧⲙⲛ̄ⲧϩⲏⲕⲉ (4) ⲡⲉϫⲉ ⲓⲥ̅ ϥⲛⲁϫⲛⲁⲩ ⲁⲛ

6 ⲛ̄ϭⲓ ⲡⲣⲱⲙⲉ ⲛ̄ϩⲗ̄ⲗⲟ ϩⲛ̄ ⲛⲉϥϩⲟⲟⲩ ⲉϫⲛⲉ
ⲟⲩⲕⲟⲩⲓ ⲛ̄ϣⲏⲣⲉ ϣⲏⲙ ⲉϥϩⲛ̄ ⲥⲁϣϥ̄

8 ⲛ̄ϩⲟⲟⲩ ⲉⲧⲃⲉ ⲡⲧⲟⲡⲟⲥ ⲙ̄ⲡⲱⲛϩ̅ ⲁⲩⲱ
ϥⲛⲁⲱⲛϩ̅ ϫⲉ ⲟⲩⲛ̄ ϩⲁϩ ⲛ̄ϣⲟⲣⲡ‘ ⲛⲁⲣ̄ ϩⲁ

Figure 35 Gospel of Thomas. Facsimilie of the first edition published by E.J. Brill (Leiden) and Harper and Row (New York) in 1959. The first page of the text is represented. This edition preceded a more extensive work published simultaneously in German, French and English. The original text is in Coptic, a script created by second century Christian missionaries in Egypt. They used the Greek alphabet to transliterate the Egyptian language of the time.

alike. Besides, the document contains contradictions and in another passage cites Thomas and Judas as two different individuals in a list of apostles: "Thomas and Matthew . . . and Judas the brother of James" (Acts of Thomas 1). Still more surprising, Jesus is depicted as selling his own brother, "Judas-Thomas," as a carpenter slave to a merchant from India. The Acts of Thomas is therefore not a reliable source for deciding whether Didymos Judas Thomas was the twin brother of Jesus. What may be said with some degree of probability is that a Judas non-Iscariot and Thomas were the same person. He could have been the brother of Jesus, twin or not; but more likely he was the Twin of James. Some European scholars argue that the name Didymos derives from the Milesian shrine of Didymes and that Thomas could have been a native of Miletus in western Asia Minor raised in the shrine.

Certain *logia** have a simpler form than their parallels in the Synoptics; some scholars qualify this shorter form as more "primitive." For example, take Gospel of Thomas 63:

> Jesus said, "There was a rich man who had much money. He said, 'I will use my money to sow, reap, plant and fill my storehouses with crops and I will lack nothing.' This is what he thought in his heart. But that night he died. Who has ears, let him hear."

To consider this simpler version as more primitive than its parallel in Luke 12:16-21 involves two assumptions: a)the oral and written traditions always expanded and never abbreviated an original saying; and b) Jesus uttered only dry parables and stern aphorisms and would not use words like "drink" "be merry," "fool" nor draw any conclusion himself as he does according to Luke's text. Neither of these assumptions may be valid. The second does not allow for Jesus to have had the character of a Semitic speaker or storyteller addressing a crowd.

Gospel of Thomas 8 is a fish parable comparable to Matt. 13: 47–50:

> And he said, "The man is like a wise fisherman who cast his net into the sea; he pulled it up from the sea full of small fish; among them he found a large (and) good fish. That wise fisherman threw all the small fish back into the sea, he chose the large fish without regret. Who has ears, let him hear."

In this case we have two different scenes. In Gospel of Thomas 8 there is a single fisherman with a throw net; in Matthew a team of fishermen pulls ashore a seine or dragnet (*see* FISHING, NETS). Both stories may be authentic because Jesus was so much involved with fishing. The fisherman of Thomas acted as a true professional; he returned to the water the small fish that still had to grow (he would catch them later) and kept the large one that was sufficient to feed himself and his family. It is a story that the population of the lake area would certainly have understood.

Other sayings without any context that could help to elucidate the message seem rather meaningless, even in a purely Gnostic theology. Such is the case for the Gospel of Thomas 89:

> Jesus said, "Why do you wash the outside of the cup? Do you not understand that he who made the inside is also he who made the outside?"

It may be a shorter form of Matthew 23:25 = Luke = Q 11:39-41, but it seems incomplete. The first sentence could have been: "Why do you wash the outside and not the inside?" and the lesson would have been: "Care as much for your inner virtues as you do for your outside appearance because God made both." Matthew's form, in a context of opposition, makes more sense.

It is a formidable task to sort out what is a genuine saying of the historical Jesus from what is not. In the absence of well established and testable criteria, insight can be gained by examining Jesus' context. In our search for Jesus' concept of the Kingdom or reign of God, two sayings in the Gospel of Thomas seem to reinforce or clarify concepts appearing in the canonical Gospels:

> His disciples said to him "When will the Kingdom come?" [Jesus said:] "It will not come by waiting for it. They will not say, 'See, here,' or 'See, there.'

But the Kingdom of the Father is spread upon the earth and men do not see it." (Gospel of Thomas 113).

Jesus said, "If your leaders say to you, 'See, the Kingdom is in heaven,' then the birds . . . will precede you. If they say to you, 'It is in the sea,' then the fish will precede you. But the Kingdom is within you and it is outside of you" (Gospel of Thomas 3, first half).

These sayings are strikingly coherent with Luke 17:20-21; Mark 1:15; 12:34; Matthew 12:28; Luke 10:9, 11; 11:20; John 3:3. They indicate that Jesus' concept of the Kingdom, if eschatological, was not cataclysmic-apocalyptic. It was probably quite different from the concept contained in some Son-of-Man sayings (see SON OF MAN) and in Qumranite writings (see DEAD SEA SCROLLS). The historical Jesus probably did not expect a cataclysmic end of the world, but rather the end of an era and of his contemporaries' wrong attitude toward God. This, of course, did not preclude his anticipation of a political disaster such as the destruction of the Temple (see CONSTRUCTION, and EXORCISM).

Another remarkable feature is that, like Q, the sayings collection of the Gospel of Thomas does not pay much attention to the Crucifixion and its redeeming effect. Instead, as in John and as suggested by some passages in the Synoptics, salvation is to be found in Jesus' words, by following his teaching:

And he said, "Whoever finds the explanation of these words will not taste death" (G. Thomas 2).

Jesus said, "You have desired many times to hear these words which I speak to you and you have no other from whom to hear them" (G. Thomas 38, first half).

Jesus said, "I took my stand in the middle of the world and in flesh I appeared to them; I found them all drunk, I found none athirst among them. And my soul was afflicted for the sons of men because they do not see that they came empty into the world (and that) they seek to go out of the world still empty. But now they are stunned. When they have shaken off their wine, then they will repent" (G. Thomas 28).

Several passages in the Synoptics and John can be compared with these sayings: Matthew 13:19; Mark 4:14; Luke 8:11; John 1:1, 14; 6:63, 68; 8:51–52. But Matthew 24:35 is the most suggestive: "Heaven and earth will pass away, but my words will not pass away." From the beginning of Christianity, a number of Jesus' followers apparently did not believe that he sacrificed himself on the cross for their redemption but rather that he brought them "words of life" for their salvation.

It has long been noted that Jesus had a favorable attitude toward women and the Gospel of Thomas provides the names of two of Jesus' first female disciples:

Salome said, "Who are you, man, and whose [son]? You did take place upon my bench and eat from my table" . . . [Salome said:] "I am your disciple." (61) Simon Peter said to them, "Let Mary go out from among us, because women are not worthy of life." Jesus said, "See, I shall lead her, and I will make her male so that she too may become a living spirit, resembling you males. For every woman who makes herself male will enter the Kingdom of Heaven" (Gospel of Thomas 114).

This Salome may be the "mother of the sons of Zebedee" (Matt. 27:56) and the same as the Salome mentioned in Mark 15:40-41 and John 16:1. Mary could be either Mary Magdalene, who is said to have experienced the first appearance of the resurrected Jesus (John 20:11-18), or Mary of Bethany, "who sat at the Lord's feet and listened to his teaching" (Luke 10:39). *Logion* 114 is the last saying of the collection and may be seen as its conclusion. It obviously indicates a sense of masculinity as the norm. Men are seen as the only humans who can become "living spirits," and a woman must thus become a man to attain eternal life. But, at least, the Jesus of Gospel of Thomas will guide her, which may have been a novel idea at the time. The saying does witness to a conflict in the early Church regarding the role of women.

BIBLIOGRAPHY

Guillaumont, A. H-Ch. Puech, G. Quispel, W. C. Till, and Y. 'Abd Al Masih. *The Gospel According to Thomas*. New York: Harper and Row, 1959.

Kloppenborg, J. S., W. M. Meyer, J. J. Patterson, and M. G. Steinhauser. *Q Thomas Reader*. Sonoma, Calif.: Polebridge Press, 1990.

Layton, B., ed. *Nag Hammadi Codex II, 2–7 Together with Gospel According to Thomas, Gospel According to Philip, Hypostasis of the Archons, and Indexes*. Nag Hammadi Studies 20. Leiden: E. J. Brill, 1989.

Meyer, W. M. "Making Mary Male: The Categories 'Male' and 'Female' in the Gospel of Thomas." *New Testament Studies* 31 (1985): 554–70.

Pagels, E. *The Gnostic Gospels*. New York: Random House, 1979.

Puech, H.-Ch. "Une collection de paroles de Jésus récemment retrouvée: L'Evangile selon Thomas." *Comptes-rendus de l'Académie des Inscriptions et Belles-Lettres*. Paris: Institut de France, 1957.

Quispel, G. "The Gospel of Thomas and the New Testament." in *Vigilae Christianae* 11 (1957): 189–207.

Robinson, J. M. and H. Koester. *Trajectories through Early Christianity*. Philadelphia: Fortress Press, 1971.

Hebron

Importance

An intact building dating from the time of Herod may give an idea of the appearance of the Temple retaining wall.

Scripture Reference

Mark 13:1.

General Information

Hebron may be one of the most ancient cities in Judea. Also called Kiriath-arba (Gen. 23:2), it is situated between Jerusalem and Beer-Sheba, 20 miles south of Jerusalem at an important intersection of north-south and east-west roads. It is considered a Levitical city and a city of refuge (Josh. 21:13). Abraham is said to have built an altar to God at He-

bron ("Oaks of Mamre, which are at Hebron," Gen. 13:18) and to have bought the field and the cave of Machpelah near Hebron from Ephron the Hittite, son of Zohar (Gen. 23:9-19), as a family burial place. Abraham, Isaac, Rebekah, Leah, and Jacob are said to have been buried there. The place has been revered for the ancestral tombs to this day and is known as the "Tombs of the Patriarchs" (Haram el-Khalil in Arabic). The wall built around it in Herod's time still stands today in perfect condition and bears witness to Josephus' statement that the construction was of "fine marble and exquisite workmanship" (*War* 4, 9.7/531–532).

When David moved his headquarters from Hebron to Jerusalem, the Tombs of the Patriarchs may have lost some of their popularity. But Herod, almost one thousand years later, revived or perhaps began the cult of the patriarchs, as part of an effort to reduce the influence of the priesthood in Jerusalem.

Archaeological Data

The remarkable Herodian wall was built with the same care and technique as the wall of the Second Temple; its very large stones were skillfully cut, dressed, and put together. The enclosed area measures 160 x 90 feet; the wall is 8 feet thick and some of its blocks are 22 feet long and 5 x 5 feet in section. Its upper half is decorated by regularly spaced pilasters, probably similar to those that adorned the upper part of the Temple platform wall. A parapet with battlements was built on top of the wall in medieval times.

Implications for Jesus Research

Although the Tombs of the Patriarchs, as they are called, were close to the area where Jesus may have withdrawn after his baptism (*see* QUMRAN), there is no indication that he visited them. (The Gospels record several instances in which Jesus mentioned the three patriarchs together: Matt. 8:11; 22:32; and Luke 13:28.) The Hebron wall enclosure provides extant evidence of the remarkable skills of Herod's engineers and builders.

Aerial View of Herodium, Seen from the West. *(The north is on the left)*

BIBLIOGRAPHY

Brunot, A. "Mamre/Hebron." *Le Monde de la Bible* 17 (1981): 46–48.

Jacobson, D. M. "The Plan of the Ancient Haram el-Khalil in Hebron." *Palestine Exploration Quarterly* 113 (1981): 73–80.

Miller, Nancy. "Patriarchal Burial Site Explored for the First Time in 700 Years." *BAR* 11 (1985): 26–43.

Ofer, A. "Hebron." *NEAEHL* 2: 606-9.

Herodium

Importance

Herodium contains a synagogue from a period just after the time of Jesus.

General Information

Herodium is the name of a fortress and palatial complex built by Herod between the hill country of Judea and the desert, 3 miles southeast of Bethlehem. In 40 B.C.E., when Herod was fleeing before the Parthians, he defeated a band of rebels who attacked him near the site of the future fortress. Perhaps this event was a factor in his decision to erect a stronghold there, on two adjacent hills. Herod had the top of the eastern hill removed; with the material collected in truncating the first hill he built up the other one, reinforcing its top with retaining walls. The fortress is circular in shape with a double fortification wall and four towers located at the cardinal points. The eastern tower is fully circular and may have stood 130 feet above the original mountain top; the other ones were half cir-

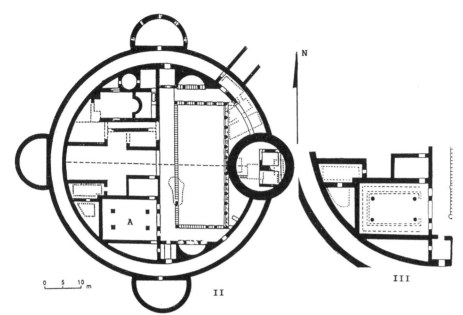

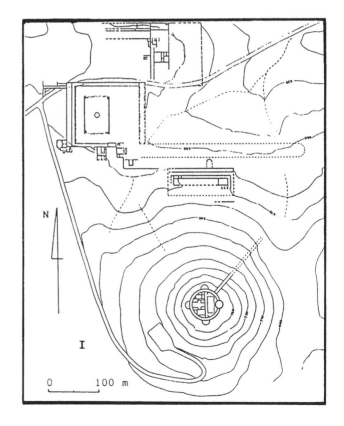

Figure 36 Herodium.
I: General map of the area with Lower Herodium in the north.
II: Plan of the fortress-palace
A: Triclinium III: Enlargement of the triclinium after its transformation. Three rows of masonry benches were added along the walls. By analogy with Masada, it may be considered that the fighters of the First Revolt (66-70 C.E.) made the addition. *(After G. Foerster and E. Netzer)*

cular. Their foundations were made of solid masonry, and rooms were built above. Inside the fortress were a magnificent peristyle on the eastern side and a triclinium—a large rectangular room with three rows of columns parallel to three sides—on the western side. The latter served as a dining room, with living quarters and a bath next to it (*see* fig. 36).

In Arabic the site is known as Jebel Fureides, "hill of the little paradise." Perhaps this is based on a name used by Herod himself, because he ordered that he be buried there, to make sure that he would rest in paradise. Against this hypothesis, some scholars argue that *Furadeis* is more probably a corruption of *Herodium*. He may have been buried in the large circular tower, but his remains have not been recovered.

Herodium was part of a chain of fortresses and the administrative center of a Judean subdistrict or toparchy. In addition to the palace fortress, Herod built a town of the same name at the foot of the mountain. The purpose of the entire project of Herodium, including the lower city, is still being debated. Scholars have suggested several reasons for its existence, all related to Herod the Great's personality:

- a memorial to Herod's crucial battle and victory on the site,
- a memorial to Herod's name,
- a palace complex,
- a fortress,
- Herod's burial place,
- the capital of the toparchy.

Whatever the purpose of the enormous complex at Herodium, it is obvious that it represents an ambitious plan, superbly implemented.

The rebels of the First Jewish War fought desperately at Herodium, but it fell to Lucilius Bassus in 72 C.E., one year before the fall of Masada. The Bar Kokhba fighters of the Second War later occupied the site. They again used the synagogue that the first fighters had built in the triclinium, or perhaps they built it themselves. They also developed an elaborate system of tunnels and caves, beneath the buildings. Later Christian hermits settled in the ruins for a time.

Archaeological Data

V. Corbo, who later worked at Capernaum, excavated the fortress and palace of Herodium (1962–67) with the financial support of the Italian Ministry of Cultural Relations. The work continued (1968–69) under the direction of G. Foerster on behalf of the Department of Antiquities and Museums of Israel. The excavators recognized three levels of occupation: the period from Herod to the First Jewish War, the Bar Kokhba War, and the period of Christian hermits. The size of the structure is impressive: the outer wall has a diameter of 180 feet, and the inner wall of 150 feet. The fighters of the Bar Kokhba War, or perhaps those of the First Jewish War (see MASADA), added rows of stone benches along three walls of the triclinium to transform it into a synagogue or assembly hall. A number of *ostraca*, graffiti, and coins attest to the occupation of the site at this time. The Christian hermits left traces of some dwellings and many inscriptions and coins.

E. Netzer's excavations of the town (1972, 1973, 1978, 1980, 1982, 1983) uncovered many features, including a main stairway leading from lower Herodium to the fortress, a large palace, a balcony adjacent to the large palace, a 380 yards (350 meters) long esplanade, a monumental building at the end of the esplanade, a few other public buildings, a pool, and another structure having a smaller pool in its center.

Implications for Jesus Research

The synagogue or assembly hall of Herodium along with those of Gamla and Masada are the only ones chronologically close enough to the time of Jesus to suggest what the synagogues he visited were like (*see* GAMLA and MASADA). Some scholars argue that these buildings were not limited to liturgical use but were more general places of meeting used for several purposes in addition to prayer. Not many communities could have afforded two such buildings. The liturgical use of these buildings may be indicated by the fact that *miqvaot* (*see* RITUAL BATHS) have been found in the vicinity of the buildings of Gamla and Masada; in the latter, a room with fragments of biblical scrolls was found incorporated in the main room.

The Herodium fortress was visible for miles around and dominated the area south of Jerusalem. The Antonia, the three high towers of Herod's palace in Jerusalem, the fortresses over Jericho, and Herodium meant that Roman eyes watched over Jewish life in the very heart of Judea and Jerusalem. The very thought of such Roman presence must have been unbearable (*see* MASADA) to many and led to the emergence of Zealot rebels on the one hand and collaborators on the other. Jesus shaped his own response in contrast to these two extreme groups.

BIBLIOGRAPHY

Eshel, H. and I. Ben-Nun. "The Other Herodium and the Tomb of Herod." *Teva Va'aretz* 24 (1982): 65–68 (Hebrew).

Short Reports on the Fourth to Sixth Seasons of Excavations: "Herodium 1980, 1982/1983." *Excavations and Surveys* 1 (1982): 40–42; *Excavations and Surveys* 2 (1983): 47–49.

Jacobson, D. M. "The Design of the Fortress of Herodium." *Zeitschrift des deutschen Palästina-Vereins* 100 (1984): 127–36.

Foerster, G. "The Synagogues at Masada and Herodium." *Ancient Synagogues Revealed*, ed. H. I. Levine. Jerusalem: Academic Press and the Israel Exploration Society, 1981, 24–29.

Netzer, E. *Herodium.* Jerusalem, 1980 (Hebrew).

———. *Greater Herodium* (Qedem 13) Jerusalem: Qedem 13, 1987.

———. "L'Herodion." *Le Monde de la Bible* 17 (1981): 16–21.

———. "Herodion. A Multi-purpose Architectural Compound." *Cathedra* 11 (1982): 201–9 (Hebrew).

———. "Searching for Herod's Tomb." *BAR* 9.3 (1983): 30–51.

———. *Herodium: An Archaeological Guide.* Jerusalem: Cana, 1987.

Netzer, E. and G. Foerster. "Herodium." *NEAEHL* 2: 618-26.

Tsafrir, Y. "Herod's Architecture and Roman Technology in its Formation." *Cathedra* 15 (1980): 56–60 (Hebrew).

Yankelevitch, R. "Herodium: Har Ha-Melekh." *Cathedra* 20 (1981): 23–28 (Hebrew).

Hippos/Susita

Importance

The "city set on a hill" that Jesus used as an image could have been Hippos, which was detached from its background and clearly visible from the Capernaum area, especially at night.

Scripture Reference

Matt. 5:14.

General Information

Hippos was a Greek city of the Decapolis set on a rounded hill above the southeastern shore of the Sea of Galilee. It was protected by deep gorges except on the southeast where a ridge linked it with the plateau above the Sea of Galilee. The city was founded during the Hellenistic period; its Greek name, Hippos, is the translation of the Aramaic *Susita,* "horse." In being derived from the name of an animal this unusual place name is similar to Gamla, Aramaic for "camel" (*see* GAMLA). Its fate followed that of other cities of the Decapolis: conquered by Alexander Jannaeus, liberated by Pompey, granted to Herod by Augustus with Gadara (*see* GADARA), and finally placed under the jurisdiction of the governor of Syria. Hippos had its own mint and its own calendar, with the first year being the year of Pompey's conquest. During the First Jewish War, it was attacked by the rebels and, as a result, its Greek citizens slaughtered the Jewish inhabitants as they did in several other Greek cities, including Gadara (Josephus, *War* 2, 18.1/457–60). During the Byzantine period it became an episcopal see.

Archaeological Data

The Department of Antiquities and Museums of Israel conducted a survey and several excavations from 1951 to 1955, and the general plan of the city was revealed. Hippos was a fortified city with circular towers reinforcing its walls. A main street, the typical Roman *cardo,* ran between two gates. A long aqueduct brought spring water to the city, and in the center was a large underground public cistern. A public bath was built during the Byzantine period, when Hippos also had at least three churches and a cathedral. At the foot of the hill, facing Tiberias, was a harbor; a trade route went between Damascus and Tiberias via Hippos, and the Talmud refers to Hippos' commercial prosperity (*see* fig. 4).

Implications for Jesus Research

In the Gospels one statement may refer to Hippos: "a city built on a hill cannot be hid" (Matt. 5:14b). At night, the lights of Hippos were visible from all around the Sea of Galilee, especially from Bethsaida, Capernaum, and the site traditionally known as the Mount of Beatitudes. (In daylight haze usually blurs the lines of the hill.) Perhaps because he often used images from the environment to illustrate his teachings, Jesus may have been inspired by the lights of Hippos across the sea and used the comparison to impress on the minds of his disciples that they were "the light of the world" (Matt. 5:14a) and that their light should "shine before others." (Matt. 5:16). In 1990, the Jesus Seminar analyzed the pericope* Matthew 5:14-16 and gave it the following ratings: *pink*: 5:14b, 5:15b; *black*: 5:14a, 5:16—which means that Jesus would have used an image without turning it into a metaphor. This view seems improbable for it does not fit with what seems to be Jesus' style of teaching.

BIBLIOGRAPHY

Chronique Archéologique (no author's name). "Susita-Hippos." *Revue Biblique* 63 (1956): 99.

Epstein, C. "Hippos (Sussita)." *NEAEHL* 2: 634-36.

Negev, A. "Hippos." *AEHL*, Rev. Ed. New York: Thomas Nelson, 1986. 1972.

Tzaferis, V. "Sussita Awaits the Spade." *BAR* 16 (1990): 51–58.

House

Importance

The Gospels frequently show Jesus and his disciples either as guests in houses or as homeowners, and Jesus used the term in a number of sayings.

Scripture References

Matt. 5:15; 7:25, 27; 9:6; 10:6, 12, 27; 12:4, 25, 29, 44; 13:57; 15:24; 20:11; 24:17, 43; 26:18; Mark 2:1, 11, 26; 3:25, 27; 6:4, 10; 9:33; 10:10, 29; 13:15; 14:3, 14; Luke 1:23, 56; 5:24, 25, 29; 6:3-5, 48: 7:6, 36; 8:27, 39, 41, 9:61; 10:5, 7, 38; 11:24; 16:27; 18:14; 19:5; 22:11; John 2:16; 4:53; 7:53; 8:35; 11:20; 12:3; 14:2; G. Thom. 33, 35, 48, 64, 71, 97, 98.

General Information

The word *house* used for designating a dwelling, a temple, a family, a household, a clan, or a dynasty is a common biblical term and appears no less than sixty-two times in the Gospels. Nevertheless, while the construction techniques, plans, and styles of ancient public buildings have been well documented through excavation of palaces, temples, synagogues and other large structures, relatively little attention has been given to domestic buildings, especially those of the lower classes. It is only recently that the remains of houses dating from the first century B.C.E. to the fourth century C.E. have been excavated in Israel at sites such as Capernaum, Chorazin, Gamla, Bethsaida, Qatzrin, Sepphoris, and Jerusalem.

The extent of the excavation at those sites provides a fairly accurate idea of what houses were like in the first century. For houses built on level ground, the floor plan was similar to that of the Roman *insula*: a series of rooms built around a courtyard. The number of doors and windows was kept to a minimum and many rooms had only one door. Several considerations mandated this type of architecture: simplicity of construction, safety, and protection against summer heat and bad weather conditions. Because stone was abundant in Palestine, it was widely used as a building material: dark basalt in Eastern Galilee and the Lower Golan, and limestone almost everywhere else, except in the Negev and in some places such as Jericho, where mud brick was the only practical and affordable material (*see* CONSTRUCTION, CITIES).

Roofs, usually flat, were normally made of wooden beams bearing rods placed across, side by side, then covered with clay and flattened with a roller. A light superstructure could be added to form one or more upper rooms. Where it was possible, as in Eastern Galilee and the Lower Golan, stone beams were used to support a full or partial second floor. In that region, the length of the roughly cut basalt beams (2 meters or 6.5 feet) restricted the width of the building. To alleviate this situation, the width was doubled and arches were built along the median of the rectangular room to support the inner extremities of the beams. These heavy beams were laid side by side to form the solid roof of the lower room and floor of the upper room. Clay was used to fill the interstices. Some expensive houses had pitched roofs covered with tiles. In ordinary houses, if there was an upper room, it was reached from the inside by a ladder or from outside by stairs. Only the houses of the wealthy had indoor stairs; they also had baths and plastered walls, often decorated with frescoes (*see* JERUSALEM, UPPER CITY). An ordinary house generally did not have a *miqveh*, "ritual bath" (the many *miqvaot* at Sepphoris may be an exception). In contrast, scores of *miqvaot* were found in the houses of the wealthy (*see* UPPER CITY) and in more modest houses at the foot of the Temple southern wall, where they were presumably rented to pilgrims (*see* JERUSALEM, CITY OF DAVID, OPHEL).

Archaeological Data

The most significant excavations of Jewish houses in Israel for the study of Jesus' environment are those of Capernaum, Gamla, Bethsaida, Chorazin, Meiron, Sepphoris, Qatzrin, and the Ophel. Because construction techniques did not change much during the first centuries of our era, and because the basic material, dark basalt, remained the same, the houses of Chorazin, Meiron, and Qatzrin, although they date from the fourth to fifth centuries C.E., provide a reasonable idea of what the houses of Jesus' time were like in Eastern Galilee. The reconstructed house and the house "under construction" in Qatzrin are certainly not far from the reality.

The "Fisherman's House" in Bethsaida, with a large courtyard where several objects testifying to fishing activities have been found, is a relatively large complex of about 20 x 15 meters (66 x 49 feet), which may have belonged to a well-to-do family.

House. *The oven. (Qatzrin)*

Domestic compounds of comparable size exist in Capernaum and Chorazin (Matt. 11:20-24; Luke 10:13-15; *see* fig. 13).

Implications for Jesus Research

Jesus, having chosen the life-style of an itinerant teacher and healer—some say Cynic—did not have a house of his own (Matt. 8:20). In cities and villages, he relied on the hospitality of others; when on his way to more distant places, he perhaps sought shelter in caves (*see* GALILEAN CAVES and JUDEAN CAVES). He was invited for dinner in the

House. *Ladder to the upper room. Note the stone stand for an oil lamp, right of the ladder. (Qatzrin)*

houses of wealthy Pharisees and tax collectors. The house of Simon the Leper in Bethany must have been of a good size to accommodate Jesus and his disciples along with the host family. So were the fishermen's houses excavated at Capernaum and Bethsaida. The house of the Last Supper with a "large upper room" was very likely the property of a wealthy family (*see* JERUSALEM, UPPER ROOM and WOOD, FURNITURE). There is not enough information to indicate the size of the house where Jesus was raised in Nazareth, but it must have been large enough for a family of at least nine (parents and five boys, and at least two daughters; Matt. 13:55-56 and parallels).

Jesus' disciples also left their homes and families to work for the Kingdom (Mark 10:28-29); some of them, such as the four fishermen and the tax collector, may have had sizeable houses. In his parables and other sayings, Jesus frequently refers to house construction and to houses as familiar settings. The number of these references indicates that most people in his audiences lived in family households. He and those of his followers who had chosen to share his lifestyle would have been the exceptions.

BIBLIOGRAPHY

Balch, D. L. "Household Codes." *The New Testament and Graeco-Roman Literature*, ed. D. E. Aune. SBL Abstracts and Seminar Papers. Atlanta: Scholars Press, 1988.

———. "Household Codes." *ABD* 3:318–20.

Ben Dov, M. *In the Shadow of the Temple.* 1982. Reprint. Jerusalem: Keter Publishing House, 1985.

de Camp, L. S. *The Ancient Engineers.* New York: Ballatine Books, 1960–88.

Herzog, Z. "Enclosed Settlements in the Negeb and the Wilderness of Beer-sheba. *Bulletin of the American Schools of Oriental Research* 250 (1983): 41–49.

Holladay, J. S., Jr. "House, Israelite." *ABD* 3: 308-18.

Hopkins, D. C. Highlands of Canaan. Sheffield: University of Sheffield Press, 1985.

Kramer, C. Village Archaeology: Rural Iran in Archaeological Perspective. New York: Ethno Academic Press, 1982.

Malherbe, A. J. The Graeco-Roman Moral Tradition and Early Christianity. Philadelphia: Fortress Press, 1986.

Mazar, A. "Three Israelite Sites in the Hills of Judah and Ephraim." *BA* 45 (1982): 167–78.

Shiloh. Y. "The Casemate Wall, the Four Room House, and Early Planning in the Israelite City." Bulletin of the American Schools of Oriental Research 268 (1987): 3–15.

Stager, L. E. "The Archaeology of the Family in Ancient Israel." Bulletin of the American Schools of Oriental Research 260 (1985): 1–35.

Summer, W. M. "Estimating Population by Analogy: An Example." Ethnoarchaeology: Implications for Archaeology, ed. C. Kramer. New York: Columbia University Press, 1979.

Jacob's Well

Importance

According to John, Jesus met a Samaritan woman there and drank water from the well.

Scripture Reference

John 4:6.

General Information

There is no reference to a well dug by or for Jacob in the Hebrew Bible. A midrash (b. Berakot R. 81, 174a), reports that Ishmael ben Jose, when going to Jerusalem, stopped at the well and had a conversation with a Samaritan regarding their respective places of prayer, Jerusalem and Mount Gerezim. Similar information is found in b. Berakot R. 32, 64a. The earliest Christian testimony to the existence of the well is given by the Bordeaux Pilgrim ca. 333. Even today, the Samaritans deny that the well dates from Jacob. Whenever it may have been dug, it no doubt was named after the patriarch because of its proximity to the field he is said to have purchased from the sons of Hamor (Josh. 24:32). The importance of the well was partly due to its location at the intersection of two main roads (see SYCHAR-SHECHEM).

Archaeological Data

The well is located inside a church built during the Crusaders period and partly restored. The property now belongs to the Greek Orthodox Church. The well is a large and deep shaft, about 7½ feet in diameter and 100 feet deep, covered with a stone slab with a hole in the center. Unfortunately, a circular wall was built on top of the slab in modern times in order to give the well an appearance familiar to western visitors. The shaft goes first through a thick layer of earth lined with masonry and then is hewn in soft rock. The water drips along the sides, which justifies the use of both the words spring (*pege,* John 4:6,14) and rain pit (*phrear,* John 4:11, 12) to identify the origin of its water; it is supplied by underground water sources and also surface water.

Implications for Jesus Research

The area where "Jacob's well" is located would have been a natural stopping place on a journey from Judea to Galilee through Samaria. The Bordeaux Pilgrim indicated the existence of plane trees at a short distance from the well. The primary author of the Fourth Gospel seems to have known about the area and chose a likely spot to set his story about Jesus' travel and encounter with people from the nearby village or small town. According to an old tradition, it was customary to meet people, especially travelers, at the town well: consider the story of Abraham's servant meeting Rebecca at a well (Gen. 24:11, 15-17) and that of Saul meeting young women at a well (1 Sam. 9:11). The dialogue between Jesus and the Samaritan woman at the well (John 4:21, 23-24) may indicate that Jesus understood God's reign differently than did John the Baptist or the Qumranites (see CAPERNAUM and DEAD SEA SCROLLS).

BIBLIOGRAPHY

Briend, J. "Puits de Jacob." Dictionnaire de la Bible, 1979.

———. "Puits de Jacob ou de la Samaritaine." Revue Biblique 65 (1958): 547–67.

Stefanovic, Z. "Jacob's Well." *ABD* 3:608–9.

Jericho

Importance

Jesus passed through Jericho, dined in Zacchaeus's house, and healed a blind man there.

Scripture References

Matt. 20:29; Mark 10:46; Luke 10:30; 18:35; 19:01.

General Information

Jericho is an oasis located six miles north of the Dead Sea where the Jordan valley reaches the Judean desert. Steep cliffs descend to a wide irrigated valley and the lowest city in the world, lying about 825 feet below sea level. The flourishing agriculture of this oasis is due to the abundance of water gushing from the springs of Ein es-Sultan (Elisha's fountains), Ein Duk, and Ein Nueima, the three springs of Wadi Qelt, and also from the spring of Anju northwest of the valley. Destruction of the ancient irrigation system and its aqueducts would turn this oasis into a desert similar to that of the Judean desert, as pictures and descriptions from the nineteenth century testify. The Hebrew Bible refers to this place as "the City of Palm Trees" (Deut. 34:3; Judg. 3:13; 2 Chron. 28:15).

According to the biblical narrative, Jericho was the first city to be conquered by the Israelites west of the Jordan River. Its miraculous conquest and destruction by the blowing of ram horn trumpets and the mighty shouts of the people is one of the most well-known biblical stories. The authenticity of the story is problematic, however, because excavations show that Jericho was no longer occupied at the time of the Israelite settlement in Canaan. Another passage in the Hebrew Bible (2 Kings 2:1-22) tells about a band ("sons") of prophets located there in the time of Elijah, who met with them before his mysterious disappearance in a whirlwind on the other side of the Jordan. His successor, Elisha, purified the water of Jericho on the way back from his final journey with his master. After the Babylonian exile, Jericho was resettled and its peo-ple participated in the reconstruction of the walls of Jerusalem (Neh. 3:2; 7:36).

Following the Persian conquest and the establishment of the satrapy* of Abar Nahara, west of the Euphrates River, large estates were taken by the king of Persia to form his private priviledged farms. They were known as *paradeisos*, and included plantations of great value, such as cedars of Lebanon (Ezra 3:7; Neh. 2:8) and persimmon or balsam trees near the Dead Sea. All of these became a royal monopoly and a source of income to the royal family. After 200 B.C.E. these properties were presumably transferred to the Seleucid kings of Syria. The Seleucid general Bacchides fortified Jericho against the Hasmoneans during their mid-second century B.C.E. revolt (Josephus, *Antiq.* 13, 1.3/15; 1 Macc. 9:50). The royal estate was probably conquered by the Hasmonean kings, who built a palace there. After the campaign of Pompey in 63 B.C.E., it fell into the hands of the Romans. As Roman ruler of the eastern empire and heir to the Hellenistic kings, Mark Antony felt free to bestow the estate to Cleopatra (34 B.C.E.); she in turn leased it to Herod the Great. Octavianus (Augustus), however, bequeathed it to Herod around 30 B.C.E.

Herod rebuilt the palaces and adorned them with lavish pools and splendid edifices. The palaces were burnt at his death, but his son Archaleus rebuilt them soon after. During the First Jewish War Vespasian stationed his troops at Jericho as he prepared to attack Jerusalem. It was still a Roman city in character when the Bordeaux Pilgrim visited it in 333 C.E. At some point thereafter the site was abandoned; a new city named Erikha, located about one mile to the east where modern Jericho now stands, was built during the Byzantine period.

Archaeological Data

The main settlement in the Oasis of Jericho has shifted to different locations through the ages. In pre-Israelite times, Tell es-Sultan was the chief area of occupation, but no strata of the Israelite periods have been found. The Hellenistic and Roman settlements were perhaps where modern Jericho is located. The Hasmonean and Herodian palaces stood at Tulul Abu el-Alayiq at the upper part of the oasis close to the eastern edges of the Judean hills, where the Wadi Qelt opens to the Jordan valley and where the ancient road led to Jerusalem (*see* fig. 37).

Tell es-Sultan has been excavated by several major expeditions: by the British in 1868 under C. Warren, in 1907–09 by the Austrian E. Sellin and the German C. Watzinger, during 1930–36 by the British J. Garstang, and again by the British from 1952 to 1958 under K. Kenyon. Kenyon's careful stratigraphic work showed no remains of Jericho from the time of early Israel (Joshua 6). She explained this absence by the practice of the local

Falahin (peasants) to fertilize their land with dirt from the mound. For this reason, the city of Joshua would have disappeared

The Hasmonean palaces of Tulul Abu el-Alayiq were excavated first by Sellin and Watzinger in the early 1900s, then by J. Kelso and D. Baramki, and by J. Pritchard in the early 1950s. The most important excavations were directed by E. Netzer from 1973 to 1987.

Netzer discovered that what was called "New Testament Jericho" was in fact a series of palaces built by the Hasmonean and Herodian kings as part of a garden city and royal estate. The founder of the larger complex was perhaps Alexander Jannaeus. Built over an area of 3 acres, it consisted in a large building (150 x 140 feet), flanked on the east by an

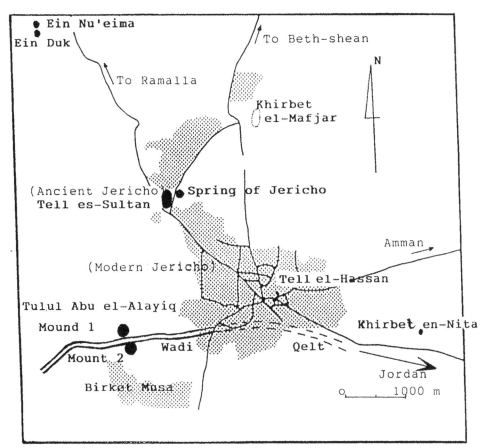

Figure 37 Jericho. Main excavation sites at or near Jericho. *(After G. Foerster).*

immense swimming pool surrounded by a wide promenade. The buildings were Hellenistic in style and adorned with designs and sculptures popular in the Hellenistic palaces of Asia Minor and Macedonia. These features included classical domestic architecture, columns in the Doric and Ionic order, and wall paintings. This indicates a Hellenistic influence on the Hasmoneans. Toward the end of their reign, they appear to have been not the Jewish redeemers from the Hellenization imposed by Antiochus IV Epiphanes but the leaders of Hellenized Jewry and all that it symbolized. This reversal, worsened by the cruelty and family feuds of their last generations, must have had a traumatic effect on the collective memory of the Jewish people.

When Herod the Great came to power, he changed the site significantly by erecting three contiguous palaces on an area of 25 acres. Netzer describes the development in the following way: Herod built the first palace in the first years of his reign, when he was only a lessee of the Hasmoneans and later of Cleopatra of Egypt. That palace, erroneously identified as a "gymnasium" in the 1950s, consisted of a large courtyard surrounded by columns. It was built at the south of the Hasmonean palace, across the Wadi Qelt. It seems that the Hasmonean family still owned the palace, thanks to their good relations with the Ptolemies. After the Battle of Actium,* Herod received Jericho and the royal estate. At this time the Hasmonean palace was destroyed either by the severe earthquake of 31 C.E. or as the result of the military struggles between Herod and Matthew Antigonus, the last of the Hasmonean rulers.

The second palace, built after this event, was different from the Hasmonean royal residence. Only the swimming pool was retained. Gardens were planted around it; the entire complex was decorated with colonnaded courtyards, pools, frescoes, and service rooms. Herod had the ruins of the old Hasmonean palace covered with dirt and planted with gardens.

The third palace, extending on both sides of the Wadi Qelt, was the largest of all. It consisted of a building erected on an artificial mound, similar to the building on the mound in the second palace. Next to it was a large sunken garden flanked by two porticos, on the east and the west, and a swimming pool east of the garden. A flight of stairs and a bridge connected the building on the top of the mound to the complex on the north side of the wadi. The northern complex consisted of a reception hall, colonnaded courtyards, and a large and lavish bathhouse. The architecture of the entire complex was Hellenistic-Roman in style. Herod employed Roman architects and construction workers, who used new Roman techniques known as *Opus Quadratum* and *Opus Reticulatum*. In comparison to the relatively modest Hasmonean palace, the Herodian complex was grandiose. Its spacious palaces and gardens and its entire presence represented a strong Hellenistic-Roman influence in the building patterns of the elite (*see* fig. 38).

Implications for Jesus Research

These examples of royal Hellenistic and Roman influence were visible to Jesus on his way from Jericho to Jerusalem. They stood in great contrast to the indigenous traditional, simple architecture as exemplified by the Qumram settlement that was just a few miles away. The builders of Qumram did not employ any Hellenistic feature in their buildings although, if they had wanted to, there were fine examples in Judea (*see* QUMRAM). Jericho was a luxuriant oasis and the Herodians still occupied the grand winter palaces built by the founder of their dynasty. The forts on top of the nearby hills certainly lodged Roman detachments. All these structures were reminders of despotism, bloody family feuds, oppression, massacres, and foreign occupation. Yet the city prospered because of the fertility of the plain and its proximity to the main trade routes. According to Luke 19:1-8, Zacchaeus was a wealthy tax collector who exacted from the people much more than the amount due (*see* TAX AND TAX COLLECTORS). Remains of sycamore wood used for timber were found in one of the Hellenistic forts. They give some credence to the vivid detail of the story describing short Zacchaeus, the tax collector, climbing up a sycamore tree to see Jesus

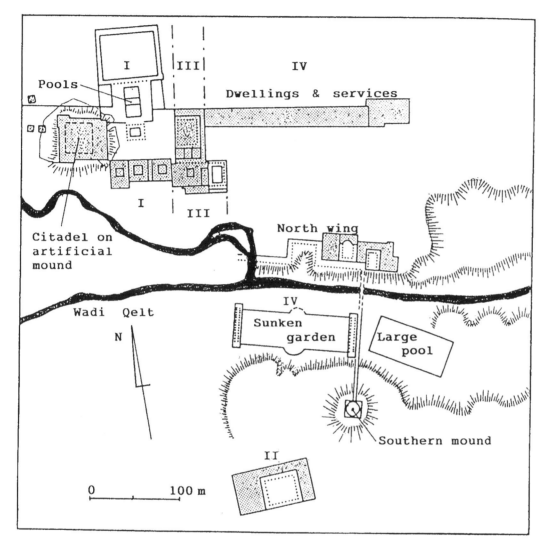

Figure 38 Jericho, Hasmonean, and Herodian Palaces. I: Hasmonean palace; II: Herod's first palace; III: Herod's second palace; IV: Herod's third palace. *(After E. Netzer)*

from a position above the heads of the crowds surrounding him (Luke 19:1-8).

In the account of Jesus' departure from Jericho on his way to Jerusalem, blind Bartimeus cried out to attract Jesus' attention. Many in the crowd rebuked him (Mark 10:48)—as the presence of large numbers of mendicants may have been considered a nuisance. Matthew expands on the story and indicates two beggars instead of one (Matt. 20:29-34), but this does not reduce the probability of the basic incident. The contrast between royal opulence and destitution of the blind and lepers, was no doubt observable in a city like Jericho. Jesus' inclination was clearly for the poor for whom he had great compassion (Matt. 25:34-40; Mark 10:21; Luke 6:20, *et passim**).

BIBLIOGRAPHY

Bartlett, J. R. *Jericho*. Cities in the Biblical World. Guildford: Surrey, 1982.

Foerster, G. "The Ancient Synagogue Inscription at Jericho and Liturgical Traditions." *Shnaton* 4 (1980): 296–98. (Hebrew, English summary).

Hachlili, R. "A Jewish Cemetery of the Second Temple Period at Jericho. *Qadmoniot* 12. (1979): 62–66 (Hebrew).

———. "A Second Temple Period Jewish Necropolis in Jericho." *BA* 43 (1980): 235–40.

———. "A Jerusalem Family in Jericho." *Eretz Israel* 15 (1981): 406–11 (Hebrew, English summary).

———. "Wall Paintings from a Monumental Jewish Tomb in Jericho in the 2nd Cent. C.E." *Nation and History. Studies in the History of the Jewish People*, edited by M. Stern. Jerusalem, 1983 (Hebrew).

———. "Did the Alphabet Have a Magical Meaning in the First Century C.E.?" *Cathedra* 31 (1984): 27–30 (Hebrew).

Hachlili, R. and A. Killebrew. "Jewish Funerary Customs During the Second Temple Period, in the Light of the Excavations at the Jericho Necropolis." *Palestine Exploration Quarterly* 115 (1983): 109–39.

Holland, T. A. and E. Netzer. "Jericho." *ABD* 3:723–40.

"Jericho Winter Palaces, 1982." *Excavations and Surveys in Israel 1983*. 50–51.

Kelso, J. L. and D. C. Baramki. *Excavations at New Testament Jericho and Khirbet en-Nilta*. Annual of American Schools of Oriental Research 29–30. New Haven: Yale University Press, 1955.

Kenyon, K. M. *Digging Up Jericho*. New York: Praeger, 1957.

Kenyon, K. M. et al. *Excavations at Jericho. III: The Architecture and Stratigraphy of the Tell*. London: British School of Archaeology in Jerusalem, 1981.

———. *Excavations at Jericho. IV: The Pottery Type Series and Other Finds*. London: British School of Archaeology in Jerusalem, 1982.

Kenyon, K. M., G. Foerster, E. Netzer and R. Hachlili. "Jericho." *NEAEHL* 2:674-91.

Merkes, D. B. "Tell es-Sultan, Site of the Old Testament Jericho." *Near East Archaeological Society Bulletin* 23 (1984): 5–34.

Netzer, E. "The Hippodrome that Herod Built at Jericho." *Qadmoniot* 13 (1980): 104–7 (Hebrew).

———. "Jericho. Les constructions hérodiennes." *Le Monde de la Bible* 17 (1981): 28–34.

———. "Recent Discoveries in the Winter Palaces of Second Temple Times at Jericho." *Qadmoniot* 14 (1982): 22-29 (Hebrew).

———. "The Winter Palace of the Judean Kings at Jericho at the End of the Second Temple Period." *Bulletin of the American Schools of Oriental Research* 228 (1977): 1–13.

Shiller, E., ed. "Jericho and Its Surroundings." *Kardom*. Jerusalem, 1983 (Hebrew).

Jerusalem, Caiaphas's House

Importance

After his arrest, Jesus was taken to Annas, the head of the priestly family then in power, and Caiaphus his son-in-law, who was High Priest from 18 to 36 C.E.

Scripture References

Matt. 26:57; Mark 14:53-54; Luke 22:54; John 18:12-14, 24.

General Information

The exact location of the house of Caiaphas is unknown. Josephus indicates indirectly that during the First Jewish War (66–73 C.E.), the High Priest resided in the Upper City, the district of Jerusalem where the ruling class and the wealthy lived (*War* 2, 17.5/426; *see* JERUSALEM, UPPER CITY). Presumably, this was also the case one generation earlier. In 333, the Bordeaux Pilgrim visited the house of Caiaphas on "Mount Zion" and in 530 Theodosius reported that "the High Priest's house was about 50 paces (120 to 150 feet) from the Holy Zion Church." Unfortunately, he did not give the location of the church nor a direction.

A clue about the location of the Holy Zion Church may be found in the Madaba Map, dated to about 560 by M. Avi-Yonah. Avi-Yonah suggests that this church was southwest of the then new Church of the Theotokos built by Justinian. The Holy Zion Church would have stood in the area of today's Dormition Church (or Church of Saint Mary). Assuming that Caiaphas's house and the Holy Zion Church were on streets set on a north-south and east-west grid (*see* JERUSALEM, STREETS AND STAIRS), the former was 120 to 150 feet either north or south or east or west of the church. This would eliminate the traditional site now buried under the structure of the Church of Saint Peter of the Cockcrow (Saint Peter in Galicantu), which is too far away—about 700 feet to the east. Yet Theodosius's statement, "the house of Caiaphas is now the Church of Saint Peter," is perplexing. The modern Saint Peter Church may not be on the site of the Saint Peter Church of Theodosius, although remains of a fifth century church were found there.

Archaeological Data

Excavations were begun in 1888 at the site of Saint Peter of the Cockcrow and ruins of the fifth-century church were discovered in 1911. The underground remains located just at the top and south of the ancient stepped street leading to the Tyropoeon Valley are impressive. Under the floor of the ancient church is a room surrounded by chambers hewn in the limestone. There are rings on one wall, and in other places various sorts of handles have been cut in the rock. It has been suggested that they were used to tie prisoners while they were scourged or beaten. One underground room with a window overlooking a pit has been interpreted as a guard room. None of these archaeological materials establish that this is the location of the fifth-century Church of Saint Peter.

In 1971, on the basis of the information in the Madaba Map and the distance given by Theodosius, M. Broshi and E. Netzer excavated an area 150 feet north of the Dormition Church and south of the present city wall in the court of the Armenian Church of Saint Savior. H. Renard had previously recognized the location of the ancient Holy Church of Zion over which the Dormition Church was built; so Broshi and Netzer used the Church of the Dormition as a point of reference. They found a stretch of a Byzantine paved street oriented north-south and a short segment of a Herodian wall. On the eastern side of the street, they unearthed remains of houses from the time of Herod located only 30 to 50 feet from another group of Herodian houses. This location thus seems to be a better candidate for the house of Caiaphas (*see* fig. 39).

Implications for Jesus Research

The house of Caiaphas was probably situated in the wealthy quarter of the Upper City. It would have been similar to those excavated in the area. All of the four canonical Gospels indicate it had a courtyard, which communicated directly with the street through a gate watched by a doorkeeper (John 18:15-16). According to the primary author of the Fourth Gospel, this doorkeeper was a woman, which would indicate that the High Priest did not use Levites or the Temple guards for his personal security (their duties were confined to the Temple: *see* TEMPLE, SERVICE AND RITUAL). If the house was of the *insula* type, there would have been several dwelling units attributed to different related families. Annas and his son-in-law Caiaphas perhaps occupied the same domestic complex. By analogy with the nearby houses of the same period, it seems improbable that there was a jail in the High Priest's house and if Jesus spent the night there, he may have been isolated in a storage room or simply guarded in a corner of the courtyard as Luke 22:61 seems to imply.

A much-debated question is the so-called "trial" of Jesus. The two independent canonical sources (Mark and John) differ. Mark describes a nocturnal hearing by assembled "high priest, chief priests, elders, and scribes" who "all condemned him as deserving death" (Mark 14:53-64). Then, "as soon as it was morning, the chief priests held a consultation with the elders and scribes and the whole council. They bound Jesus, led him away, and handed him over to Pilate" (Mark 15:1). John does not allude to such an assembly. He only says, "First they took him to Annas . . . father-in-law of Caiaphas" (John 18:12). "The high priest questioned Jesus about his disciples and about his teaching" (v. 19). "Annas then sent him bound to Caiaphas the high priest" (v. 24). "They led Jesus from Caiaphas to the praetorium" (v. 28).

Figure 39 Respective Positions of the House of Caiaphas, David's Tomb, and the Upper Room

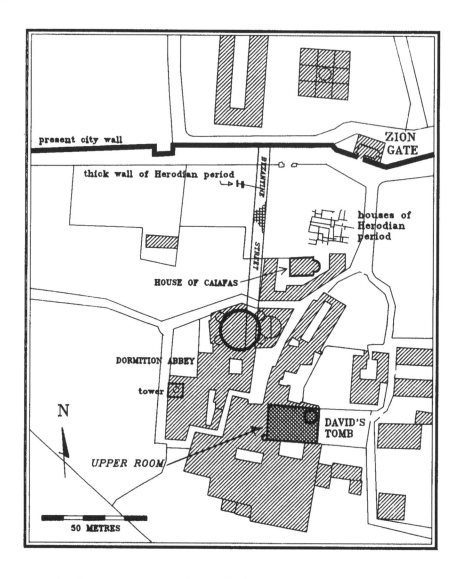

If John were the only witness among the disciples (Peter was not allowed into the High Priest's house), then his version should be preferred. Some scholars and lawyers suggest that, for legal reasons, a trial could not have occurred. Among them, Israeli Supreme Court judge Hain M. Cohn, gives the following reasons:

1. No Sanhedrin was allowed to sit as a criminal court and try criminal cases outside the Temple precincts in any private house.

2. The Sanhedrin was not allowed to try criminal cases at night: Criminal trials had to be commenced and completed during the daytime.

3. No person could be tried on a criminal charge on festival days or on the eve of a festival.

4. No person may be convicted on his own testimony or on the strength of his own confession.

5. A person may be convicted of a capital offense only upon the testimony of two lawfully qualified eyewitnesses.

6. No person may be convicted of a capital offense unless two lawfully qualified witnesses testify that they had first warned him of the criminality of the act and the penalty prescribed to it.

7. The capital offense of blasphemy consists in pronouncing the name of God, Yahweh, which may be uttered only once a year by the High Priest in the innermost sanctuary of the Temple; it is irrelevant what "blasphemies" are spoken so long as the divine name is not enunciated. (*see* THE TRIAL AND DEATH OF JESUS).

There were also practical considerations that would have made such a hasty meeting of the Jewish court impossible at short notice at the beginning of Passover. What probably happened is that, when Pilate heard that some Galilean had caused a disturbance in the Temple (*see* TEMPLE, ROYAL STOA), was called Son of David, and had followers, he summoned Caiaphas. Because he had appointed Caiaphas High Priest, he certainly could demand that his appointee find the troublemaker, arrest him and, if warranted, take legal action. Florus, in similar circumstances a few years later, used such a procedure to have rebels brought to him (*War* 2, 12.8/301–2; *see* JERUSALEM, HERODIAN and GETHSEMANE).

E. P. Sanders is probably correct in concluding that "Jesus was executed by the Romans . . . It is highly probable that he was executed for sedition or treason, as would-be-King" (*Jesus and Judaism*, 317). Perhaps the story of a trial and condemnation of Jesus by the Jewish court was a later addition, in a time of persecution, to disculpate the Romans and incline them to show tolerance toward the early Church.

BIBLIOGRAPHY

Bammel, E., ed. *The Trial of Jesus*. Studies in Biblical Theology. Naperville, Ill.: Alec R. Allenson, 1970.

Brandon, S. G. F. *The Trial of Jesus of Nazareth*. 1968. Reprint. New York: Dorset Press, 1988.

Cohn, H. H. *The Trial and Death of Jesus*. New York: Harper and Row, 1971.

Juel, D. *Messiah and Temple: The Trial of Jesus in the Gospel of Mark*. SBL Dissertation Series 31. Missoula, Mont.: Scholars Press, 1977.

Kenyon, K. M. "Excavations in Jerusalem, 1961." *Palestine Exploration Quarterly* 94 (1962): 72–89.

Power, E. "Eglise Saint-Pierre et Maison de Caiphe." *Dictionnaire de la Bible*, 1934.

———. "The Church of St. Peter at Jerusalem. Its Relation to the House of Caiaphas and Sancta Sion." *Biblica* 9 (1928): 167–86.

Sanders, E. P. *Jesus and Judaism*. Philadelphia: Fortress Press, 1985.

Jerusalem, Caiaphas's Tomb

Importance

A recent archaeological discovery attests to the existence of a High Priest named Joseph Caiaphas in the first century C.E.

Scripture References

Matt. 26:3, 57; Luke 3:2; John 11:49; 18:13, 14, 24, 28; Acts 4:6.

General Information

The High Priest Caiaphas, son-in-law of Annas, is mentioned in the New Testament and also in Josephus, who gives us his first name, Joseph. Josephus reports that the prefect of Judea, Gratus (15–26 C.E.) "deprived him [Eleazar] of it [the High Priesthood] and gave the high priesthood to Simon." Gratus seems to have appointed a new High Priest every year in several successive years, "and when he had possessed that dignity no longer than a year, Joseph Caiaphas was made his successor" (*Antiq.* 18, 2.2/35). In 36 C.E., Vitellius, the legate of Syria, at the same time that he sent Pilate back to Rome to face charges for his action against the Samaritans, "deprived Joseph who was called Caiaphas of the high priesthood and appointed Jonathan, the son of Ananus, the former High Priest, to succeed him" (*Antiq.* 18, 4.3/95).

The discovery of Caiaphas's tomb near Jerusalem contributes important information about the origin and history of his family. The discovery establishes that the name Caiaphas is spelled with the Hebrew letter *kof* and not with *caf*, as was previously supposed. This spelling led to the identification of the name with the priestly family name Pashur. The uncommon name Elioenai (Hebrew *Eliyahueini*, "Elijah, my eyes") occurs with reference to the priestly family Pashur (Ezra 10:21). Josephus mentions an "Elionaeus the son of Cantheras" as the High Priest who was appointed by Agrippa I in 44 C.E. This person is probably identical with Elionai the son of Qof, who is mentioned in the mishnah *Parah* 3:5. These two surnames have similar meaning in two languages; *qopha* (*qayapha*) in Aramaic and *cantherius* in Latin mean "basket" and "carrying." Perhaps the occupation of the family was basket making or drivers of pack asses. Some scholars suggest that Elioni was the son of Joseph Caiaphas (*see* R. Reich articles in the Bibliography).

The family originated in a village of unknown location named "Beth Meqoshesh." However, because it was customary to bury people next to their villages or on their own properties, this village may have been south of Jerusalem in the vicinity of Caiaphas's tomb.

If Caiphas and Cantheras are identical, then the reference in Talmudic literature that discloses heavy negative feelings toward the High Priests in the first century C.E. may refer to the two families that were engaged in the arrest and persecution of Jesus:

> Woe to me because of the house of Hanin (Annas of Acts 4:6), woe unto me because of the house of Katros (or "Katheras"), woe unto me because of their reed pens (libel).

No records indicate what happened to Caiaphas after he was deposed or how old he was when he died.

Archaeological Information

Significant archaeological discoveries often happen by chance, as is the case for Caiaphas's tomb. In November, 1990, during construction work done in the Peace Forest, 2,400 yards (2,200 meters) south of the Dome of the Rock (*see* fig. 40), the roof of a cave collapsed. Z. Greenhut, from the Israeli Antiquities Authority, investigated the site and found that it was a Jewish burial cave of the pre-First Jewish War period. It displayed all the features of such burial places in the Jerusalem area: a central chamber with a pit, bone repository, and *kokhim*, which, in this instance, were four in number (*see* JERUSALEM, TOMBS). Twelve ossuaries,* six of them intact, were found in the cave. Two were apparently still in the place where they were last used. Ossuary no. 6 is the most ornate. The center of the decoration contains a rectangle with small six-petaled rosettes, most of them whirled. On the back of the chest is an incised inscription: "Yehoseph the son of Qypa;" and on the narrow side: "Yehoseph the son of Qpa" is inscribed (*see* fig. 41). This ossuary contained partial remains of six individuals, including a 60-year-old male. The remains of this older person, perhaps Caiaphas, were too fragmentary to be reconstructed. In the same cave, in another ossuary containing the bones of a woman, a bronze coin of Herod Agrippa I dating to 42–43 C.E. was found in the skull. This indicates that, even in the family of the High Priest, foreign customs may have been observed: According to a Greek belief, a coin was placed in the mouth of the deceased, allowing the soul to pay Charon* for the crossing of the Styx*. The date of the coin points to a period following the Crucifixion.

Implications for Jesus Research

The Joseph Caiaphas tomb and the stone of Pilate from Caesarea Maritima (*see* PONTIUS PILATE'S STONE) provide archaeological evidence relating to the two individuals most directly involved in the arrest and crucifixion of Jesus. The core story of Jesus' condemnation and execution may be rooted in historical reality buried under layers of theological,

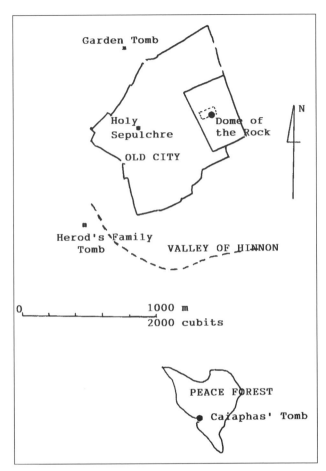

Figure 40 Caiaphas's Tomb. It was located in the south of the Temple (not in the west) and well beyond 2,000 cubits (*see* JERUSALEM, TOMBS).

christological, and ecclesiastical accretions. Noteworthy is the relatively humble tomb of a person who was the High Priest, for a lavish tomb is thought to indicate an important personality.

BIBLIOGRAPHY

Flusser, D. "Caiaphas in the New Testament." *Atiqot* 21 (1992): 81–88.

Greenhut, Z. "The Discovery of the Caiaphas Family Tomb." *The Jerusalem Perspective* 4. (1991).

———. "Burial Cave of the Caiaphas Family." *BAR* 18 (1992):28–37.

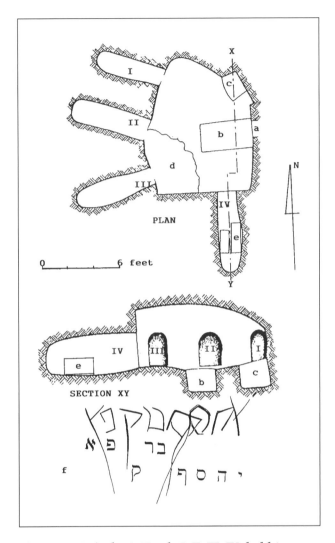

Figure 41 Caiaphas's Tomb. I, II, III, IV: *kokhim;* a: entrance; b: standing pit; c: bone depository; d: collapsed roof; e: Caiaphas's ossuary; f: one of the inscriptions with the name of Caiaphas. Modern Hebrew letters are added under each original one. The inscription reads: Joseph son of Caiaphas. *(Israel Antiquities Authority)*

———. "The 'Caiaphas' Tomb in North Talpiot, Jerusalem." *Atiqot* 21 (1992): 63–71.

Reich, R. "Caiaphas' Name Inscribed on Bone Boxes." *BAR* 18 (1992): 38–45.

———. "Ossuary Inscription from the 'Caiaphas' Tomb." *Atiqot* 21 (1992): 72–77.

Zias, J. "Human Skeletal Remains from the 'Caiaphas' Tomb." *Atiqot* 21 (1992): 78–80.

Jerusalem, City of David, Ophel

Importance

The City of David and the Ophel, south of the Temple Mount, were areas that Jesus probably traversed because they provided access to the Temple precincts.

Scripture References

Matt. 21:10, 23; Mark 11:11, 15; Luke 19:45; John 2:13-14, 23; 5:1; 7:10, 14; 8:2; 10:22; 12:12.

General Information

Originally Ophel was the name of the entire hill and spur running north-south on which ancient Jerusalem and the Temple stood. After David captured the city from the Jebusites, the name came to be applied only to the space between Jerusalem and the Temple. Ophel means "hill" or "knoll" and derives from the Hebrew or Semitic root *apl*, "to swell." Josephus renders it in Greek as *Ophlas* (*War* 5, 4.2/145) or *Ophla* (*War* 5, 6.1/254). King Jotham developed the fortifications of Jerusalem at the Ophel (2 Chron. 27:3), and Manasseh enclosed the area with a high wall (2 Chron. 33:14). It must have been a key element in the defense system of the city-Temple complex, between the two valleys of Kidron and Tyropoeon. The "Wall of Ophel" is mentioned again in Nehemiah 3:27, and Temple servants were living there in the post-exilic period (Neh. 3:26; 11:21).

After David's conquest, Jerusalem, which was not included in the territory of any tribe, became the king's property and was known as the "City of David;" when the city expanded westward and northward, the area south of the Temple Mount re-

tained this designation (*see* JERUSALEM, HERODIAN). The fortification walls followed the shape of the spur and, on the north, ran across it east-west, marking the line between the city and the "Ophel." Herod's extension of the Temple platform southward absorbed most of the Ophel. In the first century C.E. the City of David was a city within the city, still having its ancient fortification wall facing the Tyropoeon Valley on the western side of the spur. It served as a residential area where the royal house of Adiabene built palaces. On what remained of the Ophel, paved streets, terraces, and monumental stairs led to the Hulda Gates in the gigantic wall of the Temple Mount crowned in its southern side by the royal stoa which dominated the entire area (*see* TEMPLE, STOA).

Between 1968 and 1982 at the northern part of the City of David, south of the Hulda Gates, M. Ben Dov (1968–82) unearthed scores of ritual baths that give an archaeological-historical context to another discovery made more than half a century before. In 1914, the foundations of a large building interpreted as a synagogue were found in the same area; the same year, a Greek inscription on limestone and dated to the second to third centuries C.E. was recovered from a nearby cistern. It reads:

> Theodotius, son of Ventanos, priest and leader of the synagogue, son and grandson of synagogue leaders, restored this synagogue for the purpose of reading the Law and learning its commandments, and [built] the inn and guest rooms and the [ritual] baths for the visitors who need them. This synagogue was built by his forefathers, the elders and Simonides.

Theodotius could not have built all the ritual baths, but he probably restored the synagogue, the inn, and the few ritual baths attached to them. It has been suggested that this synagogue could have been that of the Freedmen of Acts 6:9. In this hypothesis, it would have been built by former war prisoners taken to Rome by Ptolemy in 63 B.C.E., or by their sons, who had been allowed to return to

The Theodotius Inscription found on Ophel in 1914.

Judea. This proposed origin of the synagogue's name may be related to a later statement of Tacitus that freed Jewish captives caused problems in Rome (*Annals* 2.85).

Archaeological Information

The City of David and Ophel have been extensively excavated since the mid-nineteenth century. Captain C. Warren was the pioneer excavator of the City of David. K. Kenyon, B. Mazar, M. Ben Dov and Y. Shiloh directed major archaeological projects. Many others have added to the data that allow us to reconstruct the City of David and the Ophel as they were before the destruction of the Temple in 70 C.E.

On the eastern side, overlooking the Kidron Valley and facing the Mount of Olives, a fortification wall with high square towers ran north-south from the eastern side of the Temple Mount to the southernmost point of the spur. How and where the fortification was connected with the eastern

wall of the Temple Mount is not clear. The wall then veered northward along the Tyropoeon Valley to return to the southern area of the Temple Mount (Ophel), but stopped short of reaching it. During the rebuilding process, Herod's architects probably razed the northwestern part of the City of David wall that was abutting the Temple in order to extend the Temple platform to the south and leave an extensive access area where large crowds of pilgrims could flow in and out during festivals. Coming out of the Temple Mount through the double gate, one would climb down the large white stairs, walk across a street and terraces paved with limestone slabs, pass an inn and a number of establishments or private homes with ritual baths and see a multitude of shops under the terraces. The Temple Mount was probably surrounded by one of the largest and most active bazaars of the Near Eastern world.

The ancient northern wall of the City of David had been razed too, and the visitor continuing his walk southward would pass the homes of various officials who had chosen to live near the Temple and the tombs of David and his descendants.

Several gates gave access to the City of David from the east and south, and from the Tyropoeon Valley and the rest of the city in the west. In the eastern wall, on the Kidron Valley, were the Fountain (or Spring) Gate near the Gihon Spring and the Casemate (or Water) Gate at the south of the spur. In the west, there was another gate giving access to the Siloam Pool in the southern area, and also probably the ancient Valley (or Western) Gate (Neh. 2:13). The latter was perhaps the 12-foot-wide gate flanked by two towers found by Crowfoot and Fitzgerald, who excavated there (1927–28). Some 80 feet below, the waters of the Gihon Spring were still flowing through the meandering tunnel of Hezekiah to the Pool of Siloam, which, according to D. Bahat (*Jerusalem*, 1989), was against the southern fortification wall of Jerusalem at the lower part of the Tyropoeon Valley in the first century C.E., and not higher, where it is now shown (*see* JERUSALEM, POOL OF SILOAM and fig. 44).

Implications for Jesus Research

When Jesus went to the Temple, he probably used the normal pilgrim access through the eastern Hulda Gates. When sojourning in the Jerusalem area, he may have come from the Mount of Olives, where the Galileans seemed to have a reserved campground (*see* MOUNT OF OLIVES), or from Bethany (*see* BETHANY). In any case, coming from the east, he would enter the city through the Fountain Gate, which was on the shortest route. Even on the occasion of his "triumphant entry" he probably did not enter through the Shushan Gate, as the Messiah would have according to common belief (*see* JERUSALEM, WALLS AND GATES). On the Ophel he could have used the ritual baths available to pilgrims.

It has been suggested that the area south of the Temple was the district of the poor. Such was not the case for the City of David nor could it have been for the Ophel, where so many ritual baths and shops were found. Except for beggars, slaves, and servants, the residents of the walled city were probably members of aristocratic, priestly, and levitical families, Temple officials, artisans, and merchants; they could not have been poor in the sense of "destitute." The poor were the hired workers and the jobless; many of them no doubt lived outside the walls in the nearby villages or in the many caves and abandoned quarries around Jerusalem. The large number of pilgrims, the on-going construction of the Temple, and the Temple service itself provided sufficient resources for artisans, builders, merchants, and their employees.

BIBLIOGRAPHY

Bahut, D. *The Illustrated Atlas of Jerusalem.* New York: Simon & Schuster, 1990.

Ben Dov, M. *In the Shadow of the Temple.* Translated by I. Friedman. Jerusalem: Keter Publishing House, 1982.

Dequeker, L. "The City of David and the Seleucid Acra in Jerusalem." The Land of Israel: Crossroads and Civilizations. *Orientalist Lovaniensia Analecta* 19 (1985): 46–57.

Franken, H. J. "The Excavations of the British School of Archaeology in Jerusalem on the South-east Hill in the Light of Subsequent Research." *Levant* 19 (1987): 129–35.

Mazar, B. "Herodian Jerusalem in the Light of the Excavations South and Southwest of the Temple Mount." *Cathedra* 8 (July 1978): 29–41.

Mazar, E. "Jerusalem, the Ophel, 1986." *Excavations and Surveys of Israel* 5 (1986): 56–58.

Mazar, E. and B. "Excavations in the South of the Temple Mount. The Ophel of Biblical Jerusalem." *Qedem* 29 (1989).

Reich, R. "Four Notes on Jerusalem III. The First Discovery of the Earliest City Wall of Jerusalem." *IEJ* 37 (1987): 163–64.

Shanks, H. "The City of David After Five Years of Digging." *BAR* 2 (1985): 22–38.

———. *The City of David: A Guide to Biblical Jerusalem.* Washington: Biblical Archaeology Society, 1973.

Shiloh, Y. "The City of David, 1978–1983." *Biblical Archaeology Today. Proceedings of the International Congress of Biblical Archaeology, Jerusalem, April 1984.* Jerusalem: Israel Exploration Society, 1985.

———. "Jerusalem, City of David, 1985." *Excavations and Surveys of Israel* 4 (1985): 52–54.

———. Excavations of the City of David I, 1978-1982. *Qedem* 19 (1984).

Jerusalem, Gehenna, Akeldama

Importance

In Israelite times the Valley of Hinnon was the site of Canaanite rituals involving child sacrifice. Later it was turned into a city dump where refuse was burnt, and under the name of Gehenna became synonymous with hell. Judas may have died in its lower part (Akeldama).

Scripture References

Matt. 5:22, 29, 30; 10:28; 18:9; 23:15, 33; 27:3-10; Mark 9:47; Luke 12:5; Acts 1:19.

General Information

The Valley of Hinnon, south and southwest of Jerusalem, marked the border between the territories of Judah and Benjamin (Josh. 15:8; 18:16). It was also known as the "Valley of the Son of Hinnon," probably so named after a family of Ben Hinnon who owned most of its land. In a certain place called Topheth in the Valley (2 Kings 23:10; Jer. 7:31), some Judeans, following the example of kings of Judah such as Ahaz (2 Chron. 28:3) and Manasseh (2 Chron. 33:6), offered their children as sacrifices to Canaanite gods. It was a time when priests were sacrificing in the Temple of Yahweh to Baal and Asherah and had instituted a male prostitution cult. King Josiah (640–609 B.C.E.) instituted a reform and destroyed all non-Yahwistic shrines (2 Kings 23:4-15); Jeremiah, who prophesied from 626 to 587 B.C.E., denounced the practices and predicted that the Valley would be called "the Valley of Slaughter" (Jer. 7:30-34; 19:1-15).

The Valley was accessed by the Potsherd or Dung Gate (see JERUSALEM, WALLS AND GATES) and was probably used in later times as a crematorium for the corpses of criminals and unclean animals, as well as a city dump for burning refuse. The term *gê hinnon*, "Valley of Hinnon" thus became a synonym for hell (Gehenna in the Gospels). According to the Talmud, there was an entrance to the underworld in the Valley of Hinnon (*b. 'Erubin* 19a). The expressions "Gehenna" and "Gehenna of fire" are both used in the New Testament to indicate the place where unrepentant sinners would be dumped (Matt. 5:22, 29, 30, *et passim*).

Akeldama, a burial ground, was also located (Acts 1:19) in the Valley of Hinnon, in its eastern part. The stories of Judas's death in Matthew 27:3-10 and Acts 1:16-19 are contradictory, but both point to an ill-famed field connected to his death either by suicide or by accident. Perhaps it was after his death that the field became known as Akeldama, which can mean "Field of Blood" or "Field of Sleeping."

Archaeological Data

No remains, such as thick layers of ashes or charred bones, have been found in the Valley of Hinnon to indicate the existence of an ancient city dump where refuse was incinerated. Many ancient Jewish and Christian tombs exist on the southern cliff of the valley, and pilgrims who died in Jerusalem were buried there up to the seventeenth century and possibly later. This custom perhaps originated because of Matthew 27:7 ("to bury foreigners"), in which case the pilgrim burials may indicate the approximate location of Akeldama.

Implications for Jesus Research

Although there is no surviving evidence of a refuse burning site in the Valley of Hinnon in the first century, the association of Gehenna with "fire" in Matthew 5:22 and 18:9 would indicate its existence at that time. Considering its infamous past and its location well below the city wall, and also the location of the Dung Gate (Potsherd Gate) and the Bethso (Latrines of the Essenes, *see* JERUSALEM, WALLS AND GATES), the Valley of Hinnon would have been a natural place for depositing and burning refuse.

The concept of eternal torment was probably not part of the Gospels' original use of Gehenna. The Hebrew Bible does not contain any specific information regarding the fate of the dead. Sheol, their last abode, was at the most a place of vegetative existence, not a place of torment. Luke 16:23, where the rich man is in torment (not necessarily eternal) in Hades, does not probably go back to Jesus. The pericope Luke 16:19-26 was rated *gray* by the Jesus Seminar in 1987. Only later in Christian tradition was the continuous burning of refuse interpreted as an eternal burning alive of sinners without destruction of the body.

BIBLIOGRAPHY

Bailey, L. "Gehenna: The Topography of Hell." *BA* 49 (1986): 187–91.

Barkay, G. "To Gehenna and Back: The Hinnon Valley, Jerusalem, Israel." *Land and Nature* 13 (1987–88): 123–29.

Fransen, P.-I. "La Vallée de la Géhenne." *Bible et Terre Sainte* 158 (Feb. 1974): 10–17.

Milikowsky, C. "Which Gehenna? Retribution and Eschatology in the Synoptic Gospels and Early Jewish Texts." *New Testament Studies* 34 (1988): 238–49.

Watson, D. F. "Gehenna" *ABD* 2:926–28.

Jerusalem, Herodian

Importance

Jerusalem was the capital of Herod's kingdom and the religious center of Palestinian and Diaspora Judaism. Jesus went to Jerusalem several times, finished his ministry and was crucified there.

Scripture References

Matt. 3:5; 4:25; 5:35; 16:21; 20:17, 18; 21:1, 10; 23:37-39; Mark 1:5; 10:32, 33; 11:1; Luke 2:22, 25, 38, 43, 45; 6:17; 9:31, 53; 10:30; 13:4; 18:31; 19:11, 28; 21:20, 24; 23:7; 24:18, 33, 47, 49, 52; John 4:20, 21, 45; 12:12.

General Information

Although the etymology of the name Jerusalem is uncertain, many scholars believe it to be a combination of two words, *yrv*, "to lay a foundation" or "to establish" and *salem*, a form of the name of the West Semitic god *Shalem* who was probably the patron god of the city. Only later was *Shalem* interpreted as *shalom*, with "Jerusalem" meaning the "city of peace" instead of "city of (the god) Shalem."

By the first century, Jerusalem had experienced a succession of constructions and destructions, including the building projects of David and Solomon and ending with the extensive work of Herod the Great. When David captured Jerusalem, the city was neither in the territory of Benjamin nor in Judah's. It was known as Jebus, the city of the Jebusites. Because David conquered it with his own mercenaries, it became a royal domain independent from tribal territories. David himself called it the "City of David" (2 Sam. 5:9), and it is so designated twenty-nine times in the Hebrew Bible. Luke calls Bethlehem the "City of David" improperly (Luke 2:4, 11). Jerusalem became the symbolic center of the kingdom when David brought to it the Ark of the Covenant, which had been captured by the Philistines (2 Sam. 6:2). Within the city, David had taken a citadel called Zion (2 Sam. 5:7; 1 Chron. 11:5), the location of which has been lost. What is called Mount Zion in Jerusalem today is not the Zion of David. Very early, Zion came to mean either the Temple Mount or Jerusalem itself. David bought a threshing floor from the Jebusite Araunah and built an altar on it (2 Sam. 24:24-25). In 2 Chronicles 3:1, the place of the threshing floor is called Mount Moriah for the first time; by reference to Genesis 22:2 it became known as the location of Isaac's interrupted sacrifice—a tradition of dubious validity (*see* SAMARIA, SAMARITANS). The Holy of Holies, or the altar of the Herodian Temple, may have been located on the spot of Araunah's threshing floor.

Solomon extended the city northward by building a new palace and the First Temple, a building that had already been planned by David. Between the City of David and the new buildings, he filled a narrow depression, known as the Millo, which was up to that time the northern limit of the city (2 Sam. 5:9; 1 Kings 9:15). In the city extension, between the Millo and the Temple-palace complex, was an area known as the Ophel (*see* JERUSALEM, CITY OF DAVID, OPHEL). By the first century, the Ophel was much smaller than in monarchic times because of the southern extension of the Herodian Temple platform; it began at the bottom of the monumental stairs at the foot of the southern wall where the Hulda Gates were located. The contour of the city wall south of the Temple followed the shape of the west bank of the Kidron just as in David's time. In 586 B.C.E. the Babylonian king Nebuchadnezzar took and destroyed the city, including the First Temple. After the Babylonian exiles returned in 538, they repaired the walls and built the Second Temple. The Birah, a fortress at the northwest corner of the Temple, was built at the same time.

Persian control of Jerusalem ended when Alexander the Great captured the city in 332 B.C.E. During the wars between the successors of Alexander the Great, Jerusalem was dominated by the Ptolemies of Egypt until the end of the third century B.C.E. In 198 B.C.E., it was captured by the Seleucids of Antioch. Under Antiochius IV Epiphanes's policy of Hellenization, a gymnasium was built below the Temple as well as a new town on the western hill, which was to be called Antioch but remained known as the Upper City.

When Antiochus IV desecrated the Temple (167 B.C.E.), the Maccabean revolt began and the Seleucids erected the fortress Akra. From the time of the liberation of Jerusalem and the rededication of the Temple by Judas Maccabee (164 B.C.E.), the city was divided between the Hellenizers and Syrians in the Upper City and the Jews in the Temple Mount and Lower City. When Simon Maccabee, brother and successor of Judas and Jonathan, took the Akra in 141 B.C.E., the city was then reunified, with the Upper City included within new fortifications. The Hasmoneans (Maccabean rulers) built a palace at the western limit of the city and a bridge between the Upper City and the Temple. The Upper City, the Hasmonean palace, and the bridge remained part of the Jerusalem of the first century C.E.

In the civil war between the sons of Jannaeus, both parties looked to the Romans for help. As a result, Pompey took Jerusalem in 63 B.C.E. and Palestine came under Roman rule. Two decades later, Herod, of Idumean origin, was appointed king by the Roman Senate. He reigned from 37 to 4 B.C.E., but first had to gain control of his kingdom, which was either in a state of rebellion in Galilee or held in part by Hasmonean pretenders (Jerusalem). He then began an ambitious building program. In Jerusalem he doubled the size of the Temple platform by extending it to the south; he built a monumental stairway at the southwestern corner of the Temple Mount; he restored the Birah and renamed it Antonia; he built a magnificent palace with three gigantic towers in the northwestern corner of the Upper City (a fourth tower, the highest, called "Psephinus," seems to have been built by Agrippa I.) He restored the Hasmonean fortifications or built new ones, forming the second wall around the upper part of the Tyropoeon Valley, a commercial district; he also built a theater in the Upper City, an amphitheater, and a hippodrome.

The Jerusalem of Jesus' time was to a great extent the product of Herod's extraordinary building projects. The only change of importance made between the death of Herod and the destruction of the Temple in 70 C.E. was the addition of an aqueduct 25 miles long by Pilate; Josephus, who give the information, does not specify the source of the water (*Antiq.* 18, 3.2/60).

Archaeological Data

Jerusalem has been the most excavated site in Israel since 1838 when E. Robinson found the Herodian arch, which bears his name today. He was succeeded by F. de Saulcy (1864), Count de Vogué, Sir C. Wilson (who found the Hasmonean arch [1864–67]), and Lieutenant C. Warren of the "Warren's Shaft" (1867). Warren also found the remains of the other end of the arch, which had a span of 39 feet. Among the many other archaeologists who have since worked in Jerusalem, the most notable would include:

- C. Clermont-Ganneau, 1871–73, stone from Temple bearing an inscription in Greek and Latin, City of David.

- F. J. Bliss and A. C. Dickie, 1894–97, identification of the southern wall of Jerusalem, Siloam Church, City of David.

- R. Weill, 1913–14, Ophel, City of David. 1925–27, wall north of the Old City.

- R. A. S. Macalister and J. G. Duncan, 1923–25, Ophel and City of David.
- J. W. Crowfoot and G. M. Fitzgerald, 1927–28, Western Gate, Ophel.
- K. Kenyon, 1962–67, Ophel, Temple wall, City of David.
- B. Mazar, 1968–82, Temple wall, southern area, and other Israeli archeologists: R. Amiram, M. Ben Dov, N. Avigad, Y. Shiloh, M. Broshi, M. Avi-Yonah, H. Geva, M. Rosen-Ayalon, D. Bahat.

Archaeological work has been very difficult and frustrating. Repeated cycles of destruction and rebuilding have eradicated many ancient remains; valleys have been filled with rubble, sometimes to a depth of 75 feet; hills have eroded; the archaeological levels have been badly disturbed; building materials have been constantly displaced and reused (*see* fig. 42). In addition, religious groups have opposed research in certain areas. Nevertheless, excavations have made important contributions to our knowledge of ancient Jerusalem and have clarified many references to the city in the Bible and in other literary sources. The results of

archaeological investigation of Herodian Jerusalem appear in the excellent reconstitution located next to the Holy Land Hotel in Jerusalem. M. Avi-Yonah supervised its construction in 1966; and it is kept up-to-date as new discoveries are made. The study of Jerusalem in connection with Jesus' life and time is reported in this volume in a number of other entries: JERUSALEM, CAIAPHAS' HOUSE; JERUSALEM, CAIAPHAS' TOMB; JERUSALEM, CITY OF DAVID, OPHEL; JERUSALEM, GEHENNA, AKELDAMA; JERUSALEM, HEROD'S PALACE; JERUSALEM, KIDRON; JERUSALEM, POOL OF BETHESDA; JERUSALEM, POOL OF SILOAM; JERUSALEM, STREETS AND STAIRS; JERUSALEM, TOMBS; JERUSALEM, UPPER CITY; JERUSALEM, UPPER ROOM; JERUSALEM, WALLS AND GATES; JERUSALEM, WATER SYSTEM. *See* also the TEMPLE entries.

Implications for Jesus Research

In Jesus' time, Jerusalem had the general configuration and appearance represented by fig. 43. Besides the Temple, which was a city and an economic entity by itself, there were ancient Jerusalem, the Lower City, the Upper City with Herod's Palace, and the New City enclosed by the second wall.

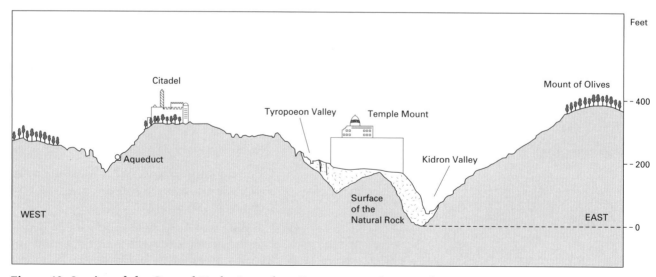

Figure 42 Section of the Ground Under Jerusalem. East-west, at the Temple Mount.

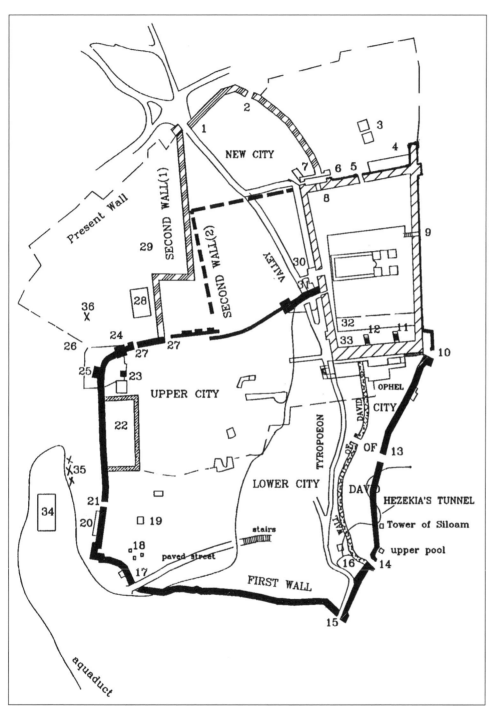

1: Ephraim or Fish Gate (Damascus Gate)
2: Gate of Benjamin
3: Pool of Bethesda
4: Pool of Israel
5: Sheep Gate?
6: Antonia
7: Strouthion Pool
8: Tadi Gate?
9: Shushan Gate (Golden Gate)
10: Horse Gate (Scape Goat Gate?)
11: Triple Hulda gate and stairs
12: Double Hulda gate and stairs
13: Spring or fountain gate
14: Casemate or water gate (King's garden area?)
15: Potsherd or Potter's Gate (Ancient Dung Gate?)
16: Pool of Siloam
17: Essenes' Gate
18: Essenes and Dyers' Quarters
19: Upper Room, New Tomb of David
20: Bethso (Essenes' Latrine)
21: Western Gate (Dung Gate)
22: Herod's Palace
23: Mariamne Tower
24: Hippicus Tower
25: Phasael Tower
26: Present Jaffa Gate
27: Possible locations of the Gannath Gate
28: Towers Pool
29: Traditional site of Golgotha
30: Warren's Gate
31: Xistos Bridge, Wilson's Arch
32: Barclay's Gate
33: Robinson's Arch
34: Snake Pool
35: Ancient Jewish Tombs
36: Hyrcanus' Monument

Figure 43 Herodian Jerusalem. A plausible rendering. Two hypothetical Second Walls are represented.

Ancient (First Temple) Jerusalem, south of the Temple, was comprised of the Ophel and City of David. Some wealthy families and also some of the priests and Levites perhaps lived in the area where the kings of Adiabene built their palaces. The ancient western wall of the City of David apparently had been restored and was used as an inner city boundary. Just west of the ancient city was the Lower City in the lower part of the Tyropoeon Valley, where the common people lived. At its southeastern extremity, according to John 9, the man born blind washed his eyes with the waters of the pool of Siloam. Jesus crossed this section of the city as he was led to the house of Caiaphas, located in the Upper City. If he climbed the stairs leading to the aristocratic quarter (*see* fig. 43), he would have seen the white structure of the theater and farther in the northwest the high silhouettes of the three high towers from the top of which it was possible to see the Dead Sea and the mountains of Moab in the east, and the Mediterranean in the west.

North of the Upper City, beyond the first wall, lay the Upper Tyropoeon or New City with its stores and markets. Outside the second wall, north of the Temple were the Pools of Israel and Bethesda (or Sheep Pool) and the sheep market. In the northwest of the second wall was the wood market and in the west, gardens and quarries with the Towers' Pool just north of the royal palace. In this area, west of the second wall, the traditional site of Golgotha has been located since the time of Constantine (*see* GOLGOTHA, TRADITIONAL SITE).

When one tries to imagine the Jerusalem of Jesus' day, it must be remembered that the present average level of the city is in some areas 45 feet above the average level of the Jerusalem of Herod. The only place certainly at the same level as 2,000 years ago is the Temple platform. Thus the Temple loomed high above the city and the Tyropoeon, Kidron, and Hinnon Valleys, which were much deeper than they are now (*see* fig. 42). The description of this majestic structure as given by Josephus is probably not exaggerated (*Antiq.* 15, 9/380–425; *see* TEMPLE, HISTORY, DESCRIPTION).

It has been suggested that all the events recorded in the Gospels in connection with the last night of Jesus in Jerusalem, all the going and coming between so many places, could not have happened in one night. (This matter is examined further under JERUSALEM, CAIAPHAS' HOUSE). Yet the distances were not so great for the people of the time for whom walking in long and swift strides was the normal way of traveling. For instance, the distance between Gethsemane and the site attributed to the house of Caiaphas could be covered in 20 minutes at their normal pace. Of course, this does not necessarily mean that all the events of Jesus' last night actually happened.

BIBLIOGRAPHY

Avigad, N. *Discovering Jerusalem*. New York: Thomas Nelson, 1980.

Avi-Yonah, N. "Excavation in Jerusalem." *Qadmoniot* 5 (1972): 70–73 (Hebrew).

Ben Dov, M. *In the Shadow of the Temple: The Discovery of Ancient Jerusalem*. Translated by I. Friedman. Jerusalem: Keter, 1982.

Davis, H. "Jerusalem Model Rediscovered." *BAR* 13 (1987): 60–62.

Jacoby, R. *Selected Plans and Illustrations. Companion to Archaeology of Jerusalem*. Jerusalem: Hebrew University, 1990.

Kenyon, K. M. "Excavation in Jerusalem 1961–67." *Palestine Exploration Quarterly* (1962–68).

Ma'oz, Z. U. "On the Hasmonean and Herodian Town-plan of Jerusalem." *Eretz Israel* 18 (1985): 46–57 (Hebrew).

Mazar, B. "Herodian Jerusalem in the Light of the Excavations South and Southwest of the Temple Mount." *Cathedra* 8 (July 1978): 29–41.

———. "Excavations Near Temple Mount Reveal Splendors of Herodian Jerusalem." *BAR* 6 (1980): 44–59.

———. *The Mountain of the Lord: Excavations in Jerusalem*. Garden City, N.Y.: Doubleday, 1975.

Safrai, S. "Jerusalem in the Time of the Second Temple." *Sepher Yerushalayim* 1 (1956): 369–91.

Shiloh, Y., B. Mazar, H. Geva, M. Ben Dov, N. Avigad, N. Rosen-Ayalon, and D. Bahat. "Jerusalem." *NEAEHL* 2:698-804.

Jerusalem, Herod's Palace

Importance

Herod's palace, which was the Jerusalem residence of the Roman prefects in the first century C.E., is one of the sites proposed for Jesus' condemnation by Pilate.

Scripture References

Matt. 27:27; Mark 15:16; John 18:28, 33; 19:9, 13.

General Information

The palace built by Herod the Great at the western edge of the Upper City, although known largely from Josephus' description rather than from archaeological materials, was a feat of architectural achievement and luxurious extravagance (Josephus, *War* 5, 4.4/176–182). It was also a strong fortress comprised of the city fortification wall itself on the western side and an inner wall 30 cubits (45 feet) high in the south and the east, with towers at regular intervals. Josephus refers to it as the "Upper Palace" (*War* 2, 17.5/429) and indicates that during the First Jewish War, which ended with the capture of Jerusalem by the Romans, priests and royal soldiers retreated to this palatial fortress. On the north side was still a stronger fortress or citadel formed by three large towers named in memory of persons dear to Herod: Hippicus, a friend slain in battle; a brother Phasael, also killed in war; and Mariamne, his Hasmonean and preferred wife, whom he had slain out of jealousy (*War* 5, 4.3–4/160–73).

According to Josephus' description, the palace contained rooms for a hundred guests, banquet halls, and cloisters, all built with rare stones and wood. Elegant furniture and gold and silver objects adorned the apartments. The palace grounds featured patios, gardens and groves, dovecotes, and ponds with bronze statues out of which water gushed forth. The towers of the northern citadel were built of large white marble blocks tightly joined together. Hippicus, at the northwest corner was a solid block, 32 feet square and 45 feet high; it was surmounted by a reservoir 30 feet high and also a two story building, 32 feet high, with battlements and turrets, for a total height of 120 feet. Phasael, in the northeast, had a solid base of 60 feet cube surmounted by a cloister and another tower for a total height of 135 feet; it was modeled after the famous Pharos* of Alexandria. The third tower, Mariamne, was probably located east of Phasael; its solid base of 30 feet cube supported a "more magnificent building," delicately adorned for a total height of 75 feet.

When Archaelus, son and successor of Herod in Judea, was deposed in 6 C.E., the palace was assigned as the prefectoral residence in Jerusalem, the normal headquarters being in Caesarea Maritima. During the prefect's absence, the palace was probably occupied by a small garrison and a group of slaves under the supervision of a steward. The permanent prefectoral representative was most likely the tribune commander of the cohort in the Antonia. At the beginning of the First Jewish War, when the Romans had evacuated Jerusalem, the rebels seized the palace, which they finally burnt, along with the upper part of the three towers (*War* 5, 4.4/182–83). After he subdued the rebellion, Titus left the towers and part of the western wall standing and installed a garrison in the southern area of the palace's ruins (*War* 7, 1.1/1–2). Successive invaders—Arabs, Crusaders, Mameluks, and Turks occupied the site and destroyed it further. Today, the only remains of Herod's magnificent palace and towers are to be found in the Citadel, just south of the Jaffa Gate, which dates mostly from the Mameluk period. What is today called David's Tower (a name given by the Crusaders) incorporates elements of the Phasael Tower.

Archaeological Data

Very few remains of Herod's enormous palace have been recovered. Bliss and Dickie in 1894 unearthed a wall in the Citadel from the Hasmonean period, which had been incorporated in a new structure.

Excavating in the same area from 1934 to 1948, C. N. Johns discovered the Hasmonean and Herodian base of David's Tower, which he identified with Phasael. The tower had been built into a previous Hasmonean wall as can be inferred from coins of Alexander Jannaeus discovered there. In 1968–69, R. Amiran and A. Eitan found the remains of a large tower preserved to a height of 10 feet. It was inside the Hasmonean fortification wall, which was also recognized by M. Broshi in 1971 when he excavated in the Armenian Garden; it was the same as the one Bliss and Dickie had previously identified. Altogether, it appears that the foundations were deep and that the palace complex was built on a platform at least 10 feet higher than the first Hasmonean construction. On the eastern side it extended probably to what is today the Street of the Armenian Patriarchate.

Implications for Jesus Research

Scholars are divided as to the location of the *praetorium*, "prefectoral residence," at the time Jesus was condemned by Pilate. The Gospels use this Latin term as well as the Greek *lithosthroton*, "stone paved area," Hebrew *gabbatha*, "elevated place," and Greek form *bematos* (from the Hebrew *bema*, "judicial bench" or "platform"), but do not indicate its location (Matt. 27:27; Mark 15:16; John 18:28, 33; 19:9, 13).

Herod's palace was almost certainly the *praetorium* in Jerusalem. According to Philo, Pilate resided in the palace at the occasion of the great feasts in the Holy City (*Delegation to Gaius*, chap. 38). Gessius Florus resided in the palace in May 66 just before the beginning of the First Jewish Revolt when he came to Jerusalem with murderous intentions and slaughtered 3,600 persons, including women and children (*War* 2, 14.8–9/301–8). Yet no specific evidence establishes that Pontius Pilate was residing in Herod's palace when he condemned Jesus to be crucified. Herod's palace was the normal prefectoral residence in Jerusalem; yet Pilate could have elected to stay in the Antonia at the time of Jesus' last Passover (*see* ANTONIA, PAVEMENT). If Jesus was sentenced to death by Pilate at

the palace, the most logical place would have been at its eastern gate opening on a square where the prefect would have had a *bema* or *sella curulis*, "judgment seat." Those who defend this hypothesis interpret the "Upper Market Place" of Josephus (*War* 2, 14.9/305) as a "large city square next to the palace." It is highly improbable that Herod would have planned a market place at one of the main gates of his palace, and that a prefect would have tolerated the gathering of crowds at his door on a regular and perhaps daily basis.

BIBLIOGRAPHY

Amiran, R. and A. Eitan. "Excavations in the Citadel, Jerusalem, 1968–1969." Preliminary Report. *Eretz Israel* 11 (1973): 213–18 (Hebrew).

Geva, H. "Jerusalem." *NEAEHL* 2:725–29.

Levine, L. I. "Symposium. Herod's Building Projects: Toward an Appraisal of Herod as a Builder." *The Jerusalem Cathedra* 1 (1981): 62–66.

Netzer, E. "Herod's Building Program." *ABD* 3:169–72.

Jerusalem, Kidron

Importance

Jesus crossed the Kidron Valley daily when he was in Jerusalem.

Scripture Reference

John 18:1.

General Information

Kidron is the name of an intermittent brook and valley on the north and east sides of Jerusalem. It separates the city and Temple from the Mount of Olives. The original meaning of the word is "dark" or "shady," which probably indicates that the valley was originally quite deep before construction projects in the area began. The present floor of the valley in places is at least 50 feet higher than the natural one, because the brook is now covered and runs underground. The bottom of the valley was filled by alluviums deposited over the course of time as well as by rubble resulting from successive destructions. The valley begins in the northwest of Jerusalem, runs east for about a mile, then turns south. In the southern corner of what is now the Old City, which coincides with the end of the ridge on which the original City of David was built, it merges with the Tyropoeon Valley (Valley of the Cheesemakers), which runs north-south and formed the western limit of the City of David. In the same southern area, coming from the west, is the Ben Hinnon Valley (*see* JERUSALEM, GEHENNA, AKELDAMA). Beyond, the Kidron continues to the southeast, passes the monastery of Mar Saba, and reaches the Dead Sea.

The Kidron and its tributaries determined the shape of Jerusalem. Originally, its deep ravine protected the City of David and the Temple from assailants coming from the east. It provided Jerusalem with its only spring, Gihon, situated on its western slope. Its water was tunnelled within the city to the Pool of Siloam by King Hezekiah (2 Chron. 32:3-5). On its eastern side, a series of tombs, some of which are monumental and almost intact after more than two millennia of existence, were hewn into its steep rocky slope.

Jesus is not the only biblical figure associated with the Kidron. When David fled before his son Absalom, he crossed the "Brook Kidron" (2 Sam. 15:23). Idols erected in the area were destroyed by righteous kings: Asa, Hezekiah, Josiah (1 Kings 15:13; 2 Kings 23:4, 6, 12; 2 Chron. 15:16; 29:16). The central part of the Kidron Valley near the city was called Jehoshaphat (Joel 3:2, 12), the place of the last judgment where the dead would be raised. Islamic tradition added the idea that everyone would have to cross the Kidron walking on the sharp edge of a sword set over it as a bridge. According to Jeremiah 31:39-40, the Kidron Valley was included in the area holy to the Lord.

Archaeological Information

The slopes of the Kidron Valley contain thousands of tombs. The following are among the most important ones existing at the beginning of the first century C.E.

In the upper valley, a magnificent tomb cave was excavated by de Saulcy in the mid-nineteenth century and erroneously attributed to the kings of Judah. In fact, this cave was prepared for queen Helena of Adiabene who was attracted to Judaism and moved to Jerusalem in 35 C.E. This tomb was so outstanding that it was visited and described by ancient authors such as Josephus, Pausanias, Eusebius, and Jerome. Indeed, this is one of the most beautiful tomb caves in Jerusalem and among the few that can be attributed with reasonable certainty to a known historical figure. Large steps descend to a spacious court in front of the cave. According to Josephus there were three pyramids on the top of the decorated façade. The cave contains several rooms with 47 burial niches. The excavations revealed rare finds, among them a sarcophagus that may be that of the queen.

Farther down the valley stand the famous tombs that are incorrectly called tombs of Jehoshaphat, Absalom, James the Lesser (Hezir), and Zechariah. The Tomb Cave of Jehoshaphat, which contains eight rooms and a decorated façade, has been dated to the first century C.E. The nearby Absalom Monument, also from the first century C.E. is a mausoleum partly rock-hewn and partly freestanding. Its features include Ionic pilasters, Doric friezes, an architrave, and a conical roof. The Tomb of James is a rock-hewn cave with a façade featuring two Doric columns carved between two pilasters. A Hebrew inscription on the architrave dated to the time of Herod the Great, identifies the tomb with the priestly family of Hezir, probably the Hazir of 1 Chronicles 24:15 and Nehemiah 10:20. The cave contains a vestibule, a court with a colonnaded façade, and a central room surrounded by rooms with *kokhim*, burial niches, (*see* JERUSALEM, TOMBS). Zechariah's Tomb is a monument hewn in the rock with no place for burials. A cube decorated with Ionian capitals, it supports an Egyptian cornice and a pyramid. No name or any attribution is written on this first-century structure, perhaps because it was never finished.

Absalom's Tomb. *It is believed that the tomb was built on the Mount of Olives in the expectation of the final resurrection, as the thousands behind it.*

Facing the Temple, half way down the Mount of Olives, is an ancient cemetery near the Franciscan chapel of Dominus Flevit ("the Lord wept"). Tombs, sarcophagi, and ossuaries dating from the second century B.C.E. to the first century C.E. and from the Late Roman period have been found there in great number. Some of the ossuaries bear names such as Martha, Mary, Simeon, John, Joseph, and Salome. This necropolis was excavated in 1953–55 by P. B. Bagatti, J. T. Milik and O. Sellers.

Implications for Jesus Research

The tomb monuments of the Kidron Valley, like many other remnants of the past, indicate that traditions do not always provide evidence of historical fact. The "Stone of Bethsaida" is a recent example of how traditions unrelated to historical reality are born (*see* BETHSAIDA). Yet, there is a tendency to accept as authentic "established tradition," especially that of Jesus' burial, which may not predate the fourth century C.E. (*see* GOLGOTHA, TRADITIONAL SITE).

Many first-century Jews, including the Qumranites, had eschatological expectations (*see* QUMRAN and DEAD SEA SCROLLS). Despite a new trend to the contrary in British and American scholarship, it is possible that Jesus too would have had such expectations. If he entered Jerusalem for his last Passover as described in the Gospels (Mark 11:7-10 and parallels), he may have been asserting through a symbolic action, that he was the Messiah. In accordance with traditional eschatological beliefs, he came from the east, from the top of the Mount of Olives, riding an ass (Zech. 9:9). He had previously raised the dead, and he crossed the Kidron to reach the Temple. It is uncertain whether he entered the Temple through the Shushan (Golden) Gate, as tradition would have it. Both Mark and Matthew indicate that he entered Jerusalem before going to the Temple; Luke could imply that Jesus entered the

Temple immediately after having wept over it (Luke 19:45); John does not specify anything. According to Matthew 21:11, the crowds said, "This is the prophet Jesus," not "the Messiah"; Luke has his Emmaus travelers use the expression "Jesus of Nazareth, who was a prophet mighty in deed and word" (Luke 24:19). This lack of consistency among the Gospels perhaps is the result of writers or editors describing Jesus' entry in a way that would make it agree with popular beliefs in order to prove that he was the expected Davidic Messiah.

Jesus would certainly have seen the recently-built mausoleums of the Kidron Valley. The names inscribed on some of the ossuaries of the Dominus Flevit cemetery do not conclusively indicate that Martha, Mary, and Simon the Leper are buried there even though the Kidron Valley was certainly used as a cemetery in the first century. The Valley may also have offered shelter to homeless hired workers, beggars, and adventurers attracted to the city, especially at the time of the pilgrim festivals.

BIBLIOGRAPHY

Avigad, N. "The Rock Carved Façades of the Jerusalem Necropolis." *IEJ* 1 (1950–51): 96–106.

Avi-Yonah, M. Review of Bagatti, P. B., and Milik, J. T., *Gli Scavi del Dominus Flevit. IEJ* 11 (1961): 91–94.

———. "A Depository of Inscribed Ossuaries in the Kidron Valley." *IEJ* 12 (1962): 1–12.

———. *Ancient Monuments in the Kidron Valley.* Jerusalem, 1954 (Hebrew).

Bagatti, B., and J. T. Milik. *Gli Scavi del 'Dominus Flevit,' Gerusalemme.* Jerusalem, 1958 (Italian).

Bagatti, B. "Nuovi apporti archeologici al Dominus Flevit (Oliveto), Studii Biblici Franciscani." *Liber Annuus* 1969, 194–236 (Italian).

Jerusalem, Pool of Bethesda

Importance

According to the Fourth Gospel, Jesus healed a paralytic at the Pool of Bethesda.

Scripture Reference

John 5:2-9.

General Information

The name "Bethesda" has different renderings in several manuscripts and ancient writings: Bethsaida, Bethzatha, Probatica. Bethsaida, "place of fishing," probably is the result of scribal error. Bethzatha is represented, with variations, in several manuscripts including *Codex Sinaiticus* (fourth century) and is used by Eusebius. In Josephus it designates the area north of the Antonia; he translates it in Greek by *Kaine Polis*, "new city" (*War* 5, 4.2/149–51). Probatica, which comes from the Greek name for sheep, was used by Jerome: "Bethesda is the pool of Jerusalem which is called Probatic, which we can translate 'Sheep Pool'" (*De situ et nom. loc. hebr.*, 23, Bethesda). Eusebius, Cyril of Alexandria, and John Chrysostom preserve the same interpretation, but associate the name with the gate leading to the Temple in the area of the pool.

Jerome describes the pool as follows:

> Bethesda, a pool of Jerusalem . . . had five porticoes; [local people] show a double pool, one of which is fed with winter rainfalls; surprisingly, the water of the other appears reddish as if tainted by blood and thus attests its ancient use by the priests who, as it is said, would come here to wash the [sacrificial] victims, and this is where its name comes from (*De Situ*, vol. 23).

Bethesda could mean "place of mercy" or "place of outpouring." A more descriptive but correct translation of John 5:2 would read, "Now in Jerusalem, by the Sheep [Gate], there is a pool called Bethesda in Hebrew." The Bordeaux Pilgrim (333) reports that he saw two pools and five porticoes there. Cyril of Jerusalem (348–386) adds that the fifth portico was in the center, and Theodosius (530) indicates that the sick came to bathe in the waters of the pool.

The pool of Bethesda is identified with a large pool located in the property of the White Fathers, close to the Church of Saint Ann, between today's Lion Gate (or Saint Stephen's Gate) and the Convent of the Sisters of Sion. The pool was constructed in the river bed of the Beth Zetha valley. This valley begins where the American Colony

Hotel is now located, crosses the city walls near the Rockefeller Museum, and joins the Kidron Valley near the Lion Gate. Several other large pools of the Beth Zetha valley include the Israel Pool, which attracted the attention of many eighteenth-century artists.

The Bethesda pool itself consisted of two pools arranged in a north-south direction with a common wall between them. The northern pool was probably constructed during the reign of the latest kings of Judah, by the end of the seventh or the beginning of the sixth century B.C.E. The southern pool was built in the beginning of the second century B.C.E. by Simon the High Priest to supply the Temple with more water (Sir. 50:3). Its reconstruction is based on the descriptions of John 5:2-4, Eusebius, and early Christian pilgrims. Later pilgrims who mention the pool were probably describing its fifth-century alteration. The original purpose of the pools was perhaps to wash the sheep brought to sacrifice in the Temple, as the name "Sheep Pool" suggests. Later it became known as a place where healings were performed by the God of the Jews and by pagan gods. When Jerusalem was rebuilt by Hadrian under the name of Aelia Capitolina, a shrine was erected there in honor of the Greco-Roman god Asclepios or Aesculapius, as indicated by a number of ex-voto* offerings presented by pilgrims who wanted to be cured or had obtained favors from the god.

Some scholars believe that the site was already dedicated to pagan gods by the time of Jesus. They point to the existence of a strong party of Jewish Hellenizers in the time of Antiochus IV Epiphanes (175–164 B.C.E.). At that time sacrifices were offered to Zeus in the Temple, and pagan shrines flourished everywhere. Even after the rededication of the Temple to Yahweh by Judas Maccabeus in 165 B.C.E., Gentiles in Jerusalem could have continued to worship their own gods, especially such a popular god as Asclepios. In any case, the advent of the Herodian rulers and, afterward, the presence of Roman governors allowed pagan cults to flourish. In the Herodian and Early Roman periods the shrine may have been dedicated either to Asclepios

or to Eshmun or Shadrapa, the Canaanite-Phoenician god of healing.

During the fifth century C.E. the pools were rebuilt and a basilica was added to commemorate the miracle performed by Jesus. The porticoes around the pool mentioned by John were removed, and the wall between the pools was reinforced. A majestic church was built over the pools, extending from the middle of the wall to some 75 feet beyond the pools. The aisles of the church were supported by arches that stood 40 feet high. Near the tomb of one of the priests of the church, which was discovered near the Lion Gate during the 1930s, was found an inscription bearing the name of the church, "Probatica"—the Sheep Pool.

The Pool of Bethesda is mentioned in the Copper Scroll from Qumran (3Q15, 57–58) dated to about 100 C.E. It lists the places in Jerusalem where treasures (probably from the Temple) were hidden. The Bethesda pool is designated with a dual plural form, a grammatical particularity of Hebrew: *beth'esdatayin*, which corresponds to "twin pool." The Scroll reads:

> Near there, at Beth'esdatayin, in the pool: Where one goes into the small pool there is a jar of aloe wood and one of white pine resin. Near there, at the western entrance of the porch of the Triclinium [dining hall] near the place of the stove are 900 talents of silver and 500 talents of gold.

The fifth century Byzantine basilica and the pool were destroyed by the Persians in 614. Later, a small chapel was built on the site. The first Church of Saint Ann was erected there by the Crusaders; Ann is the traditional name of the mother of Mary who, although her parents were said to have had a house in the area, was supposedly born in a cave near the pool. Another tradition has her born in Sepphoris.

Archaeological Data

In 1866, an ex-voto* foot was found in the ancient vaulted foundation of the Church of Saint Ann; it bears an inscription, "Ponpeia Lucilia dedicated . . . ," which Clermont-Ganneau dated to the earliest part of the second century C.E. on paleographic grounds. While working at the restoration of Saint Anne in 1871, M. Mauss first discovered elements of the pool. The 1876 discovery of the church's apse led to intermittent excavations by the White Fathers in collaboration with the archaeologists of the Ecole Biblique; the results were published in 1928 by L. H. Vincent. The White Fathers, Blondel and Pocher, began systematic excavations in 1956 under the direction of Father Rouzée from the Ecole Biblique. They unearthed the Sheep Pool and a shrine to a healing god; more specifically:

1. An immense trapezoidal cistern divided in two by a rock dike 20 feet wide, oriented east-west. The overall measurements are 135 feet in the north, 148 ½ feet in the east 142 ½ feet in the west, 196 ½ feet in the south, for a total area of over 24,000 square feet. The depth is 45 feet. At the southeast corner of the northern pool was a 50 x 20 feet cistern with a vaulted roof. The pools were probably fed by rain water and underground springs. The "stirring of the water" of John 5:7 is explained in some manuscripts of the Fourth Gospel as a certain action of an "angel of the Lord." Perhaps at the end of the rainy season, when the upper pool was full, its overflow was channeled into the lower pool and caused some turbulence. Another possibility is that one of the springs was intermittent.

2. A healing cult shrine with vaulted underground chambers, each one having a small rock-cut pool, grouped around a natural cave. Some chambers were decorated with paintings and mosaics; the water system included canals and tunnels. The complex was dated to the Early Roman period but was reused in Hadrian's time and dedicated to Asclepios as indicated by ex-voto* offerings. The small pools in the chambers were perhaps used for a ritual of underground incubation, as was commonly practiced in the healing cults, before the final ablutions.

In addition to the ex-voto* foot found in 1866, the excavated complex yielded the terra-cotta statuette of a woman with her right hand over her left breast to show the place of healing, a bas-relief in white marble showing a woman in a bath, two ex-voto boats sculptured in rock, two fragments of a small shrine to Asclepios with a representation of the sacred serpent and sheaves of wheat used in the death-life rituals of subterranean divinities.

Implications for Jesus Research

Many scholars question the reliability of the Fourth Gospel as a source of information about the historical Jesus. Yet the primary author of the Gospel of John was probably an eyewitness to several events in the life of Jesus. He was apparently well acquainted with Jerusalem and its surroundings. The Pool of Bethesda, not mentioned by the other evangelists, did exist in the first century. Jesus may have performed a healing there to demonstrate the superiority of his God over a pagan god, as may also have been the case in Phoenicia (*see* TYRE AND SIDON). The method of healing cannot be explained in modern terms. In Jesus' time many healing practices performed by physicians, priests, healers, magicians, and miracle workers were recognized and accepted by the people of his time (*see* EXORCISM; MAGIC, MIRACLES; MEDICINE, PHYSICIANS; and TRADITIONAL HEALING).

BIBLIOGRAPHY

Benoit, P. "Découvertes archéologiques autour de la piscine de Bethesda." *Jerusalem through the Ages, 25th Archaeological Convention* (1967): 48–57.

Duprez, A. "La Piscine Probatique au temps du Christ." *Bible et Terre Sainte* 86 (1966): 4–15.

Mackowski, R. M. *Jerusalem City of Jesus.* Grand Rapids, Mich.: Eerdmans, 1980.

Jerusalem, Pool of Siloam

Importance

Water from the Pool of Siloam was used in a Temple ritual of the Feast of Tabernacles. Jesus sent a blind man to wash his eyes in the pool.

Scripture Reference

John 9:7.

General Information

The Pool of Siloam is located in the Lower Ty-ropoeon Valley, west of the City of David, at the level of the southern end of the spur on which the original city was built. The name derives from the Hebrew *shiloah*, which means "aqueduct" or, more literally, "the sent [of water]" (Isa. 8:6). The pool was filled with water from the Gihon spring through a tunnel dug by King Hezekiah when the Assyrians were threatening Jerusalem (*see* JERUSALEM, WATER SYSTEM). Before the tunnel was dug the water of the Gihon was drawn directly from the spring, which had a reservoir. The water was also channeled to cultivation terraces by means of conduits either dug in the rock like tunnels or covered with slabs, depending on the terrain. Pools at the lower part of the Kidron Valley stored the unused water of the Gihon. One of them may be the Pool of Shelah (pool of the aqueduct), a reservoir of the King's Garden (Neh. 3:15), possibly the same as the King's Pool (Neh. 2:14), or Pool of Solomon (Josephus, *War* 5, 5.2/145), identified with Birket el-Hama. Some scholars, however believe that the Pool of Siloam is the same as the Pool of Shelah.

Hezekiah's tunnel was not cut in a straight line from Gihon to the Siloam Pool. The S-shape of Hezekiah's tunnel still intrigues scholars and engineers, who offer several explanations: The lack of skill and insufficient surveying techniques of the ancient engineers; and the variable hardness of the rock, which imposed changes of course.

To the first explanation it can be objected that the line of the tunnel started deliberately at each end in a direction different from that of the other terminus. Besides, the surveying methods were not so faulty considering that at the projected point of junction, the two then parallel sections were only 80 feet apart, which for a total length of 1,750 feet represents an error of 4.57 percent—quite remarkable in about 700 B.C.E. for an underground work. To the other explanation it can be answered that a variation of hardness in the rock would not justify a haphazard course. The traditional explanations for the S-shape of the tunnel cannot be sustained.

Two more plausible reasons may be offered here—a technical one and a military one. First in the technical domain, it should be recognized that the engineers probably sought to have a slow flow of water and would have lengthened the tunnel accordingly. Y. Shiloh observed that the bottom of the Pool of Siloam is only one foot below the Spring Gihon for a gradient of only 6:10,000 over 1,750 feet. Over a straight line of 1,050 feet, the shorter distance between the spring and the pool, the gradient would have been almost 1:1,000. Second, from a military perspective, the engineers may have given the tunnel a sinuous course to make an underground invasion more difficult: surprising the enemy with unexpected turns and giving the defenders more time to block the passage or prepare an ambush.

The Pool of Siloam was used as a source of water for purification in the ritual of the red heifer (Num. 19:2-10; *m. Para* 3.2) and for water of libation at the Feast of Tabernacles in late Second Temple times. Of these two rituals, the second was the most popular. The water libation was done at the beginning of the week of the feast according to Talmudic sources. On the morning of the first day the priests went in procession to the Pool of Siloam to bring water back to the Temple in sacred vessels. The procession was announced at the city gates by heralds blowing the shofar. Upon reaching the Temple, the priests circled the altar while the crowd of pilgrims waved their *lulavim,** imitating the sound of falling rain, and sang the Hallel.* The officiating priest then walked up the ramp of the altar to pour water and wine upon it, each from a silver bowl. It seems that this water libation had been imposed by the Pharisees. In protest, the Hasmonean ruler Alexander Jannaeus (104–78 B.C.E.), while officiating as High Priest at the Feast of Tabernacles, poured the water over his feet; the crowd reacted angrily and hurled their *etrogim** at him in a tempest of insults and threats. This hostility toward the non-Zadokite priests continued in the first century as attested in the Qumran literature and may relate to Jesus' action in the Temple (*see* DEAD SEA SCROLLS; QUMRAN; and TEMPLE, ROYAL STOA*)*.

The Bordeaux Pilgrim visited the site in 333 and describes the pool as surrounded by porticoes on its four sides. To commemorate Jesus' healing of the man born blind, Empress Eudocia (444–460) built the Church of Our Savior the Giver of Light over the ruins of a nympheium, "fountain," previously erected there. It stood on a small hill above the pool; it was destroyed in 614 by the Persians and replaced by the Arabs with a mosque. This last building was torn down in the eleventh century with the entire quarter south of today's southern wall.

Archaeological Information

In 1880, school boys playing in Hezekiah's tunnel found a rock slab bearing an inscription. W. F. Albright, among others, recognized its great value. It read,

> . . . when the tunnel was dug through. And this is how it was cut through: while [the men worked with their] picks, each one toward his fellow worker, and while three cubits [still remained] to be cut [through, they heard] the voice of a man calling his fellow, for there was a "zada" (split, overlap?) in the rock on the right and on [the left]. And on the day of the cutting through, the workmen struck each one toward his fellow, pick against pick. And the water started to flow from the springs to the pool, twelve hundred cubits. A hundred cubits was the height of the rock above the heads of the quarrymen (Pritchard, *Ancient Near Eastern Texts*, 321).

The slab is now in the Museum of the Ancient Orient in Istanbul where it was taken during the Ottoman rule of Palestine. The inscription can be related to the events recorded in 2 Kings 20:20 and 2 Chronicles 32:2-3.

In 1897 J. F. Bliss and A. C. Dickie discovered a courtyard about 75 feet square containing the Pool of Siloam, then reduced to 50 x 15 feet. This is all that remains today of the original pool, which was much larger, possibly as much as 80 feet square.

After her 1961–67 excavations, K. Kenyon concluded that the Pool of Siloam was not enclosed within the city walls until the first century C.E. She suggested that the water was kept in an underground cistern outside the city walls, accessible from within by means of a flight of stairs; however, no archaeological evidence substantiates this hypothesis. N. Avigad in 1979 discovered a 23-foot-wide fortification wall in the Jewish Quarter of Old Jerusalem dating from the time of Hezekiah (ca. 690 B.C.E.). He argued that this wall extended south and enclosed the Pool of Siloam, as perhaps indicated in 2 Chronicles 32:5, which specifies that Hezekiah repaired the old wall and built a new one. Kenyon noticed that there were underground channels taking excess water toward the Kidron.

Reconstructions of the pool as it was in the first century C.E. are based primarily on the excavations made by Bliss and Dickie in 1894–97. Additional information comes from excavations east of the pool. The pool was probably rebuilt with three different structures in three successive periods. This fact is sometimes overlooked, with the pool's Byzantine structure being attributed to the time of Jesus.

In order to form the pool, a wide dam was built in the valley; it was reinforced with buttresses embedded in massive foundations. Archaeology was in its infancy when Bliss and Dickie dug the pool; they may have telescoped several phases into one. Still, it is likely that the dam followed the city wall from the southeastern hill known as the City of David to the present Mt. Zion. There is no evidence that the Siloam Pool of the time of Jesus was located where it is shown today to tourists; it was probably situated under the nearby Birket el Hamra where there is now a garden (*see* fig. 44).

After the Second Jewish War (132–135 C.E.) Jerusalem was greatly altered and was renamed Aelia Capitolina. The Pool of Siloam is described in this period as sheltered in a square building; a stepped street along the Tyropoeon Valley led to it from the center of the city. Sixteen columns surrounded the pool and supported another line of sixteen, which formed an upper gallery.

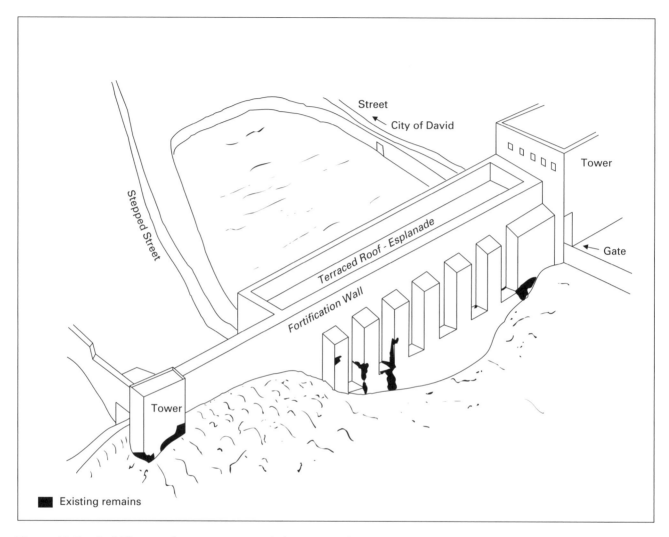

Figure 44 Pool of Siloam, First Century C.E. *(After Dan Bahat, 1989)*

This structure existed until the mid-fifth century, when it was rebuilt by Empress Eudocia. The empress added a church next to the pool. It had three aisles, and those along the walls were higher than the nave. A short flight of stairs from the southern aisle led to a stepped street alongside the pool. It descended steeply 26 feet over a distance of 82 feet. At the bottom of the stairs, eastward, a covered gallery sheltered the access to the water. About 4 feet from the walls stood a lower wall about 2.5 feet high. It may have been built to direct the fresh water arriving from the Gihon Spring all around the pool.

Implications for Jesus Research

In the early first century, the Pool of Siloam was still receiving water from the Gihon Spring through Hezekiah's tunnel as it had been for 700 years. In addition, rain water was directed to the pool through an elaborate drainage system (*see*

JERUSALEM, WATER SYSTEM). Sometimes an overflow of water was probably channeled to other reservoirs such as the Pool of Solomon.

According to John, after having received a plaster on his eyes from Jesus, the blind man found his way to the pool, washed his eyes, and recovered his sight; it seems, however, that the pool was not used for bathing. It is not certain whether it was believed that its water had healing powers as it was the case for the Pool of Bethesda (see JERUSALEM, POOL OF BETHESDA), but its purifying power is suggested by the traditions of its use in the red heifer ritual and the Tabernacles libations. The two disciples sent by Jesus perhaps met the man carrying a jar of water in the area of the Siloam Pool (Mark 14:13-14; see JERUSALEM, WALLS AND GATES; JERUSALEM, UPPER ROOM).

BIBLIOGRAPHY

Adam-Bayewitz, D. "The 'Fountain of Siloam' and 'Solomon's Pool' in First-century C.E. Jerusalem" *IEJ* 29 (1979): 92–100.

Bahat, D. *Jerusalem*. Jerusalem: Israel Exploration Society, 1989 (Hebrew).

Mare, W. H. *The Archaeology of the Jerusalem Area*. Grand Rapids, Mich.: Baker Book House, 1987.

Pritchard, J. B., ed. *Ancient Near Eastern Texts Relating to the Old Testament*. Princeton, N. J.: Princeton University Press, 1955.

Shanks, H. *The City of David: A Guide to Biblical Jerusalem*. Washington: The Biblical Archaeology Society, 1973.

Jerusalem, Streets and Stairs

Importance

Knowing about Jerusalem's street system helps to understand how large numbers of visitors moved through the city. It also helps in reconstructing Jesus' movements during his last days.

Scripture References

Matt. 26:18, 57; 27:2, 31; Mark 14:13, 53; 15:1, 20; Luke 22:10, 66; 23:1, 7; John 18:13, 24, 28; 19:17.

General Information

Because Jerusalem was built over hills and valleys, many of its streets had at least a few sections of steps. Indeed, some areas could be connected with the rest of the city only by stairs. Herod's engineers tried to alleviate this inconvenience; they also used the differences in levels to construct an effective drainage system.

Cities of the Near East grew organically, often without preplanning. The grid pattern, which was invented by Hippodamos of Milet in the fifth century B.C.E. and was in fashion in Western Asia Minor, was not widely spread in Judea and Syria until the end of the first or beginning of the second century C.E. Jerusalem thus developed without a master plan. During the reign of Herod the city expanded; it contained the old nucleus of the City of David, the Lower City, the Upper City (built during the reign of the Hasmoneans in 150 to 100 B.C.E.), and the Tyropoeon Valley, a quarter that was reshaped by Herod the Great when his engineers extended the Temple Mount. The Beth Zetha quarter at the north was probably unevenly inhabited during the first century; it was not surrounded by walls before the period of King Agrippa II (53 to ca. 100 C.E.). The few remains of the streets of Jerusalem from the time of Jesus do not allow an adequate reconstruction of their layout. They do, however, indicate that the main street was in the Tyropoeon Valley and that another street ran along the western wall of the Temple Mount. These two streets perhaps met slightly north of Robinson's Arch and continued as one street, with stairs, down to the Pool of Siloam. The northern end of the street probably reached the Damascus Gate (Ephraim Gate).

Archaeological Information

Many proposed reconstructions of Jerusalem suggest a street layout either in the Hellenistic Hippodamean grid or in the Roman pattern of Cardo and Decomanus. The first pattern is named after the Greek architect Hippodamos, who planned the port city of Athens. His grid was made of wide

Tyropoeon Valley Street.
Western Wall of the City
of David (Jerusalem
Model).

straight streets intersecting at right angles. The Romans modified the grid plan. Whenever they created new cities, they built them around two very large arteries: the *cardo maximus* (from a word that means heart) oriented north-south, and the *decomanus* oriented east-west. The other streets, also crossing at right angles, were narrower. All these reconstructions are conjectural and have little archaeological support.

During the excavations of the Upper City (*see* JERUSALEM, UPPER CITY), N. Avigad discovered foundations of an east-west street presumably part of a remodeling of the city's street pattern. Beneath the street's foundations were remains of a spacious house that had been condemned to allow for road construction. Because the excavator found the house virtually empty, he suggests that the residents of the house had been evacuated before the building was pulled down. The latest finds are from the reign of Herod the Great, indicating that the construction of the street dates to his last years or to the reign of one of his successors. It accords with Josephus's statement that, when the construction of the Temple was completed, Agrippa employed the workers to pave the streets of Jerusalem in order not to lay them off (*see* CONSTRUCTION, CITIES). Fifty-five yards of the street heading to Robinson's Arch have been excavated. The full width of the street has not been determined; 39 feet is the widest preserved area. The surface of the pavement slabs was not flat because they served as a base for a smoother pavement above.

In 1867, C. Warren discovered a stone pavement at a depth of about 13 meters from the ground surface in the southwestern corner area of the Temple. In 1968, M. Ben Dov conducted extensive excavations in the same sector and confirmed the existence of the pavement, unearthed several street sections, and reconstructed the street network in this part of the Temple district in the Herodian period. The Temple surroundings were clearly designed to handle large throngs of people. Some streets were 32 feet wide, with large sidewalks. The paving stones are unusually large and thick, and the street foundations are 20 to 65 feet deep. The size of the stones ranges from 10 to 200 square feet; the biggest ones are 1.5 feet thick and weight 19 tons. The street foundations were structured according to two different techniques: the pavement was either set over stone vaults; or it was laid over a "basement" of thick walls built on bedrock and arranged in squares of about 6 x 6 feet, filled with earth and debris. Such a pavement could have withstood heavy traffic for centuries. The streets were lined with shops constructed of large limestone blocks all in the same style. Perhaps they were built by the authorities and then sold, rented, or leased to merchants or artisans.

Along the entire length of the southern wall, about 700 feet, ran a 24-foot-wide street servicing the Hulda Gates, which gave the multitude access to the Temple. This street started from the Tyropoeon street, about 20 feet below the level of the gates, and rose in steps to become the Hulda Street. South of the gates and street was a large explanade connected with them by two monumental stairs, one about 50 feet wide below the eastern triple gate, the other about 210 feet wide under the western double gate. Under the Hulda Street were shops like those on both sides of the Tyropoeon Street. In fact, the area around the Temple was a huge cosmopolitan bazaar; even the massive supports for Robinson Arch contained four shops where stone jars, weights, and coins were found.

The Tyropoeon Street was the main artery of Jerusalem leading possibly from the Gate of Ephraim in the north (today Damascus Gate) down to the Siloam Pool in the south. It was a well-designed street, with high curbstones to keep the shops dry and a drainage system that brought rain water to the Siloam Pool. A number of smaller stepped streets branched out from the Tyropoeon and led to the Upper City in the west. The broadest one, about 15 feet wide, began in the area of Robinson's Arch and may be the street mentioned above—the one found by Avigad in the present Jewish Quarter (Upper City). In the Upper City another commercial street ran from the Gate of Ephraim to the area of what is known today as Mount Zion, where the "house of Caiaphas" was located (*see* JERUSALEM, UPPER CITY and JERUSALEM, CAIAPHAS' HOUSE).

Implications for Jesus Research

The Jerusalem of Jesus' day was designed to accommodate large crowds of visitors, especially along the arteries servicing the Temple. They swarmed on large plazas and esplanades and patronized the hundreds of shops. According to estimates based on archaeological finds and water systems, M. Ben Dov estimates at more than 150,000 the resident population of Jerusalem at that time, with an additional 100,000 visitors arriving during the pilgrimage festivals (*In the Shadow of the Temple*, 117). Estimates of Jerusalem's population, however, vary widely. One of the most conservative, that of Jeremias, suggests a maximum of 30,000 for permanent residents and perhaps 125,000 for pilgrims (*Jerusalem in the Time of Jesus*, 84).

The city, especially around the Temple, was an immense market. Jesus apparently became angry only at the merchants who traded in or even carried goods across the Temple itself. Like other pilgrims, Jesus and his disciples would have climbed the monumental stairs south of the Temple to enter through the eastern double gate in the morning; they would have exited through the western triple gate in the evening.

Because access to the Temple for ordinary pilgrims was through the Hulda Gates, and because Jesus retired at night to the Mount of Olives, his daily itinerary can be reconstructed. It is unlikely that he used the Potsherd Gate, which opened on the infamous Valley of Hinnon and would have lengthened his route (*see* JERUSALEM, GEHENNA,

AKELDAMA). The gate closer to the Temple, the Spring Gate (*see* JERUSALEM, WALLS AND GATES), which went north through the City of David and climbed the steps leading to the Hulda Gates, would have been preferable. The night of his arrest, he may have left the house of the Last Supper and taken one of the stepped streets down to the Tyropoeon, crossed the City of David, and gone out through the Spring Gate, which is the shortest route to Gethsemane. After his arrest, the soldiers may have led him into the city through the Potsherd Gate (to avoid a disturbance in the respectable quarter of David's City), taken him up the stairs to the Annas-Caiaphas house, and held him there for the rest of the night (*see* JERUSALEM, CAIAPHAS'S HOUSE).

Two possibilities for Jesus' itinerary the following morning, depending on the place where Pilate stayed, can be suggested. The normal prefectoral residence in Jerusalem was the former palace of Herod; but Pilate possibly preferred to lodge in the Antonia with the cohort in times of unrest. There, he would immediately know of any disturbance and could quickly give orders accordingly. The proponents of the traditional "Via dolorosa" route assume that the *praetorium* was in the Antonia, which is perfectly plausible. As for the terminus of Jesus' last journey, Golgotha, the current state of archaeological and historical research makes it impossible to pinpoint a location. (*See* ANTONIA; GARDEN TOMB; GOLGOTHA, TRADITIONAL SITE.)

BIBLIOGRAPHY

Ben Dov, M. *In the Shadow of the Temple.* 1982 (Hebrew). Reprint. Jerusalem: Keter Publishing House, 1985 (English).

de Camp, L. S. *The Ancient Engineers.* 1960. Reprint. New York: Ballatine Books, 1988.

Geva, H. "Jerusalem, The Second Temple Period." *NEAEHL* 2:717-29.

Jeremias, J. *Jerusalem in the Time of Jesus.* German, 1962. Philadelphia: Fortress Press, 1984.

Wilkinson, J. *Jerusalem as Jesus Knew It.* 1978. Reprint. London: Thames and Hudson, 1982.

Jerusalem, Tombs

Importance

The many ancient tombs around Jerusalem provide evidence for first century B.C.E. and C.E. Jewish burial customs and for views about eschatology, afterlife, and purity laws. Such information provides context for Jesus's beliefs.

Scripture References

Matt. 23:27; 27:60; 28:2; Mark 15:46; 16:3-4; Luke 11:44; 24:2; John 20:1.

General Information

Numerous tombs in the Jerusalem area date from the first centuries B.C.E. and C.E. Some older ones were still in use in that period. This article will not attempt to survey all the burial sites and finds; rather it will focus on burial customs related to first-century beliefs about death, resurrection, purity, and messianic expectations.

Burial sites are found everywhere around Jerusalem except west of the Temple, which is the direction from which the prevailing winds blow. Impure acts, persons, or conditions were to be located leeward, not in the west, and sufficiently distant to the north or south so that the sacred place would not be defiled by impurities the western wind might carry. For instance, the ashes of animals killed as sin offerings in the Temple (Lev. 4:1-21) as well as the sacrifices of Yom Kippur (the Day of Purgation or Atonement, Lev. 16:27) were to be carried outside the camp to "a clean place" (Lev. 4:12). A huge ash dump, 40 feet high, was discovered north of Jerusalem, beyond the third wall—not in the east, but far enough to avoid pollution carried by the prevailing western wind. In 1897, Professor Liebig of Munich analyzed its contents and found only the remains of animal flesh, bones, and teeth. The Temple Scroll stipulates that lepers and other unclean persons were to be kept east of the city (11 QTemple 46). In *The Temple Scroll* Y.

Yadin comments that it was believed that the disease of lepers was contagious and carried by the wind. He cites two rabbinic sources:

Rabbi Yohanan said: One is not permitted to pass within four cubits to the east of a leper. Rabbi Simon ben Lakhish said: Within a hundred cubits. There is no contradiction. The one who said four cubits meant when there is no wind blowing; and the one who said within a hundred cubits meant when there is a wind blowing (*Midrash Leviticus Baba Batra* 16).

Obviously, the wind was supposed to blow from the west. The other quotation comes from the Jerusalem Talmud:

Rabbi Mana would walk with people affected with boil. Rabbi Abbaya said to him: Do not walk east of him, but rather west of him (*y. Baba Batra* 3:9, 13; *The Temple Scroll*, 177).

Similarly, the Temple Scroll indicates that the latrines should be northwest of the city, far enough not to be visible, at 3,000 cubits. The War Scroll, however, gives a distance of 2,000 cubits. In reality, the *bethso*, latrines of the Essenes in Jerusalem, was in the southwest, more than 2,000 cubits from the Holy of Holies (*see* JERUSALEM, WALLS AND GATES).

Among the most important first-century burials are the following: in the north, in the Saint George's Cathedral area, the tomb of Queen Helena of Adiabene (erroneously called Tomb of the Kings) and tombs under the Dominican Ecole Biblique et Archéologique. In the northeast, on Mount Scopus: Herodian tombs where an ossuary containing the bones of a crucified man were discovered (*see* CRUCIFIXION). In the east: the many tombs of the Mount of Olives and Kidron Valley (*see* MOUNT OF OLIVES and JERUSALEM, KIDRON). In the southwest, in the area of the King David Hotel: a cluster of tombs called the Herodian Family Tomb and probably alluded to by Josephus's mention of "Herod's Monuments" (*War* 5, 3.2/108). In the southeast: the burial ground of Akeldama (*see* JERUSALEM, GEHENNA, AKELDAMA). In light of the comments

above about wind direction, the tombs to the west in the area of the Church of the Holy Sepulchre (or of the Resurrection) are unexpected. They must predate the first century C.E., as does the tomb of the Hasmonean priest and king John Hyrcanus (134–104 B.C.E.), who was buried there.

In Jesus' time there were no graves in the city itself, except for the ancient tombs of the House of David and of the prophetess Hulda (*t. Nega'im* 6). Based on the latest coins found in the Dominus Flevit necropolis (*see* JERUSALEM, KIDRON), a prohibition to build new tombs in Jerusalem was enacted after 16 C.E. Existing tombs were probably emptied at the same time to purify Jerusalem, which had grown to such an extent that many old tombs came to be included within the city walls. In connection with Numbers 19:16, in order to avoid involuntary defilement, tombs were whitewashed to make them visible even at night. The whiting was done on Adar 15 (beginning of March) to prevent impurity during the Passover (*m. Shekalim* 1:1).

Only a few sarcophagi dating from the first century C.E. have been found. Rather, most burials were carried out in two phases. First, the body was taken to the tomb and laid in a long niche (*kokh*), cut perpendicular to the wall of an underground chamber, or on a bench hewn in the rock, along a wall, frequently with an arch over it, thus the name *arcosolium* (also *kline*). Then, when the flesh had fully decomposed, usually after twelve months to three years, the bones were collected in ossuaries* made of stone or wood, the average size of which was 25 x 15 x 12.5 inches. Hewn in the rock in a cliff or on a hillside, sometimes in abandoned quarries, the typical rock-cut tomb was accessible through a low square opening normally closed with a vertical flat stone shaped like a millstone, which could be rolled back as described in the Gospels. The entrance hole opened to a chamber with *kokhim*, "niches," or *arcosolia*, "benches," in its walls. Several chambers could be connected together with tunnels and constitute underground necropolises of considerable size, as for example, the Dominus Flevit necropolis (*see* JERUSALEM,

Herod's Family Tomb, beyond the valley of Hinnon from the Jaffa Gate, Jerusalem

KIDRON), which contains more than 500 burial spots. On the northern part of the Mount of Olives is a group of tombs in a place called Karm al-Sayyid, which was previously known as Viri Galilaei because Galilean pilgrims attending festivals were thought to camp there.

To be buried in Jerusalem was considered a privilege because it was the Holy City, where the *Shekinah*, "radiant presence," of the Lord resided. Persons of great repute were buried or said to be buried there: David, Hulda, Haggai, Zechariah, Malachi, Mordecai, Simon the Just, and John Hyrcanus, among others. In the Roman Period, the lower part of the Mount of Olives facing the Temple and both sides of the Kidron Valley in the same area became choice burial grounds. It was believed that the Messiah would descend from the Mount of Olives to enter the Temple through the Shushan Gate (or Golden Gate) and raise the dead on his way (*see* JERUSALEM, KIDRON). Some historians suggest that the strength of this belief led the Ottomans to wall up the Golden Gate in 1538, to prevent the Jewish Messiah from entering the Temple platform, which was at that time in Muslim hands. It was believed that Jews who died and were buried in the Diaspora would somehow find their way back to Jerusalem through underground passages to be there for the Last Judgment. The multitude of tombs east of the Temple show how strong these messianic eschatological expectations were.

The custom of visiting a tomb three days after the funeral is well documented. In ancient times it was sometimes difficult to be certain a person was dead, and occasionally someone would be buried alive. A simple way of establishing death was to visit the tomb three days after the burial and observe the body. The Babylonian Talmud stipulates:

One should go out to the cemetery and check on the dead three days [after the funeral] and one should not fear that by doing so he follows a gentile practice. It happened that a check up after three days discovered that a certain person was buried alive. This person lived for another twenty-five years, had sons and then died (*b. Semahot* 8:1).

People were not astonished when it happened and did not necessarily see in it a divine intervention. Although this text postdates the first century, it likely reflects a tradition that goes back to that time.

Archaeological Information

The many tombs that have been discovered outside the city of Jerusalem (*see* CAIAPHAS'S TOMB) indicate that the ancient practice of double burial existed at the time of Jesus. *Kokhim* tomb caves served whole families. Other graves were used for nonresidents: pilgrims or executed persons, who were temporarily buried in Jerusalem and later removed to their family graves.

In the primary burial the corpse was placed on its back in a niche (*kokh*), or on a bench; it was not covered with soil so as to ensure rapid decay of the flesh. Clearly the body was visible for the visit specified for three days after death. There was no specific rule for placing the body, although shrouds may have been used as the Gospels indicate. No wrappings have been found in first century C.E. tombs, but that would be expected because organic materials disintegrated. Secondary burial was made when the flesh had fully decomposed. The bones were collected from the primary burial and placed into ossuaries or other niches in the tomb. It was customary at that point to anoint the bones with oil and wine. They were then arranged in a special order: The larger bones were placed at the lower level, with the smaller bones and the skull on top.

The eight hundred tombs thus far discovered in the vicinity of Jerusalem do not reflect the totality of the burials. Kloner estimates at 50 the highest average number of burials in a single tomb. The corresponding number of deaths in Jerusalem from the third century B.C.E. to the first century C.E. (period of the finds) would then be only 40,000. Kloner's estimate of the number of deaths is about 750,000 for this period; such a figure would mean that, at best, only about 5 percent of the tombs have been found. Presumably these tombs be-longed to the middle and upper classes, with the rest of the population buried in simple shallow pits that have long since disappeared.

The most common form of primary tomb burial was the *kokh*, a niche about seven feet long, perpendicular to the wall of the tomb chamber. The other major form of primary tomb burial is that of the *arcosolia*-type tombs, of which only about one hundred examples have been found. *Arcosolia* are shelves or benches carved along the walls of the main room. The ceiling of an *arcosolium* was shaped like an arch, thus the name. Most of these tombs date from the first century B.C.E. to the first century C.E. In this period the small openings leading into tomb caves were commonly obstructed with a stone block, square in shape, functioning like a plug. Circular stones rolled in a groove in front of the tomb entry were just appearing. The custom of burial in sarcophagi was rare in Jerusalem in the first century but became common in the second century C.E. and later.

The necropolis of Jerusalem formed a belt about 2 miles wide around the city walls. Of the total number of burials 39.3 percent were found in the northern zone, 16.1 percent in the eastern zone, 32.2 percent in the southern zone, and only 12.4 percent in the west. The mishnah *Baba Batra* 2:9 mentions the old custom of not burying in the west. Thus it is hardly accidental that tombs found in this area are either older than the first century C.E. or are located more than a distance of 2,000 cubits (3,000 feet) from the Temple Mount (*see* fig. 45).

Implications for Jesus Research

In the first century C.E., there were strong eschatological messianic expectations as well as belief in the resurrection of the dead. These expectations are represented in the apocalyptic literature that existed by that time: books of the Hebrew Bible (mostly Isaiah, Jeremiah, Ezekiel, Daniel and Second Zechariah), more recent writings such as 4 Ezra, Psalms of Solomon 17, the Similitudes of 1

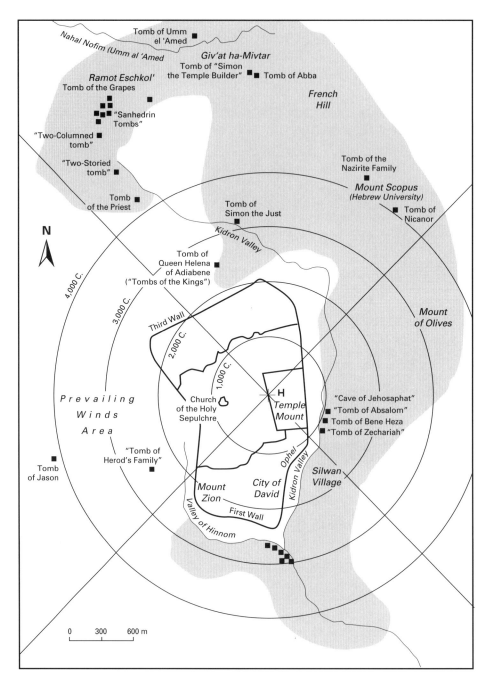

Figure 45 Distribution of Tombs according to Azimuths and Distances around Jerusalem in the Herodian Temple Period. In the western sector, no tomb is found less than 2,000 cubits (1,000 meters or 1,100 yards) from the western side of the Holy of Holies (H).

Enoch; Qumran texts (especially the War and Temple Scrolls); and perhaps the Jewish Sybilline Oracle. When the author of the Fourth Gospel has Martha say, "I know that he will rise again in the resurrection on the last day," speaking about her brother Lazarus (John 11:24), he reflects a common belief. Jesus is likely to have shared in the eschatological thought not necessarily in the apocalyptic form of the day, although some recent New Testament scholarship challenges such a possibility (see CAPHARNAUM and DEAD SEA SCROLLS).

Another issue relating to burial customs has to do with the location of the crucifixion and burial of Jesus. If burial customs in the first half of the first century C.E. preclude burials and their attendant impurities west (windward) of the Temple, then the crucifixion and burial of Jesus could not have taken place at the site of the Church of the Holy Sepulchre, which is almost exactly due west of the Holy of Holies (see GOLGOTHA, TRADITIONAL SITE). Further research about burial locations in the first century should help to establish the possibilities, or impossibilities, for Jesus' interment.

A third issue concerns the identity of the primary author of the Gospel of John. The descriptions of Jesus' tomb in all the four Gospels contain reliable information, but John offers more details. One is that it was necessary to stoop to enter the tomb (John 20:5), a fact probably provided by an eyewitness who knew the site. Another detail relates to the unnamed disciple: he entered the tomb only when he had verified that there was no corpse in it (John 20:5, 8). This would indicate that he was a priest, because entering a tomb in which there was a corpse would have defiled him for seven days (Num. 19:16) and would have prevented him from serving in the Temple during all of the Passover festival. This inference fits with the information in John 18:15 (he was related to the High Priest) and with the statement of Polycrates that John the Evangelist was "a priest wearing the sacerdotal plate" (Eusebius, *Hist.* 5, 24.3). Such information is probably the best thread to follow in the puzzling question of the identity of the Fourth Evangelist.

BIBLIOGRAPHY

Avigad, N. "A Depository of Inscribed Ossuaries in the Kidron Valley." *IEJ* 12 (1961): 1–12.

———. "The Rock Carved Facades of the Jerusalem Necropolis." *IEJ* 1 (1950–51): 96–109.

Gafini, Y. "Reinterment in the Land of Israel: Notes on the Origins and Development of the Customs." *The Jerusalem Cathedra* 1 (1981): 96–104.

Geva, H. "Jerusalem, Tomb." *NEAEHL* 2:747-57.

Hachlili, R. "Burials, Ancient Jewish." *ABD* 1: 789–94.

Kloner, A. *The Necropolis of Jerusalem in the Second Temple Period.* Ph.D diss., Hebrew University, 1980 (Hebrew, English summary).

Meyers, E. M. *Jewish Ossuaires: Reburial and Rebirth. Second Burials in their Ancient Near East Setting.* Rome: Biblical Institute Press, 1971.

Puech, E. "Ossuaries inscrits d'une tombe du Mont des Oliviers." *Liber Annuus* 32 (1982): 355–72.

Rahmani, L. V. "Ancient Jerusalem's Funerary Customs and Tombs." *BA* 44 (1981): 171–77 and 229–35; *BA* 45 (1982): 43–53 and 109–19.

Sukenik, E. L. "Jewish Tombs in the Kidron Valley." *Qedem* 2 (1945): 23–31.

Vincent, L. M. "Le Tombeau à ossuaire du Mont des Oliviers." *Revue Biblique* 11 (1902): 272–81.

Zlotnick, D. *The Tractate "Mourning" (Semahot).* New Haven: Yale University Press, 1966.

Jerusalem, Upper City

Importance

The High Priest's house and the house of the Last Supper may have been located in the Upper City, which was the quarter of the wealthy.

Scripture References

1 Macc. 12:36; 13:10; 16:23; Matt. 26:18; Mark 14:15; Luke 22:12; Acts 1:13.

General Information

The Upper City was the residential area that developed west of the Tyropoeon Valley on a hill slightly higher than the Temple Mount. It was probably first settled in the eighth century B.C.E. but may not have been enclosed with a fortification wall until the Hasmonean period (1 Macc. 12:36; 13:10; 16:23). Represented today by the Armenian and Jewish quarters of the Old City, this area also extends south of the Armenian quarter in what is now called Mount Zion (*see* figs. 47, 48). As the residential district of most of the upper class, it represented a political division that began during the Hellenistic period when the Hellenizers settled in the Upper City near a Seleucid fortress, while other Jewish groups remained in the area of the Temple. Hellenistic materials are thus found more often in the Upper City than anywhere else in Jerusalem. With the construction of his palace in the northwest of the Upper City, Herod the Great reinforced its upper class character, which it retained until its destruction by the Romans in 70 C.E.

Archaeological Data

Archaeologists have long struggled with the problem of the so-called "Invisible Wall." In the opinion of M. Avi-Yonah, shared by many others, a fortification wall existed on the eastern side of the Upper City, which overlooks the Lower Tyropoeon Valley. This opinion is based on the information that, in the First Jewish War, the rebels entrenched in the Upper City kept the Romans at bay for a full month after the Temple Mount and Lower City had fallen into the hands of Titus. Josephus, however, does not describe such a wall, nor is there any archeological evidence for its existence. Nonetheless, its hypothetical position is shown on many maps of first-century Jerusalem in encyclopedias and scholarly books; such publication, dating to as late as 1987, show a fortification wall inside the city, running along the western rim of the Tyropoeon Valley from the Gate of the Essenes to the Xystos bridge. M. Ben Dov found no evidence of such a wall in his 1968–82 excavations southwest of the Temple. Avi-Yonah finally abandoned this hypothesis before his death in 1976 (Ben Dov, pp. 116–17).

Excavations of the Upper City conducted by N. Avigad beginning in 1970 revealed several large private houses with many ceramic objects, frescoes, and other artifacts as well as information on architecture, construction techniques, sewer systems, and urban planning in the Herodian and Roman periods. These discoveries testify to the influence of Hellenistic material culture on the upper class of first-century Palestine, as the following description of three of the houses indicates:

1. *The Palatial Mansion* (*see* fig. 46c).

The "Palatial Mansion," is a large building covering an area of about 10,000 square feet and designed like a typical roman *insula*. A courtyard in the center links three surrounding units. A doorway on one side opens to a passage with a mosaic floor leading to several rooms. On another side, two doorways lead into a large hall 35 feet in length; its walls are still covered with white plaster panels so skillfully cut that they have the appearance of fine stone masonry. Fragments found on the floor suggest that the ceiling was decorated with reliefs of geometric patterns. The walls of several rooms are covered with panels painted in bright, varied colors, imitating marble slabs that only emperors and kings could afford. Other walls are decorated with fruit and leaf designs either in panels or friezes. The Palatial Mansion is representative of the residence of first-century wealthy Jewish families, for many other dwellings with mosaic floors, luxurious bathrooms, steam baths with underfloor heating, and ritualistic baths were discovered.

2. *The Herodian House of the Armenian Cemetery* (*see* fig. 46a).

Although not as large as the Palatial Mansion, this building contains several fine frescoes. It was also built according to an *insula* design with a central courtyard. On one side of the house was a large room with four ovens sunk into the ground; several cupboards built into the left wall still contained dishes when the house was excavated. Stairs led from the courtyard to a large *miqveh*, "ritual bath"; at the top of the steps was a footbath to be used before descending into the ritual bath.

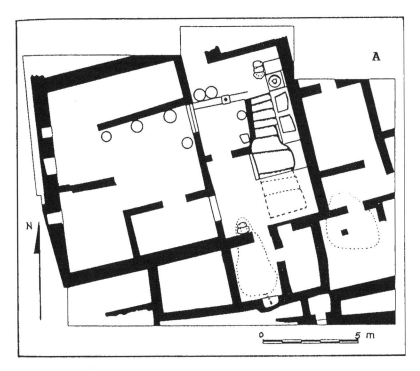

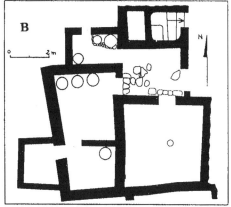

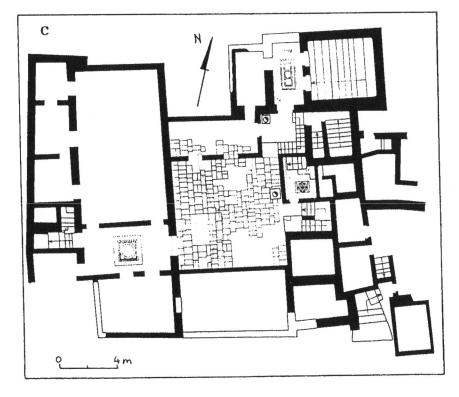

Figure 46 Upper City. Three Herodian houses. A: "Herodian House," the entrance in a courtyard was from the north; the four circles on the left represent ovens; the three blank spaces in the left wall are niches for tableware. B: Basement of the "Burnt House," where incense was probably made. C: The "Palatial Mansion" of the Herodian Quarter.

3. *The Burnt House* (*see* fig. 46b).

The basement of this house, excavated in January 1970, measures about 1,000 square feet and is well preserved. Its designation—Burnt House—derives from the fact that it was buried under a great quantity of ash, burnt wood, and soot. Its basement contained several workrooms, a kitchen, and a *miqveh*. There were also a few ovens, some large jars, and stone tables together with cooking pots, tableware, measuring cups, stone weights, perfume vials made of clay or glass, mortars and pestles, and coins. Avigad proposed that the basement had been used to prepare incense for the Temple services; the heavy soot, which clung to everything, came from burnt oily products. Two clay inkpots found in the ruins indicated that writing—perhaps for record keeping—was a household activity.

The ruins of these houses contained numerous vessels and lamps of the Hellenistic and Roman periods: stone tables, kitchen utensils, storage jars, dishes, weights, and measures. Most of the stone tables are rectangular, 33 x 22 inches on the average. They are made of limestone slabs, cut smooth and decorated around the edges, and supported by a single stone pedestal leg. Some tables had round tops with a diameter of about 22 inches.

Coins associated with the houses date from the Ptolemaic, Seleucid, and Hasmonean periods (third to first centuries B.C.E.). On the floor of the Burnt House were coins issued by the Roman prefects of Judea; others were issued by the Jewish rebels in 67, 68, and 69 C.E. As no later coins were found, the destruction of these buildings can be connected with the events of 70 C.E. One remarkable discovery was that of a menorah, 8 inches high, chiseled on the wall of a house; it may depict the seven branched lamp-stand taken by the Romans from the Temple and represented later on the Arch of Titus in Rome (*see* the photo on page 301).

The excavators were surprised that so many vessels were made of stone instead of clay or metal. The reason for this preponderance of stone vessels may lie in the Jewish laws of ritual purity. Purity requirements applied to furniture and household utensils (Lev. 11). Washing objects completely in pure water would have been sufficient except for pottery vessels, which absorbed impure liquids and could contaminate all further contents. Consequently, clay vessels, when impure, had to be broken and no longer could be used (Lev. 11:33). Metal and stone vessels, however, were not susceptible to such contamination (*m. Kelim* 10:1; *m. Para* 3:2; *see* CANA). Because metal was very expensive and because Jerusalem quarries provided limestone in profusion, stone became the material of choice for household vessels. Stone jars in the Burnt House hold up to 17 gallons.

Implications for Jesus Research

The basic facts of the story of the wedding at Cana can be related to the large stone jars found in the Upper City of the Herodian period. The stone jars in John 2:6 must have been of the same type as those found in the Jewish Quarter excavations. The primary writer of the Fourth Gospel was clearly familiar with the details of Jewish life and customs. Jesus was acquainted with the life-style of the wealthy, as at the Cana wedding and in the homes of Zacchaeus (Luke 19:2-10) and a well-to-do Pharisee (Luke 7:36).

The most significant discovery in relation to the historical Jesus is the stone weight, bearing the name of Bar Kathros, found in the Burnt House. E. P. Sanders argues that what caused the death of Jesus was the threat of the destruction of the Temple (*Jesus and Judaism*), a threat symbolized by his overturning of the money changers' tables. Most other scholars rather see in this action a symbol of the cleansing of the Temple, that is, the removal of the corrupt priesthood. The Burnt House weight reveals that there was indeed in Jerusalem, in the first century C.E., a powerful priestly family, whose corruption and oppressive practices are bemoaned in a folk song preserved in the Babylonian Talmud and Tosepta (*b. Pesahim* 57:1; and *t. Minhot* 13:21):

Woe is me because of the House of Boethus
  Woe is me because of their slaves,
Woe is me because of the House of Hanan,
  Woe is me because of their incantations,
Woe to me because of the House of Kathros,
  Woe to me because of their pens (libels),
Woe to me because of Ishmael, son of Phiabi,
For they are High Priests, and their sons are
    treasurers,
  and their sons-in-law are trustees,
  and their servants beat the people with staves.

A Joazar and an Eleazar, sons of Boethus, were High Priests at the beginning of the first century C.E.; Ishmael, son of Phiabi, was High Priest in 15–16 C.E.; and a Simon Cantheras, another son of Boethus, was High Priest in 41 C.E. (*see* JERUSALEM, CALAPHA'S HOUSE and JERUSALEM, CAIAPHA'S TOMB). Thus, at least three members of priestly families, infamous for being corrupt and oppressive, were active in Jesus' time. This may have motivated his action against the Temple; popular anger was directed against the priesthood, not the Temple (*see* TEMPLE, ROYAL STOA).

BIBLIOGRAPHY

Avigad, N. *Archaeological Discoveries in the Jewish Quarter of Jerusalem, Second Temple Period*. Jerusalem: Israel Exploration Society and Israel Museum, 1976.

———. *Discovering Jerusalem*. New York: Thomas Nelson Publishers, 1983 (Hebrew, 1980).

———. *The Upper City of Jerusalem*. Jerusalem: Sheqmona, 1980.

———. *The Herodian Quarter in Jerusalem*. Jerusalem: Keter Publishing House and Whol Archaeological Museum, 1991.

———. "Jerusalem. Hasmonean and Herodian Periods." *NEAEHL* 2:729-35.

———. "How the Wealthy Lived in Herodian Jerusalem." *BAR* 2 (1976): 23–25.

Ben Dov, M. *In the Shadow of the Temple*. Hebrew, 1982. Jerusalem: Keter, 1985, translated by Ina Friedman.

Broshi, M. "Jewish Jerusalem. A Quarter of a Century of Archaeological Research." *Israel Museum Journal* 7 (1988): 13–23.

Netzer, E. "Reconstruction of the Jewish Quarter in the Old City." *Qadmoniot* 5 (1972): 132–35 (Hebrew).

Sanders, E. P. *Jesus and Judaism*. Philadelphia: Fortress Press, 1985.

Sofios, Y. "Keeping Up with the Bar-Kathroses." *Eretz Magazine* 3 (1988): 49–54.

Jerusalem, Upper Room

Importance
Jesus had his last meal with his disciples in an upper room in Jerusalem; after his departure his disciples met in an upper room, which could have been the same one.

Scripture References
Matt. 26:18; Mark 14:15; Luke 22:12; Acts 1:13.

General Information
According to Christian tradition, the Upper Room was located in the southern part of the Upper City, between Herod's palace and the Gate of the Essenes, on today's Mount Zion (*see* fig. 47). The Pentecost phenomenon would have taken place there, and it is where the first group of Jesus' followers resided (Acts 1:13; 2:2). The traditional site was marked in Constantine's time by the Church of Holy Sion, which appears on the Madaba Map. According to Epiphanus (315–403), Hadrian found the building of the Upper Room still standing in 135. It was identified by Cyril of Jerusalem (315–386), and the Bordeaux Pilgrim visited it in 333. A first church there may have been destroyed by Diocletian in 303. The tradition identifying the site as the place of the house of the Last Supper can be traced back to Eusebius, who wrote that the gospel spread to all nations from Mount Zion (*Demonstratia Evangelica* I.4). There is no clear evidence that the Church of Holy Sion was the successor of a house church, as can be argued for the Byzantine Octagonal Church at Capernaum (*see* CAPERNAUM).

Visitors today are shown an Upper Room in a building of the Crusaders period containing also what is said to be the Tomb of David on the ground floor. The Crusaders had erected a large church

Figure 47 Present Old City of Jerusalem and Some Locations of Interest in Its Surroundings

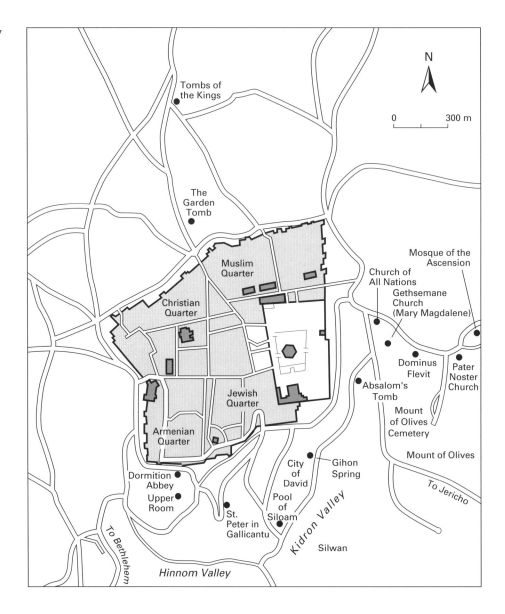

called Saint Mary in Zion on this site. When negotiations between Pope Clement VI (1342–52) and the Arabs led to an agreement that allowed the Franciscans to receive custody of the Christian sites in the Holy Land (*Custodia Terrae Sanctae*), the first project of the Franciscans was the restoration of the Upper Room. Nevertheless, it was transformed in 1523 into a mosque dedicated to the memory of *Nebi Da'ud*, "the Prophet David."

The general appearance of the Upper Room is probably the same today as it was in the sixteenth century.

Archaeological Data

In 1951, as repairs were made to the church, the Israeli archaeologist J. Pinkerfeld (Pixner, 16–24) noticed large ashlars dating from the Roman period. He identified the building as a synagogue, but J.

Finegan and B. Pixner consider it a church-synagogue of a Jewish Christian community because the Torah niche was not exactly oriented toward the Temple Mount. This reasoning, however, is not convincing and is not widely accepted.

Implications for Jesus Research

The Roman walls noted by Pinkerfeld may represent a link between the first-century house of the Upper Room and the Crusaders' building that exists today. The Upper Room may well have been in the same area as the Crusaders building, at a short distance from the Essene Quarter. This proximity between Jesus and Essenes would favor the affinities many see between early Christians and Essenes, a connection often made on the basis of textual sources (*see* DEAD SEA SCROLLS; JERUSALEM, WALLS AND GATES; QUMRAN; VITICULTURE; WOOD, FURNITURE).

BIBLIOGRAPHY

Gibson, S. "The 1961–1967 Excavations in the Armenian Garden." *Palestine Exploration Quarterly* 119 (1987): 81–96.

Mineri, S. I. "Italian Efforts to Recover the Cenacolo, 1908–1923." *Cathedra* 25 (1982): 37–64 (Hebrew).

Pixner, B. "Church of the Apostles Found on Mount Zion." *BAR* 16 (1990): 16–35.

Jerusalem, Walls and Gates

Importance

Jerusalem was a fortified city; Jesus, who predicted its destruction, was crucified outside the city wall, near a gate.

Scripture References

Matt. 23:38; 24:2; Mark 13:1-2; Luke 19:43-44; 21:20; John 19:20; Heb. 13:12-13.

General Information

Gates were constructed to control the traffic in and out of a fortified city. Because gates were a point of vulnerability at which attackers might enter, they were usually flanked by towers and had machicolations above them. At night the gates were closed and secured by heavy bars of wood or metal. The main gates opened onto a plaza that served as a place for public gatherings, official meetings, and legal business.

Jerusalem of the first century C.E. was enclosed, according to Josephus, by the first and second walls (*see* fig. 43); the third wall was not built until the reign of King Agrippa I (41–44 C.E.). The line of the first wall can be located with some certainty for most of its length. The course of the second wall is controversial because it determines whether or not the traditional location of Golgotha (Church of the Holy Sepulchure or Resurrection) is a plausible site for the Crucifixion (*see* GOLGOTHA, TRADITIONAL SITE). Josephus does accurately describe the plans of the fortifications (*War*, 5, 4.1–4/136–76). For the second wall, he simply says that it began at the Gannath (Garden) Gate, enclosed the northern quarter of the City (Upper Tyropoeon), and ended at the fortress Antonia (*War* 5, 4.2/146).

Knowing the location of the Gannath Gate, which also "belonged to the first wall," would help resolve the issue of the course of the second wall; but there is no consensus about where it was. Nehemiah reports the number and names of Jerusalem's gates when he rebuilt the city (ca. 430 B.C.E.; Neh. 2:13-16; 3). Besides the Corner Gate of 2 Kings 14:8-13, there were the Gate of Ephraim, the Old Gate, the Valley Gate, the Dung Gate, the Fountain Gate, the Water Gate, the Horse Gate, the East Gate, the Muster Gate (or Hammiphkad Gate), the Sheep Gate, and the Fish Gate (perhaps another name for the Gate of Ephraim), for a possible number of twelve, assuming there were no double names for some of them. Unfortunately, there is no precise description of the work done by the Hasmoneans and Herod the Great on the walls and gates of Jerusalem. The following list, going clockwise from Herod's palace is thus tentative: the Gannath Gate, the Gate of Ephraim, the Gate of Benjamin, the gates giving access to the Temple from outside the fortifications (Sheep Gate, Shushan [Golden] Gate and Horse Gate), then the

Fountain Gate (or Spring Gate), the Casemate Gate (or Water Gate), the Potsherd Gate (or Potter's Gate), the Essenes' Gate, and the Western (or Bethso) Gate south of Herod's palace. In addition to these eleven gates, there were gates in the western and southern walls of the City of David.

Archaeological Data

1. First Wall

About the first wall, Josephus writes (authors' wording):

> The oldest of the three walls was hard to take because of the deep valleys and high hills on which it was situated. Besides being in an advantageous position, the wall had been strongly built by David, Solomon, and their royal successors who took great pride in its construction. Starting at the north from the Hippicus Tower, it ran all the way to the colonnade and the adjacent council chamber where it met the western wall of the Temple portico. From the same tower, it went southward along the western ridge past a place called Bethso ["house of defecation, latrines"] toward the Gate of the Essenes. Then, in the south, it turned eastward above the Spring of Siloam directly to Solomon's Pool. It continued farther alongside a certain area called Ophel, going straight up in the direction of the eastern portico of the Temple." (*War* 5, 4.2/142–45).

Archaeological finds support this general description, which is illustrated in figures 43 and 48 showing the locations of the gates and other features.

Maudslay (1871–75) and Bliss and Dickie (1894–97) unearthed parts of the western and southern walls. From 1934 to 1947, when Johns excavated the Citadel (northern part of Herod's palace), he discovered the northwestern corner of the first wall and saw how the Phasael Tower of Herod was built within the first Hasmonean wall. Amiran and Eitan (1968–69) excavated a tower belonging to the same wall protruding more than 33 feet inside; they also found well-preserved rooms and an intact doorway. The Herodian builders used the existing Hasmonean walls economically, either

keeping them if they met their standards, or strengthening and rebuilding them if not.

A few features deserve special mention:

- The northern wall, from the Hippicus Tower to the Temple served as a link across the Tyropoeon Valley between the Upper and Lower Cities. At the wall's eastern end, parallel to it and built against it, was the first Hasmonean bridge over the valley, which Herod repaired and embellished. Today, in the Old City, the ancient location of this northern wall would be represented by a line between the Jaffa Gate and the Temple platform, slightly south and parallel to David Street and the Street of the Chain.

- Near the Temple, the northern part of the first wall ran along the Xystos, the covered colonnade of a gymnasium built over the ancient Hasmonean bridge. It had been erected initially by Antochius IV Epiphanes (175-164 B.C.E.) to allow young Jewish athletes to be trained in the Greek fashion (1 Macc. 1:14-15; 2 Macc. 4:11-15). In Jesus' time the Xystos was no longer used as a gymnasium; it was a covered public plaza. Josephus indicates that there was a Council (Sanhedrin) Chamber adjacent to the colonnade of the Xystos. Because the translators of the Septuagint rendered *gazith* by Xystos, Xystos could have been the Hall of Hewn Stone (*liskath-hagazith*) referred to in the Mishnah (Sanhedrin 11, 2).

- Because the Temple was a sacred area, the judgments of the Sanhedrin regarding whether priests were fit for service (*m. Middot* 5:4) must have taken place before their entrance into the holy place. Consequently, the Council Chamber must have been the Xystos hall immediately against the Temple (*see* R. M. Mackowski, *Jerusalem*, 44). Wilson's Arch indicates where this council chamber was located.

- The Xystos bridge also contained a water conduit beneath its pavement and served as an aqueduct to supply water to the Temple for ritualistic and ordinary uses.

- L. H. Vincent indicated that a gate in the western part of the first wall could have been the Dung Gate of the Herodian period, which corresponded to the Bethso of Josephus. G. Dalman had previously suggested that the word Bethso derived from the Hebrew *beith so'ah*, "house or place of excrements." Thus the latrines of the Jerusalem Essenes would have been outside their "camp" (see Deut. 23:10-15). This possibility is supported by Y. Yadin's work on the Temple Scroll and by the research of B. G. Pixner and R. M. Mackowski. The location of the latrines would have been in the area of the American Institute of Holy Land Studies, where ritual baths, pools, and channels have been found. At least one ritual bath with a divider was of a type common at Qumran. Note, however, that in the first century C.E. the name "Dung Gate" was used for the Potsherd Gate, through which refuse was removed from the city (*see* JERUSALEM, GEHENNA, AKELDAMA).

- The Gate of the Essenes was probably near the Bethso. Bliss first established its location during his 1894–97 excavations with Dickie. It was later buried under rubble and rediscovered by Pixner in the Protestant cemetery of the present Mount Zion, a few yards to the south of the tomb of the great British Egyptologist Sir William Flinders Petrie. Bliss also exposed the ancient street leading from the gate to the city. As mentioned above, a number of cisterns and baths were uncovered pointing to the existence of an Essene community.

- The line of the southern part of the first wall has been recovered with some certainty. After the Gate of the Essenes it turned eastward and crossed the lower part of the Tyropoeon Valley in the direction of the Pool of Siloam and beyond, toward the Pool

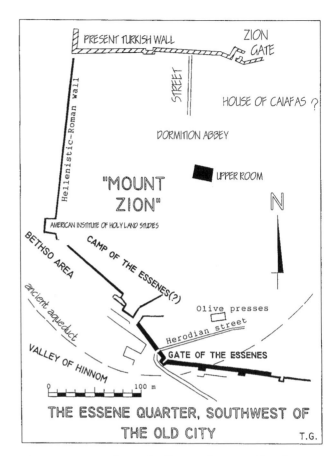

Figure 48 Jerusalem, the Essene Quarter, Southwest of the Old City

of Solomon, which is identified with Birket el-Hama, a depression south of Siloam.

- At the southeastern corner of the Ophel the first wall veered northward, following the western bank of the Kidron. Kenyon established that it ran above the older eastern wall of the Ophel of David and Solomon. It reached the level of the southeastern corner of the Temple but did not join it; it ran parallel to it. Consequently, the Temple wall was not part of the fortification system, at least in this area; rather, the Temple Mount was an enclosure within the city wall.

2. *Second Wall*

Much less information is available for the second wall. B. Hennessey, continuing the work of Hamilton who excavated in 1937–38 outside the Damascus Gate, unearthed the majestic northern triple gate of Roman Aelia Capitolina. Because roads outside Jerusalem followed roughly the same lines for several centuries, it can be inferred that there was a gate, possibly the Gate of Ephraim, at the same place in the second wall. On the western side in the area of the Church of the Holy Sepulchure, Kenyon found no wall in her excavations in the area of the traditional site of Golgotha. No other excavators have found evidence of the city wall of the first half of the first century C.E. It is thus impossible to determine whether Golgotha was outside the wall (*see* GOLGOTHA, TRADITIONAL SITE).

Figure 43 gives the two most accepted reconstructions of the course of the second wall. Both leave the traditional location of Golgotha outside the city. This wall was the northern fortification of Jerusalem from the Hasmonean-Herodian period until the building of the third wall by King Agrippa I. According to Mackowski and others, its point of departure, the Gannath Gate, would have been at the junction of Saint Mark Street and Suq el Hussor, in the quarter of the Old City known as el-Bashurah, where the *Quadrivium*, "two thoroughfare intersection," and the *Tetrapylon*, "four-column arch," of Hadrian's Aelia Capitolina were located. Israeli archaeologists excavating south of el-Bashurah, in the Jewish Quarter, discovered a large section of a paved street dating from the Byzantine period. This street probably followed the course of the street of earlier periods. If so, the corresponding street of Herodian Jerusalem would have led to a gate, the Gannath Gate, some 200 yards east of the Hippicus Tower. Not all scholars accept this theory, however; Avi-Yonah places the gate just east of the tower, which seems more likely because the gate would then have been under the direct protection of the tower. Avi-Yonah's suggestion agrees with other opinions according to which the Gannath Gate was located on the site of the Corner Gate of the Hebrew Bible.

There is no consensus about the extent of the area enclosed by the second wall. One group of scholars uses Josephus's meager information and suggests it is the area within the broken line north of the first wall on figure 43. Another group prefers a plan based on the topography of the city and remains of Herodian walls found in the northwest of the Antonia. In the latter case, the northern part of the second wall would have run on about the same line as the present northern wall in the area east of the Damascus Gate, which would have been over the ancient Gate of Ephraim or Fish Gate (Mackowski, *Jerusalem*, 67–69; Avigad and Geva, *NEAEHL*.

3. *The Gates of Herodian Jerusalem*

We have proposed that there were eleven gates in the outer fortification walls of Herodian Jerusalem: Gannath, Ephraim, Benjamin, Sheep, Shushan, Horse, Fountain, Casemate, Potsherd, Essenes, Bethso. Some scholars recognize only Gannath, Ephraim, Sheep, Fountain, Casemate, Potsherd, and Essenes, for a total of seven. Information about the Gannath, Ephraim, Bethso, and Essene Gates appears above; a few other gates will be discussed here:

- *Benjamin and Sheep Gates.* In addition to the Ephraim Gate, one or two other gates opened to the north: the Benjamin Gate at the northeastern corner of the second wall according to its larger extent and the Sheep Gate somewhere in the northern area of the Temple, east of the Antonia. Those who prefer the smaller area eliminate the Gate of Benjamin. One thing is almost certain; in Jesus' time there was a Sheep Gate, for it is the only one mentioned by name in the Gospels: "Now in Jerusalem by the Sheep Gate there is a pool, called in Hebrew Beth-Zatha "[Bethesda]" (John 5:2; *see* JERUSALEM, POOL OF BETHESDA). There was a sheep market, which still exists today, in this area; and the pool was also called the Sheep Pool. Sheep for sacrifice were taken to the Temple through this gate and possibly washed in the pool.

- *Golden (Shushan) and Horse Gates. See* TEMPLE, STAIRS AND GATES.

- *Fountain Gate.* Also known as the Spring Gate, this gate was located at one of the easiest sites to identify in that it gave access to the Gihon Spring. Kenyon, in 1961–67, found in this same area remains of a tower dating from the Jebusite and Davidic period; older ruins date to the Middle Bronze Age, testifying to occupation a millenium or more before the time of David. The Fourth Gospel does not name this gate but does mention the nearby Pool of Siloam, which was fed by water from the Gihon Spring.

- *Casemate Gate.* Another and probably more popular name for this gate was Water Gate. According to 2 Kings 25:4 and Jeremiah 39:4 and 52:7, this gate led to the king's garden outside the casemate wall at the southern end of the City of David, at the place where the Kidron, Tyropoeon, and Hinnon meet. Several reservoirs were in this area; a little farther southeast was another spring, known as the Spring of Rogel, or the Fuller's Spring.

- *Potsherd Gate.* The name Potsherd is found in Jeremiah 19:2, Dung Gate appears in Nehemiah 2:13 and 3:13, and another name was Potter's Gate. Josephus does not mention it. In 1927, J. W. Crowfoot located this gate when he unearthed a large fortification wall of the Hasmonean period. This wall fits with the information on the Madaba Map that there was a gate, in the southeastern location, which led to the ill-famed Valley of Hinnon, the Gehenna of the Gospels (*see* JERUSALEM, GEHENNA, AKELDAMA).

Implications for Jesus Research

When entering or leaving the city, Jesus walked through the Fountain Gate and Casemate Gate, opening to the Kidron valley. It is uncertain whether he entered the Temple through the Golden (Shushan) Gate when he made his official entry in Jerusalem (*see* JERUSALEM, KIDRON). When coming from or returning to Galilee through Samaria, he would have passed through the Gate of Ephraim and possibly the Gate of Benjamin. The route to Golgotha for his Crucifixion would have involved passing through either the Gannath Gate (traditional site) or the Gate of Ephraim (*see* GARDEN TOMB and GOLGOTHA, TRADITIONAL SITE).

The archaeological finds recorded above point to the probable existence of an Essene community in the southwestern area of Jerusalem close to the traditional site of the Upper Room. This proximity may relate to Mark 14:13-16 (and parallels) and suggest the location of the earliest Jewish Christian community, which could have had some affinity with the Essenes (Acts 1:13; 2:26; *see* DEAD SEA SCROLLS; QUMRAN; and fig. 48).

BIBLIOGRAPHY

Avigad, N. "Jerusalem." *NEAEHL* 2:717-25.

Benoit, P. "Les ramparts de Jerusalem." *Le Monde de la Bible* 1 (1977); 20–30.

Broshi, M. "Les murs de Jerusalem continuent de livrer leurs secrets." La recherche archéologique. *Le Monde de la Bible* 1 (1977): 48–51.

Geva, H. "The First Wall of Jerusalem during the Second Temple Period. An Architectural-Chronological Note." *Eretz Israel* 18 (1985): 21–39 (Hebrew).

———. "Jerusalem." *NEAEHL* 2:736.

Kenyon, K. *Digging Up Jerusalem.* London: Ernest Benn, 1974.

Mackowski, R. M. and Societas Jesu *Jerusalem: City of Jesus.* Grand Rapids: Eerdmans, 1980.

Shanks, H. "The Jerusalem Wall that Shouldn't Be There." Three Major Excavations Fail to Explain Controversial Remains." BAR 13 (1987): 48–57.

Yadin, Y. "The Gate of the Essenes and the Temple Scroll." *Megillath Hammigdash (The Temple Scroll).* Jerusalem: Israel Exploration Society, et al., 1977.

Jerusalem, Water System

Importance

Water in ancient Palestine was thought to have special powers and also some spiritual qualities.

Scripture References

Matt. 3:13; 15:2; Mark 1:9; 7:2; Luke 3:21; 7:44; John 1:26; 4:2,14; 5:2-6; 7:37-39; 9:7; 13:15; G. Thom. 13, 108.

General Information

The site of Jerusalem (Jebus before David's conquest) was first settled because it was on a spur between two valleys and easy to defend, and also because there was a good source of fresh water, the Gihon Spring, located in a cave on the west side of the Kidron Valley. The name Gihon comes from the Hebrew *giah*, "to gush forth". It refers to the nature of the spring, which does not flow continuously, but gushes forth several times a day. For strategic reasons when the Assyrians invaded Judea, (700–690 B.C.E.) King Hezekiah had a tunnel dug to bring the water within the walls of the city to the Pool of Siloam, in the lower part of the Tyropoeon Valley, on the west side of the City of David. The cave of the spring was obstructed so that the invaders could not divert the water (2 Kings 20:20; 2 Chron. 32:30).

As the city grew, it became necessary to increase the water supply; reservoirs and pools were built. Josephus mentions a few of these:

- The Pool of the Snake (*War* 5. 3.2/108), probably located below the southwestern corner of the city wall. It was renamed the Sultan's Pool after Suleiman the Magnificent (1520–66) restored it.
- The Towers Pool (*War* 5, 11.4/468), so named because it was just north of the three huge towers of Herod's palace. Josephus uses the Greek word *Amygdalon*, which could mean "almond" but in fact derives from the Hebrew *migdal*, "tower." Located within the Old City of Jerusalem, south of the Jaffa Gate, it is now called the "Pool of the Patriarch's Bath," perhaps because of the proximity of three patriarchates: Greek Catholic, Greek Orthodox, and Latin.

- The Strouthion Pool (*War* 5, 4.2/467), located at a diagonal from the northwestern corner of the fortress Antonia. In Greek, the name means "small bird" but, according to some scholars, it derives from the name Astarte (Ashtharah, Ashthoret), a Canaanite and Phoenician goddess. This opinion is based on the fact that the consonants *s t r t* are the same in both names.

- The Pool of Solomon (*War* 5, 11.4/145), located a short distance from the Pool of Siloam (*see* JERUSALEM, WALLS AND GATES).

Other pools and reservoirs not mentioned by Josephus are known to have existed in Jerusalem in the first century C.E.: the Pool of Bethesda and Pool of Siloam (*see* JERUSALEM, POOL OF BETHESDA and JERUSALEM, POOL OF SILOAM), the Pool of Israel just north of the Temple, which probably provided part of the water for cultic activities; pools of the Essene Quarter; and certainly others the remains of which have not been recovered.

As the city grew, water from rain and springs in the Jerusalem area became insufficient, and two aqueducts brought more water from the south. The more ancient "lower aqueduct" was the longer; its date is uncertain. The more recent "upper aqueduct" is dated to the Roman period; Roman technique is easily recognizable. It was built by Herod the Great and repaired by Pontius Pilate (*War* 2, 9.4/175–77; *Antiq.* 18, 3.2/60). The Jews protested against Pilate's initiative because he used funds from the Temple treasury to pay for it; nevertheless, this aqueduct served the Temple and its repairs were legitimate.

Archaeological Data

The Strouthion Pool, dug in the rock near the Antonia, was a large double reservoir providing water to the garrison of the fortress. It is not parallel to

An Open Section of the Aqueduct before the Old City

one of the sides of the structure, because it probably served the old fortress Birah, which was on the same location. A light bridge built over it led to the main gate of the fortress. Today this pool lies under a pavement, located in the convent of the Sisters of Sion near the *Ecce Homo* Arch, from the time of Hadrian. When he built the Roman city Aelia Capitolina over the ruins of Jerusalem, he transformed this area into a public square. The floor of the square is set on a vaulted ceiling over the pool, which measures 176 x 46 feet.

The lower aqueduct began at Ein Arrub, 15 miles south of Jerusalem, and was fed by water from two other nearby springs. According to the terrain, the aqueduct was either a channel hewn in the rock or a conduit made of plastered stones. It follows a winding route through Tekoa and Bethlehem, crosses the upper Hinnon Valley, and enters Jerusalem in the southern part of the Upper City. There, it follows the ridge of the bank of the Tyropoeon up to the location of the former northern

first wall, where its path is lost. There are indications that it brought water to the Temple through a conduit under the pavement of the Xystos Bridge (*see* JERUSALEM, WALLS AND GATES). Because of its tortuous route, the total length of this aqueduct was close to 50 miles covering a straight line distance of 15 miles.

The course of the upper aqueduct, which began 12 miles away from Jerusalem at the spring of Bir ed Daraj, was more direct. It reached a reservoir near Deir Mar Elias northeast of Tantur; or it perhaps merged with the lower aqueduct in the same area. Elaborate techniques are evident in its rock-hewn channels, stone pipes, and siphons. The stone pipes were made of large blocks with large central apertures; they were shaped in such a way that they fit tightly into each other and the joints were filled with lead or mortar to prevent leaks (*see* the photo on page 182).

By the time of the Second Temple, the Pool of Siloam had been enlarged and, in addition to the

Segments of the Stone Pipe of the Roman Aqueduct (Rockefeller Museum, Jerusalem)

water from Gihon, was filled by an elaborate drainage system that brought to it thousands of tons of rain water from November through March or April. Almost all the rain that fell on streets, plazas, squares, and esplanades was collected in tunnels carrying the water to Siloam. The system was first discovered by C. Warren and was further investigated by M. Ben-Dov. The drains, being at least 3.5 feet in height and 24 inches in width, were either tunnels carved in the limestone or channels also hewn in the rock but covered with flat or vaulted stone ceilings. The drainage system integrated natural caves and the stone vaults supporting street pavements, which were used as expansion and control chambers accessible by access holes. It is still able to absorb the water and prevent floods even in the most heavy rains (Ben Dov, 105–20).

In addition to the public water system, many houses had their own cisterns to collect rain water that fell on their rooftops. Altogether there was sufficient water to meet the needs of the Temple, of the residents, and of the pilgrims in Jerusalem. The Jews in Jerusalem as well as everywhere else in Palestine had a great concern for water and tried to assure themselves a plentiful supply for ordinary and cultic purposes.

Implications for Jesus Research

Water was precious, not only because of its primary function as a life-sustaining agent, but also because it was seen as having special powers (*see* RITUAL BATHS/MIQVAOTH) and healing virtues (*see* JERUSALEM, POOL OF BETHESDA and POOL OF SILOAM). It was also a means of expressing deference according to the protocols of hospitality: the host washed the feet of his guest or, if the visitor was of lesser status, a slave or a servant performed the rite. Although it seems that he did not require the observance of the Shammaite Pharisees as shown for instance in the controversy about hand washing (Matt. 15:2; Mark 7:2), Jesus recognized the healing virtue of water (John 9:7 and 5: 2–6) and its cleansing power; he was baptized and he let his disciples baptize (John 4:2). When he washed his disciples' feet (John 13:5) and reproached his host for not having performed this duty to him (Luke 7:44), he also recognized its symbol of hospitable deference and perfect service.

Above all, water represented spiritual nourishment; the biblical phrase "living water" (or "water of life") symbolically applied to:

- God, seen as the "fountain of living water" (Jer. 2:13; 17:13; Ps. 36:9; 42:1-2),

- The Torah, "As water is life for the world, so are the words of the Torah for the world" (Beasley-Murray, 60; also Sir. 24:23-27),

- Wisdom, "Those who drink of me will thirst for more" (Sir. 24:21; Prov. 13:14; Isa. 51:1-3),

- The Holy Spirit, "As water is given to dry land and is led over arid land so will I give my Holy Spirit to your sons and my blessing to your children's children" (Tg. Isa. 44:3); see also Isaiah 44:3 and 1QS 4:21: "Like purifying water he will sprinkle upon him the spirit of truth,"

- Salvation "With joy you will draw water from the wells of salvation" (Isa. 12:3).

The words of Jesus in John 4:14, "Those who drink of the water that I will give them will never be thirsty. The water that I will give him will become in them a spring of water gushing up to eternal life," follow in this biblical tradition.

BIBLIOGRAPHY

Barrett, C. K. *Essays on John*. Philadelphia: Westminster Press, 1982.

Beasley-Murray, G. R. *John*. World Biblical Commentary 5, 36. Waco, Tex.: Word Books, 1987.

Ben Dov, M. *In the Shadow of the Temple*. Jerusalem: Keter Publishing 1982.

Brown, R. E. *The Gospel According to John*. Vol. 1 (Anchor Bible 29). Garden City, N.Y.: Doubleday, 1966.

Bultmann, R. *The Gospel of John, a Commentary*. Philadelphia: Westminster Press, 1971.

Fortna, R. T. *The Fourth Gospel and Its Predecessor*. Philadelphia: Fortress Press, 1988.

Geva, H. "Jerusalem." *NEAEHL* 2:746-47.

Mackowski, R. M., and Societas Jesu. *Jerusalem, City of Jesus*. Grand Rapids: Eerdmans, 1980.

Milgrom, J. *Leviticus 1–16*. (Anchor Bible 3). New York: Doubleday, 1991.

Sanders, E. P. *Jewish Law from Jesus to the Mishnah*. London: SCM Press; Philadelphia: Trinity Press International, 1990.

Shiloh, Y. "Jerusalem." *NEAEHL* 2:709-12.

Wilkinson, J. *The Jerusalem Jesus Knew*. New York: Thomas Nelson, 1978.

Jordan River, Fords

Importance

Pilgrims journeying between Galilee and Jerusalem sometimes crossed the Jordan to travel on its east side; John the Baptist baptized at or near a ford in the river.

Scripture References

Matt. 3:6, 13; Mark 1:5, 9; Luke 3:3; John 1:28; 3:26; 10:40.

General Information

The Jordan River forms at the foot of Mt. Hermon at the confluence of three streams. It then flows southward along the Syro-African rift from a height of 250 feet down to 1,300 feet below sea level at the Dead Sea some 100 miles to the south. In the first century C.E. the Jordan first passed through Lake Huleh or Semechonitis, which was drained early in this century and is now being partially filled again. After leaving the Sea of Galilee at some 600 feet below sea level it follows on a meandering course, joined by several tributaries, mostly from the east, before emptying into the Dead Sea. Between these two bodies of water the river averages about 90 feet in width and is from 3 to 10 feet deep.

There is no evidence that bridges spanned the Jordan in biblical times, but ancient toponyms suggest that there were perhaps two bridges in antiquity: Jisr Benat Yakub, "Bridge of the Daughters of Jacob," just south of Lake Huleh; and Jisr el Mujami, "Bridge of the Place of Assembly," about 7 miles south of the Sea of Galilee. The river was typically crossed at fords or on rafts. There are more than twenty fords north of the Sea of Galilee but only a few between the Sea of Galilee and the Dead Sea. The Bible reports numerous struggles with much bloodshed at these spots. For example, men of Jericho attempted to cut off the retreat of spies from Israel at the Jordan fords (Josh. 2:7). After the defeat of the king of Moab, the Israelites took the fords on the way to that country and killed a great number of Moabites (Judg. 3:28-29). Gideon ordered his men to seize the fords (water) as far as Bethbarah in his struggle with the Midianites. Jephthah and the Gileadites took the fords of the Jordan as they fought off the Ephraimites (Judg. 12: 4-6).

The most important of the Jordan River fords are Jacob's Ford at the level of Hazor, north of the Sea of Galilee, the ford of the Jabbok at Wadi Zerqa (Gen. 32:22); the ford of the Armon at Wadi Muph (Isa. 16:22); the Damiya ford between Amman and Samaria; and the "fords of the Wilderness" (2 Sam. 15:28; 17:16), of which two, Mahadat el Hajalh and Mahadat el Hena, have been identified. According to tradition, Jesus was baptized at the Halajah ford (see BETHABARA).

Archaeological Data

The meandering Jordan continually changed its course over the millennia. It is difficult to identify the exact locations of the ancient fords and, except for a general survey in 1953, no excavations have been made at or near the existing fords.

Implications for Jesus Research

The Jordan had an aura of sanctity for Jesus and his contemporaries. The Israelites led by Joshua had crossed it on dry land, just as they had crossed the Red Sea, according to their Holy Scriptures. Elijah had divided its waters by smiting them with his mantle, and Elisha repeated the miraculous deed (2 Kings 2:8, 13-14). It was believed that the Jordan's water had healing powers and, in the synagogue of Nazareth (Luke 4:27), Jesus referred to the cure of the Syrian general Naaman (2 Kings 5:14). Accordingly, it was at the Jordan that John the Baptist first came forward to call for a baptism of repentance; and it was to the Jordan that Jesus went for his own baptism. A few years later, in the time of Fadus in about 44 C.E., a charismatic rebel, the would-be prophet Theudas called the people to follow him to the Jordan River, which would divide its waters at his command to allow them to cross it as their ancestors had done (Josephus, *Antiq.* 20, 5.1/97–98).

Most Galileans going to Jerusalem for the festivals preferred to avoid Samaria. They crossed the Jordan either south of the Sea of Galilee to walk along its east bank all the way; or they went to the area of Scythopolis, took the "way of the Jordan" along the west bank, and crossed it at the Damiya ford. Both routes led to the fords near Jericho, where the pilgrims entered Judea to go up to Jerusalem. Although he was apparently not afraid to go through Samaria (see SYCHAR-SHECHEM), Jesus probably also journeyed to Jerusalem along the east bank of the river.

BIBLIOGRAPHY

Glueck, N. *The River Jordan.* New York: McGraw-Hill, 1968.

"Le Jourdain." *Le Monde de la Bible* 65 (July–Aug. 1990).

Leonard, A., Jr. "The Jordan Valley Survey, 1953:" Some Unpublished Soundings Conducted by James Mellaart. *Annual of the American Schools of Oriental Research* (1992).

North, R. "Quirks of Jordan River Cartography." *Studies Historic and Archaeologic* 2 (1985): 205–15.

Van Zeist, W. "Past and Present Environment of the Jordan Valley." *Studies Historic and Archaeologic* 2 (1985): 199–204.

Judean Caves

Importance

Jesus may have found shelter in the numerous caves of Judea when he withdrew to the wilderness.

Scripture References

Matt. 4:1; 24:3; 26:30; Mark 1:12; 13:3; 14:26; Luke 4:1; 21:37; 22:39; John 8:1.

General Information

The numerous caves in Israel played an important role in the life of its people, notably in times of war and rebellion. This is especially true for the caves of the Judean desert. From the beginnings of Israelite history, they have been places of refuge (see, for example, the story of David in 1 Sam. 24:24). The twentieth-century discoveries made in caves at Qumran, Wadi Murabbaat, and the Cave of Letters have revealed how significant the Judean caves were in Jewish antiquity (*see* QUMRAN; DEAD SEA SCROLLS, and CAVE OF LETTERS).

Many of the most significant caves are found west of the Dead Sea, in the eastern slopes of the barren hills descending from a height of 3,000 feet to the seashore. The infrequent but heavy rainfalls in this area have gouged deep gorges into the porous rock, and the steep banks contain an unknown number of caves. After David and his band, after the Qumranites who slept and stored scroll jars in them, and after the Bar Kokhba warriors, Christian hermits settled in caves, but they preferred the area closer to Jerusalem.

Archaeological Data

This entry covers: 1. the caves between En Gedi and Masada, and 2. the caves of Wadi Mukhmas. (*See* also QUMRAN and DEAD SEA SCROLL). Both groups show traces of occupation in the first century C.E. The archaeological rediscovery of material from these caves is less familiar to New Testament students and to the general public than that of Qumran. The following information about each group will help remedy that situation:

1. *Caves between En Gedi and Masada.* After the discoveries of scrolls in the Qumran caves in the late 1940s, the Bedouins of the Judean desert realized that they had a fortune in their backyard, so to speak. They thus began a systematic treasure hunt in the area. In October 1951, some of them brought to the Rockefeller Museum in Jerusalem a few fragments of leather bearing Greek and Hebrew words. Upon the museum secretary's request, they led him to the location of their finds, a large cave in the Wadi Murabbaat, about halfway between Qumran and En Gedi. Believing that the Bedouins had already thoroughly searched the area, the museum official ordered no further investigation. About a month later, when R. de Vaux and L. Harding were excavating at Qumran, Kando, the Bethlehem dealer who had sold the first Dead Sea Scrolls, approached them with new fragments, assuring them that they came from nearby caves. When de Vaux noticed that they were quite different from the Qumran scrolls, he purchased a few pieces of papyrus to study and translate their inscriptions. These fragments contained two astonishing messages: "From Shimeon to Yeshua ben Galgoula, shalom." They were nothing less than fragments of letters sent by the leader of the Second Jewish Revolt, known today as Bar Kokhba. This discovery led to a systematic exploration of the area. The scores of caves that were spotted with the help of a military helicopter yielded evidence of occupation from the Chalcolithic to the Roman period.

De Vaux and Harding first explored some of the caves of Wadi Murabbaat in 1952, but the bulk of the work was done by N. Avigad, P. Bar-Adon, Y. Yadin, and Y. Aharoni in 1960 and 1961. Yadin found artifacts dating from the fourth millennium B.C.E. in the caves of Nahal Hever. On the top of the cliffs above the caves were two Roman camps, one on each side of the wadi, to keep watch over the refugees trapped below. One of these caves, which contained forty skeletons of men, women, and children, was called the "Cave of Horrors." Among the caves of Nahal Seelim (Wadi Seiyel) explored by Aharoni and Avigad, caves no. 31, "Cave of Arrows," and no. 34, "Cave of Scrolls," produced remains of the Bar Kokhba period. The former was an arsenal with numerous iron arrowheads and wooden shafts; the latter contained papyrus fragments with inscriptions in Hebrew, Aramaic, and Greek, and also the remains of phylacteries and a list of names.

Although it does not belong to the same period, another extraordinary discovery is worth mentioning. In Nahal Mishmar, in the so-called "Cave of Treasure," Bar Adon recognized two levels of occupation about 3,000 years apart. The upper level, from the Bar Kokhba period, yielded houseware, clothing, footwear, and small fragments of documents written in Greek or Hebrew. But much more important were the contents of the earlier level, dating from the Chalcolithic period. They included hundreds of copper mace-heads shaped like scepters.

2. *Wadi Mukhmas Caves.* The Wadi Mukhmas begins in the hills of Bethel and ends in the Wadi Qelt, between Ain Far and Ain Fawar, east of the villages of Jab'ah (biblical Geba) and Mukhmas (biblical Michmash) and about 5 miles west of Jericho. The high cliffs flanking the wadi make any surface communication impossible except along the bottom of the Mukhmas pass (cf. 1 Sam. 13:23). Potsherds and inscriptions indicate that the caves in this area were used up to the first century C.E., although they also must have been used during the Bar Kokhba War as well as by Byzantine monks in the sixth century according to archaeological evidence.

The caves were explored on several occasions, beginning with the Survey of Western Palestine in the 1970s. Since 1982 they have been investigated by the Institute of Cave Studies. Most of them are located in the cliffs on the northern side of the wadi, about 1.5 miles east of Mukhmas. Because they are small, most of the caves could accommo-

date only one family; yet some of them had been developed into larger dwellings by the hewing of additional rooms. Twenty-three caves were explored, most of them reached only by rock-climbing techniques. Cave no. 2 is typical of the group. It consists of one room, 11 x 8 feet, hewn in the soft rock and accessible through a vertical shaft about 10 feet high. The natural opening through which the cave was entered had been enlarged and then blocked by a wall; as a result the only access was through a tunnel about 8 feet long leading to the foot of the vertical shaft. A few steps below the entrance of the tunnel was a small cistern.

Nearly all the caves had been looted. Among the few objects retrieved was a leather sandal with double sole and straps similar to those found at Masada and in the Cave of Letters. These caves are notable for their common features: extensive hewing work, access shafts, and plastered cisterns. These features may indicate a deliberate plan to provide refuge for the local population over a period of time.

Implications for Jesus Research

Jesus lived the life of an itinerant healer, exorcist, and preacher—some would say of a Cynic philosopher (*see* GADARA). If he "had nowhere to lay his head" (Matt. 8:20), the expression could only mean that he had no fixed residence, because—besides being invited into private homes—he could sojourn in one of the many caves in the areas he traversed. These caves would have provided enough room for him and those who accompanied him. When he withdrew into the wilderness after his baptism, either in the area west of the Dead Sea or west of Jericho at a site like Wadi Mukhmas, he could have lodged in a cave as many did before and after him. Caves on the Mount of Olives offered him and his disciples shelter at night after a day of teaching in the temple. Despite this availability of caves for refuge or residence, the traditions about caves in connection with Jesus and his family probably do not reflect historical reality.

BIBLIOGRAPHY

Bar-Adon, P. "The Cave of the Treasure." *Archaeological Discovery of the Holy Land* (1967).

———. "Excavations in the Judean Desert." *'Atiqot* 9 (1989) (Hebrew).

Chronique Archéologique. "Les grottes du desert de Judée." *Revue Biblique* 69 (1962): 381–84.

Gilead, D., Y. Aharoni, J. Aviram, N. Avigad, P. Bar-Adon, J. Patrich, and E. Stern. "Judean Desert Caves." *NEAEHL* 3:816–37.

Patrich, J. "Judean Desert, Survey of Caves, 1985–1986. *Excavations and Surveys of Israel* 6 (1987–88): 66–70.

———. "Judean Desert, Secret Passages and Caves." *Excavations and Surveys of Israel* 3 (1984): 61–62.

The Society for the Research of Caves. *Migrot Zurim.* Jerusalem (Hebrew).

Machaerus (Hebrew, *Makhwar*)

Importance

Machaerus was one of Herod's palatial strongholds. His son, Antipas, had John the Baptist imprisoned and beheaded there.

Scripture References

Matt. 14:3-10; Mark 6:16-27; Luke 3:19-20.

General Information

The first fortress of Machaerus, built by the Hasmonean king Alexander Jannaeus (103–76 B.C.E.), was situated on the eastern side of the Dead Sea, in Perea, the ancient land of Moab that John Hyrcanus had conquered (Josephus, *War* 7, 6.1–2/163–177). Strabo lists it among the Hasmonean strongholds; it was used as an operational base by Aristobulus in his resistance against the Romans, and Pompey destroyed it in 64 B.C.E. (Strabo, *Geography* 16, 2–40). Herod the Great (37–4 B.C.E.) rebuilt and strengthened it; he included a magnificent palace within its walls in the same lavish style as that of Herodium and Masada. Pliny describes it as the "most important fortress of 'Judea' after Jerusalem" (*Nat. Hist.* 5, 2, 72).

After Herod's death Machaerus, with all of Perea, was given to his son Archaelaus and was later transferred to Herod Antipas in 6 C.E., when Archaelus was deposed by the Romans. In 44 C.E. Perea was added to the province of Judea; a Roman garrison occupied the fortress until the outbreak of the First Jewish War in 66 C.E. The Zealots then took possession of it but after a short siege surrendered to the governor Lucilius Bassus in 72 C.E. (*War* 7, 6.4/190–209).

Machaerus played an important role in the life of the Herodians. Herod the Great used it as one of his main strongholds and gathered enough war machines and provisions there to withstand a long siege (*War* 7, 6.2/177). Five miles away near the eastern shore of the Dead Sea was the natural spa of Calirrohe, where several pools are fed by the warm waters of some fifty springs. The name Calirrohe means "Baths of Herod" and was given to the spa because Herod took mineral baths there (*Antiq.* 17, 6.5/171). When Herod Antipas divorced his first wife, the daughter of the Nabatean king Aretas IV, she resided at Machaerus before returning to her father (*Antiq.* 18, 5.1/111–12). Antipas imprisoned John the Baptist in the fortress and had him beheaded there (*Antiq.* 18, 5.2/116–19). Machaerus was also important in Jewish tradition because it was one of the stations selected for signaling the appearance of the new moon and the beginning of the feasts (*t. Rosh Hashana* 2.2).

Archaeological Data

The fortress of Machaerus has been identified with the hill of Qsar el-Mineshke in Jordan, 5 miles east of the Dead Sea and south of Wadi Zarqa; its name is preserved in the name of the nearby village of el-Mukawer. In Greek, the name means "sword." Archaeological surveys of the site revealed walls, a bath, an approach road, and cisterns. A Roman siege system, similar to the one surrounding Masada but less developed, was also discovered.

An American, J. Vardaman, excavated at the site in 1968 and V. Corbo and the Franciscan

School of Jerusalem worked there in 1978. Five phases of occupation were recognized. The fortress built by Alexander Jannaeus measured 110 x 60 meters (360 x 196 feet). In good Hellenistic fashion, three strong square towers made up the bulk of the fortification. During the reign of Herod the Great, extensive construction took place. Walls, 2 meters (6.5 feet) thick, were erected from the northern tower and incorporated the western one. These walls were strong enough to withstand the battering rams of the time.

The fortress was occupied during the rule of the prefects (first century C.E.); the next level is attributed to the Zealots; and the last one belongs to the Roman garrison, which returned after the end of the First Jewish War.

Three stone anchors with remains of ropes attached to them, and weighing over 200 pounds each, were found in 1990 on the western shore of the sea. The ropes, dated by carbon 14, support the theory that there was boat commerce across the Dead Sea from the fourth century B.C.E. onward. An Israeli historian and economist, A. Nissembaum, suggested in 1991 that there was active boat traffic and commerce in wheat and asphalt between the southern and northern ends of the Dead Sea until the end of the Crusaders period. Such commercial use of the sea is indicated by one of the Bar Kokhba letters found by Y. Yadin in 1961. In this letter, Bar Kokhba bitterly reproaches two of his subordinates for having dealt improperly with the cargo of a ship in the port of En-Gedi (Y. Yadin, *Bar Kokhba*, 133).

Implications for Jesus Research

Two issues are related to these discoveries:

1. Some scholars claim that Herod Antipas could not have held a birthday celebration in Machaerus because it was a fortress and a prison in a remote part of his tetrarchy. Instead, he would have preferred Tiberias, his newly founded capital with a new palace. Consequently, the scene of Mark 6:16-27 and its parallel in Matthew 14:1-12 have been deemed mere inventions of the evangelists, the more so because Josephus does not offer such information. Machaerus, however, was more than a military stronghold; there was a splendid palace inside the fortress. Given its proximity to Jerusalem only 30 miles away going across the Dead Sea as opposed to 97 miles from Tiberias through Samaria or 135 miles by the safe route east of the Jordan, and given the attraction of the "Baths of Herod," it is indeed conceivable for Antipas to have invited his friends and clients to Machaerus.

Because of the importance of Machaerus, the customs of the time, and the easy communication by ship between both sides of the Dead Sea combined with a festive celebration, the beheading of John the Baptist, could have occurred in the palace-fortress. Of course, this observation hardly validates the tales of a dancing Salome or of the offer by Antipas of half of his "kingdom" and of John's head presented on a platter.

2. The story of Pilate dispatching Jesus to Herod Antipas (Luke 23:6-12) is rejected by a number of scholars as inauthentic, mainly on the basis of single attestation. As a good ruler, Antipas certainly visited the other half of his tetrarchy at least once a year and combined his visit with one of the great festivals. He may have been in Jerusalem at each Passover, after a stay at Machaerus, and met Jesus.

BIBLIOGRAPHY

Corbo, V. "La fortezza de Macheronte." *Liber Annuus* 28 (1978): 217–31.

———. "Macheronte, la reggia fortezza de Erodaina." *Liber Annuus* 29 (1979): 315–26.

———. "La fortezza de Macheronte (al Mishnaqa)." *Liber Annuus* 30 (1980): 365–76.

Loffreda, S. "Alcuni vasi ben datati della fortezza di Macheronte." *Liber Annus* 30 (1980): 377–402.

Piccirillo, M. "Le monete della fortezza di Macheronte." *Liber Annuus* 30 (1980): 403–14.

———. "Macheronte." *Le monde de la Bible* 17, (Jan.–Feb. 1981): 10–16.

Rainey, A. "Surface Remains Pertaining to the Fall of Machaerus." *Eretz Israel* 10 (1971): 264–68. (Hebrew).

Strobel, A. "Machärus—Geschichte und Ende einer Festung im Lichte archaeologisch-topographischer Beobachtungen." *Bibel und Qumran*. Berlin: Festschrift A. Bardtke, 1968.

———. "Das römische Belagerungswrerk im Machärus, Topographische Untersuchungen." *Zeitschrift des deutschen Palästina-Vereins* 90 (1974): 128–84.

Tsafrir, Y. "The Desert Fortresses of Judaea in the Second Temple Period." *The Jerusalem Cathedra* 2 (1982): 120-45.

Yadin, Y. *Bar-Kokhba*. London: Weidenfeld and Nicolson, 1971.

Magdala (Hebrew, *Migdal*; Aramaic, *Migdal Nunya*; Greek, *Taricheae*)

Importance

Magdala was a thriving city with a prosperous fishing industry in the Roman and Byzantine periods. Mary Magdalene was presumably from that city.

Scripture References

Matt. 15:39; 27:56, 61; 28:1; Mark 8:10; 15:40, 47; 16:1; Luke 8:2; 24:10; John 19:25; 20:1, 18.

General Information

Magdala is located near the present-day village of Migdal on the western shore of the Sea of Galilee, 3 miles north of Tiberias. It would be the Dalmanutha of Mark 8:10, according to some Gospel manuscripts; the name Magadan is also found in Matthew 15:39. With these two exceptions, all references to Magdala in the Gospels are indirect, through the name of Mary Magdalene (Mary of Magdala).

The city of Magdala was included in the territory of King Agrippa II by Nero (Josephus, *Antiq.* 20, 8.4/159) and was renamed *Taricheae* "salted fish." Its Aramaic name is *Migdal Nunya* (or Nunayah), "Tower of Fish" (*b. Pesahim* 46). The Talmud indicates that Magdala had a small harbor and a boat-building industry. It was a place of "wealth and depravity." During the First Jewish War, when Josephus, commander-in-chief of the rebels' army in Galilee, escaped from Tiberias, he made Taricheae-Magdala his headquarters and for-

tified it (*Life* 18, 32). Eventually, the city was besieged and captured by the Romans (*War* 3, 10:1–6/462–705). After the death of Agrippa II, it was attached to the province of Judea.

Archaeological Data

Y. Corbo and V. Loffreda excavated at Magdala between 1971 and 1974 on behalf of the Franciscan Custody of the Holy Land. They discovered Byzantine mosaic pavements, a water reservoir, a paved street, and a structure that they identified, probably erroneously, as a first-century B.C.E. synagogue. Because of its small size (the interior being 5.5 m x 6.5 m or 18 x 21 feet), they called it "mini synagoga." The interior contained seven columns organized in three rows, parallel to three walls of the room. In the northern section of the room, where there were no columns, was a flight of three steps. The building showed two phases of construction, the later one having waterways situated between the three walls and the columns. The excavators suggest that the function of the building was changed from a synagogue into a *nympheum*, that is a city fountain house, during the first century C.E. Others maintain that the building was a nympheum from its origin.

A hoard of 188 bronze coins was discovered at Magdala in 1973. Dating from the time of Nero to the reign of Elgabalos (54–122 C.E.), they were minted in the following cities: Tyre, Gadara, Acre, Beth-Shan, Tiberias, Hippos, Sepphoris, Geba, Dium, Abila, and Biblos. There is also evidence of the existence of a harbor dating from the same period. In 1986 a boat of the first century C.E. was found in the same general area (*see* BOATS).

Implications for Jesus Research

The existence of Mary Magdalene's city of origin has long been accepted. Can a correlation be made between its "depravity" and the seven demons that Jesus cast out of Mary (Luke 8:2; *see* EXORCISM)? The names of Migdal Nunya and Taricheae reflect the importance of the fishing and fish-salting industries in eastern Galilee in the time of Jesus (cf.

the fisherman's seal and fishing implements from Bethsaida; *see* BETHSAIDA).

BIBLIOGRAPHY

Avi-Yonah, M. "A Priestly List of Courses from Caesarea." *IEJ* 12 (1962): 137–139.

———. "Gazetteer of Roman Palestine." *Qedem* 5 (1976).

Brunot, A. "Magdala." *Bible et Terre Sainte* 192 (1977): 6.

Corbo, V. "Magdala." *Liber Annuus* 24. (1974): 5–37.

———. "La Citta Romana di Magdala." *Studia Hierosolymitana* (1976): 355–78.

Netzer, E. "The Synagogue of Magdala." *Synagogues in Antiquity*. Jerusalem, 1987 (Hebrew).

Meshorer, Y. *City Coins of Eretz Israel and the Decapolis in the Roman Period*. Jerusalem: Israel Museum, 1984 (Hebrew).

Strange, J. F. "Magdala." *ABD* 4:463–64.

Magic, Miracles

Importance

Jesus performed miracles and he was accused of being a magician.

Scripture References

Matt. 8:1-15, 23-34; 9:1-8, 18-34; 12:9-14, 22-24; 14:13-33; 15:21-39; 17:14-21; 20:29-34; Mark 1:23-31, 40-45; 2:1-12; 3:1-6; 4:35-41; 5:1-43; 6:30-31, 45-52; 7:24-37; 8:1-10, 22-26; 9:14-29; 10:46-52; Luke 4:33-39; 5:1-26; 6:6-11; 7:1-17; 8:22-56; 9:10-17, 37-43a; 11:14-15; 13:10-17; 14:1-6; 17:11-19; 18:35-43; John 2:11, 23-25; 4:46-54; 5:1-9a; 6:1-13, 16-21; 9:1-12; 11:1-44; Acts 3:1-10; 9:32-42; 14:8-18; 16:16-18; 19:19-20; 20:7-12.

General Information

Magic claims that it obtains by esoteric means certain results that could not be obtained by natural processes or religious rites. One alleged result is the submission of spirits or demons to the human will. A common characteristic of the techniques

and methods of magic is that there is no evident causal relation between the means and the results. Words, gestures, objects, and ingredients produce effects that cannot be rationally explained. For example, the burning of a fish's heart and liver makes a demon flee away (Tob. 8:2–3).

Anthropology and archaeology indicate that magical rites existed as long ago as prehistoric times in hunters' cultures. The oldest magical acts known to us were probably intended to figuratively surround and catch game animals. Magical circles, which became common stock-in-trade in magicians' rituals, perhaps originated with the large circle formed by hunters as they enacted the chase that would drive game into their traps. Such scenes are represented in primitive frescoes found in caves in Central Africa and elsewhere. On the walls of the caves, men without weapons are depicted dancing around animals caught in a trap or running toward it. These caves, accessible only by paths requiring difficult climbing, show no trace of occupation such as ashes or bones. Yet footprints of dancing humans were found imprinted in the hardened clay of some of the floors. Such magic perhaps antedated sacrifices as a religious rite by many millennia because the oldest altars unearthed by archaeology are much younger.

One name of Greek origin, *magos* (plural *magi*), deserves special attention. It figures in the New Testament and was widely used in the Near East and in the Greco-Roman world—with different connotations—before, during, and after the time of Jesus. Originally the *magi* formed a shamanic caste of the ancient Medes. The Greek historian Herodotus (484?–425? B.C.E.) wrote that in ancient times, they were interpreters of dreams. In the fifth century B.C.E. they became the Zoroastrian priests and astrologers of Persia. The former group of shamans had adopted the Aryan religion of the conquerors, excelled in it, transformed it, and monopolized the leadership. Their political influence became so powerful that in the fourth century C.E. they were able to institute a bloody persecution of Christians and Jews in Persia. Their influence spread in the Mediterranean world; Strabo (*Geogra-*

phy, 15. 727, 73) and Plutarch (*On Isis and Osiris*) mention them. The term *magus* became more often used for magicians who did not belong to the Zoroastrian priestly caste of Persia. Several references to Jewish *magi* can be found at about the time of Jesus: Simon Magus (Acts 8:9-24); the magus Elymas of Paphos in Cyprus (Acts 13:6-11); Atomos, another magus of Cyprus, attached to the court of the procurator Antonius Felix (52–60 C.E.) at Caesarea Maritima (Josephus, *Antiq.* 20, 7.2/142). Philo's disparaging comments on *magi* suggest that charlatans had joined their ranks, used counterfeit practices, and perverted the art. In his words, they were "mendicants, low grade women and slaves deceiving people with charms and incantations" (*Special Laws* 3.101).

Biblical Hebrew has no specific word for "magic," although it does have names for those who practiced it or a related trade: sorcerer, magician, necromancer, augur, etc. The activities of such persons are usually condemned. Because Hebrew culture contained elements related to features of Egyptian and Mesopotamian civilizations, the magical practices of those two cultures contribute to a better understanding of Hebrew attitudes toward magic and magicians. Magical practices are well attested in ancient Near Eastern sources.

The moon-god Thot of Hermopolis in Middle Egypt was said to be the inventor of magical formulae that neither gods nor people could resist. He had determined the right voice (*ma khro-u*) in terms of pitch, volume, rhythm, and the like, to be used in incantations. Women were considered especially gifted in this regard, and the queen was obligated to accompany the pharaoh to protect him while he was offering sacrifices. Magicians trained according to the precepts of Thot's school had all the other gods at their service. They could send horrifying dreams to their enemies, cause and cure diseases, produce love or hatred, and send spells. Ramses III must have been the object of magical attacks, because wax figurines and potions that magicians used against him were found in his tomb. The power of Egyptian magicians, although not as

strong as that of Moses and Aaron, is illustrated in Exodus 7–9.

In Canaan the Israelites encountered other magical traditions (Deut. 18:9), which they were told not to follow (Exod. 22:18; Deut. 18:10-12; Lev. 19:31, 20:27). The various prohibitions were attempts to stop well-entrenched popular use of magic. Even kings engaged in magic or consulted magicians. Saul, who had "expelled the mediums and the wizards from the land" (1 Sam. 28:3) had no illusions about the effectiveness of his decree. When he needed guidance regarding an upcoming military confrontation with the Philistines, he went to the witch of Endor, who conjured up the spirit of Samuel for him (1 Sam. 28:7). King Manasseh practiced soothsaying, augury, and sorcery, and dealt with mediums and wizards (2 Chron. 33:6). Isaiah of Jerusalem, in describing the anticipated deportation of the inhabitants of the Holy City, mention together: "warrior and soldier, judge and prophet, diviner and elder, captain of fifty and dignitary, counselor, the skillful magician and expert enchanter" (Isa. 3:2-3)—people who would hardly belong in the same category. This text incates that people practiced magic in Jerusalem *circa* 600 B.C.E. However, the prophets in general condemned magicians: Isaiah of Babylon (44:25); Trito-Isaiah (57:3); Jeremiah (27:9-10); Ezekiel (13:18-20; 22:28); Micah (5:12); Zechariah (10:2); Malachi (3:5). Yet the voices of the prophets were not heeded; ancient popular practices continued.

King Solomon is also linked with wisdom and magic. A wisdom figure in the Bible and in post-biblical works, Solomon had the reputation of being a magician. Josephus refers to his power (*Antiq.* 8, 2.5/45–49), and the *Testament of Solomon*, which is extant in Greek versions, praises his great wisdom. Rabbinic literature also refers to Solomon's magical power. It is said that he dominated demons by means of a seal engraved with the secret name of YHWH. Accordingly, many incantations in different countries included a reference to the seal of Solomon.

After the conquest of Alexander in the late fourth century B.C.E., Palestine became more open to Greek influence in many aspects of human activity, including magic. In the Greek tradition *goes* (plural *goetes*) was the common term for a magician, whose craft was called *goeteia*. Although Plato did not seem averse to *goeteia*, the disciples of Euripides and Socrates grouped *goetes* with "deceivers, beggars and scoundrels." Still, in his latter works, Plato prescribes that a *goes* offender should be imprisoned for life and even put to death according to the gravity of the offense (*Laws* 932).

Greece was influenced by Persian and Mesopotamian traditions after Cyrus conquered Asia Minor (540–530 B.C.E.) and brought with him the Zoroastrian *magi*. Herodotus wrote about them with some deference around 440 B.C.E. As time passed, however, the respectable *magi* were reduced to the level of the *goetes*. Both were seen as quacks, users of drugs, deceivers of the gods. This change was probably brought about by the proliferation of impostors, posing as authentic Persian *magi*, who operated in the ancient Mediterranean world. Yet, even the pure-bred *magi* were subject to severe criticism: they were said to share wives, and to have sexual intercourse with their mothers, sisters, and daughters. They were also accused of offering human sacrifices.

These accusations may have been false and malicious as were similar attacks on the early Christians. Plutarch's remark that the *magi* predicted the approaching end of the world, the destruction of the wicked, and the coming of an age of peace and happiness for the righteous is relevant to the general eschatological beliefs of the first century C.E. (M. Smith, *Jesus the Magician*, 70–72). Another famous figure, Apollonius of Tyana, performed healings and acts of magic in Jesus' time. Unfortunately, his life is known only in the writings of Philostratus, who lived two centuries after Apollonius and who embellished the story to the point of making him a divine being, a competitor of the exalted Jesus of the Christians. (For other magicians of Jesus' time, *see* SAMARIA.)

Archaeological Information

Thousands of artifacts and texts from the ancient Near East, down to the medieval periods and later, attest to the enduring popularity of magical practices. A few examples from the early Christian period indicate that Jesus was viewed by both Christians and non-Christians, as having magical powers.

From the Pereire collection in Paris comes a brown jasper stone, dated to about 200 C.E. It depicts Jesus nailed by his wrists to a cross and sitting on a peg projecting from the upright post. The legs are dangling loose, the feet slightly spread. Around the figure and on the reverse of the stone are the words, "One Father, Jesus Christ," followed by seemingly meaningless magical words.

Probably from a later date, an orange jasper in the British Museum represents a crucified figure without a cross, with a haloed head; it suggests a flying Christ. On each side, below the extended arms, are two smaller kneeling figures. Above the head, the words "Jesus M . . . " (Messiah?) can be deciphered. The reverse is inscribed with Greek magical words and signs.

Many Christian papyri and amulets in Greek and Coptic have been found in Egypt. Jesus' name is used in incantations, together with the names of Solomon, derivatives of YHWH, and names of other gods. A number of such texts are in the Bibliothèque de l'Arsenal in Paris.

Implications for Jesus Research

Was Jesus a magician? This question is difficult to answer. Two facts are certain: a) magical activity existed in his time and was linked to millennia-old magical traditions of various origins; and b) Jesus performed miracles akin to acts of magic in that no rational relation between cause and effect can explain the results. For instance, how can the mere fact of touching the hem of his garment stop a chronic hemorrhage (Mark 5:26; Luke 8:43)?

Miracles differ from ordinary acts of magic in that the beneficiary and others recognize in them, rightly or wrongly, the intervention of a supernatural power. In the Judeo-Christian tradition, miracles (also called signs or mighty works) are manifested "by the finger of God" (Luke 11:20). God is the magician. This is asserted by the talmudic tradition with the stories of two Jewish sages and miracle-workers, Honi *ha-me'ggel* (the circle drawer) and Hanina ben Dosa.

The former lived in the first century B.C.E., a contemporary of Queen Salome Alexandra, Simeon ben Shatah, Aristobulus II and Hyrcanus II. It is said of him that he caused rain to fall by praying from within a circle he drew on the ground. He was compared to "a son who importunes his father" (b. *ta'anit* 3.8). The latter, a student of Johanan ben Zakkai in Galilee, belonged to the *hasidim* mystics in the first century C.E. He too performed miracles through prayers. One of the most famous was the healing at a distance of the son of Gamaliel II. When messengers reached Gamaliel's house, they found that his son had been healed at the exact time that Hanina had said his prayer of intercession. This miracle is similar to that reported in Matthew 8:5–13 and parallels. It is debatable which one served as a model for the other. Hanina was poor and so rigorously observant that even his donkey would not eat untithed food. The talmudic tradition indicates that "compared with Ben Dosa's prayers those of the high priest himself are of no avail" (b. *ta'anit* 24b), and that with his death "wonder-workers ceased to exist" (b. *sotah* 9.15).

It is not surprising then that Jesus' opponents did not deny the miracles he performed; they only claimed that he did them by magic, by using the power of God's enemy, Satan. In his lifetime, Jesus was accused of being a magician (Beelzebul controversy, Mark 3:20-35 and parallels) and possessed by a demon (Mark 3:30; John 7:19-20; 8:35-52; 10:21). After his death, such accusations continued, as witnessed by what remains of Celsus's writings and what appears in rabbinic literature.

Celsus's original work was systematically burnt in the fourth century by the Church with many other "heretic" texts. However, Origen, in his book *Contra Celsum* (ca. 247 C.E.), quoted substantial passages from Celsus' work, which can be grouped as follows:

> Jesus was a miracle worker, a magician. He made up the story of his virgin birth, but in reality his mother was a villager making a living by spinning wool. Her husband, a carpenter, repudiated her on the charge of adultery. She lived like a tramp in shame, and secretly gave birth to Jesus, the adulterous son of a soldier name Pantera (*see* PANTERA'S TOMBSTONE). When he was a young man, Jesus who had grown up in Galilee, went to Egypt to work as a hired laborer. There he learned magic (as Moses and Aaron did). He came back to Israel with great expectations based on his newly acquired knowledge and proclaimed he was a god (*Contra Celsum* 1.28, 38).

> Once in Palestine he recruited ten (not twelve) disciples who were tax collectors and sailors of the worst kind, all illiterate. They lived as tramps, begging (1.40 ff). Jesus followed all the Jewish customs, even those about sacrifices (2.6). He was small in stature, ugly, without distinction (4.75). Deserted and betrayed by many of his disciples, he fled and was caught (2.9–12). He was tried as a bandit (2.44). At the crucifixion he opened his mouth to drink (2.37). His ministry was a failure, he persuaded no one during his lifetime (2.39, 46), but he made the correct prediction that others too, among his followers, would continue to do the same kind of magic, evil men and sorcerers, according to the plans of Satan (2.49). (M. Smith, *Jesus the Magician*, 56-60)

Rabbinic writers attributed the miracles of Jesus to sorcery or fraud:

> It has been taught: On the eve of Passover they hanged Yeshu. And an announcer went out, in front of him, for fourteen days (saying): "He is going to be stoned because he practiced sorcery" (Baraitha, b. *Sanhedrin* 43a. Tannaitic˙ period; Goldstein, 22)

> It happened with R. Elazar ben Damah who had been bitten by a snake, that Jacob, a man of Kefar Soma came to heal him in the name of Yeshu ben

Pandera; but R. Ishmael did not let him. He said, "You are not allowed, Ben Damah." He answered, "I will bring you proof that he may heal me." But he had no opportunity to bring proof for he died. R. Ishmael said, "Happy are you, Ben Damah, for you are gone in peace and have not broken the fence of the Sages" (*t. Hullin* 2, 2, 23, dated to 130 C.E. Goldstein, 32).

The grandson of R. Joshua ben Levi was choking. A certain man came and whispered to him the name of Yeshua ben Pandera. And when he came out he (R. Joshua) said to him: "What did you whisper to him?" He answered, "A certain word." He said, "It might have been better to have died than this" (*y. Sabbat*; Goldstein, 113).

These three Tannaitic texts indicate that some Jews used the services of healers or exorcists operating in the name of Jesus, thereby attributing special powers to him. Another text is also of interest:

> In the Temple was the Foundation Stone on which were engraved the letters of God's Ineffable Name. Whoever learned the secret of the Name and its use would be able to do whatever he wished . . . Yeshu came and learned the letters of the Name; he wrote them upon the parchment which he placed in an open cut on his thigh and then drew the flesh over the parchment . . . When he came to his house, he reopened the cut . . . and lifted out the writing. Then he remembered and obtained the use of the letters. (Sefer Toledoth Yeshu; Goldstein, 147).

Although this is an unreliable post-Talmudic text, it shows the reputation of Jesus as a man with mysterious power. The earliest mention of this text, which may have been written in the time of Charlemagne, is by Abogard, Bishop of Lyons (ca. 826).

Beginning with Acts, many Christian traditions assert that Jesus performed miraculous healings and so indicate that he was a miracle worker. Yet his followers maintained that he worked by the power of God. This is probably the ultimate criterion for differentiating Jesus from the other magicians of his time, especially because his chief motive was not greed but proclaiming the kingdom of God.

Another point, the appearance of the magi in the First Gospel, deserves discussion. Why did the author of Matthew include Matthew 2:1-12 in the narrative? Many reasons have been offered, but only one is based on historical facts. According to Pliny the Elder, Nero sought the power of magic to "command the gods." He invited a famous magus to come to his court. The magus Tiridates came to him with many attendants and magi. He initiated Nero in magical meals, for which the emperor was so grateful that he gave Tiridates a kingdom but he was not able to learn the art of magic (M. Smith, 72). Nero reigned from 54 to 68 C.E. The First Gospel came to its final form in about 90. Perhaps the final writer or editor included the magi incident in the narrative to demonstrate that Jesus was considered by foreign prestigious sages at least the equal of a deified Roman emperor.

To return now to the question posed earlier, "Was Jesus a magician?": it can be said that, in his Palestinian-Galilean context, he performed "mighty works." To the spectators, these miracles may have been indistinguishable from acts of magic. It is worth noting that, according to the Gospels, Jesus did not use the methods and paraphernalia of magic: stones, rings, seals, potions, parts of animals, blood, and the like. He touched, he took a patient by the hand; he uttered a command, he lifted his eyes (probably a sign of silent prayer); most of the time he did nothing that was observable, simply affirming the healing. In some case of healing, he used saliva or a plaster made of clay and spittle (*see* MEDICINE, PHYSICIANS); these are the only instances involving material elements. Although Jesus performed miracles as understood in his time, he was not a magician *stricto sensu** because he did not use procedures used by other magicians in the first century C.E.

BIBLIOGRAPHY

Cazeneuve, J. *Les rites et la condition humaine.* Paris, 1958.

Clermont-Ganneau, C. "L'envoutement dans l'antiquité et les figurines de plomb de Tell-Sandahanna." *Palestine Exploration Fund, Quarterly Statement* (1900): 332.

Garrett, *Demise of the Devil*, Minneapolis: Fortress Press, 1989.

Goldstein, M. *Jesus in the Jewish Tradition*. New York: Macmillan, 1950.

Latourelle, René. *The Miracles of Jesus and the Theology of Miracles*. New York: Paulist Press, 1988.

Levi-Strauss, C. *Anthropologie Structurale X: L'efficacité symbolique*. Paris, 1958.

Lindner, K. *La Chasse préhistorique*. Paris, 1950.

McCasland, S. *By the Finger of God*. New York: Macmillan, 1951.

Philostratus. *The Life of Apollonius of Tyana*. Loeb Classical Library.

Pritchard, J. B. ed. *Ancient Near Eastern Texts Relating to the Old Testament*. Rev. ed. Princeton, N.J.: Princeton University Press, 1955.

Rousseau, J. "Jesus in the World of Exorcism." *Jesus Seminar papers*. Sonoma, Calif.: Polebridge Press, 1992.

———. "Jesus, an Exorcist of a Kind." *SBL Seminar Papers* (1993).

Smith, M. *Jesus the Magician*. 1978. Reprint. Wellingborough, England: The Aquarian Press, 1985.

Theissen, G. *The Miracle Stories of the Early Christian Tradition*. German, 1974. Philadelphia: Fortress Press, 1983.

Masada

Importance

The excavations of Masada provide information about the Zealots and the early history of the synagogue.

Scripture References

Matt. 10:4; 11:12; Mark 3:18; Luke 6:16.

General Information

Masada is an isolated rocky plateau on the western side of the Dead Sea. Its top is nearly level and stands at an elevation of about 1,300 feet above the water. Its steep and sometimes vertical sides make access to it extremely difficult. According to Josephus (*War* 7, 8.3/285), Jonathan the priest built a fortress on the plateau and called it Masada, "Mountain Stronghold," the name by which the mount is designated today. Scholars are divided as to whether this Jonathan was the brother of Judas Maccabeus, mid-second century B.C.E., or Alexander Jannaeus whose Hebrew name was also Jonathan. In 42 B.C.E., the fortress was captured by Malichas, the enemy of Herod's father, Antipater. When Herod left Jerusalem in 41 B.C.E., fleeing from the Parthians, he took his family to Masada for their safety and continued his journey to Rome. After his return, when he had established his authority over Palestine, he built a large fortress and palaces on the plateau, which Josephus describes at length (*War* 7, 8.3–4/280–300). Before the First Jewish Revolt in 66 C.E., the fortress was occupied by a Roman garrison, which the Zealots eliminated. They held the position until May 2, 73 C.E., when it was finally taken by Flavius Silva. The besieged Zealots and their families committed mass suicide rather than surrender as their predecessors had done at Gamla 107 years before (*see* GAMLA; *War* 7, 8.6–9.2/320–406). However, a few scholars are now challenging Josephus's information about group suicide.

Archaeological Data

Masada, first identified by E. Robinson in 1838, was visited by the American missionary S. W. Wolcott in 1842, an expedition of the U.S. Navy in 1848, the French archaeologist E. de Saulcy in 1851, E. G. Ray in 1858, a survey team of the Palestine Exploration Fund in 1882, Father F. M. Abel in 1909, and the German archaeologist A. Schulten in 1931. Systematic excavations were not undertaken until 1955, when a joint expedition of the Hebrew University, the Israel Exploration Society, and the Israeli Department of Antiquities and Museums began its work. The site was first carefully surveyed. Then, under the direction of Y. Yadin, Masada was excavated (1963–65) with the help of thousands of volunteers from all over the world. Yadin identified six periods of occupation: Pre-Herodian, Herodian, pre-War, War (66–73 C.E.), Garrison, and Byzantine. The Herodian and pre-War periods correspond to Jesus' time (37 B.C.E.–66 C.E.).

The plateau, an elongated area of about 2,000 x 1,000 feet, was surrounded by a 13-foot-wide casemate wall with 110 towers 20 to 100 feet high and three gates. One gate is on the eastern side at the terminus of the "snake path" and another is on the west side near the smaller palace. The third one, on the northwest, was the Water Gate leading to the site's immense cisterns, which held more than 40,000 cubic meters (141,000 cubic feet) of water. On the northern end of the platform was the now-famous tri-terrace Herodian palace, vast storerooms, and an elaborate Roman bath.

Masada may be seen as a manifestation of Herod's character. Without the physical remains of Masada and his many other architectural projects, we would know about his personality only from texts, namely Josephus and Talmudic literature. These sources, as far as Herod the Great is concerned, have long been considered biased and problematic. Thus his massive construction programs provide another angle of vision on Herod's person and office. Masada, more than anything else, provides a strong sense of his personal impact. The entire project—a magnificent palace equipped with whatever luxury was available at the time for a royal lifestyle, in a remote part of his kingdom, on an isolated mount—was an ambitious undertaking that has never been duplicated.

The fortress is not easily accessible, yet, in addition to relying on its natural impregnability, Herod built casemate walls surrounding the plateau. The area between the northern palaces and the rest of the fortress was divided by a whitewashed wall, which served as an internal partition between the king's quarters and his subordinates. The royal palaces, set on three levels, were built on artificial fill at the northern end of the cliff; persons standing there feel suspended in air while looking out at a spectacular view. These structures perhaps served as a place of meditation, or maybe they were meant to impress and entertain guests. The most unusual feature of the northern palace is a small suspended bath at the lowest level; it is

built at the very edge of the terrace and overlooks the land and the sea below.

At the level of the storerooms, on the west side, integrated within the casemate wall but protruding in the court of the fortress is a building interpreted as a synagogue. Originally, it was a meeting room of some sort, about 36 x 45 feet including an entry hall or narthex. In the main room were five columns without built-in benches along the walls. There is no evidence that this building was at first designed as a synagogue, although Herod may have planned such a facility for the Jews of his entourage. Whatever its former use, the building was apparently modified by the Zealots so that it would be like similar buildings of the time, such as the synagogue of Gamla (*see* fig. 49; *see also* fig. 28, p. 103). They removed the partition wall and replaced it with two columns taken from the back of the building to support the ceiling. They made a smaller, inner room, and they added stone benches along the walls like the ones of the Gamla synagogue. That this modified building was used for religious purposes is indicated by the discovery of a *genizah*, "pit" (to bury discarded Hebrew Scripture), in the back room and a *miqveh*, "ritual bath," next to the main structure. Two badly damaged scrolls were found in the *genizah*; the book of Ezekiel with chapter 37 (the vision of the dry bones) almost intact, and Deuteronomy.

Implications for Jesus Research

The excavations for Masada shed light on two important issues pertaining to the time of Jesus: the features of the synagogues he visited, and the existence of the Zealots during the time of his ministry.

The Masada synagogue is similar to the buildings identified as synagogues at Herodium and Gamla (*see* HERODIUM and GAMLA). They were stone buildings with the main entry facing Jerusalem (not exactly in that direction at Masada for topographic reasons), with rows of columns, three or four built-in stepped benches along the walls, a back or side room, and at least one ritual bath nearby (*see* CHORAZIN and GAMLA). Because of

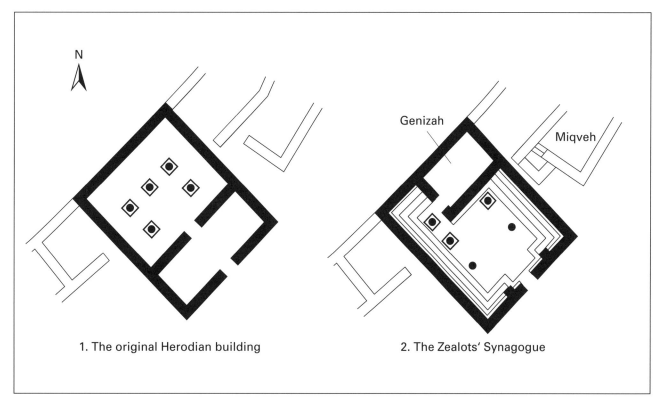

1. The original Herodian building   2. The Zealots' Synagogue

Genizah

Miqveh

N

Figure 49 The Synagogue at Masada. How the zealots changed a building into a synagogue.

the floor plan of these buildings, the healings and exorcisms Jesus performed in synagogues could be observed by all persons present, for they were sitting along the walls and facing the center. They could also respond immediately because they were facing each other. Such full visibility is probably one reason that the reality of Jesus' healings and exorcisms was not contested, even by his opponents.

The information about the Zealots in Josephus is dramatically illuminated by the Masada excavations. Because Josephus calls this group the "Fourth Philosophy" and "bandits" for the period *circa* 6 C.E. and "Zealots" for the First Jewish War, especially in Jerusalem, some scholars have suggested that the Zealots alluded to in the Gospels are a mere retrojection from the time of the First Jewish War and that the movement did not exist prior to 66 C.E. Perhaps it is the case that a strongly centralized Zealot organization did not yet exist early in the first century. Yet there is a similarity between the mentality and behavior of those inspired by Judas the Galilean and the Pharisee Saddok who "pressed hard for resistance" (Josephus, *Antiq.* 18, 1.1, 6/4–5, 23) at the time of the census in 6 C.E., and the desperate patriots of Masada. A revolutionary spirit would be occasioned in both instances. Direct continuity lies in the fact that the insurgent leaders were James and Simon, sons of Judas the Galilean, and Menahem, his grandson (or youngest son), who headed the Sicarii. Another descendant of his was Eleazar ben Jair, who was the leader of the remnant of the Sicarii at Masada (*War* 7, 8.1/253). Whatever the names given to the

Masada. *The Synagogue and its masonry benches.*

intellectual leaders and fighters of the Jewish Resistance—Fourth Philosophy, bandits, Zealots, Sicarri—the common socio-historical context is that oppression often leads to rebellion. Furthermore, even when leaders advocate only passive resistance, as has been suggested for Judas and Saddok, more violent individuals may at the same time engage in direct armed action. It is impossible to say that there was no violent spirit in Jesus' time, even if most of Herod Antipas's reign was peaceful. The Gospels themselves contain indications of violence: Gospel of Thomas 98 (the parable of the assassin), Matthew 11:12 (the violent ones who want to bring the kingdom of heaven by force), Mark 15:7 and Luke 23:19 (Barabbas, a rebel who had taken part in the insurrection in the city), and Luke 13:1 (the Galileans murdered by Pilate when they were offering their sacrifices). Jesus was faced with the problem of dealing with proponents of immediate armed rebellion while he was preaching submission to God and preparedness for the divine

rule. The rebellion of 66 and its tragic end at Masada were explosive manifestations of similar feelings of frustration and anger, which had been brewing for three generations against the Romans and their associates.

BIBLIOGRAPHY

Horsely, R. A. *Jesus and the Spirit of Violence.* San Francisco: Harper and Row, 1987.

Horsely, R. A. and J. S. Hanson. *Bandits, Prophets and Messiahs.* New York: Winston Press, 1985.

Levine, L. I., ed. *Ancient Synagogues Revealed.* Jerusalem: Academic Press and the Israel Exploration Society, 1981.

Livneh, M. and Z. Meshel. *Masada.* Jerusalem: National Parks Authority, 1965.

Netzer, E. "Masada." *NEAEHL* 3: 973–85.

———. *The Buildings, Stratigraphy and Architecture (Masada 3).* Jerusalem: Israel Exploration Society, 1991.

Silberman, N. A. "Israel: The Fall of Masada." *Between Past and Present.* New York: Doubleday, 1989.

Yadin, Y. *Masada.* New York: Random House, 1966–85.

Medicine, Physicians

Importance

Jesus performed many healings, and the Gospels refer to physicians.

Scripture References

Matt. 9:12; Mark 2:17; 5:26; Luke 4:23; 5:31; 8:43; Col. 4:14.

General Information

The Gospels and Colossians (4:14) use the Greek word *iatros*, "physician," seven times. In addition, 1 Corinthians 12:9-10 refers to "gifts of healing" and "working of miracles." From these texts it may be concluded that there were at least three kinds of healings in first-century-C.E. Palestine: those performed by physicians, those done by non-physician healers, and those associated with miracle workers. These healing practices can be set in their ancient Near Eastern and Greco-Roman context.

The practice of medicine in Mesopotamia and Egypt involved various customs and rituals, including incantations and the use of herbs and other ingredients. Because diseases were thought to be caused by demons (Mesopotamia) or evil spirits (Egypt), priests used exorcism as one method of healing. Hebrew Scripture, however, explicitly condemns magic and exorcism and ignores demons. For the ancient Israelites, disease was often viewed as the punitive consequence of a sinful situation. As such, it implied a disrupted relationship with God, who nonetheless remains the ultimate Healer (Exod. 15:26).

Priests and midwives both appear in the Hebrew Bible in connection with medical matters. Also non-priestly physicians are mentioned. For example, in 2 Chronicles 16:12 when the Judean King Asa was suffering from a severe disease in his feet (gout? arthritis? an infected wound?), he did not seek the Lord (through priests), but sought help from physicians. At the time of Ecclesiasticus (the wisdom of Jesus son of Sirach written *ca.*200 B.C.E.), physicians held a respected position in society. The passage where they are mentioned begins with this advice: "Honor physicians for their services, for the LORD created them" (Sir. 38:1-15).

Because many diseases were seen as caused by demons, exorcism became a healing practice in the late biblical period. It perhaps encroached upon the domain of the priests of YHWH, who themselves seem to have finally adopted it as indicated by the Beelzebul controversy (Mark 3:20-35 and parallels) and the involvement of the sons of Sceva (Acts 19:13-16).

Hebraic tradition was also influenced by Greco-Roman culture. In the Greco-Roman world, it was believed that the gods had healing powers. The most notable example is the Greek deity, Asklepios, who became latinized under the name of Esculapius, god of healing and patron of physicians. The Greek and then Roman practices of medicine were profoundly influenced by Hippocrates (460?–337? B.C.E.), who insisted that the physicians rely only on experience and that only what could be established by observation might be considered as truth. He thus detached himself and medicine from religion and philosophy, making the art of healing an empirical science. Hippocrates's basic principles are still valid today. Yet he and his followers were never able to eclipse the priests, who continued to perform religious healing, or the magicians. By the time of Galen (130?–200? C.E.), the most important forms of healing were still those of religion and magic.

For the physicians of the Hippocratic school and their successors, the causes of illness were cold, warmth, sun, air, and climatic conditions, which were seen as impacting the human body as divine forces independent of the gods. This was a conceptualization in which the gods or demons had no particular powers. As Hippocrates states in his treatise on *The Sacred Disease* (epilepsy): "This disease . . . comes from the same cause as others, from the things that come to and go from the body, from cold, sun and from the changing winds which are divine" ("by themselves"; Edelstein, 208).

Other ancient thinkers would go further and deny any divine quality to the sun, the moon, the earth, and all natural phenomena. They were more adamant than their Hippocratic colleagues in insisting that the processes observed in the world were not caused by a deity. Consequently, gods did not intervene in the healing of a disease. In the first century C.E., Pliny the Elder (23–79 C.E.) criticized the popular conviction that gods caused diseases:

> To believe that there are a number of gods corresponding to the virtues and vices of man . . . is still greater folly. Human nature, frail and weak, mindful of its own infirmity, has made these divisions, so that everyone might choose that which he thinks he, himself, needs the most . . . The inferior deities are arranged in classes, diseases and plagues are deified . . . to propitiate them. It was for this cause that a temple was dedicated to Fever, at the public expense, on the Palatine Hill (*Nat. Hist.* 2.15).

If the diseases could be seen as divine because they were caused by celestial bodies or the elements, they were also seen as human because it was believed that they had their origin in heredity and in the predisposition of the body's organs. In his treatise on *Prognostics*, Hippocrates advised the physician "to learn the nature of disease, how much they could be stronger than the human body, and whether there is any divine influence in them, and to learn how to forecast them" (Edelstein, 216). When the sphere of negative divine influence of celestial bodies or elements intersected with the human sphere, then disease occurred.

Greek physicians did not believe in the influence of the gods, and they also rejected the notion of demonic intervention. In this they were in agreement with the ancient Greek philosophers—Platonists, Aristotelians, and Stoics—who unanimously condemned the commonly held belief that gods or demons could be the cause of diseases. The Neo-Platonist Plotinus (205?–270? C.E.) wrote:

> They tell us they can free themselves of disease. If they mean by temperate living and appropriate regimen, they are right and in accordance with all sound knowledge. But they say that diseases are spirit-beings and boast they can expel them by formulae. This pretension may enhance their importance with the crowd gaping upon the power of magicians . . . [In fact] diseases arise from such causes as overstrain, excess, deficiency, putrid decay, . . . letting, . . . sometimes light nourishment restores the system (Psychic and Physical Treatises, *Enneades* 2.9, 16).

In the Gospels there is only one instance where the treatment of a wound is incidentally and briefly described. A traveler going from Jerusalem to Jericho was abandoned wounded on the roadside by robbers and received first aid from the good Samaritan (Luke 10:30-37). The victim was given antiseptic in the form of wine, oil was added for a soothing effect, and the wound was bandaged. Elsewhere, Jesus is shown as using spittle (Mark 8:23) or a plaster of clay and spittle (John 9:6) to cure blindness; in another instance Jesus uses salvia to cure a dumb man (Mark 7:33). These actions reflect the practices of his time, when saliva was seen as a curative agent.

Other important sources of information regarding medicine and healing in Jesus' time include the writings of Celsus, Pliny the Elder, and Josephus, and to a lesser extent some excerpts from the Dead Sea Scrolls.

Celsus (24? B.C.E.–34? C.E.), a contemporary of Jesus, gives a thorough description of the state of medical knowledge and practices of his time in *De Medicina*. His work consists of three parts: 1) how the healthy should act, 2) diseases, and 3) cures.

In the first part Celsus advises about sleeping, eating, drinking, bathing, when to force vomiting and give purgation, and how to adjust diet according to seasons. He recommends certain cures in cases of "weakness" of certain parts of the body. For instance, in cases of "head weakness," he suggests rubbing, cutting the hair, frequent walking, avoidance of hot sun, pouring cold water on the head, drinking light wine, etc.

In the second part Celsus describes symptoms of various diseases such as tuberculosis, dropsy, kidney problems, bladder disorders, phtisis, and epilepsy. There is an assumption that some substance in the body is the cause of the disease; it must be drawn out by bloodletting, purgation, cupping, rubbing, rocking, abstinence, and sweating.

In the last part of his work, Celsus describes cures according to a four-part classification of disease still meaningful today: acute, chronic, acute-chronic, and curable. For almost all internal diseases he prescribes treatments such as baths, enemas, diet, liquids, emetics, bloodletting, sweating, or cooling, and "home remedies" ranging from mustard to chicken broth. His work is particularly significant for the study of the historical Jesus, because it gives a complete overview of the medical theories and practices of the first-century Greco-Roman world.

As for Pliny, his forceful denunciation of medical abuses sheds light on some reprehensible practices of Jesus' time. According to his testimony, charlatans and quacks called themselves physicians but in fact used the techniques of magic instead of "natural remedies," thus exploiting gullible people (*Nat. Hist.* 29.1). He places most of the blame on the founders of medicine, who attributed their knowledge to the favor of gods, especially Asklepios, in order to grant to themselves prestige and sanctity. Pliny deplores the fact that the professional, scientific approach of Hippocrates had degenerated into "words devoid of meaning," with more interest in giving or listening to speeches than in search of new medicine (*Nat. Hist.* 24.6.11). The situation of the woman suffering from hemorrhages in Mark 5:26 corresponds to his criticism.

Josephus's contribution to our knowledge of medicine of the first century C.E. is contained in a short passage regarding the Essenes:

> They display an extraordinary interest in the writings of the ancients, singling out in particular those that make for the welfare of the soul and body. With the help of these, and with a view to the treatment of diseases, they make investigations into medicinal roots and the properties of stones (*War* 2, 8.6/136).

It is surprising that no texts dealing with diseases or remedies were found among the Dead Sea Scrolls. Only two published texts the *Genesis Apocryphon* (1 Qap Gen) from cave 1, and the *Prayer of Nabonidus* (4 QPr Nab) from cave 4 mention healings; one of these can also be interpreted as exorcism (*see* EXORCISM). In the first case, Abram heals Pharaoh; in the second, Daniel (presumably) heals the king of Babylon, Nebu-na'id, who retired to Teima, Arabia, in 552 B.C.E. after he had abdicated in favor of his son Bel-sur-Ussur, the Belshazzar of Daniel. In these stories, the Qumranites show two great Hebrew leaders healing two powerful monarchs, thereby demonstrating the superiority of the God of Israel. A remarkable feature in these two stories is that no medications are used; the healer or the patient prays to the God of Israel, and in one case Abram imposes his hand on the patient's head. YHWH alone is the healer. Undoubtedly the methods described in these texts were those of the Qumranites.

In Jesus' time there were physicians on duty in the Temple, possibly one for each section of priests on weekly duty (*m. Seqalim* 5.1). They were called upon when priests injured themselves in the course of their duties, many of which required physical activities (*m. Erubin* 10.13 f.). Physicians were listed among those engaged in despised trades (*m. Kiddushim* 4.14). Rabbi Judah said (ca. 150 C.E.), "the best among physicians is bound to go to Gehenna" (*m. Kiddushim* 4.14). This criticism is similar to that of Pliny's and is related to the remark about the hemorrhaging woman in Mark 5:26.

Archaeological Information

The temple of Sobek and Horus at Kom Ombo, Egypt, dates from the time of the emperor Trajan (98–117 C.E.). On its walls are depictions of medical and surgical instruments of the Roman period. They attest to aspects of applied medical knowledge in the first century C.E. and indicate that physicians were a distinct category of professionals to which Jesus did not belong. Pilgrims who came for healing left many graffiti on the walls. As was

Figure 50 Medical Instruments of the First Century C.E.: 1: speculum; 2: cup for bleeding; 3: medicine box; 4: scalpel; 5: retractor for removing arrowheads.

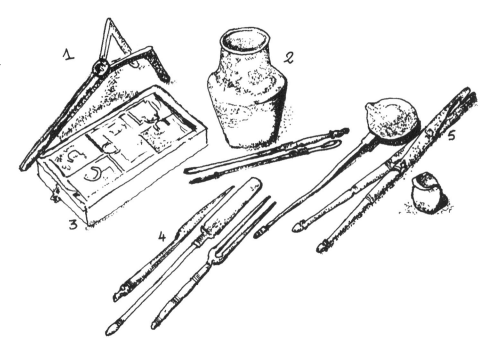

the practice in most of the Mediterranean world, patients came to spend the night in the temple precinct. When the priests of Horus, "the good physician," used their medical instruments, they probably accompanied their procedures with religious or magical rites. A number of Roman surgical instruments have been found in different ancient cities of the Roman Empire (*see* fig. 50).

Implications for Jesus Research

The information presented above makes it quite certain that Jesus was not a physician, although in three instances, two involving blindness and one dumbness, he used saliva or a plaster made of clay and spittle to effect a cure. He is not reported to have received any training in healing, nor do the Gospels have him prescribing any medications, exercises, or manipulations of joints or spine. Rather, we see him healing by virtue of a special power within him, possibly the power of God or the Holy

Spirit as expressed in the Beelzebul controversy. Although he may have prayed silently, he did not utter spoken prayers, as reported about Abram and Nabonidus in the Qumran scrolls. He made allusions to physicians by using a popular proverb familiar to his hearers. He advised lepers to see priests in order to have their healings officially recognized, but he did not encourage people to consult physicians. He did not use the magical techniques of the popular healers of his time (*see* MAGIC, MIRACLES). He is shown as truly one-of-a-kind among physicians and the other itinerant healers of Palestine; the evangelists considered his healings miracles, mighty works, or signs.

A remark must be made about the two versions of the story of the healing of the woman with menstrual hemorrhage. Luke's watering down of Mark's criticism of the greed and ineptness of the woman's physicians (she "had suffered much under many physicians, and had spent all that she had; and she was no better, but rather worse," (Mark

Moses' Seat ✦ 203

5:26) into "no one could heal her" (Luke 8:43) indicates that Luke, the physician companion of Paul, was indeed the writer, or at least an editor, of the Third Gospel.

Two issues are related to Jesus' healings: faith, and forgiveness of sin. Much has been written about the many instances in which the faith of the patient or someone else seems to be a factor in healing. Indeed, it is widely recognized by health practitioners that patients with trust in their doctors, faith in the benevolent intervention of God, or even mere confidence and optimism have an improved chance of recovery over those lacking such a mind-set.

Many Jews believed that forgiveness of sin was either concomitant with or a prerequisite of healing because diseases, woes, and afflictions were understood as the consequence of sin. In the *Genesis Apocryphon*, the healing of Pharaoh happens only when he returns Sarai to Abram. In the *Prayer of Nabonidus*, the king, when reporting his recovery, says, "A Jewish exorcist forgave my sins" (*see* EXORCISM). Prayers for both forgiveness of sin and healing survive in penitential psalms such as Psalms 25:16-18; 32:3-8; and 85:1-7. When Jesus said to the paralytic, "Your sins are forgiven," (Mark 2:5) he either simply meant "You are healed," or he associated forgiveness with healing as in Jewish tradition. The accusation of blasphemy in this case, if authentic, was unfounded (*see* JERUSALEM, CAIAPHAS'S HOUSE).

BIBLIOGRAPHY

Dupont-Sommer, A. "Exorcisme et guérisons dans les écrits de Qumran." *Vestus Testamentum Supplement* 7, (1959–60): 246-261.

Edelstein, L. *Ancient Medicine*, edited by O. Temkin and C. L. Temkin. Baltimore: Johns Hopkins University Press, 1967.

Grmek, M. D. *Diseases in the Ancient Greek World*. French, 1983. Baltimore: Johns Hopkins University Press, 1989.

Jeremias, J. *Jerusalem in the Time of Jesus*. German, 1962. Reprint. Philadelphia: Fortress Press, 1984.

Kee, H. C. *Medicine, Miracles and Magic in New Testament Times*. Cambridge: Cambridge University Press, 1986.

———. *Miracles in the Early Christian World*. New Haven, Conn.: Yale University Press, 1983.

———. "Medicine and Healing." *ABD* 4:659-64.

Latourelle, R. *The Miracles of Jesus and the Theology of Miracles*. New York: Paulist Press, 1988.

Majno, G. *The Healing Hand: Man and Wound in the Ancient World*. Cambridge: Harvard University Press, 1975.

Naveh, J. and G. S. Shaked. *Amulets and Magic Bowls: Aramaic Incantations of Late Antiquity*. Jerusalem: Magnes Press, and Leiden: Brill, 1985.

Palmer, B., ed. *Medicine and the Bible*. Exeter, England: Pater Noster Press, 1986.

Rousseau, J. *Background Information on Traditional Healing in the Time of Jesus: Investigating Ancient Healing Practices of the Bedouins*. Jesus Seminar Papers. Sonoma, Calif.: Polebridge Press, 1993.

———. "Jesus, an Exorcist of a Kind." *SBL Seminar Papers* (1993).

Sussman, M. "Sickness and Disease." *ABD* 4:6–15.

Theissen, G. *The Miracle Stories of the Early Christian Tradition*. German, 1974. Philadelphia: Fortress Press, 1983.

Vermes, G. *Jesus the Jew*. New York: MacMillan, 1973.

———. "Essenes, Therapeutai, Qumran." *Durham University Journal* June 6, 1961, 97–115.

———. "Essenes and Therapeutai." *Revue de Qumran* 3 (1962): 495–504.

Moses' Seat

Importance

According to Matthew, Jesus referred to "Moses' seat" and, according to Luke, to places of honor and best seats.

Scripture References

Matt. 23:2-3; Luke 14:7-11.

General Information

The earliest written reference to the seat of Moses is found in Matthew: "The scribes and the Pharisees sit on Moses' seat, so practice and observe whatever they tell you, but not what they do, for they do not practice what they say" (Matt. 23:2-3). Another isolated reference, in the Hebrew plural *qtdrot*, is found in Talmudic literature in the description of the seating arrangement in the first-century-C.E. synagogue of Alexandria (*t. Sukk*ot 4:6; *y. Sukk*ot 1.55a; *b. Sukk*ot 51b). The Hebrew word, derived from the Greek *kathedra*, can be applied to different kinds of seats: a) "the best seats in the synagogues" (Matt. 12:23; Mark 12:39; Luke 11:43; 20:46); these seats were probably those in the highest tier of benches along the side wall, directly across from the *bema* (*see* SYNAGOGUES); b) surprisingly, the seats of the pigeon dealers in the Temple precincts (Matt. 21:22; Mark 11:15); c) the seat of judgment (Gospel of Peter 3:7); d) the seat of an upper class woman (*m. Ketubot* 5.5; *b. Ketubot* 61a); and e) the seats of the guests waiting in the sitting room before entering the banquet hall (*t. Berakot* 4:8; *b. Berakot* 43a). The general concept tends to be that of a seat of honor. Yet such a chair could have an even more venerable function:

> Rabba said, "At first I thought that the chair (here Aramaic *corsyh*) is an accessory to an accessory . . . However, when I saw that the scroll of the Torah is actually placed in it, I came to the conclusion that it is an accessory of holiness and [that it] is forbidden [to sit in it]" (*b. Megilla* 26b–33, written ca. 300–350 C.E.).

Consequently, two important roles may be attributed to the seat of Moses (Rahmani, 1990). It was either a chair reserved for dignitaries, especially the *archisynagoges* and *hazzan* (*see* SYNAGOGUES), and elders; or it was a Torah receptacle. The second hypothesis is supported by the archaeological finds in the third and fourth century C.E. synagogues excavated at Chorazin, Hammat Tiberias, and 'En Gedi, where the seats of Moses are located in the area of the Torah shrine and show evidence that they were designed to support a scroll. A survival of this practice may exist in Samaritan and other synagogues of today, where the Torah scroll is placed vertically on a wooden chair specially made for this purpose, with a bar and an elevation across the seat to prevent the scroll from slipping or falling down when it stands upright on the ends of its rods.

Archaeological Data

In 1913, when excavating the synagogue of the Aegean island of Delos, A. Plassard unearthed a unique fragment of a marble chair, the use of which he could not at the time determine. In 1921, a stone chair of an unknown style appeared in the first synagogue excavated at Hammat Tiberias; the excavator, N. Slouschz, called it Moses' seat. Although the synagogue of Chorazin was discovered in 1869, it was only in 1927 that J. Ory of the Palestine Department of Antiquities unearthed a basalt throne decorated with a rosette on its back support.

These three chairs were free-standing; in fact, the Hammat Tiberias example was stolen, and only an incomplete description remains. At Dura-Europos and 'En Gedi, two other throne-like chairs were found attached to the synagogue structure.

The Delos marble chair probably belonged to a synagogue, possibly dating to somewhere between the first century B.C.E. and the end of the second century C.E. Probably a dignitary's seat, it is a piece of Greek art resembling the throne of the priest of Dionysos in the theater in Athens.

The drawing of the white limestone chair from Hammat Tiberias shows a piece of furniture that was not deep enough to allow a person to sit down. Furthermore, three holes set in a row parallel to the back were bored into the seat. It was almost certainly a Torah seat and undoubtedly had been set against the southern wall near the Torah shrine. Fortunately, the Galilean basalt chair from Chorazin, although slightly damaged, survived and has been published (*see* fig. 51). The four-line Aramaic inscription located on the front under the seat was written to honor and bless the memory of Yodan ben Yishma'el, who made the chair and the steps leading to it. It was found inside the synagogue in the southeastern area near the wall; it must have been originally set against the southern wall, east of and parallel to the Torah's Ark.

Implications for Jesus Research

Stone chairs are not attested in Palestinian synagogues of the first century C.E. Perhaps at that time, special seats were made of wood. Chairs and seating arrangements of the synagogues of Jesus' time may help to understand two of his sayings: Matthew 23:2 and Luke 14:7-11:

Matthew 23:2: Why does the author of Matthew mention "Moses' seat"? To what is he referring? The Fellows of the Jesus Seminar voted unanimously (abstentions not counted) for a *black* rating of Matthew 23:2 at their fall 1990 meeting. This consensus addresses the authenticity of the saying, not the existence of a seat of Moses. If there was such a seat in the synagogues Jesus visited, the question would be whether it was a seat of honor for a local priest or scribe (Matthew may have added "Pharisees" in consideration of his position against the rabbis of his time) or a Torah seat. Perhaps it served both purposes unless, as in the case of the chair found at Hammat Tiberias, the seat was not deep enough for a person to sit comfortably. Because Jesus uses the verb "sit" in Matthew's text, and also because the individuals he criticizes have to be obeyed in "what they teach" (their teaching comes from God), the following possibilities can be considered:

- After the reading of Scripture, the person interpreting the scriptural portion would sit on the seat of Moses, perhaps thereby suggesting that Moses was speaking through the mouth of that person. In this case, the seat of Moses would be a Torah chair, but a person could sit on it to expound on the Scripture just read.
- During the *haftorah*, "reading of the Prophets," as in Luke 4:17, if modern practices reflect ancient ones, the scroll from which the Pentateuchal portion had been

Figure 51 The Cathedra of Chorazin. Was it Moses' seat?

read was rolled up and set vertically on the chair with the lower ends of its wooden rods either in holes in the seat or held by an elevation of the seat or a bar. After the *haftorah*, the Torah scroll was returned to the ark and a speaker would sit on the chair to offer his exposition.

- Another possibility is that during the *haftorah* the Torah scroll was held by someone sitting the Seat of Moses.

Luke 14:7-11. This pericope was also rated *black* by the Jesus Seminar in 1990, but verse 11, "For all who exalt themselves will be humbled, and those who humble themselves will be exalted," received a *gray* rating. The advice not to seek the seats of honor in a synagogue or at a banquet was certainly not a creation of Jesus; it is found in Proverbs 25:6-7. However, there is no reason to think that he would not use familiar conventional wisdom sayings. Using such sayings would in fact help him to make his point about what the reign of God is like. The concept of wise humility continued to be advocated, as is evident in a saying dating from the early second century C.E.: "R. Shim'on ben 'Azai said: 'Descend from your place two or three steps and sit down. Better that you shall be told to ascend than to be told to descend' " (quoted by L. Y. Rahmani, 197).

BIBLIOGRAPHY

Kraeling, C. H. *The Synagogue. The Excavations at Dura-Europos, Final Report* 8-1. New Haven, Conn.: Yale University Press, 1956.

Kraus, S. "The Emperor Hadrian First of the Explorers of the Land." *Hashiloah* 19 (1921): 430, n. 5.

Levine, Lee I., ed. *Ancient Synagogues Revealed.* Jerusalem: Academic Press, 1981.

Plassart, A. "La Synagogue Juive de Delos." *Revue Biblique* 23 (1914): 523-534.

Rahmani, L. Y. "Stone Synagogue Chairs: Their Identification, Use and Significance." *IEJ* 40 (1990): 192–214.

Slouschz, N. "Les Fouilles de Tiberiade, 2ème Campagne." *Journal of the Jewish Palestine Exploration Society* (1921): 30 (Hebrew).

Vincent, L. H. "Les fouilles juives d'el Hamman, à Tiberiade." *Revue Biblique* 31 (1922): 117.

Mount Gerizim

Importance

Mount Gerizim was a place of worship for the Samaritans, who are mentioned several times in the Gospels.

Scripture Reference

John 4:20-21 ("this mountain").

General Information

Mount Gerizim, south of Mt. Ebal, rises to a height of about 2,850 feet above sea level and 700 feet above the floor of the narrow valley between it and Mt. Ebal. The two mountains mark the entrance of the pass leading to ancient Neapolis (today's Nablus). Besides Jacob's Well the other sources of water in the area are Ain Askar, south of Mt. Ebal, and a group of ten springs at the foot of Mt. Gerizim, in the southeast. In Roman times the two mountains were covered with trees. Mount Gerizim is mentioned in Joshua 8:33-34 in the narrative relating the entry of the Israelites to the Promised Land. The tribes gathered on the slopes of the two mountains to hear Joshua read the covenant document, which concludes with the blessings and curses that are the standard ending of Near Eastern treaties. In Deuteronomy (8:29), Mt. Gerizim is associated with the blessings and Mt. Ebal with the curses. An altar to the Lord was erected on Mt. Ebal according to Joshua 8:30 (cf. Deut. 27:4); but the Samaritan Torah substituted Gerizim for Ebal as the place where the altar was built. The Samaritans also believe that the near sacrifice of Isaac occurred on Mt. Gerizim, not on Mt. Moriah in Jerusalem. They contend that Abraham would have entered the Land of Canaan by the way of Shechem "at the oak (or plain) of Moreh" (Gen. 22:2) and that later on, "Moreh" was read "Moriah" (*see* SAMARIA, SAMARITANS).

After the Babylonian Exile, the returned exiles refused to let Samaritans participate in rebuilding the Temple (Ezra 4:1-3). The Samaritans then erected their own temple on Mt. Gerizim, most likely in the time of Sanballat (Neh. 4:1-9) but perhaps in the time of Darius III and Alexander in 333–32 B.C.E. (Josephus, *Antiq.* 11, 8.2–7/310, 340, 346; 12, 5.5/257, 259). Under Antiochus IV Epiphanes, the temple was dedicated to Zeus Xenios (2 Macc. 6:2; *Antiq.* 12, 5.5/261); it was destroyed by John Hyrcanus either in 128 B.C.E. (*Antiq.* 13, 9.1/255–56; *War* 1, 2.6/63) or circa 112 B.C.E. according to numismatic evidence (*see* SYCHAR-SHECHEM). Hadrian (117–138 C.E.) ordered a new temple to be erected to Zeus Hypsistos over the ruins of the Samaritan temple. The new edifice was famous for the marble stairway of fifteen hundred steps leading up to it. Later, a Byzantine church was built on the site by Zeno in 485, destroyed by the Samaritans, rebuilt, and surrounded with a defense wall by Justinian about 530. Everything was destroyed by the Arabs during their conquest of Palestine. After the collapse of the Abbasid Khalifate, the Samaritans again took possession of Mt. Gerizim. They did not rebuild their temple but established a community near the summit and still celebrate the major festivals there every year.

Archaeological Data

The northern section of Mt. Gerizim is known today as Tell er-Ras. R. Bull conducted archaeological excavations there (1964–68). He claims to have discovered the original place of worship of the Samaritans, which was built in the second century B.C.E. and is mentioned by Josephus. According to Y. Magen, however, the mound at the summit of er-Ras served as a platform for a sacred enclosure for a temple dedicated to Zeus Hypsistos and build during the Roman period. This platform measures 400 x 240 feet and rises 30 feet above its immediate surroundings. Remnants of a staircase and a causeway lead from the city of Neapolis, at the northern slope of the mountain, to the temple at er-Ras. In the south, the ruins of the Hellenistic city reach the walls of the enclosure. In the center of the enclosure there was a temple measuring 70 x 46 feet. Three flights of stairs led from the causeway to the temple inside the enclosure, which was paved with large slabs. Magen suggests that the enclosure and the temple were originally built during the reign of Antoninus Pius in the middle of the second century C.E., and not by Hadrian twenty years earlier, as suggested by ancient writers. The building was destroyed for unknown reasons at the end of the second century C.E.; it was rebuilt and significantly enlarged during the reign of Caracala at the beginning of the third century C.E.

Excavations, directed by Y. Magen, resumed in 1982 and continued for eight years on behalf of Israel's Department of Antiquities. The excavations revealed that during the early second century B.C.E., a city was erected on Mt. Gerizim, around the sacred enclosure that occupied the summit of the mountain. Although the size of the enclosure has not yet been determined, it was probably over 600 feet long and about 300 feet wide. There were two gates at the eastern wall, a fort, and perhaps another gate at the north. Near the western wall and possibly within the enclosure were public buildings. Dedicatory inscriptions were incised on the walls of the enclosure. Sixty inscriptions have been discovered so far, most of them written in Aramaic in a script that stands between Late Aramaic script and the script of the Dead Sea Scrolls. One of the inscriptions bears God's name, "Yahowa." Surprisingly, only a few inscriptions are in Greek.

During the Byzantine period, in 484 C.E., a church was erected within the enclosure by Zeno as part of his plan to oppress the Samaritans. This church was destroyed in the sixth century, rebuilt by Justinian, and demolished once and for all in the seventh century C.E. This church played a role in the Samaritan rebellion in which the Samaritan community suffered greatly.

Implications for Jesus Research

In the second century B.C.E. a town and a temple surrounded by an enclosure was built on Mt. Gerizim on the site known today as Khirbet Lozeh or Luzah and also as Givat Olam. Temple and town were both destroyed by John Hyrcanus probably between 113 and 111 B.C.E. Whether or not the temple had been rebuilt in the time of Jesus is difficult to determine. The likelihood is that it was not, because other areas nearby that have been excavated do not indicate any rebuilding during this period. The New Testament does not mention a temple on Mt. Gerizim but only a place of worship (John 4:21-22). During the first century C.E., the Samaritan enclosure was probably the only sacred area on the mount.

In the first century the most significant witness to the destroyed Samaritan temple, its huge stone altar, was visible, as it still is today. The long succession of conflicts over the sacred site was then already several centuries old. The remark that "you will worship the Father neither on this mountain nor in Jerusalem. . . . the true worshipers will worship the Father in spirit and truth" (John 4:21-23) may have been inspired by the knowledge of the rivalry between Jerusalem and the Samaritans. As in the case of Phoenicia, Caesarea Philippi, and the Decapolis, Jesus was active in the vicinity of foreign cultic sites, yet he did not condemn the worship of pagan gods; at least no such condemnation is mentioned in the Gospels.

BIBLIOGRAPHY

Adler, E. N. and M. Seligsohn. "Une Nouvelle Chronique Samaritaine." *Revue des Etudes Juives* 45 (1902).

Bull, R. J. "The Excavation of Tell er Ras on Mt. Gerizim." *BA* 31 (1968): 58–72.

Magen, Y. "The Church of Mary Theotokos on Mount Gerizim." *Christian Archaeology in the Holy Land, New Discoveries—Archaeological Essays in Honour of Virgilio C. Corbo.* Collection Major 36. Jerusalem, 1990.

———. "Gerizim, Mount." *NEAEHL* 2: 484–92.

Schneider, A. M. "Römische und Byzantinische Bauten auf dem Garizim." *Zeitschrift des deutschen Palästina-Vereins* 48 (1952): 211-34.

Stern, M. *Greek and Latin Authors on Jews and Judaism.* Vol. 2. Jerusalem: Israel Academy of Sciences and Humanities, 1980.

Mount Hermon

Importance

Mount Hermon is one of the two sites proposed for the Transfiguration; it was a long established cult place.

Scripture References

Matt. 17:1; Mark 9:2; Luke 9:28.

General Information

Mount Hermon is a large convex block that rises above the adjacent Syro-African rift. It extends over 50 kilometers (31 miles) on a north-east to south-west axis, and measures 25 kilometers (15.5 miles) at its widest point. The Hermon range is mainly of Jurassic limestone, which forms karastic landscapes. Its highest peak reaches 2,814 meters (8,500 feet) and falls steeply toward the east. The western slope, which descends in a series of terraces, enjoys abundant precipitation (dew, rain, and snow). The Barada Brook separates it from the northern Anti-Lebanon range. It borders the Damascus tableland on the east, the basalt tableland of the Golan on the south and the valley of the Senir (Ar Hasbani) and its continuation Wadi al Taym on the west. The mountain is mentioned in the Bible as marking the northern border of the tribal territory east of the Jordan River (Josh. 11:17; 12:1, 4-5) and the northern border of the half tribe of Manasseh (1 Chron. 5:23). Mount Hermon is located above the Valley of Lebanon (Josh. 11:17) and above the land or Valley of Mizpeh, where Joshua routed the Canaanite kings in the battle of the waters of Merom (Josh. 11:1-8). Prior to the Israelite settlement, it was known as the place where the Hivites resided (Judg. 3:3; Hurites according to the Septuagint). King Og of Bashan ruled over Mt. Hermon (Josh. 12:4-5); so did King Sihon of the Amorites (Josh. 13:10-11).

The toponym Hermon derives from *hrm*, which in many Semitic languages means "ban, taboo," or "consecrated" (*al-Haram* in Arabic means "sacred enclosure"). Ancient Near Eastern beliefs as in many cultures, associated high peaks and mountains with the dwelling places of gods. Hittite and biblical texts indicate that this was so for Mt. Hermon. Mursilis the Second (1344–1320 B.C.E.) called as witnesses to his peace treaty with the Amorites, Duppi-Tessub, the gods of Mount Sariyana, a synonym for Hermon (Pritchard, *Ancient Near Eastern Texts*, 205). The Bible mentions this mountain along with other places where the name of God is revered (Ps. 89:12). Ritual centers were located at the foot of Hermon: Baal Gad in the Lebanon Valley below Mt. Hermon (Josh. 11:17), and Baal Hermon (1 Chron. 5:23). Hermon was famed for its dew, which flowed over the mountains of Zion (Ps. 133:3). It was also known for its lions and leopards (Song of Sol. 4:8), as well as for its fir trees and cedars (Ezek. 27:5). It is mentioned in reference to the might of God (Ps. 29:6) and to the Jordan Valley (Ps. 42:7).

The term *hermon* is not found in ancient Near Eastern texts, but it is juxtaposed in the Bible with other toponyms that are mentioned in epigraphic records. An example is "Which Hermon the Sidonians called Sirion and the Amorites call Senir" (Deut. 3:9). It is unclear whether all three toponyms in this passage refer to the entire Anti-Lebanon range, or only to its southern spur, known today as Hermon or Jabal ash-Shaykh. The name

S[irs]on is recorded in the Egyptian execration texts of the eighteenth century B.C.E., but no settlements of that date have been found so far on this range. Hermon is contrasted with Lebanon in an Ugaritic text: "[Le]banon and its trees, Sirion and its precious cedars," (Pritchard, *Ancient Near Eastern Texts*, 134), as well as in the Hittite text mentioned above and a few times in the Bible (Ezek. 27:5; Ps. 29:6). The Bible differs from other sources with respect to the boundaries of Hermon. While the Bible sometimes includes the Anti-Lebanon range within the definition, other sources name the northern range Senir, while the name of the southern spur is still unknown. It is also possible that the names Senir, Sirion, and Hermon are general names pertaining to the entire Anti-Lebanon range, with the name Hermon also used specifically for the southern section. Another name that is associated with the Hermon, or one of its peaks, is Si'on (Deut. 4:48). Josephus does not use the name Hermon but rather Mt. Lebanon (*Antiq.* 5, 3.1/86, *et passim*). Sirion and Senir, on the other hand, are often recorded in Talmudic literature as places where sacred wine was produced (*b. Sukka* 12; *Sota* 48). It is stated that "Senir and Sirion are among the mountains of Eretz Israel" (*b. Hullin* 60).

Eusebius relates the toponym Hermon only to the southern range and testifies that: "until today the mount in front of Panias and Lebanon is known as Hermon and it is respected by nations as a sanctuary" (*Onomasticon* 20:12).

Today, Hermon is identified only with the southern spur of the Anti-Lebanon range. It is known by the names Jabal ash-Shaykh, Arabic for "the mountain of the chieftain," and Jabal al-Thal, Arabic for "the snow mountain." In Aramaic translations of the Bible, Hermon is identified as Tur Talga, "mountain of snow" (*Tg. Ongelos*; Deut. 3:9; and Song of Sol. 4:8), for the mountain is covered with snow most of the year.

Archaeological Data

The summit of the Hermon contains three peaks—in the north, east, and south-west. On the highest of these peaks, the south-western one, are the remains of a temple known as Qasr Antar or Qasr ash-Shabib. It contains an enclosure, a large basin carved in rock, and a building measuring 10 x 11 meters (33 x 36 feet). A Greek inscription invites, on behalf of the "Greatest and Holiest God," all those "who had not taken the oath" to stay away. It is interpreted as an injunction to prevent the uninitiated from reaching the sacred temple. Or it may refer to the belief that the temple should remain pure from the angels who wanted to take human wives. This temple dates from the first to the fourth centuries C.E. Surveys made after 1967 yielded a few Iron Age shards on the summit, probably indicating earlier occupation. This temple is mentioned in 1624 by a Jewish traveler, Rabbi Gershon Berabbi Eliezer.

More than twenty temples have been located in surveys of Mt. Hermon and its environs. This is a large number in comparison with other regions of the Phoenician coast. The temples appear to be the ancient cult sites of the mountain population and may represent Canaanite-Phoenician open-air shrines. During the secondary century B.C.E., chapels were carved out of the rock in the enclosures mentioned above. In the first century C.E., temples built in the classical style appeared in the complex. The pottery collected from these temples is similar to Iturean ceramics. The Itureans inhabited the mountain from the second century B.C.E. until the seventh century C.E. Because Mt. Hermon was associated with Mt. Tabor in Psalm 89:12, biblical exegesis from the medieval period sought to place Hermon next to Tabor. Consequently, the mountain south of Tabor, the hill of Moreh, was called Hermon Minor.

Implications for Jesus Research

In consideration of the proximity of Caesarea Philippi to Mt. Hermon and of the closeness between the story of Peter's confession and that of the Transfiguration in the Synoptics (there are only seven verses between the two stories in Luke, for example), it would be reasonable to situate the Transfiguration on Mt. Hermon rather than on Mt. Tabor. Tabor became the choice of the early

Church, probably because it was more accessible to pilgrims and to builders of churches and monasteries. If Jesus did go to Mt. Hermon, where a variety of pagan gods had been worshiped for centuries, he did so in the spirit of tolerance or of indifference for other religions that characterized his journeys to Phoenicia and Caesarea Philippi (*see* TYRE AND SIDON and CAESAREA PHILIPPI). The gospels do not record any word of condemnation of foreign cults. This aspect of his character deserves further research.

While the historicity of the Transfiguration cannot be ascertained (in October 1990, the Jesus Seminar rated *black* Jesus' words in Matt. 17:7), the event, as placed in the uncertain chronological order of Mark, may refer to a religious experience of Jesus and a turning point in his understanding of his mission. Followed by the other evangelists, Mark reports a series of disappointments for Jesus and journeys in foreign lands. In chapter 6 he experienced the rejection of Nazareth, the unsuccessful evangelistic mission, the beheading of John the Baptist, and the spiritual indifference of the crowds interested only in physical healing. In chapter 7 appear the journeys to Phoenicia and the Decapolis. Chapter 8 reports the misunderstanding of the religious elite and of his own disciples. At this point, after realizing his failure in Galilee and surrounding gentile territories, he may have decided to make a last desperate attempt in Jerusalem, where a true prophet [if he failed] should die (Luke 9:30; 13:33-34).

BIBLIOGRAPHY

Arav, R. "Hermon, Mount." *ABD* 3:158–59.

Aharoni, Y. "Hermon." *Encyclopedia Biblica*. Jerusalem, 1958. Vol. 3, 294-8. (Hebrew).

Appelbaum, S., S. Dar, Y. Peleg, and Y. Roth, ed. *The Hermon and Its Foothills*. Tel Aviv: Tel Aviv University Press, 1978 (Hebrew).

Avi-Yonah, M. *Carta's Atlas of the Period of the Second Temple, the Mishnah, and the Talmud*. Jerusalem: Carta, 1966.

Baldi, D. *Enchiridion Locorum Sanctorum*. Jerusalem, 1982.

Clermont-Ganneau, C. *Recueil d'archéologie orientale*. Vol. 5. Paris: E. Leroux, 1888.

Dar, S. "The Temples of Mount Hermon and Its Environs." *Abstracts of the Conference 'Greece and Rome in Eretz Israel' "*. Haifa: Haifa University Press, 1985 (Hebrew).

———. "Hermon, Mount." *NEAEHL* 2: 616–17.

Dar, S. and J. Mintzker. "A Roman Temple at Senaim, Mount Hermon." *Eretz Israel* 19 (1987): 30–45 (Hebrew).

Pritchard, J. B., ed. *Ancient Near Eastern Texts Relating to the Old Testament*. Rev. ed. Princeton, N.J.: Princeton University Press, 1955.

Mount of Olives

Importance

Jesus found shelter on the Mount of Olives, which became the traditional site of the Ascension.

Scripture References

Matt. 21:1; 24:3; 26:30; Mark 13:3; 14:26; Luke 19:29; 21:37; 22:39; John 8:1; Acts 1:12.

General Information

The Mount of Olives is a low mountain (elevation 2,500 feet) located south of Mt. Scopus near the village of et-Tur, east of the Temple on the other side of the Kidron Valley. Its Hebrew name, *har hazzêtîm*, appears as such only in Zechariach 14:4. Once in the Hebrew Bible, it is designated by a circumlocution, "ascent of Olives," upward slope, (2 Sam. 15:30), which the New Revised Standard Version renders as the "ascent of the Mount of Olives." Another reference to the Mount of Olives appears in 1 Kings 11: 7, 2 Kings 23:13, and in Ezekiel 11:23 "mountain which is east of Jerusalem" or "on the east side of the city." The mount was covered with extensive olive groves in antiquity but was deforested when Titus cut down all the trees around Jerusalem to clear the space between the city and the siege bank during the First Jewish War (Josephus, *War* 5, 12.4/523).

The mount had special sanctity in Israelite times. David went to the summit to worship God when he learned that his son Absalom had made himself king at Hebron (2 Sam. 15:32). Ezekiel saw in a vision the *shekinah*, "radiant presence," of God leaving the Temple because of Israel's sins (Ezek. 11:23) and hovering over the mount, where it would stay until the people repented. Solomon had erected places of worship, in honor of the pagan deities Chemosh and Molech (1 Kings 11:7), whose images were later destroyed by Josiah, king of Judah (ca. 640–609; 2 Kings 23:13). A chain of hilltops selected for signal fires to announce the beginning of the new moon began at the Mount of Olives. The Mishnah indicates that this beacon service extended as far as Mesopotamia. According to the Mishnah (*m. Genesis Rabba* 33:6), the dove of Noah's Ark picked up an olive leaf on the Mount of Olives. It was believed that the Messiah was to descend from the top of the Mount of Olives, on his way raise the dead buried on its slopes, cross the Kidron brook, and enter the Temple through the Shushan Gate (today's Golden Gate), which was left ajar in the expectation of his coming (*see* JERUSALEM, KIDRON).

The Mount of Olives also occupies a prominent place in the Christian tradition because Jesus withdrew and taught there during his last days in Jerusalem. It became the preferred site of the Ascension (Acts 1:9-12) over Bethany (Luke 24:50-51). A church built there by a Roman woman named Pomenia in about 387 was later destroyed but was rebuilt by the Crusaders. At some distance from this church was the Eleona (from the Greek for "olive grove"), a church built by Constantine over a cave in which Jesus was believed to have prophesied about the destruction of Jerusalem (Matt. 24:13; Mark 13:1-4). According to the apocryphal Acts of John (94–95) Jesus taught esoteric mysteries there. Eleona was thought to be the exact place of the Ascension and the future place of Jesus' return. The early bishops of Jerusalem were buried in its vicinity, but their remains have not yet been found.

The Eleona Church was destroyed by the Persians in 614, rebuilt soon after, and restored again in the twelfth century, only to suffer further destruction. Its walls were partly rebuilt in the twentieth century so as to make an enclosure around the "Cave of Christ's Teaching." Adjacent to it stands the French Carmelite Convent of the *Pater Noster*, so named because of the belief that it was at this place that Jesus taught the Lord's Prayer to his disciples in the "Cave of the Credo." Another tradition assigns a different site for the Ascension, some 230 feet from the Eleona. There, the Inbonum (Latin rendering of the Greek for "Upon the Height") Church, also called "Church of the Ascension," was built in about 375. The pilgrim Arculf reports that it was destroyed by the Persians and rebuilt in a circular form. It was destroyed again by the Arabs and rebuilt once more by the Crusaders in an octagonal form. In 1187 Salah ed Din (Saladin) transformed it into a mosque.

Archaeological Data

Early in the twentieth century, Father H. Vincent, of the Ecole Biblique et Archeologique Française of Jerusalem, was the first to excavate the remains of the Eleona Church and the Cave of Jesus' Teaching. It appeared that the church built by Constantine was a lofty structure built over the cave, but its exact design cannot be recovered because the ruins were plundered as a source of construction material. In 1910, an underground chapel that had escaped Vincent's scrutiny was discovered by the White Fathers. The chapel has a small apse at its eastern end; its location under the altar of the Constantine church indicates that the chapel predated the church. At the western end of the chapel were tombs around a chamber; they were dated to the second to third centuries C.E. No specific objects or inscriptions allow them to be identified as tombs of the first bishops of Jerusalem. Many other buildings erected by various Christian denominations and orders in different locations of the Mount of Olives testify to its importance in Christian tradition, but they have no connection with the Gospel narrative or with the historical Jesus.

Implications for Jesus Research

Incomplete as they are, the archaeological finds of the Mount of Olives point to an ancient tradition, according to which caves at the top of the Mount of

Olives had a significant role in the life of Jesus and his disciples. The cave tradition of Eleona, in this light, seems more plausible than the tradition locating the site of the Ascension at the Inbonum where, nevertheless, a large "foot print of Jesus" left in the rock when he ascended is shown to visitors. This last tradition may originate with Zechariach 14:4:

> On that day his feet shall stand on the Mount of Olives, which lies before Jerusalem on the east; and the Mount of Olives shall be split in two from east to west by a very wide valley; so that one half of the Mount shall withdraw northward, and the other half southward.

A panel of the Dura Europos Synagogue depicts this cleaving of the Mount of Olives at the end of time. If the Zechariah text made a strong impression on the Dura Europos community of the second/third centuries C.E., it may have had a similar effect on the people of early Christianity. For related information and bibliographies, *see* JERUSALEM, GETHSEMANE and JERUSALEM, KIDRON.

BIBLIOGRAPHY

Bagatti, B. "Oliviers (Mont des)." *Dictionnaire de la Bible*, 1960.

Corbo, P. V. C. *Ricerche archeologiche al Monte degli Ulivi*. Studium Biblicum Franciscarum. Collection Major 16. Jerusalem, 1965.

Chronique Archeologique. "Jerusalem, Mont des Oliviers." *Revue Biblique* 67 (1960): 249–50.

Heard, W. J. "Olives, Mount of." *ABD* 5:13-15.

Kraeling, E. G. H. "The Meaning of the Ezekiel Panel in the Synagogues at Dura." *Bulletin of the American Schools of Oriental Research* 78 (1940): 12-18.

Mount Tabor

Importance

Mount Tabor is the traditional site of the Transfiguration.

Scripture References

Matt. 17:1; Mark 9:2; Luke 9:28.

General Information

Situated in the northeastern part of the plain of Jezreel, six miles from Nazareth and twelve miles from the Sea of Galilee, Mt. Tabor is a small, isolated, rounded mountain. It is only 1,800 feet high but stands 1,200 feet above the surrounding valley and is visible from most of Galilee and Golan. According to Hosea 5:1-3, priests and members of the royal family had worshiped foreign gods ("played the harlot") on the mountain. As a prominent peak in the middle of a fertile area, it was a place of worship from ancient times. For the Israelites, it was the corner point of the territories of Zebulon, Issachar, and Naphtali (Josh. 19:12, 22, 33). In the time of Deborah, the tribes assembled at Mt. Tabor to fight the Canaanites (Judg. 4:6-14). During the Hellenistic period, the Ptolemies erected a fortress on its summit, which Alexander Jannaeus (103–76 B.C.E.) conquered. When he was preparing Galilee for the war against the Romans, Josephus built a fortification wall on the mountain (*War* 4, 1.8/56). Early Christian tradition designated Mt. Tabor as the place of the Transfiguration, and several churches were built on its top.

Archaeological Data

The summit is a fairly flat plateau, and its rectangular shape—about 900 yards long, east to west, and 450 yards wide, north to south—allows for easy construction. In 326 C.E., Helena, mother of Emperor Constantine, had a church built there. Later three small sanctuaries were erected in honor of Jesus, Moses, and Elijah. During the same period, the mountain became part of a separate administrative district known as Helenopolis. In the course of time other churches and monasteries were added. Building activity was greatly facilitated by the presence of materials from the ruins of the ancient Ptolemaic fortress. Salah ed-Din (Saladin) razed everything in 1187, the year of his victory over the Crusaders at the Horns of Hattin. His brother built a new fortress on the mountain in 1219, but it was destroyed soon after and the site was abandoned. Toward the end of the nineteenth century building activity resumed with the construction of a sanctuary and monastery by the Greek Orthodox Church. Shortly later, the Franciscans erected a basilica at the very top of Mt. Tabor. The ruins of many ancient structures, including the wall of Josephus, can still be seen.

Implications for Jesus Research

It is impossible to determine whether Mt. Tabor was the site of the Transfiguration. The early Church may have selected this location because of its easy accessibility and aesthetic appeal. Mt. Hermon would have been a more logical choice. Jesus would probably not have exposed himself at Tabor, a visible spot in the territory of Herod Antipas, who had hostile intentions against him (Luke 13:31). Hermon, in the tetrarchy of Herod Philip, was more remote and much safer.

BIBLIOGRAPHY

Briand, J. M. "Le Mont Thabor. Son histoire, ses églises," *Terre Sainte* (1990): 267–79.

Frankel, R. "Tabor, Mount." *ABD* 6:304-5.

Lewy, J. "Tabor, Tibar, Atabyros." *Hebrew Union College Annual* 23 (1950–51): 357–86.

Loffreda, S. "Una tomba Romana al Monte Tabor." *Liber Annuus* 28 (1978): 241–46.

Meistermann, B. *Le Mont Thabor. Notices historiques et descriptives.* Paris: Mersch, 1900.

Nain (Hebrew *Naim*)

Importance

According to Luke, Jesus revived a young man there. It is the southernmost point of his activity in Galilee as recorded in the Gospels.

Scripture Reference

Luke 7:11.

General Information

Mentioned only once in the gospels, Nain or Naim ("pleasant" in Hebrew) is located about five miles southeast of Nazareth; its present name is Nein. Its location on the northwest slope of "Little Hermon" (the Hill of Moreh of Judges 7:1) between Mts. Tabor and Gilboa is indeed pleasant. It overlooks the Kesulot plain with a view of Mt. Tabor and Nazareth. A small spring gushes at the outskirts of the village and pours its water into the Tebet Brook. In the first century C.E., Nain was a Jewish village located on the Via Maris between Legio and Tiberias, and on the route from Sepphoris to Scythopolis–Beth–Shean. During the Byzantine period, the village became the center of a district separate from Sepphoris and is mentioned in the list of George Cyprius. The Midrash reports it as a pleasant area; and Eusebius, Origen, and Jerome cite it in their works. In 1137 Peter the Deacon wrote, "In the village of Nain is the house of the widow whose son was brought back to life, which is now a church, and the burial place where they were going to lay him is still there to this day." Some scholars have argued that this passage reproduces a lost section of Egeria's *Travels*; if so, the testimony would date back to circa 383.

Archaeological Data

Archaeological surveys, which have been conducted on the site of Nain since the nineteenth century, have revealed remains of the Hellenistic, Roman, and Byzantine periods. During 1966–67, R. Arav excavated a tomb outside the village. The excavations revealed a typical Jewish cave tomb in use from the end of the first century B.C.E. to the end of the first century C.E. The finds enabled the excavator to identify those interred there, as well as the inhabitants of the village, as Jews.

Implications for Jesus Research

The presence of tombs dating from the first century C.E., provides a plausible background to the account of Jesus' resuscitation of a young man at Nain.

BIBLIOGRAPHY

Arav, R. "A Tomb in Naim." *Galilee Research Conference.* Haifa: University of Haifa Press, 1989: 106–18.

Avi-Yonah, M. "Gazeteer of Roman Palestine." *Qedem* 5 (1976).

Baldi, D. "Nain." *Enchiridion Locorum Sanctorum.* Jerusalem: Franciscan Publishing House (1982).

Nazareth

Importance

Jesus grew up in Nazareth and perhaps was born there.

Scripture References

Matt. 2:23; 21:11; Mark 1:24; 10:47; 14:67; 16:6; Luke 1:26; 2:51; 4:16; 4:34; 18:37; 24:19; John 1:45-46; 7:40-43.

General Information

Besides the New Testament, the earliest mention of Nazareth is by Julius Africanus (170–240 C.E.), as cited by Eusebius (*Church History* 1, 7.6–12). It must have been a very small village at the time, perhaps a satellite hamlet of Sepphoris (*see* SEPPHORIS). Built on a rocky hill, it lies in a valley near the edge of the mountain range overlooking the plain of Esdraelon to the south and southeast. In the north, the fertile Netofa Valley stretches east-west between Sepphoris and Cana. This location would explain its name, which was probably derived from the Hebrew root *nsr*, meaning "to watch" or "to guard." At an altitude of 1,300 feet, it is located some twenty miles from the Mediterranean and fifteen miles from the Sea of Galilee. According to Mark 6:2 and parallels it had a synagogue that Jesus attended (Luke 4:16). Sepphoris, only 3.5 miles away in the northwest and close to the highway from the Sea of Galilee to Ptolemais, must have exercised some influence on the life of the villagers when it was fortified and developed by Herod Antipas as the main city of Galilee from 4 B.C.E. to 19 C.E.

After the destruction of the Temple in 70 C.E., several Jewish families moved to Nazareth; among them was the priestly family of Pises, probably mentioned in 1 Chronicles 24:16 as Happizzez. An inscription unearthed by M. Avi-Yonah and A. Negev in the synagogue of Caesarea Maritima mentions Nazareth as one of the places in Galilee to which priestly families migrated after the destruction of Jerusalem by Hadrian in 135 (Whitcomb, *The Illustrated Bible Dictionary*, 1060). Eusebius in *Onomasticon* 138:24 states that Nazareth was still a small Jewish village in the fourth century. At that time a church was erected, and pilgrims came and were shown relics. In the seventh century, Nazareth and its area received the status of *polis* (Helenopolis). The pilgrim Arculf (670) indicates the existence of a church, which was later destroyed by the Muslims *circa* 700. In 1620 when the Franciscans received permission to settle in Nazareth as custodians of the holy places, development of the town into the most important Christian city in the Holy Land began.

Archaeological Data

Many holy places, especially caves, are shown in Nazareth in connection with the Gospels, but few are authentic. One that was perhaps in use in Jesus' time is known today as Mary's Well. Other archaeological remains may give some idea of what the village looked like in the first century. The few tombs dated to the first century C.E. indicate the small size of the village in Jesus' time.

Excavations made by Father P. Viaud in 1889–90, Brother B. Vlaminck in 1899, and Father B. Bagatti in 1955–70 at the traditional site of the Annunciation revealed evidence of an early cult of Mary. Many caves, cisterns, silos, wine presses, and oil vats were found, together with mosaic floors, all from the Byzantine period. Numerous inscriptions, symbols, and graffiti on walls attest to the presence of Christian pilgrims whose visits reached their peak during Crusaders times.

Today's synagogue-church may be built over the site of a small ancient synagogue that could seat forty to fifty people, appropriate in size for a village of about 500 inhabitants. There is no site corresponding to the description in Luke 4:29 of the brow of a hill from which Jesus could have been thrown headlong.

Pasture Land and Oak between Nazareth and Cana

Implications for Jesus Research

There is no doubt about the existence and location of Nazareth in the time of Jesus, and there is no reason to believe that the Greek *nazoraios* of the three later canonical Gospels, as opposed to the *nazarenos* of Mark, implied that Jesus was a member of a Jewish sect of "observants" and not an inhabitant of Nazareth. The authors of the Gospels, in whatever form they used it, understood the term as synonymous with the phrase "the one from Nazareth" (*o apo nazareth*; Matt. 12:11; Mark 1:9; John 1:45; also Acts 10:38).

Nazareth, a small village in fertile Lower Galilee, could probably not provide enough business for a *tekton*, "builder, carpenter, mason" to support his family (*see* SEPPHORIS), and Joseph may have worked in other places. In addition to its indigenous population of farmers, its favorable location may have made it the secondary residence of absentee owners of fields, orchards, gardens, vineyards, and flocks, people whose primary residences and business interests were in Sepphoris and later Tiberias, Ptolemais, and even Jerusalem. Although a small village, Nazareth was probably not an isolated place; it is unlikely that Jesus stayed there for some thirty years without contact with the surrounding world. Other traditions indicate that he may have worked as a craftsman in Egypt (*see* MIRACLES, MAGIC).

Was Nazareth the birthplace of Jesus as his very name, Jesus of Nazareth, would indicate? Mark specifies that Jesus went to preach to his own *patrida*, a Greek word that means "family from the father's side, clan, native place" (Mark 6:1). The negative question of Nathanael (John 1:45–46) and that of "some" (John 7:41-42) in the Fourth Gospel implies that Jesus was from Nazareth and Galilee, not from Bethlehem. G. Bornkamm (*Jesus of Nazareth*, 53) and R. Bultmann (*History of the Synoptic Tradition*, 32) agree that Jesus was born in Nazareth; many other New Testament scholars are of the same opinion.

An intriguing stone slab, said to have been found in Nazareth in 1878, is in the possession of the Bibliothèque Nationale in Paris (*see* the photo in Millard, 134). It came from a private collection donated in 1925 and was accompanied by a note saying, "Marble slab sent from Nazareth in 1878." It is 24 x 15 inches and bears a Greek inscription in a script that can be dated to the first century C.E. In 1930 it was translated by M. Rostovtzeff as follows:

> Caesar's order. It is my will that graves and tombs lie undisturbed forever . . . Respect for those who are buried is most important; no one should disturb them in any way at all. If anyone does, I require that he be executed for tomb-robbery.

Is there a connection between this decree and Matthew 28:13 (alleged stealing of Jesus' body by the disciples)?

BIBLIOGRAPHY

Bagatti, B. "Nazareth." *Liber Annuus* 5 (1955): 5–44.

Baldi, D. and B. Bagatti. "Excavations in Nazareth." *Studii Francescani* 9 (1937): 225–264.

Bornkamm, G. *Jesus of Nazareth*. German, 1956. Translated by I. Mcluskey, F. Mcluskey, and J. M. Robinson. New York: Harper and Row, 1960.

Bultmann, R. *History of the Synoptic Tradition*. German, 1931. Translated by John Marsh. New York: Harper and Row, 1968.

Kopp, C. *Journal of the Palestine Oriental Society* 18 (1938): 187–228.

Meyers, E. M. and J. F. Strange. *Archaeology, the Rabbis, and Early Christianity*. Nashville: Abingdon, 1981.

Millard, A. *Discoveries from the Time of Jesus*. Oxford: Lion Publishing, 1990.

Strange, J. F. "Nazareth." *ABD* 4: 1050–51.

Testa, E. *Il Simbolismo dei quideo-cristiani*. Jerusalem, 1962.

Viaud, P. *Nazareth et Ses Deux Eglises de l'Annonciation et de Saint-Joseph*. Paris, 1910.

Vlamick, G. *A Report of the Recent Excavations and Explorations Conducted at the Sanctuary of Nazareth*. Washington, D.C., 1900.

Whitcomb, J. C., Jr. "Nazareth." *The Illustrated Bible Dictionary*, 1986.

Ointments, Perfumes

Importance

The four Gospels report the anointing of Jesus by a woman.

Scripture References

Matt. 6:17; 26:6-13; Mark 14:3-9; Luke 4:18; 7:36-50; 23:56; John 11:2; 12:1-8.

General Information

In ancient Mesopotamia and Egypt the use of ointments, cosmetics, and perfumes is attested in religious rituals, magic, and medicine, as well as in the secular domain. The art of making cosmetics, ointments, and perfumes became elaborate and developed into a thriving international trade. Classical writers like Theophrastus (371–287 B.C.E.) and Pliny (23–79 C.E.) studied these substances at length. According to Herodotus,

> Arabia is the last of inhabited lands and it is the only country which produces frankincense, myrrh, cassia, cinnamon and laudanum . . . [The Arabs] procure the frankincense by means of the gum storax which the Greeks obtain from the Phoenicians and by burning it they produce spice (Herodotus 3. 107–112).

Pliny deplored the abuse of perfumes in his time:

> Perfumes serve the purpose of the most superfluous of all forms of luxury. For pearls and jewels pass to their wearers' heirs and clothes last for some time, but unguents lose their scent at once . . . Their highest usefulness is when a woman passes by, her scent may attract the attention even of those occupied in something else, and their cost is more than 400 dinarii per pound (*Nat. Hist.* 13.20–25).

> A hundred million sesterces every year, that is the sum which our luxuries and our women cost us, for what fraction of these imports, I ask you, really goes to the gods or to the powers of the lower world? (*Nat. Hist.* 6.101, 12.84).

The widespread use of ointments led to the industrial production of delicate containers that can be seen in museums everywhere: flasks, vials, and small jars. These vessels were usually made of glass or alabaster, especially in the Greek and Roman periods. Those materials were considered best for the preservation of the scent of perfume, but Pliny states that alabaster was to be preferred for ointment (*Nat. Hist.* 13.19). Oils were the vehicles through which scents were obtained and kept. The choice of the plants and spices that provided perfumes and the selection of oils to carry scents was a complicated matter, as was the processing of these materials. The sources of oils included unripe olives (*omphacium*), the seeds of grapes harvested in mid-summer, sweet almonds, cypress and alanos, light petroleum, reeds, balsam, lupine, narcissus, and more (*Nat. Hist.* 15.31).

In the Greek and Roman periods, it was believed that good ointment should be made with human spittle; certain cosmetics thus were chewed by slaves before application (for the therapeutic use of saliva *see* MEDICINE, PHYSICIANS). In order to perform this duty, slaves had to keep their mouths clean by following a special diet and chewing selected aromatics (Forbes, *Studies in Ancient Technology*, 39). Alexandria was the center of the international trade for gums and perfumes, which came from as far as India, the Himalayas, and Persia. Regional products were imported from Palestine, Syria, and Asia Minor. The production of frankincense, ointments, and perfumes was conducted on a large scale in the Canopus district of Alexandria. Special measures had to be taken in the perfume workshops to prevent pilferage by the workers:

> No vigilance is sufficient to safeguard the factories. A seal is put on the workmen's aprons, they have to wear a mask or a net on their heads, and before they are allowed to leave the premises, they have to take off all their clothes (Pliny, *Nat. Hist.* 12.59).

Ointment making was practiced by various peoples of the ancient Near East, including the Egyptians, who were great users of cosmetics, ointments, and perfumes. At feasts, they placed small cones of perfumed ointment on the foreheads of guests. Body heat slowly melted the ointment, which trickled down the faces and clothes, exhaling a pleasant odor. The Israelites too practiced anointing, and the Hebrew Bible indicates several ritual uses of ointments. Priests were anointed with a special ointment (Exod. 28:41; 29:7; 30:30-32, *et passim*), and the psalmist portrays its effect:

> *It is like the precious oil on the head,*
> *running down upon the beard,*
> *on the beard of Aaron,*
> *running down over the collar of his robes*
> (Ps. 133:2).

Two anointed places are mentioned: Bethel (Gen. 28:18) and the Tabernacle (Exod. 30:26-29). Elijah anointed Elisha (1 Kings 19:16) and was ordered by God to anoint the king of Syria. The kings of Israel were the Lord's anointed (1 Sam. 24:6, 10; 26:16-23); and several royal anointings are reported: those of Saul (1 Sam. 10:1), David (1 Sam. 16:13) on whom the Spirit of the Lord "came mightily," Solomon (1 Kings 1:39, 45), Jehu (2 Kings 9:3, 6), and Joash (2 Kings 11:12). In the same tradition, Jesus was seen as anointed directly by God "with the Holy Spirit and with power" (Acts 10:38).

In addition to their ceremonial functions, ointments were used as cosmetics to alleviate the dryness of the skin or after bathing (2 Sam. 12:20) or to prepare oneself before an amorous encounter (Esth. 2:12; Song of Sol. 1:3). The Essenes, however, may not have used oil on their bodies (Josephus, *War* 2, 8.3/123). It was customary to honor guests at a banquet by anointing their heads and feet (Deut. 33:24; Ps. 23:5; Luke 7:46). Anointing was also a sign of rejoicing (Isa. 61:3) and, as such, was omitted in time of sorrow (*b. Moed Qatan* 15b), on the day of Atonement (*m. yoma* 8.1), and in the fasts during droughts (*m. Taanit* 1. 6). By contrast, Jesus recommended paying attention to one's appearance so as to not draw attention to one's piety as in the case of fasting (Matt. 6:16-18). The bodies of Jacob and Joseph had been embalmed in Egypt before being carried to their burial place (Gen. 50:2-3, 20); the dead were anointed before entombment (Mark 14:8; 16:1; Luke 23:56; *m. Sabbat* 24.5). In order to preserve the scent until the time the ointment was to be used, the openings of the ointment jars were tightly sealed, Mary of Bethany thus had to break the neck of her alabaster jar in order to anoint Jesus' head (Mark 14:3); this procedure is mentioned in the Mishnah (*m. Kelim* 30.4).

Botanical and Archaeological Information

A number of spices and aromatic plants were used for the preparation of ointments, but the sacral ointment contained only four species to be mixed in specified proportions with olive oil: myrrh, cinnamon, kalomos and cassia. This mixture was to be blended "as by a perfumer," (Exod. 30:23-25). Stacte, onycha, galbanun, and frankincense were mixed in equal parts "as by the perfumer," with salt (Exod. 30:34) to make sacral incense. Many other substances were used for the production of ointments and perfumes. A sample of them includes:

- *Aloe* (Hebrew *ohalim* or *ohaloth*; Ps. 45:2; Song of Sol. 4:14; Prov. 7:17), which came from India and Malaya.

- *Balsam* (Hebrew *bassam*; Song of Sol. 5:1, 13; 6:13). According to Josephus, this resin was produced by the opobalsamum tree growing in the region of Mecca. Large balsam plantations existed in the region between Jericho and En-gedi in the time of the Second Temple.

- *Cassia* (Hebrew *gidda* or *gesioth*; Ps. 45:8; Ezek. 17:19). Also called cinnamon-cassia, it came from China and, according to Pliny, was sold for 1,000 dinarii a pound. The Copper Scroll mentions a "box of incense in cassia wood" (3Q15, 11. 1–4).

- *Cinnamon* (Hebrew *ginnemon*: Prov. 7:17; Song of Sol. 4:14). It came from Ceylon (Sri Lanka today).

- *Galbanum* (Hebrew *helbenah*; Exod. 30:34), also used for medication.

- *Henna* (Hebrew *kofer*; Song of Sol. 1:14; 4:13). It grows in Palestine and is used to this day as a dye for hair and nails. Egyptian mummies were painted with henna, which was also used as a medicine.

- *Frankincense* (Hebrew *lebonah*; Lev. 2:1; 14:7; 1 Chron. 9:29; Isa. 43:23; Neh. 13:9). The tree producing frankincense grows in India, Arabia, and Somalia. A very expensive ingredient, it was kept in the Temple treasury.

- *Kalamos* (Hebrew *kaneh*; Jer. 6:20; Ezek. 27:19). It was an aromatic cane that grew in India and also in the northern Jordan Valley between Lake Huleh and the Sea of Galilee.

- *Myrrh* (Hebrew *mor*; Prov. 7:7; Esth. 2:12; Song of Sol. 4:17) The sap of a small tree growing in Arabia and Africa; it was sold either in liquid or solidified form.

- *Nard* (Hebrew *nerd*; Song of Sol. 1:12; 4:13-14). This expensive perfume was extracted from two types of plants: nadala, from the Himalayas and Nepal, imported through India and Persia; and spike (Latin *spicatum*), giving the "spikenard."

Archaeological Data

A great number of containers (vials, flasks, unguentaria) and small tools for holding or applying ointments, cosmetics, and perfumes have been found in many Palestinian sites, testifying to their widespread use. Two discoveries deserve special attention: the artifacts of the "Cave of Letters" (*see* CAVE OF LETTERS) and an intact flask full of anointing oil, from one of the reexplored Qumran caves.

In the 1960 exploration of the Judean Desert Caves (*see* JUDEAN DESERT CAVES and CAVE OF LETTERS), Y. Yadin and his team found a waterskin that had been used by a woman to hide her precious possessions. Among other objects, it contained a wooden powder box, a glass vial for perfumed oil, several perfume flasks, and cosmetic tools. A mirror made of a brass disc encased in a wooden frame with a handle lay near the waterskin; both frame and handle were overlaid with red leather. The following year, another mirror identical to the first one was discovered.

One of the most interesting archaeological finds of this century in Israel was a clay flask dating from the first century. Discovered in 1988 by J. Patrich of the Hebrew University, the 7-inch-high flask was wrapped in palm leaves and buried in a three-foot-deep pit. It had two openings, one on the top of its neck for pouring and one on the side, under the handle, for filling. Both openings were tightly sealed by a hardened adipose matter, which had prevented contact of the oil with air. Mark and the Mishnah, when describing the manner of retrieving an ointment from its flask, reflect just this reality. Z. Aizenshtat and D. Ashengrau of the Casali Institute of Applied Chemistry, subjected the contents of the flask to careful and lengthy analysis. The oil had lost its scent, but they identified balsam as the main odoriferous component. The final product was heavier than water, as thick as honey, and of a reddish color as described by Pliny. The ointment probably came from En-gedi, which was famous for its balsam groves.

Implications for Jesus Research

Jesus, as is suggested in several of the entries of this book, had affinities with the Essenes but also differences. The Essenes did not use oil for the care of their bodies, but Jesus did not object to anointing. He even recommended it: "When you fast, anoint your head and wash your face, so that your fasting may not be seen by others" (Matt. 6:17-18). He also praised the women who anointed him (*see* DEAD SEA SCROLLS and QUMRAN).

All four Gospels report the anointing of Jesus by a woman. This would imply two independent attestations, Mark and John, if it is assumed, as many scholars do, that the author of John did not use the Synoptics. A third attestation would be "special Luke," because Luke introduces a different setting and a different conclusion. Nevertheless, the application of the accepted criteria for the authenticity of Jesus' sayings led the Jesus Seminar in 1987 to rate all four anointing accounts *black* by a 75 percent majority and thus to reject their authenticity. Would that decision have been different if archaeological and historical data had been integrated into the study? Let us give for comparative purposes a summary of the Gospel accounts, beginning with Mark, which is usually considered the oldest.

Mark 14:3-9. Bethany—house of Simon the Leper—a woman—alabaster jar of ointment of very costly pure nard. She broke the jar—poured it over his head—Some said (to themselves) "Why the waste? Could have been sold for more than three hundred dinarii to give to the poor"—Jesus: "You will always have the poor, you will not have me, she has pre-anointed me for burying."

Matthew 26:6-13. Bethany—house of Simon the Leper—a woman—alabaster jar of expensive ointment—She poured it over his head—The disciples said, "Why the waste? Better sell it and give to the poor"—Jesus: "You will always have the poor, you will not always have me, she has prepared my body for burial."

Luke 7:36-50. Unspecified location—house of a Pharisee (Simon, v. 40)—a woman sinner—alabaster jar of ointment—She wetted Jesus' feet with tears—wiped them with her hair—kissed them—anointed them—Jesus reproached his host, forgave the woman's sins.

John 12:1-8. Bethany, family of Lazarus—Mary took a pound of costly ointment of pure nard—anointed his feet—wiped them with her hair—Judas said, "Why was it not sold for three hundred dinarii to give to the poor?"—anti-Judas comments—Jesus: "Let her keep it for the day of my burial, the poor will always be with you but you will not always have me."

Considering these references and the evidence provided by historians and archaeology, it seems probable that Jesus was anointed several times when he was guest. Mark's account, which mentions the breaking of the jar, seems most genuine. Matthew is obviously a simplified duplication of Mark. Luke and John may refer to two other anointings, for there may have been more than one occurrence interpreted differently by the four evangelists. The name Simon was so common that the Pharisee and the Leper could well be two different persons. One disturbing factor is the discrepancy between Mark's and John's accounts, which may refer to the same event happening in Bethany. John was more familiar with the places, people, and customs of Judea than the Galileans. He had connections that the other disciples did not have, and he may have known the name and the family of the owner of the house. If it is the same event, why did he shift the anointing from head to feet? Why did he combine the story of Mark with that of Luke without regard for logic: Anointing of the head supposed a recipient sitting on a chair or bench at a table, while anointing of the feet supposed a Greco-Roman type of dining room with low tables and couches (*see* WOOD, FURNITURE). Was it to harmonize his version with the scene of the washing of the disciples' feet (John 13:5) that occasioned the difference in John? Clearly this matter needs further study.

BIBLIOGRAPHY

Corley, K. E. "The Anointing of Jesus in the Synoptic Tradition." *Jesus Seminar Papers*. Sonoma, Calif.: Polebridge Press (1994).

Dalman, G. *Arbeit und sitte in Palästina*. Vols. 4, 5 Gütersloh: Bertelsmann, 1928–42.

Forbes, R. J. *Studies in Ancient Technology*. Vol. 3. Leiden: E. J. Brill, 1955.

Harrison, R. K. *Healing Herbs of the Bible*. Leiden: E. J. Brill, 1966.

Matthews, V. H. "Perfumes and Spices." *ABD* 5:226–28.

Miller, J. I. *The Spice Trade of the Roman Empire, 29 B.C. to A.D. 641*. New York: Oxford, 1961.

Negev, A., ed. "Spices and Perfumes" *AEHL*. Rev. ed. 1986. 354–55.

Nielsen, K. "Incense in Ancient Israel." *Vetus Testamentum* Sup. 38. Leiden: Brill, 1986.

———. "Incense. *ABD* 3:404–9.

Van Beek, G. W. "Frankincense and Myrrh." *BA* 23 (1960): 69-95.

Winter, S. C. "The Anointing of Bethany, John 12:1-8." *Jesus Seminar Papers*. Sonoma, Calif.: Polebridge Press (1994).

Zohary, M. *Plant Life of Palestine: Israel and Jordan*. New York: Ronald Press, 1962.

———. *Plants of the Bible*. London, New York: Cambridge University Press, 1982.

Olive Oil Industry

Importance

The production of olive oil was a major industry in Palestine. Oil is referred to several times in the Gospels.

Scripture References

Matt. 21:1; 24:3; 25:3-8; 26:30; Mark 13:3; 14:26; Luke 7:46; 10:34; 16:6; 19:29, 37; 21:37; 22:39; John 8:1.

General Information

The most important source of oil in Palestine was the olive tree, an evergreen that grows everywhere from Judea (especially around Jerusalem) to Galilee. In the Mediterranean Basin, it belonged to the *olea europoea* family. The Palestinian olive tree produced an excellent oil and was sought by foreign buyers (Josephus, *War* 2, 21 2./590–92). According to the Mishnah, the oil of Tekoa of Galilee was the finest (*m. Menahot* 8.3).

The importance of the olive tree in the Near East is evident in its frequent appearance, along with the palm tree and some other species, as the Tree of Life in ancient art. Its importance is also marked by its presence in ancient literary productions. For example, the dove returning to Noah's Ark at the end of the flood brought back an olive leaf; the role of olive branch, and later the dove itself, as symbols of peace may be rooted in this tale.

Olive tree cultivation is simple, although the new plants must be grafted and grow slowly. Mature trees produce abundantly (up to fifteen gallons of oil every other year) for hundreds of years. They grow extremely well in the dry climate and the rocky soil of Palestine. The olives themselves were a staple food; the oil had many uses. Olive wood, hard and resistant to rot, was prized by carpenters.

Olive oil production has been a major industry in Palestine since the Bronze Age. Olive mills and presses are found all over the country, even where olive trees no longer grow. The same techniques have been used for over three thousand years. First the olives, harvested in September through December by beating the trees with rods (Deut. 24:20), were crushed under a vertical circular millstone rolling around another one, hewn to form a circular basin. A donkey could be used to move the millstone. In the process, some oil was extracted and collected in a vat through a groove in the bottom stone. Next the pulp was transferred into sacks piled up over an altar-shaped slab with grooves connected to a vat. For a few days, oil kept dripping, pressed out by the sacks' weight. The top layer in the vat was skimmed and became the "pure" or "beaten" oil required for the menorah in the Temple (Exod. 27:20, Lev. 24:2) and as an ingredient for the daily *tamid* (Exod. 29:40, Num. 28:5; *see* TEMPLE, SACRIFICIAL SYSTEM). Such fine oil was included in the payments for timber made annually by Solomon to Hiram, King of Tyre (1 Kings 5:11).

"Industrial" production came at a second stage. Long heavy beams, usually made of oak, were inserted into "pigeon holes" in the wall behind the slabs and set over the piles of sacks. These beams were so heavy that they were used as an image in the Mishnah to represent heavy weights: "as heavy as an oil press beam." Pressure was applied by hanging large stone weights at the free ends of the beams (*see* fig. 52); it was increased as needed by the addition of more weights. After separation from water by natural decantation, the oil was scooped up, strained, and poured into jars. Olive mills and presses could be owned by a landowner for his own production, by the olive grove owners of a village who would build an oil mill used in common, or by a miller who would extract oil from the crops of small farmers for a percentage of the production, usually the pure oil. Oil was an important commodity in domestic and international

Olive crusher *(Tabgah)*

trade. It was transported in pointed jars, like those used for wine (*see* VITICULTURE), and exported mainly to Egypt and Arabia, which were poor in olive trees. Olive oil was a major source of income for Palestine.

Together with grain and wine, oil was one of the three main subsistence products of ancient Palestine. The three were considered a blessing from God (Jer. 31:12; Joel 2:19), but would be taken away if Israel sinned (Deut. 28:51; Joel 1:10; Hag. 1:7-11). Kings stockpiled these precious commodities in their royal storehouses (2 Chron. 11:11; 32:28; Isa. 39:2). Olive oil was used as food, medicine, fuel for lamps, for anointing, and for sacrifices. Both biblical and rabbinic literature mention it as an ingredient in cakes and wafers. It was added to vegetable dishes and probably used for frying, although no texts document the use of certain open vessels called "frying pans" by archaeologists. As a medicine, oil softened wounds (Isa. 1:16; Luke 10:34) and, because it was perceived as a gift from God, it became a symbol of protection. Its use in healing rituals appears in the New Testament (Mark 6:13; James 5:14) and in the Talmud (*t. Sabbat* 134a). The Bible refers to oil most often in its use as an ointment. Anointing was a joyful occasion; accordingly, anointing oil was called the "oil of gladness" (Ps. 47:7 *et passim*). Kings, priests, and prophets were anointed (1 Sam. 10:1; Lev. 8:30; Isa. 61:1 *et passim*). Shields were also anointed (Isa. 21:5), probably to increase their protective power. This custom may be related to the use of oil in healings and as a protection against diseases. Guests coming to a banquet were anointed as a sign of welcome and reverence (Luke 7:46). Anointing was a sign of good will and friendship between individuals. It was recommended for personal care and Ecclesiastes 9:18 says that everyone should always have oil on the head. The pulp that remained after the extraction of the oil was used as a high-quality fuel for ovens, stoves, and kilns.

Archaeological Information

Many oil mills and presses, some dating to the first century C.E., have been found in Israel. One installation that certainly existed in Jesus' time is one of the oil mills of Gamla, which includes one crushing mill, two oil presses, and a storage vat dug into the rock. During the Early Roman period an innovation was introduced: A thick wooden screw replaced the heavy weights. This type became popular from the fourth century until modern times. In a second stage of development, a wooden screw or two directly pressed the sacks containing the crushed olives. This type was also in use in the modern period.

Oil lamps have been excavated by the thousands, those of the Roman period being among the most elaborate in design.

Implications for Jesus Research

Jesus' anointings are commented upon in OINTMENTS, PERFUMES. Here, two remarks can be made. One concerns the story of the Good Samaritan in which Luke uses the expression, "having poured oil and wine" (on the wounds of the robbers' victim; Luke 10:34). Luke is known to have made several mistakes in his writings: the dating of the census (Luke 2:1-3); "their rite of purification"

(2:22); conflation of the purification offering of a mother after childbirth with the rite of redemption of a first-born son (2:22-24); and placing the revolt of Theudas before the call of Judas the Galilean at the time of the census (Acts 5:36-37). Luke 10:34 contains another error. His reference to "oil and wine" reverses the way in which the two liquids were used medicinally: wine (or vinegar, if available) was probably poured first to clean and disinfect the wound; then the oil, which had a soothing effect, was applied. Some interpreters view the procedure as one single pouring, using a mixture of oil and wine (some kind of vinaigrette!), which could hardly have been the case. Luke 10:30b-35 received a *red* rating from the Jesus Seminar in 1986.

Another important remark concerns Jesus' attitude and comments in the Lukan story of the sinful woman anointing his feet in the house of Simon the Pharisee (Luke 7:36-50), a story that was rated *black* by the Jesus Seminar in 1987. In verse 46, Jesus makes an indirect reproach to his host for not having greeted him as he would have treated an equal or an honored guest. It seems that Jesus had not even received the marks of welcome from a slave of the host, although such a greeting would have been appropriate for a guest of inferior rank. What is worth noticing is that Jesus, in the Greek text, makes the distinction between *elaion*, "ordinary oil," and *myron*, "ointment." Did Luke know the difference? If not, the comments may come from Jesus himself.

Although his disciples used oil (Mark 6:13), Jesus himself did not use it nor any other ingredient for that matter, except saliva (*see* TRADITIONAL HEALING), in his healings. The saying of Mark 9:42 probably refers to the millstone of an oil press, since wine was pressed by foot and grain was ground by stone grinders. Because of the enormous weight of the stone tied to the neck of the offender, his fate was certainly perceived as hopeless, the more so that the vastness of the sea into which he would be thrown added to the feeling of awe.

Jesus spent his last days in Jerusalem and was arrested among olive groves and olive mills. Galilean pilgrims camped on the Mount of Olives,

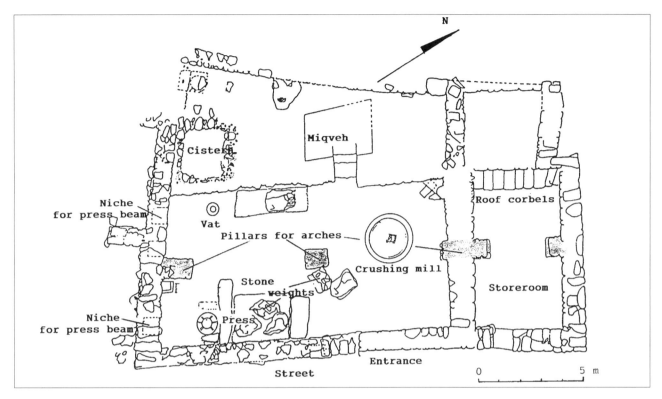

Figure 52 Plan of the Olive Press in the Industrial Area of Gamla. *(Israel Department of Antiquities and Museums)*

and on his last night Jesus retired in the Garden of Gethsemane, a name derived from the Aramaic *gatshemen*, which means "oil press" (*see* MOUNT OF OLIVES and JERUSALEM, GETHSEMANE).

BIBLIOGRAPHY

Borowski, O. *Agriculture in Iron Age Israel.* Winona Lake, Ind.: Eisenbrauns, 1987.

Dalman, G. *Arbeit und Sitte in Palästina.* Vol. 4. Gütersloh, C. Bertelsmann, 1928–42.

Dothan, T. and S. Gittin. "Miqne, Tel Ekron." *NEAEHL* 3:1057–58.

Frankel, R. *The Ancient Olive Press.* Tel Aviv: Eretz Israel Museum, 1986 (Hebrew).

Goor, A. "The Place of the Olive in the Holy Land and Its History through the Ages." *Economic Botany* 20 (1966): 233–43.

Gutman, S. "Gamala." *NEAEHL* 2:462–63.

Pantera's Tombstone

Importance

Origen (indirectly), the Talmud, and other postbiblical writings preserve a tradition that Jesus was the son of a Roman soldier named Pantera. The tombstone of a Roman soldier by that name was found in Germany.

Scripture References

Matt. 1:3, 5, 6, 18-19; Luke 1:26-27; G. Thom. 61, 105.

General Information

Two of the canonical Gospels, Matthew and Luke, state that Jesus was born of a virgin and conceived

Figure 53 Pantera's Tombstone. Found at Bingerbrück, Germany in October 1859, it reads, "Tib (erius) Jul (ius) Abdes Pantera Sidonia ann(orum) sexaginta duorum stipen (Diorum) quatraginta miles exs coh (orte) prima sagittariorum h (ic) s(itus) e(st)." Originally, the figure had an arrow in its right hand and a bow in the left. Across its breast runs the strap of a quiver. It carries a gladius to the right and a dagger to the left. Pantera came from Sidon, he obtained Roman citizenship under Tiberius, but kept "Abdes" as his name. In Aramaic, Abdes means "Servant of God." *(Drawing by Peter Engelmann, 1877. Bad Kreuznach Museum)*

of the Holy Spirit. The two other Gospels are silent about Jesus' origin. Paul, whose writings antedate Matthew and Luke by thirty to forty years, writes: "God sent his Son, born of a woman, born under the law" (Gal. 4:4) "according to the flesh" (Rom. 1:3). Although Matthew mentions a miraculous birth, he also includes in Jesus' paternal ancestry four women of questionable virtue: Tamar, who played the prostitute to bear an heir by her father-in-law Judah from within her deceased husband's family; Rahab, the prostitute and heroine of Jericho; Ruth, who lay with her kinsman Boaz to secure a marriage that would maintain family holdings; and Bathsheba, the wife of Uriah the Hittite, with whom King David committed adultery and then married after plotting the death of her husband.

The purpose of Matthew's strange genealogy is perhaps found in Origen's *Contra Celsum*. Origen reports that the pagan philosopher Celsus said that Jesus was the adulterous son of a Roman soldier. The same information is to be found in several rabbinic passages (*b. Sabbat* 104; *t. Hulim* 2,22, *et passim*), where Jesus is called by different names: Ben Panthera, Ben Pantera, Ben Pandera, Ben Stada, Balaam. The leaders of the early Church understandably tried to suppress this information, and Christian writers denounced it as a slanderous invention.

Archaeological Data

Accusations of slander subsided somewhat after 1859 when a tombstone from the first century C.E. was found at Bingerbrück in western Germany. It bears a sculpture representing a Roman archer and this epitaph: "Tiberius Julius Abdes Pantera of Sidon, aged 62, a soldier of 40 years of service, of the First Cohort of archers, lies here." The tombstone was found near the Roman border, along the Rhine, at the time of Tiberius Caesar. Bingerbrück is located where the Nahe river reaches the Rhine, 20 miles west of Mainz and about 61 miles north of the French border. Eight legions were stationed there under the command of Germanicus, son of

Nero Drusus and adopted grandson of Tiberius (Tacitus, *Annals* 1.1). Forty years of service was not unusual, although the normal enlistment contract was for twenty years. Tacitus reports that, during the mutiny following the death of Augustus, older soldiers who had served for thirty and forty years complained, showing their white hair and toothless gums (*Annals* 1.2). The Pantera tombstone can be seen today in the Bad Kreuznach Museum, a few miles from the place where it was discovered (*see* fig. 53).

Implications for Jesus Research

That the archer Tiberius Julius Abdes Pantera was from Sidon might have some bearing on the motive for Jesus' visit to the region of Tyre and Sidon (Mark 7:24, and parallels); the Gospels give no explanation for this journey. The silence of Paul, Mark, John, and even Luke in Acts about the virgin birth, and the strange Matthean genealogy, point to some kind of problem related to Jesus' origin.

An uncertain origin could explain the otherwise incomprehensible logion 105 in the Gospel of Thomas: "Whoever knows father and mother shall be called the son of a harlot." It could also explain Jesus' rejection at Nazareth, which is attested by the four evangelists. His understanding of the poor and other marginalized groups, his message to them, and his denunciation of wealth, power, and privilege would become more comprehensible if he himself would have experienced what it means to be an outcast.

What did Salome mean when she asked Jesus, "Who are you, man, and whose son? You did take your place on my bench and eat at my table" (G. Thom. 61)? Did she know of his illegitimate birth?

BIBLIOGRAPHY

Bad Kreuznach Museum. *Die Grabdenkmäler von Bingerbrück*. Bad Kreuznach: Bad Kreuznach Museum, 1986.

Goldstein, Morris. *Jesus in the Jewish Tradition*. New York: Macmillan, 1950.

Tacitus. *The Annals of Ancient Rome*. Translated by Michael Grant. New York: Dorset Press, 1984.

Pontius Pilate's Stone

Importance

The inscription on the stone testifies to the presence of Pilate in Judea in Jesus' time; his title (prefect) is clarified.

Scripture References

Matt. 27:2, 24; Mark 15:1, 5, 15, 44; Luke 3:1; 13:1; 23:12, 52; John 18:29, 33; 19:8-19, 38; Acts 3:13; 4:27; 13:28.

General Information and Archaeological Data

In addition to the Gospels, the writings of Josephus and Philo attest to the existence of Pilate as prefect of Judea (26–36 C.E.). Only in 1962 did archaeology provide tangible evidence contemporaneous with his presence in Judea. An Italian archaeological mission from the Academy of Science and Letters of Milan excavated at Caesarea Maritima (1959–64) and concentrated on the Roman theater, which at that time was buried under sand and vegetation. A. Frova, the mission director, quickly recognized that the complex structure had been modified in the fourth century into a *Kolymbêthra*, "pool for water games." In this modification, a stone had been reused as one of the steps of a stairway added to the structure. The stone bore an inscription that reads:

S TIBERIÉVM
NTIVS PILATVS
ECTVS IVDA E
É

The stone is now in the Israel Museum in Jerusalem, and a replica has been placed in the park next to the theater.

Interpretation
Several readings of the epigraph have been proposed (see Lémonon, 1981); three deserve attention; note that the accent marks a long vowel, the brackets indicate proposed missing letters, and the parentheses show restored abbreviations:

Pontius Pilate's Stone, found at Casarea Maritima

1. Reading by A. Frova:

   [CAESARIEN] S(IBUS) TIBERIÉUM
   [PON]TIUS PILATUS
   [PRAEF]ECTUS IUDA[EA]E
   [D]É[DIT]

The translation of this proposal would be "To the inhabitants of Caesarea this Tiberium, Pontius Pilate, prefect of Judea offered." The accent on the E of "TIBERIÉUM" clearly indicates a building constructed in honor of the emperor Tiberius; it has not yet been possible to determine the nature of the structure so dedicated.

2. In 1967, the Italian scholar A. Degrassi proposed the following formula, which was finally endorsed by Frova. In this reading the S of the first line is not understood as an abbreviation but as an ending:

   [DIS AUGUSTI]S TIBERIÉUM
   [.....PO]NTIUS PILATUS
   [PRAEF]ECTUS IUDA[EA]E
   [FÉCIT, D]É[DICAVIT]

This restoration of the inscription means, "To the two Augustus this Tiberium, Pontius Pilate, prefect of Judea did (or erected), (and) dedicated." "DIS AUGUSTIS" would refer to Augustus and Livia, his wife, mother of Tiberius. But as J. P. Lémonon remarks (*Pilate*, 27), is it possible that the Tiberiéum, whatever it was, be dedicated to someone other than Tiberius alone?

3. Lémonon, after a critical study of the most plausible options offered so far recognized that, in the absence of any known parallel, it is preferable not to try to reconstruct the missing part of the first line and to keep the last one as simple as possible. Thus his reading:

   [.....]S TIBERIÉUM
   [..PO]NTIUS PILATUS
   [PRAEF]ECTUS IUDA[EA]E
   [FÉCIT]

This keeps to the basic fact: " . . . this Tiberium, Pontius Pilate, prefect of Judea, did (or erected)."

Discussions will continue about the possible interpretations of the epigraph. For our purpose, we note the unanimity of the scholarship on the fact that the stone testifies to the presence of Pontius Pilate in Judea as prefect in the time of Jesus. The stone is the only contemporary witness of his existence.

Implications for Jesus Research

Pilate's stone is truly a significant archaeological discovery for the history of early Christianity, especially because it was discovered at Caesarea, the seat of Roman authority in Judea and Samaria in Jesus' time. The inscription indisputably establishes Pilate's title, which had long been debated (was he a governor, a procurator or a prefect?). The prefect had administrative, financial, military, and judicial functions. As supreme penal judge in his territory—except for recourse to the emperor himself in the case of a Roman citizen—he had the power to pronounce death sentences as he did for Jesus, and to pardon as he did for Barabbas.

Confusion about Pilate's title and function comes from the fact that, as a prefect he was also procurator in financial matters (*see* TAX AND TAX COLLECTORS). A procurator was a person who had received from another a delegation of power to manage an estate or collect income; it could be a private or public function. In public affairs, the procurators were usually chosen from among the equestrian order, which was second in rank to the senatorial order. Governors of provinces like Syria were legates belonging to the senatorial order and had authority over the legions. But Augustus, in his political and administrative reform, appointed in each province, in addition to the legate, a procurator who reported directly to the Emperor. In Egypt, the governors were prefects of equestrian rank. Judea was a hybrid creation, the governance of which was affected by the turbulence of its Jewish inhabitants. Pilate was dependent on the legate of Syria for the use of the legions, but he had *ius gladii* (originally the right to pronounce and execute the death penalty against a Roman soldier who was a Roman citizen). This right applied to the Roman officers serving in his auxiliary forces (*see* WEAPONS) and also to criminals, non-Roman citizens in the territory under his jurisdiction.

BIBLIOGRAPHY

Aziza, D. "Ponce Pilate." *L'Histoire* 70 (1984): 46–54.

Burly, E. *The Roman Army. Papers* 1929–1986. Mavors Roman Army Research. Amsterdam: J. C. Gieben, 1988.

Fuks, G. "Again on the Episode of the Gilded Roman Shields at Jerusalem." *Harvard Theological Review* 75 (1982).

Gatti, C. "A Proposito di una Rilettura dell'Epigrafe di Ponzio Pilato." *Aevum* 55 (1981): 13–21(Italian).

Jones, A. H. M. "Procurators and Prefects in the Early Principate." *Studies in Roman Government and Law*. Oxford, 1960: 115–25.

Lémonon, J. P. *Pilate et le gouvernement de la Judée*. Paris: J. Gabalda, 1981.

Pflaum, H. G. *Les Procurateurs équestres sous le Haut-Empire Romain*. 2 vols. Paris: Maisonneuve, 1950.

Schwartz, D. R. "Josephus and Philo on Pontius Pilate." *Jerusalem Cathedra* 3 (1983): 26–45 (Hebrew).

———. "Pontius Pilate." *ABD* 5:395–401.

Pottery and Glass

Importance

Most vessels used in daily life in antiquity were ceramic. The Gospels refer several times to pottery.

Scripture References

Matt. 6:30; 10:42; 20:22-23; 23:25-26; 26:23, 27, 39, 42; Mark 9:41; 10:38; 14:36; Luke 12:28; 22:17-20, 42; John 4:28; 18:11; G. Thom. 97.

General Information

Clay vessels first appeared in the Pottery Neolithic period, toward the end of prehistoric times (5500–4300 B.C.E.). Pottery then was made without the help of any mechanical tool: the clay was worked by hand on a mat, and rings of clay were put one above the other to form crude jars and bowls. The potter's wheel appeared in the following period, the Chalcolithic. At first it was a flat stone disk with a conic protuberance serving as a pivot at its center. The potter rotated it with one hand. Slow as it was, the Chalcolithic wheel allowed for the production of a variety of forms:

rounded or V-shaped bowls with flat bases, cups, drinking horns, incense bowls resting on cylindrical stands with apertures, jars of various sizes and shapes, and others. Decorative techniques and patterns were already quite elaborate.

Ceramic products were used as cooking pots and kitchen ware, storage jars, containers of different types, ovens, stoves, oil lamps, figurines, and models of houses and temples. A great variety of forms and functions developed over the centuries. Unlike metal objects, which can be melted and reused over and over again, ceramic ware is breakable; once destroyed, its shards are seldom left where the object broke but rather thrown into dumps or garbage heaps. Potsherds by the hundreds or even thousands turn up every day at most excavations. This has provided the opportunity for the historian of material culture to recognize a sequence of forms and shapes. The resulting typology serves as an essential instrument for dating and locating assemblages of ancient pottery. Because the forms and styles of ceramic vessels never were repeated, the different types were identified as characteristic of various regions, societies, and periods.

By the time of the Hellenistic Period (333–63 B.C.E.) pottery manufacture had evolved into a well-organized international industry, with large factories using techniques and producing articles that local potters tried to copy. The creativity of potters and artists is such that new models, from heavy storage jars to delicate vials and juglets, appeared almost daily.

Ceramic typology became the most common and reliable dating method in the archaeology of Palestine, where inscriptions giving absolute dates are extremely rare compared to those found in Greece, Italy, Asia Minor, Mesopotamia, or Egypt. Coins, another source of absolute dating, also are not as abundant in Palestine as in those regions and were distributed unevenly. Sir Flinders Petrie was the first to notice, while excavating Egyptian tombs, that clay vessels of different types corresponded to different historical periods. He made the same observation in southern Palestine a few years later, and in 1890 he published a method of dating by stratigraphy and ceramic typology. W. F. Albright refined and expanded Petrie's work. Publications that gave detailed descriptions, photographs, and drawings of each type of pottery for each period began to appear. Such works published by the Dominican Ecole Biblique of Jerusalem, by P. Lapp, and by R. Amiram are still used as basic references. A newer study by J. A. Blakely and W. J. Bennett provides a valuable overview of the archeological ceramics of Palestine.

Although most broken ceramic vessels were thrown on the dump heap, some were mended because they were especially valuable or because they were only cracked or chipped but not fragmented. Archaeologists everywhere in Israel have found pieces of pottery having small holes near the rim of the break, which were used for twine or wire fasteners. The larger shards of broken pots were reused as scoops, scrapers, jar lids, or as the outer lining for sewage lines, kilns, crucibles, and smelting furnaces. Pottery shards were also used as *ostraca*: potsherds inscribed in ink used for letters, school texts, receipts, and military messages. A great number of these have been found at Samaria and Lachish.

Most vessels used in the Temple were made of gold, silver, bronze, or copper; these non-absorbent materials enabled the vessels to have their ritual purity restored by washing. In certain circumstances, clay vessels were used too, as in the ceremonial cleansing of a leper after his healing (Lev. 14:5) and in the ordeal procedure of the woman suspected of adultery (Num. 5:17). Leviticus stipulates that if an unclean animal, like a mouse or a gecko, falls into a clay vessel or on an oven or a stove, the container must be broken (Lev. 11:29-35). Postbiblical halakah* goes further and ruled that even vessels used in daily life had to be destroyed if they had contained an impure substance.

Although glass objects and glaze (a coat of glass on ceramic) were known in Egypt, Persia, Greece, and Italy, they are seldom found in Palestine before the first century C.E. Originally, glass vessels cast in molds were very expensive. During the Hellenistic period, Alexandria became a leading center for glass manufacture, but few of its products, mostly wine drinking bowls, reached Palestine. With the discovery of glass-blowing in Phoenicia or Syria in the first century B.C.E. glass objects became more affordable; but the luxury glassware from Alexandria continued to be available mainly to the rich until the third century C.E. Pliny (*Nat. Hist.* 36.190), Strabo (*Geography* 16, 2.25), and Josephus (*War* 2, 10.2/189–91) all indicate that the sand of the Phoenician beaches near the mouth of the Belus river was reputed to have made the best quality glass. In fact, Phoenician glass competed with Alexandria's finest products. Jewish glass blowers worked in Sidonian glass factories, and Talmudic literature gives abundant information and rules regarding glass making. In the *haggadah**, glass-blowing is compared to the blowing of God's breath into the human body. The Talmud mentions glass objects of various types: beds, chairs, tables, bowls, spoons, jugs, lanterns, funnels, scales, weights, inkpots, rulers, and mirrors (*y. Sukka* 4 and T. Pseudo-Jonathan).

Technical and Archaeological Information

Pottery is made of clay, an hydrated silicate of alumina, usually of a reddish color in Israel though some varieties can be as light as beige. After being dug out the clay was placed in water in large basins where it was weathered and washed. Some time later, perhaps after a period of several months, the clay was trodden to remove the air and remaining impurities and to mix in the right proportion of water. At this point, temper (an additional substance such as sand or lime dust), could be added. By the first century C.E., the potter's wheel had become an elaborate instrument made of two wooden discs set at each extremity of a vertical axle. The top one, smaller, supported the clay and the larger one, at the bottom, was kept in rotation by the potter's foot. The wheel was used for making all storage and domestic items of a circular shape. Other articles like lamps, decorative slabs, and figurines were made in molds. Objects such as toys, statuettes, and one of a kind creations were shaped by hand.

After pottery had been shaped from wet clay, which was then dried, the vessels were fired in a kiln. The process required special skills for different objects and different clays; it also required different temperatures and times. Kilns could be complex structures with adjustable air vents and several firing platforms (*see* fig. 54). The potter's installation and kilns of Qumran are representative of the pottery techniques of first-century Palestine. Glaze was not used in Palestine, but some pottery was painted, usually in red or brown, either uniformly or with a variety of motifs.

A number of cuneiform texts from ancient Mesopotamia contain instructions on how to build glass furnaces and how to make glass of different quality and colors: blue, green, purple, pale blue, black, brown, red, and sapphire. They reveal a quite sophisticated technology. Remains of glass factories have been found at Tiberias, Hippos-Susita, Beth Shearim, and around the Sea of Galilee, with quantities of glass objects that are either finished or defective. These discoveries can be related to the information given in the Talmud that the thinnest and most beautiful glass was made at Tiberias (*y. Niddah* 2, *Halla* 7).

The time of Jesus coincides with the archaeological periods designated Late Hellenistic (100–63 B.C.E.) and Early Roman (63 B.C.E.–70 C.E.). During these periods there were two different trends in pottery usage: a continuation of the local pottery traditions and a growing influence of Greek techniques. In many cases, local imitations replaced the original imports from the west. The fact that different ethnic groups used similar repertoires of ceramic vessels complicates the research. Even those vessels that are recognized as imported do not always indicate their place of origin, and certainly do not prove that the people who made them moved with the vessels.

Local wares include storage jars from elongated to bag-shaped forms with sloppily attached handles. Toward the end of the Hellenistic Period the elongated flattened rim prevailed, and the first-century jars are characterized by folded "collar" rims. Wine jars imported from the island of Rhodes

Figure 54 Pottery. Artist rendering of a potter's kiln, Persian Period, as found at Tell Michal, six miles north of Tel Aviv.

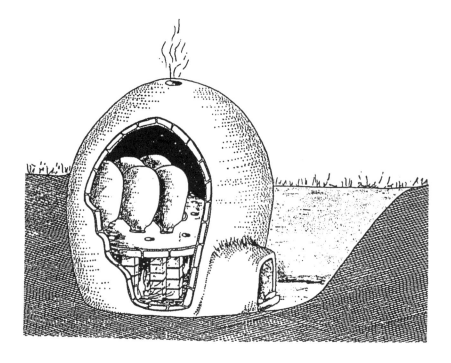

became common, especially among non-Jewish communities. They are characterized by their good-quality clay, good firing, and long handles with the imprint of the names of the producer and eponym priest. These vessels were transported by sea and were equipped with thick pointed bases that were placed in special holders in the ships. Cooking pots with thin, hard walls became common. They give a metallic sound when knocked and presumably imitate metalware. Ridges surround the walls of the vessels, which feature upright rims and two strap handles. Oil lamps were made according to two different techniques: on a potter's wheel, or in a mold. The oil lamp known as the Herodian lamp is a good example. Made on a potter's wheel, it was closed in shape, with a hole on the top for pouring oil in and a bow spout for the wick. This oil lamp was in use from the first decade B.C.E. to the end of the First Jewish War in 70 C.E. (*see* fig. 55).

Open markets and free trade within the Hellenistic kingdoms meant growing imports to Palestine. The *terra sigillata* vessels are typical imported wares, glazed in black and red, which were originally produced in Greece and Italy; but during the second century B.C.E. imitations were made and shipped to foreign markets by potters working in Asia Minor, Cyprus, Phoenicia, and North Africa. These imports made up about 5 percent of the entire ceramic production and, because they are found in almost every site of this period, were probably bought by rich and poor customers alike.

Implications for Jesus Research

The Gospels, including the Gospel of Thomas, mention or have Jesus mention the names of various clay objects used in everyday life: bowls, cups, dishes, plates, jars, and ovens. The jars are not storage jars but water jars and a jar to hold meal. (For the precious alabaster jar containing expensive ointment, *see* STONE, STONING and OINTMENTS, PERFUMES). Under JERUSALEM, POOL OF SILOAM, it is noted that the man carrying a jar of water (Mark 14:13; Luke 22:10) could have been an Essene, be-

| Storage jars | Jugs | Pots | Flasks | Juglets | Cups | Bowls and Plates | Lamps |

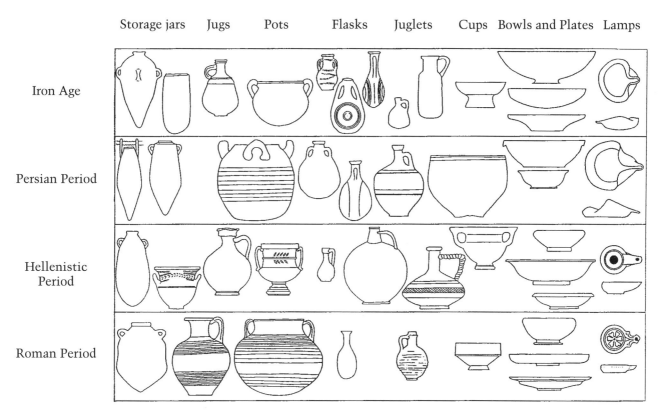

Figure 55 Pottery. Evolution of types in Israel from the Iron Age (Solomon, David) to the Roman Period. Notice the changes in lamp shapes.

cause he was doing a task normally performed by women and because the traditional site of the Upper Room is close to the ancient Essene quarters. The cup of the Last Supper may have been a cup or drinking bowl made of glass.

References to cups, dishes, and plates are found in Matthew 23:25-26, Mark 7:4, Luke 11:39-41, and the Gospel of Thomas 89 in connection with the Pharisees (or Scribes and Pharisees). The pericope Matthew 23:25-26 was given a *gray* rating by the Jesus Seminar in 1987 as well as its parallel in Luke although it is supported by the comments of Mark 7:4. The shorter form of Gospel of Thomas 89 received a *pink* rating. Gospel of Thomas 89 refers only to the material washing of the outside, while Matthew and Luke use the action in a metaphor,

the cup being the individual and the inside "greed and self-indulgence" (Matthew) or "greed and wickedness" (Luke). The genre of Near Eastern story telling in general, and the spirit and rhetoric of Jesus in particular, make it likely that in this instance he used the image of the physical act to convey an ethical or spiritual message. This issue raises the question of the authenticity of the entire twenty-third chapter of Matthew, which is often contested on the ground that the Pharisees are under severe attack. The rational of the critics is that the First Gospel was written at a time, supposedly after the Council of Jamnia, when the Pharisees and the Church of Matthew were at odds. This opinion is reflected in the ratings given by the Jesus Seminar to eighteen sayings of Jesus taken from the twenty-third chapter: 11 are *black*, 6 *gray*, and only one *pink*. The only *pink* rating is given to a saying titled "scholar privileges" (Crossan says "honors and salutations," Matt. 23:5-7):

> "They do all their deeds only to be seen by the people for they make their phylacteries broad and their fringes large; they love the place of honor at feasts, the highest seats in the synagogues, and salutations in the marketplaces and being called rabbis."

In Jesus' time the school of Shammai dominated (Hillel died ca. 10-20 C.E.) and the title "rabban" was reserved for its leader; it is uncertain whether the title "rabbi" was already given to individual teachers. Only later were they allowed to make pronouncements in their own names (Falk, 124 n. 22). Nevertheless, this fact should not invalidate the whole saying but only its last phrase.

The Pharisees of Bet Shammai were seemingly very powerful in the time of Jesus. Their spiritual ancestors had been supported by the Hasmonean rulers, especially Queen Salome Alexandra, and they had a large representation in the Sanhedrin. Even Herod who had put forty-five Sadducees to death in 37 B.C.E. spared the Pharisees because of their influence on the people. At the end of his reign, two of them, Matthias and Judas, conspired against him and provoked the incident of the golden roman eagle (*Antiq.* 17, 6, 2–4/151–67). Only then did the dying Herod dare to have the two burnt alive. In the New Testament, the influence of the Pharisees is implicitly stated in Acts 5:33–40 and 23: 6–10. In Matthew 23: 2–3, Jesus recognizes the authority of the Pharisees who sit on Moses' seat, and he enjoins his disciples and the crowds to observe and practice what they teach. That the Pharisees were leaders of the people in Jesus' time is further explicated by Josephus: "The populace gladly responded" to the call of Saddok the Pharisee and Judas the Galilean when they opposed Quirinius's decision to take a census and exact tribute in 6 C.E. (*Antiq.* 18, 1.1, 6/1–11, 23–25). In another instance, the Pharisees urged the people not to revolt against Rome at the beginning of the First Jewish Revolt (*War* 2, 17.3/411–12). Thus it is possible that Jesus could have had clashes with the Pharisees of the extremist Bet Shammai, while he probably had some affinity with the more humane Bet Hillel (Falk, 111–47). It is symptomatic that in Matthew 23 Jesus addresses scribes and Pharisees as a class, those who professed to interpret the Torah and develop the Oral Law. On these grounds it may be argued that the core of Matthew chapter 23 is authentic. The pericope Matthew 23: 29–36 may refer to the murder of some adepts of Hillel by the Shammaites in 20–10 B.C.E. (Falk, 124), but verse 34, a *post eventum*[*] prediction, and segment 35a, the curse, which may reflect a late first-century C.E. condemnation of Bet Shammai as preserved in the Jerusalem Talmud, *Berakhot* 1: 4 (Falk, 125), are probably not authentic.

BIBLIOGRAPHY

Albright, W. F. *Archaeology of Palestine*. Baltimore: Penguin, 1960.

Amiram, R. *Ancient Pottery of the Holy Land*. Jerusalem: Massada Press, 1969.

Blakely, J. A., and W. J. Bennett. *The Pottery of Palestine: Neolithic to Modern*. Winona Lake, Ind.: Eisenbrauns, 1994.

Engles, A. "3000 Years of Glassmaking." *Readings in Glass History* 1. Jerusalem: Phoenix Publications, 1973.

———. "Glassmaking in Ancient Jerusalem." *Readings in Glass History* 18. Jerusalem: Phoenix Publications, 1984.

Falk, H. *Jesus the Pharisee*. New York, Mahwah, N.J.: Paulist Press, 1985.

Forbes, R. J. "Glass." *Studies in Ancient Technology*. Vol. 5. Leiden: E. J. Brill, 1957.

Kelso, J. L. *Ceramic Vocabulary of the Old Testament*. New Haven: ASOR, 1948.

Kurinsky, S. *The Glassmakers: An Odyssey of the Jews*. New York: Hippocrene Books, 1991.

Michel, A. and J. LeMoyne. "Pharisiens." *Dictionnaire de la Bible*, 1964.

Lapp, N. "Pottery." *ABD* 5:428–44.

Lapp, P. W. *Palestinian Ceramic Chronology*, 200 B.C.–A.D. 70. New Haven: ASOR, 1961.

Neusner, J. *The Rabbinic Traditions about the Pharisees before 70*. Leiden: E. J. Brill, 1971.

Rivkin, E. "The Internal City." *Journal for the Scientific Study of Religion* 5 (1966): 225–40.

Wood, B. G. "Potter's Wheel." *ABD* 5:427–8.

Qumran

Importance

The Qumran community existed in the time of Jesus, and both John the Baptist and Jesus may have been connected with it.

Scripture References

Matt. 4:1, 11; Mark 1:12-13; 16:5; Luke 4:1; John 20:12; Acts 1:10.

General Information

Khirbet Qumran is located on the west side of the Dead Sea, above the left bank of Wadi Qumran, some 1,200 feet below sea level. Only since the Dead Sea Scrolls were found in the area has the site itself attracted attention. It was first excavated in 1951 and then from 1953 to 1956 under the direction of Father R. de Vaux, director of the Ecole Biblique et Archéologique Francaise of Jerusalem. De Vaux left his work at Tell el Far'ah (biblical Tirzah) to concentrate his efforts on Qumran. The excavations revealed the remains of a well-planned complex of buildings, cisterns, pools, canals, and ritual baths. These structures were build on a flat terrace of marl (a mixture of clay and lime). The entrance was on the north side through a large enclosure which incorporated the remains of an earlier building dating from the eighth to sixth centuries B.C.E. A three-story square tower protected the entrance.

The area around Khirbet Qumran is scorched and dry; but one-and-a-half miles to the south is the spring of Ain Feshkah. Its abundant waters allow for the irrigation of a large area. In 1958, de Vaux excavated a building there, which he dated to the same period as those of Khirbet Qumran. He concluded that the ruins of Ain Feshkah were on agricultural land used by the Qumranites to grow their own food. Nearby were found the ruins of several tanks and canals, which have been interpreted as part of a tannery where the sectaries prepared the parchment needed for their scrolls.

The oldest occupation level at Qumran dates to the Iron II period and is represented by the remains of a fortress. The next occupation level dates to the time of the Hasmonean ruler John Hyrcanus I (135–104 B.C.E.), when the Qumranites probably settled in this location. Most buildings of this level were badly damaged; they are dated by coins found in the destruction debris. In this period the settlement, including its complex water system, reached its final size and shape. It was destroyed by an earthquake and a fire in 31 B.C.E. (Josephus, *Antiq.* 14, 5.2/121; *War* 1, 9.1/370). The last period of Jewish occupation began during the time of Archelaus in or shortly after 4 B.C.E. The settlement was rebuilt according to the same ground plan as that of the previous period. In the summer of 68 C.E., during the First Jewish War, the Romans razed the complex and it was never rebuilt. The Romans occupied the site until circa 90 C.E. Judging by Bar Kokhba coins discovered in the uppermost level, it was used by the rebels during the Bar Kokhba War of 132–135.

Archaeological Data

The excavations of Qumran revealed six main periods or levels of occupation:

1. *Israelite period.* This level was not given a number in the archaeologist's listing of strata. All that remains is a fortress, dating from the eighth century to the sixth century B.C.E.

2. *Level 1a.* This level of occupation, of which little has survived, is dated to the middle of the second century B.C.E.

3. *Level 1b.* This is the main level of occupation, dated to the first half of the first century B.C.E. (*see* fig. 56). Most of the buildings at Qumran were build during this period.

Figure 56 Qumran. An artist rendering of the settlement. 1: Aqueduct entrance; 2: Ancient cistern; 3: Reservoirs and miqvaot; 4: Tower; 5: Scriptorium; 6: Kitchen; 7: Assembly hall and refectory; 8: Pantry; 9: Potters' workshop; 10: Kilns; 11: Stables. *(After R. de Vaux, Ecole Biblique et Archeologique, Jerusalem.)* Because of its layout and thin walls, the complex could not have been a fortress.

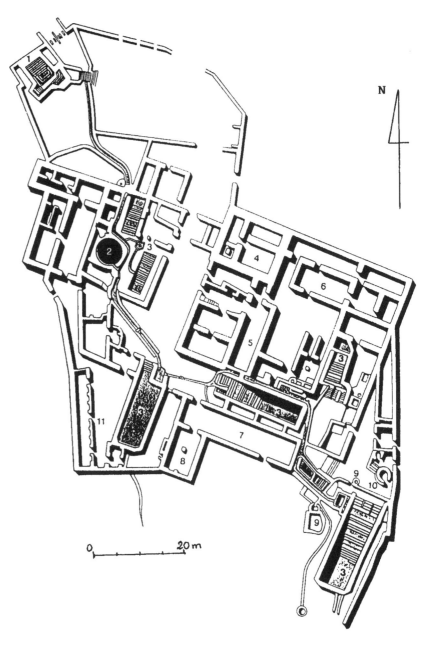

Among the most important are the refectory and the scriptorium. This level was destroyed by an earthquake in 31 B.C.E.

4. *Level 2.* Very soon after the end of level 1b, the inhabitants rebuilt the settlement along much the same lines as the previous one.

5. *Level 3.* This level was occupied by a Roman garrison after 68 C.E. Most of the buildings were in ruins during this period.

6. *Bar Kokhba War.* A few remains dating from this period were found.

South of the tower at the entrance were a number of rooms, among them potters' shops, kiln rooms, a refectory, laundry rooms, a scriptorium, and a meeting hall. An elaborate water system included a dam on the wadi, a channel hewn in rock, other channels lined with stones, cisterns, pools, and ritual baths. Various aspects of the community's life can be interpreted from the finds. Near the large hall was a smaller room used to store kitchen and tableware; more than 1,000 vessels, including 210 plates, 708 bowls, and 75 goblets, were found. In the hall were stands for jars; the hall was probably a refectory and an assembly room. No sleeping accommodations were found, but traces of occupation contemporaneous with the settlement were discovered in neighboring caves. Except for watchmen and vigils, the sectaries perhaps slept in the nearby caves or in tents on the plateau next to the buildings.

The remains of tables, benches, writing pallets, and inkpots suggest a scriptorium in which documents were written, edited, and copied. The inkpots were made of clay or bronze, and one of them contained dried ink. These artifacts, together with the existence of potters' shops and kilns, have been interpreted as evidence that the sectaries wrote or copied all or part of the scrolls hidden in jars found in the nearby caves. The jars must have been placed in the caves shortly before Vespasian attacked and razed the settlement in 68 C.E.

A cemetery containing some 1,100 tombs marked by stone heaps neatly aligned in rows existed near the settlement and, remarkably, east of the camp despite the existence of a large, level area to the west. The cemetery's location was perhaps determined by consideration of defilement from graves located windward, in accordance with information in the Temple Scroll (11QTemple 46:16-17), which prescribed the isolation of lepers and gonorrheans to the east (see JERUSALEM, TOMBS and GOLGOTHA, TRADITIONAL SITE). The skeletons were lying on their backs, heads to the south, at depths varying from 2 to 7 feet. All belonged to males; but in a side area were skeletons belonging to a few women and one child, perhaps members of servant families or families of covenanters who were married before entering the community.

Implications for Jesus Research

The discovery of the Dead Sea Scrolls and the subsequent excavations of Qumran have provided materials that shed light on Josephus, Philo, and Pliny. Archaeology alone cannot determine who the people were who settled at Qumran. It does indicate that the Qumran settlement was founded in the middle of the second century B.C.E. and that it continued with short gaps for almost two hundred years until 68 C.E. The archaeological remains suggest that settlers lived communally, rejecting whatever seemed to be Hellenistic culture. Not a single Hellenistic piece of architecture or pottery was discovered there. The identity of the sectaries is a matter of some scholarly controversy. Presumably, the study of historical and scriptural documents and of their own writings should help to establish who they were.

Their beliefs and ways of life illuminate the religious and national aspirations of at least one sectarian group, especially with regard to eschatology, from the time of Jesus. It is possible that John the Baptist and Jesus were connected with the sect, at least at some point in their lives (see DEAD SEA SCROLLS).

Two new suggestions, not yet published at the time of this writing, regarding the occupation of Qumran have been made. J. B. Humbert, Chief Archaeologist of the Ecole Biblique in Jerusalem, proposes that the settlement was Hasmonean until Pompey's conquest of Palestine (63 B.C.E.) or until the time of the war between Herod and Antigonus II (40–37 B.C.E.). According to Humbert, the Essene occupation had two phases: the first involved the continuation of Temple practices, with animal sacrifices and the construction of a Holy of Holies, whereas in the second (toward the end of the first century B.C.E.) Temple imagery was taken in a more symbolic sense and applied to the membership of the community. The "scriptorium" would date from this later phase.

A. Drori, Director of the Israeli Department of Antiquities, and Y. Magen, Archaeological Officer for Samaria and Judea, suggest that Qumran was first developed as a Hasmonean farmstead at the time when the palace of Jericho was built (*see* JERICHO). They contend that only a powerful ruler would have the resources available to build such an elaborate complex. One factor leading to this statement is the discovery of masses of buried burnt dates crushed for the production of artificial honey. Drori and Magen suggest that Herod offered the site to the Essenes, who restored it. This would explain the presence of the remains of a few women and children apart from the main burial ground there, in a celibate community.

Evidence currently available is not sufficient to enable a definitive conclusion regarding these new views.

BIBLIOGRAPHY

Callaway, P. R. "Qumran Origins: From the Doresh to the Moreh." *Revue de Qumran* 14 (1990): 637–50.

Charlesworth, James H., ed. *Jesus and the Dead Sea Scrolls*. New York: Doubleday, 1992.

Crossan, J. D. *Sayings Parallels*. Philadelphia: Fortress Press, 1986.

Davies, P. R. "How Not to Do Archaeology: The Story of Qumran." *BA* 51 (1988): 203–7.

———. *Qumran*. Cities of the Biblical World, Guildford, 1982.

de Vaux, R. "Rapports préliminaires sur les fouilles de Khirbet Qumran." *Revue Biblique* 60 (1953): 83–106; 61 (1954): 206–36; 63 (1956): 533–76; 66 (1959): 87–110, 225–54.

———. "Une hachette essenniéne?" *Vetus Testamentum* 9 (1959): 399–407.

———. *Archaeology and the Dead Sea Scrolls*. Schweich Lectures 1959. London: 1973.

———. "Qumran." *NEAEHL*.

Goranson, S. "Qumran, a Hub of Scribal Activity?" *BAR* 20.5, 37.39.

Laperrouzas, E. M. "Qumran. Archéologie du Khirbet Qumran et de la région." *Dictionnaire de la Bible*, 1979.

Murphy-O'Connor, J. "Qumran, Khirbet." *ABD* 5:590–94.

Schiffman, L. H. "Qumran." *BA* 53 (1990): 64–73.

Vermes, G. *The Dead Sea Scrolls: Qumran in Perspective.* Philadelphia: Fortress Press, 1977.

Ritual Baths (*miqvaoth*)

Importance

Knowledge of the existence and purpose of *miqvaoth* in Jesus' time may help to understand his baptism.

Scripture References

Matt. 3:1, 6, 7, 11, 13, 14, 16; 11:12-13; 14:2, 8; 17:13; 21:25; Mark 1:4, 5, 8-9; 6:14, 25; 8:28; 10:38-39; 11:30; 16:16; Luke 3:3, 12, 16, 21; 7:20, 29-30, 33; 9:19; 12:50; 20:4; John 1:26, 33; 3:22-23; 4:1-2; 10:40.

General Information

Baptism is a rite of physical cleansing by water symbolizing a religious or spiritual renewal. The name derives from the Greek verb *bapto*, "to dip", or "to immerse." Thus, the original meaning is one of immersion. Ritual bathing is not peculiar to Judaism or Christianity; similar rites can be observed in many religions, past and present, across geographical and cultural boundaries, from the Babylonian purification ritual of the cult of Enki, to the Eleusis mystery and today's Hindu immersions in the Ganges. The origins of Christian baptism, however, are found in Judaism. Jewish practices are rooted in ancient Israelite notions of purity, for which J. Milgrom's magisterial commentaries on Leviticus 1–16 and Numbers are an excellent resource. Here we will limit ourselves to a brief introduction to the scriptural notions of purity and then to the Talmudic background of baptism.

The Israelite tradition of purification by water could take different forms: washing of hands (Deut. 21:60; Ps. 73:13), sprinkling (Num. 8:7; Ezek. 36:25), and immersion. John's baptism can be seen only as immersion because of its similarity to ritual bathing of his time (as at Qumran) and because he chose sites with an abundance of water: the Jordan River and Salim near Aenon (John 3:23; *see* AENON AND SALIM). In any case, baptism belongs to the general biblical conceptualization and structure of cleanness and uncleanness. In looking at the following references to biblical instruction about purity, however, it must be remembered that the relationship of these regulations to actual practices is uncertain.

Before looking at specific items dealing with purity, it is important to note that the concept of purity is intrinsically related to holiness. God is the locus of absolute holiness and purity, and humans aspiring to holiness or approaching God's holy earthly dwelling (the Temple) had to attend to the purity of their own bodies as well as to materials with which they had contact (clothing, ritual items). Although in an ideal sense the concept of holiness in parts of the Hebrew Bible involved making all mundane or profane matters holy and pure, the reality was that there was for the most part a sense of separation between the holy and the profane and that crossing the boundary between the two involved purification so as not to contaminate or endanger the sanctity of the holy realm (*see* TEMPLE, SACRIFICIAL SYSTEM).

The priestly texts of the Pentateuch thus have precise and elaborate instructions for maintaining the holiness=purity of the sacred precincts of the Temple, and to lesser degrees, its environs in Jerusalem and in the whole land. Priests and Levites had to wash their clothes, hands, feet, or whole bodies before performing certain duties and always before approaching the altar (Exod. 30:20; Lev. 8:6; Num. 8:21). All Israelites could suffer many forms of uncleanness and were enjoined to undergo various processes of purification. Handling cleansing agents could cause uncleanliness, in which case clothes and bodies were to be washed (Lev. 16:26-28; Num. 19:6-10, 19-21; Milgrom, *Numbers*, 438–43).

Several detergents could reduce uncleanness (not to be confused with uncleanliness or physical dirtiness). Among them were blood (considered the most powerful), fire, water (used most frequently), water mixed with ashes of the Red Heifer, and others. In postbiblical times the practice of priestly cleansing was extended to the observant laity. Certain sects, like the Qumranites, observed even stricter rules. Those who followed John the Baptist submitted to a onetime initiation rite similar to the rabbinic ritual bathing of proselytes.

Although the cleansing of the whole body by immersion became important in postbiblical Judaism, there is only one instance in the Hebrew Bible of immersion, apart from any other rite, for cleansing and healing: the cure of the Syrian general Naaman, who bathed seven times in the Jordan upon the command of Elisha (2 Kings 5:9-14). Only in Josephus and in the Qumran literature is the practice of ritual bathing well documented. Josephus himself bathed day and night "for the sake of purity" during the three years that he was a follower of Bannus (*Life* 11–12).

There is abundant archaeological evidence that ritual bathing was a common practice in the first century C.E. and rules for the building of a *miqveh* appear in the Mishnah. Mishnah *miqvaoth* specifies the requirements for the construction and use of a ritual bath: it should be deep enough to allow for complete immersion, large enough to contain at least forty units of capacity called *seah* (modern equivalent unknown, perhaps a total of 200 gallons), and must be filled with running or rain water. These minimal requirements were later commented upon and expanded in rabbinic literature.

Archaeological Data

Scores of ritual baths dating from the first century B.C.E. to the second century C.E. have been excavated in Israel. Most of them comply with the recorded traditions of the Talmudic sages. By comparing archaeological evidence with the preserved tradition we may reconstruct the methods and requirements of ritual bathing in the time of Jesus. *Miqvaoth* from the time of Jesus, or slightly earlier or later, would include:

Steps of a miqueh *at* Qumran

- First century B.C.E.: Herodian Jericho.
- First century B.C.E. to first century C.E.: Arbela, Gamla, Herodium, Cypros, Machaerus, Magdala, Tiberias, Qumran.
- First century B.C.E. to second century C.E.: Masada; Herodian Quarter, Jerusalem; Ophel, Jerusalem; Essene Quarter, Jerusalem; Sepphoris.

These baths have been recognized as *miqvaoth* for three reasons: a) they are close to the Temple or a synagogue, b) they are in an Essene "camp" and met the rabbinic requirements, or c) they are in a domestic context and met all or most of the requirements. These *miqvaoth* usually are rectangular tanks, hewn in rock or dug in the ground, with stone walls; in the average, they measure 6 x 9 feet, although some may be much larger. They are lined with plaster to prevent the water from seeping into the ground or rock. The tank is about 5 to 8 feet deep, and the bottom is accessible by 4 to 8 steps although the halakhic* requirement came to be at least 6 steps. The level of the water was at least 4 feet above the bottom, which would allow complete immersion by crouching.

Nearly one hundred private *miqvaoth* in residential houses dating from the Herodian–Early Roman period were found in the excavations south of the Temple Mount in Jerusalem. According to the rules of the halakhah,* ritual bath water should be rain water or running water continuously flowing from a spring or a river. Due to the scarcity of such water in most areas, a reservoir of at least 40 *seah* was built next to the *miqveh* to hold rain water. It was called the *'otzar,* "treasury." In the case of the houses in the Temple area, the treasury was connected with the *miqveh* by a pipe 1.5 inches in diameter. To make things easier, rain water could be mixed with drawn water. Thus, when the *miqveh* had to be emptied and cleaned, it was refilled with cistern or well water, and afterward water from the treasury was added. The plaster on the walls, steps, and floors of the *miqveh* and treasury was a mixture of lime, sand, and olive oil.

Some *miqvaoth* at Qumran, and also at Jerusalem, had their stairs divided in two sections by a low partition wall. Presumably one side was used to enter the tank while in a state of impurity, and the other to climb out purified. *Miqvaoth* of this type were found in the Temple area and in the Essene quarter. In the palatial mansion of the Herodian quarter, excavated by N. Avigad, one *miqveh* was 13 x 16.5 feet, with 8 steps running along the whole length of one of the smaller sides. It was served by two doorways, one to enter and one to go out so that the exiting purified person would be separated from an entering unclean one.

The "luxury" *miqveh* of Masada (others included a much simpler one near the small synagogue) was built in accordance with the later halakhic sources. An open channel led rain water to the treasury communicating with the bath tank by an underground pipe. In order to enter the tank, the bather had to step first in a footbath. Not everyone followed the requirements regarding rain or running water. In the rich Herodian quarter of Jerusalem, for instance, many *miqvaoth* had no visible connection with a treasury near or far. Perhaps portable pipes were connected with the roof when it rained. Another suggestion is that the owners of these houses, probably members of Sadducean families, had their own tradition regarding *miqveh* use. In the Hasmonean palace of Jericho there were six *miqvaoth* receiving running water from the wadi Qelt; this large number is related to the fact that the Hasmoneans were priests.

Implications for Jesus Research

It is probable that Jesus and the disciples used the *miqveh* south of the Temple before entering through the Huldah gates (*see* JERUSALEM, CITY OF DAVID and JERUSALEM, OPHEL).

There is little doubt that in the time of John the Baptist ritual cleansing was done by complete immersion of the body and hair. It is only later that Christianity, emphasizing the symbolic character of physical cleansing, accepted that pouring water over the head satisfied the requirements for baptism (Didache 7). The person immersed had to be completely undressed, and someone would observe the immersion to verify that the body, including the hair, was completely covered with water. Because he baptized either in the Jordan or where there was plenty of water, John must have practiced full immersion, perhaps reflecting a Qumranite background (*see* DEAD SEA SCROLLS). John did not baptize as we understand it today; rather he was calling people to bathe and, at the most, verified that the immersion was complete.

Luke's portrayal of Mary as a pious woman subject to the law of *niddah* suggests that she bathed in a *miqveh* in Nazareth. According to Luke 2:22, she observed Lev. 12:2-8 regarding the purification of a woman after childbirth. Luke wrongly associates Joseph with Mary in her rite of purification by using the plural form, "their purification."

BIBLIOGRAPHY

Ben Dov, M. *In the Shadow of the Temple*. Jerusalem: Keter Publishing House, 1982 (Hebrew); 1985 [English].

Hartman, L. "Baptism." *ABD* 1:583–94.

Hübner, H. "Unclean and Clean (NT)." *A.D* 6:741–45.

La Sor, W. S. "Discovering What Jewish Miqvaot Can Tell Us about Christian Baptism." *BAR* 13 (1987): 58.

Mackowski, R. M. *Jerusalem, City of Jesus*. Grand Rapids: Eerdmans, 1980.

McRay, J. *Archaeology and the New Testament*. Grand Rapids: Baker Book House, 1991.

Milgrom, J. *Leviticus 1–16*. Anchor Bible. New York: Doubleday, 1991.

———. Numbers. The JPS Torah Commentary. New York: Jewish Publication Society, 1990.

Millard, A. *Discoveries from the Time of Jesus*. Oxford, England: Lion Publishing, 1990.

Netzer, E. "Ritual Baths during the Second Temple in Jericho." *Qadmoniot* 11 (1978): 54–59 (Hebrew).

Reich, R. "Miqva'ot (Jewish Ritual Immersion Baths) in Eretz Israel." Ph.D. diss., Hebrew University, Jerusalem, 1990 (Hebrew).

Rousseau, J. J. *Quick Notes on Miqvaoth*. Jesus Seminar Papers, February, 1992. Sonoma, Calif.: Polebridge Press, 1992.

Sanders, E. P. *Jewish Law from Jesus to the Mishnah*. Philadelphia: Trinity Press International, 1990.

Webb, R. L. *John as Baptizer: His Activity of Immersing in the Context of First-Century Judaism.* Jesus Seminar Papers, February, 1992. Sonoma, Calif.: Polebridge Press, 1992.

Wright, D. P. "Holiness (OT)." *ABD* 3:237–49.

———. "Unclean and Clean (OT)." *ABD* 6:729–41.

Samaria, Samaritans

Importance

Jesus referred to or addressed Samaritans in a manner that could have been seen as subversive by most of his Jewish contemporaries.

Scripture References

Matt. 10:5; Luke 9:52; 10:33, 37; 17:11, 16; John 4:4-40; 8:48; Acts 1:8; 8:1-14, 25; 9:31; 15:3; G. Thom. 60.

General Information

The territory known as Samaria received its name after Omri, king of the northern kingdom of Israel, transferred his capital from Tirzah (site of Tell el Farah) to a new property he bought in circa 870 B.C.E. for two talents (about 150 pounds) of silver (1 Kings 16:24) from a man named Shemer. The boundaries of the territory changed according to the political situation, but they consistently approximated that of the land attributed to the tribe of Ephraim and the half tribe of Manasseh west of the Jordan River (Josh. 16:5-10; 17:7-13). It extended about forty miles north-south, between a parallel a few miles north of Jericho to the southern part of the Plain of Jezreel or Esdraelon and about fifty miles east-west from the Jordan to the Mediterranean (*see* fig. 57).

After the fall of the northern kingdom to the Assyrians in 722/721 B.C.E., some thirty thousand Israelites (27,290 according to Sargon's Annals 11–17) were deported and scattered over the Assyrian Empire. The territory was partly repopulated with captives from Babylon, Cutha (thus the name Cutheans given by the Jews to the Samaritans), Avva, Hamath, and Sepharvaim (2 Kings 17:24). In 612 B.C.E., Samaria became a Babylonian province to which Judea was added after the fall of Jerusalem in 586 B.C.E. When Babylon was conquered by the Persians in 539 B.C.E., the territory became a satrapy* of the new empire. Judean exiles were allowed to return to their country. In 445 B.C.E., Artaxerxes sent Nehemiah, a Jewish notable from Babylon, as governor of Judea. He began to rebuild Jerusalem's walls; but Sanballat, satrap of Samaria and other officials opposed Nehemiah's projects (Ezra 4:4-24; Neh. 2:9-20; 4:1-9; 6:1-14). This may have been the beginning of the Jewish-Samaritan schism, although the Samaritans date it back to the time of Eli, when he established an "apostatic" sanctuary at Shiloh (1 Sam. 1:9). In 128 B.C.E., the Hasmonean John Hyrcanus took the cities of Samaria and Shechem, perhaps in the same year that he destroyed the Samaritan temple on Mount Gerizim (*see* MOUNT GERIZIM). He annexed the territory to the Jewish state in 111 B.C.E. When the Romans took control of Palestine in 63 B.C.E., the territory was placed under the authority of the governor of Syria. Herod the Great became king of Samaria, Judea, Idumea, and other territories in 37 B.C.E.; but his son Archelaus was deposed in 6 C.E. and from that time on the three territories were ruled as one entity by Roman prefects except for a brief period under King Agrippa I (41–44 C.E.).

The city of Samaria itself had a tumultuous history. It was built on a hill some 42 miles north of Jerusalem and about 25 miles west of the Jordan, halfway between the river and the Mediterranean coast. The hill stands at the western end of a ridge and is surrounded on the other sides by fertile valleys. It overlooks the main road connecting Jerusalem with Galilee, Phoenicia, and Damascus. It was easily defensible; its Iron Age fortification system was so strong that the city withstood attempts to capture it, as reported in 2 Kings 6:24—7:5. When the Assyrians besieged it, it took them three years before they finally captured the city (2 Kings 17:5-6) in circa 721 B.C.E.

After the death of Alexander the Great, the city passed under Ptolemaic and then Seleucid rule un-

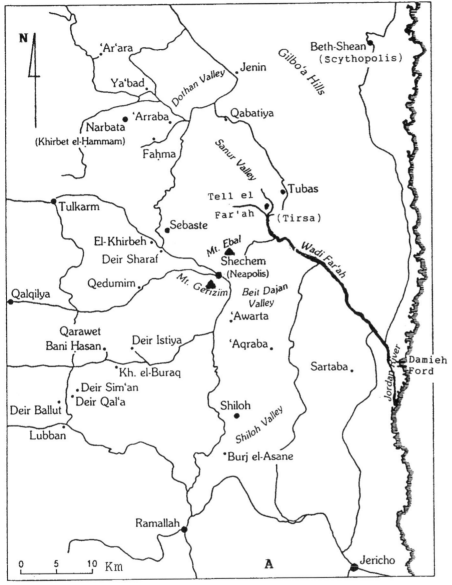

Figure 57 Samaria. (Sebaste) The region in the Roman period.

til John Hyrcanus conquered it. Herod the Great included it in his building program, probably because it had supported him in his war against Antigonus (Josephus, *Antiq.* 14, 15.3/408). In 30 B.C.E., he began major construction work and renamed the city Sebaste, from the Greek *Sebastos*, meaning Augustus, in honor of the emperor who had made him

King. The name is still preserved in Sebastiyeh, an Arab village a short distance from the ancient city. The most impressive building was a large temple, set on a platform fourteen feet high and reached by monumental stairs. Herod enclosed the city with a new fortification wall more than two miles long and strengthened by numerous towers. This

Figure 58 Samaria. (Sebaste) The temple of Augustus, Herodian period.

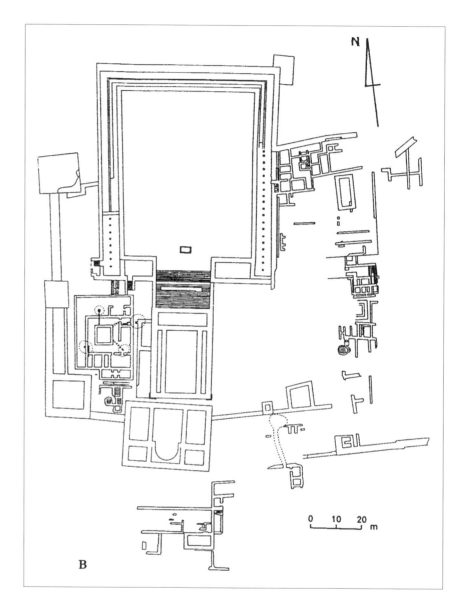

B

Sebaste was the Samaria of Jesus' and apostolic times (*see* fig. 58).

Hostility between Jews and Samaritans manifested itself in many ways over a period of several centuries. During the high priesthood of Onias, at the beginning of Seleucid rule, the Samaritans raided Judea, laid the land waste, and took Jews into slavery (*Antiq.* 12, 4.1/156). Although they were circumcised, John Hyrcanus treated the Samaritans with the same cruelty he showed toward the inhabitants of the Hellenistic cities. In return, the Samaritans supported the Seleucid Antiochus VII Sidestes (138–129 B.C.E.), who fought against John Hyrcanus. During the prefectorate of Coponius (6–9 C.E.), at the occasion of the Feast of Unleavened Bread, some Samaritans managed to enter the Temple of Jerusalem and defiled it by scattering human bones throughout the place (*Antiq.* 18, 2.2/29–30). Under Cumanus (48–52 C.E.), some Galilean pilgrims going to Jerusalem through Samaria were slain. In retaliation, the Jewish populace took arms, sacked, and burned villages in Samaria and massacred their inhabitants (*Antiq.* 20, 5.1/118–21; *War* 2, 12.3–4/232–35). It was the custom to send signals from Jerusalem to the Diaspora, along a chain of selected mountain tops, to indicate the correct moment of the beginning of the new moon so that festivals would be celebrated everywhere on the right day (*see* MACHAERUS). This system was said to have been abandoned because of "the malpractice of the Samaritans." Instead, messengers carried the information (Mishnah, *Rosh Hashanah* 1:3; 2:2).

The Samaritans, who are still represented today by a population of about five hundred, recognize only the Pentateuch as Scripture. They acknowledge only Moses as the true representative of God who lived on earth. They claim that Mount Gerizim is the authentic location of the interrupted sacrifice of Isaac and that it is the only holy site chosen by God. They believe in a final judgment when the dead will be raised and receive their reward or punishment. The last day will be ushered by the *taheb*, who is not a messiah but rather the prophet announced in Deut. 18:18. A similar eschatological figure appears in the Qumranite Rule of the Congregation (1QSa 9.2) and in the New Testament (Matt. 11:14; Mark 9:11-13; Acts 7:37, *et passim*).

The Samaritans suffered persecution under Pontius Pilate, and his excessive repression caused his banishment in 36 C.E. (*Antiq.* 18, 4.1–2/85–89). During the First Jewish War the Samaritans assembled on top of Mount Gerizim. Vespasian sent Cerealius, commander of the Fifth Legion, with a detachment of 600 cavalry and 3,000 infantry. Josephus reports that 11,600 Samaritans were slain (*War* 3, 6.32/307–15). Some Samaritans gained fame as magicians. Simon Magus (Acts 8:9-24) may be the same as Simon the Samaritan, founder of a Simonian sect that existed in the second and third

centuries C.E. (Justin Martyr, *First Apology 26; Dialogue with Trypho* 120), who was condemned by Irenaeus as heretic (*Against Heresies* 1.23). Menander, a disciple of Simon, practiced magic in Antioch; he was particularly active in the time of Claudius (41–54 C.E.; *First Apology* 26, 56). Another Samaritan sectarian, Dositheus, appeared after Jesus. He attempted to persuade the Samaritans that he was the prophet announced by Moses (Origen, *Contra Celsum* 1.57; *see* MAGIC, MIRACLES).

Archaeological Information

The first systematic excavations of the hill of Samaria were sponsored by Harvard University from 1908 to 1910. They were directed first by G. Schumacher and then jointly by G. A. Reisner and C. S. Fisher. Another series of campaigns was sponsored from 1931 to 1933 by a consortium of Harvard University, the Hebrew University of Jerusalem, the Palestine Exploration Fund, the British Academy, and the British School of Archaeology of Jerusalem. The work resumed in 1935 with the British Academy and School of Archaeology. Among the leaders of these expeditions were J. W. Crowfoot, G. M. Crowfoot, E. L. Sukenik, and K. Kenyon.

The excavators recovered building remains and artifacts dating from the Early Bronze Age to the Roman period. Among the important discoveries of the Iron Age, when Samaria was capital of the northern kingdom, were more than five hundred pieces of ivory, most of them inlays for wall paneling, furniture, boxes, and objects of toiletry. They may be remnants of Ahab's "house of ivory" (1 Kings 22:39) and of the "beds of ivory" mentioned in Amos 6:4. Another important group of finds from the Iron Age are the Samaria ostraca,* a corpus of sixty-six inscribed potsherds comprising the earliest group of ancient Hebrew writing. These ostraca probably date from the reign of Jereboam II (786–746 B.C.E.). From the Early Roman period, a large temple (70 x 85 meters, about 230 x 279 feet), probably the one built by Herod, was unearthed with its porticoes and altar (*see* fig. 58). A piece of a marble statue of an emperor, probably Augustus, was found in it. In 1965 the Jordanian Department of Antiquities under F. Zayadine conducted excavations at Samaria to improve its attraction for visitors, partly by reopening the ancient theater. J. B. Hennessey of the British School of Archaeology excavated in 1968 in order to determine the sequence and limits of the different quarters of the city in the Iron Age and Hellenistic and Roman periods. Both projects provided new information that supplemented and clarified the results of previous excavations.

In addition to the excavations, a 1962 discovery made by Bedouins, has contributed a great deal to our knowledge about the history of Samaria. In the cave of Mughâret Abu Shinjeh, in the Wadi ed-Daliyeh, about 14 kilometers (9 miles) from Old Jericho or Tell es-Sultan, they found skeletons and papyri. An ensuing excavation revealed that about two hundred citizens of Samaria—men, women and children—had died there. One document contained the name of Sanballat and allowed the excavators to date and reconstruct the events. Between the siege of Tyre and the fall of Gaza in 332 B.C.E., Alexander sent one of his generals, Parmenion, to Jerusalem and Samaria. At that time Sanballat III, governor of Samaria, died and Parmenion appointed Andromachus governor of Samaria-Judea. For the first time since Manasseh had become High Priest of the Samaritans (Ezra 10:30; Neh. 13:28-29) after his marriage to the daughter of Sanballat I, the aristocratic line of Samaritan governors was broken. The Samaritan aristocracy rebelled and burned Andromachus alive. Many of them fled to the cave. Alexander came, banished the Samaritans from the city, and replaced them with Macedonian veterans. Those in the cave were suffocated by fires set at the entrances. Then Alexander met the Jerusalem High Priest, Jaddua, who pledged loyalty. As a result, Alexander annexed three Samaritan districts to Judea: Aphrema, Lydda, and Ramathaim (Josephus, *Antiq.* 11, 8.5/333, 336; Quintus Curtius, *History* 4, 5.8).

Implications for Jesus Research

Sebaste was a beautiful and thriving city in the time of Jesus. It was cosmopolitan in character with a temple dedicated to Augustus, Greek settlers descended from Alexander's veterans, and the descendants of the various peoples relocated by the Assyrians. Descendants of those Israelites who had not been deported in 722 B.C.E. lived in the surrounding countryside.

In relation to Samaria and the Samaritans, Jesus:

- traveled through the territory of Samaria or along its border (Luke 9:52; 17:11; John 4:1-42),
- experienced hostility in a Samaritan village (Luke 9:52),
- used Samaritans as an example to his Jewish contemporaries (Luke 10:33; 17:16, 18),
- assimilated Samaritans to Gentiles or foreigners (Matt. 10:5; Luke 17:18),
- was accused of being a Samaritan (John 4:39-42).

The story of Jesus and the Samaritan woman (John 4:1-42) is generally not considered authentic by New Testament scholars. Yet the core story might be grounded in an actual incident for two reasons: the contentious character of the Samaritans for Jews of Jesus' time; and the absence of a reference to the Samaritan temple, which had been razed about 140 years before. Only a reference to the mountain as a place of worship is made. This last factor also indicates that the author of the Fourth Gospel or his source possessed accurate historical information (*see* MOUNT GERIZIM).

Samaritan religion as it exists today is rooted in that of the ancient Samaritans. This is the case at least for their views regarding the legitimate place for the Temple. In his journeys to Phoenicia, Caesarea Philipi, and the Decapolis, Jesus did not condemn different religions and foreign gods. He had a similar kind disposition toward the Samaritans. Was it because he too had suffered humiliation? (*see* PANTERA'S TOMBSTONE). It may be that his stay at Sychar was the cause for the success of Philip's evangelistic mission in Samaria a few years later (Acts 8:4-8, 25).

BIBLIOGRAPHY

Anderson, R. T. "Samaritans." *ABD* 5:940–47.

Avigad, N. "Samaria (City)." *NEAEHL* 4:1300–10.

Barag, D. "Herod's Royal Castle at Samaria-Sebaste." *Eretz Israel* 23 (1992): 293–301 (Hebrew, English summary).

Crowfoot, J. W. "Recent Discoveries of the Joint Expedition to Samaria." *Palestine Exploration Fund, Quarterly Statement* (1932): 132–33.

———. "Excavations at Samaria, 1931." *Palestine Exploration Fund, Quarterly Statement* (1932): 8–34.

Crowfoot, J. W., K. M. Kenyon, and E. L. Sukenik. *The Buildings of Samaria*. London: Palestine Exploration Fund, 1942.

Crowfoot, J. M. and G. M. Crowfoot. *Early Ivories from Samaria*. London: Palestine Exploration Fund, 1938.

Crowfoot, J. W., G. M. Crowfoot, and K. M. Kenyon. *The Objects from Samaria*. London: Palestine Exploration Fund, 1957.

Crown, A. D., et al. *The Samaritans*. Tübingen: J.C.B. Mohr, 1989.

Hall, B. W. "Samaritan Religion from John Hyrcanus to Baba Rabba." *Studies in Judaica*. Vol. 3. Sydney, Australia: University of Sydney, 1987.

Hennessy, J. B. "Excavations at Samaria-Sebaste." *Levant* 2.1 (1970): 21.

Hovers, E., A. Zertal, I. Finkelstein, S. Dar, and J. Magen. "Samaria (Region)." *NEAEHL* 6:1310–18.

Kenyon, K. M. *Royal Cities of the Old Testament*. New York: Schocken Books, 1971.

Netzer, E. "The Augusteum at Samaria-Sebaste. A New Outlook." *Eretz Israel* 19 (1987): 97–105 (Hebrew, English Summary).

Purvis, J. "Samaria (City)." *ABD* 5:914–21.

Safrai, Z. "The Samaritan Massif. A History of Settlements in the Roman and Byzantine Periods." *Shomron Studies* (1986): 127–81 (Hebrew).

Tadmor, H. "Some Aspects of the History of Samaria during the Biblical Period." *The Jerusalem Cathedra* 3 (1983): 1–11.

Tappy, R. E. *The Archaeology of Israelite Samaria*. Vol. 1. *Early Iron Age through the Ninth Century B.C.E.* Atlanta Ga.: Scholars Press, 1992.

Yeivin, Z. "Archaeological Activities in Samaria," *Eretz Shomron*. The 13th Archaeological Convention, September 1972. Jerusalem: Israel Exploration Society, 1973.

Zayadine, F. "Une Tombe du Fer II à Samarie-Sébasté." *Revue Biblique* (1968): 562–85.

———. "Samaria-Sebaste, Clearance and Excavations (October 1965–June 1967). *Annual of the Department of Antiquities in Jordan* 12–13 (1967–68): 77–86.

Sea of Galilee (*Yam Kinneret*)

Importance

Except for his journey to foreign territories, Samaria, and Judea, most of Jesus' ministry took place along the shores of the Sea of Galilee. The Gospels mention only three places in Galilee more than fifteen miles from the lake: Nazareth, Cana, and Nain.

Scripture References

Matt. 4:15, 18; 8:24, 26, 27; 13:1, 47; 14:25, 26; 17:27; 18:6; 21:21; Mark 1:16; 2:13; 4:1, 39, 41; 5:13; 6:48, 49; 9:42; 11:23; Luke 5:1, 2; 8:22, 23, 33; 17:6; 21:25; John 6:1, 16, 17, 19, 22, 25; 21:1, 7.

General Information

The Sea of Galilee is the largest body of fresh water in Israel. It was known under different names in different historical periods. The most ancient is Chinnereth or Chinneroth (Num. 34:11; Deut. 3:17; Josh. 12:3; 13:27), which was also the name of a fortified city on the northwestern shore of the sea (Josh. 11:2, 19:35), today's Tell 'Oreimeh. Because Chinnereth means "harp" in Hebrew, the lake's name may have been chosen because the Sea of Galilee is shaped like this musical instrument. Alternatively, the name may derive from the city of Kinneret on the northwestern shore.

During the Hellenistic and Roman periods, the lake, the city, and its adjacent plain were known as Gennesareth or Gennesar (1 Macc. 11:67; Matt. 13:34; Mark 6:53; Luke 5:1; *see* GENNESARETH). The Synoptics call it Sea or Lake of Galilee. No distinction is possible between the two terms because both the Hebrew *yam* and the Greek *thalassa* have this double meaning. The Fourth Gospel calls it "Lake of Tiberias" (John 6:1; 21:1) and Pliny indicates that it may also be called Lake of Taricheae, another name for Magdala (*Nat. Hist.* 5, 15.71).

The Sea of Galilee Northward, to Ginosar

The lake covers about 40,000 acres. Its surface is 640 feet below sea level, and it reaches a depth of 150 feet. Today its size is about 21 kilometers (13 miles) long north-south, and 13 kilometers (8 miles) wide in its largest part, east-west. These measurements do not correspond with those indicated by Josephus, who states that the lake was 40 x 140 stadia, i.e., 25.2 x 7.2 km (15.6 x 4.5 miles). If his numbers are correct, the lake was longer and narrower in the first century, as may well be the case, because the northern shoreline is shaped by the buildup of alluvial deposits carried by the Jordan River. This sedimentation, for example, means that the lakeside fisher's village of Bethsaida today is situated nearly 2 kilometers (1.5 miles) away from the shore (*see* BETHSAIDA)

People in antiquity believed that the Jordan River not only poured its water into the Sea of Galilee at the north but actually drove it through the lake without mixing and emerged at the south. This belief, which is recorded in Josephus and in Talmudic sources, may have been held by the inhabitants of Galilee as early as the Hellenistic period.

The wind pattern at the lake deserves comment. Because two large valleys open on the west side (Wadi Hamam and the Beit Netopha Valley), the lake is directly affected by the strong afternoon westerly breezes, especially in the summer. These breezes can come up quickly, and in a few minutes the lake can sometimes turn from a peaceful lagoon into a high sea with waves soaring up over 7 feet, making afternoon sailing extremely hazardous.

During the winter a sudden easterly wind may blow and bring high waves of 6 to 7 feet. The fishers around the lake call it *sharkiyeh*, "easterly wind." The wind is so powerful that many fish are cast onto shore and collected by the inhabitants. A similar phenomenon occurs during the summer after a particularly strong westerly wind. No experienced fisher would dare to sail in such a wind-windstorm, especially when the fish market has been supplied with fish collected from the shores. Fishers, when caught up by the storm, would do whatever is possible to return to safe harbor.

Except for several small plains on its southern, southwestern, and northwestern sides, the lake is mainly surrounded by mountains, leaving only narrow strips of land along the shore. Besides the Jordan River in the north, the lake is fed by a number of streams and underwater springs. Some of the latter give hot sulfuric waters said to have curative effects.

Depending on the amount of snow deposited during the winter on the Hermon Range, the level of the lake may vary up to ten feet. Whatever the level, fish and water fowl always remain abundant. The most productive fishing and hunting area lies at the estuaries of the Jordan, Daliyot, and other streams flowing from the Golan Heights in the region of Bethsaida, "place of fishing" or "place of hunting" (*see* BETHSAIDA). In Jesus' time, fishing had developed into an export business as testified by the very names of Taricheae, "drying and salting," and Migdal Nunya, "tower of fishers" (*see* MAGDALA), and by the discovery of a fisherman's seal at Bethsaida. Commercial sailing was also an important part of the economic life, especially the grain traffic from Hippos' harbor and Tiberias (*see* HIPPOS-SUSITA). This seafaring route was probably a branch of the Via Maris that connected Egypt and Syria. On this route travelers went from Damascus to Hippos and then, crossing the lake, to Tiberias and Ptolemais (Acco), or from Hippos to Sinaberis and to Scythopolis (Beth Shean).

The fertility of the land and the productivity of the lake meant that the region around the Sea of Galilee was a populated one. The population increased in the early first century C.E. when Herod Antipas built Tiberias in 19 C.E. and when Herod Philip developed Bethsaida-Julias a few years later, renaming it in honor of Augustus' wife Livia-Julia (*see* BETHSAIDA). According to Josephus, there were (at least) nine cities around the lake. Going clock-

wise from Tiberias one would find the following towns: Arbel, Taricheae-Magdala or Migdal Nunya, Gennesareth, Capernaum with Chorazin two miles to the north, Bethsaida with Gamla seven miles to the east in the Dalyiot Valley, Hippos-Susita ("a city on a hill"), Hamat Gader four miles southeast of the southern point of the lake, Beit Yerah or Philoteria or Sennabris on the southwestern end, Semakh (the Kefar Tsemkh of the Talmud), and Hammath-Hamman one mile south of Tiberias. The most important Jewish settlements were located north of Tiberias, and this is where Jesus was most active. There is no archaeological evidence of the existence in Jesus' time of a town (Gergesa?) at the location of Kursi where the incident of the demoniac living in a cemetery and the drowning pigs is said to have happened (*see* EXORCISM).

Archaeological Data

Except for Hippos and its harbor, which lies under water a few hundred yards south of En-Gev, many of the cities around the Sea of Galilee have been excavated. The most recent one began in 1987 at Et Tell-Bethsaida and will continue at least until 1996. The most significant finds are synagogues, a boat, and fishing implements dating from the first century C.E. (*see* TIBERIAS, MAGDALA, GENNESARETH, CAPERNAUM, CHORAZIN, BETHSAIDA, GAMLA, DECAPOLIS, HIPPOS, GADARA, BOATS, FISHING, NETS).

Archaeological surveys around the Sea of Galilee have revealed sixteen ancient harbors (*see* fig. 4, p. 23). They are, going clockwise: Kefar Akavia, on the northeastern shore; Kursi; Ein Gofra, and Ein Gev, presumably the anchorage of Hippos (Susita). Near the modern Kibbutz Haon are the remains of a large and massive anchorage, which served probably the town of Gadara. West of this place are the remains of the anchorage of Philoteria. The town of Sennaberis also had a large anchorage. The harbor of Tiberias has not yet been found. Farther north are the harbors of Gennesar, Tabgha, and Capernaum. Between Capernaum and Bethsaida are remains of what may have been a first-century C.E. anchorage.

Implications for Jesus Research

In the time of Jesus, the Sea of Galilee was the most important economic center of northeastern Palestine and was connected by roads with Syria and Mesopotamia through the Via Maris linking Damascus to Ptolemais, Caesarea Maritima, and Joppa. It offered easy access to Phoenicia, Asia Minor, Samaria, Judea, and the rest of the Mediterranean world. It was a rich fishing and agricultural area. Archaeology has revealed many witnesses to a prosperous agrarian, commercial, and industrial life: bones of cows, sheep, and goats in residential areas, eastern *terra sigillata* pottery from Asia Minor, Rhodean wine jars, local pottery, coins from Tyre, fishing implements, anchors, remains of a boat, Greek and Roman pottery and glass, wine presses, olive oil presses, and more.

In looking at the world of Jesus form textual and archaeological data, it appears that he was a fisherman or artisan who became an itinerant healer, exorcist, and preacher. His strongest followers were fishers; he was not afraid to sail across the lake; he did not fear storms on the water as a peasant might have (*see* FISHING, NETS). That the four Gospels contain over seventy-six references to the sea, fishing, and sailing suggests that activities on or around the water were a major part of Jesus' life. Yet the information given in Matthew 13:55 and Mark 6:3 about Joseph and Jesus being artisans or construction workers can not be lightly discarded. Jesus perhaps worked at boat building or repairs (*see* BOATS, FISHING). Before he began his ministry, he may have gone fishing with his friends Peter, Andrew, James, and John, for it is unthinkable that he appeared suddenly with no prior contact in their lives and asked them immediately to leave their families and work. The Gospel narratives mentioning sudden storms on the Sea of Galilee or an unexpected good harvest of fish are told by someone familiar with the lake. The Gospels describe Jesus sharing the life of fishers rather than of peasants. He visited villages but did not stay in them. The question of who Jesus was demands more extensive research, involving all areas of social science and focusing on the years 10 to 30 C.E.

BIBLIOGRAPHY

Dalman, G. *Arbeit und Sitte in Palästina.* Vol. 6. Gütersloh: Bertelsmann, 1939.

Dunkel, F. F. "Die Fischerei am See Genesareth und das Neue Testament." *Biblica* (1924).

Fiensy, D. A. *The Social History of Palestine in the Herodian Period.* Lewiston, N.Y.: E. Mellen, 1991.

Freyne, S. "Galilee, Sea of." *ABD* 2:899–901.

Gophen, M. and I. Gal. *Lake Kinneret.* Tel Aviv, 1992.

Meyers, E. "Galilean Regionalism as a Factor in Historical Reconstruction." *Bulletin of the American Schools of Oriental Research* 221 (1976): 93–101.

Nun, M. *The Sea of Galilee and Its Fishermen in the New Testament.* Ein Gev: Kibbutz Ein Gev, 1989.

Struthers–Malbon, E. "The Jesus of Mark and the Sea of Galilee." *Journal of Biblical Literature* 103 (1984): 363–77.

Sepphoris (Hebrew, *zippori*)

Importance

Sepphoris was the residence of Herod Antipas until 19–20 C.E. Its proximity to Nazareth may shed some light on the socio-historical background of Jesus.

General Information

Sepphoris, identified with Arabic Saffuriyeh, appears for the first time in historical records during the reign of the Hasmonean ruler Alexander Jannaeus. In 103 B.C.E. Ptolemy Latyrus attacked the city (Josephus, *Antiq.* 13, 12.5/335). After the conquest of Palestine by Pompey in 64–63 B.C.E. the city was chosen or perhaps confirmed as the capital of Galilee. When Herod the Great established his kingdom, he took Sepphoris during a snowstorm and showed little mercy to its rebellious citizens (*War* 1, 16.2/304). After his death, another revolt broke out in 4 B.C.E. and Judas, son of the Ezekias who had started the first revolt, attacked the city and looted the royal palace (*Antiq.* 17, 10.5/271–72). Varus, governor of Syria, came with his legions and auxiliary forces to Ptolemais and sent his general Gaius to conquer Galilee. Gaius set fire to Sepphoris and took all of its inhabitants into slavery. Herod's son, Antipas, became tetrarch of Galilee and Perea; he restored, developed, and fortified Sepphoris and made it his principal residence until he built Tiberias in 19–20 C.E. The city did not join in the First Jewish War of 66–70 C.E. After the destruction of the Second Temple, a number of Jews resettled there and Sepphoris became the seat of the exiled Sanhedrin. It remained an important city of the region until the fifth century—a mixed community of Jews, Romans, and Christians, and a center of Jewish religious studies and spiritual life. It was the home of the great rabbi Judah Hanasi known as Judah the Prince, president of the Sanhedrin. The Mishnah was compiled there around 200 C.E. In the fourth century, Joseph, a Jew converted to Christianity, built a church in Sepphoris; in the fifth century the city became an episcopal see. The Jewish Christians of Sepphoris as elsewhere were considered *minim*, "heretics," by the rabbis (*see* CAPERNAUM). According to a certain Christian tradition, Sepphoris was the residence of Anna and Joachim, legendary parents of Mary; a twelfth-century Crusaders Church at the site may commemorate this belief. A more popular tradition locates their residence in Jerusalem, where Mary was supposedly born in a cave (*see* JERUSALEM, POOL OF BETHESDA).

Archaeological Data

The first excavations were conducted in 1931 by L. Waterman on behalf of the University of Michigan. Under the ruins of a Crusaders' fort, partly built with Roman sarcophagi and architectural stones and renovated in the eighteenth century, the excavators found a Roman building. They also excavated a large theater that could have seated some five thousand spectators, remains of an aqueduct, a tunnel, and reservoirs.

In 1975–85, T. Tsuk surveyed the aqueduct of the site and in the 90s conducted extensive excavations of the water system north of the city. The University of South Florida, under the leadership of J. Strange, began an excavation project in 1983, that still continues. Beginning in 1985, E. Meyers and

C. Meyers of Duke University and E. Netzer of the Hebrew University also undertook new excavations that are still underway. The 1987 season yielded a well-preserved colored mosaic floor dating from the second century and representing a Dionysiac scene with a portrait of a beautiful woman crowned with a wreath. This mosaic floor is now visible in its restored villa at the site. It was discovered in a building originally two stories high, which was probably destroyed by the earthquake of 363 C.E. The room of the mosaic is thought to be the triclinium* (dining room) of a large mansion. Other remarkable mosaics, including the floor of a newly-discovered Byzantine period synagogue, were unearthed in the 1991, 1992, and 1993 seasons. Sepphoris had its own mint, and Roman coins were minted there during the reign of Caracalla (198–217 C.E.).

Archaeology indicates a close relationship between Jews and Romans in the Sepphoris area in the third century C.E. because of the proximity of Jewish dwellings to the villa with the Dionysos mosaic. Similarly, a coin of Caracalla refers to a treaty between the local council of the city and the senate of Rome. This closeness may have already existed in the first century, because, as mentioned above, the pacifist citizens of Sepphoris, also called Eirenopolis ("city of Peace") on coins minted in the year 67/68 C.E., refused to join the rebellion of 66 C.E. Nevertheless, thus far relatively few remains can be dated to the time of Jesus with certainty (*see* fig. 59).

Implications for Jesus Research

Several aspects of Sepphoris' history are significant;

- Peaceful cohabitation and even closeness between Jews and Romans in Sepphoris may go back to the first century C.E., perhaps due to the memories of the two previous repressions.

- Nazareth was only 3.5 miles from Sepphoris—a short walk of one hour for the people of the time.

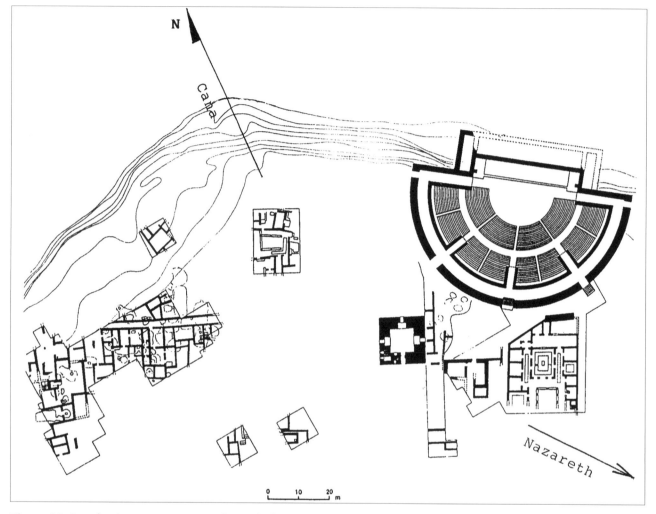

Figure 59 Sepphoris. Excavations at the end of 1992. The theater may date from the first century C.E. and could have been built by Herod Antipas; but the large mansion in the south dates from the third century. Cana is six and a half miles in the north, and Nazareth 3 and a half miles in the southeast.

- Nazareth, where Jews and priestly families settled after the destructions of 70 and 135 C.E., must have been previously known by the new settlers as a pleasant and hospitable place. Some of them may have had family estates there (*see* NAZARETH).

- Nazareth may have been too small a village to provide a livelihood for a *tekton*, "builder," and his family (*see* NAZARETH).

- There were, of necessity, commercial and agricultural dealings between Sepphoris and the neighboring villages, including Nazareth.

Assuming that Jesus was born circa 6 B.C.E., he spent his childhood and at least some of his youth near Sepphoris and may have been influenced by its culture and the contacts emerging from connections of his village to the city. He was about twelve years old at the time of the Quirinius census, which triggered the Judas-Saddok rebellion. There is no record that the people of Sepphoris joined in the revolt, which may indicate that they were on good terms with the Romans.

According to Mark 6:3 and Matthew 13:55, Joseph and his son Jesus were *tekton*, "builders," that is, construction craftsmen skilled in wood and stone work. Because a father normally taught his trade to his oldest son, Jesus would also have been a *tekton*. There is no reason to believe that the term was used figuratively to mean only "man of knowledge." As E. Meyers has suggested, Joseph and Jesus could have worked on the construction projects at Sepphoris and perhaps later at Caesarea Philipi, Tiberias, or Bethsaida-Julias. Construction workers went from place to place, even to foreign countries, where there was work. The information given by Celsus that Jesus was hired as a craftsman in Egypt seems plausible in this respect (Origen, *Contra Celsum* 28, 38).

BIBLIOGRAPHY

Meshorer, Y. "Sepphoris and Rome." *Greek Numismatics and Archaeology: Essays in Honor of Margaret Thompson* Belgium: Cultura Press, 1979: 139–71.

Meyers, C. L. *ASOR Newsletter* 39.2 (1988).

Meyers, E. M., E. Netzer, and C. L. Meyers, *IEJ* 35 (1985): 295–99; 37 (1987): 275–78; 40 (1990): 219–22; in *BA* 49 (1986): 4–19; 50 (1987): 223–31; in *Excavations and Surveys of Israel* (1988–89): 169–73.

———. *Sepphoris*. Winona Lake: Eisenbrauns, 1992.

Miller, S. *Studies in the History and Tradition of Sepphoris*. Leiden: Brill, 1987.

Strange, J. F. Articles in the *IEJ* 32 (1982): 254–55; 34 (1984): 51–52, 269–70, 278–80; 38 (1988): 188–90; in *Excavations and Surveys of Israel* 9 (1989–90): 19–20.

Tsuk, T. Articles in *Excavations and Surveys of Israel* 1 (1982): 105–7; 9 (1989–90): 20.

———. "The Aqueducts of Sepphoris." *The Aqueducts of Ancient Palestine*. Jerusalem: Yad Yitzhak Ben Zvi, 1989: 101-3.

Waterman, L., *et al. Preliminary Report of the University of Michigan Excavations at Sepphoris, Palestine in 1931*. Ann Arbor: University of Michigan Press, 1937.

Weiss, Z. "Sepphoris." *NEAEHL* 4:1324–28. 1993.

Shepherding

Importance

Raising domestic animals was a major economic activity in Palestine; the Hebrew Bible and the New Testament both use a number of images and allegories derived from the shepherd's life.

Scripture References

Matt. 7:15; 9:36; 10:6; 12:11-12; 15:24; 18:12-14; 25:32-33; 26:31; Mark 6:34; 14:27; Luke 2:8, 18, 20; 12:32; 15:3-7; John 2:14-15; 10:1-16, 26-27; 21:15-17.

General Information

Since earliest times animal husbandry was an important part of the subsistence economy of Palestine. Sheep were especially valuable as a source of meat, milk, wool, and skins. In the sacrificial system, sheep were the most common victims. They were required for the *tamid*, "daily sacrifice," and many special offerings (*see* TEMPLE, SACRIFICIAL SYSTEM). Because sheep always need care for their survival, the relationship between shepherd and flock was perceived as symbolic of the relationship between God and the people as expressed in the familiar language of Psalm 23 (23:1-2). In the Roman period there were two types of shepherding activity: that of the nomads living in tents in the Judean Desert—a life-style still surviving in some Bedouin tribes—and that of the settled farmers who continued raising sheep and goats. The sheep of Palestine probably belonged to the Syrian family *Ovis orientalis vignei* or *Ovis laticaudata*, with large tails considered as gourmet pieces.

The goat was also a source of wealth valued for its meat, milk, skin, and hair. The goat of Jesus' time most likely belonged to the Syrian family *Capra hircus mambrica*. It grazed on steep hill slopes, while sheep stayed below; and it could cause erosion by uprooting the plants it ate. Perhaps because of its role in the Yom Kippur, "Day of Atonement" ritual, when the scapegoat, symbolically laden with the sins of Israel, was sent to the satyr-demon Azazel in the desert, the black Palestinian goat became the symbol of evil and was associated with Satan as implied in the final judgment scene of Matthew 25:31-41.

Among nomadic groups the flock owner or members of the family tended the animals. In settled farms either a member of the owner's family or a hired herdsman performed that task. Nonfarmers, merchants, priests, artisans, and others could also own flocks tended by servants or hired workers. Usually there was one shepherd for one hundred animals. By the postbiblical period, hired shepherds had bad reputations, for Talmudic writings list them among despised trades. In the Babylonian Talmud (*b. Sanhedrin* 25b) they occupy fifth position after dice gamblers, usurers, trainers of racing pigeons, and dealers in produce of the sabbatical year (Jeremias, 303). Most shepherds were apparently not as saintly as Rabbi Akiva who, as a youth, tended the sheep of ben Kalha Shaboa, a rich merchant of Jerusalem. The Talmud, reflecting perennial traits, considered them dishonest thieves, leading their flocks to graze on other people's land and pilfering the produce of their animals. Consequently it forbade buying wool, milk, or kids from them (Jeremias, 304–5). A rabbinical saying specified, "For herdsmen, tax collectors and publicans, repentance is hard" (Jeremias, 311). Worst of all, they were accused of bestiality, a sexual perversion condemned by Leviticus 16:23.

Shepherds led their flocks by walking ahead of them, in contrast with butchers who drove them to slaughter. They had individual vocal signals to call their own sheep, and it was effective even if the animals were mixed with other flocks. The sheep recognized and obeyed the voice of their own shepherds. Domesticated sheep could not fend for themselves and had to be led to pasture and water. Shepherds were expected to see that they had food and water; they had to account for the animals in their charge. When a sheep stumbled into a ditch or crevice, the shepherd pulled it out with a crook, or curved staff. If the sheep was injured the shepherd carried it to a safe place across his shoulders, according to the familiar image, and attended to its wounds. In order to protect the flock against thieves and many predators, including wolves, hyenas, jackals, bears, and leopards, shepherds were often armed with a slingshot, a rod or club, and a knife.

Sheep and goats grazed on two kinds of pasture land. During the winter, flocks stayed within a few miles of the villages in daytime. Every night they were brought back to the enclosures of individual farms or put together in a communal fold kept by a guard or doorkeeper (John 10:1-3). In the spring and summer, the flocks were driven to higher pastures, in the mountains of Upper Galilee, Samaria, and Judea. There, shepherds found large caves or built sheepfolds of dry stones to keep out the wild beasts. In that case, they slept at the "door," which was only an opening in the wall without a gate (John 10:7, 9). After the wheat harvest in June, the sheep were allowed to graze in the fields and eat what was left of the harvest and the lower parts of the stalks cut by the harvesters' sickles. In the process they fertilized the soil. Shearing occurred twice a year, at the end of winter and at the end of the summer grazing; as in the case of the harvest, it was a festive occasion (2 Sam. 13:23). Despite the idyllic image of the relationship between shepherd and sheep in popular tradition, the reality is that the animals were raised to be sold, offered as sacrifice, sheared, and eaten.

Shepherding was so much a part of the life of Israel that the word *sheep* and its cognates, *lamb*, *ewe*, and *ram*, appear more than five hundred times in the Bible. In biblical imagery, God, the king, leaders, and in the New Testament, Jesus were allegorized or symbolized as shepherds. The leaders of the people were not always the good "shepherds" they should have been, and many prophets are critical of the corrupt leaders (Ezek. 34, Jer. 23, Zech. 11:4-16). Ezekiel, for example, asserts that God would one day take control, watch personally over the people, and assume the role of the good shepherd (Ezek. 34:11-16). There was also injustice among the sheep, the stronger ones pushing the weaker and eating their feed. So God would "judge between the fat sheep and the lean sheep" (Ezek.

34:17-24). The same imagery is found in the Fourth Gospel (John 10:1-16).

Archaeological Information

U-shaped iron shears have been discovered in excavations. Ancient dry stone enclosures are found in the mountains and are still used, as are caves large enough to shelter many animals. Such a cave, which was subsequently used as a secret Christian place of worship, has been identified near Tekoa, five miles southeast of Bethlehem.

Implications for Jesus Research

While shepherding was an ancient and widespread activity in Palestine, the Gospels contain proportionally far fewer references to sheep and shepherds than to fishing and boats, in which only a small portion of the population was involved (*see* AGRICULTURE, CEREALS; similar observation is made there). Jesus was more familiar with fishermen's life than with peasants' life.

The account of Jesus' birth in Luke, if considered authentic, would indicate that Jesus was born in June, after the wheat harvest when sheep were allowed into the fields to graze (Luke 2:8). The symbolic date of December 25, chosen only in the fourth century, corresponds to the date of the Roman Saturnalia and to the greatest celebration of the cult of Mithra, when the days were lengthening. This date in the month of Chislev was also near the time of the Feast of Dedication which became Hanukkah, the Festival of Lights, after the destruction of the Temple. As in many other instances, the church adopted and reinterpreted feasts and other customs from the religions of the people it converted.

The widespread image of raising sheep and goats provides an argument against the theory that Palestine was plagued by endemic poverty in the time of Jesus (*see* AGRICULTURE, CEREALS).

While many commentators do not make the distinction between mountain and village sheepfolds, the author of the Fourth Gospel knew the difference (John 10:1-3 versus 10:7, 9). He also knew about shepherds and thieves (John 10:1-16). As observed elsewhere in this work, he or his source possessed an accurate knowledge of the country, its people, and their life.

In consideration of the importance of sheep and the familiarity of the people with them, sayings attributed to Jesus in which the words *sheep* and *shepherd* are found may have a higher probability of authenticity. Nevertheless, this should not be a determining factor, if isolated, because the evangelists also were certainly familiar with shepherding and used its vocabulary.

BIBLIOGRAPHY

Beasley-Murray, G. R. *John.* Word Bible Commentary, vol. 36. Waco, Tex.: Word Books, 1987.

Brown, R. E. *The Gospel According to John.* 2 volumes. Garden City, N.Y.: Doubleday, 1966–70.

Bultmann, R. *The Gospel of John, Commentary.* German, 1964. Translated by G. M. Beasley-Murray, et al. Philadelphia: Westminster, 1971.

France, R. T. *Jesus and the Old Testament.* Downers Grove, Ill.: InterVarsity Press, 1972.

Frimage, E. "Zoology." *ABD* 6:1109–67.

Jeremias, J. *Jerusalem in the Time of Jesus.* German 1962. Philadelphia: Fortress Press, 1984.

Slaves and Servants

Importance

Jesus referred to slaves, servants, and hirelings and advocated mutual servanthood among his followers. He understood himself as a servant.

Scripture References

Matt. 3:5; 8:6-9, 13; 10:24-25; 18:23, 26-35; 20:27; 21:34-36; 22:1-13; 23:11; 24:45-51; 25:14-30; 26:51; Mark 1:20; 10:44; 12:2-5; 14:47; Luke 1:54; 2:29; 7:3, 7-8; 12:35-40, 41-48; 14:21; 15:17, 19; 17:7-10; 19:12-24; 20:10-11; John 8:34-36; 10:12-13; 13:16; 15:15, 20; 18:10, 36.

General Information

For millennia, the only form of energy available for human labor was that provided by humans themselves. In the fourth millennium B.C.E. animals began to be domesticated and trained to do the most arduous tasks. Except for sailing it was only in the late first millennium B.C.E. that people learned to harness the power of water and wind to satisfy an increasing demand for energy. The Roman engineer Vitruvius was the first (late first century B.C.E.) to write a treatise on the use of natural power. As technology developed, human labor became more oriented toward the tertiary sector (commerce and services). By the Roman period, human energy was provided by persons of different origin and status: owner and *paterfamilias** and members of their families, slaves, indentured servants, salaried individuals hired for a long period, freed slaves, hirelings or day laborers engaged for a specific task.

Slavery, the ownership of human beings by others, temporarily or for life, is ancient, but its regular use as a source of labor may date back to the time when agricultural settlements appeared. A large corpus of legislation, some of it as old as the late third millennium or early second millennium B.C.E. (for example, Ur-Nammu Code, Code of Hammurabi) bears witness to the economic importance of servitude. The purpose of such legislation was to assure the highest possible profitability of the institution.

> As a class and as individuals, slaves are always exploited, but the individual slave is frequently in a good position to provide the master with a poor return on his investment, to cheat him, to rob him, damage his property, or make him liable to others for property damage . . . and even assault and kill him. Moreover, the slave, exploited himself, has the clearest reason to exploit the master. The main question, then, is how to maximize the benefits of slavery for the owner (Watson, 1).

For the Israelites, the laws of servitude are found in Exodus 21, Leviticus 25, and Deuteronomy 15 and 21:10-14. The distinction in biblical terminology between slave, bondman or bondwoman, servant, and hireling is not always clear. In the Hebrew Bible, slaves are most often designated by the term *avd*, "male slave," and *'mh*, "female

slave," but *mgnt csf*, "bought with money," *nar*, "young man," and *nfs*, "person," are also used. A distinction is made between a Hebrew slave, "your brother, a Hebrew man or a Hebrew woman" (Deut. 15:12), and a foreign slave captured in war, or imported from abroad, or bought from among the sojourners. "Servant" was probably meant when the word *msrt* was used. This referred to a free servant, because it designated the servants of the Lord, priests and Levites (Exod. 28:35; Ezra 8:17; Isa. 61:6; Ezek. 44:11; Joel 1:9; 2:17), and officers of the king (1 Chron. 27:1). No distinction is made between the long-term servant and the short-term hireling and the word *scyr* applied to both (Exod. 12:45; Job 7:1; Mal. 3:5, *et passim*).

New Testament terminology is also confusing. For slave, *pais*, "boy," designates a slave or a worshiper (Matt. 8:6, 8-9, 13: Acts 4:27, 30) and is used interchangeably with *doulos*, "slave." *Diaconos* most likely refers to a free servant, because it is used for a king's servant and a follower of Jesus (Matt. 20:26; 22:13; 23:11; Mark 9:35; Rom. 13:14; 2 Cor. 6:4, *et passim*). The domestic servant, who was probably a live-in, is called *oiketes* (Luke 16:13; Acts 10:7)

The usual supply of slaves in antiquity was from wars or raids in foreign territories. In Sumerian texts slaves are designated as "males" or "females from a foreign country." The Israelites too took captives of war as slaves (Num. 31:9, 17-18, 25, 32; Deut. 20:10-14; 2 Chron. 28:8-15, *et passim*). Slaves were also purchased from traders, as may have been the case of the Egyptian slave Jarha (1 Chron. 2:34). In times of economic difficulty, a debtor could sell or indenture himself or even his children into servitude (Exod. 21:7-11; Deut. 15:12-18; Amos 2:6) Redemption was always possible, however, and every Hebrew slave had to be released during the sabbatical and Jubilee years (*see* below). A slave who loved the master and who could not achieve economic autonomy could become a bondman or bondwoman for life (Exod. 21:6; Deut. 15:16-17).

The slave laws show that, although they were legally chattel (a slave was "his master's money," Exod. 21:21), such persons in ancient Israel were considered as human beings. Excessive violence by the master led to the freeing of the slave (Exod. 21:26-27) or punishment of the abuser (Exod. 21:20). Besides brutality, there were other grounds for freeing a slave. Those who had sold themselves were automatically released during the year of the Jubilee (Lev. 25:39-43, 47-55) or after six years of service (Exod. 21:2-4; Deut. 15:12). A Hebrew girl sold as a slave had to be released if she had ceased to "please her master"; if she was bought for a son, the buyer had to treat her as a daughter (Exod. 21:7-11). A Hebrew slave fleeing from a foreign country back to the homeland had the right of asylum (Deut. 23:15-16).

A slave was allowed to accumulate wealth and even own slaves (2 Sam. 9:10). If a Hebrew sold himself to a non-Hebrew owner, his relatives could redeem him, or he could redeem himself with the *peculium* (savings or profits he had accumulated). There were industrial slaves slated for forced labor in construction work, in mines, quarries, and mills; but there were also slaves, the *nethinim* (Ezra 2:43-58; Neh. 7:46-60; 11:3) dedicated to the Temple, and domestic slaves who enjoyed a more normal form of life. All slaves and servants, even foreigners, participated in certain religious observances and were granted the Sabbath rest (Gen. 17:13, 27; Exod. 12:44; Lev. 22:11; Deut. 5:14-15, *et passim*).

Perhaps the most important aspect of slavery in the Hebrew Bible is the recognition that the proto-Israelites of Moses' time and before were enslaved in Egypt. Many Pentateuchal laws have motive clauses, urging generosity in remembrance of the slavery of the ancestors.

Slavery was a major socio-economic element of Roman and Italian life. Toward the end of the first century B.C.E. it is estimated that there were two to three million slaves in Italy, that is, between 35 and 40 percent of the total population. They came from all conquered or subjugated peoples, from Britain and Germany to the Near East and North Africa. The racial origins of slaves were thus diverse, as also were their occupations, which included positions or professions of prestige and trust (business agents, preceptors, physicians, property managers, and accountants) as well as menial labor. Once freed, there was no limit to what a former slave might accomplish in Roman society. Pliny reports that in 8 B.C.E. a freed slave executed a will by which he left 4,116 slaves, 3,600 pairs of oxen, 257,000 other animals and sixty million sesterces in cash. By comparison, the minimum annual income required to access senatorship was one million sesterces (*Nat. Hist.* 33.135).

In Roman culture as well as in Palestine, although slaves were legally objects, their human nature was recognized. In many instances they were treated as part of the family and became dear friends, adopted sons, or beloved wives or concubines. Legal decisions, wills and other private documents, and inscriptions on tombs provide abundant evidence of such possibilities. The overall good disposition toward slaves, besides the fact that they were assets to be preserved, came from the awareness that such dependence was an unfortunate state that could befall anyone as the result of war, piracy, or economic disaster. Even in Roman law, slaves could obtain freedom and citizenship after six years of work.

Archaeological Information

Natural forces of wind and water, in addition to human and animal power were used as sources of energy in first-century Palestine. In Caesarea Maritima tide water was channeled to flush the sewers of the city. The Magdala mosaic (*see* BOATS) shows that sails were used concurrently with oars to propel boats. Remains of water mills were found on a dam built on the Crocodile River for the creation of a reservoir to provide Caesarea with additional fresh water. Although the structure itself dates to the second century C.E., the technique was known since at least the first century B.C.E. (Strabo,

Geographia 12, 3, 40). A number of large grain grinders and olive crushers that could be operated by animals have been discovered.

There were also mechanical alternatives to human physical power; machines like cranes and winches facilitated work requiring great amounts of energy (*see* CONSTRUCTION). Nevertheless, human energy was still essential, and some of it was supplied by slavery or servitude. Besides abundant literary evidence, many tomb inscriptions found in Italy and in the ancient Roman world indicate the existence of slavery in the first century C.E.

Implications for Jesus Research

After the end of the Hasmonean and Herodian Wars and with the *Pax Romana** imposed on Palestine, there were no more opportunities for the Jews to capture prisoners of war. Jewish slaves and servants provided most of the work force. Jewish slaves served as such only for a limited number of years unless they wanted to remain with the same owner as bondmen or bondwomen, with assured food and lodging and half the salary of a hired servant (Deut. 15:11). Besides purchase, which was always available, the greatest source of foreign slaves was through procreation—children from a foreign slave mother.

During Jesus' lifetime, the construction projects relevant to him included: the continuation of the work on the Temple in Jerusalem, in Galilee, the building of Sepphoris, and of Tiberias, and in 29–30 C.E., the enlargement of Bethsaida (*see* TEMPLE, CONSTRUCTION; SEPPHORIS; TIBERIAS, and BETHSAIDA). These projects probably involved slave labor. Most of the workers Jesus encountered were agricultural and domestic slaves and hired servants, like the hired hands of the fishing boat owners he knew at Bethsaida and Capernaum (Mark 1:20). Slavery was part of the socio-economic fabric of the time, and Jesus mentions in a matter of fact manner the *doulos*, "slave," of a small farmer (Luke 17:7-10).

The healing of the centurion's slave or official's son deserves attention (Matt. 8:5-13; Luke 7:1-10; John 4:46-47). The distribution of the terms used to designate the healed person is as follows:

	pais, "boy"	*doulos*, "slave"	*uios*, "son"
Matthew	3	1	0
Luke	1	3	0
John	2	1	4

Because *pais* was used as a synonym of *doulos* (*see* GENERAL INFORMATION), the Q* source probably refers to a slave. John uses the three terms, with a higher frequency for *uios*. Considering that John was written toward the end of the first century C.E., when Greco-Roman customs prevailed, it is possible that *son* was also used as a synonym for *slave*. In Roman law children and slaves had the same status, both were property of the *paterfamilias,** both had the duty of obedience and service, and both could be sold. A slave could be adopted as son and heir, as was the case in the ancient Near East (Gen. 15:2-4). Adoption of a slave entailed automatic manumission and citizenship, and the rights to act on behalf of the *paterfamilias** were identical for son and slave (Watson, 27, 46–47, 90, 93). Consequently, there may be no contradiction in the apparent difference of relationship between the centurion or official and the healed person. John's official may well have adopted his slave.

A frequent commandment in Jesus' teaching is to be servant or slave to one another or to all. It may derive from his own understanding of himself as the Suffering Servant of Deutero-Isaiah (42:1-4; 49:1-6; 52:13—53:1-12). What role did he see for himself in the presence of the helpless crowds? "When he saw the crowds, he had compassion for them, because they were harassed and helpless, like sheep without a shepherd" (Matt. 9:36 and parallels). "Sheep without a shepherd" is an expression found frequently in the Hebrew Bible (Num. 27:17; 1 Kings 22:17; 2 Chron. 18:16; Ezek. 34:5-7; Zech. 10:2; cf. Judith 11:19). Jesus thus continued an old tradition of compassion for the underprivileged. What could he do to relieve the misfortune of those who did not even have the security slaves enjoyed? Sacrifice himself?

BIBLIOGRAPHY

Bartchy, S. S. "Slavery (Greco-Roman)." *ABD* 6:65–73.

Bradley, K. R. *Slaves and Masters in the Roman Empire.* New York, 1987.

Crossan, J. D. *The Historical Jesus. The Life of a Mediterranean Jewish Peasant.* San Francisco: Harper and Row, 1991.

Dandamayev, M. A. "Slavery (Ancient Near East; OT)." *ABD* 6:58–65.

David, J. *The People of the Mediterranean: An Essay in Comparative Social Anthropology.* The Library of Man. London: Routledge and Kegar Paul, 1977.

Finley, M. J. *Ancient Slavery and Modern Ideology.* New York: Viking Press, 1980.

Garnsey, P. and R. Saller. *The Roman Empire: Economy, Society and Culture.* Los Angeles, 1987.

Harris, W. V. "The Roman Father's Power of Life and Death." *Studies in Roman Law in Memory of A. Arthur Schiller.* Edited by R. S. Bagnall and W. V. Harris. Leiden: E.J. Brill, 1986.

Hopkins, J. *Conquerors and Slaves.* Cambridge: Cambridge University Press, 1978.

Kirschenbaum, A. *Sons, Slaves and Freedmen in Roman Commerce.* Washington, D.C., 1987.

Klasser, W. "Jesus and the Messianic War." *Early Jewish and Christian Exegesis.* Studies in Memory of William Hugh Brownlee. Edited by G. A. Evans and W. F. Stinespring. Atlanta, Ga.: Scholars Press, 1987.

Theissen, G. *Sociology of Early Christianity.* Translated by J. Bowden. Philadelphia: Fortress Press, 1978.

Watson, A. *Roman Slave Law.* Baltimore: Johns Hopkins University, 1987.

Sodom and Gomorrah

Importance

Jesus used the popular image of Sodom and Gomorrah, the sinful cities destroyed by God, to condemn the unrepentant cities or people of his time.

Scripture References

Matt. 10:15; 11:24; Luke 10:12; 17:29; Rom. 9:29 (Isa. 1:9).

General Information

Sodom and Gomorrah were two of the five "cities of the Plain" [of Siddim, "the Salt Sea"] where Lot decided to move his tent (Gen. 13:12). The other three cities were Ad'mah, Zeboi'im and Be'la or Zo'ar (Gen. 14:2). Biblical tradition suggests that this plain was fertile, "well watered everywhere like the Garden of the Lord" (Gen. 13:10). According to the narrative of Genesis 18 and 19, God decided to destroy Sodom and Gomorrah; it gives a graphic account of the mores of the people and how the two cities were incinerated by brimstone and fire "out of heaven." Subsequent generations of Israelites and Jews viewed the two cities as symbols of human sin and divine wrath.

Several ancient writers—Strabo, Diodorus, Josephus, and Tacitus—reflect the biblical account (Gen. 19:24-28) in indicating that the cities were destroyed by fire. They probably knew that the region was rich in bitumen, asphalt, petroleum, and natural gas liberated by the tectonic movements of the Syro-African rift in which the area is located; modern geological surveys have found such mineral products. A conflagration whether caused by human ignorance, or war, or by a stroke of lightning "out of heaven" (Gen. 19:24) could be seen from afar. Abraham, who was near Hebron, noticed that the smoke went "up like the smoke of a furnace" (Gen. 19:28). It is possible that the language of fire and smoke simply is used to graphically symbolize destruction, no matter what the cause.

Archaeological Data

Because of a new irrigation system reducing the amount of fresh water flowing to the Dead Sea, the level of the sea is much lower now than it was at the turn of the century; beginning in 1979, a large area south of the el-Lisan peninsula turned into dry land. W. Rast and T. Schaub explored the exposed

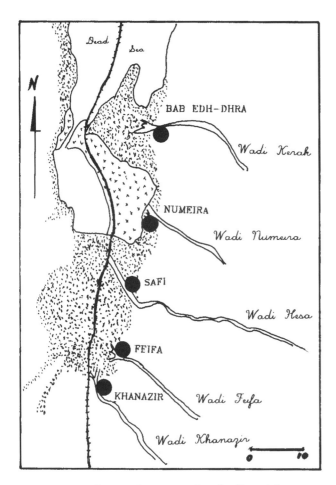

Figure 60 Sodom and Gomorrah. The five cities.

shops of Jerusalem. An investigation revealed that the origin was Bab edh-Dhra. P. W. Lapp, director of the American School of Oriental Research in Jerusalem, mounted an archaeological expedition, which worked at the site from 1965 until 1969. It became evident that it was an Early Bronze Age city that had been destroyed by fire. In 1973, W. Rast of Valparaiso University, Indiana, and R. T. Schaub of Indiana University, Pennsylvania, discovered another city, Numeira, some 12 kilometers (7.8 miles) south of Bab edh-Dhra; it had been burnt in the same period. In 1975 they began to excavate the two sites, which both were buried under soft charcoal. At Bab edh-Dhra the excavators found a city with a temple and a vast necropolis with more than 20,000 elaborate tombs, more than 500,000 buried individuals, and more than 3 million vessels, according to their estimates.

M. D. Coogan of Harvard joined the team in 1979 and supervised the work at Numeira, which, he confirmed, was destroyed by a raging fire about 2,350 B.C.E. Most interesting, south of Numeira, three other Early Bronze Age cities were discovered in a north-south alignment with Bab edh-Dhra and Numeira: Safi, Feifa, and Khanazir. Were these five cities the cities of the Valley of Saddim? Each of them lies near the mouth of a river and a spring, which would fit the description of Genesis 13:10. The Madaba Map shows Safi and identifies it as Zo'ar, one of the five cities of the Valley of Saddim. The town of Feifa also shows signs of violent destruction by fire. Accordingly, some scholars believe that these five cities are those of Genesis 13:12 and 14:2. It must be noted that the names of Sodom, Gomorrah, and Zo'ar have been found separately in different Ebla tablets discovered in 1974–76 and dated to the mid-third millennium B.C.E., but there is no evidence that they are the same three cities with the same names that were among the five cities of the Plain of Saddim (*see* fig. 60).

Implications for Jesus Research

Even if the five cities excavated or discovered by Rast, Schaub, and Coogan were not the five cities

sea floor and concluded that "it could not have contained cities at any time during the historical period." This is especially true for the Early Bronze Age (*ca.* 3,000 B.C.E.), when cities were usually built on elevated sites for the purpose of protection.

In 1924 A. Mallon, S.J., a member of the W. F. Albright and M. G. Kyle team, discovered the ancient city of Bab edh-Dhra at the eastern land base of the el-Lisan peninsula at an elevation of about 550 feet above the waters of the Dead Sea. His discovery was forgotten until 1964, when large quantities of Early Bronze Age pottery appeared in the of Genesis 14:2, it seems likely that a fiery devastation certainly happened in the area circa 2,300 B.C.E. Whether or not such an event can be linked with the Genesis narrative, the reputation of Sodom and Gomorrah as violently destroyed cities emerged and persisted. The tradition used by Jesus was familiar to his listeners. In 1989, the Jesus Seminar rated *black* the four sayings of Jesus referring to Sodom and Gomorrah or to Sodom alone (Luke 10:12 = Matt. 10:15; Matt. 11:24; Luke 17:29) Like most storytellers, he used images borrowed from daily life, popular sayings, and authoritative quotations. Such images would evoke strong responses from his audience.

BIBLIOGRAPHY

Forbes, R. J. *Bitumen and Petroleum in Antiquity*. Vol. 1 in *Studies in Ancient Technology*. Leiden: E. J. Brill, 1955.

Harland, J. P. "Sodom and Gomorrah." *BA* 5 (1942): 17–32.

Negev, A. "Sodom." *AEHL*, 1972.

Rast, W. E., et al. "Sodom and Gomorrah." *The Annual of American Schools of Oriental Research* 43 (1976): 1–60; 46 (1979): 1–190.

Sarna, N. "Abraham in History." *BAR* 3 (1977): 5–9.

Schaub, R. T. Preliminary Report of the 1981 Expedition to the Red Sea Plain in *Bulletin of the American Schools of Oriental Research* 254 (1984): 35, 60.

———. "Bab edh-Dhra." *NEAEHL* 1: 130–36.

Shanks, H.. "Have Sodom and Gomorrah Been Found?" *BAR* 6 (1980): 26–36.

———. "*BAR* Interviews Giovanni Pettinato." *BAR* 6 (1980): 46–52.

Son of Man

Importance

The expression Son of Man is frequently used by Jesus in the Gospels, a number of those times in an apocalyptic context.

Scripture References

See table 7 on page 260.

General Information

The problem of the meaning of the expression *Son of Man* either as an eschatological-apocalyptic title or as a substitute for a personal pronoun to designate oneself or another is one of the most difficult in Jesus research. A complete bibliography of all the books, essays, and articles written on the subject would be enormous. Our purpose here is simply to present one piece of archaeological information and to underscore the dichotomy in the Synoptics* between "Son of Man" and "Kingdom or Reign of God" in order to suggest further research.

G. Vermes shows that the expression *Son of Man* was used toward the beginning of the Common Era a) as a substitute for a masculine indefinite pronoun and b) more specifically as a circumlocution in the Palestinian Aramaic language when the saying was embarrassing for the speaker for reason of modesty or reserve, or when the saying referred to death or humiliation.

The examples he gives are not older than the second century C.E., but languages and dialects were stable enough to allow us to suggest that in the first century C.E. Jesus routinely used this form of self-designation. An Aramaic text of Jesus' time uses the expression *son of man* as equivalent to *man* in a non-apocalyptical context (*see* Archaeological Information below). In the Hebrew Bible the expression is used mostly by Ezekiel, who places it in God's mouth when God addresses him; he uses it more than ninety times. It is found only sixteen times in the rest of the Hebrew Bible; in the Gospels it appears more than sixty-five times.

Vermes and other scholars have noticed several interesting facts:

- In the New Testament the expression *Son of Man* is used only in the Gospels, except for one exception in Acts (Stephen's speech, 7:56); it is not used at all by Paul.

- In the Synoptics* only Jesus uses the term with the one exception of the angel in Luke

Table 7 The Son of Man Sayings in the Synoptics

Mark	Matthew	Luke	Son of Man Saying	Apocalyptic	Jesus' Self-designation
2:10	9:6	5:24	authority to forgive		X
	(5.11, "my")	6:22	reviled because of Son of Man		X
	8:20 =	Q = 9:58	nowhere to rest		X
	10:23		flee when Son of Man comes	X	?
	10:32-33("I")=	Q = 12:8–11	speak against Son of Man		X
	11:19 =	Q = 7:34	drinking and eating		X
2:28	12:8	6:5	Lord of the Sabbath	?	?
	12:37		sows the good seed		X
	12:40 =	Q = 11:30	sign of Noah	X	X
	13:41		will send his angels	X	?
8:27 ("I")	16:13	9:18 ("I")	who is the Son of Man		X
	16:27		is to come with his angels	X	?
8:31; 9:31; 10:33	17:22; 20:18; 26:2	9:22; 9:44; 18:31	to be delivered (prediction)		X
9:1 (Kingdom)	16:28	9:56	no death before	X	?
9:9	17:9		tell no one before raised		X
9:12			Elijah first, Son of Man must suffer	X	X
10:45			came to serve		X
	18:11 (?)	19:10	came to save the lost		X
	24:27 =	Q = 17:24	will come with lightning	X	?
	24:37, 39 =	Q = 17:22,26, 30	day of the Son of Man	X	?
		18:8	will he find faith?	X	?
13:26	24:30	21:27	coming in clouds	X	?
	25:31		in his glory (to judge)	X	?
14:21	26:24	22:22	betrayed, woe to betrayer		X
14:41	26:45		betrayed at Gethsemane		X
		22:48	by Judas, with a kiss		X
14:62	26:64	22:69 24:7	at right hand of power; angel speaking	X	?
			TOTAL	12	17

24:7, who quotes Jesus. He employs it either to designate himself or another being, who could be a heavenly figure.

- In John, the expression is always understood as designating Jesus.

- Despite Daniel 7:13 referring to "one like a son of man" (RSV; cf. NRSV, "one like a human being"), Jewish apocalyptic literature seldom uses the expression *Son of Man* to designate the Messiah, if at all. On that point, Vermes affirms that *Son of Man* is never a titular term in Jewish literature (*Jesus and the World of Judaism*, 96). The use of *Son of Man* as a messianic title is most likely a post-crucifixion Christian creation.

- The Gospel of Thomas, which some suppose to antedate Mark, uses the term only once in a nonapocalyptic sense as a self-designation by Jesus in logion 86, a close parallel to Matthew 8:20 = Q* = Luke 9:58 ("Foxes have holes").

How can this particular use of *Son of Man* in a titular sense in some Synoptic* passages be explained? The table on the opposite page may suggest a direction for investigation.

Counting parallel sayings as one, twenty-seven sayings can be recognized as being said by Jesus and one by an angel at the tomb. In seventeen of them, Jesus refers (or probably refers) to himself; ten are undetermined, standing either for Jesus or a heavenly figure. These seventeen instances of *Son of Man* as self-designation by Jesus are evenly distributed among the three Synoptics*: thirteen times in Matthew, ten times in Luke, and eight times in Mark, the oldest Gospel. When sorted according to their apocalyptic overtone, twelve sayings can be isolated with a dramatically different distribution: ten in Matthew, seven in Luke, and only three in Mark. The apocalyptic emphasis is obviously post-Markan.

As M. Borg observes ("Temperate Case," 90), it is striking that the expressions "kingdom or reign of God"—the heart of Jesus' message—and *Son of Man* are never found in the same logion.* More intriguing, only the *Son of Man* sayings have an element of imminence in them; only they are indisputably apocalyptical. By contrast, the kingdom or reign of God does not imply a cataclysm; it is already here, near at hand. One exception can be noted: Mark 9:1, "Truly, I tell you, there are some standing here who will not taste death until they see that the kingdom of God has come with power." But the term "with power" does not necessarily imply apocalypse, final judgment, and destruction by fire. Obviously the concepts *Son of Man* and "kingdom or reign of God" belong to two different traditions.

In the Gospel of John, the expression *Son of Man* always stands for Jesus, the one who comes from heaven and will return to it; it is not an apocalyptic figure, with perhaps the exception of John 5:27.

- 1:51   Angels upon the Son of Man.
- 3:13-14 Son of Man from heaven to be lifted up.
- 5:27   Son of God = Son of Man = judge.
- 6:27   The food the Son of Man will give.
- 6:53   Unless you eat the flesh . . .
- 6:62   If you saw the Son of Man ascending.
- 8:28   You will know I am the Son of Man.
- 12:23   The Son of Man is to be glorified.
- 12:34   People ask, "Who is this Son of Man?"
- 13:31   Now is the Son of Man glorified.

The expression *Son of Man* of the Fourth Gospel can be seen as a development of the tradition of the Jesus who proclaimed the kingdom and as a stage toward the Gnostic Jesus (*see* GOSPEL OF THOMAS).

Archaeological Data

In several instances, Dead Sea Scrolls texts use *Son of Man* as an equivalent of "man" as in one of the *hôdayôt*, "Thanksgiving Hymns":

I know that righteousness is not of man
And perfection of way not of the son of man.
To the Most High God belong all righteous deeds.

(1QH4: Vermes, *The Dead Sea Scrolls*, 177).

Another case deserves special attention because it figures in a context of exorcism and healing, activities exercised by Jesus. Among the manuscripts of cave 4 at Qumran were the fragments of an Aramaic text called "The Prayer of Nabonidus." It was first published by J. T. Milik in 1956. A. Dupont-Sommer revised the translation and published a commentary, "Exorcismes et guérisons dans les écrits de Qumran" (*see* EXORCISM). In the text, Nabu-na'id, the last king of the Neo-Babylonian dynasty is speaking:

> I was struck during seven years and [my face] was no more like that [of a son of man]. But I prayed the [Most High God] . . . . [And I wrote this:] "I was struck with a malignant inflammation at Teiman [and my face] was no more like that of the sons of men." (as reconstructed by Dupont-Sommer, translated by J. Rousseau).

This text dated to the first century B.C.E. to first century C.E. (the event itself dates from the sixth century B.C.E.), gives evidence that the expression *son of man* was used in a non-eschatological context and was equivalent to "man" around the time of Jesus. This lends support to Vermes' proposal that *habu gabra*, "that man," and *bar nash/a*, "the son of man," were synonymous. "I" can be substituted for "son of man" in the Gospels in a majority of instances (*see* table above).

Implications for Jesus Research

The conclusion that the concepts "Son of Man" and "kingdom or reign of God" belong to two different traditions seems clear. Can it then be determined which concept is the oldest and which emerged later?

The consensus among New Testament scholars is that Mark was written in about 70 C.E. (probably earlier, *see* CONSTRUCTION, CITIES; CAMPS, SIEGE BANKS; and COINS AS HISTORICAL DOCUMENTS), and Luke and Matthew in about 90 C.E. What events

between 60 and 90 C.E. could have stimulated some Christian scribes to add most of the contents of the thirteenth chapter of Mark and to emphasize apocalypticism in the later Synoptics? Qumran was destroyed by the Romans in 68; Jerusalem was conquered and the Temple razed in 70; Essenes and Zealots took refuge in Masada, the last point of resistance, which fell in 73. The survivors of the Essenes in that disastrous period may have realized that their hopes had been shattered. If the Temple defiled by a corrupt priesthood had been destroyed as expected, it could not be rebuilt according to their own conception. The Messiah had not come, and Belial and the *kittim*, "Romans," were triumphant. It is probable that some Essenes at that time renounced their role of eschatological warriors and joined the Jewish Christian movement, in which former followers of John the Baptist had already introduced an apocalyptic influence (cf. Matt. 3:7-12 = Q = Luke 3:7-9). Their scribes perhaps developed the concept "Son of Man–Messiah," who would come and at last vindicate them. The original message of the Kingdom of God was blurred. At the same time Paul's theology of a resurrected Christ and his second coming was spreading.

A plausible scenario is that the confluence of the two doctrines produced the basic tenets of Christian beliefs found in the Synoptics* before the end of the first century C.E. The Fourth Gospel, which bases salvation on believing and obeying Jesus' commandments (John 1:1, 14; 6:63, 68; 8:51; 14:15, 23; 15:18), may be closer to the original message of Jesus than the Synoptics with their theology of redemption through his sacrifice on the cross.

BIBLIOGRAPHY

Borg, M. J. "A Temperate Case for a Non-Eschatological Jesus." *Forum* 2 (1986).

———. *Conflict, Holiness and Politics in the Teachings of Jesus.* New York: Edwin Mellen Press, 1984.

Donahue, J. R. "Recent Studies on the Origin of 'Son of Man' in the Gospels." *Catholic Biblical Quarterly* 48 (1986): 584–607.

Dupont-Sommer, A. "Exorcismes et guérisons dans les éscrits de Qumran." *Supplément to Vetus Testamentum* 7 (1959): 246–61.

Hare, D. R. A. *The Son of Man Tradition*. Minneapolis: Fortress Press, 1990.

Lindars, B. *Jesus, Son of Man*. Grand Rapids: Eerdmans, 1984.

Mickelburg, G. W. "Son of Man." *ABD* 6:137–50.

Milik, J. T. "The Prayer of Nabonidus." *Revue Biblique* 43 (1956): 407–11, 415.

Perrin, N. *Rediscovering the Teachings of Jesus*. New York: Harper and Row, 1967.

———. *Jesus and the Language of the Kingdom*. Philadelphia: Fortress Press, 1976.

Robinson, J. M. *A New Quest of the Historical Jesus*. London: SCM Press, 1959.

Tatum, W. B. *In Quest of Jesus, A Guidebook*. Atlanta, Ga.: John Knox Press, 1982.

Vermes, G. *The Dead Sea Scrolls in English*. London: Penguin Books, 1987. (First ed. 1962).

———. *Jesus and the World of Judaism*. Philadelphia: Fortress Press, 1983.

———. *Jesus the Jew*. 1974. Reprint. Minneapolis: Fortress Press, 1981.

———. "The Present State of the 'Son of Man' Debate." *Journal of Jewish Studies* 29 (1978).

———. "The Use of *bar nash/bar nasha* in Jewish Aramaic." *An Aramaic Approach to the Gospels and Acts*. 1967. Reprint. Oxford: Clarendon Press, 1979.

Stone, Stoning

Importance

Stones and rocks are ubiquitous in Israel; for millennia they have provided implements and articles used in everyday life. The Gospels use them in metaphors and also in reference to stoning.

Scripture References

Matt. 3:9; 4:3; 7:9, 24; 16:18; 21:35, 44; 23:37; 24:2; 26:7; 27:51, 60, 66: 28:2; Mark 5:5; 13:1-2; 14:3; 16:3; Luke 3:8; 4:3; 6:48; 7:37; 8:6, 13; 11:11; 19:40, 44; 20:6, 17-18; 21:6; 23:53; 24:2; John 1:42; 2:6; 8:5, 7, 59; 10:31-33; 11:8, 38-39; Acts 7:58; 14:19; G. Thom. 77.

General Information

The rocky foundation of Palestine either forms the surface of the land itself or is never very far below soils that may form the surface. The most common rock types are:

- The limestone of the Lower and Middle Upper Cretaceous, the dominant ground base of Judea, which provides building stones of high quality such as those taken from the Solomonic and Herodian quarries of Jerusalem.

- The uppermost Cretaceous (Senonian) light chalk, too soft for building material and yielding infertile soils. Its softness facilitates soil erosion. Its one practical advantage is that it wears quickly to form valleys, where animal and human traffic can form fairly smooth hard surfaces. Many of Palestine's roads developed this way, such as the Megiddo Pass across the hills of Carmel.

- The Lower Tertiary (Eocene) hard limestone of Lower Galilee, Central Samaria, and Shephelah, which yields good building materials.

- The volcanic basalt of eastern Galilee and the Golan, which provided very durable building stones for the construction of Capernaum, Chorazin, and Bethsaida, the three cities where Jesus performed many healings (Matt. 11:21-23 and parallel in Luke).

The character of the rock formations lent itself to the creation of an almost infinite number of natural and artificial caves and galleries (*see* GALILEAN CAVES and JUDEAN CAVES). It also allowed for digging countless cisterns and storage pits, some of colossal proportions. Surface stones are so abundant everywhere that they provided accessible material for the construction of dwellings and of dry-laid walls to enclose vineyards and orchards. Missiles for stoning, slingshots, and catapults were instantly available. Other uses included the construction of public buildings, fortifications, roads and streets, and courts. Stones were also used to seal caves, tombs, and wells, and to make slabs for decoration and inscriptions. Piled up in cairns or erected as columns or pillars, they served as landmarks and as commemorative stelae. Large stones were hewn into hollow, cylindrical sections fitting into each other like pipes to form aqueducts. Sarcophagi and ossuaries* were often made of stone.

Long before pottery was invented, stones were shaped into implements of all sorts, such as mills, mangers, anchors, millstones, grinders, mortars and pestles, tools, plummets, loom weights, bowls and cups, and knives and other cutting instruments. Semiprecious stones were used for jewelry and for ceremonial adornments. Ointment and perfume flasks were made of alabaster, hematite, or serpentine; expensive tables, large jars, and delicate articles were cut in marble and fine limestone. Stone weights and measuring cups, because of the precision of the artistry involved, were often considered precious objects.

Two types of expensive stone, marble and alabaster, are recovered archaeologically in Palestine and are mentioned in the Bible. Marble, a form of crystallized limestone, does not exist in Israel. Herod used white, gray, and red marble extensively in his monumental construction projects. He imported it from Italy and the Greek Islands as well as red granite from Egypt. The Temple of Jesus' days had slabs and columns of marble. Because of its high price, even the wealthy could afford only small marble objects; the inner walls of their residences were painted to imitate it (see JERUSALEM, UPPER CITY). Alabaster, a soft, clear stone with veins, first appeared in Palestine mostly in perfume flasks as an import form Egypt (Pliny, *Nat. Hist.* 13.4). Its nature varies according to its origin: in Egypt it is calcium carbonate; in the Jordan Valley, calcium sulfate or gypsum. The techniques of manufacture also differed. In Egypt the cavity of the flask was drilled; in Palestine it was hollowed out with chisels.

The durability, weight, strength, and barrenness of stones led to their symbolic use in metaphors with both positive and negative connotations. In the Gospels stones represent sterility (Matt. 3:9), inedibility (Matt. 4:3; 7:9), indifference and inability to speak (Luke 19:40); or they denote solidity (Matt. 7:24-25; 21:42) or a cornerstone (Matt. 21:42; Luke 20:17-18).

Stoning, a common form of execution prescribed in the ancient world, was still practiced in Jesus' time. Pentateuchal texts mention it as punishment for a number of offenses, "to purge the evil from Israel": child sacrifice (Lev. 20:2-5), divination (Lev. 20:27), breaking the Sabbath (Num. 15:32-36), incitement to idolatry (Deut. 13:6-10), worship of idols (Deut. 17:2-7), prophesying in the name of a false god (Deut. 13:1-5), insubordination of a son (Deut. 21:18-21), and adultery (Deut. 22:21-23). Stoning usually took place outside the city (Lev. 24:14; Deut. 22–24), although Deut. 22:20-21 may indicate stoning at the door of a house. Before stoning, witnesses placed their hands on the offender's head (Lev. 12:14) as a symbol for transferring communal guilt to the culprit; then they cast the first stone, after which the rest of the people threw stones until death occurred (Lev. 4:15; 16:21). Examples of ancient prosecution and stoning are found in Leviticus 24:10-16, 23 and 1 Kings 21:8-14.

In the time of Jesus, the legal procedure was probably closer to that of the Mishnah (*m. Sanhedrin* 6:1-4). It allowed for new evidence in favor of the offender until the last minute and for confession before death. According to this text the condemned was first stripped of his garments and thrown down from a platform nine feet high by the first witness. If he survived the fall, the second witness cast a heavy stone on his chest and, if death did not occur at this point, all those present stoned him. After stoning, the body was hanged on a tree (cf. Deut. 21:22-23). According to John, Jesus was threatened with stoning several times (John 8:59; 10:31-33; 11:8). Spontaneous lynching and murder was sometimes done by stoning (Luke 20:6; Matt. 12:35, and Josephus, *War* 2, 12.1/225 [against

Roman soldiers] and 2, 17.1/406 [against Agrippa II]).

Archaeological Information

Stone objects of different sizes and shapes are recovered in many excavations and surface surveys: millstones; grain grinders; olive crushers; milestones; furniture and houseware of marble, limestone, and basalt; stone anchors in the Sea of Galilee and in the Dead Sea. Typical of the first century C.E. are circular flat stones used to close tombs, and stone ossuaries in which a second burial of the dead was made when the body had fully decomposed (*see* JERUSALEM, TOMBS). Marble columns, presumably dating from Herod's Temple, have been found reused in various places in Jerusalem, especially at the Dome of the Rock. Archaeologists have found hundreds of alabaster flasks from all periods. These include Palestinian vases from the Greco-Roman Period, many of which come from Beth-Shean and Jericho. Very common in Jerusalem are soft limestone vessels dating from the third century B.C.E. to the first century C.E.

Implications for Jesus Research

The discussion of the woman or women anointing Jesus with perfumed oil contained in an alabaster flask is treated under OINTMENTS, PERFUMES. Here the focus is kept on stoning, which raises two vexing questions in connection with the gospels:

* Who had the right to condemn Jesus to death?
* What is the degree of authenticity of the pericope now attached to the Fourth Gospel in John 7:53—8:11 (the adulterous woman)?

In John 18:31, Pilate says, "Take him yourselves and judge him according to your law." The religious leaders answer, "We are not permitted to put anyone to death." Pilate apparently had given or recognized the right of the religious authority to pronounce and execute a death sentence in certain cases. Peter's second trial (Acts 5:17-33), execution

of Stephen (Acts 7:57-60) and Paul's recognition of the right of the Jewish Court to pronounce and execute a death sentence (Acts 26:10) support the existence of this power. The *Tosepta** and the Mishnah* report of religious executions by stoning and burning (*t. Sanhedrin* 10:11; *m. Sanhedrin* 7:2).

The new High Priest, Ananus the Younger, thought he had this right: in 62 C.E. in the interim between the death of the prefect Festus and the arriving of his successor, Albinus, he convened the Sanhedrin in order to condemn James the brother of Jesus and others (Josephus, *Antiq.* 20, 9.1/200–3), but Agrippa II deposed him from the High Priesthood. The evidence contained in the Mishnah, *Tosepta*, Acts, and Josephus suggests that in the first century C.E. the Jewish court could decree capital punishment in religious matters but not in political ones or when the public order was threatened. In the dialogue of John 18:31, Pilate implied that the offense was a religious crime, and the religious authorities that it was a political one. Jesus was condemned for political reasons, as is well established by the Roman sentence and method of execution, and by the titulus on the cross, "Jesus, King of the Jews." There probably was no judgment by the Jewish court as described by the Synoptics.

This point of view has been convincingly argued by several writers, one of the most authoritative being the Israeli Supreme Court Judge and Minister of Justice H. H. Cohn, a specialist in ancient Jewish law, (*see* JERUSALEM, CAIAPHAS' HOUSE). It is highly probable that the High Priest became involved after a demand by Pilate that a Jew who seemed to be a threat to the peace of the country be arrested and brought to him. Several examples of such a collaboration are given by Josephus. Cumanus (48–52 C.E.) arrested and reprimanded the notables of several villages for having failed to pursue and arrest the robbers who had attacked Stephen, a slave of Caesar (*War* 2, 12.2/229). In 63 C.E. magistrates brought to Albinus a certain Jesus ben Ananias, a peasant prophet who for nights and days had cried out announcing the doom of Jerusalem (*War* 6, 5.3/302–94). In June 66 C.E. Florus, who had been insulted after he had plundered the Temple treasury, ordered the High Priest and the nobles to arrest and deliver to him the offenders, otherwise the leaders would be punished (*War* 2, 14.8/301–2). On the evidence of Josephus, as has been maintained by several scholars, it seems that one of the main concerns of the Gospel writers was to disculpate the Romans from having executed Jesus (*see* JERUSALEM, CAIAPHAS' HOUSE).

The "floating pericope" of the Adulterous Woman recorded in the Fourth Gospel, in John 7:53—8:11, is a moving story with a strong message; it has an intriguing history and deserves special attention. The text is missing from all early Syriac and Coptic fragments and is conspicuously absent from Papyrus 66 (third century C.E.), which contains the sections 6:11, 35—14:26 of John. It appears for the first time in Greek in the fifth-century Codex Bezea; later, one group of manuscripts places it at the end of John, and another after Luke 21:38. Some commentators like Bultmann and Beasley-Murray ignore it altogether; von Campenhausen rejects it; verses 8:7, 10 and 11 were rated *black* by the Jesus Seminar in 1991. Nevertheless, the authenticity of this tradition has strong supporters, the first one being Augustine (354–430). Among modern scholars, U. Baker, R. E. Brown, J. Jeremias, T. W. Manson, and H. Riesenfeld all regard the pericope as genuine. Because of its highly offensive character, the story must have been detached from the main gospel tradition by early scribes, preserved as an isolated anecdote, and then brought back into the main corpus. Although it exists only in one single source (with minor variations) from an unknown origin, the story meets several important criteria of authenticity: agreement with the Jewish context of Jesus' time, and agreement with some characteristic Gospel features:

- Use of dilemma: Question to Jesus about the payment of the tribute (Matt. 22:16-22 and parallels), and Jesus' question about the Messiah (Matt. 22:41-46 and parallels), Jesus' question regarding John the Baptist (Matt. 21:25-26 and parallels).

- Absence of condemnation of sinners as in Luke's stories of the Prodigal Son and the Sinful Woman anointing Jesus' feet.

- Favorable attitude of Jesus toward women.

- Offensive character of Jesus' action for his contemporaries.

- Embarrassment for the early Church: Jesus seems to condone adultery.

The enigmatic writing of Jesus on the ground (John 8:6, 8) has been the object of much speculation. Here we will simply observe that the act itself was possible, because the construction of the courts was completed only in 63 C.E. under Agrippa II (*Antiq.* 2, 9.7/219). Obviously, the Court of the Gentiles was the last one to be completed. Circa 30 C.E., it was not yet paved, and its surface was made of hardened earth. Stones and discarded pieces of hewn limestone blocks or slabs were certainly available for spontaneous or judicial stoning. These observations contribute to the sense of authenticity of the basic story.

BIBLIOGRAPHY

Beasley-Murray, G. R. *John.* Word Bible Commentary, Vol. 36. Waco, Tex.: Word Books, 1987.

Ben-Dor, I. "Palestinian Alabaster Vases." *Quarterly, Department of Antiquities of Palestine* 11 (1944): 93–112.

Blinzler, J. "The Jewish Punishment of Stoning in the New Testament Period." *The Trial of Jesus.* Edited by E. Bammel. Studies in Biblical Theology, Second Series, 13. London: SCM Press Ltd., 1970.

Brown, R. E. *The Gospel According to John.* 2 Vols. Anchor Bible 29, 29A. Garden City, N.Y.: Doubleday, 1966–70.

Bultmann, R. *The Gospel of John, Commentary.* German 1964. Translated by G. R. Beasley-Murray et al. Philadelphia: Westminster, 1971.

Cohn, H. H. *The Trial and Death of Jesus.* New York: Harper and Row, 1967.

Cope, L. *John 8:7c.* Jesus Seminar Papers. Sonoma, Calif.: Polebridge Press, 1991.

Ducan, J., and M. Derrett, "Law in the New Testament: The Story of the Woman Taken in Adultery." *New Testament Studies* 10 (1963–64): 1–26.

Frymer-Kensky, T. "Pollution, Purification and Purgation in Biblical Israel." *The Word of the Lord Shall Go Forth.*

Edited by C. L. Meyers and M. O'Connor. Winona Lake, Ind.: Eisenbrauns, 1983.

Manson, T. W. "The pericope de Adultera (John 7, 53—8, 11)." *Zeitschrift für die neutestamentliche Wissenschaft* 44 (1952–53): 255–56.

Negev, A. "Stone Implements."*AEHL*, (1972): 299.

Westbrook, R. "Punishment and Crimes." *ABD*.

Sychar-Shechem

Importance

According to the Gospel of John, Jesus met a woman from Sychar and was invited by the villagers to stay there.

Scripture Reference

John 4:5

General Information

Scholars have not agreed about the location of Sychar. It was first identified with the village of Askar, about one mile north of Jacob's Well. This opinion was based on Epiphanus who named two different cities, Sychar and Shechem (*Versio Antiqua*, 253), on the report of the Bordeaux Pilgrim (333) who located Sychar one mile away from Shechem, and on a comment from Eusebius quoted by Jerome: "Sychar is before Neapolis (Nablus) near the piece of land given by Jacob to his son Joseph" (*Di Situ et Nom. Loc. Hebr.* 279; ca. 400). It was recognized that the name "Sychar" was the result of a transcription error: the Sinaitic Syrian text of John reads Shechem instead of Sychar, and Jerome had already reported the error in *Quaest. in Gen.* 373. The excavations of Tell Balatah, 1.5 miles southeast of Nablus in the eastern part of the passage between Mt. Ebal and Mt. Gerizim, showed that Sychar is to be identified with Balanos Sikimon, a nearby Samaritan place of worship. It appeared that Shechem and Sychar were one and the same city in the area of Jacob's Well (*see* JACOB'S WELL), 40 miles north of Jerusalem and 5.5 miles southeast of Samaria.

Shechem played a prominent role in Israelite history in the Bible. Located in the hill country near the border between Ephraim and Manasseh (Josh. 20:27; 1 Chron. 7:28), at the foot of Mt. Gerizim, it is the first city of the Land of Canaan mentioned in Genesis. There Abraham encamped "at the oak of Moreh" and built an altar to the Lord (Gen. 12:6-7). According to Gen. 33:20 Jacob buried the "strange gods" there and built another altar at the same place. The book of Joshua reports that at the beginning of the Israelite settlement, Joshua called all the tribes there to renew their covenant with God (Josh. 8:30-35; 24:1-28). After Solomon's death and the Israelite rejection of Rehoboam as king at Shechem, Jereboam became king and made the city his capital for some time (1 Kings 12:15). In postexilic times, Shechem was the chief city of the Samaritans, who erected their temple on nearby Mt. Gerizim. The Hasmonean John Hyrcanus destroyed the city and temple circa 107 B.C.E. (Josephus, *Antiq.* 13, 9.1/255). During the First Jewish War Vespasian set his camp near Shechem. A new city was built in the area and named Flavius Neapolis in his honor when he became emperor Flavius Vespasianus (69–79). The Mishnah (*m. Menahot* 10.2) indicates that wheat was brought to Jerusalem from Shechem.

Archaeological Data

Biblical Shechem has been identified with Tell Balatah as a result of the excavations undertaken by C. Watzinger (1907–9) and later by C. Watzinger, E. Sellin, *et al* under the auspices of the German Society of Scientific Research (1913–14, 1926–28, 1932, and 1934). Excavations were resumed from 1956 to 1973 by G. E. Wright on behalf of the Drew-McCormick Archaeological Expedition and the American Schools of Oriental Research. The excavators identified twenty strata at Balatah, from the Chalcolithic (3,600 to 3,200 B.C.E.) to the Hellenistic periods (330 to ca. 110 B.C.E.) They discovered elaborate fortification systems, large buildings, and quantities of artifacts. The Middle Bronze Age II (1700–1550 B.C.E.) was particularly well represented. The fortress-temple of that period, a monumental structure of 84 x 68 feet with walls 17 feet wide, is an impressive building. It has been suggested that this is the temple of Baal-berith (Judg. 9:46) and the "Tower of Shechem" destroyed by Abimelech (Judg. 9:45-49). During the Hellenistic period Shechem was a prosperous city that the Samaritans viewed to be the rival of Jerusalem. Its ruins yielded coins dating from the fourth century to 107 B.C.E., suggesting that the final destruction by John Hyrcanus (134–104) happened toward that later date. It was never restored, but a village was built near its site.

Implications for Jesus Research

By the first century C.E., neither a biblical nor a Samaritan Shechem existed. In its stead a small town, possibly the Sychar of John 4:4-6, was built at walking distance from Jacob's Well, which was located at the intersection of two roads, one going east-west around Ebal, the other one oriented north-south leading from Jerusalem to Samaria and beyond. The author of the Fourth Gospel was apparently familiar with the topography of the region. He knew that Jesus' route would have avoided the road to Samaria, a mostly gentile city renamed Sebaste by King Herod, and traveled eastward, leaving Ebal on the left. Even if the dialogue between Jesus and the Samaritan woman (*see* JA-COB'S WELL) is not original, the story of Jesus' journey and stay in the village cannot be dismissed as inauthentic. One of Josephus' comments is relevant to Jesus' journey: "It was absolutely necessary for those who would go quickly to pass through [Samaria], for by that road you may go in three days from Jerusalem to Galilee" (*Life*, 52).

Besides Luke's references (Luke 10:33 and 17:16), two other passages in the Fourth Gospel imply that Jesus had some affinity with the Samaritans: John 8:48, "Are we not right in saying that you are a Samaritan and have a demon" (which could refer to magical practices); and John 11:54, "[Jesus went] to a town called Ephraim," which originally could have been "a town in Ephraim," the small town rebuilt near the ruins of Shechem, where he had been welcomed (*see* SAMARIA, SAMARITANS).

BIBLIOGRAPHY

Campbell, E. F. "Shechem." *NEAEHL* 4:1345–54.

Campbell, E. F. and J. F. Ross. "The Excavation of Shechem and Biblical Tradition." *BA* 26 (1963): 1–27.

Cole, D. P. *Shechem I*. Winona Lake, Ind.: Eisenbrauns, 1994.

Fowler, M. D. "A Closer Look at the Temple of el-Berith at Shechem." *Palestine Exploration Quarterly* 115 (1983): 49–53.

Geva, S. "A Fragment of a Tridacna Shell from Shechem." *Zeitschrift des deutschen Palästina–Vereins* 96 (1980): 41–47.

Klamer, C. "A Late Bronze Age Burial Cave near Shechem." *Qadmoniot* 14.53–54 (1982): 30–34 (Hebrew).

Magen, I. "Neapolis." *NEAEHL* 4:135b–59.

Margain, J. "Un anneau samaritain provenant de Naplouse." *Syria* 6 (1984): 45–47.

Shekhem (Nablus). *Excavations and Surveys of Israel* 2 (1983): 90–92.

Stern, E. "Archaemenian Tombs at Shechem." *Qadmoniot* 13. (1980): 101–3 (Hebrew). *Levant* 12 (1980): 90–111.

Toombs, L. E. "Shechem." *ABD* 5:1174–86.

Wright, G. E. *Shechem: A Biography of a Biblical City*. New York: McGraw–Hill, 1965.

Synagogues

Importance

Jesus performed an important part of his ministry in synagogues.

Scripture References

Matt. 4:23; 6:2, 5; 9:35; 10:17; 12:9; 13:54; 23:6, 34; Mark 1:23, 29, 39; 3:1; 5:22, 36, 38; 6:2; 12:39; 13:9; Luke 4:15, 16, 20, 33, 38, 44; 6:6; 7:5; 8:41; 11:43; 12:11; 13:10; 20:46; 21:12; John 6:59; 9:22; 12:42; 16:2; 18:20; Acts 6:9; 9:2, 20; 13:5, 14, 15, 43; 14:1; 15:21; 17:1, 17; 18:4, 7, 8, 17, 26; 22:19; 24:12; 26:11.

General Information

The term *synagogue* appears fifty-six times in the New Testament. It derives from the Greek *synagogé*, which means "place of gathering." In the Septuagint,* it translates both the Hebrew words *adh*, "congregation," and *qhl*, "assembly." In the Aramaic translation of the Hebrew Bible, *adh* is rendered by *knisht'*, "gathering," from which comes the *knst hgdlh*, "the great synagogue"; it designates an assembly for worship and biblical instruction. In the New Testament, Josephus, and Philo, the term *synagogue* is most often used to designate a place of gathering for Scripture reading (New Testament) or other meetings (Josephus). Josephus explicitly refers to two synagogue buildings in Palestine in the first century C.E.: Tiberias (*Life* 54–55) and Caesarea (*War* 2, 14.4–5/285, 289). He mentions a scroll of the Torah (*War* 2, 14.5/291–92) as being in the synagogue of Caesarea.

The numerous references to synagogues in the Gospels and Acts indicate that the institution was well developed in Jesus' time, both in Palestine, especially in Galilee, and in the Diaspora. During the twentieth century, the number of ancient synagogues discovered in Palestine increased to a total of more than one hundred, over half of them located in Galilee and the Golan. The number is even greater in the Diaspora. Nevertheless, only one building recognized as a synagogue, the one at Gamla, is firmly dated to the time of Jesus; two others, at Masada and Herodium, may have existed in his time but the remains are slightly later. The Theodotus inscription discovered in Jerusalem in 1914 refers to one of the synagogues existing in the city in the first century B.C.E., the synagogue of the freedmen (Acts 6:9; *see* JERUSALEM, CITY OF DAVID, OPHEL). Josephus, Philo, and rabbinic literature have information relevant to that given in the New Testament. In Jerusalem alone there would have been several hundred synagogues (*see* JERUSALEM, CITY OF DAVID, OPHEL). Many of them served groups of different origins. Acts 6:9 names Cyrenians, Alexandrians, Cilicians, and people from Asia besides the synagogue of the Freedmen serving slaves freed from Rome or their descendants.

None of the literary sources relates the origin of the institution, except for religious traditions stating that it goes back to the time of Moses, which is of course impossible. The first buildings used as places of worship may have appeared during the Babylonian Exile to provide for community gathering. It is also possible that, outside Palestine, Israelites or Judeans had already started building synagogues before the Exile. After the return from Babylon, meetings for prayer and study may have continued in local towns and villages, apart from the sacrificial rituals and festivals observed in the Temple of Jerusalem.

The Mishnah contains no specific rules regarding the location, orientation, and architecture of synagogues. A few rules in the *Tosepta** may be contradictory. For instance, one reference indicates that those praying should turn their faces toward the Temple (*Berakot* 3. 15.16); some interpreters conclude that the wall facing the main entrance should be in the direction of Jerusalem. Another reference prescribes that the entrance should stand in the east, as it was for the biblical tent of meeting (*t. Megilla* 4.22). In fact, the door of the Gamla synagogue (*see* GAMLA) is oriented toward the south, in the direction of Jerusalem, but it seems that the builders had no other choice because of topographic constraints. There was no Torah shrine built into the walls of the Gamla synagogue. Because in early rabbinic sources, the terms *aron*, "ark," and *tevah* (from a word meaning "chest") are both used to designate the place where the Torah scroll was kept, it is possible that the Torah was taken from a side room and brought into the synagogue at the proper time. The frieze found at Capernaum, which depicts an ark with wheels, adds to this hypothesis. Apparently, it is only in the third and fourth centuries C.E. that fixed niches for the Torah were built into the walls of synagogues (*see* CAPERNAUM).

Besides the chest or ark containing the Torah, the most important feature of the synagogues as they appeared in the third and fourth centuries were the *bema*, an elevated podium from which Scripture was read and comments made, and the *kathedra*, a seat of honor placed toward the center of the building (*see* MOSES' SEAT). The people in the first century structures were seated on built-in masonry benches, set in two or three stepped rows along the walls. Others may have sat on mats or rugs on the floor. With such a floor plan, most participants could easily follow the reading or discussion in the center and see the faces of almost all other members of the congregation. Interactions among worshipers were thus facilitated, as may be reflected in the reactions of the people to Jesus' healing and preaching in synagogues, as depicted in the Gospels. Later (second century onward) basilical synagogues rarely have more than one bench along the walls.

The *rosh hakeneset*, "head of the synagogue," was possibly called *archisynagogos* in Greek. In the Diaspora some of them may have been women in the second to sixth centuries C.E. The leader apparently determined who read the Torah and the Prophets and who spoke (Acts 13:15; *m. Sota* 7. 7.8). According to the *Tosepta* (*t. Megilla* 4.21), the leader did not read the Torah unless invited by the congregation; thus the leader was more of a coordinator and an administrator than a liturgist. Another important leader was the *hazan*, but the role of such a figure is difficult to determine exactly, because the term itself carries different meanings connected with the concept of service. The *hazan* could have been the assistant of the archisynagogos or simply a sexton. In early rabbinic writings the *hazan* seems to play the role of an assistant in the most important ceremonies (Luke 4:20; *Sipre Numbers* 39). In the Mishnah (*m. Makkot* 3.12) the *hazan* is shown as the executioner of the sentence of scourging; according to the *Tosepta* and Jerusalem Talmud he blew the trumpet from the roof of the synagogue to announce the beginning of the Sabbath and festivals (*t. Sukka* 4.199, *y. Sabbat* 16). In these last two functions the *hazan's* role was that of a subordinate. It must be pointed out that these titles come from later sources and are not attested in the first century C.E.

Archaeological Information

Fig. 61 shows the locations of the most important excavated synagogues dating from the first century B.C.E. to the fourth or fifth centuries C.E. in Palestine and neighboring countries. The highest concentrations are in Galilee-Golan and Judea, but numerous inscriptions testify to the existence of synagogues in Samaria. Although only a few of these excavated buildings existed in the first century C.E., there is little doubt that each community had such a building as indicated by the Gospels. As noted above, there may have been up to 480 synagogues in Jerusalem alone. R. Pinhas quoted R. Moshaya in the Jerusalem Talmud as saying:

> There were four hundred eighty synagogues in Jerusalem, each of which had a *bet sefer* and a *bet talmud*. The *bet sefer* was for [the study of] the Bible, and the *bet talmud* for [the study of] the Mishnah, and Vespasian destroyed them all (*y. Megilla* 3.1.73a).

This may not be an exaggeration because only ten male Jews were required to form a synagogue. (For more detailed information about the excavated synagogue buildings of Jesus' time, *see* GAMLA; HERODIUM; and MASADA).

Implications for Jesus Research

Archaeological evidence can be related to the reports in the Gospels that Jesus ministered in synagogues. If the floor plans of these synagogues were the same as that of Gamla, he was the center of focus when healing or speaking in the middle of the congregation, which was seated on benches built along the walls or on the floor.

The most important activity in the synagogue was, of course, the reading of the Torah. According to Josephus:

> He [Moses] appointed the Law to be most excellent and a necessary form of instructions, ordaining, not that it should be heard once for all or twice or on several occasions, but that every week men should desert their other occupations and assemble to listen to the Law and obtain a thorough and accurate knowledge of it (*Against Apion* 2.175).

This statement is duplicated by Acts 15:21: "For from early generations Moses has had in every city those who proclaim him, for he has been read every Sabbath in the synagogues."

However, according to L. I. Levine in *Ancient Synagogues Revealed*, at least eight other different

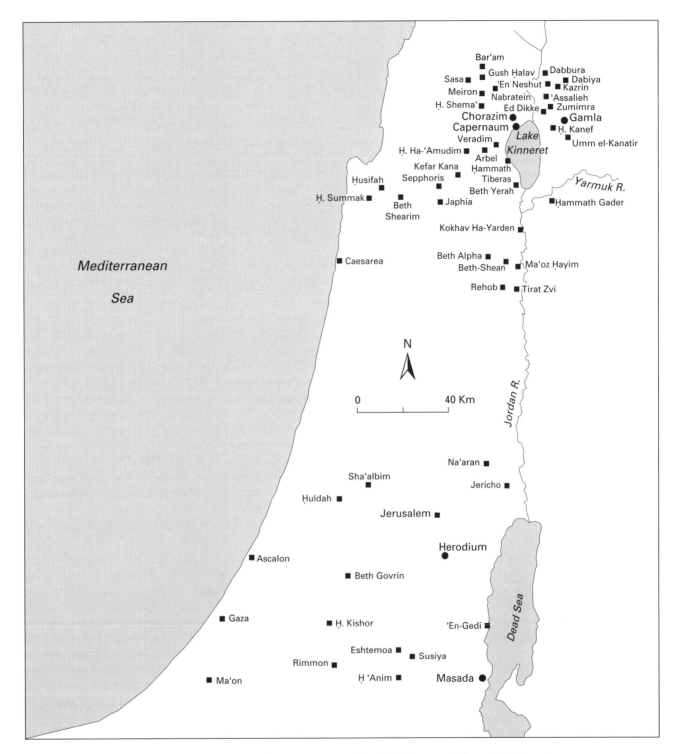

Figure 61 Synagogues. Main excavations of synagogues in Israel, Golan, and Samaria. Note the concentration in Galilee and Golan. The black dots refer to synagogues discussed in this book.

activities also took place in a first-century C.E. synagogue:

1. Prayer during the Sabbath and holidays and perhaps every week day.

2. Learning, as testified by the Theodotius inscription.

3. Community meals, as testified by Josephus, rabbinic literature, and archaeology: a triclinium or dining hall is mentioned in synagogue inscriptions found at Caesarea and Stoi in Yugoslavia. Thus community meals existed at places other than at Qumran, and perhaps Jesus followed a well-established tradition when he compared the kingdom of God to a banquet.

4. Collection and keeping of communal funds, especially for charitable purposes.

5. Sessions of communal law courts. Physical punishments were inflicted on offenders within the synagogue. Consequently, when Jesus is reported as saying, "They will hand you over to councils; and you will be beaten in synagogues" (Mark 13:9; Matt. 10:17), it is probably not a "prediction after the fact" as maintained by some New Testament scholars. The Jesus Seminar, in March of 1989, voted *black* on this saying. The practice of scourging as punishment is in texts other than the Gospels: Deut. 25:1-3; 2 Cor. 11:24; Josephus, *Antiq.* 4. 8/21–23.

6. Meetings of the General Assembly, as illustrated by the political meetings in the synagogue of Tiberias in 66–67 C.E. to decide whether the city would submit to Vespasian before he attacked it (Josephus, *Life* 54–55).

7. Lodging of travelers as attested by the Theodotius inscription, a practice also recorded in the Beth Shean synagogue.

8. Residence of synagogue officials, especially the *hazan*.

The fact that Jesus was authorized to read the Prophets (Luke 4:16) and speak to the congregation shows that he would not have been an illiterate or marginal Jew. As it is not reported in the Gospels that he was beaten in synagogues for his healings or unorthodox comments, his behavior must have been within the parameters of synagogue activity.

BIBLIOGRAPHY

Ancient Synagogues Symposium. University of Haifa: Reuben and Edith Hecht Museum, 1987.

Brooten, B. J. *Women Leaders in the Ancient Synagogues. Inscriptional Evidence and Background Issues.* Brown Judaic Studies, vol. 36. Chico, Calif.: Scholars Press 1982.

Chen, D. "The Design of the Ancient Synagogues in Galilee." *Liber Annuus* 38 (1988): 247–52.

Dothan, M. "Research of Ancient Synagogues in Eretz-Israel." *Thirty Years of Archaeology in Eretz Israel*, 1948–1978. Jerusalem: Israel Exploration Society, 1981 (Hebrew).

Finkelstein, L. F. "The Pharisaic Leadership after the Great Synagogues (170 B.C.E.–135 C.E.)." *The Hellenistic Age.* Vol. 2, *The Cambridge History of Judaism.* Cambridge: Cambridge University Press, 1989.

Foerster, G. "Synagogue Studies: Methodology and Excavations." *Zeitschrift der deutschen Palästina-Vereins* 105 (1989): 129–35.

Gutman, S. *Ancient Synagogues: The State of Research.* Ann Arbor: University of Michigan Press, 1981.

———. "La Synagogue de Gamla." *Ariel* 52 (1982): 18–25.

Ilan, Z. "A Survey of Ancient Synagogues in Galilee." *Eretz Israel* 19 (1987): 170–98.

Levine, L. I., ed. *Ancient Synagogues Revealed.* Jerusalem: The Israel Exploration Society, 1981.

———. *The Synagogue in Late Antiquity.* Philadelphia: ASOR, 1987.

Levine, L. I. and I. Magen. "Synagogues." *NEAEHL* 4.

Machlili, R. "Synagogue." *ABD* 6:251–63.

Ma'oz, Z. U. "Ancient Synagogues of the Golan." *BA* 51.2 (1988): 116–28.

Ma'oz, Z. U. and A. Killebrew. "Ancient Synagogue and Village." *BA* 51 (1988): 5–20.

Meyers, E. M. and D. Barag. "Meiron." *NEAEHL* 3:1026–27.

Meyers, E. M. and C. L. Meyers. *Excavations at the Ancient Synagogue of Gush Halav.* Meiron Excavation Project 5. Winona Lake, Ind.: Eisenbrauns and ASOR, 1990.

———. "The Synagogue in the Second Temple Period." *Eretz Israel* 23 (1992): 320–26 (Hebrew, English summary).

Tannery, Leather

Importance
Jesus refers to leather objects, wineskins, and sandals.

Scripture References
Matt. 3:11; 9:17; 10:10; Mark 1:7; 2:22; 6:9; Luke 3:16; 5:37–38; John 1:27; Acts 10:6; 12:8.

General Information
Leather was one of the earliest and most useful materials available to humankind. It was first used in the form of raw hides and skins dried in the sun. The quantities of scrapers and cutting tools found at many prehistoric sites testify to this early use. According to the Hebrew Bible (Gen. 3:21), the first gift that God offered Adam and Eve was to make "garments of skins" for them. Despite this exalted association of God with the making of leather garments, tanning later became a despised trade (*see* below).

The uses for skins and leather were practically unlimited. They were a means of protection for the body and objects, they served as containers, they functioned as monetary units, they were the object of commerce and a means of wealth accumulation. There were tanned ram and goat skins to cover the tabernacle (Exod. 25:5, *et passim*; Num. 4:25). Tents, helmets, shields, caps, girdles, and the aprons of artisans were made of leather, as were quivers, sheaths, waterskins, and wineskins. Its most prominent use was for shoes, boots, and sandals to which several references are made in the Bible (Gen. 14:23; Ezek. 16:10; Amos 2:6; Mark 1:7, *et passim*). Sandals played a part, in a way not quite comprehensible, in the punishment of a man who would not perform his levirate duty (Deut. 24:9) and in the ceremony of redeeming and exchanging (Ruth 4:7). The halakha* makes several references to the trade of shoemaker (*t. Kelim* B. 4. I. 18, *et passim*).

Tannaitic* and Talmudic writings, which may reflect earlier traditions, indicate that because of working on dead animals and because of the stench of the tanning ingredients, the craft of tanners was categorized as a despised trade. The Babylonian Talmud lists tanners in tenth position (*b. Kiddushin* 82a Bar.) and the Mishnah lists them third after dung collectors and copper smelters (*Ketubot* 7. 18). The tanner was considered as being in a permanent state of impurity because he flayed dead animals, handled fresh bloody skins, and collected dog dung for dehairing them (*b. Berakot* 25a; *t. Kiddushin* 2.2, *et passim*). To avoid pollution, a tannery had to be build on the east side of the city, that is leeward, and at least fifty cubits away from its limits (*m. Baba Batra* 2.9).

A synagogue could not be sold to become a tannery (*m. Megilla* 2.2). The Babylonian Talmud says, "The world cannot do without herbalists and tanners, happy is he who prepares spices, woe to him whose craft is tanning" (*b. Pesahim* 65a, *et passim*). Peter, when he lodged in the house of Simon the tanner in Joppa (Acts 10:6), had no qualms about being in contact with someone who worked with the fresh skins of dead animals. Either the talmudic view had not yet emerged or the view was not widely held, or Peter as an individual did not agree with that view.

Technical and Archaeological Data
A distinction is usually made between "hides," the pelts of large animals such as cattle, camels, and horses, and the "skins" of smaller animals like sheep, goats, rabbits, birds, and fish. Hides and skins have three natural layers:

- the epidermis, or outer layer, made mostly of dead cells at the surface and living ones at the base,
- the corium or derma, the middle layer, of which the leather is made; formed by cell products condensing in fibers in which cells are scattered,
- the innermost layer made of flesh or adipose tissue.

The purpose of the tanner's work was to isolate the corium in order to keep it in a durable and usable form; this was achieved by a series of three operations:

- cleansing of the skin by washing and beating, removal of the epidermis and flesh, and preparing the corium fiber to receive the tanning agent,
- tanning (curing), that is making the corium putrefaction-proof and water resistant; to this end certain chemicals were used: tannin, salt, fish oil, and smoke,
- finishing by rolling, greasing, dyeing, and other operations, which gave the final product a more attractive appearance.

Parchment was obtained by salting the skins of goats or sheep, stretching them on frames, and treating them with flour. The Qumranites may have had their own parchment factory at Khirbet Ein Feskha (*see* DEAD SEA SCROLLS and QUMRAN).

Usually, the soles of shoes were made of one layer of leather like the top; but the military boot of the Romans, the *caliga*, had a sole made of two or more layers. Those boots were produced in special factories. Quantities of intact samples have been found in Roman army camps; and they are mentioned by Roman writers such as Juvenal and Pliny (Forbes, 59–60). Women's shoes could have cork or wooden soles nailed under the leather sole; they were sometimes dyed in bright colors or embroidered and covered with stones.

In the Cave of Letters (*see* CAVE OF LETTERS and JUDEAN CAVES), a water skin made of goat hide was found in a deep crevice. It had been used as a woman's bag and contained objects that were precious to its owner: balls of dyed wool, beads, cosmetic tools, and perfume flasks. In another crevice was a basket full of other artifacts, among them a pair of nearly intact sandals. Similar sandals were found in other Judean caves and at Masada; the soles are made of leather, and thongs starting between the big and second toes reach to the back of the heel (see the photo on this page). Another cache yielded a leather purse containing legal documents (*see* CAVE OF LETTERS).

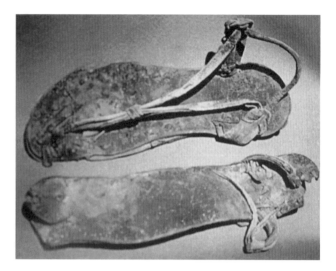

Sandals found almost intact in the "Cave of Letters"

Implications for Jesus Research

The sayings of Jesus contain familiar images that the audience would understand. "No one puts new wine into old wineskins" was a popular saying with a strong evocative power. The pressure of the gas coming from the fermentation of the new wine was too high for an old wineskin, which would burst at the seams (*see* VITICULTURE). The hearers could visualize the spilled wine and the ruined wineskin. They would immediately understand that Jesus' new teaching could not be absorbed without adjustments to old concepts. At the social level also, his teaching called for a change in the interpretation of the law and perhaps in society. The old system would have to be torn down to be replaced by the rule of God.

A problem arises regarding the instructions about sandals Jesus gave to his disciples when he sent them on their evangelistic mission. The Synoptic Gospels contain contradictory statements:

- Matthew 10:9-10: "Take no gold, . . . no bag, . . nor two tunics, nor sandals."

- Mark 6:8-9: "He ordered them to take nothing for their journey; . . . but to wear sandals."
- Luke 9:1-5: no mention of sandals.
- Luke 10:4-11: "Carry no purse, no bag, no sandals."

Mark's version, assumably the most ancient, seems to conform more to reality in its instruction to wear sandals. Even for people with thick layers of corns or calluses on their soles, journeying barefooted on the rocky soil of Galilee would have been hardly possible. The negative instruction not to take sandals, if authentic, perhaps should be understood as meaning not taking a spare pair. An argument against the authenticity of Matthew's set of instructions is the inclusion of the interdiction to carry gold, for it is quite unlikely that Jesus and his disciples had gold in their treasury. The Jesus Seminar rated Mark's version, as well as Matthew 10:10a, *gray* in 1989, thus ignoring the discrepancy between wearing or not wearing sandals and the improbability that the disciples had gold available (*see* COINS AND MONEY). These instructions to travel empty-handed are similar to the Essenes' way of journeying. They would carry no baggage because they relied on the hospitality of other Essenes who lived in nearly every town (*see* TEXTILES, DYEING; HOUSE; and DEAD SEA SCROLLS).

The attitude of Peter, who lodged in the house of Simon the tanner, may reflect Jesus' own support for the equal rights of sinners and outcasts. Another remark can be made in connection with the special character of the tanner's trade. As seen above, a tannery could not exist west of the city, because the prevailing winds would carry the stench and impurity to its population. This is coherent with the general rule that no source of impurity, especially tombs, could be windward of the city and sanctuary. This fits with the suggestion that the execution of criminals and the burial of the dead could not happen west of the city in the first century C.E. (*see* JERUSALEM, TOMBS and GOLGOTHA, TRADITIONAL SITE).

BIBLIOGRAPHY

Forbes, R. J. *Studies in Ancient Technology.* Vol. 5. Leiden: E. J. Brill, 1957.

Jeremias, J. *Jerusalem in the Time of Jesus.* German, 1962. Philadelphia: Fortress Press, 1984.

Yadin, Y. *Bar Kokhba.* London: Weindenfeld and Nicolson, 1971–78.

Tax and Tax Collectors

Importance

Jesus associated with tax or toll collectors, one of whom became a disciple.

Scripture References

Matt. 9:10-11; 10:3; 11:19; 17:24-27; 18:17; 22:15-22; Mark 2:14-17; 12:13-17; Luke 3:12-13; 5:27-32; 15:1; 18:10-13; 19:2, 8; 20:20-26; 23:2; G. Thom. 100.

General Information

As in all polities, many forms of taxation developed in Israel during the monarchy. These were distinct from Temple and priestly taxes.

- Contribution of services, in addition to those already provided by conquered peoples (2 Sam. 20:24; 1 Kings 5:13; 9:20; 12:4, 18; 2 Chron. 2:2, 17-18; 8:7-10).
- Contribution of food (1 Kings 4:7).
- Tolls collected from traders and caravans (1 Kings 10:14-29; 2 Chron. 9:13-28).

Other royal revenues included tribute exacted from subject peoples, gifts offered by vassals, spoils of war, and profit from the king's properties, businesses, and mines. The first property tax mentioned in the Bible is that assessed by King Jehoiakim of Judah on land owners in order to pay tribute to Pharaoh Neco (2 Kings 23:35).

Usually, the ruler of a conquered or vassal country in the ancient Near East was responsible for the payment of tribute to the suzerain; but the Persians introduced a new system. Appointed governors, satraps,* paid predetermined sums to their king; in return, they levied taxes on every person, land owner or not: "tribute, custom, or toll" (Ezra 4:13; 7:24). That every one was normally subject to taxation is seen in the decision of Artaxerxes to exempt priests, Levites, and all Temple personnel (Ezra 7:24). The satraps also collected wine, grain, and money (forty shekels of silver daily) for their own benefit (Neh. 5:15). When Nehemiah was appointed governor, he did not levy the satrap's allotment for himself; instead, he supplied food for one-hundred-fifty officials and also foreign visitors, for which purpose he received one ox, six sheep, fowls, and skins of wine every day (Neh. 5:17-18). Some Jewish officials (Neh. 5:1) took advantage of economic difficulties to force the people to mortgage their properties at high interest rates and even to sell their children as slaves when a famine arose. Nehemiah reacted by ordering the profiteers to return to the people "their fields, their vineyards, their olive orchards, and their houses, and the interest on money, grain, wine, and oil" they had been exacting from them (Neh. 5:11-12). It is significant that Nehemiah took this action after there had been "a great outcry of the people and of their wives against their Jewish brothers" (Neh. 5:1). When injustice and exaction became intolerable, the people appealed to their leader.

Unlike the Persian rulers, the succeeding Ptolemaic and Seleucid kings did not appoint tax agents. Instead, they farmed out the right to collect taxes to the highest bidder (Josephus, *Antiq.* 12, 4.1–5/154–85). Like other conquerors, the Romans exacted tribute and other taxes from the peoples they subjugated. After Pompey took control of Palestine in 63 B.C.E., the Jews had to pay more than 10,000 talents (*Antiq.* 15, 4.5/77–79). Caesar lightened the burden imposed by the Seleucids and probably by the Hasmoneans (*see below*).

Herod instituted a sales tax (*Antiq.* 17, 8.4/205) in addition to the tax in nature levied on crops. He collected the tribute due to the Romans and most likely was allowed to keep a fraction of it. At his death his sons were authorized to collect a tribute from their peoples: Archelaus, 600 talents (400 according to *War* 2, 6.3/97), Antipas, 200, and Philip 100 (*Antiq.* 17, 11.4/317–20).

After the banishment of Archelaus in 6 C.E. and the establishment of a direct rule over Judea-Samaria-Idumea, the Roman tax system was extended to this part of Palestine. It included the ancient *tributum soli*, "tax on the ground," which probably passed from Archelaus to the *Fiscus Caesaris*, "imperial treasury." Under the Seleucids tribute amounted to one-third of the grain harvest. In order to assess it accurately Caesar ordered the establishment of an official cadastre; the work was completed under Augustus. For Palestine Caesar reduced the burden by not requiring the tribute in the sabbatical year and by reducing it to 25 percent on the first following productive year. As need for revenue increased, the value of personal property was added to the value of the real property: furniture, slaves, and money.

Augustus added a *tributum capitis*, a tax on the person. For Palestine it was based on the census of 6 C.E. ordered by Quirinius, legate of Syria. In theory a new census was to be taken every five years. After the upheaval caused by this first census (*Antiq.* 18, 1.1/1–10) there is no record of another such registration. Local authorities were probably responsible for keeping the information current. If the same rules as the ones existing in Syria applied, all men 14 to 65 and women 12 to 65 years of age were subject to the *tributum capitis*. Its amount was probably one dinarius, one day's wage for an agricultural worker (F. M. Heichelheim, 237).

The Roman tax system also included indirect duties:

- The *portorium*, a tax *ad valorem*, "based on value," on the transportation of goods, including slaves and animals. It took the form of a user's fee for spots in public markets, certain roads, bridges, and of customs duties at border crossings and sea ports. Its usual rate was 2.5 percent—thus its other name of *quadragesima*.

- The *vicesima hereditatium*, an "inheritance tax," created by Octavian in 6 C.E. with other taxes on transfer of real property.

- The *centensima rerum venalium*, a "sales tax," instituted by Augustus. There already had been a tax of 4 percent on the sale of slaves since 7 C.E.

- A business license fee appeared under the name of *aurum negotiatorium*. It was levied on merchants, artisans, and members of professional or craft guilds.

Another important source of revenue for the state or its ruler derived from leasing the *ager publicus*, public domain: conquered land leased for cultivation, grazing, mines, or estates such as that of Salome bequeathed to the emperor (Pliny, *Nat. Hist.* 12:111–23). Corvées were organized as needed for the construction of roads, fortifications, and public buildings, and personal requisitions could be ordered (Matt. 5:41; 23:32, and parallels). Some cities received the right to collect their own *portorium*, which came in addition to that instituted by the state. In Jerusalem, a tax on homes (*Antiq.* 19, 6.3/299) may have been collected for the maintenance of the wall (*m. Baba Batra* 1.5).

Thus, the Roman tax system at the beginning of the first century C.E. was quite elaborate. With a series of national, regional, and local layers, it was comparable to those existing today in most Western countries. Although direct information is lacking, it is generally assumed that most of the Roman tax system applied directly to the subprovince of Judea, and that Antipas and Philip instituted identical systems in their territories. The Jews had the additional ancestral burden of the tithe on all crops to be paid to the priests and Levites, the half-shekel Temple tax paid by all Jewish males, and the mandatory offerings (*see* TEMPLE, SACRIFICIAL SYSTEM and TEMPLE, TREASURY).

In Judea, a subprovince somewhat independent from Syria, the tribute was probably collected directly under the authority of the prefect who, in this aspect, acted as a procurator (*see* PILATE'S STONE). Some prefects may have transferred the burden to the High Priest. Toll on personal property was more difficult to collect and so was farmed out to local *architelones*, "chief tax collectors" like Zacchaeus, residing in a main center of commercial activity, in his case in Jericho (Luke 19:2-10). In Judea there was no central publican as in Italy and senatorial provinces; the situation was comparable to that of Syria and Egypt. The financial procurators, prefects of Egypt and Judea, and procurators assigned to the Legate of Syria, made decisions in matters of taxation, including the inheritance tax. They established the structure of the tax base and were receivers and payers. One of their most important duties was to assure the timely payment of the troops' salaries.

There were certainly abuses by tax collectors and financial procurators (*Antiq*, 18, 6.5/172–78; *War* 2, 14.1/272–76; Philo, *Legatio ad Caius*, 199). Tiberius made efforts to limit such corruption (Tacitus, *Annals* 5.6); Suetonus quotes him as saying "a good shepherd does not flay his flock" (*Tiberius* 32). In the Gospels and in rabbinic literature, the tax collectors are associated with robbers, sinners, prostitutes, and Gentiles (Matt. 9:10-11; 11:19; 18:17; 21:3; Mark 2:15-16; Luke 5:30; *m. Nedarim* 3.4; *t. Baba Kama* 94a; cf. *b. Sanhedrin* 25b).

Archaeological Information

Ostraca* found at Samaria and Tell ed-Duweir mention payments in kind made to the king of Israel. Jar handles unearthed at Gibeon and Lachish bear the imprint of seals stating, *lmlk*, "to the king." The excavation season of 1989 at Bethsaida yielded a similar jar handle. Its seal imprint represents a man kneeling with raised hands, the inscription is the same. These finds date to the eighth century B.C.E. and relate to a provincial tax system. Many Roman coins bearing the profile of Tiberius, the Roman emperor at the time of Jesus, were found in Israel. They are dinarii similar to that presented to Jesus in his dispute with representatives of the religious establishment about the legitimacy of paying taxes to Rome (Matt. 22:15-22 and parallels; *see* COINS AND MONEY).

Implications for Jesus Research

At the beginning of the first century C.E., the people of Judea complained to the emperor about the excessive taxes imposed on them by Herod the Great and Archelaus; they even requested that their country be annexed to the province of Syria under Roman rule (*Antiq.* 17, 11.2/304–14; *War* 2, 6.2/84–92). But between 6 C.E. and the time of the Crucifixion, there is no evidence of rebellion or recourse to the sovereign for redress of oppressive taxation as in the times of Rehoboam (1 Kings 12:1-2) and Nehemiah (*see* General Information above). The revolt of 6 C.E., caused by the first Roman census, was as much religious and nationalistic as economic (*Antiq.* 18, 1.1/1–10). The only other insurrection that is mentioned during Jesus' life is that caused by the ruthlessness of Pilate, who came into power in 26 C.E. (Mark 15:7). During the same period, the reigns of Antipas in Galilee and Philip in Gaulanitis seem to have been rather uneventful. There is no basis for claiming that the people of Palestine were in a state comparable to that of the serfs of seventeenth-century France. The socioeconomic reality of Palestine during Jesus' time needs to be investigated more carefully.

Many estimates of the tax burden have been made. One such estimate, in the case of a small farmer, gives the following results, which we provide here to encourage further research.

Taxation by the Romans and Tetrarchs

1. *Tributum soli* on crops. Yearly average, excluding the sabbatical year:

$$\frac{25\% + 5 \times 33\%}{6} = 31.7\%$$

estimated at 60% of all crops and income = 19%

2. *Tributum capitis*, for a family of six.
   6 dinarii of income for 250 days (one worker assumed) = 1%

3. Sales, inheritance taxes. Total impact = 5%
4. *Portorium*. Total impact = 4%
5. Gifts to official = 3%
   Total civil taxes = 32%

Traditional Jewish Taxes

6. Tithes on all crops. Total impact = 8%
7. Half-shekel (2 dinarii) tax on males = 1%
8. Sacrifices. Total impact = 3%
   Total Jewish taxes = 12%

Forced exactions

9. Officials' persecution, banditry = 5%
   Total burden = 49%

This total is comparable with what is paid today in Western countries, when all direct and indirect taxes at all levels of government are added up. A male day laborer paid only the *tributum capitis*, the half-shekel tax, and the price of the small offerings required of the poor.

Jesus did not advocate rebellion against the payment of the tribute to Rome. His answer, "Render to Caesar the things that are Caesar's and to God the things that are God's" (Mark 12:15) may reflect an attitude of indifference to the dominion of a foreign power in that God allowed it to be. As S. G. C. Brandon remarked, this saying could have been interpreted as an interdiction for paying the tribute on the reasoning that, because everything belonged to God, nothing belonged to Caesar, who should not receive anything (*Jesus and the Zealots*, 345–47). This correlates with the witnesses' statement of Luke 23:2: "We found this man . . . forbidding us to give tribute to Caesar." A suggestion of C. A. Evans is worth considering. In his article "Opposition to the Temple," he proposes that Jesus intended to point out the offense caused by the image of the emperor on the Roman dinarius. He suggests that, because of the commandment "You shall not make for yourself an idol" (Exod. 20:4), observant Jews would refuse to possess such an image. This is not convincing, however, because the half-shekel Temple tax had to be paid with Tyrian coins bearing the image of the pagan god Melkart (*see* TEMPLE, TREASURE and COINS AND MONEY).

In contrast with the Sadducees, Pharisees, and Essenes, and in accord with the attitude of John the Baptist, Jesus did not ostracize anyone. Admission to the kingdom or eternal life was based on repentance and submission to the will of God. His concern was for those at the bottom of the socio-economic ladder, the "sheep without a shepherd" (Matt. 9:36) and all sinners, including tax collectors. He was probably not a social activist or a militant extremist. If he was implicated in an insurrection, it may only have been by accident (*see* WEAPONS AND ARMORS).

BIBLIOGRAPHY

Benoit, P. "Quirinius." *Dictionnaire de la Bible*, 1977.

Brandon, S. G. F. *Jesus and the Zealots*. New York: Scribner's Sons, 1967.

Bruce, F. F. "Render to Caesar." *Jesus and the Politics of His Day*. Edited by E. Brammel and C. D. F. Moule. Cambridge: Cambridge University Press, 1984.

Crossan, J. D. *The Historical Jesus*. San Francisco: Harper and Row, 1991.

Evans, Craig A. "Opposition to the Temple: Jesus and the Dead Sea Scrolls." *Jesus and the Dead Sea Scrolls*. Edited by James H. Charlesworth, 235–53. The Anchor Bible Reference Library. New York: Doubleday, 1992.

Hart, H. St. J. "The Coin of 'Render unto Caesar.' " *Jesus and the Politics of His Day*. Edited by E. Bammel and C. F. D. Moule, Cambridge: Cambridge University Press, 1984.

Horsley, R. A. "High Priests and the Politics of Roman Palestine." *Journal for the Study of Judaism* 17 (1986): 30–31.

———. *Jesus and the Spiral of Violence*. San Francisco: Harper and Row, 1987.

Jagersma, H. *A History of Israel from Alexander the Great to Bar Kokhba*. Philadelphia: Fortress Press, 1985.

Lémenon, J. P. *Pilate et le gouvernement de la Judée*. Paris: J. Gabalda, 1981.

McLean Harper, G. Jr. "Village Administration in the Roman Province of Syria." *Yale Classical Studies* 1 (1928): 105–68.

Snell, D. C. "Taxes and Taxation." *ABD* 6:338–40.

Temple, History, Description

Importance

The Temple was the center of Jewish national, religious, and political life. It symbolized God's presence among the people. Jesus visited it several times and taught there daily during his last days in Jerusalem.

Scripture References

There are numerous references to Herod's Temple in the New Testament, among them Matt. 4:5; 21:12; 24:1; 27:51; Mark 11:15; 11:27; 13:1; 15:38; Luke 1:8-11; 4:9; 19:45; 20:1; 21:5; 23:45; John 2:14; 10:23; Acts 3:2, 10, 11; 5:12.

General Information

Because the Temple was the most important monument and the most significant national and religious institution for the Jews of the first century C.E., information about it helps to understand Jesus' relationship to it. Although, after the Exile, Temple sacrifice had lost some of its importance in favor of prayer and the study of Torah, the Temple remained the only place where certain cultic ceremonies and practices were observed; it was the point of convergence of tens of thousands of pilgrims during the great festivals. Although in the time of Jesus political leadership and judicial prerogatives had ceased to be held by the priesthood, recognition of the Temple's importance continued. The times for prayers in the synagogues, for example, corresponded to the times of sacrifices, and the worshipers turned toward the Temple (*m. Berakot* 4:5). Only in radical groups like the Qumranites had the Jerusalem Temple lost its prestige.

In addition to the present article several other entries concern the Temple:

- Royal Stoa,
- Sacrificial System,
- Service and Ritual,

- Solomon's Portico,
- Stairs and Gates,
- Treasury,
- Trumpeting Place,
- Warning Signs.

Five important sources—the Bible, the Books of Maccabees, Josephus (*War* book 5, chap. 5; *Antiq.* book 15, chap. 11), the Dead Sea Scrolls, and the Mishnah (tractates *Middot, Tamid, Yoma, Sheqalim*)—provide data that, when combined with archaeological discoveries, inform us about Herod's Temple.

Brief History. The Temple Jesus knew was the Temple of Herod, or "Third Temple," sometimes referred to as successor to the Second Temple. The First Temple, which King Solomon began to build in 957 B.C.E. (1 Kings 5–8; 2 Chron. 2–7), after several modifications, was destroyed by the Babylonians in 587 B.C.E. It was set in an enclosure 500 cubits (861 feet as estimated by L. Ritmayer) square, north of the Ophel. The same enclosure was used by Zerubbabel to build the Second Temple, which was rededicated in 515 B.C.E. In the course of its long life, Zerubbabel's Temple was probably modified, damaged, or even destroyed several times. The Seleucid rulers erected the fortress Akra to keep watch over the Temple. Its location has been debated, but on the basis of a subterranean pool identified as the Akra cistern mentioned in the Mishnah (*m. 'Erubin* 10:14), J. Schwartz and L. Ritmayer suggest, as does B. Mazar, that the fortress was standing against the southern wall, on the highest point of the Ophel. After he conquered Jerusalem in 141 B.C.E., Simon Maccabee razed the Akra and used its blocks of stone to build a new wall and extend the Temple platform about 135 feet to the south (*Antiq.* 13, 6.7/217). This proposal can be related to a verse of 1 Maccabees: "He [Simon] strengthened the fortifications of the temple hill alongside the citadel, and he and his men lived there" (1 Macc. 13:52, NRSV).

In 20–19 B.C.E., almost five centuries after the dedication of the Second Temple, Herod the Great undertook a vast project of embellishing the Temple itself and of enlarging and beautifying the Temple Mount. Herod's architects expanded the platform to the north, west, and south over a total area of more than 35 acres. It corresponded approximately (the northern limits are not well ascertained) to the present Haram esh-Sheriff, which incorporates most of its foundations and some of its retaining walls. In this as in all his building endeavors Herod made a point of creating something bigger and more beautiful than what existed in his time. The largest monumental platform known in the Greco-Roman world at the end of the first century B.C.E. was the esplanade of the palatial compound of Persepolis, which measures 450 by 300 meters (1476.45 by 984.3 feet). The Herodian platform according to the estimate of F. G. Hollis was 1041 feet in the north, 1556 feet in the east, 929 feet in the south and 1596 feet in the west or an average of 1576 x 985 feet, which is 100 feet longer than the Persepolis platform. The entire Temple complex was larger than any other holy structure built by the Romans at the time or by their predecessors anywhere else in the known world, including Egypt, Carthage, Syria, and Mesopotamia.

When Herod decided to rebuild the Temple, he sought to forestall any objections of the priests or people, who might be concerned that the Temple service would be disrupted. He began by accumulating all the necessary materials and he made careful preparations before tearing down any existing structures (*Antiq.* 15, 11.2/389–90). Although it was a totally new sanctuary, the work was conducted in such a way that the service was never interrupted, and because only they could enter the sacred area, Herod had one thousand priests trained beforehand as masons and builders. The sanctuary itself was built in eighteen months (*Antiq.* 15, 420), but work was still going on in the surrounding porticoes some time before the First Jewish Wars, which broke out in 66 C.E. (*Antiq.* 20, 219–21). The height of the sanctuary was increased by 40 cubits, its width by 30 cubits, and its façade was completely redone. Only stones of the purest white were used, and many parts were plated with gold and silver (*War* 5, 5.6/222). Its splendor was unequaled: "He who has not seen the Temple of Herod has never seen a beautiful building in his life." (*m. Baba Batra* 4 a). Herod build a large flight of stairs over an arch to connect the southwestern corner of the Temple esplanade with the Lower City, and another one at the southeastern corner.

The Temple was treated differently by the existing political powers at different periods. After the Greek conquest, the High Priest Simon II the Just, son of Onias, was able to fortify the sanctuary circa 180 B.C.E. (Sir. 50:1-4). He also built a reservoir "like the sea," which may be the Pool of Bethesda (*see* POOL OF BETHESDA). At first the Hellenistic successors of Alexander respected the Temple and made generous gifts for its maintenance and service; the Temple officials and scribes were exempted from the payment of the royal tax (*Antiq.* 12, 3.3/140–42: 13, 6.7/213; 2 Macc. 3:2-3). But Antiochus IV Epiphanes reversed the situation drastically. In 169 B.C.E., after returning from Egypt, he entered the sanctuary and took away all its holy vessels. In 167 he erected an altar to Zeus on the altar of Yahweh, and the sacred services ceased until Judah Maccabee took Jerusalem in 165 (1 Macc. 4:58; 2 Macc. 1:9; 2:18) and rededicated the Temple to God. This first ceremony is traditionally claimed to be the origin of the feast of Hanukkah.

Under the Romans trouble began with Pompey, who entered the Holy of Holies in 63 B.C.E.; he did not seize anything, however (*War* 1, 6.6/152–53). When Crassus, then governor of Syria, went to war against the Parthians he stole 2,000 silver talents and all the gold from the Temple Treasury (*Antiq.* 14, 7.1/105–9). More difficulties occurred under the Roman prefects of Judea, especially in the times of Pontius Pilate, Varus, and Gessius Florus, who was mostly responsible for the beginning of the First Jewish War. Finally the Romans conquered Jerusalem and its last fortress, the Temple, which was destroyed in 70 C.E. The menorah and some cultic objects were taken as spoil by the conquerors and are represented on a relief still visible on Titus' Arch in Rome.

Toward the end of the Second Temple or during the time of the Third there were other Jewish sanctuaries. The best known is the Temple of the Samaritans on Mt. Gerizim (*see* Mount Gerizim), erected after the people of Samaria were refused the right to participate in the building of the Second Temple (Ezra 4:1-3). Under Antiochus Epiphanes it was dedicated to Zeus in 167 B.C.E. as was the Jerusalem Temple. It was razed by John Hyrcanus at the same time as Samaria in 108–107 B.C.E. (Antiq. 13. 10.3/281).

Hundreds of papyri discovered near the turn of the century at Elephantine, an island in the Nile near Aswan, revealed the existence of a Hebrew-Aramaic community there in the Persian period. It had its own Temple erected to the god Yahu, probably the same as Yahweh. The papyri were published in 1906, 1911, and 1953 by different scholars. The Elephantine temple, destroyed by the Egyptians in 410 B.C.E., was rebuilt later by permission of the governor of Judea under the provision that animal sacrifices would not be offered. Another temple in Egypt is known from Josephus. Onias III, son of Simon II the Just, of the lineage of Zadok, was High Priest in the time of Seleucus IV Philopater (187–175 B.C.E.), but he turned his allegiance to the Ptolemies of Egypt. When Antiochus IV Epiphanes became king in 175 B.C.E., Onias fled to Egypt and requested from Ptolemy VI Philometor permission to build a Temple to Yahweh in Leontopolis, in the Nile Delta, in the *nomos* of Heliopolis. This favor being granted to him, he built a temple and organized its service with the cooperation of the priests and Levites of the Egyptian Diaspora (Antiq. 13, 3.1–3/62–73; War 7, 10.3/427–32).

Description. In order to extend the Temple esplanade to twice its size, Herod's engineers carried out a titanic enterprise. They first hewed away the rock at the northwest corner of the mount to a depth of 58 feet and extended the enclosure to the fortress Antonia, which had been built earlier. On the northeastern corner they filled a small valley going to the Kidron, and for this purpose built a wall 124 feet high and filled the space created with earth. At the southeastern corner the ground level was 154 feet lower than the planned extension of the platform. There the space was filled with rocks and earth to a height of 98 feet, and on this raised surface they built immense vaults over a distance of 290 feet to support the new esplanade. These cave-like structures at the southeastern corner of the Temple Mount are improperly called "Solomon's Stables." Most of the structure of the new Temple Mount was in fact comprised of retaining walls that were formidable ramparts but also had artistic merit: the white stone blocks were carefully embossed, and the upper part of the wall was decorated with pilasters in the same fashion as the wall of Machpelah at Hebron (see HEBRON). There were embrasures and battlements guarded by Levites especially at the corners and gates.

The largest part of the Temple precincts was opened to all, including foreigners—thus its name, Court of the Gentiles. It was surrounded by porticoes made of two rows of marble columns 25 cubits (38 feet) high, supporting cedar beams and a flat roof. On the same side as the Golden Gate in the east, and facing the sanctuary, was Solomon's Portico (John 10:23; Acts 3:11; 5:12), possibly so-called because it incorporated portions of walls dating from the First Temple. There, Jesus and the apostles after him held meetings. It was also called the "Street of the Lord's House" because of its location opposite the sanctuary. In the south, much higher than the other porticoes, stood a stoa in the form of a huge basilica called the "Royal Portico" or "Royal Stoa" (see TEMPLE, ROYAL STOA). In this vast area crowds gathered to listen to rabbis and other speakers and to deal with merchants and money changers.

Toward the center of the Temple precincts but more to the north, was the sacred core surrounded by a stone lattice or balustrade (soreg) about 2.5 feet high according to the Mishnah (m. Middot 2:3), but probably higher, because signs bearing a warning to Gentiles were attached to it (see JERUSALEM, WARNING SIGNS). Josephus, who indicates a height of 3 cubits (about 4.5 feet, War 5, 5.2/193), probably preserves a more accurate

record. Inside the soreg, fourteen steps led to a platform enclosed by a high rampart 10 cubits (15 feet) thick. Inside the rampart, the space was occupied from east to west by the Court of Women, the Court of Israel, and the Court of the Priests, in which stood the sanctuary. The Court of Women was quite large, 135 cubits (202 feet) square; at each of its corners was a chamber 40 cubits (60 feet) square: the Chamber of the Nazirites in the southeast, Chamber of Oil in the southwest, Chamber of the Lepers in the northwest, Chamber of Wood in the northeast. On the eastern side of the Court of Women fifteen semi-circular steps led to Nicanor's Gate, which was 115 cubits (172 feet) high. Its doors were overlaid with embossed bronze decorations of Corinthian style. It is probably the gate referred to by Josephus as the "Corinthian Gate" (War 5, 5.3/204). All the other gates of the sanctuary were plated with silver and gold.

Behind Nicanor's Gate, only men had access to the Court of Israel, a narrow area 135 cubits (202 feet) wide but only 11 cubits (17 feet) deep in front of the Court of the Priests. Under the floor of the Court of Israel, the Levites stored musical instruments in special chambers. A wall 66 feet high surrounded the two courts of the sanctuary; on its upper part hung spoils taken from Israel's enemies by the Hasmoneans and Herod the Great. Non-priests could go beyond the limits of the Court of Israel into the Court of the Priests to lay their hands on sacrificial animals and wave the parts to be burnt (m. Kelim 1:8); they could also enter the Court of the Priests on some other occasions (see Implications below).

The Court of the Priests measured 187 x 135 cubits (290 x 202 feet). It contained the Temple itself, the altar of burnt offerings, the laver holding the water used by the priests to wash their hands and feet, the slaughtering place with its six rows of four rings for tying animals (thus 24 animals could be killed at the same time), and marble pillars supporting cedar beams on which the carcasses were hooked for skinning. In the slaughtering area stood tables for the preparation of the sacrifices: removing limbs and cutting out viscera and fat. Outside

The Temple Complex with the Walls of the Court of Women in the Center.
On the right (north) is the Antonia (Jerusalem model).

the sanctuary the main feature was the altar, 32 cubits square and 16 cubits (24 feet) high. Its exact location has been disputed, but it was probably centered on the threshing floor of Araunah, where David had built the first altar (2 Sam. 24:18, 25). Like ancient Canaanite altars, it had a small protuberance (horn) at each corner. A ramp on the southern side gave access to the top. The previous altar, which had been defiled by the cult of Zeus under Antiochus Epiphanes, had been torn down by Judah Maccabee and its stones stored in one of the main chambers existing within or against the walls of the Court of Priests (*see* TEMPLE, WALLS AND GATES).

The Temple building had a flat roof with golden spikes to keep the birds away; it included the sanctuary on the eastern side and the Holy of Holies in the west. Its façade was larger than the main body,

100 cubits (150 feet) wide and 100 cubits (150 feet) high, while the rest of the building was as high but only 70 feet wide; for this reason the Mishnah (*m. Middot* 4:7) compares it to a lion "narrow in the rear and broad in the front." At the façade stood four pillars as represented on the silver tetradrachmas of Bar Kokhba (*see* MASADA). The entrance to the sanctuary, or main hall of the Temple, was 40 cubits (60 feet) high and 20 cubits (30 feet) wide; it was reached by a few steps and was closed by an immense curtain. Behind the curtain was a hall extending left and right all the way across the wider part of the building, but like the Court of Israel, it was only 11 feet deep. On its cedar beams hung golden crowns with golden chains that the young priests would climb to clean the crowns. From the entrance hall a double gate, the "Great Gate" of the Temple, opened to the sanctuary. When this gate

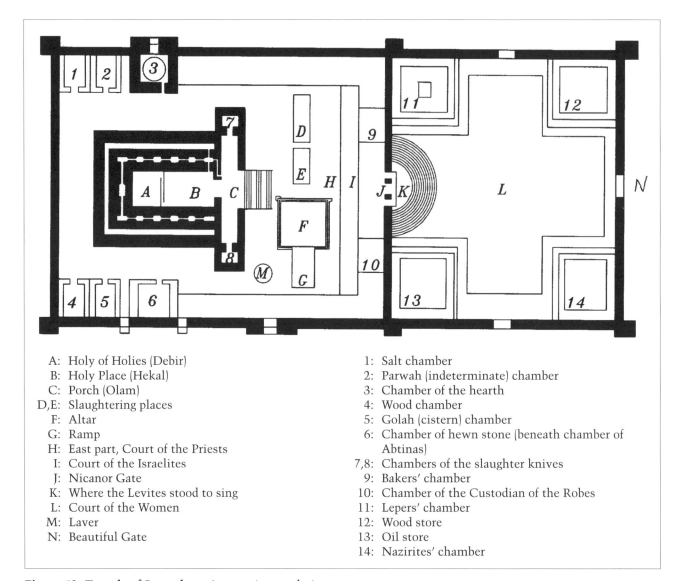

A: Holy of Holies (Debir)
B: Holy Place (Hekal)
C: Porch (Olam)
D,E: Slaughtering places
F: Altar
G: Ramp
H: East part, Court of the Priests
I: Court of the Israelites
J: Nicanor Gate
K: Where the Levites stood to sing
L: Court of the Women
M: Laver
N: Beautiful Gate

1: Salt chamber
2: Parwah (indeterminate) chamber
3: Chamber of the hearth
4: Wood chamber
5: Golah (cistern) chamber
6: Chamber of hewn stone (beneath chamber of Abtinas)
7,8: Chambers of the slaughter knives
9: Bakers' chamber
10: Chamber of the Custodian of the Robes
11: Lepers' chamber
12: Wood store
13: Oil store
14: Nazirites' chamber

Figure 62 Temple of Jerusalem. A tentative rendering.

was opened or shut, it is said that the noise of the hinges was heard as far as Jericho (*m. Tamid* 3:8). Over the gate was displayed the golden vine on which the priests hung presents of gold, shaped in the form of leaves and grapes (*m. Middot* 3:8).

Three stories of rooms lined each side of the Temple, which reduced its inner dimensions. The sanctuary was 40 x 20 cubits (60 x 30 feet), and its walls were plated with gold. It contained the altar of incense, the table of the bread of the presence, the golden menorah (lampstand), and the instruments necessary for its service. One of the marble slabs on the floor of the sanctuary was removable; beneath it was dust to be used in mixing the water of bitterness, which was given as an ordeal ritual to women suspected of infidelity. This took place near Nicanor's Gate, in the Court of Women. The 20 cubit (30 feet) square Holy of Holies, which communicated directly with the outer sanctuary but was separated from it by a large double curtain, was empty. It was supposed to hold the Ark of the Covenant, but that object had disappeared, perhaps when Jerusalem fell to the Babylonians (587 B.C.E.), or even earlier when Pharaoh Shishak raided Jerusalem in the tenth century B.C.E. The Holy of Holies was believed to be the earthly dwelling place of the divine presence, and the High Priest alone entered it only once a year on Yom Kippur, the "Day of Purgation," to offer incense and seek atonement for the people (see TEMPLE, SERVICE AND RITUAL). For this solemn occasion he set aside his rich vestments and wore white linen clothes, as did the other priests (Lev. 16:4).

Administrations and Judiciary. During the first half of the first century B.C.E., the High Priest was appointed by the Roman prefect of Judea or by the legate of Syria (*Antiq.* 18, 2.2/34-35). He was the head of the Temple and did not belong to any division; he could offer animal sacrifices and incense at his discretion but only at the appropriate times on the Sabbath and festivals. He alone could perform certain rites like the offering of incense and pronouncing the name of God on Yom Kippur, and the burning of the Red Heifer. He read the Torah at the end of the sabbatical years. He wore a special garment of blue, purple, and scarlet with fittings of gold; his breastplate bore the names of the twelve tribes of Israel on twelve precious stones. These vestments were kept in the fortress Antonia when not in use, a custom initiated by John Hyrcanus for reasons of security, so that no one could usurp his functions. The *segan,* deputy High Priest (also called *strategos*), was the chief of the priests and came second in rank; his role was to supervise the daily Temple service. During the existence of the Third Temple, the Chief of the Priests may have been recruited from the Pharisees. The Romans always chose the High Priest from members of the

priestly oligarchy until they relinquished this right to Herod of Chalchis, and then to Herod Agrippa, who nevertheless continued the tradition. Between 6 and 67 C.E. sixteen High Priests, out of eighteen, belonged to only five families. During this period, there is evidence of greed and corruption in the High Priesthood. Josephus reports that, in the time of Agrippa, the High Priest Ishmael, son of Phiabi, sent his servants to seize the tithes of the priests on the threshing floors (*Antiq.* 20, 8.8/181). So did Ananias and others to the point that some priests died of starvation (*Antiq.* 20, 9.2/206-7). The same kind of oppression is recorded in the Babylonian Talmud (*b. Pesahim* 57.1) and *Tosepta* (*t. Minhot* 13.21; see JERUSALEM, UPPER CITY). It is no accident that the first victim of the *sicarii* was Jonathan the High Priest (*War* 2,13.3/256).

The office of priest was hereditary; adolescent males of priestly families in theory could participate in the service but, in fact, had to reach the age of twenty before joining in the rituals. (The minimum age of twenty was also required of the Essenes joining Qumran; see DEAD SEA SCROLLS.) Priests alone could enter the sanctuary and approach the altar; they officiated at the daily services and gave the blessings. They could perform all the tasks assigned to the Levites but even then they kept their privileged status. Priests were divided into *mishmarot,* "divisions," serving one week at a time. When their turn of service came their tasks were assigned by lots, the ultimate form of egalitarian organization—letting God decide. Pilgrim priests from the Diaspora could join their divisions on duty, except for those who had "corrupted" themselves by serving in the heretic temple of Leontopolis in Egypt. Those priests who could not take part in the ritual because of physical imperfections could nonetheless assist in the work of their divisions, bless the people, and receive their share of the sacrifices, that is, their income.

In the course of time, the Levites from whose tribe the priests, descendants of Eleazar son of Aaron, had originated, were deprived of their traditional duties. Into the Third Temple they served as singers and gatekeepers. They were in charge of checking persons entering the Temple enclosure. They too were divided in 24 divisions and provided a continuous guard of the Temple; they locked and opened the gates at the appointed times. According to Josephus, upon a special request of the Levites, the Sanhedrin authorized the singers of hymns to wear the priestly white linen clothes (*Antiq.* 20, 9.6/216–17).

Certain other functions were given to Temple officials chosen from priestly families. By order of importance were two *katolikim* or *catholicos*, "controllers of the Treasury," seven *amarkelim*, "trustees," three *gizbarim*, "treasurers." In regard to the Temple service, each week supervisors instructed and watched over the divisions of priests and Levites. Many functions were hereditary and were held by certain families. The Mishnah gives the names of fifteen officers who were probably serving during the time of Agrippa. Among these were: Yohanen ben Phinehas in charge of the tokens exchanged for money to buy sacrifices (which indicates that the commerce of sacrificial animals was controlled by the High Priesthood); Ben Ahijah, health officer; Gabinimus, Temple crier; Ben Geber in charge of the gates; Ben Babi, in charge of the menorah wicks; Ben Arza, choir master; the Garmu family in charge of the bread of the presence; the Abtinas family in charge of the incense; and Phineas in charge of the priestly garments (*m. Sheqalim* 5, 1).

The captain of the guard had an important role. He organized the watch and disciplined priests and Levites who did not fulfill their responsibilities. Each watch was composed of three priests and twenty-one Levites; the priests guarded three of the chambers in the sanctuary and Levites were distributed among gates and corners of the Temple Mount and Temple Court, two chambers and the back of the Holy of Holies. Besides these small groups of Levites there was apparently no permanent armed guard under a commander answering to the High Priest, as might be implied by Matthew 27:65, where Pilate refers to "a guard of soldiers."

The Supreme Jewish Council, the Sanhedrin, derives its name from the Greek *sunedrion*, "seating together, assembly." It was composed of 71 members; there were also two small courts of 23 members each. The Supreme Council had judiciary, legislative, and executive powers. Its membership consisted of both Sadducees and Pharisees. It was convened and presided over by the High Priest, and vacancies were filled by co-optation, which made this body relatively independent from Roman and religious authorities. There were no meetings on the Sabbath and on feast days, and a capital case could not be examined on the eve of the Sabbath or festivals or at night. Moreover, it was illegal to pass a death sentence on the same day as the trial (*m. Sanhedrin* 5). These rules cast serious doubts on the authenticity of the trial of Jesus as reported in the Synoptic Gospels. The account of the Fourth Gospel, which mentions only an informal inquiry by the High Priest seems more in line with the reality. In light of these rules, the problem of whether the Sanhedrin had the right to sentence Jesus to death becomes a moot question (*see* JERUSALEM, CAIAPHAS'S HOUSE).

Archaeological Data

While the platform walls of the Herodian Temple are still visible, and capitals, sections of columns of the porticoes, and some inscriptions have been recovered, nothing belonging with certainty to the Temple itself has been found.

Each entry pertaining to the Temple complex includes a section giving archaeological information.

Implications for Jesus Research

Jesus was in the category of Israelites, thus neither priest nor Levite. As such, provided he was in a state of ritual cleanliness approved by a Levite at one of the gates, he could go beyond the *soreg* (balustrade) into the Court of Women and Court of Israel in order to offer sacrifices or gifts, or simply to observe and pray. He could also serve in the Temple area with the priests on duty as a representative of the Galilean community and participate in the prayer during the services (*ma'amadot*). The same privileges applied to his disciples. Apart from these regulated activities, which gave laity access to the Court of the Priests, the people came mostly to observe the services, to receive the priestly benediction, and to prostate themselves before God. The Mishnah (*m. Middot* 2:3) indicates that thirteen prostrations were made in commemoration of the thirteen breaches opened in the *soreg* by the High Priest Alcimas who was appointed in 161 B.C.E. by Demetrius I. They were repaired later by Jonathan, first Hasmonean High Priest (152–142). Even if they were ritually clean Jews could immerse themselves in a ritual bath before entering the Temple Court (*y. Yoma* 3:3, 40). All visitors removed their shoes or sandals when entering the Temple Mount and many dressed in white for the occasion. People visiting the Temple did not turn their backs to it; entering by the triple Hulda Gate, they moved counterclockwise around the Temple Court and then exited through the Double Gate. There is no reason to suppose that Jesus did not follow such customs.

Although the Gospels and Acts indicate that Jesus, when in Jerusalem, centered his activity on the Temple, as did the first Jewish Christians, there is no evidence that Jesus or the disciples offered sacrifices or gifts, or even entered the Court of Israel. Only Acts mentions that Peter and John entered the Temple enclosure (Acts 3:3) and thus had just immersed themselves in a ritual bath. Did Jesus, who did not require his disciples to wash their hands before eating (Matt. 15:2; Mark 7:2), immerse himself before entering the Temple? The fact that he heard the call of John the Baptist and went to the Jordan indicates that he respected traditional rules, if not the precepts of the Pharisees (Mark 7:7-8), as he did also for the payment of the half-shekel tax (Matt. 17:27), and in observing Passover (Matt. 26:17-19 and parallels). Thus he probably followed the customs of the time and bathed as did other pilgrims (*see* RITUAL BATHS, *MIQVAOT*).

Rabbis taught and merchants and money changers exercised their trades in the porticoes and Royal Stoa (*see* TEMPLE, ROYAL STOA), some remnants of which have been discovered in excavations. According to the Gospels Jesus preferred to stay in these areas, which were open to all, where syna-gogue-like meetings were held, and where he had more freedom to speak and act. He may have held his sessions in Solomon's Portico, where his immediate successors probably continued a tradition he had established (Acts 3:11; 5:12). He would have been facing the sanctuary and from there and could watch people as they put money in the treasury (Mark 12:41; *see* TEMPLE, TREASURY). The Fourth Gospel (along with Acts) is the only one that mentions Solomon's Portico by name (*see* TEMPLE, SOLOMON'S PORTICO).

The existence of colossal buildings made of large, beautiful stones is reflected in remarks such as those found in Mark 13:1 and Luke 21:5. According to John 2:20 the building activity in the Temple area had been going on for 46 years. In light of the probable time when this remark was made (27–28 C.E.), it corresponds to the time given by Josephus for the beginning of the construction (20–19 B.C.E.). The primary author of John was apparently well aware of the events of Jesus' life, especially those that took place in Judea.

Although Jesus ostensibly reacted against the mercantile practices authorized or even encouraged by the high priesthood on the Temple Mount, it seems that he did not have any objection to the religious tradition embodied in the Temple service. He did not oppose the payment of the per-capita tax; he encouraged a healed leper to show himself to the priest and make an offering (Matt. 8:4; Lev. 14:4). Above all, Jesus visited the Temple. In this regard, he is to be strongly differentiated from the Qumranite sect. Also, while the Qumranites conceived a post-eschatological temple (11Q Temple, *see* DEAD SEA SCROLLS), Jesus may have referred only to a symbolic temple (Mark 14:58 and parallels) or no temple at all (John 4:21-24).

When Peter healed a man who was lame at the Beautiful Gate in the name of Jesus (Acts 3:1-10) and said "I have no silver or gold," he was perhaps inspired by the gates of the Temple enclosure, which were plated with these precious metals. This remark supports the view that the Beautiful Gate was the first gate of the Temple Courts, opening in the east and leading to the Court of Women. This area, with its flow of pious people, was a natural place for a beggar to stay. Nicanor's Gate, between the Court of Women and the Court of Israel would not fit with the text. It was opened only to men, which meant less traffic; moreover, it was plated with embossed bronze, not with silver and gold.

BIBLIOGRAPHY

Ben Dov, M. *In the Shadow of the Temple: The Discovery of Ancient Jerusalem*, translated by I. Friedman. Jerusalem: Keter, 1982.

Broshi, M. "The Role of the Temple in the Herodian Economy." *Journal for the Study of the New Testament* 30 (1987): 3–20.

Busink, T. *Der Tempel von Jerusalem*, 2 vols. Leiden: Brill, 1970–80.

Cohn, E. W. "Second Thoughts about the Perforated Stone on the Haram of Jerusalem." *Palestine Exploration Quarterly* 114 (1982): 143–46.

Comay, J. *The Temple of Jerusalem*. New York: Holt, Rinehart and Winston, 1975.

Einstein, J. D. and G. A. Banton. "Temple." *The Jewish Encyclopedia* 12, 1906.

Friedman, R. E. "The Tabernacle in the Temple." *BA* 44 (1980): 241–48.

Gutmann, J. ed. *The Temple of Solomon*. Missoula, Mont: Scholars Press, 1976.

Jacobson, D. M. "Ideas Concerning the Plan of Herod's Temple." *Palestine Exploration Quarterly* 112 (1980): 33–40.

Kaufman, A. S. "Where the Ancient Temple of Jerusalem Stood. Extant 'Foundation Stone' of the Ark of the Covenant is Identified." *BAR* 9 (1983): 40–59.

Klein, M. C. *Temple Beyond Time: The Story of Solomon's Temple at Jerusalem*. New York: Reinhold, 1970.

Laperrousaz, E. M. "La discontinuité (seam, straight joint) visible prés de l'extrémité sud du mur oriental du Haram esh-shérif marque-t-elle l'angle sud-est du 'Temple de Solomon'?" *Vetus Testamentum* 38 (1988): 399–406.

———. "Herod's Mighty Temple Mount." *BAR* 12.6 (1986): 40–49.

———. "King Solomon's Wall Still Supports the Temple Mount." *BAR* 13.3 (1987): 34–44.

Mazar, B. *The Mountain of the Lord: Excavating in Jerusalem*. Garden City, N.Y.: Doubleday, 1975.

———. "Le mur du temple." *Bible et Terre Sainte* 122 (June 1970): 8–15.

———. "Excavations Near Temple Mount Reveal Splendors of Herodian Jerusalem." *BAR* 6.4 (1980): 44–59.

———. "The Temple Mount." Proceedings of the International Congress of Biblical Archaeology. (1984): *Biblical Archaeology Today* (1985): 463–68.

Meyers, C. "The Elusive Temple." *BA* 45 (1979): 33–41.

———. "Temple, Jerusalem." *ABD* 6: 350–69.

Patrich, J. "The Structure of the Second Temple. A New Reconstruction." *Qadmoniot* 21 (1988): 56–57 (Hebrew).

Ritmayer, K. and L. "Reconstructing Herod's Temple Mount in Jerusalem." *BAR* 15 (1989): 23–48.

Ritmayer, L. "Locating the Original Temple Mount." *BAR* 18 (1992): 24–45.

Stein, M. "How Herod Moved Gigantic Blocks to Construct Temple Mount." *BAR* 7 (1981): 42–46.

Sporty, D. "The Location of the Holy House of Herod's Temple: Evidence from Post-Destruction Period." *BA* 53 (1990): 194–204; 54 (1991): 28–35.

Ussishkin, A. "Temple Mount." *Encyclopedia Judaica* 15 (1971).

Wightman, G. J. "Temple Fortunes in Jerusalem." *Bulletin of the Anglo-Israel Archaeological Society* 9 (1989–90): 29–40.

Wright, G. E. "God Amidst His People: The Story of the Temple, The Rule of God." *Essays in Biblical Theology*. New York: Doubleday, 1960.

———. "The Temple in Syria-Palestine." *BA* 7 (1944): 65–77.

Yadin, Y. *Temple Scroll*. 3 vols. Jerusalem: Israel Exploration Society *et al*, 1977–83.

Zimmerman, M. A. "Tunnel Exposes New Areas of Temple Mount." *BAR* 7 (1983): 34–41.

Temple, Royal Stoa

Importance

Jesus drove out the merchants and overturned the money changers' tables in or near the royal stoa.

Temple Royal Stoa Seen from the Solomon Portico. *Note the landings of the steps from the two Hulda gates. (Jerusalem Model)*

Scripture References

Matt. 21:12-16; Mark 11:15-17; Luke 19:45-48; John 2:13-16.

General Information

The Greek *stoa* refers to a colonnade or to an area enclosed by or containing rows of pillars. In the Greco-Roman world it was a place of gathering for merchants, local people, visitors, and pilgrims. Such structures were built in the vicinity of temples or other public areas in large cities like Rome, Athens, Atticus, and even Sebaste (Samaria). The royal stoa of Jerusalem stood at the southern part of the Court of Gentiles, at a distance from the Temple sanctuary. Most discussions of the Temple's stoa are based on Josephus's description:

> The fourth front of the [court], facing south, also had gates in the middle, and had over it the Royal Portico, which had three aisles, extending in length from the eastern to the western ravine. It

was not possible for it to extend farther. And it was a structure more noteworthy than any under the sun. For while the depth of the ravine was great, and no one who bent over to look into it from above could bear to look down to the bottom, the height of the portico standing over it was so very great that if anyone looked down from its rooftop, combining the two elevations, he would become dizzy and his vision would be unable to reach the end of so measureless a depth. Now the columns [of the portico] stood in four rows, one opposite the other all along—the fourth row was attached to a wall built of stone, and the thickness of each column was such that it would take three men with outstretched arms touching one another to envelop it; its height was twenty-seven feet, and there was a double moulding running round its base. The number of all the columns was a hundred and sixty two, and their capitals were ornamented in the Corinthian style of carving, which caused amazement by the magnificence of its whole effect. Since there were four rows, they made three aisles among them, under the porticoes. Of these the two side ones corresponded and were made in the same way, each being thirty feet in width, a stade in length, and over fifty feet in height. But the middle aisle was one-and-and-half times as wide and twice as high, and thus it greatly towered over those on either side. The ceiling (of the porticoes) was ornamented with deeply cut wood carving representing all sorts of different figures. The ceiling of the middle aisle was raised to a greater height, and the front wall was cut at either end into architraves with columns built into it, and all of it was polished, so that these structures seemed incredible to those who had not seen them, and were beheld with amazement by those who set eyes on them (*Antiq.* 15, 11.5/411–16, translated by Ralph Marcus, Loeb Classical Library).

Herod's stoa probably did not contain shops. It had four rows of columns, of which the fourth was attached to the southern wall of the enclosure. There was no wall at the north row within a Roman basilica; but the structure had three aisles with the center one similar to a nave, wider and higher than the two side aisles. Herod's stoa resembled in this sense a Roman basilica. Roman temples known as Caesareums* were built at the same period in different parts of the empire; they contained such basilica porticoes. The first one was built by Julius Caesar and was dedicated to the worship of the emperor. Similar buildings were erected in Antioch, Palmyra, Alexandria, Pisidia, Smyrna, and Cyrene. If Herod's stoa was a type of Caesareum,* then it contained also an exedra,* a semicircular wall with benches at one of its ends where the supervisors of the building could be seated.

Josephus reports that this building deserved more attention than any other building under the sun, for it was undoubtedly the longest building of his time. Furthermore, it was not built on solid rock but was founded on gigantic blocks, which formed the retaining walls, immense dirt fills, and a complicated set of underground halls with two large thoroughfares, all under the portico. To add to the luxurious impression and to give easy access to the building, Herod added two flights of stairs leading from the area at the bottom of the southern wall to the stoa. It was a masterpiece of construction, sure to impress all who saw it.

Archaeological Data

In his excavations in the southwestern area of the Temple Mount, B. Mazar found several fragments of columns with a diameter of 4 feet 7 inches, which corresponds to a circumference such that three men joining hands could embrace it, just as described by Josephus. Mazar also found Corinthian capitals and pieces of carved panels, cornices, friezes, and stone sundials, probably all thrown down into the valley from the top of the Temple platform when the Romans demolished the buildings in 70 C.E.

Some of these can be seen today in the plaza of the Jewish quarter and north of the el Aqsa Mosque on the Temple Mount. These remains, whether or not they belong to the stoa, bear witness to the size and beauty of the structures built by Herod, who sought to create monuments larger and more beautiful than any others of his time.

Implications for Jesus Research

The information given by Josephus, together with archaeological data, allows for a fairly accurate reconstruction of the site where Jesus performed his symbolic cleansing of the Temple. The stoa, like other structures of its kind, was made for everyday activities: trading, the purchase of sacrificial animals, exchanging money, making deals, storytelling, and group meetings. During the festivals it was undoubtedly a crowded place despite its gigantic size, and traders tended to move into the Court of Gentiles toward the opening of the Temple platform where the stairs of the Hulda Gates landed. This movement was probably allowed by the High Priesthood for some compensation. Under these circumstances, Jesus' indignation can be understood. By overturning the tables of the money changers he was not predicting the destruction of the Temple, as some scholars have argued. Rather, his act must have been a symbol of needed cleansing and also an act of protest against the corruption of the High Priesthood, as is attested in Josephus (*Antiq.* 20, 8.8/174–81) and popular lore (*b. Pesahim* 57a; *t. Minhot* 13:21; *see* JERUSALEM, UPPER CITY).

There are scholarly controversies about the fact that Jesus acted violently without being arrested immediately by the Temple guard. A look at the plan of the area to re-create the scene helps to understand what happened. The highest concentration of merchants and animals was probably between the two openings leading to the Hulda Gates. Jesus arrived by the eastern stairs like everyone; he probably hurried toward the western stairs, pushed aside merchants and animals, and overturned the money changers' tables that were in his way. Then he merged with the outgoing crowd and disappeared in the underground stairs leading to the Double Gates. The whole sequence took no more than a few minutes, and the disturbance created by this lightning-fast action would not have reached the Temple authorities quickly enough for them to have arrested him.

BIBLIOGRAPHY

Barrois, G. *Jesus Christ and the Temple.* Crestwood, N.Y.: St. Vladimir Seminary Press, 1980.

., M. "Herod's Mighty Temple Mount." *BAR* 12 (1986): 40–49.

———. *In the Shadow of the Temple.* Jerusalem: Keter Publishing House, 1982.

Hamilton, N. Q. "Temple Cleansing and Temple Bank." *Journal of Biblical Literature* 83 (1964): 365–72.

Horbury, W. "New Wine in Old Wineskins: IX. The Temple." *Expository Times* 86 (1974–75): 36–42.

Mazar, B. *The Mountain of the Lord.* Garden City, N.Y.: Doubleday, 1975.

———. "The Temple Mount." *Biblical Archaeology Today. Proceedings of the International Congress of Biblical Archaeology, Jerusalem, April 1984.* Jerusalem: Israel Exploration Society, 1985.

Moloney, F. J. "Reading John 2:13–22: The Purification of the Temple." *Revue Biblique* 97 (1990): 432–52.

Sanders, E. P. *Jesus and Judaism.* Philadelphia: Fortress Press, 1985.

Temple, Sacrificial System

Importance

Sacrifices, offered daily, were the most visible forms of communal and individual worship and of economic support for the Temple and its personnel.

Scripture References

Matt. 5:23-24; 8:2-4; 12:3-5; 23:18-20; Luke 2:22-23; Acts 21:26; 1 Cor. 9:13; Heb. 5:1-3.

General Information

The origins of sacrifice among ancient peoples have been studied by anthropologists since the mid-nineteenth century, but there is no consensus on how or why it developed and what it meant. Sacrifice is a complicated phenomenon, and probably no one explanation would suffice. Many ancient peoples believed that the gods needed to consume food to maintain their divine powers. Vestiges of such beliefs are found in expressions such as Psalm 78:25 ("bread of angels") and Wisdom of Solomon 16:20 ("food of angels"). Such beliefs are also reflected in the custom of burning animal fat on the altar to produce a pleasing odor to the Lord (Lev. 3:4, *et passim*). A phrase such as "all fat is the Lord's" (Lev. 3:16) indicates that fat, among other parts of animal's bodies, was considered a divine food. Sacrificial offerings thus symbolized sustenance given to the divine ruler. In any case, for the Israelites as for other ancient peoples, sacrifice provided a way for the people to relate to their deity.

Ancient Near Eastern people sought to serve the gods and treat them like kings, providing them not only with a steady flow of victuals but also with all the care given to earthly sovereigns: attendance when getting up in the morning, washing, dressing, praising, attendance when going to sleep at night. In Israelite Temple activities YHWH was treated in similar fashion, although the symbolic meaning attached to the various rituals probably was different than for other peoples.

An elaborate system of animal sacrifice and agricultural offerings developed in ancient Israel, as part of the socio-economic regulation of national life, and as a way of supporting the ruling caste (*see* TEMPLE, TREASURY and TAX AND TAX COLLECTORS). The complex regulations found in the Hebrew Bible for preserving the sanctity of everything brought before the Lord, and the stipulation of what those things were, were expounded upon later, after the destruction of the Temple, in rabbinic literature. Here, they are briefly presented according to the following categories: daily sacrifices, tributary offerings, expiatory offerings, votive and thanksgiving offerings, peace offerings, freewill offerings, miscellaneous offerings.

Daily Sacrifices. The *tamid*, "daily sacrifice," consisted of two whole lambs accompanied by offerings of cereal and libations of wine. The animals were entirely burnt except for the hides, which were given to the priests. A male lamb was offered every morning and afternoon. On the Sabbath, two more lambs were added; on other holidays, the sacrifice was complemented with the sin offering of one goat. On the New Moon, the daily sacrifice included two young bulls, one ram, and seven male lambs. The same number of animals was required for each day of Passover and Pentecost (*m. Sebuʿot*, "Feast of Weeks of First Fruits"). For Rosh ha-Shanah, "New Year" (first day of the seventh month) and Yom Kippur, "Day of Purgation," the sacrifices were reduced to one bull, one ram and seven male lambs; but on Yom Kippur two sin offerings were added, one for the sins of the High Priest and one for the sins of the people. The highest consumption of animals occurred at Sukkot, "Feast of Tabernacles or Booths": thirteen young bulls, two rams, and fourteen male lambs on the first day; the number of bulls reduced by one on each successive day until only seven were sacrificed on the seventh day. On the eighth day the sacrifices were reduced to the level of Rosh ha-Shanah and Yom Kippur. In addition, one goat was sacrificed as a sin offering on each day of Sukkot. Every whole burnt sacrifice was accompanied by a prede-

termined amount of cereal offering usually presented in the form of a mixture of fine flour, olive oil, and frankincense baked in loaves, wafers, or lumps. The quantities were fixed in relation to the size of animal sacrificed, decreasing from bull to lamb.

Tributary Offerings. In agricultural societies such offerings may have been viewed as a tribute due to the God-king who owned the land, flocks, and herds, and who caused the rains to fall, the seeds to germinate, and the cattle to reproduce and multiply. Because the first child in a family, the first of a flock to be born, or the first of a crop to be harvested symbolized all that was expected to come, special ceremonial attention was paid to the first-born or harvested of humans, plants, and animals. Even though the first-born males of humans and animals were thought to belong to God, first-born male children and male unclean animals could be redeemed for a ransom (Exod. 13:12-15, 34:19-20; Lev. 27:26; Num. 18:15-17; Deut. 14:23; 15:19-20). The first fruits of the crop (Exod. 22:29; 23:19; 34:26), and the best part of grain, olive oil (virgin oil), new wine, new shorn wool, and the first cake of meal after the grain was collected from the threshing floor also belonged to God and were part of sacrificial offerings. The quantities of these first products are not specified in the biblical texts, but later were fixed as a tithe (tenth) of the harvest.

Expiatory Offerings. J. Milgrom's extensive work on Leviticus and Numbers illuminates the concepts involved in the Israelite sacrificial system, especially in matters of sin and purification offerings (*see* Bibliography). Milgrom makes the point, not often recognized, that the object of the purification brought about by a sacrifice was not the sinner or the unclean person but the Temple or the altar. It was an ancient belief that an offense created a physical miasma that would permeate the sanctuary and pollute it. Evidence of this belief is found in other Near Eastern cultures. Certain practices, such as incantations and the smearing of purifying substances, especially blood, on the horns of the altar, were considered efficacious in maintaining the purity and thus the sanctity of the sacred precinct.

Humans' sins and impurities thus had the potential to defile the Temple. Priests offered purification sacrifices in order to keep the sanctuary free from the pollution caused by sin, for God would not abide in a polluted Temple (which resulted from sinful behavior). God might even leave and abandon Israel to its doom, as in the time of Ezekiel (Ezek. 11:23). But God would return to the Temple if the people repented (Ezek. 43:2-5; Isa. 40:5). Pollution of the sanctuary came either from physical or moral impurity. Leviticus 4 lays forth procedures for people who had sinned inadvertently. The blood of the sacrifice cleansed the sanctuary, but the inadvertent sinner was purified by remorse. If the cause of the impurity was physical, the person was cleansed by ablution (Milgrom, *Numbers*, 444–47). Those guilty of committing sins of which they were aware paid stipulated penalties and then brought guilt offerings that the priests used to make atonement on behalf of the guilty individuals (Lev. 6:1–8).

It was believed that there were three degrees of impurity that could pollute the sacred area of Tabernacle or Temple, according to the degrees of sanctity of that area:

1. Individuals' involuntary sins and physical impurity polluted the altar area, which could be purified or, more accurately, purged by smearing the horns of the altar or its base with the blood of the sacrifice.

2. The inadvertent sin of the High Priest and the involuntary sins of the people of Israel as a whole polluted the main sanctum or sanctuary, which could be purified by the High Priest, who placed blood on the sanctuary's altar and sprinkled some of it on the curtain separating the sanctuary from the Holy of Holies.

3. Unrepented sin polluted the whole sacred area, including the most sacred part of it, the Holy of Holies. In accordance with Numbers 15: 30–31, the wanton sinner was "cut off"

from the people, which meant banishment or execution. In both cases, the sinner could not offer a sacrifice and the removal of the impurity caused by such sin was effected only at the annual purgation of the Holy of Holies, on Yom Kippur (*see* fig. 63).

Among the expiatory sacrificial procedures were the *hatta't*, "sin offering," "decontaminating sacrifice," *asham*, the "guilt offering," and the scape goat ritual of Yom Kippur. The importance of the sin offering was proportionate to the rank of the offender: The High Priest and the community each offered a young bull, a ruler brought a male goat, an ordinary man, a female goat, or a lamb. Poor people could bring a pair of doves or pigeons, one being burnt with its feathers as a whole offering and the other being presented as a sin offering. In case of extreme poverty, a tenth of an *ephah* of fine flour was accepted (an *ephah* was about one half of a bushel). The person offering the sacrifice laid one hand on the head of the animal to be slaughtered as a way of identifying it with himself (Lev. 4:4, *et passim*). The blood was collected and, according to the circumstances presented above, applied to the horns of the altar, or sprinkled on its side in the case of birds, or brought into the outer sanctum of the Temple to be offered on the altar of incense and sprinkled on the inner curtain. The suet of the entrails, the kidneys, and the appendage of the liver were burnt on the altar, and the flesh was kept for the priests to be eaten within the Temple Court. In the case of the bulls offered by the High Priest and the people, the whole carcass was burnt outside "the camp."

Not to be confused with the sin offering was the guilt offering (*asham*), which did not bring purification or reparation. It was a fine imposed on a person who had defrauded or caused material damage to someone else, including God (Lev. 5:16-17; 14:12-13; Num. 6:12; Ezra 10:19). This fine came above the amount of money or property in kind to be restituted and was fixed at one fifth of the amount defrauded, of the loss incurred, or of the damage caused. People with leprosy and Nazirites

Figure 63 How the Temple Was Purged from the Pollution Caused By the Sins of God's People. (*Adapted from J. Milgram Leviticus 1-16*)

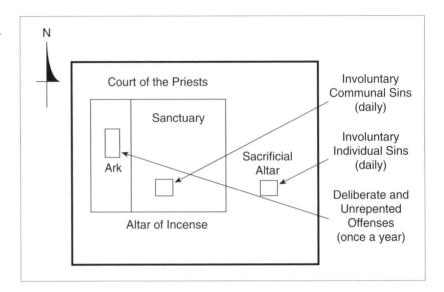

who had become defiled during the period of their vows were considered to have defrauded God by depriving him of service rightly due; they had to pay a fine. In each case the guilty person had to confess the sin, make full restitution, pay the fine, and offer the *asham* sacrifice. For cleansed lepers and Nazirites having broken their vows, the guilt offering was a lamb. The entrails and fat were burnt on the altar, the blood sprinkled around it, and the rest of the animal kept by the priests to eat. In the case of cleansed lepers some of the blood was applied to the tips of their right ears, right thumbs, and right big toes (Lev. 14:2–5).

The rite of the scapegoat on Yom Kippur was observed for the removing of the sins of the people. The scapegoat was not a substitute for the lives of human offenders that God could have claimed in retribution; rather, it was a vehicle for carrying the sins of all Israel away to a solitary land (Lev. 16:22), in the territory of "the satyr demon Azazel" (Milgrom, *Numbers*, 446). In fact, two *hatta't* goats were required, one for the regular sin sacrifice to purge the sanctuary of "Israel's impurities" (Lev. 16:22), and the other, the scapegoat, to carry away "all of Israel's transgressions" (Lev. 16:21). Because of its character of collective elimination of the

community's offense it involved a confession of sin by and for all the people and a public ceremony.

Besides these three main subcategories of expiatory sacrifices several purification rituals required whole burnt and sin offerings; childbirth (Lev. 12: 6–8), unclean issues (Lev. 15: 14–15), hemmorhages (Lev. 15: 29–30), and defilement during the period of a Nazirite's vows (Num. 6: 10–11). Moreover, additional meal offerings were presented for the cleansing of a leper (Lev. 14: 10, 20, 21, 31) and for the completion of a Nazirite vow (Num. 6: 15-17).

Votive and Thanksgiving Offerings. Votive offerings were made as the consequence of a contract presented to God by the supplicant for the fulfillment of a request. They are mentioned incidentally in Leviticus 7:16, 22:21, Numbers 15:3, and more specifically in the method of valuation (Lev. 27:1-29) and in the rules of the vows (Num. 30:2-16). The votive offering could be presented either at the time of the vow or when the request had been granted. Thanksgiving offerings were spontaneous expressions of gratitude when a favor had been received without a prior contract with the deity or even without a request. According to Leviticus 7:12-14, cakes and bread were offered for thanksgiving with the sacrificial animal; this kind of offering was eaten by the offerer and was sometimes categorized as a type of peace offering.

Peace Offerings. Peace offerings were communal offerings (Lev. 3:1-16; 7:11-36) which, besides the fat and viscera burnt on the altar and the priests' portion, were eaten by the offerer and his family and the Levite in the community (Deut. 12:12, 18-19). There were few restrictions regarding the kind of animal to be sacrificed, except that it should be from the herd or the flock and without blemish. The animal was not slaughtered in the abattoir north of the altar but at the door of the sanctuary. The priest could share his portion, comprised of the breast and right thigh and of a cake, with his family in any ritually clean place. However, the offerer and his household had to eat the peace offering "before God" (Deut. 12:7, *et passim*), that is, in or near the Court of Women. Ritual peace offerings took place in certain circumstances: completion of a Nazirite's vow, celebration of *shavuot*, "Feast of Weeks," and consecration of a priest. Peace offerings were also given at the occasion of certain events of national importance: military victory (1 Sam. 11:15), end of a famine or plague (2 Sam. 24:25), recognition of a new king (1 Kings 1:9, 19, 23), and Israel's reconsecration to God under King Hezekiah (2 Chron. 29:31-36).

Freewill Offerings. These offerings were voluntary. They could be presented at pilgrimage festivals. 2 Chronicles 35:8 reports that King Josiah and his officers offered thousands of animals to be eaten by the people at Passover. When animals were involved in freewill offerings, the rules regarding the absence of imperfections were less stringent than for prescribed offerings (Lev. 22:23).

Miscellaneous Offerings. Many other offerings are mentioned in the Pentateuch: meal and libation offerings, wave-offerings (waving the priest's portion of the peace offering), and so on.

The sacrificial system as set forth in the Pentateuch would have involved the slaughter of hundreds of thousands of animals every year in the holy precincts (*see* TEMPLE, SERVICE AND RITUAL for an estimate of the number of sacrifices for Passover alone). Such large numbers make us question whether, in reality, sacrifices were made as the texts describe them. The texts may represent an ideal structure that was never carried out in all its details. Most scholars recognize that the canonical presentation of the sacrificial system is one or more steps removed from actual cultic practice.

Archaeological Data

Nothing remains from the altar of the Jerusalem Temple, which is known only through descriptions. Examples of Israelite altars found at Beersheba, Arad, and other sites may give an idea of what it looked like with a protuberance at each corner. The remains of the altar or "high place" at Dan may have been visible in the first century C.E.

Implications for Jesus Research

Despite the problems brought about by a powerful High Priesthood appointed by the Romans and with the exception of such groups as the Qumranites, acceptance of the Temple and its sacrificial system, in whatever form it existed, was probably still strong in the time of Jesus (Acts 3:1, 9, 11, *et passim*). The Pharisees had made changes in Temple procedures, with Scripture readings and priestly prayers added to the sacrificial service (*see* TEMPLE, SERVICE AND RITUAL).

According to Luke, Jesus' parents observed the commandment to offer sacrifices after childbirth at the end of the mother's impurity period, and they redeemed their first-born male infant (Luke 2:22-23). They also went to Jerusalem every year for the Passover (Luke 2:41), and they apparently began to take Jesus with them when he reached religious maturity at age twelve (Luke 2:42). Jesus continued in the tradition of his parents and people (John 2:13, 23; 5:1; 7:10-11, 37; 10:20).

The interpretation of Jesus' symbolic action in the Temple as a cleansing (Matt. 21:12 and parallels) must take into account that sin offerings were made to cleanse the Temple and the altar from impurities caused by the transgressions of the people. It was not likely to have been an action symbolizing the destruction of the Temple, as argued by some scholars; rather it was a symbolic action against a corrupt priestly oligarchy (*see* JERUSALEM, UPPER CITY and TEMPLE, HISTORY, DESCRIPTION). Prophetic symbolic actions, as practiced in ancient Israel, acted out the event announced by the prophet in a manner easily understood by the people. An example of a prophetic act symbolizing destruction was Jeremiah's breaking of a jar (Jer. 19:10-13); the overturning of tables or the driving out of merchants and animals were unlikely to represent destruction.

Matthew reports that Jesus healed a leper and told him to show himself to the priest and offer the required sacrifice (Matt. 8:2-4); the command is repeated by Luke but without the order to bring a sacrifice (Luke 17:14). On this ground alone, Luke's story seems less plausible. The sacrifice that the cleansed leper would offer fell in the category of *asham* offering: paying a fine for having been unable to serve God because of physical impurity. The order given by Jesus can be seen as a recognition of the role of the priesthood and the sacrificial system. Although Jesus had no regard for the corrupt priestly oligarchy, he accepted the traditional system as practiced at the end of the Second Temple period. To this view, however, it may be objected that Jesus' command was given only for the well-being of the healed leper and his social rehabilitation.

In light of the rules pertaining to sacrifices a question arises regarding the killing of the fatted calf and the rejoicing in honor of the Prodigal Son (Luke 15:23). Would a Jew privately kill a choice fatling usually reserved for Temple sacrifice without offering what was due to God, the priest, and the Levite in the community? Some Jews probably would have offered a thanksgiving or a peace sacrifice for such a great occasion and brought the fatling and his whole household to Jerusalem for a celebration "before God." Because this story dates to a generation or so after the destruction of the Temple, when sacrifices could no longer be offered, it may be that the author of Luke retrojected into the time of Jesus the customs of his own time. A story originating with Jesus would probably have had a more traditional tone (cf. Matt. 8:1-4). It is also remarkable that no praise is offered to God in the Prodigal Son story and only merrymaking is mentioned. On the other hand, Jesus had relationships with nonobservant people and addressed them according to their own way of living and speaking.

BIBLIOGRAPHY

Anderson, G. *Sacrifices and Offerings in Ancient Israel: Studies in Their Social and Political Importance.* Atlanta, Ga.: Scholars Press, 1987.

———. "Sacrifices and Sacrificial Offerings (OT)." *ABD* 5: 870–86.

Biran, A. "Dan." *NEAEHL* 1: 328

Chilton, G. *The Temple of Jesus: His Sacrificial Program within a Cultural History of Sacrifice.* Pennsylvania State University, 1992.

Frymer-Kensky, T "Pollution, Purification and Purgation in Biblical Israel." *The Word of the Lord Shall Go Forth.* Edited by C. L. Meyers, and M. O'Connor, Winona Lake, Ind.: Eisenbrauns, 1983.

Levine, B. A. *Leviticus.* The J.P.S. Torah Commentary. Philadelphia: Jewish Publication Society, 1989.

———. *Numbers 1–20.* Anchor Bible 4. New York: Doubleday, 1993.

Milgrom, J. *Numbers.* The JPS Torah Commentary. Philadelphia: Jewish Publication Society, 1990.

———. *Leviticus 1–16.* Anchor Bible 3. New York: Doubleday, 1991.

Sanders, E. P. *Jewish Laws from Jesus to the Mishnah.* 1985. Reprint. Philadelphia: Fortress Press, 1987.

———. *Judaism, Practice and Belief* 63 B.C.E.–66 C.E. London: SCM. Philadelphia: Trinity Press International, 1992.

See Bibliography under TEMPLE, SERVICE AND RITUAL.

Temple, Service and Ritual

Importance

According to Luke Jesus may have been related to a priestly family. Polycrates of Ephesus says that John the Evangelist was a priest wearing the sacerdotal plate (Eusebius, *Hist.* 5, 24); moreover, John

18:19 indicates that the Beloved Disciple was related to the High Priest.

Scripture References

Matt. 5:23; 23:18-20, 35; Luke 1:5, 8-10, 23; John 18:19.

Situation at the Time of the Third Temple

With the exception of the temple of Hieropolis in Egypt (*see* TEMPLE, HISTORY, DESCRIPTION), the Temple of Jerusalem was the only official place for offering sacrifices to YHWH. The sacrificial order probably was based on Pentateuchal texts, with a few additions to the festivals: the Maccabean Triumph celebrated on Nicanor's Day, the thirteenth of Adar and immediately followed by *purim*, a feast commemorating the deliverance of the Jews by Esther from a massacre plotted by Haman; *Hanukkah*, the Feast of Dedication, beginning on the twenty-fifth of Kislev in celebration of the rededication of the Temple by Judah Maccabee in 165 B.C.E.; and the rite of water libation on Sukkot, the Feast of Booths.

Prayers and readings of Scripture had been systematically included in the daily ritual, probably under pressure from Pharisees who found increasing support among the ordinary priesthood, as can be seen in the case of Josephus who was at the time a priest and a Pharisee. Detailed descriptions of the sacrificial system as it was probably practiced before the destruction of the Temple in 70 C.E. are found in the tractate *Tamid* of the Babylonian Talmud and elsewhere.

The basis of the whole system was the *tamid*, double daily sacrifice, one at dawn and the other in the afternoon. These two sacrifices framed the sacrificial rites of the day, even in the most solemn circumstances. Liturgical components accompanied or supplemented the offerings: at the beginning of the day, after the incense offering, the priests gave the priestly blessing in unison (*b. Tamid* 7:2); later they recited the *shema** followed by its blessings, the Ten Commandments, and excerpts from the *amidah*, "service of prayer." On the Sabbath, at the change of priestly units, the outgoing priests blessed the incoming ones: "May he who has caused his name to dwell in this place cause to dwell among you love, brotherhood, peace and friendship" (*b. Tamid* 5:1). The Levites recited the psalm of the day with accompaniment of music; nonpriestly representatives of the people joined the priests to pray and read from the Bible when the sacrifices were completed.

Daily Service

Every day, early in the morning, one of the priests on duty was the first to get up and bathe. At cockcrow, a chief priest arrived, knocked at the door of the Chamber of the Hearth (*see* fig. 62), and asked for the priest who was up and ready for service. This priest cast lots to choose who among his colleagues would serve for the day. Then the chief priest took the keys of the Temple and entered the inner court with the other priests following him in a procession led by two torchbearers. All daily tasks were assigned by lots. The priest in charge of the ashes operated a winch to draw water for the laver from an underground cistern, then the other priests washed their feet and hands (*see* fig. 64). He then took a *mahtah*, "silver shovel," climbed the ramp of the altar, and brought it down to deposit it in a heap on the court floor. The other priests, having finished washing their hands and feet, took larger shovels and removed the rest of the ashes. When the heap of ashes had reached a certain level it was taken outside the city, presumably to the ash dump found north of the third wall (*see* JERUSALEM, TOMBS).

With the completion of the preparatory rituals, the priests again gathered together and lots determined who would slaughter the *tamid* lamb, who would sprinkle the blood, who would tend the golden altar of incense and menorah, and who would help in the sacrifice. When the tasks had been so distributed, one priest climbed to the top of a tower to observe the light of the new dawn growing in the east until it reached Hebron, probably in reverence for the ancestors buried there (*see* HEBRON). At that precise moment he would make the announcement, "*Barkai*, the morning light has appeared, even to Hebron." This was the signal for

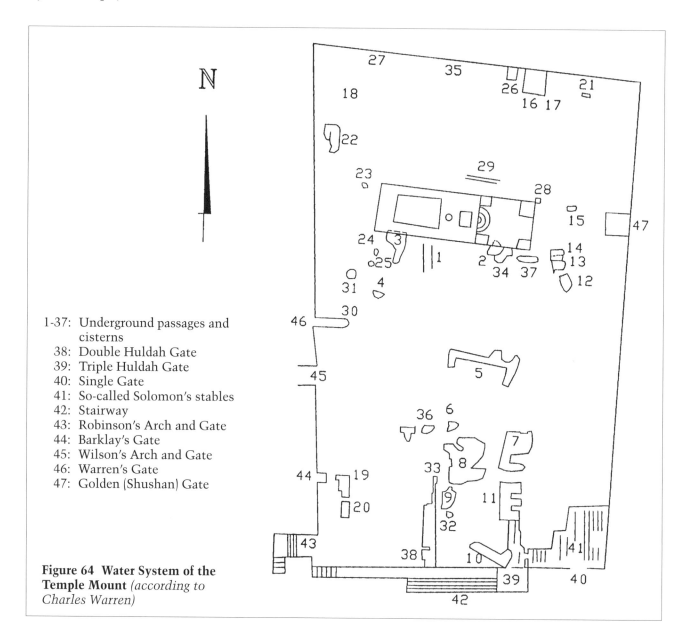

N

1-37: Underground passages and
        cisterns
  38: Double Huldah Gate
  39: Triple Huldah Gate
  40: Single Gate
  41: So-called Solomon's stables
  42: Stairway
  43: Robinson's Arch and Gate
  44: Barklay's Gate
  45: Wilson's Arch and Gate
  46: Warren's Gate
  47: Golden (Shushan) Gate

**Figure 64 Water System of the
Temple Mount** *(according to
Charles Warren)*

the chief priest to order a lamb to be brought from
the Chambers of the Lambs situated at the northeastern corner of the sacred precincts. Gold and silver vessels were then taken out from the Chamber
of Vessels. The lamb was examined by torchlight,
for it was still dark inside the high walls of the

Temple court; when it was ascertained that it was
unblemished, it was given water to drink from a
golden cup and taken to the abattoir. After it was
killed, priests designated for this task removed the
hide and cut the carcass into pieces, which were
placed on the lower half of the altar ramp (*kebesh*)

together with the freshly baked cake offering. Meanwhile, other priests performed the service of the menorah and altar of incense in the outer sanctum.

This second series of tasks being completed, all the priests assembled once more and recited the morning prayers: one blessing, the Ten Commandments, three parts of the *shema*,* and three benedictions (*b. Tamid* 3:1-9; 4:1-3). After the prayers, lots were cast again to designate those who would offer the incense (Luke 1:9) and those who would carry the sacrifice to the top of the altar. At this time, a large gong was struck, its sound reverberating throughout Jerusalem and beyond. This signaled that the time of the morning offering had come and called the Levites to gather for hymn singing. Immediately after the hymns, at the time of the incense burning, the Israelites of the *ma'amad*, "lay delegation," gathered for prayer in the Temple court. According to Luke 1:10 and Judith 9:1, Jews outside the Temple also prayed at that time. When incense had been burnt in the outer sanctum, all the priests except for the High Priest, who bore God's name on an inscribed plate on his turban, assembled on the steps of the porch, facing east, and pronounced the blessing over the people, saying the sacred name, raising their hands over their heads. When they heard God's name, all in the Temple court prostrated themselves. Only after this ritual were the pieces of the sacrifice carried to the top of the altar and thrown into the pyre; the meal offering was burnt immediately after. The shofar was sounded, and the libation of wine was poured on the altar, and cymbals were struck. The Levites began to sing the psalm of the day, their melody punctuated at certain pauses by a blast of the shofar at the sound of which the people prostrated themselves. The psalm concluded the morning sacrifice ritual.

The daily service continued with the afternoon *tamid*. Individual sacrifices could be offered until half past the eighth hour (about 2:30 P.M.). After the afternoon *tamid* the gates of the Temple and the Temple court were closed. A few priests remained to keep the fire going and offer the pieces of sacrifices that had not been burnt during the day. The other priests retired in the Chamber of the Hearth and some in the Chamber of the Flame, also located on the northern side of the Temple court. The Chamber of the Hearth was the larger and had a domed roof. It was the normal quarters of the division on duty, half of its area extended outside the holy precincts on a platform called the *hel*. There, in daytime, the priests could come in turns to sit down and warm their bare feet and hands. At night, older priests slept on couches along the walls and the younger ones on cushions on the floor. During the night, the keys of the Temple were kept under a marble slab of the floor. A priest slept there until the chief priest came in the morning and began the daily routine again.

Special Celebrations

On the Sabbath individual sacrifices were not offered. As much of the work as possible was done for the daily ritual the day before. A *musaf*, "additional sacrifice," of two sheep was offered on the Sabbath. The Bread of the Presence was replaced on that day as the priestly unit changed. The priests of the *mishmar*, "new division," arrived before the morning prayer to receive the blessing from the outgoing division. The first task of the new division—the replacement of the Bread of Presence—came immediately after the *musaf*. Four priests entered the sanctuary to remove the bread of the preceding Sabbath and also the censers. Four other priests followed them, two carrying twelve freshly baked loaves taken from a marble table in the entrance hall and two carrying two new censers filled with frankincense. In changing the bread, they were careful to always keep twelve loaves on the table. As one was removed it was simultaneously replaced with a fresh one. The bread of the previous Sabbath was divided among the priests of the two divisions.

Special dispositions had to be taken for the great festivals when tens of thousands or more pilgrims swarmed into Jerusalem from all over the Roman world. Each festival had its specific *musaf*; but the most important additional sacrifices came from the pilgrims: peace offerings and whole burnt offerings. The ashes from the altar were removed on the eve of the feast and the gates of the Temple were unlocked at midnight to be opened at daybreak. In order to allow everyone to see the Temple vessels, the gates and curtain of the building were kept wide open.

The Feast requiring the greatest amount of work for the priesthood was *Pesah*, Passover, because every family was supposed to sacrifice and eat of a lamb. Those who did not belong to a large family banded together by groups of ten to twenty people to share a lamb (Josephus, *War* 6, 9.3/425). On the eve of Passover the afternoon *tamid* was offered at the eighth hour (about 2:00 P.M.) instead of the ninth and a half hour, and the family Passover sacrifices began immediately after. Worshipers were admitted by groups, each group being as large as the Temple court could hold. When the court was filled, its gates were closed and a priest blew the shofar. The offerers killed their own lambs and the priests collected the blood, passing their basins to another priest when they were full, and receiving empty basins to continue the operation without interruption. A steady flow of blood was thus thrown against the base of the altar. As groups succeeded one another the Levites sang songs of praise (*Hallel*; Pss. 113-18). The people took their slaughtered lambs with them, roasted them, and ate them after dark. The Talmud reports that when King Agrippa once requested that a kidney of each slaughtered lamb be set aside to evaluate the number of participants in the Passover Festival, 600,000 animals were counted (*b. Pesahim* 64b), which seems impossible, because it would have meant a number of worshipers between 6 and 12 million. According to Josephus, more than 3 million Jews participated in the Passover of 65 C.E. (*War* 2, 14.3/280; cf.6, 9.3/423-27), which seems a much inflated figure. On the third day of Passover, according to the prescriptions of the Pharisees, the *omer*, a special offering of freshly harvested barley, was brought to the Temple, ground into flour, and mixed with oil and frankincense. Only a handful was burnt at the altar, the remainder was eaten by the priests.

For *Shavuot*, Pentecost or Feast of Weeks, according to Leviticus 23:16-20, two loaves of bread were brought to the Temple, waved in front of the sanctuary, and eaten by all the priests present. The Pharisees extended to a full week the time during which the Jews could offer sacrifices and bring their first fruits to the Temple. Mishnah *Bikkurim* 3:3 indicates that the first fruits were brought in a procession led by an ox, which was later slaughtered as a peace offering.

During the eight days of *Sukkot*, the Feast of Booths, a large number of collective sacrifices were offered (Num. 29:12-35; *see* TEMPLE, SACRIFICIAL SYSTEM) and the entire *Hallel* was sung every day to the accompaniment of flute. On the first seven days a libation of water was added to the morning libation of wine (*see* JERUSALEM, POOL OF SILOAM, and the reaction of the Maccabean High Priest Alexander Jannaeus against this practice). This was not a biblical prescription but was imposed by the Pharisees against the will of the Sadducean priests "in order that the new rainy season be blessed" (*b. Rosh Hashanah* 16a).

Music, both choral and instrumental, was part of the Temple ritual, especially for the *tamid* and *musaf* sacrifices and the offerings of the people. Hymns were taken from biblical poems such as Exodus 15, Deuteronomy 32:1-43, and Psalms. The Mishnah indicates that lyres, flutes, and cymbals were played at the offering of the *tamid* and during the festivals. The Septuagint* and several *baraitot* (pieces of ancient tradition appearing in the Talmuds) give the names of the psalms sung by the Levites on each day of the week and on some of the holidays. For instance, "The earth is the Lord's" (Ps. 24) was sung every Sunday, and the songs of ascent (Pss. 120-134) were sung during the celebration of *sho'evah*, "water drawing," at the Feast of Booths. According to the Mishnah there were never fewer than twelve Levites in the choir, and children participated in the singing for the inclusion of higher notes (*Arakim* 3:3-6).

The Menorah on the Arch of Titus in Rome.

Faithfulness of the Priests

During the last days of the Temple, despite food scarcities caused by the Roman siege, the *tamid* continued to be offered; but when the daily offerings did cease the people grieved (Josephus, *War* 6, 2.1/94). Josephus reports that one priest, Jesus son of Thebuthi, who had access to the Temple sanctuary, and Phineas, the Treasurer, bought their lives and freedom by looting the Temple and giving Titus many precious objects (*War* 6, 9.3/387-91). These two incidents were exceptions. Most priests present in the Temple were slain (*War* 6. 5.1/271); others climbed to the roof of the Temple, removed the spikes from it, and hurled them at the Romans below. Two among them threw themselves into the fire and burnt with the Temple; the rest stayed until the end and were killed (*War* 6, 5.1/278-80).

Archaeological Information

No objects from the Temple service have survived, only representations, many of which postdate the first century C.E., have been found: the menorah and other cultic objects on the Arch of Titus in Rome; a representation of the menorah on a wall of the Herodian Quarter in Jerusalem; the menorah, a shofar, and an incense shovel on ancient synagogue mosaic pavements; the menorah on coins of Antigonus; and the table of the Bread of the Presence on other coins (*see* fig. 65).

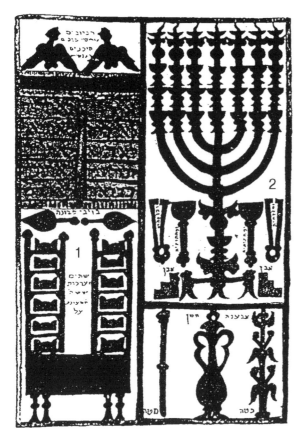
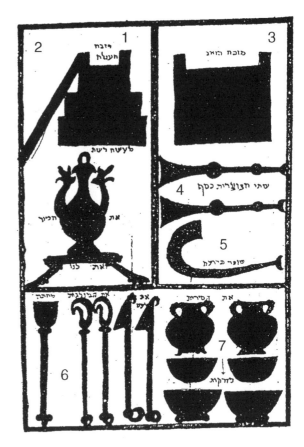

Figure 65 Temple Service and Ritual. Furniture and utensils of the Temple according to an illuminated Hebrew manuscript of the Bibliotheque Nationale, Paris.1: Showbread table and shovels; 2: Menorah and its instruments; 3: Altar of burnt offering and its ramp; 4: trumpets; 5: Shofar; 6: Altar tools; 7: Vessels for libations.

A unique bronze shovel with two attached intact incense cups was excavated from the Cave of Letters by Y. Yadin and his team in 1960-61 (*see* CAVE OF LETTERS). Perhaps it was saved from the Temple destruction in 70 C.E., or it may at least be identical to those used in the Temple. While charcoal was burning in the shovel, incense kept in the cups was sprinkled over it from time to time (Y. Yadin, 109).

Implications for Jesus Research

The existence of an elaborate Temple ritual in the time of Jesus is well attested both in Josephus and in early rabbinic literature. Presumably, these sources reflect a situation not too different from reality.

The gospels indicate that the poor could be faithful observants (Mark 12:41; Luke 2:24) and, as seen above, Josephus reports that the people grieved when sacrifices ceased. Jesus is unlikely to have opposed the Temple ritual and the priestly service; there is nothing derogatory in his references to the altar (Matt. 5:23-24; 23:18-20, 35). If we accept the proposition that Jesus' action in the Temple was directed against the priestly oligarchy alone, he then was not opposed to sacrifices offered as acts of devotion nor to the priestly service. Rather, he confronted those scribes and Pharisees who, in his view, misled the people and also the Sadducees who were part of the oligarchy. The only recorded but indirect critique of ordinary priests and Levites is to be found in the story of the Good Samaritan (Luke 10:31-32).

Jesus may have been inspired by the classical prophets who spoke out against the sacrificial ritual and whose voices are echoed in the Psalms and wisdom literature: Isaiah 1:11-17, Jeremiah 6:20; 7:21-23; Hosea 6:6; Amos 5:21-27; Micah 6:6-8; Psalms 40:6; 50:8-15; and Proverbs 21:3. Those prophets, however, actually were criticizing offerings made without proper devotion to God's commandments, not the sacrifices themselves: "I cannot endure solemn assemblies with iniquity" (Isa. 1:13); "Remove the evil of your doings . . . learn to do good, seek justice, rescue the oppressed, defend the fatherless, plead for the widow" (Isa. 1:16-17); "These people honor me with their lips, while their hearts are far from me" (Isa. 29:13); "Obey my voice, and I will be your God" (Jer. 7:23); "Let justice roll down like waters" (Amos 5:24); "Do justice, . . . love kindness, . . . walk humbly with your God" (Mic. 6:8). Jesus was thus acting in good prophetic tradition when he encouraged a leper to offer the proper sacrifice and when he observed the Passover meal, although the lamb may have been provided by his host. His disciples and immediate successors continued his acceptance of the Temple and its service; Jesus probably encouraged such an attitude.

John indicated that Jesus went to the Temple early in the morning when in Jerusalem (John 8:2); he was there with the crowd of pilgrims for the offering of the incense, the prayers, and prostrations.

There is no reason to question John's authenticity in this regard. (see fig. 67 for a representation of the Qumranites' ideal eschatological temple).

BIBLIOGRAPHY

Bagatti, B. *Recherche sur le site du temple de Jeruslem (1er–7ème siecles)*. Jerusalem: Franciscan Printing Press, 1979.

Chilton, B. *The Temple of Jesus: His Sacrificial Program within a Cultural History of Sacrifice*. University Park: Pennsylvania State University, 1992.

Clements, R. E. *God and Temple*. Oxford: Basil Blackwell, 1965.

Haran, M. *Temples and Temple Service in Ancient Israel*. Oxford: Clarendon, 1978.

Har-El, M. "Water of Purification, Hygiene and Cult at the Temple in Jerusalem." *Eretz Israel* 19 (1987): 310-13 (Hebrew).

Levine, M. *The Tabernacle: Its Structure and Utensils*. Tel Aviv: Melehet Hamishkhan, 1969.

Patrich, J. "The Mesibah of the Temple According to the Tractate Midot." *IEJ* 36 (1986): 215-33.

Yadin, Y. *Bar-Kokhba*. London: Weidenfeld and Nicolson, 1971.

Temple, Solomon's Portico

Importance
Solomon's portico was a gathering place for teachers and speakers.

Scripture References
John 10:23; Acts 3:11; 5:12.

General Information
According to Josephus, there was a double colonnade running along the sides of the Temple platform (*War* 5, 5.2/190). The columns were white marble monoliths 25 cubits (about 37 feet) high and supported a roof of finely carved cedar wood. The width of the porticoes was 30 cubits (45 feet), and they extended for a total length of six stada

(about 3600 feet), providing shelter against rain and sun for thousands of people. Josephus, in his description of the Temple, does not call Solomon's portico by name. Yet in mentioning that 18,000 workers were laid off when all the work on the Temple Mount was completed under King Agrippa II (*Antiq.* 20, 9.7/219), he indicates that a colonnade 400 cubits (600 feet) long stood on the eastern side and dated from the time of Solomon. People requested that Agrippa demolish and rebuild it in order to provide new jobs for the unemployed workers. Instead he decided to pave the city with white stone slabs. Because the original portico of Solomon was probably destroyed by the Babylonians with the rest of the Temple in 586 B.C.E., it must have been rebuilt by Zerubbabel before 515 B.C.E.

It is possible that Herod and those who continued his construction work kept the old elements and were satisfied to harmonize them with the remaining buildings.

Archaeological Information

Among the many columns taken from the Temple ruins and used to build new structures—churches and mosques—it is impossible to identify any that would have come from Solomon's portico. Still, it is likely that some of those architectural elements once were part of that structure.

Implications for Jesus Research

The Fourth Gospel indicates that Jesus walked in Solomon's portico in winter at the occasion of the Feast of Tabernacles. John is the only Gospel giving the name of Solomon's portico in connection with Jesus. We have already noted that the author of the Fourth Gospel seems to have a better knowledge than the other Gospel writers of the Palestine of Jesus, of the Temple, and of the way of life of the people. In many instances, he may even have been an eye-witness.

When Jesus was sitting down "opposite the treasury" (Mark 12:41), he was probably in front of the immense gate leading to the Court of Women where thirteen collection boxes stood (*see* TEMPLE, TREASURY). If some of these boxes were located at the entrance to the Court, someone sitting "opposite the treasury" in Solomon's portico could see people put money in them.

Solomon's portico would have been a likely setting for Jesus' teaching and other activities in the Temple, for it opened on the Court of the Gentiles but faced the Temple itself. According to Acts 3:11 and 5:12, people gathered around the Apostles in Solomon's portico; Jesus' former disciples continued a tradition probably begun by their master.

BIBLIOGRAPHY

Laperrousaz, E. M. "King Solomon's Wall Still Supports the Temple Mount." *BAR* 13 (1987): 34-44.

Temple, Stairs and Gates

Importance

Knowing the location of the entries to the Temple Mount helps visualize Jesus' paths when he went there.

Scripture References

Matt. 4:5; 12:6; 23:16, 17, 21; 24:1; Mark 11:16; Luke 2:37; 4:9; John 2:15, 20.

General Information

Two literary sources give information about the peripheral ways of access to the Temple: Josephus (*Antiq.* 15, 11.5/410-11), and the Mishnah (*m. Middot* 1.1, 3). They refer to different gates in the outer walls of the Temple Mount; in the light of archaeological materials, they seem to complement each other, with some overlap. Josephus lists several gates, four on the western side and others (an unspecified number) on the southern side. He does not mention any gate in the eastern and northern sides; while reporting the Roman attack of 70 C.E. (*War* 6, 4.1/222), however, he incidentally mentions a northern gate, which would correspond to the Tadi Gate of the Mishnah.

Mishnah *Middot* refers to five gates, with only one on the western side, probably the gate corresponding to Wilson's Arch, through which the priests entered to serve their week of duty (*see* JERUSALEM, WALLS AND GATES). *Middot* indicates two more gates in the south: one in the east (Shushan) and one in the north (Todi). Josephus gives a more detailed description of the gate located in the southern part of the western wall:

> Now, in the western side of the Temple Mount were four gates; the first led to the king's palace and went to a passage over the intermediate valley [Tyropoeon]; two more led to the suburbs of the city; and the last led to the other city where the roads descended into the valley by a great number of steps, and up hill again for the city lay over-against the valley along the entire southern quarter (*Antiq.* 15, 11.5/410).

This last description corresponds to the gate and stairs located at Robinson's Arch and excavated by B. Mazar. It was the gate giving access to the royal portico, above the southern wall of the Temple Mount. The existence of the three other western gates can also be related to archaeological discoveries. From south to north they are Barclay's Gate, the gate corresponding to Wilson's Arch, and Warren's Gate (*see* fig. 64).

In the south the greatest flow of visitors would have been through the Hulda Gates, named after the woman who prophesied in the days of King Josiah and who authenticated as God's word a document found in the Temple. The Mishnah indicates that there were two sets of stairs: the Triple Gate in the east, through which worshipers entered the Temple, and the Double Gate in the west, used only to exit. Behind the two Hulda Gates and under vaulted and decorated ceilings were stairs and ramps leading to the Court of the Gentiles, just north of the royal portico. One of these ramps still exists today behind the Double Gate, under the floor of the el Aqsa Mosque (*see* fig. 66).

On the northern side, in the vicinity of the Antonia was the Tadi Gate, which the general public did not use according to the Mishnah. It may have been the gate through which the High Priest went

to take and then return his sacred garments, which were in the custody of the civil power from the time of Hyrcanus until 36 C.E. when Vitellius, the legate of Syria, deposed Pilate and returned the priestly robes to the Jews (Josephus, *Antiq.* 15, 11.4/407-8). The inner Temple and the Antonia were probably connected by an underground passage called *nisos* in the Mishnah.

Excavations revealed an unnamed gate in the eastern wall, close to the southeastern corner of the Temple Mount. It led to a storeroom of the temple treasury known as the Chamber of Utensils (*m. Shekalim* 6) into which donors could enter directly. In the same area is an arch spring identical to that of Robinson's Arch on the western side. It can be identified as the ramp of the scapegoat (Lev. 16:20-22) mentioned in the Mishnah (*m. Shekalim* 6.2 and *Yoma* 4.2).

Because the Temple was built on a hill between two deep valleys, it was accessible only by ramps and stairways. The most remarkable were the monumental staircase leading to the royal portico, the wide steps below the Hulda Gates, and the arch supporting the stairs going down from the gate of the scapegoat. Stairs provided access to the Shushan Gate; but because they are now under a cemetery, it is impossible to excavate them. On the western side stairs led to the gates known today as Warren's and Barclay's Gates. As for the gate corresponding to Wilson's Arch located between these last two, it was accessed by a bridge connecting the Temple with the Xystos, the Upper City, and the royal palace (*see* JERUSALEM, HERODIAN). Worshipers literally had to "ascend the hill of the Lord" (Ps. 24:3 and others).

Archaeological Data

In the nineteenth century four American and British archaeologists discovered or identified on the western side of the Temple Mount the arches and gates that bear their names. They are, south to north: Robinson's Arch (1838), Barclay's Gate (1848), Wilson's Arch (1864-67), and Warren's Gate (1870). Located 267 feet north of the southern corner of the Temple Mount, Barclay's Gate is one of

Figure 66 The Hulda Gates. A: Temple Gate (entry); B: Double Gate (exit); C: Tunnel to the Court of Women; D: Royal Stoa.

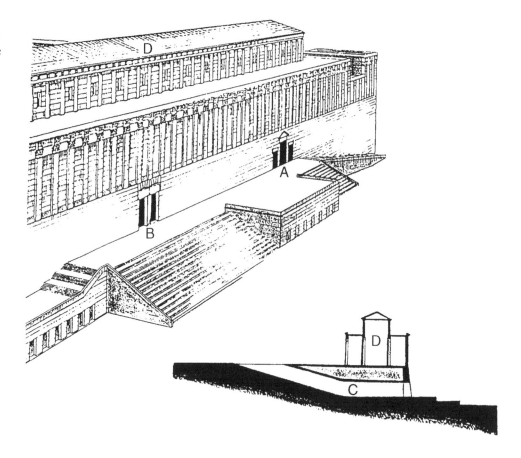

two gates that led to the suburbs according to Josephus. It was called the Coponius Gate, probably after Coponius (6-9 C.E.), the first procurator who ruled over Judea after Archelaus was deposed. Some scholars doubt that a gate to the most sacred place of the Jews would be named after a pagan ruler. Yet it is to be noted that the Shushan Gate was named after the capital city of a Persian emperor, Darius. Coponius, after succeeding a Herodian tyrant, may have made a gesture of goodwill toward the Jews and was perhaps thus memorialized in a gate name. Behind this gate are a corridor and a staircase turning southward at a right angle up to the Temple platform.

The gate of Wilson's Arch stood 325 feet north of the southwestern corner of the Temple Mount, just north of today's Western Wall. It opened at the eastern end of the bridge of the Xystos, the gymnasium built by Antochius Epiphanes (175-164 B.C.E.; *see* JERUSALEM, WALLS AND GATES), and was connected to the royal palace by a street or underground passage running along the northern wall. W. F. Stonespring in the mid-1960s showed that Wilson's Arch was structurally connected to the Temple platform; it thus dates to the time of Herod's construction of the Temple (began in 20-19 B.C.E.). Excavating in the southwestern area of the Temple Mount in the late 1960s, B. Mazar found that Robinson's Arch spanned a distance of 42 feet to a pier set in a direction perpendicular to the Western Wall. He also discovered a series of arches descending along the southern wall down to the level of the Herodian street, paved with large white stone slabs, that C. Warren had detected in 1867 at

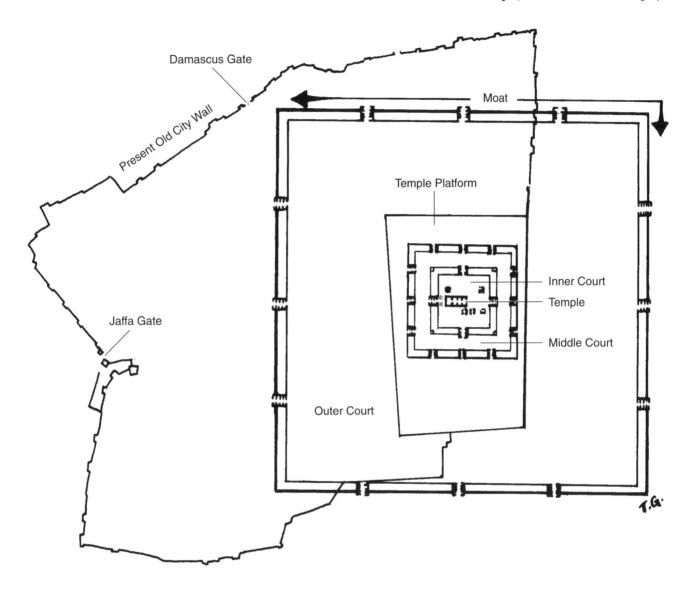

Figure 67 The Qumranite Eschatological Temple, Almost as Large as Jerusalem Old City. Temple Scroll, 11QT, 30-4b. This mythological temple has twelve gates named after Israel's tribes.

the bottom of a shaft dug at the foot of the Temple Mount. These arches supported the monumental stairway leading from the Double Hulda Gate to the street following the course of the Tyropoeon Valley.

On the southern side of the Temple Mount, the two Hulda Gates are visible today in their rebuilt, walled-in form, attributed to Suleiman the Magnificent in the mid-sixteenth century. Still farther to the east and close to the southeastern corner is the

The monumental stairs leading to the southwestern stoa entrance. (Jerusalem Museum)

single gate, which opens into a large vaulted area incorrectly called Solomon's Stables (*see* Fig. 67). Its vaults support the Temple platform and its halls, which extend 260 feet westward and 200 feet northward may have been used as storerooms or temporary stables for sacrificial animals. The Knights Templar kept horses there.

The Shushan Gate was probably under the present Golden Gate, of the Byzantine or Umayyad period, and would have been located some 1,020 feet from the southeastern corner of the Temple Mount. Probes made in 1971 and 1972 by J. Fleming and others located the top of an arch below the Golden Gate, thereby lending support to the hypothesis that the Shushan Gate was at this location.

Implications for Jesus Research

In the first century C.E. it was believed that the Messiah would come down the Mount of Olives and enter through the Shushan Gate, which was left ajar in this expectation (*see* JERUSALEM, KIDRON). The description in Mark 11:1-10 (and its parallels) of the "triumphant" entry of Jesus into Jerusalem reflects this popular expectation. The Gospel account may be a creation of the author of Mark, who gave a christological tone to his story, because it is nowhere specified that Jesus entered through the Shushan Gate as he would have if, by his attitude and actions, he had claimed to be the Messiah. The wording of Mark 11:11a,b indicates that he did not: "Then he entered Jerusalem [not the Temple], and went [from Jerusalem] into the temple." Once in the Temple he did nothing right away: "and when he had looked around at everything, as it was already late, he went out to Bethany with the twelve." One of the strongest criteria, the criterion of "embarrassment" for the early Church points toward the authenticity of this abstention from a messianic claim.

It is possible to reconstruct Jesus' path when he went to the Temple from the Mount of Olives. He would have entered through the Fountain Gate by the Gihon Spring, gone northward in the City of David, reached the *miqvaoth* area in the Ophel, and perhaps bathed in one of the ritual baths rented to the pilgrims (*see* RITUAL BATHS). Then he would have climbed the wide steps leading to the Triple Gate, entered into the vaulted stepped corridor, and continued climbing to the Court of the Gentiles, just north of the Royal Stoa. There he would have seen the merchants selling birds and animals for sacrifices and also the money changers who were there to offer Tyrian coins to people delinquent in paying the half-shekel tax. The money changers should have been in the royal portico but probably went beyond their assigned space to come closer to the prospective customers; such aggressiveness evoked Jesus' violent reaction (Mark 11:15-17 and parallels). In any case, Jesus would have continued northward toward Solomon's portico, perhaps to listen to speakers and to speak himself.

The Gospels do not mention that Jesus ever entered the Court of Israel or the Court of the Priests to offer a sacrifice. He may have entered the Court of Women, because it is in this court that the thirteen collection boxes were located (*see* TEMPLE, TREASURY) and because it is reported that he watched people giving money (Mark 12:41). In that case he would have entered through one of the doors of the *soreg*, the latticed stone wall or balustrade between the Court of Gentiles and the Temple itself, on which warning signs were posted (*see* WARNING SIGNS). One of the Levites on watch at the door would have inquired to verify that he was a Jew in a state of ritual purity. Otherwise he could have watched from the Court of Gentiles through the wide main gate, perhaps the "Beautiful Gate" of Acts 3:2, 10 east of the Court of Women. When leaving, he would not have retraced his steps, it being inappropriate to turn one's back to the Temple. Instead, he would have continued northward and then proceeded counterclockwise around the walls of the sanctuary, perhaps prostrating himself thirteen times as did the other worshipers, according to rabbinic sources (*y. Middot* 2:2; *y. Shekalim* 6:1).

BIBLIOGRAPHY

Busink, T. A. *Der Tempel von Jerusalem. Von Solomo bis Herodes*, 2 vols. Leiden: E. J. Brill, 1970–1980.

Comay, J. *The Temple of Jerusalem*. New York: Holt, Rinehart and Winston, 1975.

Crowfoot, J. W. V. "Excavations in the Tyropeon Valley, Jerusalem 1927." *Annual of the Palestine Exploration Fund* (1929).

Flemming, J. "The Undiscovered Gate Beneath Jerusalem's Golden Gate." *BAR* 9 (1983): 24-37.

Hollis, F. J. *The Archaeology of Herod's Temple*. London: Dent, 1934.

Mackowsky, R. M. *Jerusalem City of Jesus*. Grand Rapids, Mich.: Eerdmans, 1980.

Magan, Y. "The Gates of the Temple Mount According to Josephus and the Mishnah." *Cathedra* 14 (1980): 41-53 (Hebrew).

Mazar, B. *The Mountain of the Lord: Excavating in Jerusalem*. Garden City, N.Y.: Doubleday, 1975.

Temple, Treasury

Importance

The Temple was an economic center supported by the donations of the people; its treasury is mentioned by name four times in the Gospels.

Scripture References

Matt. 17:27; 27:6; Mark 12:41; Luke 21:1; John 8:20.

General Information

The Temple Treasury was a major financial institution, collecting resources from all over the country and from the Diaspora and redistributing its wealth in various economic sectors and geographical areas. Its sources of income were numerous; contributions were large and small, individual and collective. Several types of contribution are known from ancient sources:

- *Contributions from foreign kings.* Ptolemy II Philadelphus, for example, offered gifts of gold and silver, which Josephus describes at length (*Antiq.* 12, 2.7-10/57-84); Seleucus IV paid for the cost of all sacrifices (2 Macc. 3:3); Antiochus donated 20,000 silver shekels, wheat, flour, salt, material, and cedar wood for repairs (*Antiq.* 12, 3.3/140-41). Many others gave lavishly according to Josephus, Philo, and 1 and 2 Maccabees.

- *Gifts of immovable property.* Many houses and tracts of land dedicated to the Temple were sold, with the proceeds going to the Treasury (*m. 'Arakin* 8; *t. Shekalim* 2:15).

- *Half-shekel tax.* All Jewish males aged 20 and over were expected to pay the half-shekel tax once a year (see Exod. 30:14-15). This tax, which provided the steadiest flow of income, was supplemented by the contributions of persons not obligated to pay the half-shekel tax and by wealthy people who offered gold coins as an additional contribution. This money coming to Jerusalem from all over the Roman world aroused the greed of local officials in places where the coins were collected or through which they passed. To avoid thefts, Temple collections were escorted by military detachments under Julius Caesar and Augustus. In Judea, every year on the first of Adar (mid-February), the Jerusalem High Court sent messengers to cities and villages in order to remind the people that the taxes were due in the Treasury by the first of Nissan (end of March, beginning of April; *y. Shekalim* 1:1, 45d). The tax had to be paid in Tyrian coins, which were of the highest quality. Tables of money changers were set up throughout the land on the fifteenth of Adar and in the Temple on the twenty-fifth. Collection containers or boxes, shaped like trumpets (*shofarot*), were installed in the country for the occasion; in the Temple thirteen *shofarot* stood all year round in the Court of Women, each of them bearing an inscription indicating the object of the collection (*y. Shekalim* 6:1, 5; Josephus, *War* 5, 5.2/200).

- *Votive offerings.* The revenue generated by the "vows of valuations" and other votive offerings

(Lev. 27, *m. 'Arakin* 24a) was kept in a special Treasury chamber earmarked for Temple repairs.

- *Free-will offerings.* Several sorts of free-will offerings, such as anonymous gifts from those who wanted to give alms secretly and donations of gold and silver vessels, were kept in special chambers.

- *Deposits.* The Temple Treasury also functioned as a bank for safe deposits. People believed that God would protect valuables stored in the Temple. According to Josephus, enormous amounts of wealth accumulated there in that way (*War* 6, 5.2/282).

Priests or members of priestly families were appointed as treasurers to pay for the multifarious expenses of the Temple. They purchased animals for the regular sacrifices and for the private sacrifices of pilgrims unable to bring unblemished live animals with them. They compensated blemish inspectors and those who instructed priests on the proper way to slaughter the sacrificial animals. The Temple service required the purchase of many other goods and materials of the best quality. Wine and fine flour came mostly from Judea, olive oil from Galilee, calves from Sharon, rams from Moab, and lambs from Hebron; doves were raised on the Mount of Olives: the barley for the Omer had to be grown in the Land of Israel. The imported ingredients and herbs for incense were expensive and had to be carefully selected. Maintenance and repair for such a large complex as the Temple Mount and its structures were costly. In addition, construction expenses continued until circa 60 C.E.

Archaeological Information

Ezra 2:69 reports that some of the heads of families returning from exile gave a total of sixty-one thousand darics (*darkemonim*) of gold in free-will offerings for the rebuilding of the Temple. As gold coins the darics could not have been Greek drachmas, which were made of silver; thus they must have been Persian gold drachias. Archaeological excavations have not revealed any such coin in Israel, and thus the information in Ezra has been called into question. As for the *shofarot*, "treasury boxes," they are known only from literary sources and pictures (*see* COINS AND MONEY).

Implications for Jesus Research

The Gospels mention Jesus in connection with the Temple Treasury and the payment of the half-shekel per capita tax. The Greek word *gazophylakeiou*, "treasury," as found in Mark 12:41 and Luke 21:1, may refer to the *shofarot* of the Court of Women. Although Jesus had access to the Court of Israel, it seems he did not enter even the Court of Women, which was opened to all Jews, women and men. In connection with the Treasury and the half-shekel tax, it appears that Jesus was aware of the practices of his time although the Gospels indicate that he did not condone all of their aspects. This observation applies to a number of other Gospel details that can be related to information provided by archaeology, historical accounts, and rabbinic writings; as noted elsewhere, the Gospels often contain reliable information.

BIBLIOGRAPHY

Anderson, G. *Sacrifices and Offerings in Ancient Israel: Studies in Their Social and Political Importance*. Atlanta, Ga.: Scholars Press, 1987.

Jeremias, J. *Jerusalem in the Time of Jesus*. German, 1962. Philadelphia: Fortress Press, 1984.

See Bibliographies under COINS AND MONEY; TAX AND TAX COLLECTORS; TEMPLE, SACRIFICIAL SYSTEM.

Temple, Trumpeting Place

Importance

The trumpet was blown at the major points of the Temple service.

Scripture References

Matt. 24:31; 1 Cor. 15:52; 1 Thess. 4:16.

General Information

The term *trumpet* is used in English translations of the Bible for two different wind instruments. One is the *shofar*, a word related to the Akkadian *shapparu*, "wild goat" whose males had large horns curved backward. Trumpets so designed were made of curved animal horns. Another trumpet was the *hazozrah*, a straight instrument made of silver, copper, or gold. The *hazozrah* (Num. 10:1-10), was used in the liturgy by the priests (usually in pairs) to announce sacrifices and ritual acts; on special occasions, 120 or more of these trumpets were blown.

The *shofar* is the instrument most often mentioned in the Hebrew Bible. It is first named in Exodus 19:16, where it is said that God appeared to the Hebrews amid thunder and lightening at Mount Sinai and that the people heard "a very loud shofar blast" and "trembled." According to Leviticus 25:8-10, the *shofar* was sounded at the jubilee to "proclaim liberty throughout the land to all its inhabitants." It was blown on the New Year, *Rosh Hashanah*, which is also known as *Yom teru'ah*, "a day of blowing" (Lev. 23:24; Num. 29:1). It announced festivals like the New Moon, and it marked the beginning and end of the sabbath. Rabbinic tradition mentions three kinds of trumpet (*shofar*) signals:

teqiah, "hit," blowing from a lower to higher note;
terua, "alarm," staccato;
shevarim, "danger," tremolo.

The War Scroll (1QM; 4Q 491-96, Col. 3) indicates that there were several other forms of signals. In addition to cultic functions, the *shofar* was used for military musters and battle signals.

Archaeological Data

In 1970 a large limestone slab was found by Israeli archaeologists at the foot of the southwestern corner of the Temple Mount. It had probably been thrown down from the top during the demolition of the Temple by Titus in 70 C.E. It bears a Hebrew inscription, which reads: *lbyt htqyh lhk . . .*, "place

Figure 68 A broken slab reading "Place of Trumpeting" was found in the southwestern corner of the Temple Mount.

of trumpeting." This inscription undoubtedly relates to the tradition in the first century C.E., of the sounding of the trumpet in the Temple (*see* fig. 68).

Implications for Jesus Research

The sounding of the *shofar* and of trumpets accompanied certain cultic activities and festivals. There were probably several locations in the Temple walls or towers where the *shofar* was sounded. On the northeastern tower, for example, the beginning of the New Moon and feasts was signaled by *shofar* via Herodium and Machaerus as far as Babylon (*see* MACHAERUS).

The sounding of the trumpet became associated with apocalyptic visions (*see* War Scroll, Matt. 24:31, and 1 Cor. 15:52). Yet Mark 13:26-27 does not mention the sounding of trumpets when the Son of Man comes "in clouds with great power and glory." This omission may be accidental, or it may

indicate that the passage is not authentic. When Matthew reproduced the pericope from Mark, he may have added the trumpet reference in accord with conceptions current at the time.

BIBLIOGRAPHY

Demsky, A. "When the Priests Trumpeted the Onset of the Sabbath." *BAR* 12 (1986): 50-52.

Jones, I. "Music and Musical Instruments." *ABD* 4:930-39.

See Bibliography under TEMPLE, SERVICE, AND RITUAL.

Temple, Warning Signs

Importance

The Temple platform was open to everyone, but the area around the Temple itself was accessible only to Jews.

Scripture References

Matt. 8:10-12; 21:31.

General Information

Like all such sacred enclosures, the Temple involved a hierarchy of accessibility. The sacred area around the Temple itself could be entered only by Jews who were ritually clean. The Court of Women was opened to all ritually pure Jews, regardless of age and sex. Only men could enter the Court of Israel. Only priests and Israelites offering animal sacrifices or members of the *ma'amadot* (*m. kelim* 1:8; *mishmarot* and *ha'amadot*) could enter the Court of the Priests. Priests alone could enter the main room (outer sanctum) of the Temple where the altar of incense, the menorah, and the showbread table were set; and only the High Priest could enter the Holy of Holies (inner sanctum), once a year on the Day of Purgation.

The Temple walls were surrounded by the *soreg*, a stone balustrade or lattice wall ten handbreadths (about 40 inches) wide according to the Mishnah (*m. Middot* 2:3), or three cubits (about 5 feet) high, according to Josephus. The *soreg* incorporated pillars at regular intervals; these bore stone slabs inscribed in Greek or in Latin with a warning: "No Gentiles should go beyond the sign under penalty of death!" (Josephus, *War* 5, 5.2/193; *Antiq.* 15, 11.5/418). This injunction applied even to Roman citizens. Josephus also writes that "This enclosure (of the Court of Women) had on the eastern side a large gate through which those who were ritually clean came in together with their wives, but the Temple, further inside, was not allowed to the women."

Archaeological Data

In 1871, C. Clermont-Ganneau discovered an intact slab, bearing the warning inscription in Greek; it is now in a museum in Istanbul. A fragment of another slab, also inscribed in Greek and large enough to be identified with certainty as the warning sign, was found in 1935 outside the Lion or Saint Stephen's Gate (*see* the photo on this page).

Implications for Jesus Research

Prescriptions of hierarchy or differential access to certain places or practices and the general stratification of Palestinian society can both be contrasted with the kingdom of God proclaimed by Jesus, which was open to everyone who repented. There were no sacrifices to be offered and no purity laws to be observed. Jesus' kingdom involved an inner purity, or a purity of the heart; repentant prostitutes and tax collectors gained entry without any further formality. Jesus gave Samaritans, Gentiles and a "prodigal son" as models. This was certainly a subversive teaching in the eyes of the priestly establishment and of most Pharisees, although its equalitarian aspect would have resonated with many others.

BIBLIOGRAPHY

Segal, P. "The Penalty of the Warning Inscription from the Temple in Jerusalem." *IEJ* 39 (1989): 89-94.

Broken part of a soreg *warning sign in Greek.*

Textiles, Dyeing

Importance

The Gospels contain a number of references to garments and linens.

Scripture References

Matt. 5:40; 6:28; 9:16, 20-21; 10:10; 14:36; 21:8; 22:11-12; 23:5; 24:18; 25:36, 43; 27:35, 59; Mark

2:21; 5:15, 27-28; 6:9; 9:3; 10:50; 11:7-8; 13:16; 14:51-52; 15:17, 20, 24, 46; 16:5; Luke 2:7, 12; 3:11; 5:36; 7:25; 8:27, 35; 16:19; 19:35; 22:36; John 11:44; 13:4; 19:23, 40; 20:5-7; 21:7.

General Information

The making of textiles is an ancient activity that can be traced back to prehistoric times. The domestication of sheep and goats is as ancient as the Neolithic, when the spinning and weaving of wool and hair was already practiced. In Mesopotamia, the Near East, and Greece wool was the most important of animal fibers. Camel hair is also attested. Wool and shearing are frequently mentioned in the Hebrew Bible: lambs provided clothing (Prov. 27:26); women bought wool and flax (Prov. 31:13); a poor man could warm himself in the fleece of a rich man's sheep (Job 31:20); every year the king of Moab gave to the king of Israel a tribute of 100,000 lambs and the wool of as many rams (2 Kings 3:4)—the first fleece of the sheep was offered to the priests (Deut. 18:4).

Wool came in a variety of natural colors, from clear white to dark brown with many shades between. It was also dyed in blue, red, and a combination of the two that could imitate the expensive purple of Tyre (*see* TYRE AND SIDON). Dyers clustered in certain cities and in a certain quarter of Jerusalem (in the south of the Upper City) where there was enough water for their work, but wool was probably sent to Tyre for dyeing in purple (Ezek. 27:19). Pure white wool was compared with snow (Ps. 147:16; Isa. 1:18; Dan. 7:9). Pliny devotes a long passage to sheep and wool (*Nat. Hist.* 8).

In Palestine flax was grown for the production of "fine linen" with which priests' garments were made (Exod. 25:4; 28:8, 15, 39, Lev. 6:10; 16:4, 23, 36 *et passim*). Several other references are made to flax and linen in the Bible and rabbinic literature. Rahab hid two Israelite spies among stalks of flax that were drying on her roof (Josh. 2:6). Spinning was usually a woman's task (Hos. 2:5, 9; Prov. 31:13); but specialized garments may have been produced by male artisans: the king of Tyre sent Huramabi, a man skilled at working in precious materials and fine linen to Solomon (2 Chron. 2:13-14). Isaiah 19:9 refers to workers in combed flax without indication of gender.

The flax grown in Palestine was of good quality (Pausanias 5, 5.2); the center of its production, Arbel in Galilee, was highly regarded (*M. Ketubot* 5.9). Clements of Alexandria indicates that the Hebrew linen was of the same quality as the Egyptian (*Paedagogus* 2, 10.15). Palestine did not export in large quantities, however, and international buyers had to find additional supplies of linen in Tyre, Byblos, and Beirut. Normally linen was not dyed, except for some threads colored blue for decorative purpose. Flax was the most important fiber of Palestine. The climate was too dry to allow for cotton cultivation; as a result, cotton is seldom mentioned in Hebrew literature. The biblical stipulation that fibers of different nature should not be used together in a garment (Lev. 19:19 and Deut. 22:11) is perhaps explained by a surviving ancient tradition: Wool was considered ritually unclean by the Egyptians and is never found in their temples and tombs. Philostratus wondered about this practice:

> In what way is linen better than wool? Was not wool taken from the back of the most gentle of animals, from a creature that the gods who did not disdain to be shepherds beloved . . . On the other hand flax is sown and grown eveywhere and gold is never mentioned in connection with it (as opposed to the golden fleece). However, because it is not plucked from the back of a living animal, the Indians regard it as pure, and so do the Egyptians, and I, myself, and Pythagoras on this account, have adopted it for our garments when we discuss praying or offering sacrifice (*Apollonius* 8, 7.5).

The dyes available in antiquity were not very pure, and the techniques for making them were not sophisticated. Dyers' formulas were family secrets handed down from generation to generation; some have been preserved. Red dyes were mostly made of kermes and cochineal extracted from female insects of the coccida family; the final color could vary from pink to scarlet. A cheaper red dye was madder extracted from the roots of *rubia tinctorium*, a perennial vine that grows in the Near East. Blue dyes were all of vegetable origin, with Indian indigo not yet cultivated in first century C.E. Palestine. Purple, the most precious dye, was produced by certain mollusks: welks (a variety of mussel), the *murex brandaris*, and *murex trunculus*. Variations in factors such as salt content and exposure to sunlight meant that the final color ranged from deep purple to purplish red. Experiments showed that the liquid extracted from 12,000 mollusks produced only 1.5 grams of pure purple dye; this explains why a pound of Tyrian purple cost the equivalent of 10,000 dollars (1994 value).

Most terms found in ancient texts to designate the varying shades of blue, purple, scarlet, and crimson cannot be translated accurately; thus the corresponding colors cannot be identified with certainty. As R. J. Forbes notes (*Studies in Ancient Technologies*, vol. 4, 119), it is impossible to say exactly what kind of *hyakinthos*, "blue" and *porphyra*, "purple" fabrics Judas Maccabee took from the Syrians (1 Macc. 4:23; 8:14; 10:20; 11:58; 2 Macc. 4:38). The exact colors of the "blue" threads in the tassels of the Hebrew *talithoth*, "mantles" (Num. 15:38), the color of the garments of the kings of Midian (Judg. 8:26), the colors used in the Tabernacle (Exod. 26:36; Lev. 14:4, *et passim*), and the color of the "scarlet" or "purple" robe or cloak placed on Jesus' shoulders at the time of his trial cannot be determined.

Josephus indicates that the wool shops and clothes makers were located in the "new town" of Jerusalem (*War* 5, 8.1/331), in the area north of the Antonia and Second Wall (*see* JERUSALEM, WALLS AND GATES). Some professions pertaining to textile and related industries may not have been held in high esteem. The Mishnah lists flax-combers, tanners, weavers, tailors, launderers, and sellers of purple wool among those engaged in despised trades. For the weavers, it was because weaving was normally done by women (Jeremias, 303–310).

Archaeological Information

The Gezer Calendar, found at Gezer during the 1902-9 Macalister excavations and dated to the late tenth century B.C.E., mentions the "hoeing up of flax" as an important part of the agricultural year. The cultivation of flax in Israelite times is not well documented archaeologically. However, the fact that the Rahab story mentions flax stalks would suggest that, at least in the Jordan Valley, flax was grown. Cultivation of this plant remained strong in that area until the fourth century C.E. In any case, wool was far more common in Palestine than linen, which remained a special and costly fabric. The loom weights, spindle whorls, dye vats, and other artifacts of textile production found in Palestine probably were used chiefly for processing wool.

Since the early 1950s, following the discovery of the Dead Sea Scrolls and other manuscripts, the caves in the Judean Desert have been systematically explored. In the process, pieces of textiles, including linen, have turned up in caves near Qumran, at Murabba'at, and in Nahal Hever. The most important and best-preserved collection was found in the Cave of Letters in Nahal Hever, explored by Y. Yadin in 1960 and 1961. During the Bar Kokhba Revolt (132-35 C.E.) insurgents were trapped in the cave and eventually died of starvation. They had brought with them and hidden their most precious possessions, including rugs, tunics, mantles, bundles of wool dyed in purple, spinning whorls and skeins of yarn, and a child's linen shirt. A total of 43 natural colors and dyes have been recognized. Some of the dyes and mordants were of high quality. None of the fabrics were made of mixed fibers; the weavers who made the textiles and those who wore them apparently followed the prescriptions of Lev. 19:19 and Deut. 22:11.

Implications for Jesus Research

How did Jesus usually dress?

Mark 5:27-30 is not explicit enough to give any valuable indication. According to the Transfiguration scene (Matt. 17:02 and parallels), Jesus' garments became "dazzling white," which may suggest that they were already white, and possibly made of linen. From the crucifixion scene, it seems that Jesus had five pieces of clothing, including a seamless tunic (John 19:23). They would have been an outer garment, a tunic or cloak, a head cloth, a loin cloth, and a pair of sandals. Because the tunic and sandals were of greater value than the other pieces, casting lots for their distribution was justified (see TUNIC WITHOUT SEAM, DICE). The exact color of the "scarlet" robe or cloak given by derision to Jesus at the time of his condemnation by Pilate (Matt. 27:28 and parallels) cannot be determined.

The information that Jesus' garments had been taken by the soldiers, and relevant material found in the Fourth Gospel (John 20:5-7), allow some observations to be made about the burial customs of the Jews in the time of Jesus:

- Bodies were placed in burial chambers for rapid decomposition (see JERUSALEM, TOMBS).

- No remains of textiles have been found in the first-century Jewish tombs of Jerusalem.

- Jesus probably was not buried with new garments, but rather with a simple shroud perhaps made of two sheets as indicated by the plural *othonia*, "sheets." John mentions a "napkin" or "kerchief" that was placed on Jesus' head, but such a practice is not otherwise attested in Palestine.

- In consideration of the first remark above, a statement that Joseph of Arimathea brought a large quantity of spices "to combat the inevitable decomposition of the corpse" does not fit with the Jewish customs of the time.

White garments may have had a particular significance among the Jewish people of the first century C.E. The candidate Essene was presented with a small mattock, a loin cloth and a white garment (Josephus, *War* 2, 8.7/137-38; 1QS 6:14-23). Other figures connected with the death of Jesus wore white garments, as he probably did: the young man at the tomb (Mark 16:5), the two men, "dazzling," (Luke 24:4), and the two other men of Acts 1:10 at the Ascension. The traditional explanation is that these mysterious figures represent angels. Another suggestion is that similarities in dressing and in other matters, such as rules of hospitality and methods of healing and exorcism, indicate the existence of certain links between Jesus and the Essenes (see DEAD SEA SCROLLS; EXORCISM; HOUSE; TANNERY, LEATHER).

BIBLIOGRAPHY

Barber, E. J. W. *Prehistoric Textiles*. Princeton, N.J.: Princeton University Press, 1991.

Borowski, O. *Agriculture in Iron Age Israel*. Winona Lake, Ind.: Eisenbrauns, 1987.

Danker, F. W. "Purple." *ABD* 5:557-60.

Douglas, E. R. "Dress and Ornamentation." *ABD* 2:232-38.

Forbes, R. J. *Studies in Ancient Technologies*, V4 Leiden: E. J. Brill, 1956.

Jensen, L. B. "Royal Purple of Tyre." *Journal of Near Eastern Studies* 22 (1963): 104-18.

Jeremias, J. *Jerusalem in the Time of Jesus*. German, 1962. Philadelphia: Fortress Press, 1984.

Yadin, Y. *Bar Kokhba*. London: Weidenfeld and Nicolson, 1978.

Tiberias (Hebrew, *tveria*)

Importance

Tiberias became the capital city of Galilee at the time of Jesus' adult life.

Scripture References

John 6:1, 23; 21:1.

General Information

Tiberias, situated on the western shores of the Sea of Galilee, was founded in 18 or 19 C.E. by Herod Antipas, tetrarch of Galilee and Perea, to replace Sepphoris as his main residence. Antipas named it in honor of emperor Tiberius (14–37 C.E.). Avi-Yonah dated the foundation of the city to 18 C.E. by associating it with Tiberius' sixtieth birthday; based on numismatic evidence, E. Schurer, G. F. Hill, and Y. Meshorer prefer 19 C.E. The proximity of hot springs, still used today, made the site all the more attractive, but when the construction of the city was started, an ancient necropolis appeared, which made the city unclean for Jews (even today, *cohanim*, descendants of priestly families, avoid the southern road leading to Tiberias; because of this problem a bypass was built just for them in 1991–92). Thus, in order to populate his new city, Antipas recruited soldiers, non-Jews, freed slaves, landless people, the poor, and Jews who did not care about the purity issue to settle there. He even transferred people by force from his other domains (Josephus, *Antiq*. 18, 2.3/36–38). At first Tiberias was probably an unwalled city; only during the reign of emperor Septimus Severus (193–211 C.E.) was it strongly fortified. Antipas erected a number of large buildings: his palace on a hill, a stadium, a synagogue, and a fortress in the north; the town center grew on a narrow stretch of land between the hills and the lake shore.

Tiberias received the status of a *polis* (city with some autonomy); it was governed by a council of six hundred, an archon, and a committee of ten (Josephus, *War* 2, 21.3–8/595–637). It minted its own bronze coins and used its own calendar, beginning on the day of its foundation. In 61 C.E. Tiberias, together with Magdala-Taricheae and Bethsaida Julias, were detached from Galilee and given to Agrippa II by Nero (*Antiq*. 20, 8.4/158–59). During the First Jewish War, the city remained loyal to Agrippa and surrendered to Vespasian, avoiding destruction. After the fall of Jerusalem in 135, Tiberias was "paganized" by Hadrian but rapidly became an important center of Judaism. The peak of the city's fame took place between the Late Roman period and the Middle Ages, beyond the focus of our study. It is to be noted, however, that beginning circa 150 C.E. the city served as the seat of the Sanhedrin. It was also the official residence of the Patriarchs (the presidents of the San-hedrin), probably from the time of R. Judah HaNasi and the seat of the Great Academy (Yeshiva), supervised by rabbis Yohanan, Bar Napha, and Resh Lakish, among others. It is also the place where the Palestinian or Jerusalem Talmud was compiled (ca. 420 C.E.), and where the Hebrew vowel punctuation system (masoretic system) was invented. Archaeological discoveries from this period include a few synagogues, bath houses, and residential quarters. There are also remains left by the non-Jewish population, notably a monastery on the top of Mt. Berenice. The coins minted in Tiberias testify to a non-Jewish presence; they depict the temple dedicated to the cult of the emperor, Hygeia, the goddess of the warm springs of Hammath, Tyche the city goddess, and Serapis.

Archaeological Data

The city of Tiberias actually consists of two adjacent towns, Hammath (the Greek derivation for Emmaus meaning "hot springs"), and Tiberias proper, situated a little farther north. A settlement at Hammath existed long before Herod Antipas founded the nearby Tiberias. The Bible refers to a place named Hammath among the fortified towns of Naphtali, probably around the Sea of Galilee (Josh. 19:35), together with Kinneret (Tel Rureime), Rakkat (Tel Quneitra) and Zer or Zed (Bethsaida?). Although Iron Age remains have not been found at Hammath, this site may be the biblical Hammath, simply because there is no Hammath elsewhere in the vicinity.

Excavations begun in 1921 at Hammath and at Tiberias indicate that Hammath was founded earlier than Tiberias; it dates from the Hellenistic period, probably from the first century B.C.E., or possibly earlier. A public building, which lies underneath a fourth-century C.E. synagogue, may be attributed to this period. The function of this building has not been determined, but the presence of Corinthian and Doric architectural elements suggest that it was a gymnasium.

By the time Josephus, in the second half of the first century C.E., Hammath and Tiberias were united. The twin sites featured splendid buildings including a palace, *thermae*, "hot baths," an agora, a *boulotherion*,* a stadium, strong fortification walls, and a fortress. Almost none of these has been discovered as yet. The only remains of the Herodian city found so far are the southern city gate and a paved street called the "Cardo" by the excavator, G. Foerster. The city gate was set between two round towers and flanked by two large columns on high pedestals, as was typical of the Late Hellenistic–Early Roman urban military fortifications. The street leading from the gate into the city was paved with basalt slabs laid partly obliquely, as in Roman streets. The walls adjacent to the towers were found to be of a much later period. Archaeologists believe that the gate and the paved road date from the foundation of the city, namely the years 18–19 C.E. Although there is no definite proof that the Roman city was fortified, such a possibility should not be totally dismissed. During the Roman period there was a large open space between the city gate and the closest city buildings, perhaps because the town of this period was not densely populated.

Implications for Jesus Research

At the time of Jesus' ministry, Tiberias was the new residence of Herod Antipas, "that fox" (Luke 13:32). The Gospels do not indicate that Jesus visited the city. He may have avoided it for two reasons: its uncleanness resulting from the presence of burials, and the presence of Antipas and his guard.

Joanna, one of the women following Jesus, was probably from Tiberias as she was the wife of Chuza, Herod Antipas's steward (Luke 8:3). Recalling that it was a pagan city, the fact that boats came from Tiberias to the place where Jesus had fed the multitude may indicate that Gentiles and other unbelievers were attracted to him, certainly because of his reputation as a healer and miracle worker, and perhaps because he was seen as a prophet (John 6:14). His influence on non-Jews is reflected in other passages of the Gospels (Matt. 4:25, *et passim*).

BIBLIOGRAPHY

Foerster, G. *Revue Biblique* 82 (1975): 105–7.

———. *Qadmoniot* 10 (1977): 87–91 (Hebrew).

Foerster, G. and F. Vitto. "Tiberias." *NEAEHL* 4:1464–73.

Hill, G. F. *Catalogue of the Greek Coins of Palestine in the British Museum.* Bologna, 1965.

Strange, J. F. "Tiberias." *ABD* 6:547–49.

Yardeni, A. "The Synagogue at Hammat Tiberia (Stratum II)." *Eretz Israel* 23 (1992): 320–26 (Hebrew, English summary).

Traditional Healing

Importance

Healing is the activity of Jesus most often reported in the Gospels. His methods may be better understood in the light of popular traditional healing.

Scripture References

Matt. 4:23-24; 8:1-15; 9:1-8, 12, 18-26; 10:8; 11:2-6; 15:29-31; 20:29-34; Mark 1:29-31, 40-45; 2:1-12, 16-17; 3:1-6; 5:21-23, 25-43; 7:31-37; 8:22-26; 10:46-52; Luke 4:23, 38-39; 5:12-16, 17-26, 30-32; 6:6-11; 7:1-23; 8:40-55; 10:7-9; 18:35-43; John 5:2-16; 9:1-12; 11:1-45.

General Information

In Palestine, as in the rest of the Greco-Roman world, healing was performed by different practitioners applying various methods according to diverse sets of beliefs. Among ancient methods were those of the priests whose healing practices sometimes involved elaborate rituals. Perhaps even older and certainly more popular were the methods of traditional or folk healers, examined in this entry. Scientific medicine based on observation goes back to Hippocrates (460?–377? B.C.E). Working in more mysterious ways and having great influence on the people were exorcists, magicians, and miracle workers, who also claimed that they could heal sufferers from their ailments (*see* EXORCISM; MEDI-

CINE, PHYSICIANS; MAGIC, MIRACLES). Distinctions between categories were not clear-cut; adherents of different methods could use the same plants, prayers, and incantations. Thus the category of healing is based more on beliefs and principles rather than methods. Priests and their clients believed that the gods performed the healing; traditional healers used ancient practices based on superstitions and folk medicine. Physicians and surgeons had a more scientific approach; exorcists, magicians, and miracle workers invoked supernatural powers, which could be good or evil. In his first letter to the Corinthians, Paul recognized two of the practitioners we have mentioned, the miracle worker and the [traditional] healer (1 Cor. 12:28).

The methods of traditional healing did not involve special paraphernalia, such as amulets, magic bowls, surgical instruments, and magic dolls, that might be recovered through field archaeology. Thus, it is necessary to turn to ethnoarchaeology in order to study ancient healing practices that may still survive in some cultures. For example, some customs of the Bedouins still living in the Middle East and in North Africa may go as far back as the second millennium B.C.E. The traditional healers of Jesus' time perhaps used some of the healing techniques still practiced among today's Bedouins.

Anthropological and Technical Information

From 1949 to 1958, one of the authors (J. Rousseau) had the opportunity to study the healing practices of the Bedouins of North Africa, some of which resembled those of the country herbalists and healers of Mediterranean Europe. Later, in 1987, Aref Abu Rabia of Beer-Sheba presented to the Albright Institute in Jerusalem a monograph on the healing practices of the Bedouins of the Negev. Most of the content of this section is comprised of what direct observation (in 1949–58) and the Abu Rabia monograph have in common. In addition, two methods involving the use of minerals and observed in North Africa are also included.

Bedouins' basic beliefs regarding illness and healing include the following:

- All things that happen to humans, both good and evil, come from the will of God; therefore a person must accept one's fate with faith, patience, courage, and long-suffering. This belief is based on a strong monotheism and in a form of submissive wisdom not foreign to that of Job.
- God creates health and illness or allows them to come through the natural or supernatural powers he created.
- Most diseases are sent as a punishment for sin.
- God heals through the mediation of a gifted person—a physician or a traditional healer.
- A healthy life can result from living by three simple rules:

  1) observe the basic principles of hygiene, religion, and social behavior;
  2) avoid all foods and beverages that are harmful, and places and relationships that can be dangerous;
  3) maintain good relationships with neighbors in accordance with the laws and commandments of the Koran.

These basic beliefs have some similarities with those of early Judaism: God is the one supreme power from whom everything emanates. Sin is thought to be related to illness. Observance of the commandments, dietary rules, and keeping good relationships with neighbors are the conditions of a healthy life.

In general, Bedouins prefer traditional healers to physicians, but a physician is consulted when the traditional healer does not succeed. The practitioners of traditional healing represent several specialties: dervish, amulet writer, cauterizer, healer of broken bones, herbalist, and specialist in medicinal spices. Certain places such as holy tombs, jujube tree groves, the seas, and the tombs of ancestors are deemed to have healing powers.

A distinction is made between preventive and curative practices. Amulets borne on the body, reading verses of the Koran, taking vows, visiting tombs of saints, prophets, or ancestors, outwitting the "evil eye," and observing the basic rules are considered preventive practices. Medicines and observance of various practices after the illness has struck are considered curative.

Because it is the object of a wide-spread and strong belief among the Bedouins, the evil eye deserves special attention. It is seen as a spell cast by a devil or by a person who, just by looking at the victim, can cause harm. It is thought to originate in meanness, covetousness, jealousy, and other negative feelings. The practitioners of traditional medicine use different measures against the evil eye.

Preventive Measures. There are several ways to ward off the evil eye:

• Hanging blue beads on an infant's head while chanting Koran verses. This is usually done by the mother or the grandmother, who may put alum (double sulfate of potassium and aluminum) in the beads so that, if the evil eye appears, it will use up its power on the alum by grinding it into a powder rather than attacking the child.

• Hanging amulets on adults to repel the evil eye, devils, or evil spirits and diseases from the bearer. The *khatib*, "amulet writer," writes the text in ink on a piece of paper, folds it in a triangle, wraps it in cloth or leather and places it on the customer, usually hanging it around the neck or attaching it to an arm. The amulet can also be placed under the pillow of the person to be protected if the action of "earth devils" (genies) is feared or if insomnia or nightmares are to be fought. Only the amulet writer knows the text and its meaning; no one else is supposed to open the amulet under penalty of terrible punishments inflicted by the devils. The art of amulet writing is a jealously guarded secret passed from father to son.

• Reciting Koran verses; it is a general panacea used alone or in combination with other methods.

Curative Practices. How can someone attacked by the evil eye be cured? A woman, usually the mother or grandmother of the patient, takes three pieces of alum and places them in the tent fire. After a while she removes them and examines their shape. One of the pieces, according to its shape, will indicate who is the source of the evil eye: man, woman, or devil. It is said that a woman of experience can even give the name of the person who cast the spell. When the reading is completed, she crushes the three pieces of alum in her hand. Then, with her hand holding the crushed alum, she makes circles around the head of the patient, asking Allah to heal the person and eliminate the spell. As a conclusion, she reads aloud verse 2:256 of the Koran:

> Allah is the only God, there is no other than him, the Living, the Inchangeable. Neither slumber nor sleep can overcome him. All that is in heaven and on earth belongs to him. Who may intercede with him without his permission? He knows what is before people and what is behind them, and men grasp of his knowledge only what he lets them learn. His throne covers the heavens and earth and he is never weary of protecting them. He is the Most High, the Sublime.

This verse can be written and placed on one arm as an amulet.

When the reading is completed, the woman smears some of the alum powder on the forehead, elbow, and heel of the patient and then throws the rest behind the tent while she commands the evil eye to depart. Then she ties a kerchief around the patient's head and gives her a cup of tea; the patient rests in bed until healing is completed.

Among the practitioners, the dervish is the most respected figure. Originally, a dervish was a member of a Muslim religious order from Kenya or Anatolia; in the present Bedouin tradition, he is a wise old man, righteous, religious, reliable, and considered to be in close contact with Allah through angels. Like the art of writing amulets, the knowledge of the dervish is transmitted from father to son. Some dervishes practice traditional healing and are consulted on various matters such as health, marriage laws, and identifying thieves. They can treat scorpion stings and snake bites. To do so the dervish first drinks olive oil, takes a sharp knife and heats it in the fire, makes a cut on the spot of the bite or sting, and sucks out blood and venom while chanting Koran verses. He gives the patient olive oil to drink followed by goat milk or tea; the patient should not drink water for two days.

One popular method of healing is to visit certain tombs: holy tombs (tombs of saints or *marabouts*), tombs of prophets, and tombs of ancestors. Any action that may resemble an act of worship or ostensible sorrow is forbidden: weeping, kneeling, scratching of the face, lamenting, lighting candles, and prayers of request. The purpose of such visits is to be reminded that there is no escape from death, to learn to accept one's fate, and to be inspired by the saintly life or lessons of the venerable dead. Nevertheless, women do visit certain *marabouts* to pray in order to be cured of sterility.

The use of music in healing and exorcism is popular in many cultures, including that of the Bedouins. Usually, it takes the form of night drumming while Koran verses are read, the patients sit together around a fire, and incense is burnt.

The most characteristic forms of traditional healing come from the symbiosis of the Bedouins with their environment. It finds its expression in many ways: responsible use of their scarce sources of water, good land management, choice of sites for pitching their tents according to seasons, use of the desert flora for their personal care and for feeding animals, use of animals and animal products. The most common use of natural resources for healing involves medicinal plants, the properties of which have been known in many cultures over several millennia. Wherever they may live, the Bedouins make medicinal plants the bulk of their pharmaceutical resources; they also use animals and animal products as well as some minerals.

Medicinal Plants. The following list consists of ten plants likely to have been known in ancient Palestine for their medicinal properties:

• Colocynth or bitter apple (*Citrullus Colcynthus*), a plant of the gourd family. Its fruit contains a bitter spongy pulp used as a purgative. A small amount of the pulp is mixed with water and drunk.

• Chamomile (*Matricaria Chamomilla*). The leaves are boiled in water and the decoction is drunk to relieve sore throats and colds. It is also used during menstruation and for pain in the kidneys and urinary tract.

• Onion (*Allium Cepa*). The bulb and leaves are eaten as a cure for colds. Onion juice is smeared on the mouth, nose and hands of children to protect them from diseases. A plaster made of onions cooked in oil is applied on wounds to disinfect them and to draw pus. Onion peels are applied on scorpion stings and snake bites to draw out the poison.

• Fenugreek (*Trigonalla Foenum Graecum*). A leguminous plant, the seeds are ground to powder and mixed with water for the treatment of stomach ache and diabetes. It is believed that fenugreek stimulates the secretion of milk in nursing mothers. Bedouin women drink it in high concentration, and also recite verses from the Koran, after the menstrual period, in order to increase the probability of a pregnancy.

• Mandragora or Mandrake (*Mandragra Officinalis*), similar to the Chinese ginseng. The fruit, eaten during the menstrual period while reciting verses from the Koran is considered a remedy for sterility. The Bedouins consider it a holy plant, and they take great care not to damage or destroy it. In the Bible, mandrake is known as "love plant" (Gen. 30:14-16; Song of Sol. 7:13).

• Ginger (*Zingiber Officinalis*). The rhizome of this plant has a hot, spicy taste; it is used in cooking and traditional medicine. Crushed into powder, it is drunk with tea as a remedy for colds, sore throats, liver problems, hoarseness and intestinal gas. Bedouin men drink it in tea as an aphrodisiac.

• Cumin (*Cuminum Cyminum*). An umbelliferous plant resembling fennel, its fruit and seeds are aromatic and carminative (they eliminate gases).

The seeds are used to flavor food, and nursing mothers take them to enhance lactation. It is considered a good remedy for stomach ache and gases in the digestive system.

• Lemon (*Citrus Limonum*). One of the most ancient and popular remedies, lemon is added to tea as a medication for colds, sore throats, nausea, dizziness, stomach aches, and diarrhea.

• Sage (*Salvia Triloba*) is an aromatic herb. Its leaves are boiled in water and the concoction is drunk as a remedy for stomach ache and gases, diarrhea, and indigestion. It is said to ease menstrual pains and is considered a menstrual regulator.

• Jujube tree (*Ziziphus Spina Christi Lotus*) or Christ's thorn. This is a plant of the genus Zizyphus, which comprises spiny bushes or trees of the buckthorn family; its edible fruit is called jujube. Bedouins consider it as a holy plant, make vows in its name, slaughter sheep and goats and read Koran verses next to it. To mark their good will and devotion to Allah, they hang pieces of white cloth on it as a sign that they have made their pilgrimage there. Eaten in large quantities, its fruit is said to cure diarrhea. Bedouin women believe that going to the jujube tree and eating its fruit while reading the Koran will increase the probability of pregnancy.

Animals and Animal Products. Many of the existing uses may have originated in ancient magical practices.

• Camel milk. The Bedouin believe that the camel's milk makes men strong and virile. It is given to children with liver problems and to persons bitten by snakes or stung by scorpions. Camel milk is said to restore old men's potency.

• Camel urine is used as a disinfectant for wounds; it is also thought to prevent dandruff and to strengthen the hair roots.

• Donkey milk is given to children as a remedy for stammering.

• Donkey meat is cooked and given to women who have a "devil" in them, leading them to madness and even causing their children's death.

• Donkey dung is collected, dried, kept for about a year and then boiled in water; it is used to wash wounds.

• Goat milk is considered good for snake bites and scorpion stings.

• Hedgehog. The animal is burnt with its spines, and the patient inhales the smoke as a remedy for malaria.

• Hyena flesh. The flesh is boiled and eaten as a remedy for stomach ache accompanied with bloody stools, and for asthma.

• Hyena blood is said to be a remedy for senility.

• Hyena hair is burnt on coals and the smoke is inhaled as a cure for smallpox.

• Meloe. The meloe is a genus of coleopterous insects of the *cantharidae* family; it is an oil or blister beetle. These insects execrete a liquid, with an offensive taste and smell, that contains cantharidin, an ingredient used in the preparation of aphrodisiacs. Bedouin women crush the beetle with oil and form a suppository inserted in the vagina as a remedy for barrenness.

• Porcupine blood is drunk as a remedy for heart pain and to strengthen heart muscles.

• Scorpion. In order to immunize a child against scorpion stings, a yellow scorpion is burnt and its ashes are placed on the nursing mother's nipples. It is believed that, as the infant suckles, it becomes immune to scorpion poison.

Minerals. The following two examples come from direct observation in North Africa and are not listed in Abu Rabia's monograph.

• Clay. A certain sandy-colored clay is used to absorb pus from boils; in one night a large boil is completely drained of its pus. The clay is mixed with water to form a paste applied to the boil; it is kept in place by means of a bandage.

• Crude oil (petroleum). Crude oil seeping from the ground in some *oueds* (wadis or valleys) is collected and used to treat the skin ailments of humans and also of animals such as camels, mules, horses, and asses. This method may have been used in Palestine because asphalt from the southern part of the Dead Sea was the object of trade with the rest of the country (*see* MACHAERUS).

Implications for Jesus Research

Traditional healing uses available natural resources. It has the use of plants in common with ancient medicine; the use of animal products and incantations with magic; the use of prayer and Scripture reading with religious healing.

The Gospels do not indicate that Jesus used any of the ingredients of traditional healing such as leaves, seeds, roots and fruits of plants; agricultural products like wine, vinegar, and olive oil; flesh, milk, blood, viscera, hair, urine, excrements of animals; minerals such as clay, stones, sulfur, salt, and crude oil. In one instance he uses a plaster made of earth and saliva. John 9:6-7 states that "he spat on the ground and made mud with the saliva and spread the mud on the man's eyes, saying to him, 'Go, wash in the pool of Siloam' . . . Then he went and washed and came back seeing."

A common disease in the Near East, then and now, is trachoma, an infection of the conjunctiva, which causes suppuration and inflammation of the eyelids. The eyelids become so swollen that the ill person cannot open them. The plaster used by Jesus would have absorbed the pus; after the washing with clean water, the inflammation would have diminished and the eyelids would have opened. This treatment, however, would not destroy the germs causing the infection; the relief would have been only temporary. While traditional Bedouin healing did not use saliva, Jesus used it in other instances: the healing of the man who was blind at Bethsaida (Mark 8:22-26) and the healing of the deaf man with a speech impediment (Mark 7:32-35; Matt. 15:29-31). In Greco-Roman culture it was believed that saliva had healing properties, and Jesus' method was coherent with the practices of the time.

Pliny the Elder reports that saliva, among other body liquids, was a potent remedy: "The best of all safeguards against serpents is the saliva of a fasting human being" (*Nat. Hist*. 30). Other uses included spitting on epileptics during a seizure, spitting in one's hand to increase the force of a blow, and applying saliva to boils, leprous sores, and eye ailments. In this last instance, the saliva of a fasting woman was seen as a potent medication for treating watery eyes (Kee, *Medicine, Miracle and Magic*, 104). Tacitus describes Vespasian moistening with saliva the eyes and cheeks of a blind and crippled follower of Serapis; the eyesight of the man was restored (Kee, 83). In his attempt to show that Jesus was a magician, M. Smith says that:

> fluid could help to make the contact closer; the readiest form of fluid was spittle, and both spittle and the act of spitting were commonly believed to have magical powers; so we find Jesus, like other magicians, smearing spittle on his patients or using salva made with spittle. (*Jesus the Magician*, 128)

Smith, however, misrepresents the facts. There is no evidence that magicians used saliva in Jesus' time; on the contrary, as seen above, saliva was used as a medication. The last part of Smith's statement should read: "were commonly believed to have *healing* powers: so we find Jesus, like other *healers*, using spittle on his patients . . . "

In looking at the nature of the ailments cured, it is clear that Bedouin traditional healing is most concerned with sterility, menstrual problems, impotence, digestive problems, colds, sore throat, death and illnesses of young children, scorpion stings, and snake bites. In contrast, Jesus healed the blind, the lame, the deaf, the mute, the paralytic, the epileptic, the crippled, and lepers. In only one instance is it reported that he healed (unknowingly) a woman with a menstrual hemorrhage (Matt. 9:20-22 and parallels). Jesus specialized in infirmities and ailments that were perceived as incurable. This fact, combined with a method that used no rituals, paraphernalia, or ingredients of any kind, give his healings the character of miracles as claimed by the Gospels. In short, Jesus does not seem to have the characteristics of a traditional healer. In other entries, it is shown that he was neither a physician nor a magician as they were understood in his time. Jesus' techniques of healing were sui generis*, perhaps closer to those of the Qumranites than to any other group or practitioners of his time (*see* EXORCISM; MEDICINE, PHYSICIANS; DEAD SEE SCROLLS).

BIBLIOGRAPHY

Abu Rabia, A. *Healing Practices of the Negev Bedouins*. Jerusalem: Albright Institute, 1987.

Baily, C. and A. Danin. "Bedouin Plant Utilization in Sinai and the Negev." *Economic Botany*: 35.2,145–62.

Baldensperger, L. and G. Crowfoot. *From Cedar to Hyssop*. London: Sheldon Press, 1932.

Canaan, T. "Plant-Lore in Palestine Superstition." *The Journal of the Palestine Oriental Society* 8 (1928): 129–68.

Duke, J. A. *Medicinal Plants of the Bible*. New York: Trado-Medic Books, 1983.

Edelstein, L. *Ancient Medicine*. 1967. Reprint. Translated by C. L. Temkin. Baltimore: The Johns Hopkins University Press, 1987.

Feldman, D. M. *Health and Medicine in the Jewish Tradition*. New York: Crossroad, 1986.

Feliks, J. *Plant World of the Bible*. Ramat Gan, 1968 (Hebrew).

3M. Nature and Man in the Bible. London: Soncino Press, 1981.

Grmek, Mirko D. *Diseases in the Ancient Greek World*. French, 1983. Translated by M. Mueliner and L. Mueliner. Baltimore: The Johns Hopkins University Press, 1989.

Hareuveni, A. "Herbal Medicine among the Palestinian Arabs." *Harefuah* 3:113–27 (Hebrew).

Harrison, R. K. *Healing Herbs of the Bible*. Leiden: E. J. Brill, 1966.

Kee, H. C. *Miracle in the Early Christian World*. New Haven: Yale University Press, 1983.

———. *Medicine, Miracle and Magic in New Testament Times*. Cambridge, Mass.: Cambridge University Press, 1986.

Latourelle, R. *The Miracles of Jesus and the Theology of Miracles*. Mahwah, N.Y.: Paulist Press, 1988.

Levi, S. *Religious Life and Customs among the Bedouins of Southern Sinai*. Jerusalem: Ministry of Education, 1980 (Hebrew).

Njidat, A. "Medicinal Herbs Among Njidat Tribes." *Teva' Vaaretz* (1981) (Hebrew).

'Othman, A. "Vegetal Treatment in Palestine Countryside." *Society and Heritage* 6 (1976): 72–91.

Palvitz, D. "Herbal Medicine and Its Value in Western Medicine." *Mada'* 6: 264–70 (Hebrew).

Pillsbury, B. L. *Traditional Health Care in the Near-East*. Washington D.C.: U.S. Agency for International Development, 1978.

Rousseau, J. J. "Jesus, an Exorcist of a Kind." *SBL Seminar Papers* (1993).

———. *Background Information on Traditional Healing in the Time of Jesus: Investigating Ancient Healing Practices of the Bedouins*. Jesus Seminar papers. Sonoma: Polebridge Press, 1993.

Smith, M. *Jesus the Magician*. U.S., 1975. Reprint. Wellingborough, Great Britain: The Aquarian Press, 1985.

Theissen, G. *The Miracle Stories of the Early Christian Tradition*. Translated by Francis McDonald. Philadelphia: Fortress Press, 1983.

Thomsen, M.-L. "The Evil Eye in Mesopotamia." *Journal of Near Eastern Studies* 51 (1992): 15–32.

Vermes, G. *Jesus the Jew*. Philadelphia: Fortress Press, 1983.

World Health Organization. *The Promotion and Development of Traditional Health Medicine*. Technical Report Series 622. Geneva, 1978.

Tunic without Seam, Dice

Importance

According to John, Jesus' tunic had no seam. This may indicate the social level of some of his supporters.

Scripture References

Matt. 27:35; Mark 15:24; Luke 23:34; John 19:23-24.

General Information

Although those condemned to crucifixion were normally led to the execution ground and hanged on the cross naked, it seems that, out of respect for Jewish beliefs, the Romans in Palestine let their victims be clothed (*see* CRUCIFIXION). The Gospels indicate that Jesus' garments were given back to

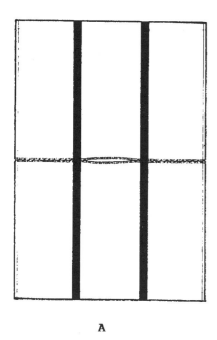

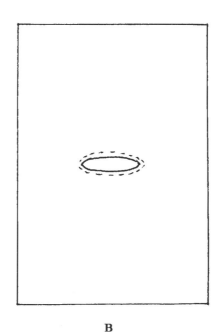

Figure 69 A: Regular Tunic with Clavi as Found in the Cave of Letters. It is made of two pieces of cloth sewn together with a slit left open for the head. **B: The Tunic without Seam of Jesus.** It was weaved in one piece on the loom and a hole for the head was cut and hemmed afterward.

A

B

him after the scourging; and John adds the information that his tunic was of a special kind, "seamless, woven in one piece from the top." Normally, a tunic was made of two square or rectangular sheets of the same width, sewn together to form a long piece. A slit was left in the seam for the head. The sides were also sewn together except at the top, where a hole was left for the arms. A more expensive type of tunic, probably worn by the High Priest (Josephus, *Antiq.* 3, 7.4/161), was made of only one long piece of cloth, folded in two, with a hole cut in the middle for the head (*see* fig. 69).

The Mishnah and Talmud refer to the common two-piece tunic: "two leaves of a *halug* [tunic], on one of which a defect is visible, the other is ritually clean" (*m. Nega'im* 9.9). "R. Jose said: and the opening of a *halug* which is made of two leaves" (*y. Sabbath* 15a); more explicitly "Which is the unskilled and which is the skilled [tailor]? R. Jose ben Haninah said: he who matches the *clavi* (*see* Archaeological Information below) is the skilled one and he who does not match them is the unskilled" (*y. mo'ed Qaṭan* 80d). A seamless tunic was probably a rare possession.

Jesus' precious tunic was attributed to one of the soldiers by lots. When the Gospels use the expression *casting lots*, "throwing dice" is probably meant since soldiers carried dice to play when off duty.

Archaeological Information

In 1960, in the cave of Letters (*see* CAVE OF LETTERS), Y. Yadin found a large number of sheets with two parallel bands woven of weft threads having different colors from those of the web. Among them were several sets of double sheets. Each set had two different colors, one for the sheets, another one for their bands. They were sewn together along one selvage; but between the bands, the sheets remained unsewn, leaving a slit for the head. These tunics, with two parallel bands running down from the shoulders, back and front, are the oldest ones of the Roman period so well preserved. They indicate that the Jews whose clothes were preserved in the Cave of Letters wore the typical Roman *tunica* with two *clavi* (color bands). The width of the bands indicated the rank of the wearer: the larger the band, the more important the person was.

Roman dice are well represented in archaeological finds. They were made of bone and were marked like modern ones. Several pairs were found in individual graves of Jason's Tomb in Jerusalem, which was used in the first centuries B.C.E. and C.E. The Romans may have adopted this game from the Greeks: a third century B.C.E. statuette from Tanagra in Greece represents a woman throwing dice; it can be seen in the Musée du Louvre in Paris.

Implications for Jesus Research

The author of John who, in many instances shows awareness of details about places and customs of Palestine, is the only evangelist to indicate that Jesus' tunic was seamless. If he is correct, then Jesus was wearing an expensive piece of clothing. Was it offered to him by wealthy people he knew? The Gospels offer several possibilities: Joanna, wife of Chuza (Luke 8:3), Simon the Pharisee, Zacchaeus, Joseph of Arimathea, Nicodemus, Mary and Martha of Bethany, and Matthew Levy, the tax collector who became his disciple.

It has been suggested that John gave the information about the seamless tunic in order to confer upon Jesus the dignity of a High Priest, because the High Priest wore a seamless robe. But nowhere else does the Fourth Gospel attempt to use such an image for Jesus.

BIBLIOGRAPHY

Beasley-Murray, G. R. *John*. World Bible Commentary 36. Waco, Tex.: Word Books, 1987.

Yadin, H. *Bar Kokhba*. 1971. Reprint. London: Weidenfeld and Nicolson, 1978.

Tyre and Sidon

Importance

Tyre and Sidon were cities of Phoenicia, a territory adjacent to Galilee. Jesus referred to these two cities, preached to listeners from them, and visited Sidon.

Scripture References

Matt. 11:21-22; 15:21; Mark 3:8; 7:24, 31; Luke 4:26; 6:17; 10:13-14; Acts 12:20; 21:7; 27:3.

General Information

Phoenicia, the coastal land stretching northward from Palestine, between the Mediterranean and the mountain ranges of Lebanon, extended at the peak of its prosperity from the region of Dora in the south to Ugarit in the north. Dora (Dor) and other Philistine cities became Sidonian colonies during the Persian period. The Phoenician economy was based on maritime trade and industries such as fishing, production of purple dye from the murex shell, jewelry, metal work, weapons, glass, pottery, and the like. From 1150 to 853 B.C.E., the Phoenician cities had autonomous status and founded colonies along the Mediterranean coast. Among these was Carthage in Tunisia, which became the archrival of Rome. Like most of the other areas of the Near East, Phoenicia fell under the yoke of Assyria (841–627 B.C.E.) and then submitted to Babylon and Persia.

Sidon was the first Phoenician city to explore the sea, and its shipmasters became expert in celestial navigation. It established ties with Greece and gained fame from the work of its artisans in gold, silver, copper, textiles, and dyes. The Sidonians probably invented glass blowing and developed a prosperous glass industry. The Israelite king, Ahab, married Jezebel, daughter of Ethbaal, king of Sidon. She brought her own traditions with her when she came to Israel and as a result came into mortal conflict with Elijah (1 Kings 19:1—22:38; 2 Kings 9). Sidon was conquered and burnt by the Persians in 351 B.C.E. but surrendered without battle to Alexander in 333 B.C.E. When Pompey took the city in 64 B.C.E. he granted it autonomy and the privilege of minting coins.

According to Herodotus, Tyre was founded circa 2,700 B.C.E., a date that accords well with the early third millennium ruins discovered there. It is mentioned in the Execration Texts of Egypt (ca. 1,850 B.C.E.) and in various Assyrian and classical sources. The name *Tyre* means "rock," and in fact the harbor city was built on a rock island located 16 miles north of Ptolemais (the Acre of the Crusaders; today's Acco) near the border of the ancient territory of the tribe of Asher and 25 miles south of Sidon. After the decline of Egyptian power, Tyre became the dominant city of Phoenicia and established commercial ties with all the known world. Its main harbor, protected by a breakwater 820 yards long and 9 yards thick, was built by King Hiram (981–947). King David turned to Tyre to obtain cedar, masons, and carpenters to built his palace (2 Sam. 5:11). Solomon renewed the ties with Hiram of Tyre when he undertook the building of the First Temple (1 Kings 5:1-6). In return for Hiram's cooperation Solomon gave him the land of Cabul with twenty cities in the territory of Asher (northwestern Galilee). Nehemiah 13:16 reports that Tyrians were among those selling merchandise in Judea and Jerusalem. In Second and Third Temple times, the only currency accepted for the payment of the half-shekel Temple tax was Tyrian coinage because of its high standard and its high percentage of pure silver (98 percent, *see* TEMPLE, TREASURY). Usha, the mainland city associated with the seaport of Tyre, was connected with the island for the first time by Alexander. His goal was to take the harbor, so he built a mole half-a-mile long and 200 feet wide; it took seven months before he could conquer Tyre. The Christian writer Origen was buried in Tyre in 254 C.E.

Archaeological Information

Sidon was built on small hill protruding into the sea; its hinterland was a fertile plain. There were two harbors, one each on the northern and southern sides of the hill. A large mound near the city wall is a deposit of millions of murex shells, which testifies to the importance of Sidon's purple dye industry. Excavations were difficult because the ancient site of Sidon is obscured by medieval and modern constructions. In 1855 the sarcophagus of Eshmunezer, a fifth-century B.C.E. Sidonian king, was discovered. This led to a search for the necropolis of the town. In 1877, the famous marble sar-

cophagus known as the Sarcophagus of Alexander was unearthed. It actually belonged to King Abdalonymos, the last Sidonian ruler, who died in 320 B.C.E. Fashioned in Attic style, its reliefs show hunting scenes and a battle in which Alexander appears.

The southern necropolis contains tombs dating from the Iron Age to the Byzantine period. A Persian period temple dedicated to Eshmun, a god of healing, was excavated 5 kilometers northwest of Sidon (*see* JERUSALEM, POOL OF BETHESDA).

Although the excavations of Tyre by M. Chebab unearthed Phoenician structures, none of them provided information about the palaces of the Tyrian kings. The great temple of the god Melkart has not been discovered. Melkart, identified with Hercules by the Greeks, was the chief god of Tyre. Melkart's portrait appears on Tyrian shekels of the Greco-Roman period.

Both aerial photography and underwater archaeology in the harbors have been used to explore ancient Tyre and Sidon. Tyre had two harbors, the Sidonian harbor in the north and the Egyptian harbor in the south. They were probably built in the Hellenistic period and equipped with well-constructed landing piers. The Egyptian quay was over 750 meters (2,470 feet) long and 8 meters (29 feet) wide. During the Roman period, a colonnade 10 meters (33 feet) wide connected the two harbors. A theater in the city was probably extant during the Hellenistic period. In the second century C.E. the city was partly renovated and a temple built. An aqueduct brought water to the city from the springs of Ras el Ain, some 12 kilometers away.

Implications for Jesus Research

Many biblical prophets, echoed by the Psalms, castigate Tyre and occasionally Sidon (Isa. 23:1-17; Jer. 25:22; 27:3; 47:4; Ezek. 26:2-9; Joel 3:4-8; Amos 1:9-10; Zech. 9:2-4; Pss. 45:12-13; 83:7). Centuries later Jesus apparently saw them differently; he compared them favorably with the unrepentant cities of Galilee (*see* BETHSAIDA; CAPERNAUM; CHORAZIM), visited Phoenicia, and perhaps entered Sidon. If Tyrians (and others) were still selling their merchandise in Judea and Jerusalem on the sabbath (Neh. 13:16), Jesus is not reported to have opposed their trade, although he opposed selling and money exchanging in the Temple. The reasons for such an attitude are unknown. As for his journey, if his only reason for visiting Phoenicia had been his personal safety, the Decapolis—which he also visited—was closer and as safe as the Gentile coastland. Why then did Jesus visit Phoenicia? Three suggestions may be offered:

1. The principal temple of Sidon was that of Eshmun, the god of healing. Perhaps, by exorcising a demon out of the daughter of the Phoenician woman (Matt. 15:21-28; Mark 7:24-31), Jesus wanted to show Gentiles the supremacy of the God of the Jews, even in a domain in which the power of another god was recognized (see JERUSALEM, POOL OF BETHESDA).

2. Among his listeners were Phoenicians (Mark 3:8; Luke 6:17); he may have wanted to extend his teaching and influence to their country.

3. Mark specifically indicates that Jesus visited Sidon (Mark 7:31, "went through Sidon"). If this is the case, it would be the only large city that Jesus visited besides Jerusalem. Could there be a connection between this visit and the fact that Tiberius Julius Abdes Pantera was from that city (see PANTERA'S TOMBSTONE)?

BIBLIOGRAPHY

Bikay, P. M. *The Pottery of Tyre*. Warminster: Aris and Phillips, 1978.

Danker, F. W. "Purple." *ABD* 5:557–60.

Edwards, D. R. "Tyre." *ABD* 6:686–92.

Hanson, R. S. *Tyrian Influence in Upper Galilee*. Cambridge, Mass.: ASOR, 1980.

Jensen, L. B. "Royal Purple of Tyre." *Journal of Near Eastern Studies* 22 (1963): 104–18.

Jidejian, N. *Tyre through the Ages*. Beirut: Dor El-Mashreq, 1969.

———. *Sidon through the Ages*. Beirut: Dor El-Mashreq, 1971.

Poidebard, A. *Un grand port disparu: Tyros*. Paris: Librairie Orientale R. Geuthner, 1939.

Schmitz, P. C. "Sidon." *ABD* 6:17–18.

Viticulture

Importance

Viticulture was an essential part of Palestine's agrarian economy. Jesus used the biblical imagery of vineyard, vine, and grapes; he was accused of being a "glutton and a drunkard;" and he may have taken wine as the symbol of a "New Covenant."

Scripture References

Matt. 7:16; 9:17; 20:1-15, 22-23; 21:28-31, 33-41; 26:27-29; 27:34; Mark 10:38-39; 12:1-9; 14:23-25; 15:23; Luke 5:37; 6:44; 7:33-34; 13:6-7; 20:9-16; 22:17-18; 23:36; John 2:1-10; 4:46; 15:1-5; 19:29-30.

General Information

Since the dawn of history, vineyards have been a major source of food and drink in the Near East. The grapevine and its products thus figure prominently in ancient art and literature. Egyptian tomb paintings from the third millennium B.C.E., reliefs found in Ashurbanipal's palace at Nineveh (ca. 640 B.C.E.), show scenes of grape harvesting and use vines as decorative motifs. According to the Greeks, wine was first produced in India and then spread to the west by Dionysos. Indeed, the Hebrew word for wine, *yayin*, may derive from Hittite, an Indo-European language. In the Hebrew Bible, Noah is said to have been the first human to plant a vineyard (Gen. 9:20-22). According to Numbers (13:21-23), the spies sent by Moses into the land of Canaan came back with a cluster of grapes so heavy that two men were needed to carry it on a pole resting on their shoulders. Ancient Egyptian inscriptions from the Old Kingdom refer to the wine of Canaan; and the Egyptian prince Sinuhe mentions the grapes of Syria and of the land of Israel in a document dating to circa 1780 B.C.E. Jacob's blessings to Judah (Gen. 49:11) also indicate the antiquity of Palestine's reputation for having good vineyards.

Grapevines grew abundantly in Palestine, mostly on hillsides, the flat land being reserved for wheat and barley. Stone walls were built around vineyards to protect them from thieves and wild animals; in addition, some owners erected watchtowers. Vines were planted in parallel rows eight to ten feet apart, and forked sticks supported the grape clusters. Outside vineyards, individual vines grew near trees and houses, or in arbors (1 Kings 4:25; Micah 4:4; Zech. 3:10). When the grapes were formed, the vine was pruned in order to increase its yield (Isa. 18:5; John 15:2). A rich landowner could employ a farmer or rent his vineyard to tenants (Song of Sol. 8:11; Matt. 21:34). As in the case of wheat, barley, and olives, gleaners were allowed to gather fallen grapes or those left by harvesters (Lev. 19:10; Deut. 24:21). Vineyards were to lie fallow during the sabbatical year and were not to be used for other plants (Deut. 22:9), but by the Roman period there may have been an exception for fig trees (Luke 13:6).

The grape harvest began toward the end of August or in September. Grapes could be eaten as fruit, dried into raisins, boiled and thickened into a syrup used as *dibbes*, "honey," or made into wine. For the preparation of raisins, grapes were spread out in the sun on a house top or in a courtyard (Pliny, *Nat. Hist.* 16). Raisin cakes, rich in iron, minerals, and sugar, were a highly nutritious food; and travelers took them, along with dried figs or dates, on trips. At vintage time, workers carried the grapes in baskets to the winepress, either a natural flat rock or a large basin hewn in a rock. The juice, extracted by stone presses or by bare-foot treading, was collected through a channel into a vat, also hewn into the rock, below the level of the floor of the winepress. The liquid, or must, was left to settle overnight, with the fermentation beginning about six to twelve hours after pressing. The following day, the new wine was collected into jars plugged with clay stoppers; the jars were then stored in caves, cellars, or cisterns, and the fermentation continued. A hole was bored in the shoulder of the jar to allow the fermentation gas to be re-

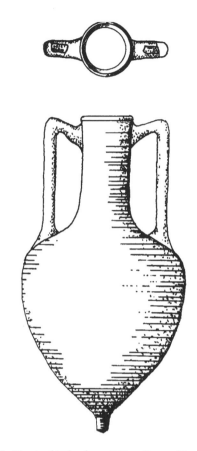

Figure 70 Typical Rhodean Wine Jar as Found in Many Sites in Hellenistic-Roman Palestine. Note the seal imprints on the tops of the handles.

leased. When fermentation was completed, the hole was sealed and, for commercial production, the origin, quality of the wine, and the name of the producer were imprinted on the seal. Because of the pressure of the fermentation gas, new wine could not be put in old wineskins, which would burst at the seams.

Wine was probably part of the daily diet and was offered at banquets. The Hebrew word for banquet, *mishteh*, is from the word meaning "to drink"; it indicates that without wine there was no rejoicing. Offerings of wine accompanied sacrifices and were poured as libations at the foot of the altar in the same manner as blood (*see* TEMPLE, SACRIFICAL SYSTEM). Concurrently with vinegar, wine was used to disinfect wounds (Luke 10:34) and was also considered as medicine. It was traded in large quantities, either as import or export. Along with other things, Solomon gave to Hiram, King of Tyre, 20,000 baths (110,000 gallons) of wine in payment for timber from Lebanon (2 Chron. 2:8-10, 15). Well regarded foreign wines were imported from the islands of Rhodes, Chios, Cos, Lesbos and other Greek islands and Italy. In the Roman period wine was transported in large jars with long pointed bases that were placed in rows of circular holes bored in planks and set at the bottom of shipholds. Wine could be mixed with spices that made it more intoxicating. Mixed with myrrh or gall, it was used as analgesic (Matt. 27:34; Mark 15:23). The word "wine" was used in poetry as a metaphor of sensuality (Song of Sol. 4:10; 7:7, 9).

"Vineyard," "vine," and "wine" are as frequently used as "sheep" and "shepherd" in biblical imagery. "Vineyard" and "vine" can symbolize Israel, which was "planted" by God (Ps. 80:8-13). She was first a "choice vine, from pure stock" but turned "degenerate, and [became] a wild wine" (Jer. 2:21). "Vine" could represent individuals (Ezek. 17:1-8), and it was a symbol of prosperity (1 Kings 4:25; 2 Kings 18:31; Deut. 7:13). Over the Great Gate of the Herodian Temple was displayed a gigantic golden vine on which the priests hung presents of gold shaped in the form of leaves of grapes (*m. Middot* 3:8, *see* TEMPLE, HISTORY, DESCRIPTION). Drunkenness was condemned by the prophets (Isa. 5:11–13; 28:1–3 *et passim*); the priests on duty at the Temple as well as the Nazirites were forbidden, by law or vow, the consumption of wine (Lev. 10:9; Ezek. 44:21; Num. 6:3). The kings of Israel and Judah owned large vineyards and storage facilities for taxes paid in kind (1 Chron. 12:40; 2 Chron. 11:11).

The economy of the Hellenistic period created open markets into all of the eastern Mediterranean basin and in the Hellenistic *oikoumene*.* The markets were not limited to local commerce, but were open to all producers and traders. This arrangement encouraged farmers to specialize in indigenous growths, to exchange their products in the markets, and to purchase goods that were produced elsewhere. As a result olives and grapes were extensively planted almost everywhere in Palestine, Syria, southern Anatolia, Greece, and Italy. Wine and olive oil industries were the major sources of wealth. Following biblical tradition, Jesus' parables and allegories use vineyard, vine, and wine imagery: the kingdom is a vineyard ("laborers for his vineyard," Matt. 20:1-16; the "two sons," Matt. 21:28-32; "the wicked tenants," Matt. 21:33-41, and parallels), he is the "true vine," and God is the "vinegrower" (John 15:1-11). Such imagery appears in other sayings: "The fig tree in the vineyard" (Luke 13:6-9), "the new wine in an old wineskin" (Matt. 9:17). Jesus may well have compared his body to bread and his blood to wine (Mark 14:22-25 and parallels; *see* UPPER ROOM).

Archaeological Information

A large number of archaeological finds attest to the importance of viticulture in first-century Palestine as well as other periods. Hundreds of winepresses, wine jars, and drinking cups have been discovered throughout the country. Many of the eighth century B.C.E. Samaria ostraca refer to wine (*see* SAMARIA, SEBASTE), as do some papyri of postbiblical periods from Nessana, a prosperous Nabatean town of the west central Negev.

Many reliefs and mosaic pavements in ancient churches and synagogues feature decorative motifs inspired by vines and wine. Thousands of jar handles bearing seal imprints from Rhodes, the Greek islands, and Italy provide evidence that foreign wines were imported (*see* fig. 70). At Qalandia, in a large garden north of Jerusalem, numerous wine presses, and a storage room with a large number of wine amphoras were discovered. Until the Hellenistic period, wine and olive oil were probably produced in the same installation. Grapes were pressed during the late summer and olives during the fall and early winter. Eventually, because of the growing production, two separate installations appeared.

Implications for Jesus Research

Because wine was forbidden to the Nazirites, it is possible that John the Baptist, who did not drink wine, had taken the Nazirite vow (Num. 6:2-12; Matt. 11:18). Jesus probably did not abstain from wine as indicated by the Gospel accounts of the Last Supper. Consequently, Jesus' remark in Matthew 11:18-19, that he was seen as a glutton and drunkard, may be authentic, especially because this statement meets the criterion of "embarrassment" used by the Jesus Seminar to identify authentic sayings. Nevertheless, in 1989 the Jesus Seminar gave it a *gray* rating, which means that the saying would probably not be authentic.

Jesus may have had a good knowledge of viticulture. His description of the preparation of a vineyard for production conforms with existing practices (Matt. 21:33 and parallels): after a vineyard was planted, a hedge was set around it, a winepress was hewn, and a watchtower erected. According to the Gospels, he was aware of problems of the absentee owner who leaves his property to tenants and cannot collect his share of the produce (Matt. 21:34-39 and parallels). Jesus' remark about new wine in an old wineskin shows an awareness of practical problems due to wine fermentation; or he used a popular saying based on the well-known effects of the fermentation.

The Fourth Gospel tends to be viewed as irrelevant to historical Jesus research. Yet, our study shows that the primary writer of John knew the people and the territory of Palestine very well. This is certainly the case with respect to viticulture. Familiarity with the beneficial effect of pruning (John 15:2) is evident in a metaphor attributed to Jesus: the vine represents Jesus, and the branches are the disciples who cannot bear fruit if they are cut off from the vine.

There has been considerable disagreement among scholars and theologians about what is sometimes called the "prayer of institution," the saying of Jesus at the Last Supper, and its meaning. It is found in 1 Cor. 10:16 and 11:23-26, and in the Synoptics, but Luke's version is reworded in such a way that it cannot be used to evaluate the authenticity of the saying. External data are of little help in determining what Jesus meant when he used the words "wine," "cup," "[new] covenant" and "blood" at the "Last Supper." Only three elements are well established:

1. The Greek word *deipnon*, "supper," found in Greek writings, papyri, and various inscriptions, was used for cultic meals of communion between gods and humans.

2. The covenant, a solemn promise, was made binding by an oath or by a symbolic action such as a common meal with the drinking of wine from the same cup.

3. The Qumranites, contemporaries of Jesus with whom he had some affinities (*see* DEAD SEA SCROLLS; EXORCISM; TRADITIONAL HEALING; and MEDICINE, PHYSICIANS), understood themselves as being in a "new covenant" with God (cf. Jer. 31:31-34) and had common meals in the expectation of the final banquet with God or the messiah(s) (*Damascus Document*, CD).

Whether Jesus made a covenant with his disciples to the effect that they would continue to have common meals in remembrance of him, or brokered a "(new) covenant" between God and his followers, is not clear. He may have compared the wine of the cup to blood, because, as we have seen above, libations of wine were poured at the foot of the altar in the same manner as was sacrificial blood. The assimilation of wine to blood and bread to body may not have been complete, because in the original gospel texts (presumably Aramaic), the copula "is" does not exist. That is, what is translated "this is my blood" could as well be "this is like my blood." In an interpretation quite different from the traditional one, the Didache refers to the communion bread as a symbol of unity and not as sharing the body of Christ:

Regarding the Eucharist. Give thanks as follows:

First concerning the cup:

"We give you thanks, our Father, for the holy wine of David, your servant, whom you have made known to us through Jesus, your servant. To you be the glory for ever."

Next concerning the broken bread:

"We give you thanks, our Father, for the life and knowledge which you have given to us through Jesus, your servant. To you be the glory for ever. As this broken bread was scattered over the hills and then, when gathered became one loaf, so may your church be gathered from the ends of the earth into your Kingdom. For yours is the glory and the power through Jesus Christ forever." (Did. 9:1-4)

Dogmatists and fundamentalist critics explain that this text was used only for "agape meals, not for communion." Others claim that the text only gave prayers to be said before the communion itself, which was reserved for the baptized, in a different room where the catechumens were not admitted. Because the Didache gives instructions for baptism, because it contains no other text dealing with communion, and because the words "cup" and "broken bread" appear in the text, Didache 9:1-4 may present a communion formula coming from a different tradition than the one generally recognized. The expression "holy vine of David" most likely refers to Jesus as a fruitful descendant of David and echoes the metaphor of John 15:1.

BIBLIOGRAPHY

Billiard, R. *La vigne dans l'antiquité.* Lyon, 1913.

Borowski, O. *Agriculture in Iron Age Israel.* Winona Lake, Ind.: Eisenbrauns, 1987.

Dalman, G. *Arbeit und Sitte in Palästina.* Vol. 4. Reprint. Gütersloh: Hildesheim, 1964.

Dommershausen, W. *"yayin." Theological Dictionary of the Old Testament* 6:59–64. Grand Rapids, Mich.: Eerdmans, 1990.

Forbes, R. J. *Studies in Ancient Technology.* Vol. 3. Leiden: E. J. Brill, 1955.

Frankel, R. *The History of Wine and Oil Production in Galilee in the Biblical, Mishnaic and Talmudic Periods.* Ph.D. diss., Tel Aviv University, 1984 (Hebrew).

Goor, A. "The History of Grape Vine in the Holy Land." *Economic Botany* 20 (1966): 46–66.

Jacob, I. and W. "Flora." *ABD* 2:803-817.

Kleist, J. A. "The Didache." *Ancient Christian Writers.* Westminster, Md.: Newman Press, 1946.

Léon-Dufour, X. *Sharing the Eucharist Bread.* French, 1982. Trans. M. O'Connell. New York: Paulist Press, 1987.

Weapons

Importance

Jesus lived in a country under military occupation, and weapons provided imagery for some of his sayings. Several of his disciples may have carried swords.

Scripture References

Matt. 10:34; 26:47, 51-52, 55; Mark 14:43, 47-48; Luke 2:35; 22:36, 38, 52; John 18:10-11; G. Thom. 98.

General Information

In 63 B.C.E., Palestine came under Roman dominion and was placed among the territories attached to Syria whose legate was also commander-in-chief of the legions stationed in his province. From 6 C.E. to the First Jewish War, Judea, which included Samaria and Idumea, became a prefectoral subprovince with special status (*see* PONTIUS PILATE'S STONE). This direct rule was interrupted only during the short reign of Agrippa I (41–44 C.E.). If the prefects did not have authority over the legions, they had the power to recruit their own auxiliary units. According to Josephus and H. G. Pflaum's research, there were two *alae* (literally "wings," squadrons of cavalry), one in Sebaste (*ala* Sebastenorum) and one in Caesarea (*ala* Caesariensium), and four auxiliary cohorts under their command (*Antiq.* 20, 6.1/122; *War* 2, 12.5/236; Pflaum, "Judée" in *les procurateurs*). In addition, client rulers had to maintain an army that would support Roman forces if required.

The superiority of the Roman military organization, tactics, and armaments led local rulers such as Antipas and Philip to adopt Roman military techniques. War implements became fairly standardized and, at the same time, diversified according to their special purposes.

The legion, an independent tactical unit of about six thousand men included heavy infantry, light infantry (*velites*, who disappeared as a class category with Marius' reform, 107–100 B.C.E.), cavalry, artillery, engineers, administrators, medical staff, and other specialists. During operations, auxiliary troops recruited locally could double the number of its soldiers. The standard armament was as follows:

1. Heavy Infantry
   * *Hasta*, "lance," a thrusting weapon.
   * *Pilum*, "javelin," a throwing weapon about 6.5 feet long, half for the shaft and half for the blade. Each legionary had two; their range was from 35 to 70 yards.
   * *Gladius*, "short sword," with a blade of about 20 inches.
   * *Scutum*, "rectangular shield" about 48 x 30 inches. It was made of wood covered with leather.
   * *Armor* made of metal blades. The officers wore the *lorica squamata* made of metal scales.
   * *Cassis*, "helmet," with flaps protecting the cheeks.

2. Light Infantry. Its special weapons were:
   * *Parma*, the circular shield of the *velites*.
   * *Galea*, a leather helmet.
   * *Funda*, a sling. Its maximum range was about 200 yards.
   * *Arcus*, bow, with arrows 24 inches long.

3. Cavalry. It had two special weapons:
   * *Parma*, circular shield, same as the *velites'*.
   * *Contus*, a light spear used for thrusting or throwing.

4. Artillery. Each legion had perhaps up to sixty pieces.
   * *Balista*, large crossbow throwing heavy spears.
   * *Catapulta*, machine with a swinging arm hurling stone balls.
   * *Onager* or *scorpio*, a light piece on cart wheels working like a small catapult with a sling at the end of the arm.

In the military domain as in others, the Romans made the most of the science and technology of their time.

Archaeological Information

Archaeological discoveries made throughout the countries that the Romans occupied complement and illustrate the ancient literary evidence describing their weaponry. In Israel, catapult balls, spear and arrow heads, armor scales, and sword blades have been found at Gamla, Masada (*see* GAMLA, MASADA), and in other places where the Romans fought the Jews.

The archaeological and literary data are further enhanced by sculptures and monuments, such as the Arch of Titus in Rome, the Triumphant Arch of Orange in France, ancient tombs (*see* PANTERA'S TOMBSTONE), and reliefs, which provide abundant graphic documentation. The combination of all these sources allows for an accurate knowledge of Roman weapons of the first century C.E. (*see* figs. 71, 72).

Implications for Jesus Research

Among the weapons duplicated or imported from the Roman arsenal by local rulers, and sometimes captured by rebels, the *gladius* was perhaps the most popular. Its size, between that of the traditional sword and the dagger, made it easy to conceal under a coat or in the packs of beasts of burden. In the parable of the assassin (G. Thom. 98), the weapon alluded to may well have been such a sword, which was designed for close combat.

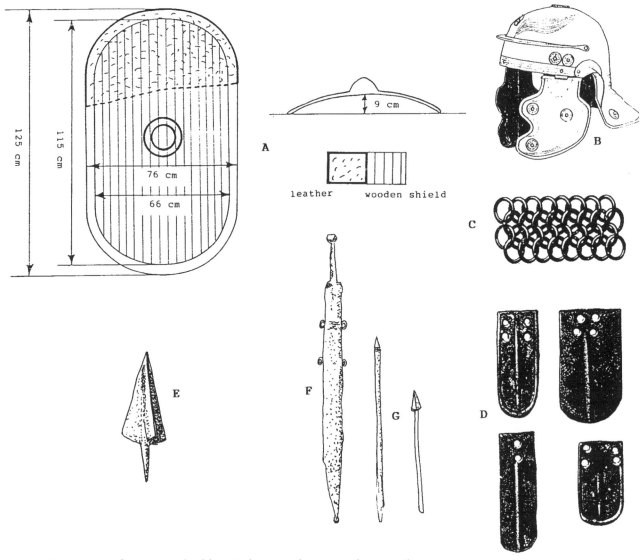

Figure 71 Roman Infantry. A: Shield; B: Helmet, early imperial; C: Mail;
D: Armor scales; E: Arrowhead; F: Gladius; G: Arrows.

Jesus used the image of the sword as a symbol of division on his account within families: "Do not think that I have come to bring peace to the earth; I have not come to bring peace, but a sword" (Matt. 10:34; Luke 12:51). Is this an original saying or a retrojection of the situation that existed in the early Church? Does it reflect disagreement among Jesus' followers? Or does it evoke apocalyptic images rooted in Jewish future expectations? Considering the propensity of Jews to argue and fight between themselves over rules, principles, and ideologies as abundantly demonstrated by the history of the period, it would have been an appropriate image to use; the more so that it was already re-

Figure 72 Roman Cavalry. Top: Relief from the tombstone of T. Flavius Bassus. Bottom: Reconstructed typical Tiberio-Claudian harness. The prefects of Judea had two *alae* of auxiliary cavalry under their command.

flecting an existing situation: Jesus and his followers had left their own families, and his brothers were not supportive of his actions. Nevertheless, this saying was rated *black* by the Jesus Seminar in 1989, although only 50 percent of the fellows voted for that color, because of the weighted system used.

The question about whether or not Jesus was involved with some of his disciples in the insurrection mentioned in Mark 15:7 needs to be examined. It has been proposed that Jesus and Barabbas

were the same person because, in some manuscripts, the full name of the insurgent is given as Jesus Barabbas (Jesus, son of the father). Nevertheless, Jesus (Yehoshua) was such a common name that this argument is of little value. Besides, it would presuppose a gross distortion of the accounts of Jesus' last days, which otherwise are fairly consistent in the four canonical Gospels and in harmony with what Acts and Paul say on the subject. According to Luke, Jesus advised those of his disciples who did not have swords to buy some (22:36) and shortly afterwards said that two were enough (22:38). All canonical gospels report that at the time of Jesus' arrest one disciple cut off the ear of the High Priest's slave with a sword (Matt. 26:51 and parallels).

Both Luke 22:36 and 38 were rated *black* by the Jesus Seminar in 1987. Nevertheless, considering the circumstances of the time, the presence of at least one armed disciple at Gethsemane, and above all the criterion of embarrassment, an argument can be made for the authenticity of Luke 22:36. As embarrassment became a factor, the author or editor of the Third Gospel would have added verse 38. Although Jesus' main concern was not a national or political uprising, he lived among people who resented Roman dominion and the corruption of the High Priesthood. Because he came to Jerusalem with a group of Galileans at a time when there had been an insurrection, Pilate may have required the Jerusalem authorities to find him so that he could be arrested and interrogated. Florus used such a procedure at the beginning of the First Jewish Revolt of 66 C.E. (*War* 2, 14.8, 9/301–2, 305).

The similarity between the Roman shields of the end of the Republic and the Early Empire and those described in the War Scroll provides a possible time frame for the dating of the latter (*see* DEAD SEA SCROLLS).

BIBLIOGRAPHY

Bisley, E. *The Roman Army. Papers 1929–1986.* Mavors Roman Army Researches 4. Amsterdam: J. C. Gieben, 1988.

Coulston, J. C., ed. "Military Equipment and the Identification of Roman Soldiers." *Proceedings of the Fourth Roman Military Equipment Conference.* Biblical Archaeology Reports, International Series 394. Oxford, 1988.

Davies, R. W. *Service in the Roman Army.* Edited by D. Breeze and V. A. Maxfield. Edinburgh, 1989.

Gichon, M. "The Success of the Roman Legions: Military Analysis in Josephus' Wars of the Jews." *Cathedra* 21 (1981): 3–22.

Horsley, R. A. *Jesus and the Spiral of Violence.* San Francisco: Harper and Row, 1987. Reprint, Minneapolis: Fortress Press, 1993.

Horsley, R. A. and J. S. Hanson. *Popular Movements at the Time of Jesus.* New York: Winston Press, 1985.

Klasser, W. "Jesus and the Messianic War." *Early Jewish and Christian Exegesis.* W. H. Brownlee Homage Series 10. Atlanta, Ga.: Scholars Press, 1987.

Luttwah, E. N. *The Grand Strategy of the Roman Empire.* 1976. Reprint. Baltimore: Johns Hopkins University Press, 1988.

Maddin, R., J. D. Muhly, and T. Stech. "Armor Scales from Masada: A Metallurgical Study." *IEJ* 33: 108–9.

Pflaum, H. G. *Les procurateurs équestres sous le haut empire Roman.* 2 vols. Paris: Maisonneuve, 1950.

Schatzan, T. "The Armies of the Hasmoneans and Herod." *Antiquitas Judaeorum* 26.7, 1992.

Yadin, Y. *The Art of Warfare in Biblical Lands.* 2 vols. New York: McGraw-Hill, 1963.

Weights and Measures

Importance
The Gospels mention measures and distances.

Scripture References
Matt. 5:15, 41; 7:2; 13:33; 23:32; Mark 4:21, 24; Luke 6:38; 11:33; 13:21; 16:6-7; John 2:6; 12:3; 19:39.

General Information
Systems of weights and measures require a stable political authority to impose the use of units duplicating official standards in public and private affairs. Such conditions existed in Mesopotamia, Egypt, and in the Greco-Roman world. The Israelites had several systems that shared features of those used in neighboring areas. The results of the research on weights and measures are only indicative, based on averages, and summarized in the following tables. Modern equivalents are given in units of the International System: meters, liters, and grams. For conversion into the American system, use the tables at the end of the book.

In the evaluation of the distances of tombs from the western wall of the Sanctuary, we estimate the value of 2,000 cubits to be 1,000 meters (1 cubit = 0.5 m; *see* GOLGOTHA, TRADITIONAL SITE and JERUSALEM, TOMBS).

Measures of Length and Distances. In the Greco-Roman world, there were several values of the foot: Olympic = 0.32045 m, Alexandrian = 0.308 m, Epidaurus = 0.30 m, Delphic = 0.196 m. Those more widely used were the Alexandrian foot for a stadium of 185 m, and the Delphic foot for a stadium of 177.6 m.

The Roman mile was a hybrid unit worth either 5,000 Delphic feet of 0.296 m. or 8 Alexandrian stadia of 185 m (*see* tables 8, 9).

Measures of Capacity. There is some uncertainty about the measurement of capacity, for which there are two sets of loosely defined units—one for grains and another for liquids (*see* table 10).

Measures of Weight. This was the most complex system. In Palestine there were two types of weights: the anepigraphic (without any mark) usually made of stone, and the epigraphic marked with a sigla. The sigla ठ used for the standard basic unit is the most numerous and belongs to the most homogenous system. Its average value corresponds to a shekel of 11.424 grams. It is the system represented below; the first table shows the system of the common *mina* of 50 shekels, the second one is for the system using a *mina* of 60 shekels.

In the second system of weights, the fractional units of the shekel had the same value as in the first (*see* table 11).

Table 8 Measures of Length

Units	Common Value	Ezekiel Measure	Egyptian Cubit Long	Egyptian Cubit Short	Ratio
cubit	.44425 m	.512829 m	.525 m	.450 m	1
hand	.22212 m	.25914 m	.2615 m	.225 m	2
palm	.07404 m	.08638 m	.0875 m	.075 m	6
inch	.01851 m	.021595 m	.021875 m	.01875 m	24

Table 9 Measures of Distance

Units	Alexandrian Measures	Delphic Measures	Syro-Phoenician Long	Syro-Phoenician Short	Ratios		
mile	1,480 m	1,480 m	1,572.7 m	1,537.5 m	1		
stadium	185 m	177.6 m	213 m	205 m	7.5	1	
fathom	1.85 m	1,776 m	2.13 m	2.05 m	750	100	
pace			1.065 m	1.025 m	1,500	200	
cubit	0.462 m	0.444 m	0.5328 m	0.525 m	3,000	400	1
foot	0.308 m	0.296 m	0.3552 m	0.341 m	4,500	600	1.5

Table 10 Measures of Capacity

Grain	Liquid	H.B. System (I. Benzinger)	Persian-Hellenistic (Albright)	Ratio
homer	kor	364.41 Liters	218.31 Liters	1
letech		182.2 l	109.15 l	2
ephah	bath	36.44 l	21.83 l	10
seah		12.148 l	7.28 l	30
	kin	6.074 l		60
omer, issaron		3.644 l	2.183 l	100
qab		2.0248 l	1.21 l	180
	log	0.5062 l	1.303 l	720

Archaeological Information

Stone or metal weights, measuring cups, and cubit rods have been found in the Near East and in Palestine. Such artifacts can be seen in Jerusalem in the Burnt House, the Herodian house in the Jewish Quarter, and the Israel Museum. Roman milestones have also been discovered. One was found near Capernaum; it can be seen on the Franciscan property (*see* CAPERNAUM). In 1993 two hemispheric basalt weights were found in Bethsaida.

Implications for Jesus Research

The following words for measure and measurements are found in the Gospels. Except for "bath"

Table 11 Measures of Weight

Units	Weights	Ratios			
talent, kikkar	34.272 g	1			
mina, maneh	571.2	60	1		
shekel	11.424 g	3,000	50	1	
beka	5.712 g	6,000	100	2	
gerah	0.571 g	60,000	1,000	20	
Units	Weights	Ratios			
talent, kikkar	41,126.4 gr	1			
mina, maneh	685.44	60	1		
shekel	11.424	3,600	60	1	
beka	5.712	7,200	120	2	
gerah	0.571	72,000	1,200	20	

Table 12 Measures in the Gospels

Greek Term	Corresponding Hebrew	Corresponding English	References
sata		measures	Matt. 13:33
metron		measure	Matt. 23.32; Luke 6:38; John 3:34
metrates		measures	John 2:6
batous	bath		Luke 16:6 (applied to oil)
korons	kor		Luke 16:7 (applied to wheat)
litra		pint	John 12:3; 19:39
modion		bushel	Matt. 5:15; Mark 4:21; Luke 11:33
milion		mile	Matt. 5:41

and "kor" they derive from Greek or Roman units.

In reference to Luke 16:7, it is to be noted that "kor" normally designated a measure of liquid; for wheat, the equivalent "homer" would have been preferred (*see* table 12).

The Q saying Luke 6:38 = Matt. 7:2 deserves special attention.

Luke 6:38a: Give, and it will be given to you.
　6:38b: A good measure, pressed down, shaken together, running over, will be put into your lap;

6:38c: for the measure you give will be the measure you get back.

Matt. 7:2a: For with the judgment you pronounce you will be judged,

　7:2b: and the measure you give will be the measure you get.

In 1989, the Jesus Seminar rated Matt. 7:2a and Luke 6:38a and b *black*, and Matt. 7:2b and Luke 6:38c *gray*. In 1990 Matt. 7:2b was unanimously changed to *black*, while its parallel Luke 6:38c remained *gray*.

Our position, in such a case, is that this kind of minute analysis is meaningless. The complete texts were written in Greek some three hundred years after the original saying was uttered, probably made in Aramaic, with an intervening period of oral tradition. Still, Luke's version may reflect an authentic saying of Jesus on the basis of its accurate description of the action.

BIBLIOGRAPHY

Archer, G. L. "The Chronology and Metrology of the Old Testament." *Expositors Bible Commentary* 1. Grand Rapids, Mich.: Zondervan, 1979.

Eran, A. "The Weights." *'Atiquot* 15 (1982): 91–100.

Foster, L. A. "The Chronology and Metrology of the New Testament." *Expositors Bible Commentary* 1 (1979): 591–613.

Kloner, A. "Lead Weights of Ben Kosba's Administration." *Eretz Isrsael* 20 (1989): 345–51 (Hebrew).

Powell, M. A. "Weights and Measures." *ABD* 6:897–908.

Qedar, S. "Two Lead Weights of Herod Antipas and Agrippa II and Early History of Tiberias." *Israel Numismatic Journal* 9 (1986–87): 29–35.

Reed, W. L. "Weights and Measures." *The Interpreter's Dictionary of the Bible* 4. New York: Abingdon Press, 1962. 828–39.

Scott, R. B. Y. "The Hebrew Cubit." *Journal of Biblical Literature* 77 (1958): 205–14.

———. "Weights and Measures of the Bible." *BA* 22 (1958): 22–40.

Trinquet, J. "Métrologie Biblique." *Dictionnaire de la Bible*, 1957.

Wood, Furniture

Importance

Like stone and clay, wood was one of the most important materials in Palestine. Trees, wood, and furniture are frequently mentioned in the gospels.

Scripture References

Matt. 3:10; 7:17-19; 8:11; 9:6, 10; 12:33; 13:32, 15:27; 21:8, Mark 2:9, 11; 7:28; 11:8; 14:12; Luke 3:9; 5:29; 6:43-44; 8:16; 10:8; 11:7, 37-38; 13:19; 14:12; 16:21; 17:6, 7, 34; 21:29; 22:14, 21, 30; 23:31; John 5:9-12; 12:2; 13:28; G. Thom. 77.

General Information

Wood was abundant in ancient Palestine, but over the centuries the devastation of wars and the general use of wood for fuel led to the present barrenness. For example, during the siege of Jerusalem, Vespasian and Titus cut down all the trees around the city. During the Ottoman period, the Turks razed entire forests to provide fuel for their trains. As a result, the landscape of Israel today is quite different from that of Palestine during the Roman Period.

In antiquity, the availability of wood meant that it was widely used in building, for implements and furnishings, and for a variety of household objects. Local oaks and olive trees provided most of the wood used for making furniture, tools, agricultural implements, carts, and boats. Because large structures required long pieces of timber, David, Solomon, and Herod imported cedar from Lebanon for their construction projects; those who could afford it certainly followed their example on a smaller scale. Other materials, such as stone, metals, and even ivory (1 Kings 10:18, *et passim*) were also used. In the houses of the rich, furniture was elaborate and often incorporated artistic embellishments, as is clear from discoveries at sites such as Herculaneum, Pompei, and the Herodian Quarter of Jerusalem (*see* JERUSALEM, UPPER CITY). The furniture of an ordinary house was rather simple: a table, a few chairs or stools and benches, sometimes beds and chests. People usually slept on the floor or on stone or brick benches attached to the walls and covered with mats or animal skins. They probably slept wrapped in their garments, their heads resting on a pillow or a rolled piece of clothing or a bag. Only the wealthy slept on actual beds, some of which were quite costly (Prov. 7:16-17; Amos 6:4). Such items were probably made according to the Egyptian style: a wooden platform supported by metal legs.

At mealtime Jesus' contemporaries probably sat at a table or on the floor around a mat, wooden board, rug, or animal skin. The rich would have adopted the Roman way of eating, on dining couches, which the Romans themselves had copied from the Greeks and modified by adding a back support. Oil lamps placed on lampstands or shelves provided light. Furniture was mostly simple and utilitarian.

Archaeological Information

The discovery of a first-century boat under the waters of the Sea of Galilee at Ginnosar in 1986 gave precious information on the kinds of wood that were used in Palestine in Jesus' time (*see* BOATS) for construction purposes. The species identified were:

- *Conifers*: Cedrus Libani Laud, imported cedar from Lebanon for the fore part of the keel and most of the strakes (hull planks).

  Pinus Halepensis, Aleppo pine, a common tree in Palestine, used only for one strake.

- *Broad-leafed trees*: Ziziphus Spina-Christi (Jujube, Christ's thorn), a large tree; its preferred habitats are in the Galilee and Jordan Valley. It was used for the aft part of the keel.

  Quercus Libani or Quercus Ithaburensis. Laboratory analysis could not differentiate the two species, but it was probably the latter, which was common in the forests of the Dan Valley, Hula Plain, Upper Jordan Valley, Central Galilee, Samaria, and Gilead. Most frames and a few strakes were made of this wood, as well as all tenons and pegs. This was the common oak.

  Salix (willow), a local tree, only one frame.

  Crataegus (hawthorn), local tree, one frame.

  Cercis Siquastrum (redbud), local tree, one frame.

Local wood was clearly used as much as possible, for this boat and for everything made of wood. The most favored source of wood was the oak tree, which covered Galilee and other regions of Palestine, and gave a high density, durable wood. Acacia, another hardwood tree growing in desert areas, also was used in buildings and for furniture, as was the wood of olive trees, cypress trees, the Aleppo pines, poplars, tamarisks, and willows.

A good reconstruction of furniture and wood implements as they may have existed in the first century C.E. can be seen in the restored fifth-century house at Qatzrin in the Golan.

Implications for Jesus Research

Three questions may be considered with respect to the historical Jesus in relation to wood and furniture:

- Jesus' original trade,
- The "beds" carried by paralytics upon Jesus' commands,
- The setting of the Last Supper.

According to two of the Synoptics Jesus was a "carpenter" (Mark 6:3), a son of a "carpenter" (Matt. 13:55). The latter designation reflects the fact that occupations were typically transmitted within families. The Greek *tekton* is usually translated by "carpenter" in English, but the original meaning was broader as seen in *architekton*, master builder, from which we have "architect." The *tekton* was a construction craftsman able to work with wood, stone, and bricks. Jesus may have worked as a construction worker and as a boat builder or repairman (*see* NAZARETH; SEPPHORIS; and BOATS). Celsus, as quoted by Origen, indicates that Jesus went to Egypt where he worked as a hired laborer (*Contra Celsum* 28, 38).

The "beds" that the paralytics carried after their healing may have been of two different types. Matthew (9:2, 6) uses the word *klines* (from which, through the Latin *reclinare* we have "recline"). This "bed" was a light couch, not heavier than a modern stretcher. Mark and John use the term *krabaton*, (Mark 2:4, 9, 11 and John 5:8, 9, 10 *et passim*)—from which the French has "grabat" through the Latin *grabatos*—which designates a cheap mattress, like a bag filled with straw. The last term is probably more accurate, because it is used by the oldest Gospel and by John who is usually familiar with details about the country, the people, and their customs. The object so designated must have been a mat easily rolled up and light to carry.

In Christian art, Jesus and his disciples are usually represented sitting at a table in Last Supper scenes in much the same way as people sit for meals in western countries. In some modern reconstructions, they are shown as following the Roman custom, reclining around a U-shaped table as in a triclinium. The two models are equally possible and need to be considered in relation to the locale and the person who offered the "upper room." To look at the site of the meal, one begins with Mark 14:13-15:

> Go into the city, and a man carrying a jar of water will meet you; follow him, and wherever he enters, say to the owner of the house, "The Teacher asks, Where is my guest room where I may eat the Passover with my disciples?" He will show you a large upper room furnished and ready; there prepare [the meal] for us.

Because Jesus and his disciples probably either camped on the Mount of Olives or lodged at Bethany in the house of Simon the Leper (Mark 14:3 and parallels), they would have entered the city either through the Fountain Gate (by the Gihon Spring) or the Casemate Gate (also called Water Gate, by the King's Garden) or, perhaps, the Potsherd Gate (near the Pool of Siloam; see JERUSALEM, WALLS AND GATES). In each case, it was a logical location to meet someone carrying a water jar. Because that person was a man, he could have been the slave of a rich homeowner residing in the City of David, south of the Temple, or one of the Essenes, a celibate, from the Essene Quarter in the southern part of the Upper City, in the area of the traditional site of the Last Supper (see UPPER ROOM).

If the host was a rich man, he could have adopted the Roman dining style, and the upper room would have been furnished with a low U-shaped table and dining couches as was the case in the house of the Pharisee where the woman "stood behind him at his feet" (Luke 7:38). The information given by Luke is understandable only if Jesus was lying on a couch with his feet away from the table; the woman could not have been under the table with Jesus sitting on a chair. If the host was the head or the hostel manager of the local Essene community, then the furniture would more likely have been in the traditional Jewish mode: table and chairs or benches. On the other hand, if the host was one of his secret disciples and a member of a priestly family, perhaps John Mark and his mother as suggested by John 18:17, Acts 6:7; 12:12 and Eusebius in his *Church History* as he quotes Polycrates (3, 31 and 5, 24), then the first option seems likely. This suggestion would cohere with Matt. 8:11 (the final banquet with Abraham, Isaac and Jacob) and 9:10, which use the Greek "recline," as well as Mark 2:15 and Luke 5:29, under different forms.

BIBLIOGRAPHY

Carcopino, J. *La vie quotidienne à Rome à l'apogée de l'empire.* Paris: Hachette, 1939.

Daniel-Rops, H. *Daily Life in the Time of Jesus.* Translated by P. O'Brian. New York: Hawthorn Books Inc., 1962.

Eusebius. *The History of the Church from Christ to Constantine.* Translated by C. A. William. New York: Dorset Press, 1965.

Parker, J. J., M. C. Tenney, and W. White, Jr. *Daily Life in Bible Times.* New York: Thomas Nelson, 1982.

Taussig, H. "The Meals of the Historical Jesus." *Jesus Seminar Papers.* Sonoma, Calif.: Polebridge Press, 1994.

Werker, E. "Identification of Wood." *The Excavation of an Ancient Boat in the Sea of Galilee (Lake Kinneret).* 'Atiqot 19 (1990): 65–76.

✦ Tables ✦

343

Table 13 Archaeological Periods in Palestine

Prehistoric Times

Period	Geological Epoch	Approximate Dates (B.C.E.)
Lower Paleolithic	Middle Pleistocene (Quaternary)	1,000,000–120,000
Middle Paleolithic	Upper Pleistocene (Quaternary)	120,000–45,000
Upper Paleolithic		45,000–18,000
Epipaleolithic(Mesolithic)		18,000–8,300
Prepottery (Neolithic)	Holocene	8,300–5,500
Pottery Neolithic		5,500–4,500
Chalcolithic		4,500–3,300

Historical Times

Bronze Age (Canaanite Period)

Early Bronze Age	I A–B	3300–3000 B.C.E.
Early Bronze Age	II	3000–2700
Early Bronze Age	III	2700–2200
Middle Bronze Age	I (EB IV–Intermediate Bronze)	2200–2000
Middle Bronze Age	IIA	2000–1750
Middle Bronze Age	IIB	1750–1550
Late Bronze Age	I	1550–1400
Late Bronze Age	IIA	1400–1300
Late Bronze Age	IIB	1300–1200

Iron Age (Israelite Period)

Iron Age	IA	1200–1150
Iron Age	IB	1150–1000
Iron Age	IIA	1000–900
Iron Age	IIB	900–700
Iron Age	IIC	720–586

Neo-Babylonian Period   587–538

Persian Period I   538–450

Persian Period II   450–332

Hellenistic Period

Early Hellenistic period	332–167
Late Hellenistic period	167–37

Roman and Byzantine Periods

Early Roman period	37 B.C.E.–132 C.E.
(Heriodian period, 37 B.C.E–70 C.E.)	
Late Roman period	132–324
Byzantine period	324–638

Early Arab to Ottoman Periods

Early Arab period (Umayyad and Abbasid)	638–1099
Crusaders and Ayyubid periods	1099–1291
Later Arab period (Fatimid and Mameluke)	1291–1516
Ottoman period	1516–1917

Note: Periods may vary slightly according to archaeological schools.

Table 14 Chronology from the Exile to 50 B.C.E.

Date	Palestine	Egypt	Mesopotamia & Persia	Anatolia & Syria	Greece & Rome
600 B.C.E.	Destruction of Jerusalem and exile of Judah, 587 Ezekiel *Babylonian Captivity* Edict of Cyrus allows return of Jews, 538 *Persian Period* Zerubbabel Temple rebuilt, 520–515 Ezra's mission, 458?? Nehemiah comes to Juday, 445 (440?)	Egypt under Persian rule, 525–401 Unsuccessful revolt Return to native rule	*New Babylonian Empire* Nebuchadnezzar II, 605–562 *Persian Empire* Cyrus, 550–530 Babylon falls, 539 Cambyses, 520-522 Darius I, 522–486 Xerxes I, 486–465 Artaxerxes I Darius II, 433–404	Syria and Anatolia under Persian rule Phoenicians provide fleet for Persian attacks on Greece	Solon's judicial reforms, ca. 590 Rome ruled by Etruscan kings *Roman Republic* established, 509 Persian Wars, 499–479 Thermopylae-Salamis, 480 Pericles, 461–429 Herodotus
400 B.C.E.	Ezra's mission, 398? *Alexander* Palestine passes under Alexander's rule and Hellenization begins, 332 Ptolemaic Egyptian rule, 312	Persian rule, 342–332 Alexander conquers Egypt, 332 Ptolemy I, 323–284 *Ptolemaic Kingdom* Alexandrian Jews translate Pentateuch into Greek (250?) Ptolemy V, 203–181	Artaxerxes III, 358–338 Alexander invades Persia, 331 Seleucid rule Parthians and Bactrians gain independence ca. 250	Alexander takes Tyre, 332 Seleucid rule Seleucus I, 312–280 *Seleucid Empire* Antiochus I, 280–261 Seleucus II, 246–226 Antiochus III (The Great), 223–187	Socrates' death Sack of Rome by Gauls Philip II of Macedon Alexander the Great, 336–323 *Alexander's Empire* Wars of the Diodochi First and Second Punic Wars Hannibal in Italy, 218

continues on page 346

Table 14   Chronology from the Exile to 50 B.C.E. *(continued)*

Date	Palestine	Egypt	Mesopotamia & Persia	Anatolia & Syria	Greece & Rome
200 B.C.E.	Palestine comes under Seleucid Syrian control, 198		*Parthian Empire*	Battle of Magnesia, 190	Spain annexed by Rome
				Antiochus IV (Epiphanes), 175–163	Roman Expansion
	Maccabean Period	Ptolemy VI, 181–146			
	Judas Maccabeus leads revolt of Jews, 166–160		Mithridates I, 171–138		Third Punic War
	Temple rededicated, 164	Antiochus IV campaigns in Egypt		Antiochus V, 163–162	Romans destroy Carthage and
	Jonathan, 160–142			Demetrius I, 162–150	Corinth, 146
	Simon, 142–134	Ptolemy VII, 146–116			
	John Hyrcanus I, 134–104			Demetrius II, 145–139	Reforms of the Gracchi
				Tyre independent	
	Aristobulus I, 104–103		Mithridates II, 124–88		
400 B.C.E.		Ptolemy VIII, 116–81		Mithridatic Wars	
	Alexander Jannaeus, 103–76				
			Tigranes of Armenia		Sulla dictator 82–79
	Alexandra, 76–67	Ptolemy XI, 81–80		Antiochus XIII, 68–67	
	Aristobulus II, 67–63		Phrates III, 70–57		
	Pompey takes Jerusalem for Rome, 63				
	Hyrcanus II, High Priest, 63–40		Orodes I, 57–38		*First Triumvirate* Pompey's campaigns in Asia, 68–63
	Antipater governor, 55			Anatolia and Syria under Roman control	
		Cleopatra VII, 51–30	War with Rome, 55–38; Crassus defeated		Caesar's Gallic Wars, 58–51

Table 15 Chronology from 50 B.C.E. to Bar Kokhba

Date	Palestine	The West	The East
50 B.C.E.	*Roman Rule* Caesar in Judea, 47 Parthian invasion, 40 Antigonus, 40–37 Herod the Great, 37–4 B.C.E. Herod's Temple begun, 18 Birth of Jesus, 7–4 B.C.E. (?) Archelaus, 4 B.C.E.–6 C.E.	Death of Pompey, 48 Death of Caesar, 44 *Second Triumvirate* Battle of Phillippi, 42 Battle of Actium, 31 Augustus, first emperor, 27 B.C.E.–14 C.E. *Roman Empire*	*Parthian Empire* Phraates, 37–32 Parthians defeat Antony, 36
0	 Roman prefects, 6–41, 44–67 Pontius Pilate, 27–37 Death of Jesus, 30 C.E. (?) Herod Agrippa I, 41–44 Paul's first journey, Council at Jerusalem, 46/47 (?)	Varus defeated in Germany, 9 Tiberius, 14-37 Gaius (Caligula) 37–41 Claudius, 41–54 Conquest of Britain begun, 43	 Artabanus II, 10–40

50 C.E.
 	
100 C.E.
 	
135 C.E.
	Antonius Felix, 52-60
	Imprisonment of Paul, 58 (?)
	Porcius Festus, 60–62
	Paul sent to Rome, 60 (?)
	Gessius Florus, 64–66
	First Jewish Revolt, 66–73
	
	Destruction of Jerusalem, 70
	Fall of Masada, 73
	
	Jewish center at Jamnia
	
	Jewish uprisings in Palestine, Egypt,
	  Mesopotamia, 116–117
	
	Bar Kokhba Revolt, 132–135
	Jerusalem razed, Aelia Capitolina
	  built on site
		Nero, 54–68
		
		First persecution of Christians, 64
		Galba, Otho, Vitellius, 68/69
		
		Vespasian, 69–79
		
		Titus, 79–81
		
		Domitian, 81–96
		
		Nerva, 96–98
		Trajan, 98–117
		
		Campaigns in Dacia, 101-107
		
		Hadrian, 117–138
			Vologases I, 51–80
			
			Parthian War with Rome, 53–63
			
			Osroes (Chosroes), 89–128
			
			Conquest of Nabateans by Romans
			
			Trajan invades Parthia, 114
			
			Territory lost to Romans is regained
			  by the Palestinians, 118

Table 16 Rulers of the Greco-Roman World and of Palestine

Seleucid Kings of Syria

Seleucus I Nicator	311–281 B.C.E.
Antiochus I Soter	281–261
Antiochus II Theos	261–246
Seleucus II Callinicus	246–225
Seleucus III Soter	225–223
Antiochus III the Great	223–187
Seleucus IV Philopator	187–175
Antiochus IV Epiphanes	175–164(?)
Demetrius I Soter	162–150
Alexander Balas	150–145
Demetrius II Nicator	145–140
Antiochus VI Epiphanes	145–142
Antiochus VII Sidetes	138–129
Demetrius II Nicator	129–125
Cleopatra Thea	126
Cleopatra Thea and Antiochus VIII Grypus	125–121
Seleucus V	125
Antiochus VIII Grypus	121–96
Antiochus IX Cyzicenus	115–95
Seleucus VI Epiphanes Nicator	96–95
Demetrius III Philopator	95–88
Antiochus X Eusebes	95–83
AntiochusXI Philadelphus	94–83
Philip I Philadelphus	
Antiochus XII	87–84

The Ptolemies of Egypt

Ptolemy I Soter	304–282 B.C.E.
Ptolemy II Philadelphus	285–246
Ptolemy III Euergetes	246–221
Ptolemy IV Philopator	221–205
Ptolemy V Epiphanes	205–180
Ptolemy VI Philometor	180–145
Ptolemy VII Neos Philopator	145
Ptolemy VIII Euergetes II	170–116
Ptolemy IX Soter II	116–107
Ptolemy X Alexander I	107–88
Ptolemy IX Soter II (restored)	88–81
Ptolemy XI Alexander II	80
Ptolemy XII Neos Dionysos	80–51
Cleopatra VII Philopator	51–30

Overlapping dates usually indicate coregencies.

Roman Emperors, to Constantine

Augustus	27 B.C.E. –14 C.E.
Tiberius	14–37 C.E.
Caligula	37–41
Claudius	41–54
Nero	54–68
Galba	68–69
Vespasian	69–79
Titus	79–81
Domitian	81–96
Nerva	96–98
Trajan	98–117
Hadrian	117–138
Antonius Pius	138–161
Lucius Verus	161–169
Cammadus	176–192
Septimius Severus	193–197
Clodius Albinus	193–197
Pescennius Niger	193–194
Caracalla	198–217
Geta	209–212
Macrinus	217–218
Diadumenianus	218
Elagabalus	218–222
Severus Alexander	222–235
Maximinus	235–238
Philip the Arab	244–249
Decius	249–251
Trebonianus Gallus	251–253
Valerian	253–260
Gallienus	253–268
Aurelius	268–270
Aurelian	270–275
Probus	276–282
Diocletian	284–305
Maximianus	286–305
Constantius I	293–306
Galerius	293–311
Constantine I	306–337

The Hasmonaeans

Jonathan	152–142 B.C.E.
Simon	142–134
John Hyrcanus	134–104
Aristobulus	104–103
Alexander Jannaeus	103–76
Salome Alexandra	76–67
Aristobulus II	67–63
Hyrcanus II	63–40
Matthias Antigonus	40–37

The Herodians

Herod I (the Great)	37–4 B.C.E.
Archelaus	4 B.C.E.–6 C.E.
Herod Antipas	4 B.C.E.–39 C.E.
Herod Philip	4 B.C.E.–34 C.E.
Herod Agrippa I	41–44
Agrippa II	53–100 (?)

The Prefects

Coponius	ca. 6–9 C.E.
M. Ambibulus	9–12
Annius Rufus	12–15
Valerius Gratus	15–26
Pontius Pilatus	26–36
Marcellus	36–37
Cuspius Fadus	41–?
Tiberius Alexander	?–48
Ventidius Cumanus	48–52
Antonius Felix	52–60
Pordius Festus	60–62
Albinus	62–64
Gessius Florus	64–?

Table 17 The Maccabean (Hasmonean) Dynasty

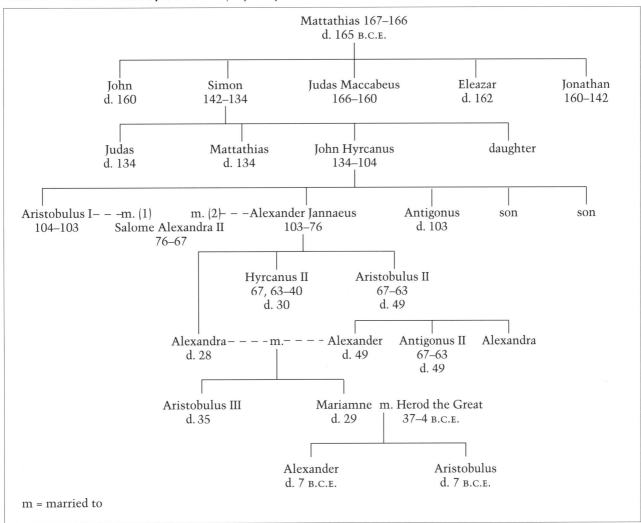

Table 18 The Herodian Dynasty

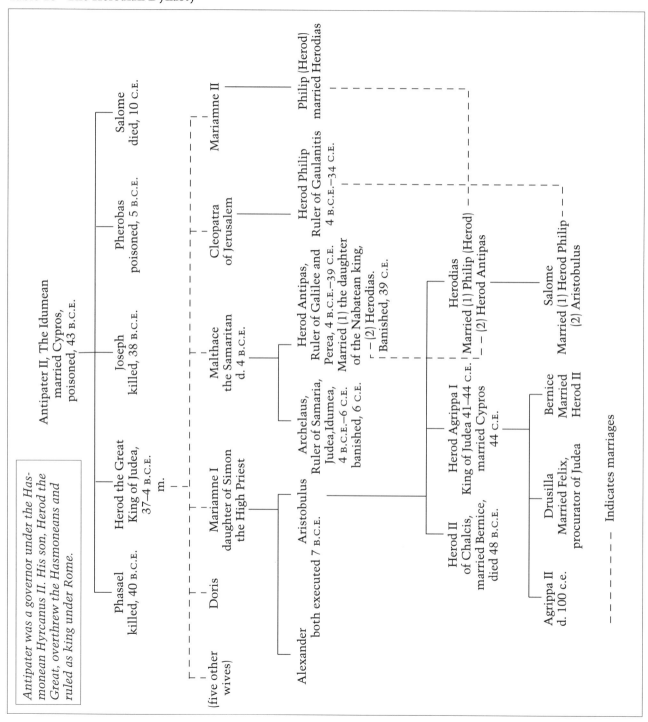

Antipater was a governor under the Hasmonean Hyrcanus II. His son, Herod the Great, overthrew the Hasmoneans and ruled as king under Rome.

Antipater II, The Idumean
married Cypros,
poisoned, 43 B.C.E.

Phasael
killed, 40 B.C.E.

Herod the Great
King of Judea,
37–4 B.C.E.
m.

Joseph
killed, 38 B.C.E.

Pherobas
poisoned, 5 B.C.E.

Salome
died, 10 C.E.

Doris

Mariamne I
daughter of Simon
the High Priest

Malthace
the Samaritan
d. 4 B.C.E.

Cleopatra
of Jerusalem

Mariamne II

(five other
wives)

Alexander

Aristobulus
both executed 7 B.C.E.

Archelaus,
Ruler of Samaria,
Judea,Idumea,
4 B.C.E.–6 C.E.
banished, 6 C.E.

Herod Antipas,
Ruler of Galilee and
Perea, 4 B.C.E.–39 C.E.
Married (1) the daughter
of the Nabatean king,
–(2) Herodias.
Banished, 39 C.E.

Herod Philip
Ruler of Gaulanitis
4 B.C.E.–34 C.E.

Philip (Herod)
married Herodias

Herod II
of Chalcis,
married Bernice,
died 48 B.C.E.

Herod Agrippa I
King of Judea 41–44 C.E.
married Cypros
44 C.E.

Herodias
Married (1) Philip (Herod)
—(2) Herod Antipas

Agrippa II
d. 100 C.E.

Drusilla
Married Felix,
procurator of Judea

Bernice
Married
Herod II

Salome
Married (1) Herod Philip
(2) Aristobulus

– – – – –   Indicates marriages

Table 19   The High Priests of Jerusalem from 200 B.C.E. to 70 C.E.

Simon the Righteous	after 200 B.C.E.	6. Joseph, son of Elam	5
Onias II	to 175	7. Joezer, son of Boethus	4
Jesus (Jason)	175–172	8. Eleazer, son of Boethus	from 4 B.C.E.
Menelaus	172–162	9. Jesus, son of See	until 6 C.E.
Jacim (Alcimus)	162–159	10. Annas	6–15
		11. Eshmael b. Phiabi I	ca. 15–16

The Eight Maccabean High Priests (152–37 B.C.E.)

Jonathan	152–143[2] B.C.E.	12. Eleazar, son of Annas	ca. 16–17
Simon	142[1]–134	13. Simon, son of Kamithos	17–18
John Hyrcanus I	134–104	14. Joseph Caiaphas	ca. 18–37
Aristobulus I	104–103	15. Jonathan, son of Annas	37
Alexander Jannaeus	103–76	16. Theophilus, son of Annas	from 37
Hyrcanus II	76–67, 63–40	17. Simon Kantheras, son of Boethus	from 41
Aristobulus II	67–63	18. Matthias, son of Annas	
Antigonus	40–37	19. Elionaius, son of Kantheras	ca. 44
		20. Joseph, son of Kami	

The Twenty-eight High Priests from 37 B.C.E. to 70 C.E.

1. Ananel	37–36 B.C.E., 34 B.C.E.	21. Ananias, son of Nebedaius	47–55 or more
2. Aristobulus III, the last Maccabean	35	22. Ishmael b. Phiabi II	until 61
3. Jesus, son of Phiabi	to ca. 22	23. Joseph Qabi	until 62
4. Simon, son of Boethus	ca. 22–5	24. Ananus, son of Ananus	62
5. Mattaiah, son of Theophilus 5–4		25. Jesus, son of Damnaius	ca. 62–65
		26. Joshua b. Gamaliel	ca. 63–65
		27. Matthias, son of Theophilus	65–67
		28. Pinhas of Habta	67–70

Table 20 The Family Tree of Jesus, according to the Gospels, Romans, and Eusebius

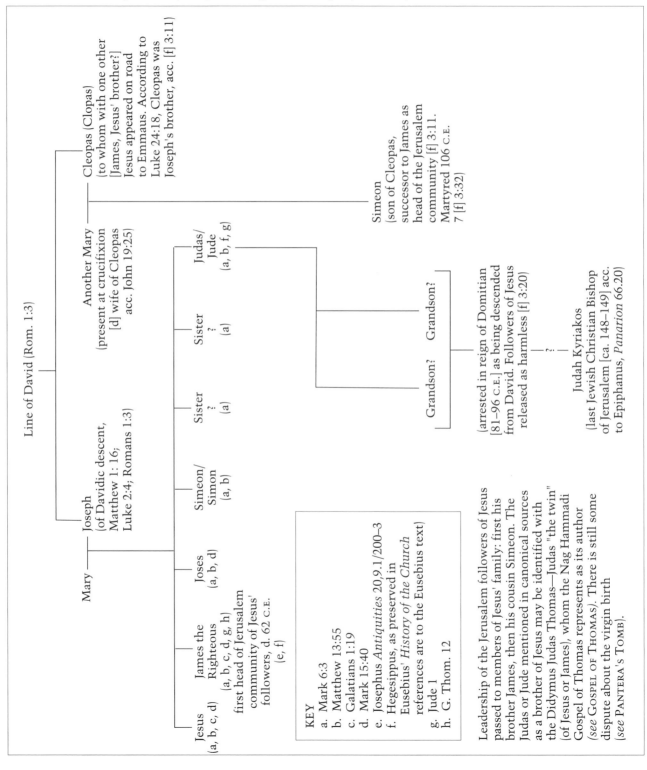

Table 21 Orders and Tractates of the Mishnah and Talmud

	Mishnah Chapters	Babylonian Talmud Pages	Jerusalem Talmud Pages	Content
1. Zeraim Order (Division of Agriculture {"seeds"})				
Berakhot (Ber.)	9	64	68	Prayers, benedictions
Pe'ah	8		37	Laws of gleanings and charity
Demai (Dem.)	7		34	Doubtfully tithed produce
Kilayim (Kil.)	9		44	Various kinds of seeds, trees, and animals
Shebi'it (Seb.)	10		31	Laws of the sabbatical year
Terumot (Ter.)	11		59	Contributions to the priests
Ma'aserot (Ma'as.)	5		26	Tithes for the Levites and the poor
Ma'aser Sheni	5		33	The second tithe and bringing it to Jerusalem
Hal'ah (Hal.)	4		28	The dough offering to the priests
'Orlah ('Or.)	3		20	Prohibition against harvesting trees for four years
Bikkurim (Bik.)	3		13	Offering of the first fruits at the Temple
2. Moed Order (Division of Appointed Times)				
Sabbat (Sabb.)	24	157	92	Sabbath laws
Iruvin	10	105	65	The laws of permissible limits on the Sabbath
Pesahim (Pesah.)	10	121	71	Laws of *hametz* and *matzah* and the paschal sacrifice
Shekalim	8		33	The shekel dues for the Temple and Temple ceremonies
Yoma	8	88	42	Sacrifices and the fast on Yom Kippur
Sukkah (Sukk.)	5	56	26	The building of a *sukkah*, the four species, and the festival in the Temple
Besa	5	40	22	General festival laws
Rosh Hashanah (Ros Has.)	4	35	22	Fixing the months and years, blowing the *shofar*, and the Rosh Hashanah prayers
Ta'anit (Ta'an.)	4	31	26	The regular fast days
Megillah (Meg.)	4	32	34	Laws of Purim
Mo'ed Qatan (Mo'ed Qat.)	3	29	19	Laws of the intermediate festival days
Hagigah (Hag.)	3	27	22	*Halakhot* for pilgrimage festivals
3. Nashim Order (Division of Women)				
Yebamot (Yebam.)	16	122	85	Levirate marriage, prohibitions on marriage, testimony on the death of the husband
Ketubot (Ketub.)	13	112	72	The marriage contract and special agreements
Nedarim (Ned.)	11	91	40	Various types of vows
Nazir	9	66	47	The *nazirite* laws
Sotah	9	49	47	Laws concerning an adultress, murder in which the perpetrator is unknown, and war
Gittin (Git.)	9	90	54	Divorce, writing and sending the *get*
Kiddushim	4	82	48	The marriage act, laws of genealogy

continues on page 354

Table 21 Orders and Tractates of the Mishnah and Talmud (continued)

	Mishnah Chapters	Babylonian Talmud Pages	Jerusalem Talmud Pages	Content
4. Nezikin Order (Division of Damages)				
Baba Kama	10	119	44	Direct and indirect damages
Baba Metzia	10	119	37	Losses, loans, work, and wage contracts
Baba Batra (B. Bat.)	10	176	34	Partnership, sales, promissory notes, and inheritance
Sanhedrin (Sanh.)	11	113	57	Various types of courts, criminal law, principles of faith
Makkot (Mak.)	3	24	9	Punishment by flagellation
Shebu'ot (Sebu.)	8	49	44	Oaths
'Eduy'ot ('Ed.)	8			A collection of testimonies on various subjects
'Abodah Zarah ('Abod. Zar.)	5	76	37	Keeping one's distance from idolatry and idolators
'Abot	5			Ethics and *derekh eretz*
Horayot	3	14	19	Erroneous rulings of the courts and their rectification
5. Kodashim Order (Division of Holy Things)				
Zebahim (Zebah.)	14	120		Laws of sacrifice
Menahot (Menah.)	13	110		Meal offerings, *tzitzit*, *tefilin*
Hullin (Hul.)	12	142		Laws of ritual slaughter and dietary laws
Bekhorot (Bek.)	9	61		The first-born child and animal, defective animals
'Arakhin ('Arak.)	9	34		Valuation of Temple offerings and soil
Temurah (Tem.)	7	34		Substituting an animal offering
Keritot (Ker.)	6	28		Sins requiring extirpation and sacrifices for them
Me'ilah (Me'il.)	6	22		Sins of sacrilege against Temple property and atonement for them
Tamid	6	8		Daily sacrifices in the Temple
Middot (Mid.)	5			Measurements of the Temple
Kinim	3			What to do when various sacrifices have been mixed
6. Toharot Order (Division of Purities)				
Kelim	30			Various types of utensils and their sensitivity to pollution
Oholot (Ohol.)	18			Laws of the uncleanliness of the dead
Nega'im (Neg.)	14			Laws regarding leprosy
Parah	12			Preparation of the ashes of the red heifer and purification after contact with the dead
Toharot (Tohar.)	10			Various laws of purification
Miqwa'ot (Miqw.)	10			Laws of the *miqva'ot* for purification
Nidah (Nid.)	10	73	13	Ritual impurity of the woman
Mahkshirin (Maks.)	6			Ways in which foods become ritually unclean
Zabim	5			Gonorrhea and purification from it
Tevul Yom	4			Discussion of various kinds of ritual uncleanliness
Yadayim (Yad.)	4			Ritual uncleanliness of the hands
'Uqsin ('Uq.)	3			Categorization of things that are susceptible to ritual uncleanliness

Table 22 Common Conversions of Weights and Measures

All archaeologists have adopted the International System of Measures (formerly metric system). This table allows American readers to make conversions whenever they do not appear in the entries. Israeli archaeologists sometimes use an additional unit for area measurement, the dunam, which is a quarter of a hectare or 0.6178 acres.

To change	to	multiply by	To change	to	multiply by
acres	hectares	.4047	liters	quarts (dry)	.9081
bushels (U.S.)	hectoliters	.3524	liters	quarts (liquid)	1.0567
centimeters	inches	.3937	meters	feet	3.2808
cubic feet	cubic meters	.0283	meters	yards	1.0936
cubic meters	cubic feet	35.3145	metric tons	tons (long)	.9842
cubic meters	cubic yards	1.3079	metric tons	tons (short)	1.1023
cubic yards	cubic meters	.7646	miles	kilometers	1.6093
feet	meters	.3048	millimeters	inches	.0394
gallons (U.S.)	liters	3.7853	ounces avdp.	grams	28.3495
grains	grams	.0648	pecks	liters	8.8096
grams	grains	15.4324	pints (dry)	liters	.5506
grams	ounces avdp.	.0353	pints (liquid)	liters	.4732
hectares	acres	2.4710	pounds ap or t	kilograms	.3732
hectoliters	bushels (U.S.)	2.8378	pounds avdp.	kilograms	.4536
inches	millimeters	25.4000	quarts (dry)	liters	1.1012
inches	centimeters	2.5400	quarts (liquid)	liters	.9463
kilograms	pounds ap or t	2.6792	square feet	square meters	.0929
kilograms	pounds avdp.	2.2046	square meters	square feet	10.7639
kilometers	miles	.6214	square meters	square yards	1.1960
liters	gallons (U.S.)	.2642	square yards	square meters	.8631
liters	pecks	.1135	tons (long)	metric tons	1.0160
liters	pints (dry)	1.8162	tons (short)	metric tons	.9072
liters	pints (liquid)	2.1134	yards	meters	.9144

Table 23 Straight Line Distances between Main Points in Palestine (Miles)

	Beersheba	Bethsaida	Caesarea Maritima	Caesarea Philippi	Cana	Capernaum	Chorazin	Dan	Gadara	Gamla	Jericho	Jordan River	Jerusalem	Machaerus	Magdala	Masada	Mt. Gerizim	Mt. Hermon	Mt. Tabor	Nain	Nazareth	Ptolemais	Qumran	Samaria	Sepphoris	Sidon	Tiberias	Tyre
Beersheba	0																											
Bethsaida	127	0	47	24	21	4	3		19	7	76		83		9		56	28	22	25	25	33	83	53	24	46	11	35
Caesarea Maritima	88	47	0	71								39	56								25	26		24	28	76	23	57
Caesarea Philippi	150	24	71	0		27		3	43	25	99		109					6	48		46	44		75	43	27	34	30
Cana		21			0	18							75		16					15	9			40	6		16	
Capernaum		4		27	18	0	2		18	10	71	3	82		4		53	32	18	23	20	30		48	6	46	7	36
Chorazin		3				2	0					3	84		6													
Dan	146	23		3				0				3	106															
Gadara		19		43		18			0	17	57	7	67	77										45			19	
Gamla	129	7		25		10			17	0	84	7	84			114												
Jericho	58	76		99		71			57	84	0	6	14	24		40		84			58		10	31			66	
Jordan River			39			3	3	3	7	7	6	0	19	23		20	20				17	33		22				
Jerusalem	46	83	56	109	75	82	84	106	67	84	14	19	0	27	77	34	30	112	65	60	65	82	14	35	69	124	74	104
Machaerus	54	95							77		24	23	27	0		23							15				88	
Magdala		9			16	4	6						77		0												4	
Masada	24									114	40	20	34	23		0	23						31					
Mt. Gerizim		56				53						20	30			23	0				36			7				
Mt. Hermon		28		6		32					84		112					0						81				
Mt. Tabor		22		48		18							65						0		6			31			11	
Nain					15	23							60						6	0	6			27			15	
Nazareth		25	25	46	9	20					58	17	65				36		6	6	0	22		31	4	58	15	42
Ptolemais		33	26	44		30						33	82								22	0			18	45	28	25
Qumran	53	83									10		14	15		31							0					
Samaria		53	24	75	40	48					31	22	35				7	81	31	27	31			0			44	70
Sepphoris		24	28	43	6								69								4	18			0	54	16	37
Sidon		46	76	27		46							124								58	45			54	0	55	19
Tiberias		11	23	34	16	7					66		74	88	4				11	15	15	28		44	16	55	0	40
Tyre		35	57	30		36							104								42	25		70	37	19	40	0

✦ Historical Synopsis ✦

from Salome Alexandra to Masada

(*Italics* indicate uncertain dates)

76–67 B.C.E. Reign of Salome Alexandra, widow of the Hasmoneans Aristobulus I (104–103 B.C.E.) and Alexander Jannaeus (103–76). Her brother, Simeon ben Shetah, leader of the Pharisees and former president of the Sanhedrin, restores Pharisaic supremacy in religious and political affairs. During this period, the Pharisees establish their school system and execute some of their persecutors (*see* CRUCIFIXION).

67–63 Fratricidal war for power between Salome's two sons, Hyrcanus II and Aristobulus II.

63 While in Damascus, during the war against the Parthians, Pompey, commander of the Roman legions in Syria, receives three delegations: one from Hyrcanus II, one from Aristobulus II, and one from the Pharisees. The Pharisees ask for the abolition of Hasmonean rule and the return to the former Zadokite line of High Priests. Aristobulus II flees to Jerusalem and settles in the Temple, preparing for a siege. The Pharisees and supporters of Hyrcanus II open the gates of Jerusalem to Pompey, who captures the Temple after a three month siege. Twelve thousand Jews are killed; Pompey enters the Holy of Holies but does not plunder it. Hyrcanus II is appointed High Priest and ethnarch under the control of Scaurus, legate of Syria. Aristobulus is taken to Rome as a prisoner with his sons, but one of them, Alexander, escapes.

57 Alexander attempts to gain power. He is defeated by Gabinus, legate of Syria, and Mark Antony.

56 Aristobulus II and his other son, Antigonus, escape from Rome and start a new revolt. They surrender at Machaerus (*see* MACHAERUS). Alexander tries again but is defeated at Mount Tabor (*see* MOUNT TABOR). Gabinus goes to Jerusalem and organizes the local government according to the wishes of Antipater, father of Herod.

54 Gabinus is replaced by Crassus, who loots the Temple in order to finance the war against the Parthians. Crassus is defeated and killed.

53–51 Crassus is succeeded by Cassius as legate of Syria. At the request of Antipater, he represses a popular uprising in Galilee. Thirty thousand Jews are sold into slavery.

49 Roman civil war of Pompey against Julius Caesar. Pompey is defeated and assassinated. Antipater and Hyrcanus II submit to Caesar (Aristobulus II and Alexander were killed by Pompey's partisans). Hyrcanus II is appointed High Priest and ethnarch with hereditary rights. Antipater is appointed procurator of Judea with Roman citizenship. He appoints his older son Phasael governor of Jerusalem, Judea, and Perea.

47–46 Antipater appoints his second son Herod governor of Galilee. Herod captures the rebels' leader, Ezekias, and puts him and his men to death. Hyrcanus summons him to appear before the Sanhedrin to account for the executions. But Herod, backed by Sextus Caesar, legate of Syria, arrives with a strong bodyguard. He leaves as appointed governor of Coele-Syria and Samaria.

44 Death of Julius Caesar.

43 Revolt in Judea and Galilee led by Antigonus. Herod defeats the rebels and banishes Antigonus. He becomes engaged to Mariamne, daughter of Alexander, father of Antigonus.

42 Cassius and Brutus are defeated by Mark Antony and Octavian. Herod and Phasael offer allegiance to Mark Antony and are appointed cotetrarchs of Judea.

40 Antigonus reappears, backed by the Parthians. Phasael and Hyrcanus II are taken prisoners. Antigonus cuts Hyrcanus's ear to prevent him from being appointed High Priest again. Phasael commits suicide (*Antiq.* 14.379 or is assassinated by the Parthians, *Antiq.* 15.367–368).

40–37 Reign of Antigonus, appointed High Priest and king by the Parthians. Herod escapes to Rome via Masada, where he leaves his family in safety. He gains the support of Antony and Octavian and is elected king of Judea by the Senate in 40 B.C.E. (*see* HERODIUM; MASADA).

39–37 Herod lands at Ptolemais, collects an army, captures Jaffa, frees his family from Masada, and withdraws to Galilee, where he puts down another insurrection. He besieges Jerusalem with the help of the Roman army. A great massacre occurs, Antigonus is beheaded, Herod marries Mariamne and takes possession of his kingdom.

37 B.C.E. – 4 C.E. Reign of Herod the Great. He begins by executing forty-five Sadducee supporters of Antigonus and confiscating the silver and gold of the wealthy. He creates a new aristocracy and reduces the power of the Sanhedrin to religious matters. He favors the Essenes and Pharisees, who are not forced to take an oath of allegiance to him. The function of High Priest is no longer hereditary; he appoints seven different ones during his reign, the first one being Ananel from Babylon. He initiates a grandiose building program. He experiences great domestic troubles with ten wives and fifteen children. (*See* ANTONIA; CAESAREA MARITIMA; CAESAREA PHILIPPI; HEBRON; HERODIUM; JERICHO; JERUSALEM, HERODIAN; JERUSALEM, HEROD'S PALACE; MASADA; TEMPLE, HISTORY; TEMPLE, ROYAL STOA; TEMPLE, STAIRS AND GATES).

36 B.C.E. The sixteen-year-old Aristobulus is appointed High Priest upon the insistence of Alexandra, Herod's mother-in-law. After his popular welcome at the feast of Pentecost, Herod has him drowned at Jericho.

31 Battle of Actium. Herod pays allegiance to Octavian, who will be Emperor Augustus. Herod executes Mariamne, whom he suspects of adultery.

20 Beginning of the extension and beautification of the Temple. Probable date of the birth of Philo Judaeus of Alexandria. Hillel and Shammai become leaders of the Pharisees.

7 Herod has his sons from Mariamne, Alexander and Aristobulus, executed.

7–4 Probable time of the birth of Jesus.

5 Execution of Antipater, another son of Herod.

4 Final illness of Herod. Incident of the Golden Eagle in the Temple. The Pharisees Judas and Matthias are executed by Herod. General uprising put down by Varus, legate of Syria. Herod's kingdom is divided among three of his sons: Archelaus (Judea), Antipas (Galilee and Perea), and Philip (Herod) (Banias territory and Golan).

6 C.E. Archelaus is deposed. Roman prefects rule over Judea (*see* TABLE 16, RULERS OF THE GRECO-ROMAN WORLD AND OF PALESTINE). Quirinius, legate of Syria, orders a census. This causes strong opposition under the leadership of Judas the Galilean and the Pharisee Saddok. Then follows a period of relative peace until the time of Pontius Pilate.

6–15 Annas is High Priest.

7 During the rule of Coponius, the Samaritans defile the Temple by throwing in dead men's bones (*see* SAMARIA, SAMARITANS).

8 Possible date of the birth of Apollonius of Tyana, famed philosopher, healer, and miracle worker. He is deified after his death.

14 Death of Augustus. Tiberius becomes emperor.

18–36/37 Joseph Caiaphas is High Priest (*see* CAIAPHAS'S HOUSE; CAIAPHAS'S TOMB).

19 Foundation of Tiberias by Herod Antipas (*see* TIBERIAS).

26 Pontius Pilate is prefect of Judea (*see* PONTIUS PILATE'S STONE).

28 Jesus joins the movement of John the Baptist. John is imprisoned. Jesus starts his own movement.

29 John the Baptist is beheaded (*see* MACHAERUS).

29–30 Herod Philip gives the status of *polis* to Bethsaida and renames it Julias (*see* BETHSAIDA; COINS AS HISTORICAL DOCUMENTS).

30 Insurrection; Barabbas and Jesus are arrested, Jesus is crucified. Rabbi Gamaliel is in Palestine.

33 Martyrdom of Stephen.

34 Death of Herod Philip.

35 Paul's conversion.

36 Pontius Pilate is deposed after his massacre of innocent Samaritans.

36/37 Caiaphas removed from the High Priesthood by Vitellius, legate of Syria.

37 Death of Tiberius, succeeded by Caligula.

37–38 Birth of Josephus.

39 Pogrom of Alexandria. Flaccus, prefect of Egypt, attempts to impose the cult of Caligula upon the Jews. Philo leads a delegation to Rome to ask Caligula himself for a special exemption. The problem is solved when Caligula is murdered; he is succeeded by Claudius. Herod Antipas is banished to Gaul.

41 Under the rule of the prefect Cuspius Fadius, appearance of the pseudo-messiah Theudas. Fadius decapitates him and sends his head to Rome.

41–44 Agrippa I is King of Judea. He is succeeded by Tiberius Alexander, new prefect of Judea.

42 Paul begins his missions.

42–44 James, son of Zebedee is executed by Agrippa I. Peter is arrested and imprisoned, and then escapes.

43–44 or 48–49 "Apostolic Council" in Jerusalem.

47 The prefect Tiberius Alexander crucifies James and Simon, sons of Judas the Galilean (*see* CRUCIFIXION; MASADA).

48 Claudius gives to Agrippa II, son of Agrippa I, the kingdom of Herod of Chalcis, and later a larger domain to which Nero will add parts of Galilee and Perea. Agrippa II is a strong supporter of Roman rule and intervenes in Temple affairs.

63 James, brother of Jesus, is executed by the High Priest Annas II.

64 Gessius Florus is appointed prefect of Judea. His persecutions and exactions cause the First Jewish War of 66–70.

66 Beginning of the First Jewish War. Cestius Gallus, legate of Syria, is first defeated. Josephus is appointed commander-in-chief of the rebels' army in Galilee. Indecisive battle of Bethsaida against Agrippa II's army. Vespasian arrives in Galilee with the Roman legions (*see* BETHSAIDA; EXORCISM).

67 Capture and destruction of Gamla. The rebels under Josephus are defeated at Jotapata after a forty-seven-day-siege. Josephus is made prisoner by Vespasian (*see* GAMLA).

68 Destruction of Qumran (*see* QUMRAN).

69 Vespasian is made emperor; Josephus is freed.

70 Titus besieges and captures Jerusalem. The Temple is razed and burned.

73 Last episode of the First Jewish War: capture and destruction of Masada (*see* MASADA).

73–74 Publication of the *War of the Jews* by Flavius Josephus.

✦ Glossary ✦

Actium (Battle of) In 31 B.C.E., naval battle between Octavian and Antony at the entrance of the Arta Gulf in Greece. Octavian's Commander Agrippa won, and Octavian, future Augustus, exercised dominion over the Roman World.

A fortiori (Latin). For a stronger or superior reason; all the more.

A priori (Latin). From cause to effect; deductively.

Boulotherion (Greek). Building where the *boule*, local governing assembly of a city, met.

Caesareum (Latin). Building, usually a temple, dedicated to the Roman Emperor.

Century (Latin). Infantry unit of eighty to one hundred men commanded by a centurion.

Charon (Greek). In Greek mythology, the son of Erebus and Nox, who ferried the souls of the dead across the river Styx to Hades for a fee.

De visu (Latin). Seen by one's own eyes.

Didache (Greek). Instructions for Christians written in Greek around the turn of the second century C.E. It is also known as the Teaching of the Twelve Apostles.

Ecofact. Article of economic significance such as textile, object of leather, tool, or food item.

Eschatology (Greek). A belief about the end of the world or time. It is not necessarily apocalyptic, that is, about a revelation or a cataclysm.

Et passim (Latin). And more.

Exedra (Greek). Antichamber or outdoor area of a meeting hall where people could sit and converse.

Ex vaticinum (Latin). From the prophecy.

Ex-voto (Latin). Object placed in a temple, shrine, or church as the consequence of a vow or in gratitude for a healing or favor obtained.

Gemara (Hebrew). Commentary or interpretation of the Mishnah. Both Mishnah and Gemara are part of the Talmud.

Haggadah (Hebrew). Explanation of Hebrew Scripture in the form of story, legend, anecdote, or parable; about two thirds of the Babylonian Talmud is *Haggadah*.

Halakah (Hebrew). Any normative Jewish legal material or statements of law; about one third of the Babylonian Talmud is *Halakah*.

Hallel (Hebrew). Praise. Part of Jewish services in which Psalms are recited or sung. It is believed that they were Psalms 113 to 118 of the modern numbering.

Haram esh-Sharif (Arabic). "Noble Sanctuary." Modern Arabic name for the Temple Mount.

Hebrew Bible. Canon of Hebrew Scripture as completed at Jamnia in about 90 C.E. It is divided in three parts: Torah or Pentateuch, Prophets, and Writings. The canons of the Christian Old Testament, although based on the Hebrew Bible, differ from it in order and contents. Most of the references in this book derive from the American Protestant canon, the Geneva Protestant canon, and from the Roman Catholic canon.

Hypogeum (Greek). Tomb hewn underground as opposed to a tomb in a natural or hewn cave.

Insula (Latin, pl. Insulae). Living complex usually built around a courtyard for a large family. City block with multiple domestic units.

Koine (Greek). Attic dialect that incorporated Ionic elements. It became the lingua franca of the Hellenistic and Roman world.

Lingua Franca (Latin). Common language in a large area of peoples originally having different dialects.

Lituus (Latin). Hooked stick of a Roman augur.

Logion (Greek, pl. *logia*). An independent saying as in the Gospel of Thomas.

Lulav (Hebrew, pl. *lulavim*). Branch of palm tree, one of the four elements needed for the celebration of the Jewish Feast of *Sukkoth* (Feast of Booths, or Tabernacles).

Maccabees/Hasmoneans. Jewish dynasty founded by the priest Mattathias I who began the rebellion against Antochius IV Epiphanes in 167 B.C.E. The nickname Maccabee (probably "hammer") was given to Judah, the first of Mattathias's sons, who succeeded him.

Midrash (Hebrew). Exposition of Hebrew Scripture either in halakic or haggadic form.

Mishnah (Hebrew). Ancient Jewish laws and traditions edited and compiled in about 200 C.E. by Rabbi Judah the Prince but containing earlier traditions. It is composed of sixty-three tractates divided into six orders or divisions. It forms the first and most ancient part of the Talmud (*see* table 21).

Mithra. Iranian god also found in India in the Vedic era (ca. 1,300 B.C.E.). In the Hellenistic period its cult spread with significant changes to Asia Minor and reached Rome in the first century B.C.E. There it became one of the most important cults and a rival of Christianity. Mithra was usually represented with a Phrygian hat while sacrificing a bull. The cult included seven degrees of initiation, holy meals, and the sacrifice of animals.

Muristan (Persian). Hospital. Today it designates an area south of the Church of the Holy Sepulchre, by the Lutheran Church of the Redeemer. It is the location of the ancient Roman forum and the place where Charlemagne, who had a friendly relationship with the caliph Harun er-Rashid, built a hospital for Christian pilgrims at the beginning of the ninth century C.E.

Necropolis (Greek). City of the dead. Large burial ground.

Oikoumene (Greek). The general binding of humankind geographically, culturally, politically, and spiritually. This was the ideal of Alexander the Great that was taken over in the concept of the Pax Romana. The original meaning was "inhabited world" and the English "ecumenic" derives from it.

Ossuary. From the Latin "os" (bone). Receptacle for the bones of a decomposed corpse. Placing the bones of a dead person in an ossuary constituted a second burial.

Ostracon (Greek, pl. ostraca). Piece of broken pottery with written words on it.

Paterfamilias (Latin). Head of a household, not necessarily the father or grandfather of all. He had power of life and death over every member of the household, without recourse to judicial authorities.

Pax Romana (Latin). The peace imposed by the Roman senate or emperor on dominated peoples. If accepted, those submitting to it could gain many advantages, including Roman citizenship.

Pharos (Greek). The tower and lighthouse of the harbor of Alexandria built by Ptolemy II on the island of the same name. The light, reflected by mirrors, was seen at sea at a great distance. The tower collapsed in 1302, more than fifteen centuries after its construction.

Phylactery (Greek). Originally meant "fort." Strip of parchment, papyrus, or paper containing the words of Deuteronomy 6:8 or parallels. By extension, small leather case containing these Hebrew Scripture passages, attached to the forehead and arms by observant Jews during prayers.

Post eventum (Latin). After the event.

Praetorium (Latin). Originally, the place where the praetor, one of Romes highest magistrates, exercised his power. The meaning of the term expanded to designate the place where Roman rulers outside Rome discharged their functions.

Propylaeum (Greco-Roman, pl. Propylaea). A vestibule before a Greco-Roman building.

Q. From the German "Quelle" or "source." The expression probably was first used in 1890 by Johannes Weiss. It designates the hypothetical source of the Jesus sayings that Matthew and Luke have in common and are not to be found in Mark. When "Q" is used to designate a verse, it is followed by the Lukan verse number.

Sapiential. From Latin "sapiens" or knowledge. Having, providing, or expounding knowledge.

Satrap. From Persian. Name of the governor of a province of the Persian Empire (satrapy).

Septuagint. Name given to the Hebrew Bible translation in Greek. According to legend the work was done in Alexandria about 250 B.C.E. by seventy scholars in seventy days. The name is signified by the Roman numerals LXX.

Shema. First word of the Jewish call to listen to the Torah: *Shema Yisrael Adonai Eloheinu Adonai Eḥad*, or "Hear, O Israel: The Lord is our god, the Lord is One." (Deut. 6:4). It is the title of the fundamental monotheistic statement of Judaism inscribed in phylacteries and is recited in unison in public liturgy.

Soreg (Hebrew). Latticed stone fence or balustrade surrounding the Herodian Temple building beyond which non-Jews could not go.

Spina (Latin). In a Roman hippodrome the spina was the central wall separating the two parallel straight sections of the track.

Stricto sensu (Latin). In the strict sense of the term; strictly speaking.

Styx (Greek). In Greek mythology, the Styx was the river separating the world of the living from the world of the dead. The souls crossed it in Charon's boat to reach their final abode.

Sui generis (Latin). Of its own kind, unique.

Synoptics (from the Greek). That which gives a general view of the whole. Name used to designate the first three Gospels because of their similarities.

Tannaitic (Aramaic). Tannaitic refers to the period 70–200 C.E., when the *tanna'im* (teachers) collected the tradition of the Mishnah. The rabbis who wrote the *Gemara* are known as *amora'im* (explainers, interpreters).

Targum (Hebrew). Aramaic translation of the Hebrew Bible.

Tetrastyle (Greek). Building with four columns.

Tosepta or tosefta (Hebrew). Collection of Tannaitic *beraitot* (sing. *beraita*), or "additions," arranged according to the orders of the Mishnah.

Triclinium (Greco-Latin). Originally a long couch extending around three sides of a dining table for reclining at meals. Later the name was used to designate the Roman dining room itself.

Vaticinum ex et post eventu. Prophecy made from and after the event.

General Bibliography

This general bibliography complements the specialized bibliographies found at the end of each article.

ARCHAEOLOGY

Aharoni, H. *The Archaeology of the Land of Israel.* Hebrew, 1978. Philadelphia: Westminster/John Knox, 1982.

Albright, W. F. *From the Stone Age to Christianity.* Garden City, N.Y.: Doubleday, 1957.

Ben-Tor, A., ed. *The Archaeology of Ancient Israel.* New Haven: Yale University Press, 1992.

Ceram, C. W. *Gods, Graves and Scholars.* German, 1949. New York: Random House, Vintage Books, 1986.

Kenyon, K. M. *Archaeology in the Holy Land.* 1960. Reprint. New York: Thomas Nelson, 1985.

Mazar, A. *Archaeology of the Land of the Bible.* New York: Doubleday, 1990.

Moorey, P. R. S. *A Century of Biblical Archaeology.* Louisville, Ky.: Westminster/John Knox, 1991.

Shanks, H., Ed. *Ancient Israel.* Washington, D.C.: Biblical Archaeology Society, 1988.

ATLASES, DICTIONARIES, AND ENCYCLOPEDIAS

The Anchor Bible. Garden City, N.Y.: Doubleday, 1964–1990.

Anchor Bible Dictionary. Garden City, N.Y.: Doubleday, 1992.

Archaeological Encyclopedia of the Holy Land. New York: Putnam's Sons, 1972.

Atlas of Israel. Amsterdam: Elsevier, 1970.

Biographie Universelle. 43 vol. Graz, Austria: Akademische u. Verlagsanstalt, 1966–70.

Dictionnaire de la Bible. Paris: Letouzey and Ané, 1895–1993.

Encyclopedia Judaica. Jerusalem: Keter Publishing House; New York: Macmillan, 1972.

The Harper Atlas of the Bible. New York: Harper and Row, 1987.

The International Critical Commentary. Edinburgh: T. and T. Clark, 1979.

The Interpreter's Dictionary of the Bible. Nashville: Abingdon, 1962. Sup 1976.

The Jewish Encyclopedia. New York: KTAV, 1906.

The New Encyclopedia of Archaeological Excavations in the Holy Land. New York: Simon and Schuster, 1993.

The Theological Dictionary of the New Testament. Grand Rapids, Mich.: Eerdmans, 1974.

Women's Bible Commentary. Louisville, Ky.: Westminster/John Knox, 1992.

HISTORICAL, RELIGIOUS, AND SOCIAL BACKGROUND OF JESUS

Bammel, E. and C. Moule, eds. *Jesus and the Politics of His Days.* 1984. Reprint. Cambridge: Cambridge University Press, 1988.

Cartlidge, D. R. and D. L. Dungan, eds. *Documents for the Study of the Gospels.* 2d ed., rev. and enl. Minneapolis: Fortress Press, 1994.

Cohen, S. J. D. *From the Maccabees to the Mishnah.* Philadelphia: Westminster, 1987.

Collins, J. J. *The Apocalyptic Imagination.* New York: Crossroad, 1987.

Eckardt, A. R. *Reclaiming the Jesus of History.* Minneapolis: Fortress Press, 1992.

Feldman, L. H. and G. Hata. *Josephus, the Bible and History.* Detroit: Wayne State University Press, 1988.

Hengel, M. *Judaism and Hellenism.* German, 1973. Philadelphia: Fortress Press, 1988.

Hoehner, H. W. *Chronological Aspects of the Life of Christ.* Grand Rapids, Mich.: Zondervan, 1977.

Horsley, R. A. and J. S. Hanson. *Bandits, Prophets and Messiahs.* New York: Winston Press, 1985.

Jagersma, H. *A History of Israel from Alexander the Great to Bar Kochba.* German, 1985. Philadelphia: Fortress Press, 1986.

Jeremias, J. *Jerusalem in the Time of Jesus.* German, 1962. Philadelphia: Fortress Press, 1984.

Kee, K. C. *Jesus in History.* 1970. Reprint. New York: Harcourt Brace Jovanovich, 1977.

Murphy, F. J. *The Religious World of Jesus.* Nashville: Abingdon, 1991.

Neusner, J. *Messiah in Context.* Philadelphia: Fortress Press, 1984.

Patai, R. *The Messiah Texts.* Detroit: Wayne State University Press, 1979.

Reicke, B. *The New Testament Era.* German, 1964. Philadelphia: Fortress Press, 1989.

Russell, D. S. *The Jews from Alexander to Herod.* 1967. Reprint. London: Oxford University Press, 1991.

Safrai, S. and M. Stern. *The Jewish People in the First Century.* 2 vols. Philadelphia: Fortress Press, 1974, 1987.

Sanders, E. P. *Jewish Law from Jesus to the Mishnah.* Philadelphia: Trinity Press International, 1990.

Simon, M. *Jewish Sects at the Time of Jesus.* French, 1960. Philadelphia: Fortress Press, 1967.

Whittaker, M. *Jews and Christians. Greco-Roman Views.* Cambridge: Cambridge University Press, 1984.

JESUS THE MAN

Beaude, P. M. *Jesus de Nazareth.* Paris: Desclée, 1983.

Boers, H. *Who Was Jesus?* San Francisco: Harper and Row, 1989.

Borg, M. *Jesus: Conflict, Holiness and Politics.* New York: Edwin Mellen, 1984.

Bornkamm, C. *Jesus of Nazareth.* German, 1956. New York: Harper and Row, 1960. Minneapolis: Fortress Press, 1995.

Charlesworth, J. H. *Jesus within Judaism.* New York: Doubleday, 1988.

Conzelman, H. *Jesus.* German, 1959. Philadelphia: Fortress Press, 1973.

Crossan, J. D. *The Historical Jesus.* San Francisco: Harper, 1991.

——. *Jesus. A Revolutionary Biography.* San Francisco: Harper, 1994.

Falk, H. *Jesus the Pharisee.* New York: Paulist Press, 1985.

Fredricksen, P. *From Jesus to Christ.* New Haven, Conn.: Yale University Press, 1988.

Freyne, S. *Galilee, Jesus and the Gospels.* Philadelphia: Fortress Press, 1988.

Goldstein, M. *Jesus in the Jewish Tradition.* New York: Macmillan, 1950.

Hagner, D. A. *The Jewish Reclamation of Jesus.* Grand Rapids, Mich.: Zondervan, 1984.

Horsley, R. *Jesus and the Spiral of Violence.* 1984. Reprint. San Francisco: Harper and Row, 1988.

Matthews, S. *Jesus on Social Institutions.* Philadelphia: Fortress Press, 1971. First edition, 1928.

Meier, J. P. *A Marginal Jew.* New York: Doubleday, 1991, Vol 2, 1994.

Meyer, B. F. *The Aims of Jesus.* London: SCM Press, 1979.

Robinson, J. M. *A New Quest of the Historical Jesus.* 1959. Reprint. Philadelphia: Fortress Press, 1983.

Sanders, E. P. *Jesus and Judaism.* Philadelphia: Fortress Press, 1985.

Schleiermacher, F. *The Life of Jesus.* Philadelphia: Fortress Press, 1975.

Schweitzer, A. *The Quest of the Historical Jesus.* German, 1906. Introduction by J. Robinson. New York: Macmillan, 1968.

Theissen, G. *The Shadow of the Galilean.* Philadelphia: Fortress Press, 1987.

Vermes, G. *Jesus and the World of Judaism.* England, 1983. Philadelphia: Fortress Press, 1984.

———. *Jesus the Jew.* 1973. Reprint. Philadelphia: Fortress Press, 1988.

———. *The Religion of Jesus the Jew.* Minneapolis: Fortress Press, 1993.

TEXTS AND CRITICISM

Abernathy, D. *Understanding the Teachings of Jesus.* New York: Seabury, 1983.

Aune, D. E. *The New Testament in Its Literary Environment.* Philadelphia: Westminster, 1987.

Black, M. *An Aramaic Approach to the Gospels and Acts.* 1946. Reprint. London: Oxford University Press, 1979.

Bruce, F. F. *Jesus and Christian Origins outside the New Testament.* Grand Rapids, Mich.: Eerdmans, 1974.

Bultman, R. *Theology of the New Testament.* German, 1951. New York: Charles Scribner's Sons, 1972.

Conzelman, H. *An Outline of the Theology of the New Testament.* New York: Harper and Row, 1969.

Crossan, J. D. *Four Other Gospels.* (Gospel of Thomas, Egerton Papyrus, Secret Mark, and Gospel of Peter). Minneapolis: Winston Press (Seabury), 1985.

———. *Saying Parallels.* Philadelphia: Fortress Press, 1986.

Dibelius, M. *From Tradition to Gospel.* New York: Charles Scribner's Sons, 1967.

Funk, R. W., R. W. Hoover, and the Jesus Seminar. *The Five Gospels.* New York: Macmillan, 1993.

Goehring, J. E., C. W. Hedrick, J. T. Sanders, and H. D. Betz, eds. *Gospels Origins and Christian Beginning.* In honor of James M. Robinson. Sonoma, Calif.: Polebridge Press, 1990.

Henneke, E. *New Testament Apocrypha.* German, 1959, 1961. Philadelphia: Westminster Press, 1963, 1964.

James, M. R. *The Apocryphal New Testament.* 1924. Reprint. Oxford: Clarendon, 1980.

Jeremias, J. *New Testament Theology. The Proclamation of Jesus.* New York: Charles Scribner's Sons, 1971.

———. *The Parables of Jesus.* German, 1954. New York: Charles Scribner's Sons, 1972.

Malina, B. J. and R. L. Rohrbaugh. *Social Science Commentary on the Synoptic Gospels.* Minneapolis: Fortress Press, 1992.

Miller, R. J., ed. *The Complete Gospels.* Sonoma, Calif.: Polebridge Press, 1992.

Patterson, S. J. *The Gospel of Thomas and Jesus.* Sonoma, Calif.: Polebridge Press, 1993.

Perrin, N. *Rediscovering the Teachings of Jesus.* New York: Harper and Row, 1967.

Reicke, B. *The Roots of the Synoptic Gospels.* Philadelphia: Fortress Press, 1985.

Robinson, J. M., ed., *The Nag Hammadi Library.* San Francisco: Harper and Row, 1978.

Robinson, J. M. "The Son of Man in the Sayings Gospel Q." *Tradition and Translation—Festschrift for Carsten Colpe.* Berlin and New York: Walter de Gruyter, 1994.

Sanders, J. A. *From Sacred Story to Sacred Text.* Philadelphia: Fortress Press, 1987.

Stein, H. *The Synoptic Problem* 1987. Reprint. Grand Rapids, Mich. :Baker Book House, 1989.

Strocker, W. D. *Extracanonical Sayings of Jesus.* Atlanta, Ga.: Society of Biblical Literature, 1989.

Theissen, G. *The Gospels in Context.* German, 1989. Minneapolis: Fortress Press, 1991.

✦ Index of Scriptures Cited ✦

This index does not include the topical references given at the beginning of each entry.

Jeremiah (cont.)
25:22	327
27:3	327
31:12	221
31:31-34	83, 331
31:39	153
31:40	153
32:24	36
47:4	327

Ezekiel
4:2	36, 73
11:23	210, 211, 293
12:13	96
13:18-20	191
16:10	273
17:1-8	330
17:17	36
17:19	218
17:20	96
21:22	36
23:28	191
26:2-9	327
26:5	96
26:14	96
27:5	208, 209
17:19	218, 314
34:5-7	256
34:11-16	252
34:17-24	253, 253
36:25	236
43:2-5	293
44:11	254
44:21	330
47:10	96

Daniel
7:9	314
7:13	82, 261
11:15	36

Hosea
2:5	314
2:9	314
5:1-3	212
6:6	303
13:15	87

Joel
1:9	254
1:10	221
2:17	254
2:19	221
3:2	153
3:4-8	327
3:12	153

Amos
1:9-10	327
2:6	273
5:21-27	303
5:24	303
6:4	243, 339

Micah
4:4	9, 329
5:2-4	17
5:12	191
6:6-8	303

Habakkuk
1:14-15	96

Zechariah
3:10	9, 329
9:2-4	327
9:9	19, 154
10:2	191, 257
11:14-16	252
14:4	210, 212

Malachi
3:1-5	82
3:5	191, 254

Apochrypha

Tobit
8:2-3	89, 190

Wisdom of Solomon
16:20	291

Sirach
24:21	183
24:23-27	183
38:1-15	199
50:1-4	281
50:3	156

1 Maccabees
1:14-15	176
4:23	315
4:58	281
8:14	315
9:2	99
9:50	132
11:34	87
11:58	315
11:67	245
12:36	170
13:10	170
13:52	280
16:23	170

2 Maccabees
1:9	281
2:18	281
3:2-3	281
3:3	310
4:11-15	176
4:38	315

New Testament

Matthew
1:5	17
2:6	17
2:11	18
3:6	82
3:7-12	82, 262
3:9	264
4:3	264
4:15	100
4:23-25	92
4:25	86, 318
5:14b	127
5:14-16	128
5:15	128
5:22	145
5:23-24	303
5:26	58
5:29	145
5:30	145

✦ Index of ✦
Early Jewish Writings Cited

✦ Index of Ancient Writers Cited ✦

✦ Index of Names, ✦ Places, and Subjects